EYEWITNESS TRAVEL

NEW YORK CITY

MAIN CONTRIBUTOR: ELEANOR BERMAN

DK

LONDON, NEW YORK,
MELBOURNE, MUNICH AND DELHI
www.dk.com

PROJECT EDITOR Fay Franklin
ART EDITOR Tony Foo
EDITORS Donna Dailey, Ellen Dupont, Esther Labi
DESIGNERS Steve Bere, Louise Parsons, Mark Stevens
EDITORIAL ASSISTANT Fiona Morgan

CONTRIBUTORS
Lester Brooks, Patricia Brooks, Susan Farewell, Cheryl Farr Leas

PHOTOGRAPHERS
Max Alexander, Dave King, Michael Moran

ILLUSTRATORS
Richard Draper, Robbie Polley, Hamish Simpson

US EDITOR
Mary Sutherland

This book was produced with the assistance of
Websters International Publishers.

Reproduced by Colourscan (Singapore)
Printed and bound by L.Rex Printing Co. Ltd, China.

First American Edition, 1993
11 12 13 14 10 9 8 7 6 5 4 3 2 1

Published in the United States by
DK Publishing,
375 Hudson Street, New York, New York 10014

Reprinted with revisions 1994, 1995, 1996, 1997, 1999, 2000,
2001, 2002, 2003, 2004, 2005, 2006, 2007, 2008, 2009, 2010, 2011

Copyright © 1993, 2011 Dorling Kindersley Limited, London.

Published in Great Britain by Dorling Kindersley Limited.

A CATALOG RECORD IS AVAILABLE
FROM THE LIBRARY OF CONGRESS.

ISSN: 1542-1554
ISBN: 978-0-75666-918-8

FLOORS ARE REFERRED TO THROUGHOUT IN ACCORDANCE WITH AMERICAN USAGE; IE
THE "FIRST FLOOR" IS AT GROUND FLOOR LEVEL

Front cover main image: Statue of Liberty

MIX
Paper from
responsible sources
FSC
www.fsc.org FSC™ C018179

**The information in this
DK Eyewitness Travel Guide is checked annually.**
Every effort has been made to ensure that this book is as up-to-date
as possible at the time of going to press. Some details, however, such
as telephone numbers, opening hours, prices, gallery hanging
arrangements, and travel information are liable to change. The
publishers cannot accept responsibility for any consequences arising
from the use of this book, nor for any material on third party
websites, and cannot guarantee that any website address in this book
will be a suitable source of travel information. We value the views and
suggestions of our readers very highly. Please write to: Publisher,
DK Eyewitness Travel Guides, Dorling Kindersley, 80 Strand, London
WC2R 0RL, Great Britain, or email: travelguides@dk.com.

CONTENTS

**Baseball star
Babe Ruth
(1895–1948)**

INTRODUCING
NEW YORK

South Manhattan skyline

Chinatown, Lower East Side

Trump Tower, Upper Midtown

The New York City Ballet

Riverfront promenade in Brooklyn

TRAVELERS' NEEDS

Bagel from a New York deli

SURVIVAL GUIDE

Solomon R. Guggenheim Museum, Upper East Side

HOW TO USE THIS GUIDE

This Eyewitness Travel Guide helps you get the most from your stay in New York with the minimum of practical difficulty. The opening section, *Introducing New York*, locates the city geographically, sets modern New York in its historical context and describes the highlights of the year. *New York at a Glance* is an overview of the city's attractions. Section two, *New York Area by Area*, guides you through the city's sightseeing areas. It describes all the main sights with maps, photographs and detailed illustrations. In addition, seven planned walks take you step-by-step through special areas.

Well-researched tips on where to stay, eat, shop, and on sports and entertainment are in section three, *Travelers' Needs*. *Children's New York* lists highlights for young visitors, and section four, *Survival Guide*, shows you how to do everything from mailing a letter to using the subway.

NEW YORK AREA BY AREA

Manhattan has been divided into 15 sightseeing areas, each described separately. Each area opens with a portrait, summing up the area's character and history and listing all the sights to be covered. Sights are numbered and clearly located on an *Area Map*. After this comes a large-scale *Street-by-Street Map* focusing on the most interesting part of the area. Finding your way around each area is made simple by the numbering system. This refers to the order in which sights are described on the pages that follow.

Sights at a Glance lists the sights in the area by category, including: Historic Streets and Buildings, Modern Architecture, Museums and Galleries, Churches, Monuments, and Parks and Squares.

The area covered in greater detail on the *Street-by-Street Map* is shaded red.

Numbered circles pinpoint all the listed sights on the area map. Trump Tower, for example, is ❷

1 The Area Map

For easy reference, the sights in each area are numbered and located on an Area Map. To help the visitor, the map also shows subway stations, heliports and ferry embarkation points.

Photographs of facades and distinctive details of buildings help you locate the sights.

Color-coding on each page makes the area easy to find in the book.

Street by Street: Upper Midtown

UPPER MIDTOWN

SIGHTS AT A GLANCE

GETTING THERE

SEE ALSO

2 The Street-by-Street Map

This gives a bird's-eye view of the heart of each sightseeing area. The most important buildings are illustrated, to help you spot them easily as you walk around.

A locator map shows you where you are in relation to surrounding areas. The area of the *Street-by-Street Map* is shown in red.

Trump Tower ❷ is also shown on this map.

UPPER MIDTOWN

LOCATOR MAP

KEY

A suggested route for a walk takes you past some of the area's most interesting sights.

Travel tips help you reach the area quickly by public transportation.

Stars indicate the sights that no visitor should miss.

NEW YORK AT A GLANCE

Each map in this section concentrates on a specific theme: *Museums, Architecture, Multicultural New York,* and *Celebrated New Yorkers.* The top sights are shown on the map; other sights are described on the two pages following and cross-referenced to their full entries in the *Area by Area* section.

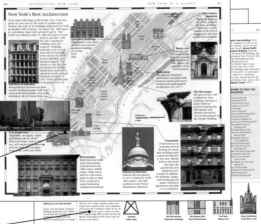

Each sightseeing area is color-coded.

The theme is explored in greater detail on the pages following the map.

3 Detailed information on each sight

All important sights in each area are described in depth here. They are listed in order, following the numbering on the opening Area Map. Practical information is also provided.

PRACTICAL INFORMATION

Each entry provides all the information needed to plan a visit to the sight. The key to the symbols is inside the back cover.

Address

Map reference to Street Finder at back of book

Sight Number

Trump Tower ❷

725 5th Ave. **Map** 12 F3.
Tel 832-2000. **M** 5th Ave-53rd St.
Garden level, shops open 10am–6pm
Mon–Sat. **Building open** 8am–10pm
daily. **Adm free.** See **Shopping** p311.
📷 ♿ Concerts. 🍴 🔲 📶

Opening hours

Services and facilities available

Telephone number

Nearest subway station

4 New York's major sights

These are given two or more full pages in the sightseeing area in which they are found. Important buildings are dissected to reveal their interiors; museums have color-coded floor plans to help you find particular exhibits.

The Visitors' Checklist provides the practical information you will need to plan your visit.

The facade of each major sight is shown to help you spot it quickly.

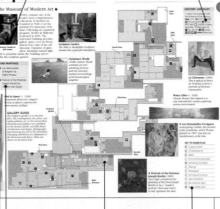

Stars indicate the most important exhibits or works of art on display inside, or the most interesting architectural details of the building.

A color key helps you find your way easily around the collection.

Floors are referred to in accordance with American usage, i.e., the "first floor" is at ground level.

INTRODUCING
NEW YORK

FOUR GREAT DAYS IN NEW YORK

At first glance New York may seem a bit overwhelming, but these four great days are planned to give you a taste of the Big Apple, with much of the city's best in architecture, shopping, museums, and fun. Each day offers a mix of things to see and do, and the schedules are not meant to be rigid – you'll find ample time to explore places that catch your fancy. All sights mentioned are cross-referenced so that you can find more information, check what's nearby, and tailor the day. Prices show the cost for two adults or for a family of two adults and two children including lunch.

Chrysler pinnacle

CITY LANDMARKS

- A tour of the UN
- Modern, Art Deco, and Beaux Arts edifices
- Lights of Times Square
- Empire State Building

TWO ADULTS allow at least $120

Morning
Start at the East River with a guided tour of the **United Nations headquarters** (see pp160–63), with its striking modern architecture. Then head to 42nd Street, detouring into the unique residential enclave of **Tudor City** (see p158), and dropping in to admire the Art Deco interior of the **Chrysler Building** (see p155). Next is **Grand Central Terminal**, a great Beaux Art landmark (see pp156–7). Admire the Main Concourse and explore the shopping gallery, colorful food market, and a food court with everything from sushi to Southern barbecue to New York cheesecake. Another lunchtime option is chowder or a platter of Long Island oysters at the **Grand Central Oyster Bar** (see p306).

Afternoon
Back on 42nd Street is another Beaux Arts creation, the **New York Public Library** (see p146; free one-hour tours at 11am and 2pm Tue–Thu). The marble halls, stairways, Main Reading Room and Periodicals Room are highlights. Check your e-mail for free in the Bill Blass Public Catalog Room. Look out also for current exhibits. Behind the library is **Bryant Park** (see p145), a welcome oasis of green in midtown. Ahead is New York's most famous crossroads, **Times Square** (see p147), gateway to the glittering neon of Broadway. Just beyond is 42nd Street, now a bright avenue of restored theaters, giant movie palaces, and Madame Tussaud's Wax Museum, with many true-to-life celebrities. Hail a cab to the **Empire State Building** (see pp136–7) and end the day with a fine twilight view of the city from the 86th-floor observatory.

Glistening Prometheus Statue and Lower Plaza at Rockefeller Center

ART AND SHOPPING

- A morning of modern art
- Lunch at Rockefeller Center
- Fifth Avenue shopping
- Tea at The Pierre

TWO ADULTS allow at least $135

Morning
The spectacular **Museum of Modern Art** (MOMA) (see pp172–5) will easily fill your morning with its wonderful art. Allow a couple of hours to enjoy its great works, including Van Gogh's *The Starry Night* and Claude Monet's *Water Lilies*, as well as Picasso's *Les Demoiselles d'Avignon*, to name just a few. Don't miss the design exhibits on floor three; one of MOMA's best-known facets. Leave the museum and stroll over to the **Rockefeller Center** (see p144) for lunch at the Rock Center Café, where you can watch the ice skaters in winter.

The neon lights of Times Square, the city's famous crossroads

◁ New York harbor and 42nd Street in 1946

In summer the rink is transformed into a leafy garden, where you can dine at the Rink Bar.

Afternoon

After lunch head for **St. Patrick's Cathedral** *(see pp178–9)*, the largest Catholic cathedral in the US and one of the city's finest places of worship. Then continue along **Fifth Avenue** for an afternoon of upscale shopping. Saks Fifth Avenue is just across the street from St. Patrick's at 50th Street. Heading uptown, the temptations include a dizzying variety of glitzy shops, such as Cartier (52nd St), Henri Bendel (55–56th sts), Prada, Tiffany (57th St), and Bergdorf Goodman (57–58 sts). End the day on 61st Street with a final splurge – enjoy a cocktail at **The Pierre** *(see p289)*.

HISTORIC NEW YORK

- **A boat trip to Ellis Island and the Statue of Liberty**
- **Lunch at Fraunces Tavern**
- **A tour of Old New York**

TWO ADULTS allow at least $120

Morning

At Battery Park, board the ferry to the **Statue of Liberty** *(see pp74–5)* and on to **Ellis Island** *(see pp78–9)*, the point of arrival for many immigrants (round trip includes both stops). On your return, exit the park at **Bowling Green**, the city's oldest park *(see p73)*. Walk to the **Fraunces Tavern Block Historic District** *(see p76)*, New York's last block of 18th-century commercial buildings. The recreated Tavern includes a museum of the revolutionary period and a restaurant that

Central Park, a vast area of fun rides, animals, and places to play

Statue of Liberty

is the perfect choice for an atmospheric lunch.

Afternoon

A block away is Stone Street Historic District, rebuilt after a fire in 1835. Look for **India House** *(see p56)*, once the New York Cotton Exchange, now **Harry's Café**. Take William Street to Wall Street and **Federal Hall** *(see p68)* with exhibits on the US Constitution. Nearby is the **New York Stock Exchange** *(see pp70–71)* and **Trinity Church** *(see p68)*, built in 1839. Go up Broadway to **St. Paul's Chapel** *(see p91)*, miraculously unscathed after the World Trade Center fell behind it. Ahead is **City Hall** *(see p90)*. Finally, head for the **South Street Seaport Historic District**, heart of the 19th-century port *(see pp82–3)*, with a view of the awesome **Brooklyn Bridge** *(see pp86–9)*.

A FAMILY FUN DAY

- **A morning in Central Park**
- **Lunch at the Boathouse**
- **Dinosaurs at the American Museum of Natural History**

FAMILY OF 4 allow at least $175

Morning

Central Park *(see pp205–9)* was made for family fun. Ride the vintage Carousel, watch model boats in action at Conservatory Pond, visit the Zoo, then watch the animal parade on the Delacorte clock on the half hour. There are themed playgrounds to please all ages: Safari at West 91st Street (2–5 years); Adventure at West 67th Street (6–12 years). The Swedish Cottage Marionette Theater, at West 79th, presents classic fairy tales at 10:30am and noon Tue–Fri (Wed also 2:30pm) and 1pm Sat; book ahead. Rent bikes or take a boat out on the lake, then lunch at the Boat House, which has a view of the lake. In winter, you can ice skate at the Wollman rink.

Afternoon

Depending on ages and interests, choose between the interactive **Children's Museum** *(see p219)*, or the famous dinosaurs and dioramas at the **American Museum of Natural History** *(see pp216–17)*. Finish up on West 73rd Street for a "wee tea" at Alice's Tea Cup.

Ellis Island, the view greeting early immigrants to New York

Putting New York on the Map

New York is a city of eight million people, covering 301 sq miles (780 sq km). The city gives its name to the state of New York, the capital of which is Albany, 156 miles (251 km) to the north. New York is also a good base from which to visit the historic towns of Boston and Philadelphia, as well as the nation's capital, Washington, DC.

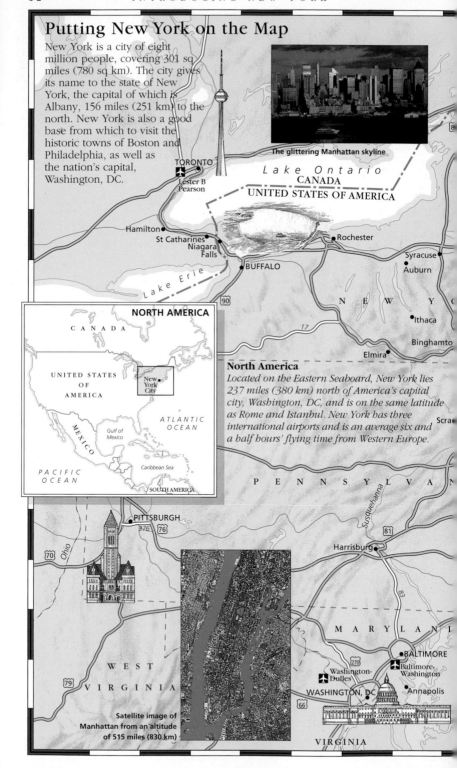

The glittering Manhattan skyline

TORONTO

Lester B
Pearson

Lake Ontario

CANADA
UNITED STATES OF AMERICA

Hamilton

St Catharines
Niagara
Falls

BUFFALO

Lake Erie

Rochester

Syracuse
Auburn

N E W Y

Ithaca

Binghamto

Elmira

North America

Located on the Eastern Seaboard, New York lies 237 miles (380 km) north of America's capital city, Washington, DC, and is on the same latitude as Rome and Istanbul. New York has three international airports and is an average six and a half hours' flying time from Western Europe.

Scra

NORTH AMERICA

C A N A D A

UNITED STATES
OF
AMERICA

New
York
City

M E X I C O

Gulf of
Mexico

ATLANTIC
OCEAN

Caribbean Sea

PACIFIC
OCEAN

SOUTH AMERICA

P E N N S Y L V A N

Susquehanna

PITTSBURGH

Ohio

Harrisburg

W E S T

V I R G I N I A

M A R Y L A N

BALTIMORE

Washington-
Dulles

Baltimore-
Washington

WASHINGTON, DC

Annapolis

VIRGINIA

**Satellite image of
Manhattan from an altitude
of 515 miles (830 km)**

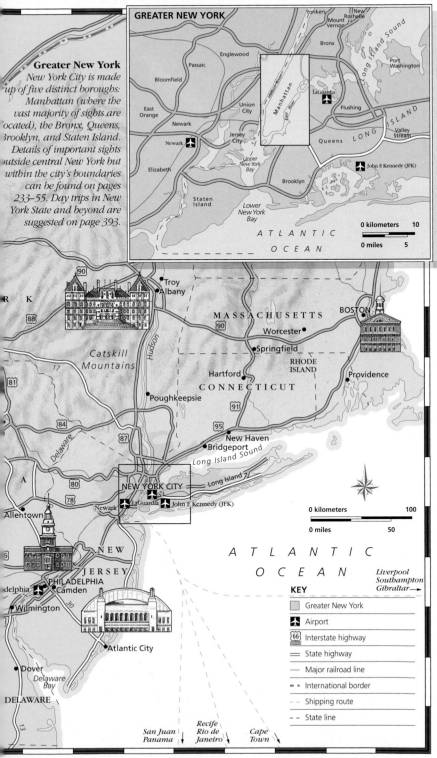

Greater New York
New York City is made up of five distinct boroughs: Manhattan (where the vast majority of sights are located), the Bronx, Queens, Brooklyn, and Staten Island. Details of important sights outside central New York but within the city's boundaries can be found on pages 233–55. Day trips in New York State and beyond are suggested on page 393.

GREATER NEW YORK

0 kilometers 10
0 miles 5

0 kilometers 100
0 miles 50

KEY

- Greater New York
- ✈ Airport
- 66 Interstate highway
- = State highway
- — Major railroad line
- ▪ ▪ International border
- - - Shipping route
- – – State line

Manhattan

This guide divides Manhattan into 15 areas, each with its own chapter. Many of New York's oldest and newest buildings rub shoulders in Lower Manhattan. It is from here, too, that you can take the Staten Island ferry, for breathtaking views of the city's famous skyline and the Statue of Liberty. Midtown includes the Theater District and Fifth Avenue's glittering shops. Museum Mile, alongside Central Park on Upper East Side, is a cultural paradise. To the north lies Harlem, America's most famous black community.

Grand Central Terminal
This Beaux Arts station has been a gateway to the city since 1913. Its concourse is a vast pedestrian area with a high-vaulted roof (see pp156–7).

Morgan Library & Museum
One of the world's finest collections of rare manuscripts, prints, and books is on display in this palazzo-style building (see pp164–5).

Statue of Liberty
Presented as a gift from the French to the American people in 1886, this towering statue has become a symbol of freedom throughout the world (see pp74–5).

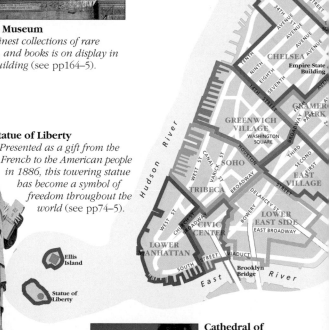

Cathedral of St. John the Divine
When it is finished, at some time after the mid-21st century, this great cathedral will be the largest in the world. It is also a theater and music venue (see pp226–7).

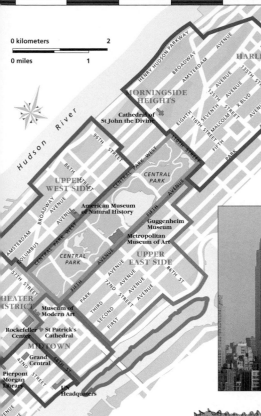

0 kilometers 2
0 miles 1

United Nations
New York is the headquarters of the global organization set up to preserve world peace and security (see pp160–63).

Empire State Building
This is the tallest skyscraper in New York and a symbol of the city. Built in the 1930s, it has since attracted more than 110 million visitors (see pp136–7).

KEY

▢ Major sight

Metropolitan Museum of Art
With a stunning collection of artifacts dating from prehistoric times to the present, this is one of the world's greatest museums (see pp190–97).

Brooklyn Bridge
This bridge spans the East River between Manhattan and Brooklyn. Built in 1883, it was the largest suspension bridge and the first to be constructed of steel (see pp86–9).

Solomon R. Guggenheim Museum
A masterpiece of architecture by Frank Lloyd Wright, this unique building contains a fine collection of 19th- and 20th-century painting (see pp188–9).

THE HISTORY OF NEW YORK

From its first sighting almost 500 years ago by Giovanni da Verrazano, New York's harbor was the prize that all of Europe wanted to capture. The Dutch first sent fur traders to the area in 1621, but they lost the colony they called New Amsterdam to the English in 1664. The settlement was re-christened New York and the name stayed, even after the English lost the colony in 1783, at the end of the Revolutionary War.

A shell-work cloak worn by an Indian chief

THE GROWING CITY
In the 19th century, New York grew rapidly and became a major port. Ease of shipping spawned manufacturing, commerce was king and great fortunes were made. In 1898, Manhattan was joined with the four outer boroughs to form the world's second-largest city. From 1800 to 1900, the population grew from 79,000 to 3 million people. New York City became the country's cultural and entertainment mecca as well as its business center.

THE MELTING POT
The city continued to grow as thousands of immigrants came seeking a better life. Overpopulation meant that many at first lived in slums. Today, the mix of cultures has enriched the city and become its defining quality. Its eight million inhabitants speak some 100 languages.

Manhattan's skyline took shape as the city grew skyward to make space for its ever-increasing population. Throughout its history, the city has experienced alternating periods of economic decline and growth, but in both good times and bad, it remains one of the world's most vital cities.

The following pages illustrate significant periods in New York's history.

A deed signed by New Amsterdam's last Dutch governor, Peter Stuyvesant, in 1664

◁ The southern half of Manhattan and part of Brooklyn in 1767

Early New York

Indian husk mask

Manhattan was a forested land populated by Algonquian-speaking Natives when the Dutch West India Company established a fur trading post called New Amsterdam in 1625. The first settlers built houses helter-skelter, so even today the streets of Lower Manhattan still twist. Broadway, then called by the Dutch name *Breede Wegh*, began as an Indian trail known as the Weekquaesgeek Trail. Harlem has also kept its Dutch name. The town was unruly until Peter Stuyvesant arrived to bring order. But the colony did not produce the expected revenues, and in 1664 the Dutch let it fall to the English, who renamed it New York.

GROWTH OF THE METROPOLIS

■ 1664   □ Today

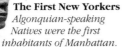

Seal of New Netherland
The beaver pelt and wampum (Indian shell beads) on the seal were the currency of the colony of New Netherland.

FIRST VIEW OF MANHATTAN (1626)
The southern tip of Manhattan resembled a Dutch town, down to the windmill. Although shown here, the fort had not yet been built.

The First New Yorkers
Algonquian-speaking Natives were the first inhabitants of Manhattan.

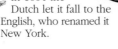

Iroquois Pot
Iroquois Indians were frequent visitors to early Manhattan.

Indian Village
Some Algonquians lived in longhouses on Manhattan before the Dutch arrived.

Dutch ships

Native canoe

TIMELINE

1524 Giovanni da Verrazano sails into New York harbor

1625 Dutch establish first permanent trading post

1626 Peter Minuit buys Manhattan from the Natives

1653 Wall is built for protection from attack; adjacent street is called Wall Street

1600	1620	1640

1609 Henry Hudson sails up the Hudson River in search of the Northwest Passage

1625 First black slaves brought from Africa

1643–45 Indian skirmishes end with temporary peace treaty

1647 Peter Stuyvesant becomes colonial governor

1654 First Jewish settlers arrive

Dutch Delftware
Colonists brought this popular tin-glazed earthenware pottery from Holland.

Manhattan Skyline
The Strand, now Whitehall Street, was the site of the city's first brick house.

Tiger **timbers**

WHERE TO SEE DUTCH NEW YORK

Dug up by workmen in 1916, these remnants of a Dutch ship, the *Tiger*, which burned in 1613, are the earliest artifacts of the period and are now in the Museum of the City of New York *(see p199)*. Rooms in this museum, as well as in the Morris-Jumel Mansion *(see p235)* and the Van Cortlandt House Museum *(see p240)*, display Dutch pottery, tiles and furniture.

Purchase of Manhattan
Peter Minuit bought the island from the Natives in 1626 for $24 worth of trinkets.

Dutch windmill

Fort Amsterdam

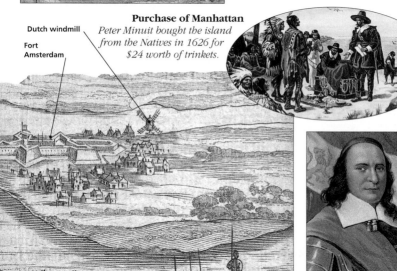

Peter Stuyvesant
The last Dutch governor was a tyrant who imposed strict laws – such as an edict closing all the city's taverns at 9 o'clock.

1660 First city hospital established

1664 British forces oust Dutch without a fight and change name to New York

1676 Great Dock built on East River

1698 Trinity Church dedicated

1660

1680

1700

The surrender of New Amsterdam to the British

1680s Bolting Laws give New York exclusive right to process and ship grain

1683 First New York city charter established

1689 Merchant Jacob Leisler leads revolt against taxes and takes over the city for two years

1693 Ninety-two cannons installed for protection; area becomes known as the Battery

1691 Leisler sentenced to death for treason

Colonial New York

Colonial gentleman

Under British rule, New York prospered and the population grew rapidly. The bolting of flour (grinding grain) was the main commercial enterprise. Shipbuilding also flourished. As the city prospered, an elite emerged that could afford a more refined way of life, and fine furniture and household silver were made for use in their homes during the Colonial period. During more than a century of governing New York, Britain proved more interested in profit than in the welfare of the colony. The Crown imposed hated taxes, and the spirit of rebellion grew, although especially in New York, loyalties were divided. On the the eve of Revolution, New York was the second-largest city in the 13 colonies, with 20,000 citizens.

Colonial currency

GROWTH OF THE METROPOLIS

◼ *1760*   □ *Today*

Bedroom

Dining room

Colonial Street
Pigs and dogs roamed free on the streets of Colonial New York.

Kas
This Dutch-style pine wardrobe was made in New York's Hudson River valley around 1720.

Shipping
Trade with the West Indies and Britain helped New York prosper. In some years, 200 or more vessels visited the port.

TIMELINE

1702 Lord Cornbury appointed Colonial governor; he often wore women's clothes

1711 Slave market set up at the foot of Wall Street

1720 First shipyard opens

| 1700 | 1710 | 1720 | 1730 |

1710 Iroquois chief Hendrick visits England

1732 First city theater opens

1725 *New York Gazette*, city's first newspaper, is established

Captain Kidd

The Scottish pirate William Kidd was a respected citizen, lending a block and tackle to help build Trinity Church (see p68).

VAN CORTLANDT HOUSE

Frederick Van Cortlandt built this Georgian-style house in 1748 on a wheat plantation in what is now the Bronx. Today a museum (see p240), it shows how a well-to-do Dutch-English family once lived.

West parlor

WHERE TO SEE COLONIAL NEW YORK

Colonial buildings are open to the public at Historic Richmond Town on Staten Island *(see p254)*. Fine examples of Colonial silver and furniture are on display at the Museum of the City of New York *(see p199)*.

Richmond Town General Store

Colonial Kitchen

Plain white cheese, called "white meat," was often served in place of meat. Waffles, introduced by the Dutch, were popular. Fresh fruit was rare, but preserved fruits were eaten.

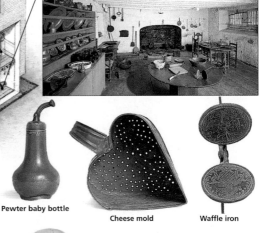

Pewter baby bottle

Cheese mold

Waffle iron

Sucket fork, for eating preserved fruits

Decorative Carvings

A face carved in stone peers over each of the front windows.

1734 John Peter Zenger's libel trial upholds freedom of the press

1741 Slave uprising creates hysteria; 31 slaves are executed, 150 imprisoned

1754 French and Indian War begins; King's College (now Columbia University) founded

British soldier

1759 First jail built

1740

1750

1760

1733 Bowling Green becomes first city park; first ferries to Brooklyn

King's College

1762 First paid police force

1763 War ends; British gain control of North America

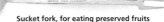

Revolutionary New York

George Washington, Revolutionary general

Dug up into trenches for defense, heavily shelled by British troops and scarred by recurring fires, New York suffered during the American Revolution. But despite the hardships, many continued to enjoy cricket games, horse races, balls and boxing matches. After the British took the city in 1776, it became their headquarters. The Continental army did not return to Manhattan until November 25, 1783, two years after the fighting ended.

GROWTH OF THE METROPOLIS

☐ 1776   ☐ Today

Battle Dress
The Continental (Patriot) army wore blue uniforms, while the British wore red.

British soldier

TOPPLING THE KING
New Yorkers tore down the statue of King George III in Bowling Green and melted it down to make ammunition.

Soldier's Haversack
American soldiers in the War of Independence carried their supplies in haversacks.

Battle of Harlem Heights
Washington won this battle on September 16, 1776. But he did not have enough troops to hold New York so retreated, leaving it to the British.

American soldier

Patriot

Death of a Patriot
While working behind British lines in 1776, Nathan Hale was captured and hanged by the British without trial for spying.

TIMELINE

1765 British pass Stamp Act; New Yorkers protest; Sons of Liberty formed

1767 New duties imposed with Townshend Act; after protests, the act is repealed

1770 Sons of Liberty fight British in the "Battle of Golden Hill"

1774 Rebels dump tea in New York harbor to protest taxes

1760

1770

1780

St. Paul's Chapel

1766 St. Paul's Chapel completed; Stamp Act repealed; Statue of George III erected on Bowling Green

General William Howe, commander in chief of the British troops

1776 War begins; 500 ships under General Howe assemble in New York harbor

Fire Fighters

Fires had long threatened the city, but during the war a series of fires nearly destroyed it. In the wake of the patriot retreat, on September 21, 1776, a devastating fire razed Trinity Church and 1,000 houses.

Leather fire bucket

Flags of the Revolution

Washington's army flew the Continental colors, with a stripe for each of the 13 colonies and a Union Jack in the corner. The Stars and Stripes became the official flag in 1777.

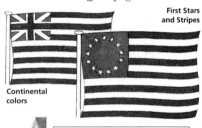

First Stars and Stripes

Continental colors

Statue of George III

General Washington Returns

Washington received a hero's welcome when he reentered New York on November 25, 1783, after the British withdrawal.

Cheering patriots

WHERE TO SEE THE REVOLUTIONARY CITY

In 1776, George Washington used the Morris-Jumel Mansion in upper Manhattan as a headquarters *(see p235)*. He also slept at the Van Cortlandt House *(see p21 and p240)*. After the war he bade farewell to his officers at Fraunces Tavern *(see p76)*.

Morris-Jumel mansion

1783 Treaty of Paris signed, US wins independence; British evacuate New York

1789 George Washington inaugurated as first president at Federal Hall

1790 US capital is moved to Philadelphia

1794 Bellevue Hospital opens on the East River

1801 *New York Post* founded by Alexander Hamilton

1790

1800

1785 New York named US capital

1784 Bank of New York chartered

1792 Tontine Coffee House built – first home of the Stock Exchange

1791 New York Hospital, city's oldest, opens

Washington's inauguration

1804 Vice President Aaron Burr kills political rival Alexander Hamilton in a duel

New York in the 19th Century

Firmly established as the nation's largest city and preeminent seaport, New York grew increasingly wealthy. Manufacturing increased due to the ease of shipping; tycoons like John Jacob Astor made millions. The rich moved uptown; public transportation followed. With rapid growth came fires, epidemics and financial panics. Immigrants from Ireland, Germany, and other nations arrived. Some found prosperity; others crowded into slums in Lower Manhattan.

Governor De Witt Clinton

GROWTH OF THE METROPOLIS

■ 1840   □ Today

Sheet Music
The Stephen Foster ballad Jeanie With the Light Brown Hair *was popular at this time.*

Croton Distributing Reservoir was built in 1842. Until then, New Yorkers had no fresh drinking water – they relied on deliveries of bottled water.

Omnibus
The horse-drawn omnibus was introduced for public transportation in 1832 and remained on New York streets until World War I.

Keeping Fit
Gymnasiums such as Dr. Rich's Institute for Physical Education were established in New York in the 1830s and 1840s.

TIMELINE

1805 First free state schools established in New York

1811 Randel Plan divides Manhattan into grid pattern above 14th Street

1812–14 War of 1812; British blockade New York harbor

The Constitution, *most famous ship in War of 1812*

1835 Much of old New York razed in city's worst fire

1810

1820

1830

1807 Robert Fulton launches first steamboat, on the Hudson River

1822 Yellow fever epidemic; people evacuate to Greenwich Village

1823 New York surpasses Boston and Philadelphia to become nation's largest city

1827 New York abolishes slavery

1837 New Yorker Samuel Morse sends first telegraph message

The Brownstone
Many brownstone row houses were built in the first half of the century. The raised stoop allowed separate entry to the parlor and ground-floor servants' quarters.

Crystal Palace was an iron and glass exhibition hall erected for the 1853 World's Fair.

NEW YORK IN 1855
Looking south from 42nd Street, Crystal Palace and the Croton Distributing Reservoir stood where the main public library and Bryant Park are today.

THE PORT OF NEW YORK
New York's importance as a port city grew by leaps and bounds in the early 19th century. Robert Fulton launched his first steamboat, the *Clermont*, in 1807. Steamboats made travel much quicker – it now took 72 hours to reach Albany, which was both the state capital and the gateway to the West. Trade with the West by steamboat and canal boat, and with the rest of the world by clipper ship, made the fortunes of many New Yorkers.

The steamboat *Clermont*

Crystal Palace in Flames
On October 5, 1858, New York's Crystal Palace exhibition hall burned to the ground, just as its predecessor in London did.

Grand Canal Celebration
Ships in New York harbor lined up to celebrate the 1825 Erie Canal opening. In connecting the Great Lakes with Albany, on the Hudson River, the canal opened a water link between the Midwest and the Port of New York. New York realized huge profits.

1849 Astor Place riots; ships set sail for California Gold Rush

1851 *New York Times* first published

1861 Civil War begins

1863 Draft riots last four days, many die

1853 New York hosts World's Fair

1857 Financial panic and depression

1865 Abraham Lincoln lies in state in City Hall

1840

1850

1860

Early baseball player

1845 New York Knickerbockers, first organized baseball team chartered

Clipper ship card

1858 Vaux and Olmsted design Central Park; Macy's founded

Crowds in Central Park

1842 Croton Reservoir built

FREE TRADE

The Age of Extravagance

Industrialist Andrew Carnegie

As New York's merchant princes grew ever wealthier, the city entered into a gilded era during which many of its most opulent buildings went up. Millions were lavished on the arts with the founding of the Metropolitan Museum, Public Library and Carnegie Hall. Luxury hotels like the Plaza and the original Waldorf-Astoria were built, and elegant department stores arose to serve the wealthy. Such flamboyant figures as William "Boss" Tweed, political strongman and king of corruption, and circus man Phineas T. Barnum were also larger than life.

GROWTH OF THE METROPOLIS
☐ 1890   ☐ Today

Overlooking the Park
The Dakota (1880) was the first grand luxury apartment house on the Upper West Side (see p218).

Palatial Living
Mansions lined Fifth Avenue. When it was built in 1882, W.K. Vanderbilt's Italianate palace at 660 Fifth Avenue, was one of the farthest north.

Fashion City
Lord & Taylor built a new store on Broadway's Ladies' Mile; 6th Avenue between 14th and 23rd streets was known as Fashion Row.

BATHING SUITS.

A GREAT SPECIALTY AT
LORD & TAYLOR'S, Broadway and 20th Street, N.Y
CHEAPEST AND BEST QUALITY OF BATHING SUITS IN THE CITY.

THE ELEVATED RAILROAD
By the mid 1870s, elevated railroads or "Els" ran along 2nd, 3rd, 6th and 9th avenues. They made travel faster, but left noise, grime and pollution in their wake.

TIMELINE

1867 Brooklyn's Prospect Park completed

1868 First elevated railroad built on Greenwich Street

1870 J.D. Rockefeller founds Standard Oil

1871 The first Grand Central Depot opens on 42nd St.; "Boss" Tweed is arrested and imprisoned

1877 A.G. Bell demonstrates the telephone in New York

1865   1870   1875

1869 First apartment house built on 18th Street; Black Friday financial crisis hits Wall Street

The interior of the Stock Exchange

1873 Banks fail: Stock Exchange panics

1872 Bloomingdale's opens

1879 St. Patrick's Cathedral completed; first city telephone exchange opened on Nassau Street

Mark Twain's Birthday
Mark Twain, whose 1873 novel The Gilded Age *portrayed the decadent lifestyle of New Yorkers, celebrated his birthday at Delmonico's.*

WHERE TO SEE THE AGE OF EXTRAVAGANCE

The Gold Room in the Henry Villard Houses *(see p176)* is a good place to experience the city's past. Formerly the Music Room, it is now an upscale bar called Gilt. The Museum of the City of New York also has period rooms *(p199)*.

Elevated train

Streetcar

Bowery

Rural Fifth Avenue
This painting by Ralph Blakelock shows a shanty-town at 86th Street. Today it is one of New York's most expensive addresses.

The Tweed Ring
William "Boss" Tweed led Tammany Hall, which dominated city government. He stole millions in city funds.

Nast's cartoon of "Boss" Tweed

Tammany Tiger
The Museum of the City of New York has "Boss" Tweed's cane, which sports a gold Tammany Tiger mascot on its handle.

1880 Canned fruits and meats first appear in stores; Metropolitan Museum of Art opens; streets lit by electricity

1883 Metropolitan Opera opens on Broadway; Brooklyn Bridge completed

1886 Statue of Liberty unveiled

1891 Carnegie Hall opens

1880

1885

1890

1888 Great Blizzard dumps 22 in (56 cm) of snow

1890 First moving picture shows appear in New York

Grand display of fireworks over Brooklyn Bridge, 1883

1892 Cathedral of St. John the Divine begun; Ellis Island opens

New York at the Turn of the Century

Horse-drawn carriage

By 1900, New York was a hub of American industry: 70% of the country's corporations were based there, and the port handled two-thirds of all imported goods. The rich got richer, but in the crowded slums, disease spread. Even so, immigrants kept their rich traditions alive, and political and social reform emerged. In 1900, the International Ladies' Garment Workers' Union was founded to battle for the rights of the women and children who toiled in dangerous factories for low wages. The Triangle Shirtwaist Factory fire in 1911 also sped reform.

GROWTH OF THE METROPOLIS
▢ *1914*   ▢ *Today*

Gateway to America
Almost five times as crowded as the rest of New York, the Lower East Side was the most densely populated place in the world.

Crowded Conditions
Tenements were unhealthy and overcrowded. They often lacked windows, air shafts or proper sanitary facilities.

WHERE TO SEE TURN-OF-THE-CENTURY NEW YORK
The Lower East Side Tenement Museum *(see p97)* has exhibits on tenement life.

Tailor's scissors

Hip bath

Inside a Sweatshop
Workers toiled long hours for low wages in the overcrowded sweatshops of the garment district. This view of Moe Levy's shop was taken in 1912.

Streetcars on Broadway

TIMELINE

1895 Olympia Theater is first to open in the Broadway area

1898 Five boroughs merge to form world's second-largest city

1901 Macy's opens Broadway department store

1895

1896 First bagel served in a Clinton Street bakery

1897 Waldorf-Astoria Hotel opens: the largest hotel in the world

1900 Mayor Robert Van Wyck breaks ground for city's first subway with silver shovel

1900

1903 Lyceum Theater opens – oldest Broadway house still in use

FLATIRON BUILDING

Overlooking Madison Square where Broadway, Fifth Avenue and 23rd Street meet, the 21-story tower was one of the city's first skyscrapers (1902). Triangle-shaped, it was dubbed the Flatiron Building (see p127).

Underlying steel structure

Elaborate limestone facade

Only 6 ft (185 cm) wide at apex of triangle

Supper in the Saddle
Decadent parties were all the rage. C.K.G. Billings's horseback dinner at Sherry's restaurant in 1903 was the talk of all New York.

Plaza Promenade
The section of Fifth Avenue in front of the Plaza Hotel was considered the most elegant in the city.

Ventilated hairpiece

High Fashion
In 1900 styles were stiff, with wire hoops and bustles worn beneath ornate dresses. Later, clothes became softer and more practical.

Long bustle

Wire hoops

1906 Architect Stanford White shot at Madison Square Garden, which he had built in 1890

1909 Wilbur Wright flies first plane over New York

1910 Pennsylvania Station opens

1913 Woolworth Building is world's tallest; new Grand Central Terminal opens; Harlem's Apollo Theater opens

1905 First crossing of the Staten Island Ferry

1907 First metered taxicabs; first Ziegfeld Follies

1911 Triangle Shirtwaist Factory fire kills 146 sweatshop workers; New York Public Library completed

Woolworth Building

New York Between the Wars

Entrance card to the Cotton Club

The 1920s were a time of high living for many New Yorkers. Mayor Jimmy Walker set the pace, whether squiring chorus girls, drinking in speakeasies or watching the Yankees. But the good times ended with the 1929 stock market crash. By 1932, Walker had resigned, charged with corruption, and one-quarter of New Yorkers were unemployed. With Mayor Fiorello La Guardia's 1933 election, New York began to recover and thrive.

GROWTH OF THE METROPOLIS

◼ *1933*   ◻ *Today*

Exotic Costumes
Chorus girls were a major Cotton Club attraction.

THE COTTON CLUB
This Harlem nightclub was host to the best jazz in town, as first Duke Ellington and then Cab Calloway led the band. People flocked from all over the city to hear them.

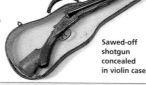

Defying Prohibition
Although alcohol was outlawed, speakeasies – semi-secret illegal drinking dens – still sold it.

Home-Run Hitter
In 1927, baseball star Babe Ruth hit a record 60 home runs for the Yankees. Yankee Stadium (see p241) became known as "the house that Ruth built."

Sawed-off shotgun concealed in violin case

Gangsters
Dutch Schultz was the kingpin of an illegal booze racket.

TIMELINE

1918 End of World War I

1919 18th Amendment bans alcohol, launches Prohibition Era

1920 US women get the vote

1920

1924 Novelist James Baldwin is born in Harlem

1925 *The New Yorker* magazine is launched

1926 Jimmy Walker becomes mayor

Opening of the Holland Tunnel

1925

1927 Lindbergh flies across the Atlantic; first talking movie, *The Jazz Singer,* opens; Holland Tunnel opens

1929 Stock market crash; Great Depression begins

1930 Chrysler Building completed

1931 Empire State Building becomes world's tallest

1930

Big Band Leaders
Banned from many downtown clubs, black artists like Cab Calloway starred at the Cotton Club.

Broadway Melodies
The 1920s were the heyday of the Broadway musical, with a record number of plays opening.

THE GREAT DEPRESSION

The Roaring Twenties ended with the stock market crash of October 29, 1929, which set off the Depression. New York was hard hit: squatters' shacks sprang up in Central Park and thousands were out of work. But art flourished as artists went to work for the Works Projects Administration (WPA), creating outstanding murals and artworks throughout the city.

Waiting to receive benefits in 1931

Breakfast menu

Lindbergh's plane, *Spirit of St. Louis*

Lindbergh's Flight
New Yorkers celebrated Lindbergh's nonstop solo flight across the Atlantic in 1927 in a variety of ways, including a breakfast in his honor.

Rockefeller Center
Millionaire John D. Rockefeller drives the final rivet to celebrate the opening of Rockefeller Center on May 1, 1939.

Mass Event
Forty-five million people visited the 1939 World's Fair in New York.

1933 Prohibition ends; Fiorello LaGuardia begins three terms as mayor

1940 Queens-Midtown Tunnel opens

1942 Times Square blacked out during World War II; Idlewild International Airport (now JFK) opens

1935

1940

1945

1936 Parks Department headed by Robert Moses; new parks created

1939 Rockefeller Center is completed

1941 US enters World War II

1944 Black leader Adam Clayton Powell elected to Congress

Postwar New York

Since World War II, New York has seen both the best of times and the worst. Although established as the financial capital of the world, the city itself almost went bankrupt in the 1970s. In 2008 the collapse of the Wall Street bank Lehman Brothers precipitated the worst financial crisis since 1929. Since the early 1990s, New York has seen a dramatic drop in the crime rate and an increase in the restoration of such landmarks as Grand Central Terminal and the "new" Times Square. This constant rebuilding is emblematic of the city's position as the cultural and financial hub of the United States.

BILTMORE THEATER

1967 Hippie musical *Hair* opens on Off-Broadway, then transfers to the Biltmore Theater

1971 Pop artist Andy Warhol has a retrospective show of his work at the Whitney Museum

1953 Merce Cunningham founds dance company

1975 Federal loan saves New York from bankruptcy

1945 End of World War II

1954 Ellis Island closes

1966 Newspaper and transit strikes

1981 New York regains solvency

1946 UN headquarters established in New York

1959 Guggenheim Museum opens

1945	1950	1955	1960	1965	1970	1975	1
MAYORS:	IMPELLITERI	WAGNER		LINDSAY		BEAME	KOC
1945	1950	1955	1960	1965	1970	1975	1

1947 Jackie Robinson, first black baseball player in the major leagues, signs with Brooklyn Dodgers

1963 Pennsylvania Station razed

1973 World Trade Center completed

1964 New York World's Fair; race riots in Harlem and Bedford-Stuyvesant; Verrazano Narrows Bridge links Brooklyn and Staten Island; Beatles play at Shea Stadium

Souvenir scarf

1968 20,000 anti-establishment hippies gather in Central Park; student sit-ins at Columbia University

Andy Warhol with actresses Candy Darling and Ultra Violet

1983 Economic boom: property prices skyrocket; Trump
Tower completed by real estate tycoon Donald Trump,
who symbolizes the "yuppie" wealth of the 1980s

1988 Twenty-five percent
of New Yorkers live
below the poverty line

1990 David Dinkins, New York's
first black mayor, takes office;
Ellis Island reopens as an
immigration museum

2001 Terrorist attack on the World Trade Center; Mayor
Giuliani is a great support to the people of New York.
President George W Bush declares war on terrorism

2009 US Airways flight
1549 crash-lands in the
Hudson River. All 155
passengers survive

1987 Stock
market crash

1994 Rudolph Giuliani
takes office as mayor

1985	1990	1995	2000	2005	2010	2015
	DINKINS	GIULIANI		BLOOMBERG		
1985	1990	1995	2000	2005	2010	2015

1986 Shock of corruption
scandals rock Mayor Koch's
administration; Centennial
of Statue of Liberty

2000
Population
reaches just
over 8 million

2003 A major power outage on August 14 leaves
50 million people in the North East (including
New York City), mid-West, and ports of Canada,
blacked out for up to 24 hours

2002 The lights go on
in a regenerated 42nd
Street, which crosses
Broadway at Times
Square. Along with
neighboring Chelsea
and its cutting-edge
galleries, the area
out-shines SoHo as
the city's chic spot

1995 The neglected Chelsea Piers
are renovated and open as a
mammoth sports and entertainment complex *(see p138)*

NEW YORK AT A GLANCE

There are almost 300 places of interest described in the Area by Area section of this book. They range from the bustling New York Stock Exchange *(see pp70–71)* to Central Park's peaceful Strawberry Fields *(see p208)*, and from historic synagogues to dazzling skyscrapers. The following 14 pages provide a time-saving guide to New York's most interesting sights. Museums and architecture each have a section, and there are guides to the people and cultures that have given the city its unique character. Each sight is cross-referenced to its own full entry. Below are the top ten tourist attractions to start you off.

NEW YORK'S TOP TEN   TOURIST ATTRACTIONS

Ellis Island
See pp78–9.

Empire State Building
See pp136–7.

South Street Seaport
See pp82–4.

Rockefeller Center
See p144.

Museum of Modern Art
See pp172–5.

Central Park
See pp204–9.

Metropolitan Museum of Art
See pp190–97.

Statue of Liberty
See pp74–5.

Brooklyn Bridge
See pp86–9.

Chinatown
See pp96–7.

New York's Best: Museums

New York's museums range from the vast
scope of the Metropolitan Museum to the personal
treasures of financier J. Pierpont Morgan's own
collection. Several museums celebrate New York's
heritage, giving visitors an insight into the people
and events that made the city what it is today.
This map features some highlights, with a
detailed overview on pages 38 and 39.

Museum of Modern Art
Picasso's Goat *(1950) is
among the impressive
collection in the
renovated and
expanded
Museum of
Modern
Art.*

***Intrepid* Sea-Air-
Space Museum**
*This naval museum
also traces the
progress of
flight explo-
ration. The large air-
craft carrier housing the
museum returned to Pier 86
in late 2008 after renovation.*

**Morgan Library
& Museum**
*One of the world's
finest collections of
manuscripts, prints
and books includes
this rare French
Bible from 1230.*

**Merchant's
House
Museum**
*This perfectly
preserved
1832 house
belonged to
a wealthy
trader.*

Ellis Island
*This museum vividly re-
creates the experiences
of many millions of
immigrant families.*

Upper
West Side

Theater
District

Chelsea
and the
Garment
District

Lower
Midtown

Gramercy
and the
Flatiron
District

Greenwich
Village

SoHo and
TriBeCa

East
Village

Lower East
Side

Lower
Manhattan

Seaport
and the
Civic
Center

Ellis
Island

HUDSON RIVER

EAST RIVER

| 0 kilometers | 2 |
| 0 miles | 1 |

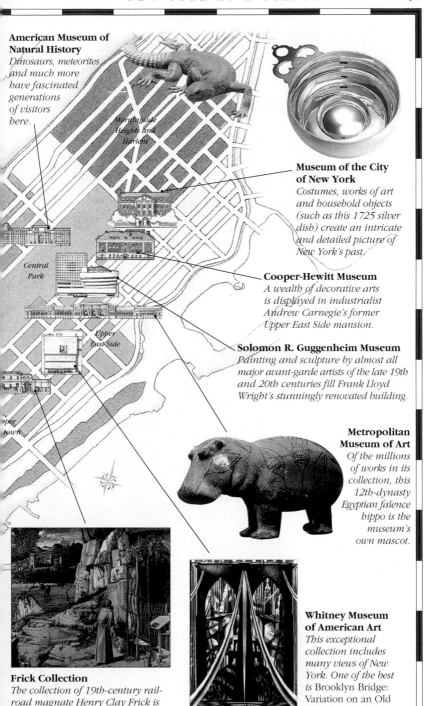

American Museum of Natural History
Dinosaurs, meteorites and much more have fascinated generations of visitors here.

Morningside Heights and Harlem

Central Park

Upper East Side

per town

Museum of the City of New York
Costumes, works of art and household objects (such as this 1725 silver dish) create an intricate and detailed picture of New York's past.

Cooper-Hewitt Museum
A wealth of decorative arts is displayed in industrialist Andrew Carnegie's former Upper East Side mansion.

Solomon R. Guggenheim Museum
Painting and sculpture by almost all major avant-garde artists of the late 19th and 20th centuries fill Frank Lloyd Wright's stunningly renovated building.

Metropolitan Museum of Art
Of the millions of works in its collection, this 12th-dynasty Egyptian faïence hippo is the museum's own mascot.

Frick Collection
The collection of 19th-century railroad magnate Henry Clay Frick is displayed in his former home. Masterpieces include St. Francis in the Desert (about 1480) by Giovanni Bellini.

Whitney Museum of American Art
This exceptional collection includes many views of New York. One of the best is Brooklyn Bridge: Variation on an Old Theme (1939), by Joseph Stella.

Exploring New York's Museums

Richmond Town tobacco tin

You could devote an entire month to visiting New York's museums and still not do them justice. There are more than 60 museums in Manhattan alone, and half that number again in the other boroughs. The wealth of art and the huge variety of offerings – from Old Masters to old fire engines, dinosaurs to dolls, Tibetan tapestries to African masks – is equal to that of any city in the world. Note that some museums close on Monday as well as on another day. Many stay open late one or two evenings a week, and some have one evening when admission is free. Not every museum charges for admission, but donations are always welcome.

PAINTING AND SCULPTURE

New York is best known for its art museums. The **Metropolitan Museum of Art** houses an extensive collection of American art, as well as world-famous masterpieces. **The Cloisters**, a branch of the "Met" in Upper Manhattan, is a treasury of medieval art and architecture. The **Frick Collection** has a superb display of Old Masters. In contrast, the **Museum of Modern Art (MoMA)** houses Impressionist and modern paintings. **The Whitney Museum of American Art** and the **Solomon R. Guggenheim Museum** also specialize in modern art, the Whitney's biennial show being the foremost display of work by living artists. Today's cutting-edge art is at the **New Museum of Contemporary Art**, while the work of craft artists can be seen at the **American**

Folk Art Museum. The **National Academy Museum** displays a collection of 19th- and 20th-century art, donated by academy members. In Harlem, the **Studio Museum** shows the work of black artists.

CRAFTS AND DESIGN

If you are interested in textiles, porcelain and glass, embroideries and laces, wallpaper, and prints, visit the **Cooper-Hewitt Museum**, the decorative arts outpost of Washington's Smithsonian Institution. The design collections at **MoMA** trace the history of design from clocks to couches. The **Museum of Arts and Design** offers the finest work of today's skilled artisans in mediums from furniture to pottery, and the **American Folk Art Museum** presents folk forms, from quilts to canes. Silver collections are notable at the **Museum of the City of New York**. The fine displays of native art at the **National Museum of the American Indian** include jewelry, rugs and pottery.

PRINTS AND PHOTOGRAPHY

The **International Center of Photography** is the only museum in New York that is totally devoted to this medium. Collections can also be seen at the **Metropolitan Museum of Art** and MoMA, and there are many examples of early photography at the **Museum of the City of New York** and **Ellis Island**.
  Prints and drawings by such great book illustrators as Kate Greenaway and Sir John Tenniel are featured at the **Morgan Library & Museum**. The **Cooper-Hewitt Museum** has examples of the use of prints in the decorative arts.

FURNITURE AND COSTUMES

The annual exhibition of the Costume Institute at the **Metropolitan Museum of Art** is always worth a visit. Also impressive is the American Wing, with its 24 rooms of original furnishings tracing life from 1640 to the 20th century. Period rooms depicting New York in various settings, beginning with the 17th-century Dutch, are on display at the **Museum of the City of New York**. There are also some house museums that give a realistic picture of life and furnishings in old New York. The **Merchant's House Museum**, a preserved residence from 1832, was occupied by the same family for 98 years. **Gracie Mansion** was the residence of mayor Archibald Gracie, who bought it in 1798 from a shipping merchant, and it is open periodically for public tours. The **Theodore Roosevelt Birthplace** is the brownstone where the 26th president of the United States grew up, and the **Mount Vernon Hotel Museum** was an early 19th-century resort.

Corn husk doll, American Museum of Natural History

The Peaceable Kingdom (c.1840–45) by Edward Hicks, at the Brooklyn Museum

HISTORY

Palm pistol at the New York City Police Museum

American history unfolds at **Federal Hall**, the United States' first capitol, where George Washington took his oath as America's first president on the balcony in April 1789.

Visit the **Fraunces Tavern Museum** for a glimpse of colonial New York. **Ellis Island** and **Lower East Side Tenement Museum** re-create the hardships faced by immigrants. The new **Museum of Jewish Heritage** in Battery City is a living memorial to the Holocaust. The **New York City Fire Museum** and the **New York City Police Museum** chronicle heroism and tragedy, while the **South Street Seaport Museum** re-creates early maritime history.

TECHNOLOGY AND NATURAL HISTORY

Forest-dwelling bonga, American Museum of Natural History

Science museums hold exhibitions from nature to space-age technology. The **American Museum of Natural History** has vast collections covering flora, fauna and cultures from around the world. Its Rose Center/Hayden Planetarium offers a unique view of space. The *Intrepid* **Sea-Air-Space Museum** is a repository of technology that chronicles military progress. It is based on the decks of an aircraft carrier.

If you missed a classic Lucille Ball sitcom or footage of the first man on the moon, the place to visit is the **The Paley Center for Media**, which holds these and many other classics of TV and radio.

ART FROM OTHER CULTURES

Egyptian mummy, Brooklyn Museum

Artwork of other nations is the focus of several special collections.

Oriental art is the specialty of the **Asia Society** and the **Japan Society**. The **Jewish Museum** features major collections of Judaica and has changing exhibitions of various aspects of Jewish life. **El Museo del Barrio** is dedicated to the arts of Puerto Rico, including many Pre-Columbian Taino artifacts. For an impressive review of African-American art and history, visit the **Schomburg Center for Research in Black Culture**. Finally, the **Metropolitan Museum of Art** excels in its multicultural displays, ranging from the art of ancient Egypt to that of contemporary Africa.

LIBRARIES

New York's notable libraries, such as the **Morgan Library & Museum**, offer superb art collections as well as a chance to view pages from ancient manuscripts and rare books. The **New York Public Library**'s collection includes historic documents and manuscripts of many famous works.

BEYOND MANHATTAN

Other museums worth a visit include the **Brooklyn Museum of Art**, with a huge collection of artifacts from across the world and over one million paintings. The **Museum of the Moving Image** in Queens has a unique collection of motion-picture history. The **Jacques Marchais Museum of Tibetan Art** is a rare find on Staten Island as is **Historic Richmond Town**, a well-restored village dating from the 1600s.

New York's Best: Architecture

Even when following world trends, New York has
given its own twist to the turns of architectural
fashion, the style of its buildings influenced by both
geography and economy. An island city, with space
at a premium, must look upward to grow. This
trend was reflected early on with tall, narrow town
houses and later with
the city's apartment
buildings and sky-
scrapers. Building
materials such as cast-
iron and brownstone
were chosen for their
local availability and
practical appeal. The
result is a city that has
developed by finding
flamboyant answers to
practical needs. A more
detailed overview of
New York's architecture
is on pages 42 to 43.

Apartment Buildings
*The Majestic is one of five
Art Deco twin-towered
apartment buildings
on Central
Park
West.*

Cast-Iron Architecture
*Mass-produced cast-iron was often
used for building facades. SoHo has
many of the best examples, such as this
building at 28–30 Greene Street.*

Post-Modernism
*The quirky, yet elegant, shapes
of buildings like the World
Financial Center, built in 1985
(see p69) mark a bold departure
from the sleek steel-and-glass
boxes of the 1950s and 1960s.*

Theater
District

Chelsea
and the
Garment
District

Greenwich
Village

Gramercy
and the
Flatiron
District

SoHo and
TriBeCa

East
Village

Lower
East Side

Lower
Manhattan

Brownstones
*Built from local sand-
stone, brownstones
were favored by the
19th-century middle
classes. India House,
built in a Florentine
palazzo style on Wall
Street, is typical of
many brownstone
commercial buildings.*

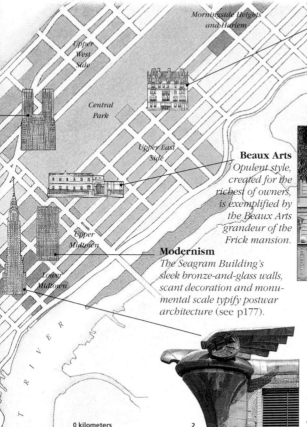

Morningside Heights and Harlem

Upper West Side

Central Park

Upper East Side

Upper Midtown

Lower Midtown

EAST RIVER

0 kilometers 2

0 miles 1

19th-Century Mansions

The Jewish Museum (see p186), formerly the home of Felix M. Warburg, is a fine example of the French Renaissance style that typified these mansions.

Beaux Arts

Opulent style, created for the richest of owners, is exemplified by the Beaux Arts grandeur of the Frick mansion.

Modernism

The Seagram Building's sleek bronze-and-glass walls, scant decoration and monumental scale typify postwar architecture (see p177).

The Skyscraper

The glory of New York architecture, these buildings expressed a perfect blend of practical engineering skill together with fabulous decoration, such as this gargoyle on the Chrysler Building.

Federal Architecture

Federal style was popular in civic architecture of the 19th century; City Hall combines it with French Renaissance influences.

Tenements

Constructed as an economic form of housing, for many these buildings were a stark introduction to new lives. Mainly built on the Lower East Side, the apartments were hopelessly overcrowded. In addition, the buildings' design, with inadequate air shafts, resulted in apartments with little or no ventilation.

Exploring New York's Architecture

A Federal-style front door

During its first 200 years, New York, like all of America, looked to Europe for architectural inspiration. None of the buildings from the Dutch colonial period survive in Manhattan today; most were lost in the great fire of 1776 or torn down to make way for new developments in the early 1800s. Throughout the 18th and 19th centuries, the city's major architectural trends followed those of Europe. With the advent of cast-iron architecture in the 1850s, the Art Deco period and the ever-higher rise of the skyscraper, New York's architecture came into its own.

FEDERAL ARCHITECTURE

This American adaptation of the Neoclassical Adam style flowered in the early decades of the new nation, featuring square buildings two or three stories tall, with low hipped roofs, balustrades and decorative elements – all carefully balanced. **City Hall** (1811, John McComb, Jr. and Joseph François Mangin) is a blend of Federal and French Renaissance influences. The restored warehouses of **Schermerhorn Row** (c. 1812) in the Seaport district are also in Federal style.

BROWNSTONES

Plentiful and cheap, the brown sandstone found in the nearby Connecticut River Valley and along the banks of the Hackensack River in New

A typical brownstone with stoop leading up to the main entrance

Jersey was the most common building material in the 1800s. It is found all over the city's residential neighborhoods, used for small homes or small

apartments – some of the best examples of brownstone can be found in **Chelsea**. Because street space was limited, these buildings were very narrow in width, but also very deep. A typical brownstone has a flight of steps, called a stoop, leading up to the living floors. Separate stairs lead down to the basement, which was originally the servants' quarters.

TENEMENTS

Tenements were built to house the huge influx of immigrants who arrived from the 1840s up to World War I. The six-story blocks, 100 ft (30 m) long and 25 ft (8 m) wide, offered very little light and air except from tiny side-wall air shafts and windows at each end, leaving the middle rooms in darkness. The tiny apartments were called railroad flats after their similarity to railroad cars. Later designs had air shafts between buildings, but these helped the spread of fire. The **Lower East Side Tenement Museum** has scale models of the old tenements.

CAST-IRON ARCHITECTURE

An American architectural innovation of the 19th century, cast iron was cheaper than stone or brick and allowed ornate features to be prefabricated in foundries from molds and used as building facades. Today, New York has the world's largest concentration of full and partial cast-iron facades. The best, built in the 1870s, are in the **SoHo Cast-Iron Historic District**.

The original cast-iron facade of 72–76 Greene Street, SoHo

BEAUX ARTS

This French school of architecture dominated the design of public buildings and wealthy residential properties during New York's gilded age. This era (from 1880 to about 1920) produced many of the city's most prominent architects, including Richard Morris Hunt (**Carnegie Hall**, 1891; **Metropolitan Museum of Art**, 1895), who in 1845 was the first American architect to study in Paris; Cass Gilbert (**Custom House**, 1907; **New York Life Insurance**

ARCHITECTURAL DISGUISES

Some of the most fanciful forms on the New York skyline were devised by clever architects to disguise the city's essential but utilitarian – and rather unattractive – rooftop water tanks. Look skyward to discover the ornate cupolas, spires and domes that transform the most mundane of features into veritable castles in the air. Examples that are easy to spot are atop two neighboring Fifth Avenue hotels: the Sherry Netherland at 60th Street and the Pierre at 61st Street.

Standard water tower

The Dakota Apartments, built in 1884, on the Upper West Side across from Central Park

buildings resembled castles and châteaux, and were built around courtyards not visible from the street. Favorite landmarks are the five **Twin Towers** on Central Park West, the San Remo, Eldorado, Century, the Beresford, and the Majestic. Built during the peak of Art Deco (1929 to 1931), they create the distinctive skyline seen from the park.

Empire State Building (1931) was completed. Both are Art Deco classics, but it was Raymond Hood's **Group Health Insurance Building**, formerly the McGraw-Hill Building, that represented New York in 1932 in the *International Style* architectural survey.

The World Trade Center *(see p72)* was New York's tallest building until September 2001 *(see p54)*. It represented the "glass box" Modernist style, now superseded by the Post-Modern style, such as the **Citigroup Center** (1977).

Building, 1928; the **US Courthouse**, 1936); the teams of Warren & Wetmore (**Grand Central Terminal**, 1913; **Helmsley Building**, 1929); Carrère & Hastings (**New York Public Library**, 1911; **Frick Mansion**, 1914); and McKim, Mead & White, the city's most famous firm of architects (**Villard Houses**, 1884; **United States General Post Office**, 1913; **Municipal Building**, 1914).

APARTMENT BUILDINGS

As the city's population grew and space became ever more precious, family homes in Manhattan became much too expensive for most New Yorkers, and even the wealthy joined the trend toward communal living. In 1884 Henry Hardenbergh's Dakota *(see p218)*, one of the first luxury apartment buildings, started a spate of turn-of-the-century construction on the Upper West Side. Many of the

SKYSCRAPERS

Although Chicago gave birth to the skyscraper, New York has seen some of the greatest innovations. In 1902 Daniel Burnham, a Chicago architect, built the **Flatiron Building**, so tall at 300 ft (91 m) that skeptics said it would collapse. By 1913, the **Woolworth Building** had risen to 792 ft (241 m). Soon, zoning laws were passed requiring "setbacks" – upper stories were stepped back to allow light to reach street level. This suited the Art Deco style. The **Chrysler Building** (1930) was the world's tallest until the

Art Deco arched pattern on the spire of the Chrysler Building

245 Fifth Avenue (Apartment Building)

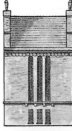

60 Gramercy Park North (Brownstone)

The Pierre (Beaux Arts)

Sherry Netherland Hotel (Beaux Arts)

Multicultural New York

Wherever you go in New York, even in pockets
of the hectic high-rise city center, you will find
evidence of the richly ethnic flavor of the city.
A bus ride can take you from Madras to Moscow,
Hong Kong to Haiti. Immigrants are still coming to
New York, though numbers are fewer than in the
peak years from 1880 to 1910, when 17 million
people arrived. In the 1980s, a million newcomers,
largely from Caribbean countries and Asia, arrived
and found their own special corner of the city.
Throughout the year you will encounter crowds
celebrating one of many festivals. To
find out more about national
celebrations and parades,
see pages 50 to 53.

Hell's Kitchen
*For a while called "Clinton"
to reflect a new neighborhood
mix, this was the first home
of early Irish immigrants.*

Little Ukraine
*Services are held at T.
Shevchenko Place as
part of the May 17
festivities to mark the
Ukrainians' conversion
to Christianity.*

Little Korea
*Not far from Herald
Square is a small Korean
enclave with a variety
of restaurants.*

Little Italy
*For ten days in September, the Italian
community gathers around the
Mulberry Street area, and the streets
are taken over by the celebrations of the
Festa di San Gennaro.*

Chinatown
*Every year,
in January
or February,
Mott Street
is packed
as residents
celebrate the
Chinese
New Year.*

*Theater
District*

*Chelsea
and the
Garment
District*

*Gramercy
and the
Flatiron
District*

*Greenwich
Village*

*SoHo and
TriBeCa*

East Village

*Seaport
and the
Civic
Center*

*Lower
Manhattan*

*Lower East
Side*

The Lower East Side
*The synagogues around
Rivington and Eldridge
streets reflect the
religious traditions of
this old Jewish area.*

0 kilometers   2

0 miles   1

Harlem
The Sunday morning gospel service at the Abyssinian Baptist Church is one of Harlem's finest.

El Barrio
The vibrant Hispanic community of Harlem's El Barrio district is centered around the street market, La Marquetta.

Yorkville
Only a few cafés and bierkellers remain to keep the flavor of this former uptown German district. The Steuben Day Parade is still held here each September.

Little India
The restaurants of East 6th Street offer Eastern atmosphere at affordable prices.

Upper East Side
The magnificent St. Nicholas Russian Orthodox Cathedral on East 97th Street is a reminder of the dispersed White Russian community. Mass is held in Russian each Sunday.

Exploring New York's Many Cultures

Stained glass at the Cotton Club

Even "native" New Yorkers have ancestral roots in other countries. Throughout the 17th century, the Dutch and English settled here, establishing trade colonies in the New World. Soon America became a symbol of hope for the downtrodden elsewhere in Europe. Many flocked across the ocean, some penniless and with little knowledge of the language. The potato famine of the 1840s led to the first wave of Irish immigrants, followed by German and other European workers displaced by political unrest and the Industrial Revolution. Immigrants continue to enrich New York in countless ways, and today an estimated 100 languages are spoken.

Turkish immigrants arriving at former Idlewild Airport in 1963

THE JEWS

There has been a Jewish community in New York since 1654. The city's first synagogue, Shearith Israel, was established by refugees from a Dutch colony in Brazil and is still active today. These first settlers, Sephardic Jews of Spanish descent, included such prominent families as the Baruchs. They were followed by the German Jews, who set up successful retailing enterprises, like the Straus brothers at Macy's. Russian persecution led to the mass immigration that began in the late 1800s. By the start of World War I, 600,000 Jews were living on the Lower East Side. Today, this area is more Hispanic and Asian than Jewish, but it holds reminders of its role as a place of refuge and new beginnings.

THE GERMANS

The Germans began to settle in New York in the 18th century. From John Peter Zenger onward *(see p21)*, the city's German community has championed the freedom to express ideas and opinions. It has also produced giants of industry, such as John Jacob Astor, the city's first millionaire.

THE ITALIANS

Italians first came to New York in the 1830s and 1840s. Many came from northern Italy to escape the failing revolution at home. In the 1870s, poverty in southern Italy drove many more Italians across the ocean. In time, Italians became a potent political force in the city, exemplified by Fiorello La Guardia, one of New York's finest mayors.

THE CHINESE

The Chinese were late arrivals to New York. In 1880, the population of the Mott Street district was a mere 700. By

Eastern States Buddhist Temple, in central Chinatown *(see pp96–7)*

the 1940s, they were the city's fastest-growing and most upwardly mobile ethnic group, extending the old boundaries of Chinatown and establishing new neighborhoods in parts of Brooklyn and Queens. Once a closed community, Chinatown now bustles with tourists exploring the streets and markets, and sampling the creative cuisine.

THE HISPANIC AMERICANS

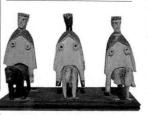

Hispanic religious carving at El Museo del Barrio *(see p231)*

Puerto Ricans were in New York as early as 1838, but it was not until after World War II that they arrived in large numbers in search of work. Most live in El Barrio, formerly known as Spanish Harlem. Professionals who fled Fidel Castro's Cuba have moved out of the city itself but are still influential in Hispanic commerce and culture. Parts of Washington Heights have large Dominican and Colombian communities.

THE IRISH

The Irish, who first arrived in New York in the 1840s, had to overcome harsh odds. Starving and with barely a penny to their names, they labored hard to escape the slums of Five Points and Hell's Kitchen, helping to build the modern city in the process. Many joined the police and fire-fighting forces, rising to high rank through dedication to duty. Others set up successful businesses, such as the Irish bars that act as a focus for the now-scattered New York Irish community.

THE AFRICAN AMERICANS

Perhaps the best-known black inner-city community in the Western world, Harlem is noted for the Harlem Renaissance of writing *(see pp30–31)* as much as it is for great entertainment, gospel music and soul food. The move of black African Americans from the South to the North began with emancipation in the 1860s and increased markedly in the 1920s, when Harlem's black population rose from 83,000 to 204,000. Today Harlem is undergoing revitalization in many areas. The African American population has also dispersed throughout the city.

THE MELTING POT

Other New York cultures are not distinctly defined but are still easily found. Ukrainians gather in the East Village, around St. George's Ukrainian Catholic Church on East 7th Street. Little India can be spotted by the restaurants along East 6th Street. Koreans own many of the small grocery stores in Manhattan, but most tend to live in the Flushing area of Queens. The religious diversity of New York can be seen in the Islamic Center on Riverside Drive, the

A woman celebrating at the Greek Independence Day parade

Russian Orthodox Cathedral on East 97th Street *(see p199)*; and the new Islamic Cultural Center on 96th Street – Manhattan's first major mosque.

THE OUTER BOROUGHS

Brooklyn is by far the most international borough of New York. Caribbean newcomers from Jamaica and Haiti are

The New York police, a haven for Irish Americans

one of the fastest-growing immigrant groups. West Indians tend to cluster along Eastern Parkway between Grand Army Plaza and Utica Avenue, the route of the lavish, exotically costumed West Indian Day Parade in September. Recently arrived Russian Jewish immigrants have turned Brighton Beach into "Little Odessa by the Sea," and the Scandinavians and Lebanese have settled in Bay Ridge and the Finns in Sunset Park. Borough Park and Williamsburg are home to Orthodox Jews, and Midwood has an Israeli-Middle East accent. Italians live in the Bensonhurst area. Greenpoint is little Poland, and Atlantic Avenue is home to the largest Arab community in America.

The Irish were among the earliest groups to cross the Harlem River into the Bronx. Japanese executives favor the more exclusive Riverdale area. One of the most distinctive ethnic areas is Astoria, Queens, which has the largest Greek population outside the mother-land. Jackson Heights is home to a large Latin American quarter, including 300,000 Colombians. Indians also favor this area and neighboring Flushing. But it is the Asians who have transformed Flushing, so much so that the local train is popularly known as "The Orient Express."

NEWCOMERS WHO MADE THEIR MARK see also pp48–9.

The dates mark the year these immigrants entered the US via New York.

- **1893** Irving Berlin (Russia), musician
- **1894** Al Jolson (Lithuania), singer
- **1896** Samuel Goldwyn (Poland), movie mogul
- **1902** Joe Hill (Sweden), labor activist
- **1903** Frank Capra (Italy), film director
- **1904** Hyman Rickover (Russia), developer of nuclear submarine
- **1906** "Lucky" Luciano (Italy), gangster (deported 1946)
- **1908** Bob Hope (England), comedian
- **1909** Lee Strasberg (Austria), theater director
- **1912** Claudette Colbert (France), film star
- **1913** Rudolph Valentino (Italy), film star
- **1921** Bela Lugosi (Hungary), star of *Dracula*
- **1923** Isaac Asimov (Russia), scientist and writer
- **1932** George Balanchine (Russia), ballet choreographer
- **1933** Albert Einstein (Germany), scientist
- **1938** von Trapp family (Austria), singers

1890	1895	1900	1905	1910	1915	1920	1925	1930	1935	1940

Remarkable New Yorkers

New York has nourished some of the best creative talents since the beginning of the 20th century. Pop Art began here, and Manhattan is still the world center for modern art. The alternative writers of the 1950s and '60s – known as the Beat Generation – took inspiration from the city's jazz clubs. And as it is the financial capital, many leading world financiers have made New York their home.

Pop artist Andy Warhol

WRITERS

Novelist James Baldwin

Much great American literature was created in New York. *Charlotte Temple, A Tale of Truth,* first published in 1791 by Susanna Rowson (c. 1762–1824), was a tale of seduction in the city and a best-seller for 50 years.

America's first professional author was Charles Brockden Brown (1771–1810), who came to New York in 1791. The novels of Edgar Allan Poe (1809–49), the pioneer of the modern detective story, expanded the thriller genre. Henry James (1843–1916) published *The Bostonians* (1886) and became the master of the psychological novel, and his friend Edith Wharton (1861–1937) became known for her satirical novels about American society.

American literature finally won international recognition with Washington Irving's (1783–1859) satire, *A History of New York* (1809). It earned him $2,000. Irving coined the names "Gotham" for New York and "Knickerbockers" for New Yorkers. He and James Fenimore Cooper (1789–1851), whose books gave birth to the "Western" novel, formed the Knicker-

bocker group of US writers. Greenwich Village has always attracted writers, including Herman Melville (1819–91) whose masterpiece, *Moby Dick* (1851), was very poorly received at first.

Jack Kerouac (1922–69), Allen Ginsberg, and William Burroughs all went to Columbia University and drank at the San Remo Café in Greenwich Village. Dylan Thomas (1914–53) lived at the Chelsea Hotel *(see p139).* Novelist Nathanael West (1902–40) worked in the Gramercy Park Hotel, and Dashiell Hammett (1894–1961) wrote *The Maltese Falcon* while living there. James Baldwin (1924–87), born in Harlem, wrote *Another Country* (1963) on his return to New York from Europe.

ARTISTS

The New York School of Abstract Expressionists founded the first influential American art movement. It was launched by Hans Hofmann (1880–1966) with Franz Kline and Willem de Kooning, whose first job in America was as a house-painter. Adolph Gottlieb, Mark Rothko (1903–70), and Jackson Pollock (1912–56) went on to popularize this style. Pollock, Kline and de Kooning all had their studios on the Lower East Side.

Pop Art began in New York in the 1960s with Roy Lichtenstein and

Andy Warhol (1926–87), who made some of his cult films at 33 Union Square. Keith Haring (1958–90) was a very prolific graffiti artist who gained fame for his Pop Art murals and sculptures.

Robert Mapplethorpe (1946–89) acquired notoriety for his homoerotic photos of men. Jeff Koons was part of the Neo-Pop or Post-Pop movement of the 80s.

The illusionistic murals by Richard Haas enliven many walls throughout the city.

ACTORS

In 1849 the British actor Charles Macready started a riot by saying Americans were vulgar. A mob stormed the Astor Place Opera House, where Macready was playing Macbeth, police opened fire, and 22 rioters were killed.

In 1927 Mae West (1893–1980) spent 10 days in a workhouse on Roosevelt Island and was fined $500 for giving a lewd performance in her Broadway show *Sex.* Marc Blitzstein's radical pro-labor opera *The Cradle Will Rock* produced by Orson Welles (1915–85) and John Houseman (1902–88), was immediately banned and the show had to move to

Vaudeville actress Mae West

another theater. The actors managed to get around the ban by buying tickets and singing their roles from the audience.

The musical has been New York's special contribution to the theater. Florenz Ziegfeld's (1869–1932) *Follies* ran from 1907 to 1931. The opening of *Oklahoma!* on Broadway in 1943 began the age of musicals by the famous duo Richard Rodgers (1902–79) and Oscar Hammerstein, Jr. (1895–1960).

Off Broadway, the Province-town Players at 33 MacDougal Street were the first to produce Eugene O'Neill's (1888–1953) *Beyond the Horizon* (1920). His successor as the major innovative force in US theater was Edward Albee, author of *Who's Afraid of Virginia Woolf?* (1962).

MUSICIANS AND DANCERS

Leonard Bernstein (1918–90) followed a long line of great conductors at the New York Philharmonic, including Bruno Walter (1876–1962), Arturo Toscanini (1867–1957) and Leopold Stokowski (1882–1977). Maria Callas (1923–77) was born in New York but moved to Europe.

Carnegie Hall *(see p148)* has featured Enrico Caruso (1873–1921), Bob Dylan and the Beatles. A record concert attendance was set in 1991 when Paul Simon drew a million people for his free concert in Central Park.

The legendary swinging jazz clubs of the 1930s and 1940s are now gone from 52nd Street. Plaques on "Jazz Walk" outside the CBS building honor such

Josephine Baker

famous performers as Charlie Parker (1920–55) and Josephine Baker (1906–75).

Between 1940 and 1965, New York became a world dance capital, with the establishment of George Balanchine's (1904–83) New York City Ballet and the American Ballet Theater. In 1958, choreographer Alvin Ailey (1931–89) set up the American Dance Theater, and Bob Fosse (1927–87) changed the course of musicals.

INDUSTRIALISTS AND ENTREPRENEURS

Tycoon Cornelius Vanderbilt

The rags-to-riches story is an American dream. Andrew Carnegie (1835–1919), "the steel baron with a heart of gold," started with nothing and died having given away $350 million. His beneficiaries included public libraries and universities throughout America. Many other foundations are the legacies of wealthy philanthropists. Some, like Cornelius Vanderbilt (1794–1877), tried to shake off their rough beginnings by patronizing the arts.

In business, New York's "robber barons" did what they liked with apparent impunity. Financiers Jay Gould (1836–92) and James Fisk (1834–72) beat Vanderbilt in the war for the Erie Railroad by manipulating stock. In September 1869 they caused Wall Street's first "Black Friday" when they tried to corner the gold market, but fled when their fraud was discovered. Gould died a happy billionaire, while Fisk was killed in a fight over a woman.

Modern entrepreneurs include Donald Trump *(see p33)*, owner of Trump Tower, and the late Leona and Harry Helmsley. After Leona passed away in August 2007, the bulk of the Helmsley's $4-billion estate was left to a charitable trust.

ARCHITECTS

Cass Gilbert (1858–1934), who built such Neo-Gothic sky-scrapers as the Woolworth Building of 1913 *(see p91)* was one of the men who literally shaped the city. His caricature can be seen in the lobby, clutching a model of his masterpiece. Stanford White (1853–1906) was as well known for his scandalous private life as for his fine Beaux Arts buildings, such as the Players Club *(p128)*. For most of his life, Frank Lloyd Wright (1867–1959) spurned city architecture. When he was persuaded to leave his mark on the city, it was in the form of the Guggenheim Museum *(pp188–9)*. German-born Ludwig Mies van der Rohe (1886–1969), who built the Seagram Building *(p177)*, did not believe in "inventing a new architecture every Monday morning," although some might argue that this is just what New York has always done best.

Musical producer Florenz Ziegfeld

NEW YORK THROUGH THE YEAR

Springtime in New York sees Park Avenue filled with blooms, while Fifth Avenue goes green for St. Patrick's Day, the first of the year's many big parades. Summer in the city is hot and humid, but it is worth forsaking an air-conditioned interior to step outside, where parks and squares are the setting for free open-air music and theater. The first Monday in September marks Labor Day and the advent of the orange-red colors of autumn. Then, as Christmas nears, the shops and streets begin to sparkle with dazzling window displays.

Dates of the events on the following pages may vary. For details, consult the listings magazines *(see p377)*. NYC & Co., part of the New York Convention and Visitors Bureau *(see p371)*, issues a useful quarterly free calendar of events.

SPRING

Every season in New York brings its own tempo and temptations. In spring, the city shakes off the winter with tulips and cherry blossoms in the parks and spring fashions in the stores. Everyone window shops and gallery hops. The hugely popular St. Patrick's Day Parade draws the crowds, and thousands don their finery for the Easter Parade down Fifth Avenue.

Inventive Easter bonnets in New York's Easter Parade

MARCH

St. Patrick's Day Parade
(Mar 17), Fifth Ave, from 44th to 86th St. Green clothes, beer and flowers, plus bagpipes.
Greek Independence Day Parade *(Mar 25)*, Fifth Ave, from 49th to 59th St. Greek dancing and food.
New York City Opera Spring Season *(Mar–Apr)*, Lincoln Center *(p350)*.
Ringling Bros and Barnum & Bailey Circus *(Mar–Apr)*, Madison Square Garden *(p135)*.

Yellow tulips and cabs shine on Park Avenue

EASTER

Easter Flower Show *(week before Easter)*, Macy's department store *(pp134–5)*.
Easter Parade *(Easter Sun)*, Fifth Ave, from 44th to 59th St. Paraders in costumes and outrageous millinery gather around St. Patrick's Cathedral.

APRIL

Cherry Blossom Festival *(late Mar–Apr)*, Brooklyn Botanic Garden. Famous for Japanese cherry trees and beautifully laid out ornamental gardens.
Annual Earth Day Festival Activities *(varies)*.
Baseball *(Apr–May)*, Major league season starts for Yankees and Mets *(p360)*.
New York City Ballet Spring Season *(Apr–Jun)*, New York State Theater and Metropolitan Opera House in Lincoln Center *(p214)*.

MAY

Five Boro Bike Tour *(early May)*, a 42-mile (68-km) ride ending with a festival with live music, food and exhibitions.
Cuban Day Parade *(first Sun)*, a carnival on Sixth Ave, between 44th St and Central Park South.

Parading in national costume on Greek Independence Day

International Food Festival and Street Fair *(mid-May)*, from W 37th to W 57th St. Ethnic foods, music, and dance.
Washington Square Outdoor Art Exhibit *(usually last two weekends May; also Sep)*.
Memorial Day Activities *(last weekend)* A parade down Fifth Ave, festivities at South Street Seaport.

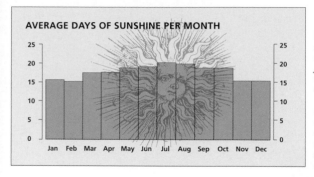

AVERAGE DAYS OF SUNSHINE PER MONTH

Jan Feb Mar Apr May Jun Jul Aug Sep Oct Nov Dec

Days of Sunshine
New York enjoys long hours of summer sun from June to August, with July the month of greatest sunshine. The winter days are much shorter, but many are clear and bright. Autumn has more sunshine than spring, although both are sunny.

SUMMER

New Yorkers escape the hot city streets when possible, for picnics, boat rides, and the beaches. Macy's fireworks light up the Fourth of July skies, and more sparks fly when the New York Yankees and Mets baseball teams are in town. Summer also brings street fairs, outdoor concerts, and free Shakespeare and opera in Central Park.

Policeman dancing in the Puerto Rican Day Parade

JUNE

Puerto Rican Day Parade *(early Jun)*, Fifth Ave, from 44th to 86th St. Floats and marching bands.
Museum Mile Festival *(second Tue)*, Fifth Ave, from 82nd to 105th St. Free entry to museums.
Central Park Summerstage *(Jun–Aug)*, Central Park. Music and dance of every variety, almost daily, rain or shine.
Metropolitan Opera Parks Concerts. Free evening concerts in parks throughout the city *(pp350–51)*.
Shakespeare in the Park *(Jun–Sep)*. Star actors take on the Bard at Delacorte Theater, Central Park *(p347)*.

Lesbian and Gay Pride Day Parade *(Jun)*, from Columbus Circle along Fifth Ave to Washington Sq *(p115)*.
JVC Jazz Festival *(mid–late Jun)*. Top jazz musicians perform in various halls in the city *(p353)*.

JULY

Macy's Firework Display *(Jul 4)*, usually the East River. This is the undisputed high point of the city's Independence Day celebrations, featuring the best fireworks in town.
American Crafts Festival *(mid-Jun–early Jul)*, Lincoln Center *(p214)*. Displays of high-quality crafts.
Mostly Mozart Festival *(end Jul–end Aug)*, Avery Fisher Hall, Lincoln Center *(pp350–51)*.
NY Philharmonic Parks Concerts *(late Jul–early Aug)*. Free concerts in parks throughout the city *(p351)*.

Festivities at a summer street fair in Greenwich Village

Lincoln Center Festival *(Jul)*, Dance, opera, and other performing arts from around the world.

AUGUST

Harlem Week *(mid-Aug)*. Films, art, music, dance, fashion, sports, and tours.
Out-of-Doors Festival *(Aug)*, Lincoln Center. Free dance and theater performances *(p346)*.
US Open Tennis Championships *(late Aug–early Sep)*, Flushing Meadows *(p360)*.

Crowds of spectators flock to the US Open Tennis Championships

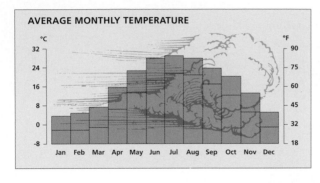

AVERAGE MONTHLY TEMPERATURE

°C / °F chart with months Jan Feb Mar Apr May Jun Jul Aug Sep Oct Nov Dec

Temperature
The chart shows the average minimum and maximum temperatures for each month in New York. With top temperatures averaging 84° F (29° C), the city can become hot and humid. In contrast, the months of winter, although rarely below freezing, can seem bitterly cold.

AUTUMN

Labor Day marks the end of the summer. The Giants and the Jets kick off the football season, the Broadway season begins and the Festa di San Gennaro in Little Italy is the high point in a succession of colorful neighborhood fairs. Macy's Thanksgiving Day Parade is the nation's symbol that the holiday season has arrived.

SEPTEMBER

Richmond County Fair
(Labor Day weekend), in the grounds of Historic Richmond Town *(p254)*. New York's only authentic county fair.
West Indian Carnival
(Labor Day weekend), Brooklyn. Parade, floats, music, dancing, and food.
Brazilian Festival
(early Sep), E 46th St, between Times Sq and Madison Ave.

Exotic Caribbean carnival costume in the streets of Brooklyn

Brazilian music, food, and crafts.
New York is Book Country *(mid–late Sep)*, Fifth Ave, from 48th to 59th Sts. Book fair.
Festa di San Gennaro *(third week)*, Little Italy *(p96)*. Ten days of festivities and processions.
New York Film Festival *(mid-Sep–early Oct)*, Lincoln Center *(p214)*. American films and international art films.
Von Steuben Day Parade *(third week)*, Upper Fifth Ave. German-American celebrations.
American Football *(season begins)*, Giants Stadium, home to the Giants and the Jets *(pp360–61)*.

OCTOBER

Columbus Day Parade *(2nd Mon)*, Fifth Ave, from 44th to 86th Sts. Parades and music to celebrate Columbus's first sighting of America.
Pulaski Day Parade *(Sun closest to Oct 5)*, Fifth Ave, from 26th to 52nd Sts. Celebrations for Polish-American hero Casimir Pulaski.
Halloween Parade *(Oct 31)*, Sixth Avenue, Greenwich Village. Brilliant event with fantastic costumes.
Big Apple Circus *(Oct–Jan)*, Damrosch Park, Lincoln Center. Special themes are presented each year *(p365)*.
Basketball *(season begins)*, Madison Square Garden. Local team is the Knicks *(pp360–61)*.
New York City Marathon *(early Nov)*. From Staten Island through all the city boroughs.

Huge Superman balloon floating above Macy's Thanksgiving Day Parade

NOVEMBER

Macy's Thanksgiving Day Parade *(fourth Thu)*, from Central Park West and W 79th St to Broadway and W 34th St. A joy for children, with floats, huge balloons, and Santa.
Rockefeller Center Ice Skating Rink *(Oct–Mar)*, Open to the public. You can skate beneath the famous Christmas Tree.
Christmas Spectacular *(Nov–Dec)*, Radio City Music Hall. Variety show, with the Rockettes.

Revelers in Greenwich Village's Halloween Parade

AVERAGE MONTHLY RAINFALL

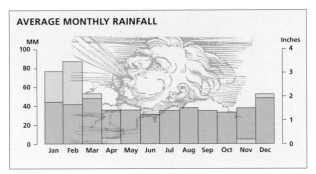

MM
100
80
60
40
20
0

Inches
4
3
2
1
0

Jan Feb Mar Apr May Jun Jul Aug Sep Oct Nov Dec

Rainfall
March and August are the months of heaviest rainfall in New York. Rainfall in spring is usually unpredictable, so be prepared. Sudden heavy snowfalls in winter can cause chaos in the city.

☐ Rainfall

☐ Snowfall

WINTER

New York is a magical place at Christmas – even the stone lions at the Public Library don wreaths for the occasion, and shops become works of art. From Times Square to Chinatown, New Year celebrations punctuate the season, and Central Park becomes a winter sports arena.

Statue of Alice in Wonderland in Central Park

DECEMBER

Tree-Lighting Ceremony *(early Dec),* Rockefeller Center *(p144).* Lighting of the giant Christmas tree in front of the RCA Building.
Messiah Sing-In *(mid-Dec),* Lincoln Center *(p214).* The audience rehearses and performs under the guidance of various conductors.
Hanukkah Menorah *(mid–late Dec),* Grand Army Plaza, Brooklyn. Lighting of the huge menorah (candelabra) every night during the eight-day Festival of Lights.
New Year's Eve. Fireworks display in Central Park *(pp206–7);* festivities in Times Square *(p147);* 5-mile (8-km) run in Central Park; poetry reading in St. Mark's Church.

JANUARY

National Boat Show *(Jan),* Jacob K. Javits Convention Center *(p138).*
Chinese New Year *(late Jan/Feb),* Chinatown *(pp96–7).* Dragons, fireworks, and food.
Winter Antiques Show *(Jan),* Seventh Regiment Armory *(p187).* NYC's most prestigious antiques fair.

Chinese New Year celebrations in Chinatown

FEBRUARY

Black History Month. African-American events take place throughout the city.
Empire State Building Run-Up *(early Feb).* Runners race to the 102nd floor *(pp136–7).*
Lincoln and Washington Birthday Sales *(Feb 12–22)* Big department stores sales throughout the city.
Westminster Kennel Club Dog Show *(mid-Feb),* Madison Square Garden *(p135).* Major dog show.

PUBLIC HOLIDAYS

New Year's Day (Jan 1)
Martin Luther King Jr. Day (3rd Mon, Jan)
President's Day (mid-Feb)
Memorial Day (end May)
Independence Day (Jul 4)
Labor Day (1st Mon, Sep)
Columbus Day (2nd Mon, Oct)
Election Day (1st Tue, Nov)
Veterans Day (Nov 11)
Thanksgiving Day (4th Thu, Nov)
Christmas Day (Dec 25)

The giant Christmas tree and decorations at Rockefeller Center

The Southern Tip of Manhattan

This view of Lower Manhattan, seen from the Hudson River, encompasses some of the most striking modern additions to the city skyline, such as the distinctively topped quartet of the World Financial Center. You will also catch glimpses of earlier Manhattan: Castle Clinton set against the green space of Battery Park and, behind it, the Custom House building. From 1973 until September 2001 the area also boasted the World Trade Center. Its landmark towers were destroyed in a terrorist attack on the city. The 1 World Trade Center building (formerly known as Freedom Tower), on the northwest corner of the WTC site, is due for completion in late 2013.

LOCATOR MAP

▪ *The Southern Tip*

WORLD TRADE CENTER REDEVELOPMENT SITE

On September 11, 2001, two planes bound for Los Angeles were hijacked and targeted at the World Trade Center. Hundreds of people died in the impact, but thousands more were killed when the twin towers collapsed. Two other planes were also hijacked that morning; the first struck the Pentagon, while the second came to ground near Pittsburgh. The death toll exceeded the number of troops killed in the Revolutionary War *(see pp22–3)*, and comparisons were made with the bombing of Pearl Harbor. Images of the destruction were seen across the world, drawing support for a "war against terrorism." Currently being constructed on the site is 1 World Trade Center (formerly called Freedom Tower). At 1,776 ft (541 m), its proposed height in feet refers to the year of the Declaration of Independence.

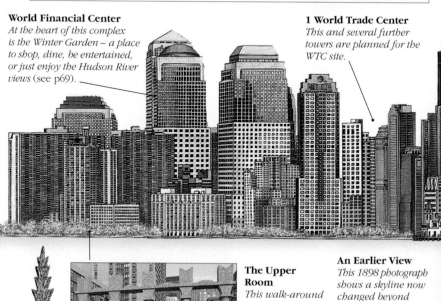

World Financial Center
At the heart of this complex is the Winter Garden – a place to shop, dine, be entertained, or just enjoy the Hudson River views (see p69).

1 World Trade Center
This and several further towers are planned for the WTC site.

The Upper Room
This walk-around sculpture by Ned Smyth is one of many works of art in Battery Park City (see p72).

An Earlier View
This 1898 photograph shows a skyline now changed beyond recognition.

Detail from The *Upper Room*

Skyscraper Museum

Located at the southern tip of Battery Park City, the Skyscraper Museum celebrates and explores New York's rich architectural heritage.

US Custom House

This magnificent 1907 Beaux Arts building now houses the Museum of the American Indian (see p73).

East Coast War Memorial

In Battery Park, a huge bronze eagle by Albino Manca honors the dead of World War II.

26 Broadway

The tower of the former Standard Oil Building resembles an oil lamp. The interior is still decorated with company symbols.

Bank of New York

17 State Street

26 Broadway

1 Liberty Plaza

Liberty View

Castle Clinton

US Custom House

American Merchant Mariners' Memorial (1991)

This sculpture by Marisol is on Pier A, the last of Manhattan's old piers. The pier also has a clock tower that chimes the hours on ships' bells.

Shrine of Mother Seton

The first US-born saint lived here (see p76).

Lower Manhattan from the East River

At first sight, this stretch of East River shoreline, running up from the tip of Manhattan Island, is a seamless array of 20th-century office buildings. But from sea level, streets and slips are still visible, offering glimpses of old New York and the Financial District to the west. On the skyline itself, a few of the district's early skyscrapers still proudly display their ornate crowns above their more anonymous modern counterparts.

LOCATOR MAP

■ East River View

India House
The handsome brownstone at One Hanover Square is one of the finest of its kind.

Vietnam Veterans' Plaza
An engraved green-glass memorial dominates the former Coenties Slip, a wharf filled in to make a park in the late 19th century (see p76).

Hanover Square
A statue of one of the Dutch mayors, Abraham De Peyster, sits near the house where he was born in 1657.

One New York Plaza

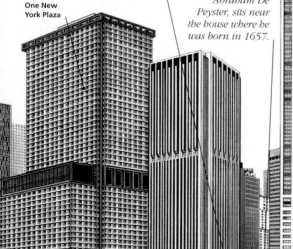

55 Water Street

Barclay's Bank Building

Downtown Heliport
Air-Sea Rescue and sightseeing flights operate from here.

Battery Maritime Building
This historic ferry terminal serves only Governors Island (see p77).

Delmonico's
This upscale steakhouse draws many carnivores.

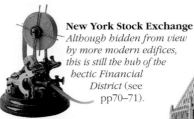

New York Stock Exchange
Although hidden from view by more modern edifices, this is still the hub of the hectic Financial District (see pp70–71).

40 Wall Street
In the 1940s, the pyramid-topped tower of the former Bank of Manhattan was hit by a light aircraft.

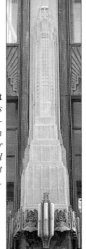

70 Pine Street
Replicas of this elegant Gothic-style tower can be seen near the Pine and Cedar Street entrances.

Bank of New York
This serene 1928 interior is part of the bank set up in 1784 by Alexander Hamilton (see p23).

Morgan Bank
Columns from lobby to rooftop are the theme of this striking modern building.

1 Financial Square

New York Stock Exchange

Chase Manhattan Bank Tower

120 Wall Street

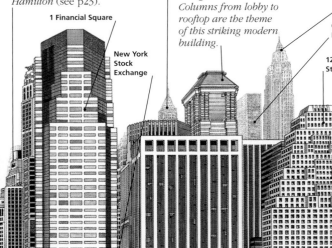

100 Old Slip
Now in the shadow of One Financial Square, the small palazzo-style First Precinct Police Department was the city's most modern police station when it was built in 1911.

Citibank Building

Carved medallion, 100 Old Slip

Queen Elizabeth Monument
The ocean liner that sank in 1972 is remembered here.

South Street Seaport

As the Financial District ends, the skyline, as seen from the East River or Brooklyn, changes dramatically. The corporate head-quarters are replaced by the piers, low-rise streets and warehouses of the old seaport area, now restored as the South Street Seaport *(see pp82–3)*. The Civic Center lies not far inland, and a few of its monu-mental buildings can be seen. The Brooklyn Bridge marks the end of this stretch of skyline. Between here and midtown, apartment blocks make up the majority of riverside features.

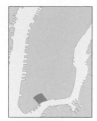

LOCATOR MAP

South Street Area

Stonework on the Woolworth Building

Pier 17
A focal point of the Seaport, this traditional-style leisure pier is packed with shops, vendors, and restaurants.

Woolworth Building
The handsomely decorated spire marks the headquarters of F.W. Woolworth's empire. It is still the finest "cathedral of commerce" ever built (see p91).

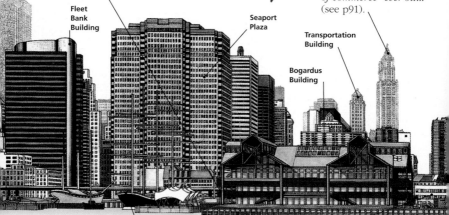

Fleet Bank Building

Seaport Plaza

Transportation Building

Bogardus Building

Maritime Crafts Center
At Pier 15, craftspeople demonstrate traditional seafaring skills such as woodcarving and model-making.

Titanic Memorial
The lighthouse on Fulton Street commemorates the sinking of the Titanic, the largest steam ship ever built.

Police Plaza

Five in One (1971–4), in Police Plaza, is a sculpture by Bernard Rosenthal. It represents the five boroughs of New York.

United States Courthouse

The Civic Center is marked on the skyline by the golden pyramid of architect Cass Gilbert's courthouse (see p85).

Municipal Building

Among the offices of this vast building is the Marriage Chapel, where weddings "at City Hall" actually take place. The copper statue on the skyline is Civic Fame by Adolph Weinman (see p85).

Surrogate's Court and Hall of Records

Archives dating back to 1664 are stored and displayed here (see p85).

Verizon Telephone Company

Police Plaza

Pace University

Southbridge Towers

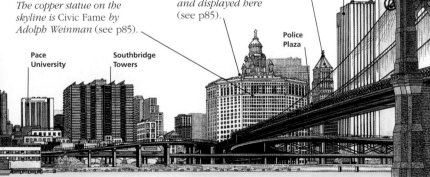

Con Edison Mural

In 1975, artist Richard Haas re-created the Brooklyn Bridge on the side wall of a former electrical substation.

Brooklyn Bridge

Views of, and from, the bridge have made it one of New York's best-loved landmarks (see pp86–9).

Midtown Manhattan

The skyline of Midtown Manhattan is graced with some of the city's most spectacular towers and spires – from the familiar beauty of the Empire State Building's Art Deco pinnacle to the dramatic wedge shape of Citicorp's modern headquarters. As the shoreline progresses uptown, so the architecture becomes more varied; the United Nations complex dominates a long stretch, and then Beekman Place begins a strand of exclusive residential enclaves that offer the rich and famous some seclusion in this busy part of the city.

LOCATOR MAP

■ *Midtown*

Chrysler Building
Glinting in the sun by day or lit up by night, this stainless-steel spire is, for many, the ultimate New York skyscraper (see p155).

Grand Central Terminal
Now dwarfed by its neighbors, this landmark building is full of period details, such as this fine clock (see pp156–7).

Empire State Building
At 1,250 ft (381 m), this was the tallest building in the world for many years (see pp136–7).

MetLife Building

The Highpoint

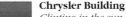

Tudor City
Built in the 1920s, this complex is mock Tudor on a grand scale, with over 3,000 apartments (see p158).

United Nations
Works of art from member countries include this Barbara Hepworth sculpture, a gift from Britain (see pp160–63).

1 and 2 UN Plaza
Angular glass towers house offices and the UN Millennium Plaza Hotel (see p158).

General Electric Building
Built of brick in 1931, this Art Deco building has a tall spiked crown that resembles radio waves. (see p176).

Waldorf–Astoria
The splendid interior of one of the city's finest hotels lies beneath twin copper-capped towers (see p177).

Citigroup Center
St. Peter's Church nestles in one corner of the Citigroup Center, with its raked tower (see p177).

Rockefeller Center
The outdoor skating rink and walkways of this complex of office buildings, shops, and eateries are a great place to people watch (see p144).

The Nail, by Arnaldo Pomodoro, St. Peter's Church, Citicorp Center

General Electric Building

100 UN Plaza

866 UN Plaza

Trump World Tower

St. Mary's Garden
The garden at Holy Family Church is a peaceful haven.

Japan Society
Japanese culture, from avant-garde plays to ancient art, can be seen here (see pp158–9).

Beekman Tower
Now an all-suite hotel, this Art Deco tower was built in 1928 as a hotel for women who were members of US college sororities.

NEW YORK
AREA BY AREA

LOWER MANHATTAN

The old and the new converge at Lower Manhattan, where Colonial churches and early American monuments stand in the shadow of skyscrapers. New York was born here, and this was the site of the nation's first capitol. Commerce has also flourished here since 1626, when Dutchman Peter Minuit purchased the

Minuit memorial on Bowling Green

island of Man-a-hatt-ta from the Algonquian Indians for goods valued at $24 *(see p19)*. A number of buildings are currently under development on the site of the World Trade Center *(see p54)*, including Freedom Tower. Upon completion, this will soar to 1,176 feet high. Visitors are advised to call all sights in the area to check opening times.

Trinity Church at the foot of Wall Street

SIGHTS AT A GLANCE

Historic Buildings and Important Sites
Battery Maritime Building 16
Federal Hall 2
Federal Reserve Bank 1
Fraunces Tavern Museum 13
New York Stock Exchange pp70–71 3
World Trade Center Site 6

Museums and Galleries
Castle Clinton National Monument 20
Ellis Island pp78–9 18
Museum of Jewish Heritage 21
Skyscraper Museum 8
US Custom House 11

Monuments and Statues
Charging Bull 9
Statue of Liberty pp74–5 17

Parks and Squares
Battery Park 19
Bowling Green 10
Vietnam Veterans' Plaza 14

Boat Trips
Staten Island Ferry 15

Churches
Saint Elizabeth Ann Seton Shrine 12
Trinity Church 4

Modern Architecture
Battery Park City 7
World Financial Center 5

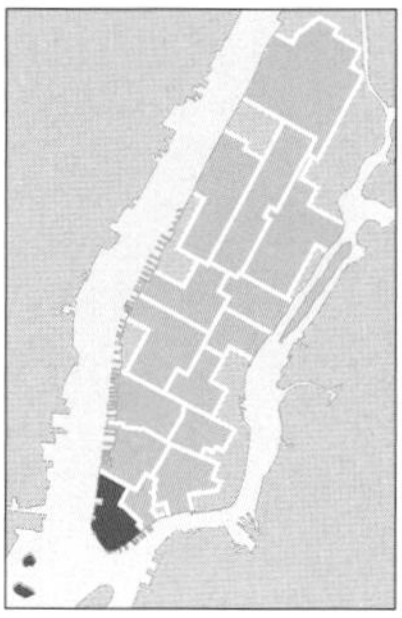

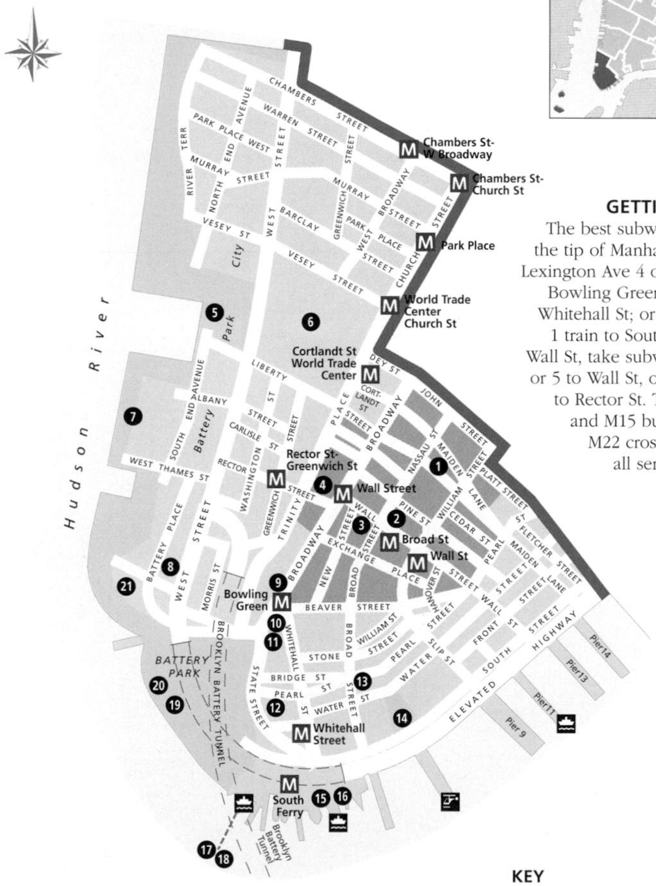

GETTING THERE

The best subway routes to the tip of Manhattan are the Lexington Ave 4 or 5 trains to Bowling Green; R or W to Whitehall St; or the 7th Ave 1 train to South Ferry. For Wall St, take subways 2, 3, 4, or 5 to Wall St, or 1, R, or W to Rector St. The M1, M6, and M15 buses and the M22 crosstown route all serve the area.

SEE ALSO

- ***Street Finder,*** maps 1, 2
- ***Where to Stay*** p280
- ***Restaurants*** p296

0 meters 500

0 yards 500

KEY

- Street-by-Street map
- [M] Subway station
- ⛴ Ferry boarding point
- 🚁 Heliport

Street by Street: Wall Street

No intersection has been of greater importance to the city, past or present, than the corners of Wall and Broad streets. Three important sites are located here. Federal Hall National Monument marks the place where, in 1789, George Washington was sworn in as president. Trinity Church is one of the nation's oldest Anglican parishes. The New York Stock Exchange, founded in 1817, is to this day a financial nerve center whose ups and downs cause tremors around the globe. The surrounding buildings are the very heart of New York's famous financial district.

The Marine Midland Bank rises straight up 55 stories. This dark, glass tower occupies only 40% of its site. The other 60% is a plaza in which a large red sculpture by Isamu Noguchi, *Cube*, balances on one of its points.

Trinity Building, an early 20th-century Gothic skyscraper, was designed to complement nearby Trinity Church.

The Equitable Building (1915) deprived its neighbors of light, prompting a change in the law: skyscrapers had to be set back from the street.

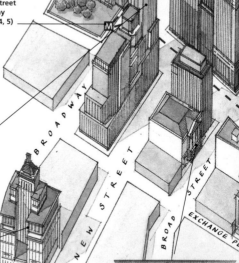

★ **Trinity Church**
Built in 1846 in a Gothic style, this is the third church on this site. Once the tallest structure in the city, the bell tower is now dwarfed by the skyscrapers that surround it. Many famous early New Yorkers are buried in the churchyard ❹

Wall Street subway (lines 4, 5)

The Irving Trust Company, built in 1932, has an outer wall patterned to look like fabric. In the lobby is an Art Deco mosaic in shades of flame and gold.

26 Broadway was built as the home of the Standard Oil Trust. An oil lamp rests on top of it.

New York Stock Exchange ★
The hub of the world's financial markets is housed in a 17-story building constructed in 1903 ❸

The Liberty Tower
is clad in white
terracotta and is in
the Gothic style.
It was later
turned into
apartments.

**The Chamber
of Commerce**
is a fine Beaux
Arts building
of 1901.

STAR SIGHTS

★ Federal Hall

★ Federal Reserve
Bank

★ New York
Stock Exchange

★ Trinity Church

LOCATOR MAP
See Manhattan Map pp14–15

KEY

– – – Suggested route

| 0 meters | 100 |
| 0 yards | 100 |

**Chase Manhattan Bank and
Plaza** has the famous Jean
Dubuffet sculpture, *Four
Trees*, located in the plaza.

**★ Federal
Reserve Bank**
*In the style of
a Renaissance
palace, this
is a bank for
banks. US
currency is
issued here* ❶

Louise Nevelson Plaza
is a park containing Nevelson's
sculpture *Shadows and Flags.*

WALL ST

Wall Street is named for the wall that
kept enemies and warring Indians out
of Manhattan – the street is now the
heart of the city's business center.

**Wall Street in
the 1920s**

★ Federal Hall
*Built as the US Custom
House in 1842, this
classical building, refurbished in 2006, usually
houses an exhibit about
the Constitution* ❷

Federal Reserve Bank ❶

33 Liberty St. **Map** 1 C2. **Tel** (212) 720-6130. Ⓜ Fulton St–Broadway Nassau. ◯ 8:30am–5pm Mon–Fri. ⬤ public hols. 🚫 ♿ 🎫 free (reservations required). **www**.newyorkfed.org

Entrance to Federal Reserve Bank

This is a government bank *for* banks – it is one of the 12 Federal Reserve banks, and therefore issues US currency. You can identify bank notes originating from this branch by the letter B in the Federal Reserve seal on each note.

Five stories below ground is one of the largest storehouses for international gold. Each nation's hoard is stored in its own compartment within the subterranean vault, guarded by 90-ton doors. Payments between nations used to be made by physical transfers of gold. An exhibition of "The History of Money," with 800

items, runs from 10am to 4pm. Designed by York & Sawyer in the Italian Renaissance style, the 1924 building occupies a full block and is adorned with fine wrought-iron grillwork.

Federal Hall ❷

26 Wall St. **Map** 1 C3. **Tel** (212) 825-6888. Ⓜ Wall St. ◯ 9am–5pm Mon–Fri. ⬤ public hols. 📷 ♿ 🎫 10am, 1pm, 3pm. 🖥 www.nps.gov/feha

A bronze statue of George Washington on the steps of Federal Hall marks the site where the nation's first president took his oath of office in 1789. Thousands of New Yorkers jammed Wall and Broad Streets for the occasion. They roared their approval when the Chancellor of the State of New York shouted, "Long live George Washington, President of the United States."

The present structure, renovated in 2006, was built between 1834 and 1842 as the US Customs House. It is one of the finest Classical designs in the city. Display rooms off the Rotunda include the Bill of Rights Room and an interactive computer exhibit about the Constitution.

New York Stock Exchange ❸

See pp70–71.

Trinity Churchyard

Trinity Church ❹

Broadway at Wall St. **Map** 1 C3. **Tel** (212) 602-0800. Ⓜ Wall St, Rector St. ◯ 7am–6pm Mon–Fri, 8am–4pm Sat, 7am–4pm Sun (church); 7am–4pm (5pm DST) Mon–Fri, 8am–3pm Sat & pub hols, 7am–3pm Sun (churchyard). 🏛 12.05pm Mon–Fri, 9am & 11:15am Sun. 📷 except during services. 🎫 2pm daily; also Sun after 11:15am service. **Concerts** see details online. 🏛 🖥 www.trinitywallstreet.org

This square-towered Episcopal church at the head of Wall Street is the third one on this site. Designed in 1846 by Richard Upjohn, it was among the grandest churches of its day, marking the beginning of the best period of Gothic Revival architecture in America. Richard Morris Hunt's design for the sculpted brass doors was inspired by Lorenzo Ghiberti's *Doors of Paradise* at the Baptistery in Florence.

Restoration has uncovered the original rosy sandstone, long buried beneath layers of city grime. The 280-ft (86-m) steeple, the tallest structure in New York until the 1860s, still commands respect despite its towering neighbors.

Many prominent early New Yorkers are buried in the graveyard: statesman Alexander Hamilton; steamboat inventor Robert Fulton; and William Bradford, founder of New York's first newspaper in 1725.

Marble-columned rotunda within Federal Hall

World Financial Center ❺

West St. **Map** 1 A2. **Tel** (212) 945-2600. Ⓜ A, C and J, M, Z, and 2, 3, 4, 5 to Fulton St, E to WTC Station, R, W to Cortlandt St and 1 to Rector St. 🖼 ♿ 🍴 🖥 🏛 **www**.worldfinancialcenter.com

A model of urban design by Cesar Pelli & Associates, this development is a vital part of the revival of Lower Manhattan, and its damage in the World Trade Center attack was attended to as a matter of urgency. Four office towers soar skyward, housing the headquarters of some of the world's most important financial companies. At the heart of the complex lies the dazzling Winter Garden, a vast glass-and-steel public space (all 2,000 panes of glass had to be replaced), flanked by 45 restaurants and shops, opening onto a lively piazza and marina on the Hudson River. The sweeping marble staircase leading down to the Winter Garden often doubles as seating for free arts and

Main floor of the Winter Garden

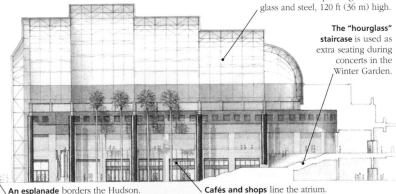

The atrium is a sparkling vault of glass and steel, 120 ft (36 m) high.

The "hourglass" staircase is used as extra seating during concerts in the Winter Garden.

An esplanade borders the Hudson.

Cafés and shops line the atrium.

events, varying from classic to contemporary in music, dance and theater. Sixteen *Washingtonia robusta* palm trees, 40 ft (15 m) high, have been replaced in this contemporary version of the "palm court" of yesteryear.

Inaugurated in 1988, the building has been hailed as the Rockefeller Center of the 21st century.

World Financial Center viewed from the Hudson River

New York Stock Exchange ❸

In 1790, trading in stocks and shares took place haphazardly on or around Wall Street, but in 1792, 24 brokers who traded at 68 Wall Street signed an agreement to deal only with one another: the basis of the New York Stock Exchange (NYSE) was formed. The NYSE has weathered a succession of alternating slumps ("bear markets") and booms ("bull markets"), growing from a local marketplace into a financial center of global importance. Membership is strictly limited. In 1817, a "seat" cost $25; in the "bullish" years of the late 1990s, the prices ran as high as $4 million. In 2006, the NYSE became a for-profit public company, and all the seats were exchanged for cash and stock settlements. Traders now buy one-year licenses.

Ticker-tape Machine
Introduced in the 1870s, these machines printed out up-to-the-minute details of purchase prices on ribbons of paper tape.

Computerized stock tickers
flash a steady stream of prices as fast as the human eye is able to read them.

WHAT A TRADING POST DOES

The 17 trading posts each consist of 22 groups, or "sections," of traders and technology, each trading the stock of up to 10 listed companies. Commission brokers work for brokerage firms, and rush between booth and trading post, buying and selling securities (stocks and bonds) for the public. A specialist trades in just one stock at a time, quoting bids to other brokers, and independent floor brokers handle orders for busy brokerage firms. Clerks process the orders that come into the trading post via SuperDOT computer into the Exchange's Market Data System. The pages help on the busy exchange floor, bringing orders from the booths to the brokers and specialists. Post display units

Trading post

show stock prices, and flat screens show prices and trades for the specialist. As of January 24, 2007, all NYSE stocks can also be traded via an electronic hybrid market.

The 48-Hour Day
During the 1929 Crash, stock exchange clerks worked nonstop for 48 hours. Their mood stayed cheerful despite the panic outside.

VISITORS' CHECKLIST

20 Broad St. **Map** 1 C3. *Tel* (212) 656-3000. M 2, 3, 4, 5 to Wall St, R, W to Rector St. M1, M6, M15. visitors' gallery closed to the public for security reasons. for educational purposes only. Highly restricted. www.nyse.com

Public viewing gallery

Trading post

Trading Floor
On a typical day, some 3.5 billion shares are traded for more than 2,000 listed companies. The advanced electronics that support the Designated Order Turnaround (SuperDOT) computer are carried above the chaos of the trading floor in a web of gold piping.

Great Crash of 1929
On Tuesday, October 29, over 16 million shares changed hands as the stock market crashed. Investors thronged Wall Street in bewilderment but, contrary to popular myth, traders did not leap from windows in panic.

Members' entrance, Wall Street

TIMELINE

1792 Buttonwood Agreement signed on May 17

1844 Invention of the telegraph allows trading nationwide

1867 Ticker-tape machines introduced

1903 Present Stock Exchange building opens

1976 DOT system replaces ticker tape

1981 Trading posts upgraded with electronic units

1987 "Black Monday" crash, October 19. Dow Jones Index drops 508 points

1750	1800	1850	1900	1950	2000	2010

1817 New York Stock & Exchange Board created

Crowds gather outside during the 1929 Crash

1863 Name changed to New York Stock Exchange

1865 New Exchange Building opens at Wall and Broad Streets

1869 "Black Friday" gold crash, September 24

1929 Wall St. Crash, October 29

2001 After 8 years of bull markets, economy falters after September 11

2006 The NYSE merges with Archipelago Holdings to become a for-profit public company

World Trade Center Site ❻

Map 1 B2. Ⓜ *Chambers St, Rector St.* ◯ *Viewing wall on Church St.* **www**.panynj.gov/wtcprogress **www**.renewnyc.org **Tribute WTC Visitor Center** *120 Liberty St.* **Tel** *1-866-737-1184.* ◯ *10am–6pm Mon–Sat (from noon Tue), noon–5pm Sun.* 🎦 📷 **www**.tributewtc.org

Immortalized by film-makers and photographers, the twin towers of the World Trade Center dominated the skyline of Manhattan for 27 years, until September 2001's terrorist attack *(see p54)*. The enormous weight of each building was supported by an inner wire cage, which melted from the heat of the fire caused by the two passenger aircraft that were flown into the towers.

These towers were part of a buildings complex consisting of six office blocks and a hotel, connected by a vast underground concourse lined with shops and restaurants. A bridge linked the complex to the World Financial Center

(see p69), which survived the attack. The World Trade Center was home to some 450 companies with 50,000 employees. Large numbers of visitors used to come to see the views from the observation deck or the rooftop promenade at Two World Trade Center. The elevator took 58 seconds to reach the 107th floor. At One World Trade Center, this speedy ascent could be taken to the Windows on the World restaurant on the 107th floor. One memorable day at the Center was on August 7, 1974, when Philippe Petit stepped onto a tightrope

between the two towers and entertained crowds of office workers for almost an hour with a high-rise balancing act.

Buildings are beginning to reoccupy "Ground Zero". Plans to erect a skyscraper, designed by architect Daniel Libeskind, have been controversial. Several memorials and a museum are also being worked on and are planned to open in 2013.

The Tribute WTC Visitor Center, on the south side of the site, pays homage to the victims, survivors, and rescue efforts of September 11. They also offer walking tours.

Philippe Petit about to step out between the two towers in 1974

Battery Park City ❼

Map 1 A3. Ⓜ *1 to Rector St.* 📷 ♿ 🍴 📱 **www**.batteryparkcity.org

Governor Mario Cuomo set the tone for this project in

Battery Park City esplanade

1983 when he urged the developers, "Give it a social purpose – give it a soul." The ambitious neighborhood is on 92 reclaimed acres (37 ha) along the Hudson River.

The restaurants, apartments, sculptures, and gardens are built on a human scale.

Battery Park City is designed to house more than 25,000 people. The most visible part of it is the World Financial Center *(see p69)* and total costs are estimated at $4 billion.

The 1.2-mile (2-km) walk along the river offers unobstructed views of the Statue of Liberty.

Skyscraper Museum ❽

39 Battery Pl. **Map** 1 A3. **Tel** *(212) 968-1961.* Ⓜ *4, 5 to Bowling Green; 1, R, W to Rector St.* ◯ *noon–6pm Wed–Sun.* 🎦 📱 **www**.skyscraper.org

Adjacent to the Ritz Carlton hotel, this museum celebrates New York's architectural heritage and examines the historical forces and individuals that shaped the

city's skyline. There is a permanent exhibition on the World Trade Center and a digital reconstruction of how Manhattan has changed over time, as well as temporary exhibitions that analyze tall buildings as objects of design, products of technology, sites of construction, real-estate investments, and places of work and residence.

The airy Skyscraper Museum

Arturo Di Modica's iconic bull statue, at the southern end of Broadway

Charging Bull 🟑

Broadway at Bowling Green.
Map 1 C4. Ⓜ *Bowling Green.*

At 1am on December 15, 1989, sculptor Arturo Di Modica and 30 friends unloaded his 7,000-lb (3,200-kg) *Charging Bull* bronze statue in front of the New York Stock Exchange. The group had eight minutes between police patrols to place the sculpture, but they managed to carry out the deed in just five. The bull was later taken away for obstructing traffic and lacking a permit. Due to the large outcry, however, the Parks Department gave it a "temporary" stomping ground on Broadway, just north of Bowling Green, where it remains to this day, the unofficial mascot of Wall Street.

Di Modica created the sculpture after the 1987 stock-market crash, to symbolize the "strength, power, and hope of the American people for the future." It took him two years to complete at a personal cost of $350,000.

Bowling Green 🔟

Map 1 C4. Ⓜ *Bowling Green.*

This triangular plot north of Battery Park was the city's earliest park, used first as a cattle market and later as a bowling ground. A statue of King George III stood here until the signing of the Declaration of Independence,

when, as a symbol of British rule, the statue was hacked to pieces and smelted for ammunition *(see pp22–3)*. The wife of the governor of Connecticut is said to have melted down enough pieces to mold 42,000 bullets.

The fence, erected in 1771, is still standing, but minus the royal crowns that once adorned it. They met the same fate as the statue. The Green was once surrounded by elegant homes. Beyond it is the start of Broadway, which runs the length of Manhattan and, under its formal name of Route 9, all the way north to the State capital in Albany.

Top of a column at the US Custom House

Fountain at Bowling Green

US Custom House 🕚

1 Bowling Green. **Map** 1 C4.
Ⓜ *Bowling Green.* **National Museum of the American Indian.** *Tel (212) 514-3700.*
◯ *10am–5pm daily (to 8pm Thu).*
⬤ *Dec 25.* ♿ 🚻
www.nmai.si.edu

One of New York's finest Beaux Arts designs, this 1907 granite palace by Cass Gilbert is a fitting monument to the city's role as a great seaport, decorated by the best sculptors and artists of the time. Forty-four Ionic columns stand guard, with an ornate frieze. Heroic sculptures by Daniel Chester French depict four continents as seated women: Asia (contemplative), America (facing optimistically forward), Europe (surrounded by symbols of past glories) and Africa (still sleeping).

Inside, murals by Reginald Marsh decorate the fine marble rotunda, showing the progress of ships into the harbor. Opposite the entrance is a portrait of movie star Greta Garbo giving a press conference on board ship. In 1973 the US Customs Service moved out, leaving the building empty but for a small bankruptcy court.

The Custom House took on a different function in 1994, when the George Gustav Heye Center of the **Smithsonian National Museum of the American Indian** was unveiled on three floors of the building. The museum's outstanding collection of about a million artifacts along with an archive of many thousands of photographs, spans the breadth of the native cultures of North, Central and South America.

Exhibitions include works by contemporary Native American artists as well as changing displays drawn from the permanent collection.

Statue of Liberty ⑰

A gift from the French to the American people, the statue was the brainchild of sculptor Frédéric-Auguste Bartholdi and has become a symbol of freedom throughout the world. In Emma Lazarus's poem, which is engraved on the base, Lady Liberty says: "Give me your tired, your poor,/ Your huddled masses yearning to breathe free." Unveiled by President Grover Cleveland on October 28, 1886, the statue was restored in time for its 100th anniversary in 1986. The crown was closed to the public following the events of September 11, but reopened in 2009.

★ Golden Torch
In 1986, a new torch replaced the corroded original. The replica's flame is coated in 24-carat gold leaf.

The crown is the highest level open to visitors.

The frame was designed by Gustave Eiffel, who later built the Eiffel Tower. The copper shell hangs on bars from a central iron pylon.

A central pylon anchors the 200-ton statue to its base.

354 steps lead from the entrance to the crown.

Observation deck

From Her Toes to Her Torch
Three hundred molded copper sheets riveted together make up Lady Liberty.

THE STATUE
With a height of 305 ft (93 m) from ground to torch, the Statue of Liberty dominates New York harbor

★ Statue of Liberty Museum
Posters featuring the statue are among the items on display.

The pedestal is set within the walls of an army fort. It was the largest concrete mass ever poured.

The original torch now stands in the main lobby.

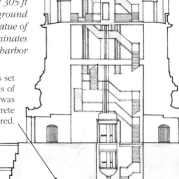

Museum

★ Ferries to Liberty Island
Ferries cross New York Harbor to Liberty Island, where the Statue offers some of the city's finest views.

Portrait of Liberty
Bartholdi's mother was the model for Liberty. The seven rays of her crown represent the seven seas and seven continents.

Making the Hand
To mold the copper shell, the hand was made first in plaster, then wood.

A Model Figure
A series of graduated scale models enabled Bartholdi to build the largest metal statue ever constructed.

FREDERIC-AUGUSTE BARTHOLDI

The French sculptor who designed the Statue of Liberty intended it as a monument to the freedom he found lacking in his own country. He said "I will try to glorify the Republic and Liberty over there, in the hope that someday I will find it again here." Bartholdi devoted 21 years of his life to making the statue a reality, even traveling to America in 1871 to talk President Ulysses S. Grant and others into funding it and installing it in New York's harbor.

STAR FEATURES

★ Ferries to
Liberty Island

★ Golden Torch

★ Statue of Liberty
Museum

Restoration Celebration
On July 3, 1986, after a $100-million restoration, the statue was unveiled. The $2-million fireworks display was the largest ever seen in America.

Saint Elizabeth Ann Seton Shrine ⑫

7 State St. **Map** 1 C4. **Tel** (212) 269-6865. Ⓜ Whitehall, South Ferry. ◯ 6:30am–5pm Mon–Fri. 🚪 8:05am, 12:15pm, 1:05pm Mon–Fri; 11am Sun. ◯

**Elizabeth
Ann Seton**

Elizabeth Ann Seton (1774–1821), the first native-born American to be canonized by the Catholic Church, lived here from 1801 to 1803. Mother Seton founded the American Sisters of Charity, the first order of nuns in the United States.

After the Civil War, the Mission of Our Lady of the Rosary turned the building into a shelter for homeless Irish immigrant women – 170,000 passed through on their way to a new life in America. The adjoining church was built in 1883. The Mission established and maintains the shrine to Mother Seton.

Fraunces Tavern Museum ⑬

54 Pearl St. **Map** 1 C4. **Tel** (212) 425-1778. Ⓜ Wall St, Broad St, Bowling Green. ◯ noon–5pm Mon–Sat. 🔵 public hols, day after Thanksgiving. 🖼 📷 groups only.

Lectures, films. 🎟 📷 www.frauncestavernmuseum.org NYC Police Museum 100 Old Slip, South St. **Map** 1 D3. **Tel** (212) 480-3100. ◯ 10am–5pm Mon–Sat. Donation suggested. 📷 groups only. www.nycpolicemuseum.org

New York's only remaining block of 18th-century commercial buildings contains an exact replica of the 1719 Fraunces Tavern where George Washington said farewell to his officers in 1783. The tavern had been an early casualty of the Revolution: the British ship *Asia* shot a cannonball through its roof in August 1775. The building was bought in 1904 by the Sons of the Revolution. Its restoration in 1907 was one of the first efforts to preserve the nation's heritage. The ground floor restaurant has wood-burning fires and great charm. An upstairs museum has changing exhibits interpreting the history and culture of early America. The **New York City Police Museum** (see p84) is at South Street. Exhibits include NYPD artifacts, interactive displays, seminars, and special events. Visit the Hall of Heroes and try your hand at the firearms training simulator.

Vietnam Veterans' Plaza ⑭

Between Water St and South St. **Map** 2 D4. Ⓜ Whitehall, South Ferry.

This multilevel brick plaza features, in its center, a huge wall of translucent green glass, engraved with excerpts from speeches, news stories, and moving letters to families from servicemen and women who died in the Vietnam war between 1959 and 1975.

Staten Island Ferry – one of the city's best bargains

Staten Island Ferry ⑮

Whitehall St. **Map** 2 D5. **Tel** 311. Ⓜ South Ferry. ◯ 24 hrs. Free. 📷 ♿ www.siferry.com

The first business venture of a promising Staten Island boy named Cornelius Vanderbilt, who later became the railroad magnate, the ferry has operated since 1810, carrying island commuters to and from

The 18th-century Fraunces Tavern Museum and restaurant

the city and offering visitors an unforgettable close-up of the harbor, the Statue of Liberty, Ellis Island and lower Manhattan's incredible skyline. The fare is still the city's best bargain: it's free.

Battery Maritime Building

11 South St. **Map** 2 D4.
M South Ferry. ● to the public.

From 1909 to 1938, the municipal terminal for ferries to Brooklyn operated here on the site of a small wharf known as Schreijers Hoek, from which Dutch Colonial ships once set sail for the mother country. At the height of the ferry era, 17 lines made regular runs from these bustling piers, which are used now only by the Coast Guard service for Governors Island.

The building was designed in 1907 and has been undergoing renovation since 2008. Arriving boats face 300-ft (91-m) arched openings guarded by tall, ornately scrolled columns and adorned with latticework, molding and rosettes typical of the Beaux Arts period. This is actually a false front of sheet metal and steel, painted green to resemble copper.

Ironwork railing on the Battery Maritime Building

Statue of Liberty ⑰

See pp74–5.

Ellis Island ⑱

See pp78–9.

Castle Clinton National Monument in Battery Park

Battery Park ⑲

Map 1 B4.
M South Ferry, Bowling Green.

Named for the cannons that once protected the harbor, the park is one of the best places in the city for gazing out to sea. Over the years, landfill has extended the greenery far beyond its original State Street boundary.

The park is rimmed with statues and monuments, such as the Netherlands Memorial

Beaux Arts subway entrance at the corner of Battery Park

Monument and memorials to New York's first Jewish immigrants and the Coast Guard. Fritz Koenig's *The Sphere*, a sculpture that once stood in the World Trade Center Plaza, is now here, serving as a memorial to those who died in the 9/11 terrorist attack.

Castle Clinton National Monument ⑳

Battery Park. **Map** 1 B4. *Tel* (212) 344-7220. M Bowling Green, South Ferry. ○ 8:30am–5pm daily. ● Dec 25. ⊡ ⬡ ▣ *Concerts.* ⬚ www.nps.gov/cacl

Castle Clinton was built in 1811 as an artillery defense post 300 ft (91 m) offshore,

connected to Battery Park by a causeway; but landfill gradually linked it to the mainland. None of its 28 guns was ever used in battle.

The fort was enclosed in 1824 to become a fashionable theater, where Phineas T. Barnum introduced "Swedish nightingale" Jenny Lind in 1850. In 1855 it preceded Ellis Island as the city's immigration point, processing over 8 million newcomers. In 1896, it became the New York Aquarium, which moved to Coney Island in 1941 (*see p249*).

Now it is a monument and visitors' center for Manhattan's National Park Service sites, with historical panoramas of the city. The complex is the departure point for the Statue of Liberty–Ellis Island ferry (*see p386*).

Museum of Jewish Heritage ㉑

36 Battery Place. **Map** 1 B4. *Tel* (646) 437-4200. M Bowling Green, South Ferry. ⬚ M1, 6, 9, 15, 20. ○ 10am–5:45pm Sun–Tue, Thu, 10am–8pm Wed, 10am–3pm Fri and eve of Jewish holidays. ● Sat, Jewish holidays, Thanksgiving. ⬚ ⬡ ⬚ ⬚ ▣ *Lectures.* www.mjhnyc.org

The museum has a core exhibition of more than 2,000 photographs, 800 artifacts, and 25 documentary films about Jewish life, before, during, and after the Holocaust. It also contains a state-of-the-art theater for films, lectures and performances; a memorial garden; classrooms; a resource center and library; a family history center; expanded gallery space for temporary exhibitions; offices; a café and event hall.

Ellis Island ⑱

Half of America's population can
trace its roots to Ellis Island, which
served as the country's immigration
depot from 1892 until 1954. Nearly
12 million people passed through
its gates and dispersed across the
country in the greatest wave of
migration the world has ever known.

Main building

The railroad office
sold tickets onward
to the final
destination.

Centered on the
Great Hall or
Registry Room,
the site today
houses the three-
story *Ellis Island
Immigration
Museum.* Much of this story is told with
photos and the voices of actual
immigrants, and an electronic database
traces ancestors. Outside, the
*American Immigrant Wall of
Honor* is the largest wall of
names in the world. No other
place explains so well the
"melting pot" that formed the
character of the nation. Visit
early to avoid the crowds.

Rail Ticket
*A special fare
for emigrants
led many on
to California.*

★ **Dormitory**
*There were
separate sleeping
quarters for male
and female
detainees.*

THE RESTORATION

In 1990 a $156-million project
by the Statue of Liberty-Ellis
Island Foundation, Inc.,
renewed several ruined buildings, replacing the copper
domes and restoring the
interior with original fixtures.

**The ferry
office** sold
tickets
to New
Jersey.

★ **Baggage
Room** *The
immigrants' meager
possessions were checked
here on arrival.*

Great Hall ★
*Immigrant
families were
made to wait for
"processing" in the
Registry Room.
The old metal
railings were
replaced with
wooden benches
in 1911.*

The metal and glass awning is a re-creation of the original.

Arrival *Steerage passengers crowd the deck as the ship approaches Ellis Island.*

Main entrance

Immigrant Family
An Italian mother and her children arrive in 1905.

STAR FEATURES

★ Baggage Room

★ Dormitory

★ Great Hall

Medical Examining Rooms
Immigrants with contagious diseases could be refused entry and sent back home.

SEAPORT AND THE CIVIC CENTER

Manhattan's busy Civic Center is the hub of the city and the state, of the federal governments' court systems and the city's police department. In the 1880s it was the heart of the newspaper publishing business as well. The area is still a handsome enclave of imposing architecture with fine landmarks from every period in the city's history, from the 20th-century Woolworth Building to 19th-century City Hall and 18th-century St. Paul's

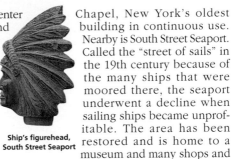

Ship's figurehead, South Street Seaport

Chapel, New York's oldest building in continuous use. Nearby is South Street Seaport. Called the "street of sails" in the 19th century because of the many ships that were moored there, the seaport underwent a decline when sailing ships became unprofitable. The area has been restored and is home to a museum and many shops and restaurants. The Brooklyn Bridge, once the largest suspension bridge in the world, lies to the north.

SIGHTS AT A GLANCE

Historic Streets and Buildings
AT&T Building **14**
Brooklyn Bridge pp86–9 **3**
City Hall **10**
Criminal Courts Building **4**
Municipal Building **7**
New York County Courthouse **5**
Old New York County Courthouse **9**
Schermerhorn Row **2**
South Street Seaport **1**
Surrogate's Court, Hall of Records **8**
United States Courthouse **6**
Woolworth Building **12**

Churches
St. Paul's Chapel **13**

Parks and Squares
City Hall Park and Park Row **11**

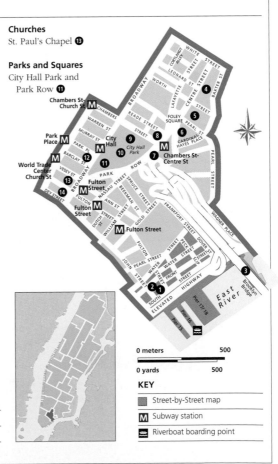

KEY

	Street-by-Street map
M	Subway station
	Riverboat boarding point

0 meters 500
0 yards 500

GETTING THERE
Many subway lines serve the area: the 7th Ave/Broadway 2 and 3 trains to Park Pl or Fulton St; the Lexington Ave 4, 5 and 6 to Brooklyn Bridge; the 8th Ave A and C to Chambers St and the R or W to City Hall. By bus take the M1, M6, M9, M15, M109 or the M22 crosstown.

SEE ALSO

◁ South Street Seaport

Street by Street: South Street Seaport

Part commercial and part historical, the development of South Street Seaport has transformed the former heart of the 19th-century port of New York, which had long been neglected, into a lively and pleasant part of the city. Tall ships are once again moored here, and shops, restaurants, and cafés abound. The South Street Seaport Museum tells the story of New York's maritime past through craft demonstrations, ship tours, and river cruises.

★ **South Street Seaport**
Once full of sailors and sailing ships, the seaport is now a lively complex of shops, restaurants, and museums ❶

Cannon's Walk is a 19th- and 20th-century block of buildings, with an outdoor café, shops, and a very lively marketplace.

The Titanic Memorial is a lighthouse built in 1913 in memory of those who died on the *Titanic*. It now stands on Fulton Street.

To Fulton St. subway (4 blocks)

Schermerhorn Row
Built as warehouses in 1813 and due to house The World Port New York exhibit, the Row contains the South Street Seaport Museum and Brookstone ❷

The Boat-Building Shop lets you watch as skilled craftspeople build and restore small wooden vessels.

At the Maritime Crafts Center woodcarvers and painters can be seen at work on models, ship carvings, and figureheads.

Ship in a bottle

The Pilothouse was originally from a steam tugboat built in 1923 by New York Central. The Seaport's admission and information center is to be found here.

STAR SIGHTS

★ Brooklyn Bridge

★ South Street Seaport

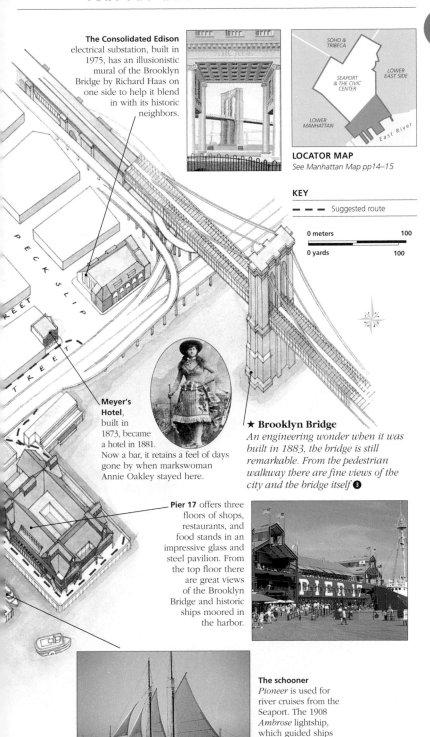

The Consolidated Edison electrical substation, built in 1975, has an illusionistic mural of the Brooklyn Bridge by Richard Haas on one side to help it blend in with its historic neighbors.

LOCATOR MAP
See Manhattan Map pp14–15

KEY

- - - Suggested route

| 0 meters | 100 |
| 0 yards | 100 |

Meyer's Hotel, built in 1873, became a hotel in 1881. Now a bar, it retains a feel of days gone by when markswoman Annie Oakley stayed here.

★ **Brooklyn Bridge**
An engineering wonder when it was built in 1883, the bridge is still remarkable. From the pedestrian walkway there are fine views of the city and the bridge itself ❸

Pier 17 offers three floors of shops, restaurants, and food stands in an impressive glass and steel pavilion. From the top floor there are great views of the Brooklyn Bridge and historic ships moored in the harbor.

The schooner *Pioneer* is used for river cruises from the Seaport. The 1908 *Ambrose* lightship, which guided ships into port, is also moored here.

The Ambrose lightship at a South Street Seaport pier on the East River

South Street Seaport ❶

Fulton St. **Map** 2 E2. *Tel* (212) SEA-PORT. Ⓜ *Fulton St.* ◯ *Nov–Mar: 10am–7pm Mon–Fri, 11am–6pm Sun; Apr–Oct: 10am–9pm Mon–Sat, 11am–8pm Sun.* ◉ ♿ ▮ *Concerts.* ▯
▯ **South Street Seaport Museum** 12 Fulton St. ▯ *(212) 748-8600.* ◯ *Apr–Dec: 10am–6pm Tue–Sun; Jan–Mar: 10am–5pm Fri–Mon.* ◉ *Jan 1, Thanksgiving, Dec 25.* ▥ ◉ ♿ ▮ *Lectures, exhibits, films.* ▯ ▯ www.southstseaport.org

The heart of New York's 19th-century seaport has been given an imaginative new lease on life. Glitzy stores and restaurants sit harmoniously beside seafaring craft, historic buildings, and museums, with spectacular views of Brooklyn Bridge and the East River from the cobblestone streets. Historic ships berthed here range from the little tugboat *W.O. Decker* to the great four-masted sailing ship *Peking*. Mini-trips on the schooner *Pioneer* are a great way to see the river.

The **Museum** covers the 12 blocks of what was once America's leading port. Not only is it home to the largest fleet of privately maintained historic vessels in the US, but there are also artifacts, artworks, and documents from the 19th- and early 20th-century maritime world.

The New York City Police Museum *(see p76)* chronicles the history of law enforcement. Exhibits include weapons, the art of fingerprinting and forensics, and the arrest records of famous criminals.

Fulton Fish Market, which was a popular attraction at Seaport for more than 150 years, moved to the Bronx in 2006.

Schermerhorn Row ❷

Fulton and South Sts. **Map** 2 D3. Ⓜ *Fulton St.*

This is Seaport's architectural showpiece. Constructed in 1811 by shipowner and chandler Peter Schermerhorn on land reclaimed from the river, the buildings were originally warehouses and counting-houses. With the opening of the Brooklyn Ferry terminus in 1814 and of Fulton Market in 1822, the block became desirable property.

The Row has been restored as part of the South Street development, and it now houses 24 museum galleries, as well as shops, and restaurants.

Brooklyn Bridge ❸

See pp86–9.

Criminal Courts Building ❹

100 Centre St. **Map** 4 F5. Ⓜ *Canal St.* ◯ *9am–5pm Mon–Fri.* ◉ *public hols.* ♿

This 1939 building is Art Moderne in style, with towers reminiscent of a Babylonian temple. The three-story-high entrance is set back in a court, behind two huge, square, free-standing granite columns – an intimidating sight for the accused. The building also houses the Manhattan Detention Center for Men, which was formerly across the street in a building known as "The Tombs" because of its Egyptian-style architecture. The nickname has stuck, although the original is long gone. An aerial walkway, or "bridge of sighs," links the courts with the correctional facility across Centre Street.

The building also houses the night courts, where cases are generally heard from 5pm to 1am on weekdays.

Entrance to the Criminal Courts Building

New York County Courthouse ❺

60 Centre St. **Map** 2 D1. Ⓜ *Brooklyn Br-City Hall.* ◯ *9am–5pm Mon–Fri.* ◉ *public hols.* ♿

Built to replace the Tweed Courthouse *(see p90)*, this county supreme courthouse was completed in 1926.

Restored buildings on Schermerhorn Row

The fluted Corinthian portico at the top of a wide staircase is the main feature of the hexagonal building. The austere exterior is offset by a circular-columned interior rotunda featuring Tiffany lighting fixtures and a series of rich marble and ceiling murals by Attilio Pusterla on themes of law and justice. Six wings radiate from the rotunda, each housing a single court and its facilities.

The courtroom drama *Twelve Angry Men,* starring Henry Fonda, was filmed here.

New York County Courthouse

United States Courthouse ❻

40 Centre St. **Map** 2 D1. Ⓜ
Brooklyn Br-City Hall. ⏲ *9am–5pm Mon–Fri.* ● *public hols.* ♿

This courthouse was the last project undertaken by noted architect Cass Gilbert, designer of the Woolworth Building *(see p91).* Begun in 1933, the year before his death, it was finished by his son. The

United States Courthouse

31-story structure is a pyramid-topped tower set on a classical temple base. The bronzework on the doors is handsome, but the interior lacks the colorful decoration Gilbert had outlined in his sketchbooks. Aerial walkways link the building with its Police Plaza Annex.

Municipal Building ❼

1 Centre St. **Map** 1 C1. Ⓜ
Brooklyn Br-City Hall. 🅾 ♿

The Municipal Building, constructed in 1914, dominates the Civic Center and straddles Chambers Street. It was McKim, Mead & White's first skyscraper and houses government offices and a marriage chapel. The exterior, in harmony with City Hall, has no excess detail to detract from the earlier building. The most notable feature is the top, a fantasy of towers capped by Adolph Wienman's statue *Civic Fame.*

A railway passage (no longer in use) through the base, and the plaza joining the Municipal Building to the entrance of the IRT subway station were built as concessions to modern transportation needs. The building has had a far-reaching influence on architectural style; the main building at Moscow University is said to have been modeled on its design.

Surrogate's Court, Hall of Records ❽

31 Chambers St. **Map** 1 C1.
Ⓜ *City Hall.* ⏲ *9am–5pm Mon–Fri.*
● *public hols.* 🅾 ♿ 📷

A Beaux Arts triumph, the original Hall of Records was begun in 1899 and completed in 1911. The elaborate columned facade is of white Maine granite, with a high mansard roof. The figures by Henry K. Bush-Brown in the roof area represent life's stages from childhood to old age; the statues by Philip Martiny over the colonnade are of notable New Yorkers such as Peter

Municipal Building

Stuyvesant. Martiny also made the representations of New York in its infancy and New York in revolutionary times at the Chambers Street entrance.

The Paris Opéra Garnier was the inspiration for the twin marble stairways and painted ceiling of the dazzling central hall. The ceiling mosaic by William de Leftwich Dodge features the signs of the zodiac and symbols of record keeping.

The restored Hall of Records holds public records dating back to 1664. A permanent exhibition, *Windows on the Archives,* features historical papers, drawings, letters and photographs illustrating what life was like in New York from 1626 to the present.

Surrogate's Court

Brooklyn Bridge ❸

Completed in 1883, the Brooklyn Bridge was the largest suspension bridge and the first to be constructed of steel. Engineer John A. Roebling conceived of a bridge spanning the East River while ice-bound on a ferry to Brooklyn. The bridge took 16 years to build, required 600 workers and claimed over 20 lives, including Roebling's. Most died of caisson disease (known as "the bends") after coming up from the underwater excavation chambers. When finished, the bridge linked Manhattan and Brooklyn, then two separate cities.

Souvenir medal cast for the opening of the bridge

BROOKLYN BRIDGE
From making the wire to sinking the supports, the bridge was built using new techniques.

Anchorage
The ends of the bridge's four steel cables are fastened to a series of anchor bars held in place by anchor plates. These are held down by giant granite vaults up to three stories high. Their vast interiors, once used for storage, are now used for summer art displays.

Granite vault

Cable to tower

Anchor bar

Caisson
The towers rose up above caissons, each the size of four tennis courts, which provided a dry area for underwater excavation. As work went on, they sank deeper beneath the river.

Shaft

Anchor Plates
Each of the four cast-iron anchor plates holds one cable. The masonry was built up around them after they were placed in position.

Anchor plates

Anchor plate

Vault

Central span is 1,595 ft (486 m) long

Vault

Roadway from anchorage to anchorage is 3,579 ft (1,091 m)

First Crossing

Master mechanic E.F. Farrington in 1876 was the first to cross the river on the bridge-in-progress, using a steam-driven traveler rope. His journey took 22 minutes.

Steel Cable Wire

Each cable contains 3,515 miles (5,657 km) of wire, galvanized with zinc for protection from the wind, rain, and snow.

Brooklyn Tower (1875)

Two Gothic double arches, each 271 ft (83 m) high, one in Brooklyn, the other in Manhattan, were meant to be the portals of the cities.

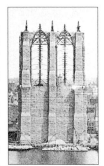

JOHN A. ROEBLING

The German-born Roebling designed the bridge. In 1869, just before construction started, his foot was crushed between an incoming ferry and the ferry slip. He died three weeks later. His son, Washington Roebling, finished the bridge, but in 1872 he was taken from a caisson suffering from the bends and became partly paralyzed. His wife, under his tutelage, then took over.

Inside the Caisson

Immigrant workers broke up rocks in the riverbed.

MAKING THE CABLES

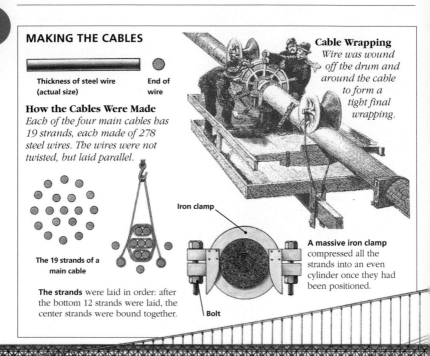

Thickness of steel wire
(actual size)

End of
wire

How the Cables Were Made
*Each of the four main cables has
19 strands, each made of 278
steel wires. The wires were not
twisted, but laid parallel.*

**The 19 strands of a
main cable**

The strands were laid in order: after
the bottom 12 strands were laid, the
center strands were bound together.

Iron clamp

Bolt

Cable Wrapping
*Wire was wound
off the drum and
around the cable
to form a
tight final
wrapping.*

A massive iron clamp
compressed all the
strands into an even
cylinder once they had
been positioned.

1983 Centennial Fireworks over the Brooklyn Bridge
Celebrating the bridge's 100th year, this display was awesome.

Bustling Bridge
*This 1883 view from
the Manhattan side
shows the original two
outer lanes for horse-
drawn carriages, two
middle lanes for cable
cars, and the elevated
center walkway.*

Panic of May 30, 1883
*After a woman tripped on the
bridge, panic broke out. Of the
estimated 20,000 people on the
bridge, 12 were crushed to death.*

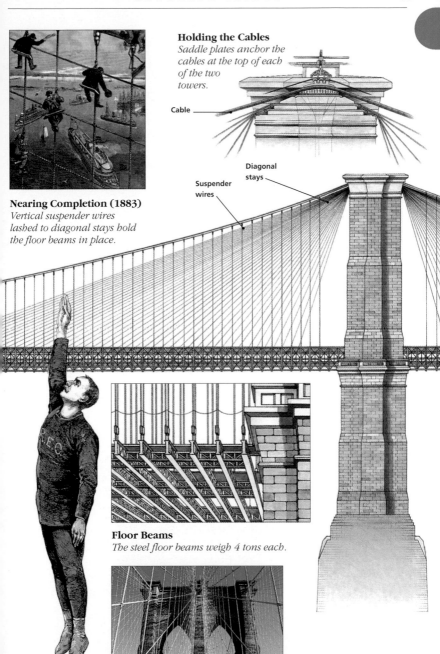

Holding the Cables
Saddle plates anchor the cables at the top of each of the two towers.

Cable

Diagonal stays

Suspender wires

Nearing Completion (1883)
Vertical suspender wires lashed to diagonal stays hold the floor beams in place.

Floor Beams
The steel floor beams weigh 4 tons each.

Odlum's Jump
Robert Odlum was the first to jump off the bridge, on a bet, in May 1885. He later died from internal bleeding.

Elevated Walkway
Poet Walt Whitman said that the view from the walkway – 18 ft (5.5 m) above the road – was "the best, most effective medicine my soul has yet partaken."

Old New York County Courthouse ❾

52 Chambers St. **Map** 1 C1.
Ⓜ *Chambers St-City Hall.*
⚑ *included in City Hall tour.*

This building is best known for the scandal it caused. It is nicknamed the "Tweed Courthouse" for the political boss who spent 20 times the budget for the building and pocketed $9 million of the total $14 million cost. "Boss" Tweed even bought a marble quarry and sold materials to the city at huge profit. Public outrage eventually led to his downfall in 1871 – ironically, he was tried in his own courthouse and died in a New York jail *(see p27)*.

After an $85 million restoration, including the 85-ft (26-m) rotunda and the grand staircase, this vibrant 19th-century landmark became the home of the Department of Education.

City Hall's imposing early 19th-century facade

City Hall ❿

City Hall Park. **Map** 1 C1. **Tel** *311.*
Ⓜ *Brooklyn Br-City Hall Park Pl.*
◯ *for prearranged tours only.* 📷
♿ ⚑ *(212) NEW-YORK.*

City Hall has been the seat of the New York city government since 1812, and is one of the finest examples of early 19th-century American architecture. A stately Federal-style building (with some influences from the French Renaissance), it was

P.T. Barnum's museum blazes in 1865 as crowds watch from City Hall Park

designed by John McComb, Jr., the first prominent American-born architect, and the French emigré Joseph Mangin.

Marble cladding was not used for the building's rear, since it was not expected that the city would ever develop farther to the north. In 1954, a program of restoration remedied this and the interior was refurbished.

Mangin is usually given credit for designing the exterior, and McComb for the beautiful interior with its fine domed rotunda encircled by 10 columns. The space beneath it opens onto an elegant marble stairway, leading to the splendid second-floor City Council chambers and the Governor's Room, which houses a portrait gallery of early New York leaders. This magnificent entrance has welcomed rulers and heroes for nearly 200 years. In 1865 Abraham Lincoln's body lay in state in this hall.

Stand on the steps and look to your right to see a statue of Nathan Hale, a US soldier hanged by the British as a spy in September 1776 during the Revolutionary War. His last words – "My only regret is that I have not more lives than one to offer in the service of my country" – won him a permanent place in the history books and hearts of America.

City Hall Park and Park Row ⓫

Map 1 C2. Ⓜ *Brooklyn Br-City Hall Park Plc.*

This was New York's village green 250 years ago, complete with stocks and whipping post. It was the scene of pre-Revolution protests against English rule, and there is a memorial to the "Liberty Poles" (symbols of revolt) on City Hall's west lawn. The Declaration of Independence was read to George Washington and his troops here on July 9, 1776.

Later, Phineas T. Barnum's American Museum at the park's southern tip drew crowds from 1842 until it burned down in 1865. The Park Row building was the site of the Park Theater. From 1798 to 1848, the best actors of the day, such as Edmund Kean and Fanny Kemble, performed there. Park Row runs along the east side of City Hall Park. Once called "Newspaper Row," it was lined with the lofty offices of the *Sun*, *World*, *Tribune*, and other papers.

Statue of Benjamin Franklin in Printing House Square

Printing House Square has a statue of Benjamin Franklin with his *Pennsylvania Gazette*.

City Hall Park is a green space, used by those working nearby as a peaceful place to sit and relax.

Woolworth Building ⑫

233 Broadway. **Map** 1 C2. ◐ *to the public.* Ⓜ *City Hall Park Pl.*

Bas-relief caricature of architect Gilbert in the Woolworth lobby

In 1879, salesclerk Frank W. Woolworth opened a new kind of store, where shoppers could see and touch the goods, and everything cost five cents. The chain of stores that followed made him a fortune and changed retailing forever.

The 1913 Gothic headquarters of his empire was New York's tallest building until 1930. It set the standard for the great skyscrapers. Architect Cass Gilbert's soaring two-tiered design, adorned with gargoyles of bats and other wildlife, is topped with a pyramid roof, flying buttresses, pinnacles, and four small towers. The marble interior is rich with filigree, sculptured reliefs, and painted decoration, and has a high glass-tile mosaic ceiling that almost seems to glow. The lobby is one of the city's treasures. Gilbert showed his sense of humor here, in bas-relief caricatures of the founder counting out his fortune in nickels and dimes; of the real-estate broker closing a deal; and of Cass Gilbert himself cradling a large model of the building. Paid for with $13.5 million in cash, the building has never had a mortgage. Woolworth's went out of business in 1997. The building is now owned by the Witkoff Group.

St. Paul's Chapel ⑬

209–211 Broadway. **Map** 1 C2. **Tel** *(212) 233-4164.* Ⓜ *Fulton St.* ◯ *10am–6pm Mon–Sat, 9am–4pm Sun.* ◑ *most public hols.* ✝ *12:30pm Wed; 8am, 10am Sun.* ◯ 📷 *by appt.* **Concerts** *1pm Mon.* www.saintpaulschapel.org

Miraculously untouched when the World Trade Center towers collapsed in 2001, St. Paul's is Manhattan's only extant church built before the Revolutionary

The Georgian interior of St. Paul's Chapel

War. It is a Georgian gem. The colorful interior, lit by Waterford chandeliers, is the setting for free concerts. The pew where newly inaugurated George Washington prayed has been preserved. In the churchyard, the Actor's Monument commemorates George F. Cooke, who played many great roles at the Park Theater; he drank himself to death at the Shakespeare Tavern on Fulton Street. The chapel's "Unwavering Spirit" exhibition chronicles the volunteer efforts after September 11.

AT&T Building ⑭

195 Broadway. **Map** 1 C2. Ⓜ *Broadway-Nassau Fulton St.* ◯ *office hours.*

This former headquarters was designed by Welles Bosworth from 1915 to 1922. The facade is said to have more columns than any other building in the world, and the interior of the building is a forest of marble pillars. The whole edifice looks like a gigantic square-topped layer cake.

A sea sprite above the door of the AT&T (American Telephone and Telegraph) Building

LOWER EAST SIDE

Nowhere does the strong ethnic flavor of New York come through more tangibly than in Lower Manhattan, where immigrants began to settle in the late 19th century. Here Italians, Chinese and Jews established distinct neighborhoods, preserving their languages, customs, foods and religions in the midst of a strange land. This neighborhood of

19th-century tin, Lower East Side Tenement Museum

low-rise buildings is steadily becoming gentrified, but the old flavor remains. The area brims with restaurants, bars, and trendy stores, but still offers some of the city's greatest bargains and has a spirit found nowhere else. The composer Irving Berlin, who grew up here, famously said: "Everybody ought to have a Lower East Side in their life."

SIGHTS AT A GLANCE

Historic Streets and Buildings
Chinatown **4**
Delancey Street **10**
East Houston Street **11**
Engine Company No. 31 **14**
Home Savings of America **1**
Little Italy **3**
Orchard Street **8**
Police Headquarters Building **2**

Puck Building **12**

Parks and Squares
Columbus Park **5**

Museums and Galleries
FusionArts Museum **19**
Lower East Side Tenement Museum **7**
New Museum of Contemporary Art **16**

Shops and Markets
Economy Candy **17**
Essex Street Market **20**
The Pickle Guys **15**

Churches and Synagogues
Angel Orensanz Center **18**
Bialystoker Synagogue **9**
Eldridge Street Synagogue **6**
Old St. Patrick's Cathedral **13**

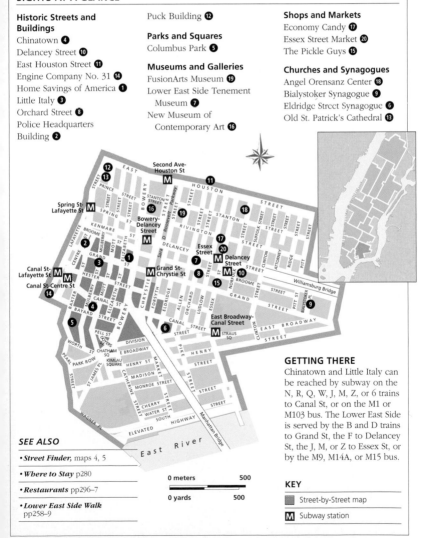

GETTING THERE
Chinatown and Little Italy can be reached by subway on the N, R, Q, W, J, M, Z, or 6 trains to Canal St, or on the M1 or M103 bus. The Lower East Side is served by the B and D trains to Grand St, the F to Delancey St, the J, M, or Z to Essex St, or by the M9, M14A, or M15 bus.

SEE ALSO

- *Street Finder,* maps 4, 5
- *Where to Stay* p280
- *Restaurants* pp296–7
- *Lower East Side Walk* pp258–9

0 meters 500
0 yards 500

KEY

Street-by-Street map

M Subway station

◁ **Dragon puppet in Chinatown at Chinese New Year**

Street by Street: Little Italy and Chinatown

New York's largest and most colorful ethnic neighborhood is Chinatown, which is growing so rapidly that it is overrunning nearby Little Italy as well as the Lower East Side. Streets here teem with grocery stores, gift shops and hundreds of Chinese restaurants; even the plainest offer good food. What is left of Little Italy can be found at Mulberry and Grand streets, where old-world flavor abounds.

★ Little Italy
The scents of Italy still waft from the restaurants and bakeries of this area, once home to thousands of immigrants ❸

The Market on Canal Street has a wide range of bargains in new and used clothes and fresh produce.

Ⓜ **Canal Street subway** (lines R, W, N, Q, 6)

★ Chinatown
Home to a thriving – and still expanding – community of Chinese immigrants, this area is famous for its restaurants and hectic street life. The area truly comes alive around the Chinese New Year in January or February ❹

The Eastern States Buddhist Temple at 64b Mott Street contains over 100 golden Buddhas.

The Wall of Democracy on Bayard Street is covered with newspapers and posters describing the situation in China.

Columbus Park
Once a slum, this park now fills with residents playing mahjong ❺

Confucius Plaza is marked by sculptor Liu Shih's monument to the Oriental philosopher.

Chatham Square has a memorial to Chinese-American war dead.

Police Headquarters Building

The dome of this Baroque civic building towers over the City Hall area. In 1973, the police moved out; ten years later the building was turned into apartments ❷

LOCATOR MAP
See Manhattan Map pp14–15

KEY

– – – Suggested route

Home Savings of America
Stanford White designed this in 1894 for the old Bowery Savings Bank ❶

Umbertos Clam House, known as the place where Mafia boss Joey Gallo was shot in 1972, once occupied this location on Mulberry Street.

| 0 meters | 100 |
| 0 yards | 100 |

★ Eldridge Street Synagogue
Built in 1887, this was the first large temple built in the US by European Jews ❻

Bloody Angle, where Doyers Street turns sharply, was the gruesome site of many gangland ambushes during the 1920s.

STAR SIGHTS

★ Chinatown

★ Eldridge Street Synagogue

★ Little Italy

Home Savings of America ❶

130 Bowery. **Map** 4 F4.
Ⓜ *Grand St, Bowery.*

Imposing inside and out, this Classical Revival building was built for the Bowery Savings Bank in 1894. Architect Stanford White designed the ornamented limestone facade to wrap around the rival Butchers' and Drovers' Bank, which refused to sell the corner plot. The interior is decorated with marble pillars and a ceiling scattered with gilded rosettes.

Detail from Home Savings of America

By the mid-20th century, the bank was a contrast to the Bowery with its vagrants and flophouses. It is now the site of opulent Capitale, and open only for private functions.

Police Headquarters Building ❷

240 Centre St. **Map** 4 F4.
Ⓜ *Canal St.* ⬤ *to the public.*

Completed in 1909, this was a fitting home for the city's new professional police force. The main portico and end pavilions have Corinthian columns and the dome dominates the skyline. However, lack of space meant the headquarters had to fit into a wedge-shaped site in the midst of Little Italy.

For nearly three-quarters of a century, this was where "New York's finest" came to work. During Prohibition, Grand Street from here to the Bowery was known as "Bootleggers' Row," and alcohol was easily obtained except when a police raid was due. The liquor merchants paid handsomely for a tip-off from inside police headquarters. The police moved to different headquarters in 1973, and in 1985 the building was converted into a luxury cooperative apartment project.

Little Italy ❸

Streets around Mulberry St.
Map 4 F4. Ⓜ *Canal St.*
www.littleitalynyc.com

The southern Italians who came to New York in the late 19th century found themselves living in the squalor of "dumbbell" apartments. These were built so close together that sunlight never reached the lower windows or backyards. With over 40,000 people living in 17 small, unsanitary blocks, diseases such as tuberculosis were rife.

Despite the privations of life on the Lower East Side, the community that grew up around Mulberry Street was lively with the colors, flavors, and atmosphere of Italy. These have lingered on, though the Italian population has dwindled to 5,000 and

Chinatown has encroached on the traditional "Little Italy."

The most exciting time to visit is during the Feast of San Gennaro around September 19 *(see p52)*. For nine days Mulberry Street is renamed Via San Gennaro. On the saint's day, his shrine and relics are paraded through the streets. Throughout the feast there is music, dancing, and sideshows, and stalls selling Italian food and drink, as well as other ethnic cuisines.

Little Italy's restaurants offer simple, rustic food served in friendly surroundings at reasonable prices. NoLIta, North of Little Italy, is filled with boutiques, shops, and cafés. The fashionable flock here for the coolest small labels.

A street scene in Little Italy

Chinatown ❹

Streets around Mott St.
Map 4 F5. Ⓜ *Canal St.*
Eastern States Buddhist Temple
64b Mott St. ⬤ *9am–6pm daily.*
www.explorechinatown.com

The Chinatown of the early 20th century was primarily a male community, made up of immigrants who had first gone to California. Wages were sent home to their families in China, who were prevented from joining them by US immigration laws. The men relaxed by gambling at mahjong. The community remained isolated from the rest of the city, financed and controlled by its own secret organizations, the Tongs.

Some of the Tongs were simply family associations who provided loans. Others, such as the On Leong and the Hip Sing, who were at war with one another, were criminal fraternities. Tiny, crooked Doyers Street was

Stonework figures adorning the Police Headquarters Building

A Chinese grocer tending his shop on Canal Street

called "Bloody Angle"; enemies were lured there and set upon by gang members waiting around the bend.

A truce between the Tongs in 1933 brought peace to Chinatown. By 1940 it was home to many middle-class families. Immigrants and businesses from Hong Kong also brought postwar prosperity to the community. Today over 80,000 Chinese-Americans live here.

Many visit the neighborhood to sample the cuisine, but there is more to do here than eat. There are galleries, antiques and curio shops, and Oriental festivals (see p53). To glimpse another side of Chinatown, step into the incense-scented Eastern States Buddhist Temple at 64b Mott Street, where offerings are piled up and over 100 golden Buddhas gleam in the candlelight.

Columbus Park ❺

Map 4 F5. **M** Canal St.

The tranquillity of Columbus Park today could not be further removed from the scene near this site in the early 1800s. The area, known as Mulberry Bend, was a red-light district, part of the infamous Five Points slum. Gangs with names like the Dead Rabbits and the Plug Uglies roamed the streets. A murder a day was common-place; even the police were afraid to pass through. Partly as a result of the writings of reformer Jacob Riis (see p49), the slum was taken down in 1892. The park is now the only open space in Chinatown.

Eldridge Street Synagogue ❻

12 Eldridge St. **Map** 5 A5. **Tel** (212) 219-0888. **M** East Broadway. ◐ 10am–4pm Sun–Thu. ◑ Fri sundown, Sat 10am onward. 🎟 🚫 📷 Every half hour from 10am until 3pm. 🖥 www.eldridgestreet.org

When this house of worship was built by the Orthodox Ashkenazi from Eastern Europe in 1887, it was the most flamboyant temple in the neighborhood. But many immigrant Jews saw the Lower East Side as just the beginning of a new life, and later moved out of this massive synagogue.

In the 1930s, the huge sanctuary, rich with stained glass, brass chandeliers, marbleized wood paneling, and fine carving, was closed. Much later a group of citizens raised funds for preservation, and the main sanctuary was reopened in 2007. The synagogue has become a vibrant cultural center, with concerts and other special programs.

Even after years of neglect, the facade, with touches of Romanesque, Gothic and Moorish designs, is impressive. Inside, the Italian hand-carved ark and sculpted wooden balcony show why this building was the pride of the area.

Lower East Side Tenement Museum ❼

108 Orchard St. **Map** 5 A4. **Tel** (212) 431-0233. **M** Delancey, Grand St. ◐ 10am–6pm daily. 📷 compulsory (book ahead). First tour: 10:30am; last tour: 5pm. ● Jan 1, Thanksgiving, Dec 25. 🎟 🚫 📹 **Lectures, films, videos**. 🖥 (daily). www.tenement.org

Street vendor's pushcart (1890s), Lower East Side Tenement Museum

The interior of this building was restored to re-create apartments as they appeared in the late 1870s, in 1916, 1918, and 1935. There were no regulations on tenement living conditions until 1879. Many rooms had no windows, and indoor plumbing was rare. The rooms give a sense of the cramped and deplorable conditions in which so many lived. The program includes the exhibit "Piecing It Together," about the area's garment history. The museum also offers superb walking tours.

Window, Eldridge Street Synagogue

Orchard Street ⑧

Map 5 A3. Ⓜ Delancey, Grand St.
See **Shopping** p320.
www.lowereastsideny.com

Jewish immigrants founded the New York garment industry on this street, named for the orchards that once stood here on James De Lancey's Colonial estate. For years the street was filled with pushcarts loaded with goods for sale. The pushcarts are long gone, and not all the shopkeepers are Jewish, but the flavor remains. On Sunday there is an outdoor market, and shoppers fill the street from Houston to Canal, looking for clothing bargains.

Orchard Street is also at the heart of the Lower East Side's gentrification. Boutiques and vintage stores nestle alongside bars, clubs, restaurants, and the boutique Blue Moon hotel, formerly a tenement.

Vegetable stall at an outdoor market in Canal Street

Mural featuring a sign of the zodiac in Bialystoker Synagogue.

Bialystoker Synagogue ⑨

7–11 Willett St. **Map** 5 C4.
Tel (212) 475-0165. Ⓜ Essex St.
✱ frequent services.
▣ prearranged only. ▣
www.bialystoker.org

This 1826 Federal-style building was originally the Willett Street Methodist Church. It was bought in 1905 by Jewish immigrants from the Bialystok province of Poland, who converted it into a synagogue. For this reason, it faces west in the tradition of Christian churches instead of east.

The synagogue has a beautiful interior, with lovely stained-glass windows, a three-story carved wooden ark, and murals representing the signs of the zodiac and views of the Holy Land.

Delancey Street ⑩

Map 5 C4. Ⓜ Essex St.
See **Shopping** p320.
Bowery Ballroom 6 Delancey St.
Tel (212) 533-2111. See website
for shows schedule. ▣ no flash.
♿ www.boweryballroom.com

Once a majestic boulevard, Delancey Street these days is little more than an obligatory entrance to the Williamsburg Bridge. The street was named for James De Lancey, whose farm was situated here in Colonial days. During the American Revolution (see pp22–3), De Lancey remained loyal to King George III. After the war, he fled to England, and his land was seized.

At 6 Delancey sits the **Bowery Ballroom**, a three-story theater completed only weeks before the stock market crash of 1929 (see p31). Throughout the Great Depression and World War II, the building was deserted. Later, it served as a retail space, housing a haberdashery, a jeweler's boutique, and Treemark Shoes, until its resurrection as a live-music venue in the late 1990s. Much of the theater's original structure is still in place, including such decorative details as the brass rails, the copper-vaulted plaster ceiling of the mezzanine bar, and the brass and iron exterior metalwork.

Live music at the Bowery Ballroom, in a stylish 1920s theater

East Houston Street ⓫

East Houston St. **Map** *4 F3, 5A3.*
Ⓜ *Second Avenue.*

The dividing line between the Lower East Side and the East Village, East Houston between Forsyth and Ludlow streets clearly demonstrates the

Trays of bagels at a traditional Jewish bakery in East Houston Street

changing mix of old and new in the area. Between Forsyth and Eldridge streets is the Yonah Schimmel Knish Bakery, a fixture for more than 90 years, still with its original showcases. Further down the block is the Sunshine Theater, constructed as a Dutch Church in the 1840s and later used as a boxing arena and a Yiddish vaudeville theater. Today it shows art films.

While much of the Jewish flavor of the Lower East Side has disappeared, there are two survivors farther along East Houston. Russ and Daughters is a culinary landmark, a third-generation family business that began on a pushcart, circa 1900. At this location since 1914, the store has seen its fortunes change with the neighborhood. It is famed for traditional smoked fish and herring, and has an impressive stock of caviar.

At the corner of Ludlow Street is perhaps the best-known survivor, the bustling Katz's Delicatessen *(see p297),* well past its 100th

birthday and still packing them in for pastrami and corned beef sandwiches.

Puck Building ⓬

295–309 Lafayette St. **Map** *4 F3.*
Ⓜ *Lafayette.* ⬡ *to the public during business hours.* **Tel** *(212) 274-8900.*

This block-square architectural curiosity was built in 1885 by Albert and Herman Wagner. It is an adaptation of the German *Rundbogenstil,* a mid-19th-century style characterized by horizontal bands of arched windows and the skillful use of molded red brick.

From 1887 to 1916 the building housed the satirical magazine *Puck,* and at the turn of the century it was the largest building in the world devoted to lithography and publishing.

Today it is the site of some of New York's most stylish parties and artiest fashion-photography shoots. The only connection remaining to the mythical Puck is the gold-leaf statue on the corner of Mulberry and Houston, and the smaller version over the entrance on Lafayette Street.

Statue of Puck on the northeast corner of the Puck Building

Facade of Old St. Patrick's Cathedral, now a parish church

Old St. Patrick's Cathedral ⓭

263 Mulberry St. **Map** *4 F3.* **Tel** *(212) 226-8075.* Ⓜ *Prince St.* ⬡ *8am–12:30pm & 3:30–6pm Thu–Tue.* ✝ *9am, noon Mon–Fri; 5:30pm Sat; 9:15am, 12:45pm Sun; Spanish: 11:30am Sun.* **www**.oldsaintpatricks.com

The first St. Patrick's was begun in 1809, and it is one of the oldest churches in the city. When fire destroyed the original in the 1860s, it was rebuilt much as it is today. When the archdiocese transferred the see to the new St. Patrick's Cathedral uptown *(see pp178–9),* Old St. Patrick's became the local parish church, and it has flourished despite a constantly changing ethnic congregation.

Below the church are vaults containing the remains of, among others, one of New York's most famous families of restaurateurs, the Delmonicos. Pierre Toussaint was also buried here, but in 1990 his remains were moved from the old graveyard beside the church to a more prestigious burial place in a crypt in the new St. Patrick's Cathedral. Born as a slave in Haiti in 1766, Toussaint was brought to New York, where he lived as a free man and became a prosperous wig-maker. He later devoted himself to caring for the city's poor, also tending cholera victims and using his money to build an orphanage. The Vatican is now considering the philanthropic Toussaint for sainthood.

Engine Company No. 31 🄬

87 Lafayette St. **Map** *4 F5.*
Tel (212) 966-4510. Ⓜ *Canal St.*
Ⓞ *to the public.*

In the 19th century, fire stations were considered important enough to merit a building of architectural importance and the Le Brun firm was the acknowledged master of the art. This 1895 station is one of their best. The building resembles a Loire château, with its steep roof, dormers and towers, seeming almost fairy tale-like in this location.

The present-day tenant is the Downtown Community Television Center, which offers courses and workshops to members. However, the building is no longer open to the public.

The Pickle Guys 🄯

49 Essex St. **Map** *5 B4.* **Tel** *(212) 656-9739.* Ⓜ *Grand St.*
Ⓞ *9am–4pm Fri, 9am–6pm Sun–Thu.* **www**.nycpickleguys.com

The scent of pickles permeates this little section of Essex Street, just as it did in the early 1900s when Jewish pickle shops filled the area. True to the old Eastern European recipe, The Pickle Guys store their pickles in barrels filled with brine, garlic and spices; this mixture preserves the pickles for months on end. Pickle varieties include full sour, three-quarters sour, half sour, new, and hot.

Facade of Engine Company No. 31, in the style of a French château

No chemicals or preservatives are added and the shop operates to strict Kosher rules.

The store also carries pickled tomatoes, pickled celery, olives, mushrooms, hot peppers, sun-dried tomatoes, sweet kraut, sauerkraut, and herring. It is run like a family business, with a friendly, chatty atmosphere, which perpetuates the neighborhood's traditions.

New Museum of Contemporary Art 🄰

235 Bowery St. **Map** *4 E3.* **Tel** *(212) 219-1222.* Ⓜ *Spring St, Bowery.* Ⓞ *noon–6pm Wed–Sun (9pm Thu, Fri).* Ⓞ Ⓞ Ⓞ Ⓞ **Lectures, readings, music.** Ⓞ **www**.newmuseum.org

Marcia Tucker left her post as the Whitney Museum's Curator of Painting and Sculpture in 1977 to found this museum. Her aim was to exhibit the kind of work she felt was missing from more traditional museums. She created one of New York's most cutting-edge exhibition spaces, which includes an innovative Media Lounge for digital art, video installations, and sound works.

The rotating collection features a wide range of art, from large-scale photographs of 1960s America to geometric abstracts. The museum takes an inclusive approach, showcasing both emerging and established artists, including Mark Rothko and Roy Lichtenstein.

The striking seven-story building, designed by Tokyo-based architects Sejima & Nishizawa, is a notable addition to this Manhattan street. It rises like a sculptural stack of glowing cubes and is the first art museum to be built in downtown Manhattan in over a century. It has 60,000 sq ft (5,574 sq m) of exhibition space, a theater, store, café, and a rooftop terrace offering stunning views of the city.

Sweets on the densely packed shelves at Economy Candy

Economy Candy 🄱

108 Rivington S. **Map** *5 B3.* **Tel** *1-800 352-4544.* Ⓜ *Second Ave–Houston St.* Ⓞ *10am–5pm Sat, 9–6pm Sun–Fri.* **www**.economycandy.com

A Lower East Side landmark since 1937, this family-owned candy store stocks hundreds of varieties of candy, nuts, and dried fruit. Lined with floor-to-ceiling shelves packed with old-fashioned dispensers, the store is one of

Entrance to The Pickle Guys' store, with traditional pickling barrels

the few businesses on Lower East Side that has remained almost unchanged in name and specialty throughout the neighborhood's fluctuating fortunes over 50 years.

This is due in no small part to Jerry Cohen's enterprise in transforming his father's "Nosher's Paradise" from a penny candy store to a national company. The shop carries sweets and treats from all over the world, as well as numerous food items dipped in chocolate and 21 colors of candy-covered chocolate buttons.

Interior of the Angel Orensanz Center, once a large synagogue

Angel Orensanz Center ⓲

172 Norfolk St. **Map** *5 B3*.
Tel *(212) 529-7194.* Ⓜ *Essex St, Delancey St.* ◯ *by appt.* ♿
www.orensanz.org

Built in 1849, this cherry-red Neo-Gothic structure was once the oldest synagogue in New York. With ceilings 54 ft (15 m) high and seating for 1500, it was also the largest in the United States at the time. It was designed by the Berlin architect Alexander Saelzer in the tradition of the German Reform movement, and closely resembles Cologne Cathedral and the Friederichwerdeschekirche in the Mitte in Berlin.

After World War II and the decline of Lower East Side's Yiddish population, the synagogue was one of

many to close. In 1986, the building was acquired by the Spanish sculptor Angel Orensanz, who turned it into an art studio. It now serves as a spiritual and cultural center with a program of artistic, musical, and literary events.

FusionArts Museum ⓳

57 Stanton St. **Map** *5 A3*.
Tel *(212) 995-5290.* Ⓜ *Second Ave-Houston St.* ◯ *noon–6pm Tue–Fri & Sun.* ◎ ♿ 🚻
www.fusionartsmuseum.org

With psychedelic metal sculptures that give a foretaste of the pieces displayed inside, the entrance to this museum is hard to miss. It is dedicated to showing "fusion art", defined as art in which various artistic disciplines, such as painting, sculpture, photography, and video, meld to form a distinct genre in themselves. The museum's location gives it access to an underground art scene that uptown contemporary art museums often neglect, and it also offers lesser-known artists the opportunity to exhibit their work in a reputable gallery.

Many New York City artists who have been creating fusion art on the Lower East Side for more than two decades have already shown their work in group exhibitions here.

Metal sculptures at the entrance of the FusionArts Museum

Essex Street Market ⓴

120 Essex St. **Map** *5 B3*.
Tel *(212) 312-3603/388-0449.* Ⓜ *Essex St, Delancey St.* ◯ *8am–7pm Mon–Sat.* ◎ 🍴
🚻 **www**.essexstreetmarket.com

The market was created in 1938 by Mayor Fiorello H. La Guardia to bring pushcart vendors together and out of the way of traffic, especially police cars and fire trucks that used the narrow streets.

Two dozen meat, cheese, produce, and spice stalls fill the market. One of the oldest vendors is Jeffrey's butcher store, which has been at the market since 1939. Also here are the Essex Restaurant, which servies Latin/Jewish fare, and Cuchifritos, an art gallery showing the work of the neighborhood's artists.

Cut of meat on a butcher's display at the indoor Essex Street Market

SOHO AND TRIBECA

Art and architecture are the twin lures that have transformed these formerly industrial districts. SoHo (south of Houston) was threatened with demolition in the 1960s until preservationists drew attention to the rare historic cast-iron architecture. The district was saved, and artists began to move into the loft

Storefront of a SoHo bakery

spaces. Galleries, cafés, shops and then boutiques followed. Brunch and gallery hopping in SoHo is now a favorite weekend outing. As rents rose, many artists were priced out of SoHo and moved to TriBeCa (Triangle Below Canal). Now, trendy TriBeCa has galleries, many restaurants, and the Tribeca Film Festival in May.

SIGHTS AT A GLANCE

Historic Streets and Buildings
Greene Street ❸
Harrison Street ❽
Haughwout Building ❶
St. Nicholas Hotel ❷
Singer Building ❹
White Street ❾

Museums and Galleries
Children's Museum of the Arts ❺
New York City Fire Museum ❼
New York Earth Room ❻

GETTING THERE
Take the F, V, B, or D subway to Broadway-Lafayette; the 6 to Bleecker St or Spring St; or the N or R to Prince St. For TriBeCa, take the 1 to Franklin St, or the 1, 2, 3, A, or C to Chambers St. Bus routes are the M1 or M6, the M21 Houston St crosstown for SoHo, and the M6 or M20 for TriBeCa.

SEE ALSO

• **Street Finder,** map 4

• **SoHo Walk** pp260–61

• **Restaurants** pp297–9

• **Where to Stay** p281

0 meters   500

0 yards   500

KEY

▢ Street-by-Street map

Ⓜ Subway station

◁ **Cast-iron facades on Greene Street**

Street by Street: SoHo Cast-Iron Historic District

The largest concentration of cast-iron architecture in the world *(see p42)* survives in the area between West Houston and Canal streets. The heart of the district is Greene Street, where 50 buildings erected between 1869 and 1895 are found on five cobblestoned blocks. Most of their intricately designed cast-iron facades are in the Neo-Classical Revival style, with Corinthian columns and pediments. Mass-produced in a foundry, they were relatively inexpensive to produce and easy to erect and maintain. Now they rare works of industrial art, well suited to the present character of this district.

West Broadway, as it passes through SoHo, combines striking architecture with a string of art galleries, shoe shops, designer boutiques, and small restaurants.

72–76 Greene Street, the "King of Greene Street," is a splendid Corinthian-columned building. It was the creation of Isaac F. Duckworth, one of the masters of cast-iron design.

The Broken Kilometer, at 393 West Broadway, is an installation by Walter De Maria *(see p107)*. Its 500 brass rods are arranged to play tricks with perspective. Laid end to end, the rods would measure 1 km.

Performing Garage is a tiny experimental theater that pioneers the work of avant-garde artists.

★ **Greene Street**
Of all Greene Street's fine cast-iron architecture, one of the best is 28–30, the "Queen," which was built by Duckworth in 1872, and has a tall mansard roof ❸

Canal Street-Broadway subway (2 blocks)

10–14 Greene Street dates from 1869. Note the glass circles in the risers of the iron stoop, which allowed daylight to reach the basement.

15–17 Greene Street is a late addition from 1895, in a simple Corinthian style.

★ Singer Building
This terra-cotta beauty was built in 1904 for the famous sewing machine company ❹

Richard Haas, the prolific muralist, has transformed a blank wall into a convincing cast-iron frontage.

LOCATOR MAP
See Manhattan Map pp14–15

KEY

– – – Suggested route

Prince Street subway station (lines N, R)

Dean & DeLuca is one of the best gourmet food stores in New York. Its range includes a global choice of coffee beans *(see p336).*

101 Spring Street, with its simple, geometric facade and large windows, is a fine example of the style that led to the skyscraper.

Spring Street subway station

St. Nicholas Hotel
During the Civil War, this former luxury hotel was used as a headquarters for the Union Army ❷

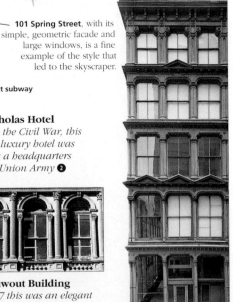

0 meters   100
0 yards   100

STAR SIGHTS

★ Greene Street

★ Singer Building

Haughwout Building
In 1857 this was an elegant store, featuring the first Otis safety elevator ❶

Haughwout Building ❶

488–492 Broadway. **Map** 4 E4.
Ⓜ *Canal St, Spring St.*

Haughwout Building facade

This cast-iron building was erected in 1857 for the E.V. Haughwout china and glassware company, which once supplied the White House. Beneath the grime, the design is superb: rows of windows are framed by arches set on columns flanked by taller columns. Mass-produced sections repeat the pattern over and over. The building was the first to use a steam-driven Otis safety elevator, an innovation that made the skyscraper a possibility.

St. Nicholas Hotel ❷

521–523 Broadway. **Map** 4 E4.
Ⓜ *Prince St, Spring St.*

English parliamentarian W. E. Baxter, visiting New York in 1854, reported of the recently opened St. Nicholas Hotel: "Every carpet is of velvet pile; chair covers and curtains are made of silk or satin damask … and the embroidery on the mosquito nettings itself

St. Nicholas Hotel in its heyday in the mid-19th century

might be exhibited to royalty." It is small wonder, then, that it cost over $1 million to build – and with profits of over $50,000 for that year it must have seemed money well spent. Its glory was short-lived, however. In the Civil War it served as a Union Army head-quarters. Afterward, the better hotels followed the entertain-ment district uptown, and by the mid-1870s the St. Nicholas had closed. There is little left on the ground floor to attest to its former opulence, but look up to the remains of its once-stunning marble facade.

Greene Street ❸

Map 4 E4. Ⓜ *Canal St.*

Haas mural on Greene Street

This is the heart of SoHo's Cast-Iron District. Along five cobblestoned blocks are 50 cast-iron buildings dating from 1869 to 1895. The block between Broome and Spring streets has 13 full cast-iron facades and from 8–34 is the longest row of cast-iron buildings anywhere. Those at 72–76 are known as the "King of Greene Street," but 28–30, the "Queen," is considered to be the finest. The architecture is best appreci-ated as a streetscape, with row upon row of columned facades. Walk into any of the galleries housed within to see the spacious interior lofts.

At the corner of Greene and Prince streets, the illusionistic muralist Richard Haas has created an eye-catching work, disguising a plain brick side wall as a cast-iron frontage. Look for the detail of the little gray cat, which sits primly in an "open window."

Singer Building ❹

561–563 Broadway. **Map** 4 E3.
Ⓜ *Prince St.*

The "little" Singer Building built by Ernest Flagg in 1904 is the second and smaller Flagg structure by this name, and many critics think it superior to the 41-story tower on lower Broadway that was torn down in 1967. The charmingly ornate building is adorned with wrought-iron balconies and graceful arches painted in striking dark green. The 12-story facade of terracotta, glass and steel was advanced for its day, a forerunner of the metal and glass walls to come in the 1940s and 1950s. The building was an office and warehouse for the Singer sewing machine company, and the original Singer name can be seen cast in iron above the entrance to the store on Prince Street.

Early electric-powered Singer sewing machine

Children's Museum of the Arts ❺

182 Lafayette St. **Map** 4 F3. *Tel*
(212) 274-0986. Ⓜ *Prince St.*
M1, M6. ◻ *noon–5pm Wed, Fri,*
Sat, Sun, noon–6pm Thu. **Theater**
workshop *1–6pm Thu.* 🎨 ♿
www.cmany.org

Founded in 1988, this
innovative museum aims to
make the most of children's
artistic potential by
providing plenty of
hands-on activities,
sing-alongs,
workshops, and
performances.
Children aged 1–12
can busy themselves
with paint, glue, paper
and other messy materials
to create their own drawings
and sculptures. For inspiration, displays of work by

**Brightly-colored exhibition space at
the Children's Museum of the Arts**

local artists are exhibited
alongside examples of
children's art from around the
world. Kids can play around
in the dressing-up room and
the ball pond, and the
museum also hosts a varied
program of events appealing
to children and families.

New York Earth Room ❻

141 Wooster St. **Map** 4 E3. *Tel*
(212) 989-5566. Ⓜ *Prince St.* ◻
noon–3pm & 3:30–6pm Wed–Sun.
♿ 📷 www.earthroom.org

Of the three Earth Rooms
created by conceptual artist
Walter De Maria, this is the
only one still in existence.
Commissioned by the Dia
Art Foundation in 1977, the
interior earth sculpture consists

of 280,000 lbs (127,000 kg) of
dirt piled 22 in (56 cm) deep
in a 3,600 sq ft (335 sq m)
room. *The Broken Kilometer,*
another sculpture by De Maria,
can be seen at 393 West
Broadway *(see p104).* It is
composed of 500 solid brass
rods arranged in
five parallel
rows.

**1901 La France
horse-drawn steam
pumper in the City Fire Museum**

New York City Fire Museum ❼

278 Spring St. **Map** 4 D4.
Tel (212) 691-1303. Ⓜ *Spring St.*
◻ *10am–5pm Tue–Sat, 10am–4pm*
Sun. ⬤ *public hols.* 🎨 📷 ♿ 🛈
www.nycfiremuseum.org

This museum is housed in
a Beaux Arts–style 1904
firehouse. New York City's
unsurpassed collection of
fire-fighting equipment and
memorabilia from the 18th
century to 1917 includes scale
models, bells, and hydrants.
Upstairs, fire engines are neatly
lined up for an 1890 parade.
An interactive fire simulation,
available for groups, gives an
insight into fire-fighting.
    The museum's first floor
features an exhibition on
9/11, filled with tributes.

Harrison Street ❽

Map 4 D5. Ⓜ *Chambers St.*

Surrounded by modern
high-rise blocks, this rare row
of eight beautifully restored
Federal town houses, with
their pitched roofs and
distinctive dormer windows,
almost seems like a stage set.
The houses were constructed
in the late 1700s and early
1800s. Two of the buildings
were designed by John
McComb, Jr., New York's first

major native-born architect,
and were moved from
Washington Street, their
original site, for preservation
purposes. The houses had
previously been used as
warehouses and were about
to be razed to the ground,
when, in 1969, the Landmarks
Preservation Commission
intervened to secure the
necessary funding to enable
them to be restored. They are
now privately owned.
    On the other side
of the high-rise
complex is
Washington Market
Park. This area was
formerly the site of
New York City's
wholesale produce
center. The market relocated
to the Bronx in the 1970s.

White Street ❾

Map 4 E5. Ⓜ *Franklin St.*

While not as fine and intricate
as some of the SoHo blocks,
this sampling of TriBeCa
cast-iron architecture shows
a considerably wide range of
styles. The house at No. 2 has
carefully balanced Federal
features and a rare gambrel
roof, in contrast with the
mansard roof of No. 17.
Numbers 8 to 10 White,
designed by Silesian-born
Henry Fernbach, in 1869,
have impressive Tuscan
columns and arches, with
Neo-Renaissance shorter
upper stories to give an
illusion of height. In contrast,
38 White is the home of neon
artist Rudi Stern's gallery, Let
There Be Neon.

**Rudi Stern's Let There Be Neon
gallery in White Street**

GREENWICH VILLAGE

New Yorkers call it "the Village," and it began as a country village, an escape for city dwellers during the yellow fever epidemic of 1822. The crazy-quilt pattern of streets, reflecting early farm boundaries or streams, makes it a natural enclave that has been a bohemian haven and home to many celebrated artists and writers.

Jazz club flag on West 3rd Street

A popular gay district is here, but the area has become mainstream and expensive. Near Washington Square, it is dominated by New York University students. Once cheaper, the East Village attracts a trendy crowd from all over the city. The Meatpacking District, which still functions as such, has become overwhelmed with smart boutiques and restaurants.

SIGHTS AT A GLANCE

Historic Streets and Buildings
75½ Bedford Street ❷
Grove Court ❸
Isaacs-Hendricks House ❹
Jefferson Market Courthouse ❽
Meatpacking District ❺
New York University ❶❺

Patchin Place ❾
St. Luke's Place ❶
Salmagundi Club ❶❶
Washington Mews ❶❹

Museums and Galleries
Forbes Magazine Building ❶⓪

Churches
Church of the Ascension ❶❸
First Presbyterian Church ❶❷
Judson Memorial Church ❶❻

Parks and Squares
The High Line ❻
Sheridan Square ❼
Washington Square ❶❼

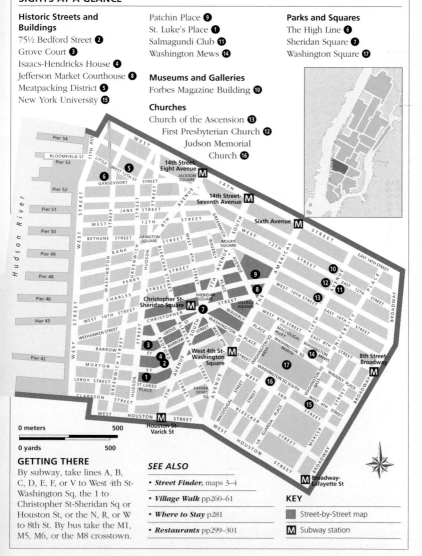

0 meters 500
0 yards 500

GETTING THERE
By subway, take lines A, B, C, D, E, F, or V to West 4th St-Washington Sq, the 1 to Christopher St-Sheridan Sq or Houston St, or the N, R, or W to 8th St. By bus take the M1, M5, M6, or the M8 crosstown.

SEE ALSO

• *Street Finder,* maps 3–4

• *Village Walk* pp260–61

• *Where to Stay* p281

• *Restaurants* pp299–301

KEY

Street-by-Street map

Ⓜ Subway station

◁ **People enjoying relaxed café culture in leafy Greenwich Village**

Street by Street: Greenwich Village

A stroll through historic Greenwich Village is a feast of unexpected small pleasures – charming row houses, hidden alleys, and leafy courtyards. The often quirky architecture suits the bohemian air of the Village. Many famous people, particularly artists and writers, such as playwright Eugene O'Neill and actor Dustin Hoffman, have made their homes in the houses and apartments that line these old-fashioned narrow streets. By night, the Village really comes alive. Late-night coffeehouses and cafés, experimental theaters and music clubs, including some of the best jazz venues, beckon you at every turn.

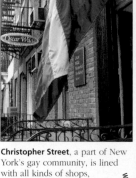

The Lucille Lortel Theater is at No. 121 Christopher Street; it opened in 1955 with *The Threepenny Opera*.

Christopher Street, a part of New York's gay community, is lined with all kinds of shops, bookstores, and bars.

Twin Peaks at No. 102 Bedford Street began life in 1830 as an ordinary house. It was rebuilt in 1926 by architect Clifford Daily to house artists, writers, and actors. Daily believed that the quirky house would help their creativity flourish.

Grove Court
Six houses dating from 1853–4 are set at the back of a quiet leafy courtyard ❸

The building on the corner of Bedford and Grove streets was used as the characters' apartment block in the TV sitcom *Friends*.

CHRISTOPHER STREET
BEDFORD STREET
GROVE STREET
BLEECKER STREET
W 4TH ST.
SEVENTH AVENUE
BARROW STREET
MORTON STREET
ST LUKE'S PLACE

No. 75½ Bedford Street
Built in 1873 in an alley, this is the city's narrowest house ❷

★ **St. Luke's Place**
This beautiful row of Italianate houses was built in the 1850s ❶

To Houston Street subway (2 blocks)

The Cherry Lane Theatre was founded in 1924. Originally a brewery, it was one of the first of the Off-Broadway theaters.

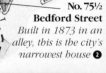

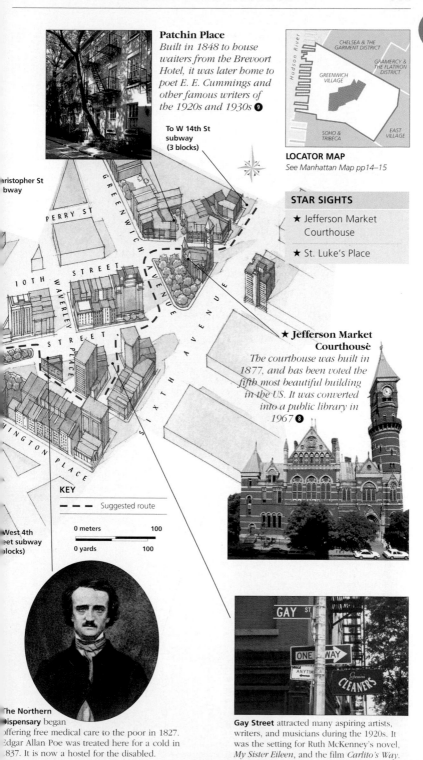

Patchin Place
Built in 1848 to house waiters from the Brevoort Hotel, it was later home to poet E. E. Cummings and other famous writers of the 1920s and 1930s ⑨

To W 14th St subway (3 blocks)

Christopher St subway

PERRY ST

GREENWICH AVENUE

10TH STREET

WAVERLEY PLACE

STREET

WASHINGTON PLACE

SIXTH AVENUE

LOCATOR MAP
See Manhattan Map pp14–15

CHELSEA & THE GARMENT DISTRICT

GRAMERCY & THE FLATIRON DISTRICT

GREENWICH VILLAGE

Hudson River

SOHO & TRIBECA

EAST VILLAGE

STAR SIGHTS

★ Jefferson Market Courthouse

★ St. Luke's Place

★ Jefferson Market Courthouse
The courthouse was built in 1877, and has been voted the fifth most beautiful building in the US. It was converted into a public library in 1967 ⑧

KEY

– – – Suggested route

West 4th Street subway (3 blocks)

0 meters 100
0 yards 100

The Northern Dispensary began offering free medical care to the poor in 1827. Edgar Allan Poe was treated here for a cold in 1837. It is now a hostel for the disabled.

GAY ST
ONE WAY
ANYTIME
Genuine CLEANERS

Gay Street attracted many aspiring artists, writers, and musicians during the 1920s. It was the setting for Ruth McKenney's novel, *My Sister Eileen*, and the film *Carlito's Way*.

Row houses on St. Luke's Place, a street with literary associations

St. Luke's Place ●

Map 3 C3. M *Houston St.*

Fifteen attractive row houses, dating from the 1850s, line the north side of this street. The park opposite is named for a previous resident of St. Luke's Place, Mayor Jimmy Walker, the popular dandy who ran the city from 1926 until he was forced to resign after a financial scandal in 1932.

In front of the house at No. 6 are the tall lamps that always identify a mayor's home in New York. More recently, the most recognizable house on the block has been No. 10, the home of the Huxtable family in *The Cosby Show* (although the series sets it in Brooklyn). This is also the block where *Wait Until Dark* was filmed, starring Audrey Hepburn as a blind woman living at No. 4. Theodore Dreiser was one of several writers, including the poet Marianne Moore, who lived here. Dreiser wrote *An American Tragedy* while living at No. 16. One block north, the corner of Hudson and Morton Streets marked the edge of the Hudson River three centuries ago.

Mayor's lamp at No. 6

75½ Bedford Street ●

Map 3 C2. M Houston St. ○ *to the public.* **www**.cherrylanetheatre.com

New York's narrowest home, just 9½ ft (2.9 m) wide, was built in 1893 in a former passageway. The poet Edna St. Vincent Millay lived here briefly, followed by the actor John Barrymore, and later Cary Grant. The three-story building, now renovated, is marked by a plaque.

Just around the corner, at 38 Commerce Street, Miss Millay founded the Cherry Lane Theater in 1924 as a site for avant-garde drama. It still premieres new works. Its biggest hit was the 1960s musical *Godspell*.

Grove Court ●

Map 3 C2. M *Christopher St/ Sheridan Sq.*

An enterprising grocer named Samuel Cocks built the six town houses here, in an area formed by a bend in the street. (The bends in this part of the Village originally marked divisions between colonial properties.) Cocks reckoned that having residents in the empty passage between 10 and 12 Grove Street would help his business at No. 18.

But residential courts, now highly prized, were not considered respectable in 1854, and the lowbrow residents attracted to the area earned it the nickname "Mixed Ale Alley." O. Henry later chose this block as the setting for his 1902 work *The Last Leaf*.

Isaacs-Hendricks House

Isaacs-Hendricks House ●

77 Bedford St. **Map** 3 C2. M *Houston St.* ○ *to the public.*

This is the oldest surviving home in the Village, built in 1799. The old clapboard walls are visible on the sides and rear; the brickwork and third floor came later. The first owner, John Isaacs, bought the land for $295 in 1794. Next came Harmon Hendricks, a copper dealer and associate of revolutionary Paul Revere. Robert Fulton, who used copper for the boilers in his steamboat, was one of Hendricks's customers.

Meatpacking District ●

Map 3 B1 M *14th St (on lines A, C, E); 8th Av L; Christopher St/ Sheridan Sq.*

Once the domain of butchers in blood-stained aprons, these days (and particularly nights) the Meatpacking District is very different. Squeezed into an area south of 14th Street and west of 9th Avenue, the neighborhood is now dotted with trendy clubs, lounges, and boutique hotels that swell with New Yorkers out for a

The mid-19th-century town houses at Grove Court

good time. The area's hipness quotient rose when Soho House, the New York branch of the London private members' club, moved in, followed by the smart Hotel Gansevoort, with rooftop swimming pool. Hip clothiers have outlets here, upscale restaurants have opened, and new nightclubs and bars pop up every month.

The High Line ❻

Map 3 B1. **Tel** (212) 500-6035. M 14th St (on lines A, C, E); 8th Av L; Christopher St/Sheridan Sq. ⏰ 7am–8pm daily. **www**.thehighline.org

Built on a disused railway line running from the Meatpacking District through West Chelsea to 34th Street, this elevated park offers a unique chance to stroll amid greenery high above the city streets, against a backdrop of the city skyline.

Sheridan Square ❼

Map 3 C2. M Christopher St-Sheridan Sq.

This square, where seven streets converge, is the heart of the Village. It was named for the Civil War General Philip Sheridan who became commander in chief of the US Army in 1883. His statue stands in nearby Christopher Park.

The Draft Riots of 1863 took place here. Over a century later, another famous disturbance rocked the square. The Stonewall Inn on Christopher Street was a gay bar that had stayed in business (it was then illegal for gays to gather in bars) by paying off the police. However, on June 28, 1969, the patrons rebelled, and in the pitched battle that ensued police officers were barricaded inside the bar. It was a landmark moral victory for the budding gay rights movement. The inn that stands today is not the original. The Village remains a focus for the city's gay community.

"Old Jeff," the pointed tower of Jefferson Market Courthouse

Jefferson Market Courthouse ❽

425 Ave of the Americas. **Map** 4 D1. **Tel** (212) 243-4334. M W 4th St-Washington Sq. ⏰ noon–8pm Mon & Wed, 10am–6pm Tue, noon–6pm Thu, 1–6pm Fri, 10am–5pm Sat. ⏺ public hols. ♿ **www**.nypl.org

This treasured Village landmark was saved from the wrecking ball and converted into a branch of the New York Public Library through a spirited preservation campaign that began at a Christmas party in the late 1950s.

The site became a market in 1833, named after former president Thomas Jefferson. Its fire lookout tower had a giant bell that was rung to alert the neighborhood's volunteer fire fighters. In 1865, the founding of the municipal fire department made the bell obsolete, and the Third Judicial District, or Jefferson Market, Courthouse was built. With its Venetian Gothic-style spires and turrets, it was named one of the 10 most beautiful buildings in the country when it opened in 1877. The old fire bell was installed in the tower. Here, in 1906, Harry Thaw was tried for Stanford White's murder (see p126).

Statue of General Sheridan in Christopher Park

By 1945, the market had moved, court sessions had been discontinued, the four-sided clock had stopped and the building was threatened with demolition. In the 1950s, preservationists campaigned first to restore the clock and then the whole building. Its renovation was undertaken by architect Giorgio Cavaglieri, who preserved many of the original details, including the stained glass and a spiral staircase that now leads to the library's dungeonlike reference room.

Facade and an ailanthus tree at Patchin Place

Patchin Place ❾

W 10th St. **Map** 4 D1. M W 4th St-Washington Sq.

One of many delightful and unexpected pockets in the Village is this tiny block of small residences. It is lined with ailanthus trees that were planted in order to "absorb the bad air." The houses were built in the mid-19th century for Basque waiters working at the Brevoort Hotel on Fifth Avenue.

Later the houses became fashionable addresses, with many writers living here. The poet E. E. Cummings lived at No. 4 from 1923 until his death in 1962. The English poet laureate John Masefield also lived on the block, as did the playwright Eugene O'Neill and John Reed, whose eyewitness account of the Russian Revolution, *Ten Days That Shook The World*, was made into a film, *Reds*, directed by Warren Beatty.

Toy battleship from the
Forbes Magazine Collection

Forbes Magazine Building ⑩

60 5th Ave. **Map** 4 E1. *Tel (212) 206-5548.* Ⓜ *14th St-Union Sq.* **Galleries** ◯ *10am–4pm Tue–Wed, Fri–Sat (times may vary). No strollers.* 🚶 *Thu groups only.* ⚙ ◯ *public hols.*

Some architectural critics have called this 1925 limestone cube by Carrère & Hastings pompous. It was originally the headquarters of the Macmillan Publishing Company. When Macmillan moved uptown, the late Malcolm Forbes moved in with his financial magazine, *Forbes.* The Forbes Magazine Galleries here show Forbes's diverse tastes, with over 500 antique toy boats; Monopoly games; trophies; 12,000 toy soldiers; and a signed copy of Abraham Lincoln's Gettysburg Address, among other historical memorabilia. Paintings, from French to American Military works, are also on display.

Salmagundi Club ⑪

47 5th Ave **Map** 4 E1. *Tel (212) 255-7740.* Ⓜ *14th St-Union Sq.* ◯ *1–5pm daily.* 🚫 **www**.salmagundi.org

America's oldest artists club resides in the last remaining mansion on lower Fifth Avenue. Built in 1853 for Irad Hawley, it now houses the American Artists' Professional League, the American Watercolor Society and the

Greenwich Village Society for Historic Preservation. Washington Irving's satiric periodical, *The Salmagundi Papers,* gave the club its name.

Founded in 1871, the club moved here in 1917. Periodic art exhibits open the late 19th-century interior to the public.

Exterior of the Salmagundi Club

First Presbyterian Church ⑫

5th Ave at 12th St. **Map** 4 D1. *Tel (212) 675-6150* Ⓜ *14th St-Union Sq.* ◯ *11:45am–12.30pm Mon, Wed, Fri, 11am–12:30pm Sun.* 🚶 *6pm Wed in chapel.* **www**.fpcnyc.org

Designed by Joseph C. Wells in 1846, this Gothic church was modeled on the Church of St Saviour in Bath, England. The church is noteworthy for its brownstone tower. The carved wooden plaques on the altar list every pastor since 1716. The south transept by McKim, Mead & White was added in 1893. The fence of iron and wood was built in 1844 and restored in 1981.

Church of the Ascension ⑬

5th Ave at 10th St. **Map** 4 E1. *Tel (212) 254-8620* Ⓜ *14th St-Union Sq.* ◯ *noon–2pm, 5–7pm daily.* 🚶 *6pm Mon–Fri, 9am, 11am Sun.* 📷 *(except during services).* **www**.ascensionnyc.org

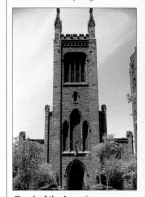

Church of the Ascension

This English Gothic Revival church was designed in 1840–41 by Richard Upjohn, architect of Trinity Church. The interior was redone in 1888 by Stanford White, with an altar relief by Augustus Saint-Gaudens. Above the altar hangs *The Ascension*, a mural by John La Farge, who also designed some of the stained glass. The belfry tower is lit at night to show off the colors. In 1844 President John Tyler married Julia Gardiner here; she lived in nearby Colonnade Row *(see p120)*.

Washington Mews ⑭

Between Washington Sq N and E 8th St. **Map** 4 E2. Ⓜ *W 4th St.*

Built originally as stables, this hidden enclave was turned into carriage houses around 1900. The south side was added in 1939. Gertrude Vanderbilt Whitney, founder of the Whitney Museum *(see pp200–01)*, once lived here.

At No. 16 is NYU's French House, remodeled in a French style. Movies, lectures, and classes in French are held here.

New York University ⑮

Washington Sq. **Map** 4 E2.
Tel *(212) 998-1212, (212) 998-4636.* Ⓜ *W 4th St.* ⊙ *8:30am–8pm Mon-Fri.* **www**.nyu.edu

Originally called the University of the City of New York, NYU was founded in 1831 as an alternative to Episcopalian Columbia University. It is now the largest private university in the US and extends for blocks around Washington Square.

Construction of the school's first building on Waverly Place sparked the Stone-cutters' Guild Riot of 1833: contractors protested the use of inmates from a state prison to cut stone. The National Guard restored order. The original building no longer exists, but a memorial with a piece of the original tower is on a pedestal set into the pavement on Washington Square South. Samuel Morse's telegraph, John W. Draper's first-ever photographic

Bust of Sylvette by Picasso, between Bleecker and West Houston streets

portrait and Samuel Colt's six-shooter were invented here.

The Brown Building, on Washington Place near Greene Street, was the site of the Triangle Shirtwaist Company. In 1911, 146 factory workers died in a fire here, leading to new fire safety and labor laws.

A 36-ft (11-m) enlargement of Picasso's *Bust of Sylvette* is in University Village.

Judson Memorial Church ⑯

55 Washington Sq S. **Map** 4 D2.
Tel *(212) 477-0351.* Ⓜ *W 4th St.* ⊙ *10am–1pm, 2pm–6pm Mon–Fri.* ✝ *Sun 11am.* **www**.judson.org

Built in 1892, this McKim, Mead & White church is an impressive Romanesque building with stained glass by John La Farge. Designed by Stanford White, it is named after the first American missionary sent to foreign soil, Adoniram Judson, who served in Burma in 1811. A copy of his Burmese trans-lation of the Bible was put in the cornerstone when the building was dedicated.

It is the unique spirit of this church, not the architecture, that makes it stand out. Judson Memorial has played an active role in local and world concerns and has been the site of activism on issues ranging from AIDS to the arms race. It is also home to avant-garde art exhibitions and Off-Off Broadway plays.

Arch on the north side of Washington Square

Washington Square ⑰

Map 4 D2. Ⓜ *W 4th St.*

This vibrant open space was once marshland through which the quiet Minetta Brook flowed. By the late 1700s, the area had been turned into a public cemetery – when excavation began for the park, some 10,000 skeletal remains were exhumed. The square was used as a dueling ground for a time, then as a site

for public hangings until 1819. The "hanging elm" in the northwest corner remains. In 1826 the marsh was filled in and the brook diverted under-ground, where it still flows; a small sign on a fountain at the entrance to Two Fifth Avenue marks its course.

The magnificent marble arch by Stanford White, was completed in 1895 and replaced an earlier wooden arch that spanned lower Fifth Avenue to mark the centenary of George Washington's inauguration. A stairway is hidden in the right side of the arch. In 1916, a group of artists led by Marcel Duchamp and John Sloan broke in, climbed atop the arch, and declared the "free and independent republic of Washington Square, the state of New Bohemia."

Across the street is "the Row." Now part of NYU, this block was once home to New York's most prominent families. The Delano family, writers Edith Wharton, Henry James and John dos Passos, and artist Edward Hopper all lived here. Number 8 was once the mayor's official home.

Today students, families and free spirits mingle and enjoy the park side by side. A few drug dealers frequent the park, but it is safe by day.

Window on the corner of West 4th Street and Washington Square

EAST VILLAGE

Peter Stuyvesant had a country estate in the East Village, and in the 19th century, the Astors and Vanderbilts lived here. But around 1900, high society moved uptown and immigrants moved in. The Irish, Germans, Jews, Poles, Ukrainians and Puerto Ricans all left their mark in the area's churches and landmarks, and the city's most varied

Mosaic, facade of St. George's Ukrainian Catholic Church

and least expensive ethnic restaurants. In the 1950s low rents attracted the "beat generation." Later, hippies were followed by punks, and experimental music clubs and theaters still abound. Astor Place buzzes with students. To the east are Avenues A, B, C, and D, an area known as "Alphabet City," which has been transformed into one of New York's trendiest areas.

SIGHTS AT A GLANCE

Historic Streets and Buildings
Bayard-Condict Building ❽
Colonnade Row ❸
Cooper Union ❶

Museums and Galleries
Merchant's House Museum ❹

Churches
Grace Church ❻
St. Mark's-in-the-Bowery Church ❺

Parks and Squares
Tompkins Square ❼

Famous Theaters
Public Theater ❷

SEE ALSO
• *Street Finder,* maps 4, 5
• *Where to Stay* pp281–2
• *Restaurants* pp301–2

GETTING THERE
By subway, the 6 train stop at Astor Place is the most convenient or the F or V to 2nd Ave for Alphabet City; the area is also served by the M9, M14A, M15, and M103 buses and the M8 crosstown bus.

KEY
▢ Street-by-Street map
Ⓜ Subway station

0 meters 500
0 yards 500

Gothic bas-relief on the facade of Grace Church

◁ **The interior of McSorley's Old Ale House**

Street by Street: East Village

At the spot where Tenth and Stuyvesant streets now intersect, Peter Stuyvesant's country house once stood. His grandson, also named Peter, inherited most of the property and had it divided into streets in 1787. Among the prize sites of the St. Mark's Historic District are the St. Mark's-in-the-Bowery Church, the Stuyvesant-Fish house and the 1795 home of Nicholas Stuyvesant, both on Stuyvesant Street. Many other homes in the district were built between 1871 and 1890 and still have their original stoops, lintels and other architectural details.

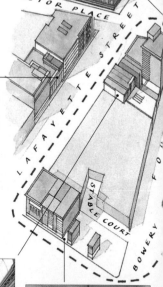

Astor Place subway (line 6)

Astor Place saw rioting in 1849. English actor William Macready, playing Hamlet at the Astor Place Opera House, criticized American actor Edwin Forrest. Forrest's fans revolted and there were 34 deaths.

Alamo is the title of the 15-ft (4.5-m) steel cube in Astor Place designed by Bernard Rosenthal. It revolves when pushed.

Colonnade Row
Now in shabby disrepair, these buildings were once expensive town houses. The houses, of which only four are left, are unified by one facade in the European style. The marble was quarried by Sing Sing prisoners ❸

Public Theater
In 1965 the late Joseph Papp convinced the city to buy the Astor Library (1849) as a home for the theater. Now restored, it sees the opening of many famous plays ❷

★ Merchant's House Museum
This museum displays Federal, American Empire, and Victorian furniture ❹

STAR SIGHTS

- ★ Cooper Union
- ★ Merchant's House Museum

★ **Cooper Union**
Founded by self-made man Peter Cooper in 1859, it still provides a free education to its students ❶

The Stuyvesant-Fish House
(1803–04) was constructed out of brick. It is a classic example of a Federal-style house.

St. Mark's-in-the-Bowery-Church
The church was built in 1799 and the steeple added in 1828 ❺

Renwick Triangle
is a group of 16 houses built in the Italianate style in 1861.

LOCATOR MAP
See Manhattan Map pp14–15

Stuyvesant Polyclinic
was founded in 1857 as the German Dispensary, and it is still a health clinic. The facade is decorated with the busts of many famous physicians and scientists.

St. Mark's Place was once the main street of hippie life. It is still the hub of the East Village youth scene. Funky shops now occupy many of the basements.

```
0 meters        100
0 yards         100
```

Little India,
the row of Indian eateries on the south side of East Sixth Street, offers a taste of India at budget prices.

KEY

– – – Suggested route

Little Ukraine is home to 30,000 Ukrainians. The hub is St. George's Ukrainian Catholic Church.

McSorley's Old Ale House still brews its own ale and serves it in surroundings seemingly unchanged since it opened in 1854 *(see p317).*

Great Hall at Cooper Union, where Abraham Lincoln spoke

Cooper Union ❶

7 East 7th St. **Map** 4 F2.
Tel (212) 353-4000. Ⓜ Astor Pl.
◯ 11am–7pm Mon–Fri, 11am–5pm
Sat, and for lectures and concerts in
Great Hall. ◯ Jun–Aug, public hols.
⊠ ♿ www.cooper.edu

Peter Cooper, the wealthy industrialist who built the first US steam locomotive, made the first steel rails and was a partner in the first transatlantic cable venture, had no formal schooling. In 1859 he founded New York's first free, non-sectarian coeducational college specializing in design, engineering, and architecture. Still free, the school inspires intense competition for places. The six-story building, renovated in 1973–4, was the first with a steel frame, made of Cooper's own rails. The Great Hall was inaugurated in 1859 by Mark Twain, and Lincoln delivered his "Right Makes Might" speech there in 1860. Cooper Union still sponsors a Public Forum.

Public Theater ❷

425 Lafayette St. **Map** 4 F2. **Tel** (212)
239-6200 (tickets). Admin (212) 539-
8500. Ⓜ Astor Pl. See also **Entertainment** p344. www.publictheater.org

This large redbrick and brownstone building began its life in 1849 as the Astor Library, the city's first free library,

The Public Theater on Lafayette Street

now part of the New York Public Library. It is a prime American example of German Romanesque Revival style.

When the building was threatened with demolition in 1965, Joseph Papp, founder of the New York Shakespeare Festival, which became The Public Theater, persuaded New York City to buy it as a home for the company. Renovation began in 1967, and much of the handsome interior was preserved during conversion into six theaters. Although much of the work shown is experimental, The Public Theater was the original home of hit musicals *Hair* and *A Chorus Line* and hosts the popular Shakespeare in the Park (in Central Park) every summer.

Colonnade Row ❸

428–434 Lafayette St. **Map** 4 F2.
Ⓜ Astor Pl. ◯ to the public.

The Corinthian columns across these four buildings are all that remain of a once-magnificent row of nine Greek Revival town houses. They were completed in 1833 by developer Seth Geer and were known as "Geer's Folly" by skeptics who thought no one would live so far east. They were proved wrong when the houses were taken by such eminent citizens as John

Jacob Astor and Cornelius Vanderbilt. Washington Irving, author of *Rip Van Winkle* and other classic American tales, lived here for a time, as did two English novelists, William Makepeace Thackeray and Charles Dickens. Five of the houses were lost when the John Wanamaker Department Store razed them in the early 20th century to make room for a garage. The remaining buildings are falling to ruin.

Merchant's House Museum ❹

29 E 4th St. **Map** 4 F2. **Tel** (212)
777-1089. Ⓜ Astor Pl., Bleecker St.
◯ noon–5pm Mon, Thu–Sun and
by appt. 🎦 ⊠ ♻ 🚫
www.merchantshouse.com

The original 19th-century iron stove in the kitchen of the Merchant's House Museum

This remarkable Greek Revival brick town house, improbably tucked away on an East Village block, is a time capsule of a vanished way of life. It still has both its original fixtures and its kitchen, and is filled with the actual furniture, ornaments, and utensils of the family that lived here for almost 100 years. Built in 1832, it was bought in 1835 by Seabury Tredwell, a wealthy merchant, and stayed in the family until Gertrude Tredwell, the last member, died in 1933. She had maintained her father's home just as he would have liked it, and a relative opened the house as a museum in 1936. The first-floor parlors are very grand, a sign of how well New York's merchant class lived in the 1800s.

St. Mark's-in-the-Bowery Church ❺

131 E 10th St. **Map** 4 F1. **Tel** (212) 674-6377. Ⓜ Astor Pl. ⏱ 8:30am– 4pm Mon–Fri (hours may vary). ✝ 6:30pm Wed, 11am Sun; in Spanish 5:30pm Sat.

One of New York's oldest churches, this 1799 building replaced a 1660 church on the *bouwerie* (farm) of Governor Peter Stuyvesant. He is buried here, along with seven generations of his descendants and many other prominent early New Yorkers. Poet W.H. Auden was a parishioner and is also commemorated here.

In 1878, a grisly kidnapping took place when the remains of department store magnate A.T. Stewart were removed from the site and held for $20,000 ransom.

The church rectory at 232 East 11th Street dates from 1900 and is by Ernest Flagg, who achieved renown for his Singer Building *(see p106)*.

Grace Church ❻

802 Broadway. **Map** 4 F1. **Tel** (212) 254-2000. Ⓜ Astor Pl, Union Sq. 🚌 M1. ✝ Jul–Aug: 10am, 6pm Sun; Sep–Jun: 9am, 11am, 6pm Sun. ♿ ♿ **Concerts.** **www**.gracechurchnyc.org

James Renwick, Jr., the architect of St. Patrick's Cathedral, was only 23 when he designed this church, yet many consider it his finest achievement. Its delicate early Gothic lines have a grace befitting the church's name. The interior is just as beautiful, with Pre-Raphaelite stained glass and a handsome mosaic floor.

The church's peace and serenity were briefly shattered in 1863, when Phineas T. Barnum

Grace Church altar and window

staged the wedding of midget General Tom Thumb here; the crowds turned the event into complete chaos.

The marble spire replaced a wooden steeple in 1888 amid fears that it might prove too heavy for the church – and it has since developed a distinct lean. The church is visible from afar, because it is on a bend on Broadway. Henry Brevoort forced the city to bend Broadway to divert it around his apple orchard.

Tom Thumb and his bride at Grace Church

Tompkins Square ❼

Map 5 B1. Ⓜ 2nd Ave, 1st Ave. 🚌 M9, M14A.

This English-style park has the makings of a peaceful spot, but its past has more often been dominated by strife. It was the site of America's first organized labor demonstration in 1874, the main gathering place during the neighborhood's hippie era of the 1960s and, in 1991, an arena for violent riots when the police tried to evict homeless people who had taken over the grounds. The square also contains a poignant monument to the neighborhood's greatest tragedy. A small statue of a boy

and a girl looking at a steamboat commemorates the deaths of over 1,000 local residents in the *General Slocum* steamer disaster. On June 15, 1904, the boat caught fire during a pleasure cruise on the East River. The boat was crowded with women and children from this then-German neighborhood. Many local men lost their entire families and moved away, leaving the area and its memories behind.

Bayard-Condict Building ❽

65 Bleecker St. **Map** 4 F3. Ⓜ Bleecker St.

The graceful columns, elegant filigreed terra-cotta facade and magnificent cornice on this 1898 building mark the only New York work by Louis Sullivan, the great Chicago architect who taught Frank Lloyd Wright. He died in poverty and obscurity in Chicago in 1924.

Sullivan is said to have objected vigorously to the sentimental angels supporting the Bayard-Condict Building's cornice, but he eventually gave in to the wishes of Silas Alden Condict, the owner.

Because this building is squeezed into a commercial block, it is better appreciated from a distance. Cross the street and walk a little way down Crosby Street for the best view.

The Bayard-Condict Building

GRAMERCY AND THE FLATIRON DISTRICT

Four squares were laid out in this area by real estate developers in the 19th century to emulate the quiet, private residential areas in many European cities. Gramercy Park, still mainly residential, was one of them. The townhouses around this square were designed by some of the

Lizard on a statue in Union Square

country's best architects, such as Calvert Vaux and Stanford White, and occupied by some of New York's most prominent citizens. Today, not far away, boutiques, trendy cafés, and high-rise apartments have taken over the stretch of lower Fifth Avenue just south of the famous Flatiron Building.

SIGHTS AT A GLANCE

Historic Streets and Buildings
Appellate Division of the Supreme Court of the State of New York **3**
Block Beautiful **11**
Con Edison Headquarters **14**
Flatiron Building **5**
Gramercy Park Hotel **12**
Ladies' Mile **6**
Metropolitan Life Insurance Company **4**

National Arts Club **8**
New York Life Insurance Company **2**
The Library at the Players **9**

Museums and Galleries
Theodore Roosevelt Birthplace **7**

Churches
The Little Church Around the Corner **16**

Parks and Squares
Gramercy Park **10**
Madison Square **1**
Stuyvesant Square **13**
Union Square **15**

SEE ALSO

- *Street Finder,* maps 8, 9
- *Where to Stay* p282
- *Restaurants* pp302–3

0 meters 500
0 yards 500

GETTING THERE
The closest subway stations are at 23rd St, where the N, R, F, V, W, and 6 trains stop, and Union Sq, for the N, Q, R, W, L, 4, 5, and 6 trains. Buses to the area include the M101–3 on 3rd Ave, the M1–3 or M5 on 5th and Madison Aves, and the M6 and M7 on Broadway.

KEY
Street-by-Street map
M Subway station

◁ Con Edison Headquarters by night

Street by Street: Gramercy Park

Gramercy Park and nearby Madison Square tell a tale of two cities. Madison Square is ringed by offices and traffic and is used mainly by those who work nearby, but the fine surrounding commercial architecture and statues make it well worth visiting. It was once the home of Stanford White's famous pleasure palace, the old Madison Square Garden, a place where revelers always thronged. Gramercy Park, however, retains the air of dignified tranquility it has become known for. Here, the residences and clubs remain, set around New York's last private park, for which only those who live on the square have a key.

Statue of Diana atop the old Madison Square Garden

★ Madison Square
The Knickerbocker Club played baseball here in the 1840s and was the first to codify the game's rules.
Today office workers enjoy the park's many statues of 19th-century figures, among them Admiral David Farragut ❶

23rd Street subway (lines N, R)

★ Flatiron Building
The triangle made by Fifth Avenue, Broadway, and 23rd Street is the site of one of New York's most famous early skyscrapers. When it was built in 1903, it was the world's tallest building ❺

A sidewalk clock found in front of 200 Fifth Avenue marks the very end of the once-fashionable shopping area, known as Ladies' Mile.

Ladies' Mile
Broadway from Union Square to Madison Square was once New York's finest shopping area ❻

Theodore Roosevelt Birthplace
The house is a replica of the one in which the 26th American president was born ❼

KEY

– – – Suggested route

0 yards   100

National Arts Club
This is a private club for the arts, on the south side of the park ❽

Appellate Court
This small marble palace is said to be the world's busiest courthouse ❸

LOCATOR MAP
See Manhattan Map pp14–15

New York Life Insurance Company
This spectacular building by Cass Gilbert bears his trade-mark pyramid-shaped top ❷

STAR SIGHTS

★ Flatiron Building

★ Madison Square

Metropolitan Life Insurance Company
Vast vaulted entrances mark each corner ❹

23rd Street subway (line 6)

Gramercy Park
Only residents can use the park itself, but all can enjoy the peace and charm of the area around it ❿

The Library at the Players
Actor Edwin Booth founded this club in 1888 ❾

The Brotherhood Synagogue was a Friends' Meeting House from 1859 to 1975, when it became a synagogue.

The Block Beautiful
This is a tree-lined stretch of East 19th Street. No particular house is outstanding, but the street as a whole is lovely ⓫

Pete's Tavern has been here since 1864. Short story writer O. Henry, a well-known chronicler of the city, wrote "The Gift of the Magi" in the second booth.

Madison Square ❶

Map 8 F4. Ⓜ *23rd St.*

Farragut's statue, Madison Square

Planned as the center of a fashionable residential district, this square became a popular entertainment center after the Civil War. It was bordered by the elegant Fifth Avenue Hotel, the Madison Square Theater, and Stanford White's Madison Square Garden. The torch-bearing arm of the Statue of Liberty was exhibited here in 1884.

The Shake Shack is a top lunchtime spot for neighborhood office workers, while the surrounding park makes for a leisurely stroll to admire the sculptures. The 1880 statue of Admiral David Farragut is by Augustus Saint-Gaudens, with a pedestal by Stanford White. Farragut was the hero of a Civil War sea battle; figures representing Courage and Loyalty are carved on the base. The statue of Roscoe Conkling commemorates a US senator who died during the great blizzard of 1888. The Eternal Light flagpole, by Carrère & Hastings, honors the soldiers who fell during World War I.

New York Life Insurance Company ❷

51 Madison Ave. **Map** 9 A3. Ⓜ *28th St.* ◯ *office hours.*

This imposing building was designed in 1928 by Cass Gilbert of Woolworth Building fame. The interior is a masterpiece, adorned with enormous hanging lamps, bronze doors and paneling, and a grand staircase leading, of all places, to the subway station.

Other famous buildings have stood on this site. Barnum's

Hippodrome was here in 1874, then the first Madison Square Garden opened in 1879. A wide range of entertainments were put on, including the prizefights of heavyweight boxing hero John L. Sullivan in the 1880s. The next Madison Square Garden – Stanford White's legendary pleasure palace – opened on the same site in 1890. Lavish musical shows and social events were attended by New York's elite, who paid over $500 for a box at the prestigious annual horse show.

The building had street-level arcades and a tower modeled on the Giralda in Seville. A gold statue of the goddess Diana stood atop the tower. Her nudity was shocking, but far more scandalous was the decadent life and death of White himself. In 1906, while watching a revue in the roof garden, he was shot dead by millionaire Harry K. Thaw, the husband of White's former mistress, showgirl Evelyn Nesbit. The headline in the journal *Vanity Fair* summed up popular feeling: "Stanford White, Voluptuary and Pervert, Dies the Death of a Dog." The ensuing trial's revelations about decadent Broadway high society leave modern soap operas far behind.

New York Life Insurance Company's golden pyramid roof

Appellate Division of the Supreme Court of the State of New York ❸

E. 25th St. at Madison Ave. **Map** 9 A4 Ⓜ *23rd St.* ◯ *9am–5pm Mon–Fri (court in session from 2pm Tue–Thu, from 10am Fri).* ● *public hols.* ✍

Appeals relating to civil and criminal cases for New York and the Bronx are heard here, in what is widely considered to be the busiest court of its kind in the world. James Brown Lord designed the small yet noble Palladian Revival building in 1900. It is decorated with more than a

Statues of *Justice* and *Study* above the Appellate Court

dozen handsome sculptures, including Daniel Chester French's Justice flanked by Power and Study. During the week, the public is invited to step inside to admire the fine interior, designed by the Herter brothers, including the courtroom when it is not in session. Among the elegant details worth looking for are the fine stained-glass windows and dome, the murals, and the striking cabinetwork.

Displays in the lobby often feature some of the more famous –and infamous – cases that have been heard in this court. Among the celebrity names that have been involved in appeals settled here are Babe Ruth, Charlie Chaplin, Fred Astaire, Harry Houdini, Theodore Dreiser, and Edgar Allan Poe.

Clock tower of the Metropolitan Life Insurance Company building

Metropolitan Life Insurance Company **4**

1 Madison Ave. **Map** 9 A4.
M 23rd St. ◯ banking hours. 🚫

In 1909, the addition of a 700-ft (210-m) tower to this 1893 building ousted the Flatiron as the tallest in the world. The huge four-sided clock has minute hands said to weigh 1000 lb (454 kg) each. The building is lit up at night, and is a familiar part of the evening skyline. It served as the company symbol "the light that never fails."
A series of historical murals by N.C. Wyeth, the famed illustrator of such classics as *Robin Hood*, *Treasure Island* and *Robinson Crusoe* (and the father of painter Andrew Wyeth), once graced the walls of the cafeteria. The building now houses First-Boston Crédit-Suisse.

Flatiron Building **5**

175 5th Ave. **Map** 8 F4. **M** 23rd St.
◯ office hours.

Originally named the Fuller Building after the construction company that owned it, this building by Chicago architect Daniel Burnham was the tallest in the world when it was completed in 1902. One of the first buildings to use a steel frame, it heralded the era of the skyscrapers.
It soon became known as the Flatiron for its unusual triangular shape, but some called it "Burnham's folly," predicting that the winds created by the building's shape would knock it down. It has withstood the test of time, but the winds along 23rd Street did have one notable effect. In the building's early days, they drew crowds of males hoping to get a peek at women's ankles as their long skirts got blown about. Police officers had to keep people moving along, and their call, "23-skidoo" became slang for "scram."
The stretch of Fifth Avenue to the south of the building, formerly rather run down, has come to life with chic shops such as Emporio Armani and Paul Smith, giving the area new cachet and a new name, "the Flatiron District."

Flatiron Building during its construction

Ladies' Mile **6**

Broadway (Union Sq. to Madison Sq.). **Map** 8 F4–5, 9 A5. **M** 14th St, 23rd St.

Arnold Constable store

In the 19th century, the "carriage trade" came here in shiny traps from their town houses nearby, to shop at stores such as Arnold Constable (Nos. 881–887) and Lord & Taylor (No. 901). The ground floor exteriors have changed beyond recognition; look up to see the remains of once-grand facades.

President Teddy Roosevelt

Theodore Roosevelt Birthplace **7**

28 E. 20th St. **Map** 9 A5. **Tel** (212) 260-1616. **M** 14th St.-Union Sq-23rd St. ◯ 9am–5pm Tue–Sat (last adm: 4pm). ● pub hols. 🚫 📷 🎥 hourly. **Lectures, concerts, films, videos.** 🔲 www.nps.gov/thrb

The reconstructed boyhood home of the colorful 26th president displays everything from the toys with which the young Teddy played to campaign buttons and emblems of the trademark "Rough Rider" hat that Roosevelt wore in the Spanish-American War. One exhibit features his explorations and interests; the other covers his political career.

Bas-relief faces of great writers at the National Arts Club

National Arts Club ❽

15 Gramercy Pk S. **Map** 9 A5. **Tel** (212) 475-3424. Ⓜ *23rd St.* ◯ *noon–5pm Mon–Fri during exhibitions.* **www**.nationalartsclub.org

This brownstone was the residence of New York governor Samuel Tilden, who condemned "Boss" Tweed *(see p27)* and established a free public library. He had the facade redesigned by Calvert Vaux in 1881–4. In 1906 the National Arts Club bought the home and kept the original high ceilings and stained glass by John La Farge. Members have included most leading American artists of the late 19th and early 20th century, who were asked to donate a painting or sculpture in return for life membership; these gifts form the permanent collection. The club is open to the public for exhibitions only.

The Library at the Players ❾

18 Gramercy Pk S. **Map** 9 A5. **Tel** (212) 228-7610. Ⓜ *23rd St.* ⬤ *except for pre-booked group tours.* 📷

This two-story brownstone was the home of actor Edwin Booth, brother of John Wilkes Booth, President Lincoln's assassin. Architect Stanford White remodeled the

building as a club in 1888. Although intended primarily for actors, members have included White himself, author Mark Twain, publisher Thomas Nast and Winston Churchill, whose mother, Jennie Jerome, was born nearby. A statue of Booth playing Hamlet is across the street in Gramercy Park.

Decorative grille at The Players club

Gramercy Park ❿

Map 9 A4. Ⓜ *23rd St, 14th St-Union Sq.*

Gramercy Park is one of four squares (with Union, Stuyvesant and Madison) laid out in the 1830s and 1840s to attract society residences. It is the city's only private park, and residents in the surrounding buildings have keys to the park gate as the original owners once did. Look through the railings at the southeast corner to see Greg Wyatt's fountain, with giraffes leaping around a smiling sun.

The buildings around the square were designed by some of the city's most famous

Fountain with sun and giraffes by Greg Wyatt in Gramercy Park

architects, including Stanford White, whose house was located on the site of today's Gramercy Park Hotel. Particularly fine are 3 and 4, with graceful cast-iron gates and porches. The lanterns in front of 4 serve as symbols marking the house of a former mayor of the city, James Harper. Number 34 (1883) has been the home of the sculptor Daniel Chester French, the actor James Cagney and circus impresario John Ringling (who had a massive pipe organ installed in his apartment).

Block Beautiful ⓫

E 19th St. **Map** 9 A5. Ⓜ *14th St-Union Sq, 23rd St.*

House facade on the Block Beautiful on East 19th Street

This is a serene, tree-lined block of 1920s residences, beautifully restored. None of them is exceptional on its own, but together they create a wonderfully harmonious whole. Number 132 had two famous theatrical tenants: Theda Bara, silent movie star and Hollywood's first sex symbol, and the fine Shakespearean actress Mrs. Patrick Campbell, who originated the role of Eliza Doolittle in George Bernard Shaw's *Pygmalion* in 1914. The hitching posts outside 141 and the ceramic relief of giraffes outside 147–149 are two of the many details to look for as you walk along the block.

Gramercy Park Hotel ⓬

2 Lexington Ave at 21st St. **Map** 9 B4.
Tel (212) 475-4320. **M** *14th St-Union Sq,
23rd St.* **www**.gramercyparkhotel.com

Located on the site of Stanford
White's house, this hotel has,
for more than 60 years, been
a home away from home for
many international visitors
and New Yorkers alike. It is
also right next to the only
private park in Manhattan.

The shabby-chic hotel drew
all types, from old matrons,
to wealthy young rock stars.
Then Ian Schrager, of Studio
54 fame, began a $200-million
renovation, in which the 185-
room hotel was given an
"eclectic-Bohemian" look by
artist Julian Schnabel. The
conversion included 23 condominiums that range in price
from $5 million to $10 million.
The elegant Rose and Jade
bars and a Chinese restaurant
are open to the public.

Stuyvesant Square ⓭

Map 9 B5. **M** *3rd Ave, 1st Ave.*

This oasis, in the form of
a pair of parks divided by
Second Avenue, was part of
Peter Stuyvesant's original
farm in the 1600s. It was still
in the Stuyvesant family when
the park was designed in
1836; Peter G. Stuyvesant sold
the land to the city for the
nominal sum of $5 (much to
the delight of those living
nearby, who saw real estate
values jump). A statue of
Stuyvesant by Gertrude
Vanderbilt Whitney stands in
the park. The park separated
the Stuyvesant area from the
poorer Gas House district.

Con Edison Headquarters ⓮

145 E 14th St. **Map** 9 A5. **M** *3rd Ave,
14th St-Union Sq.* ⬤ *to the public.*

The clock tower of this
building, which dates from
1911, is a local landmark.
Originally conceived by
Henry Hardenbergh, the

The towers of Con Edison (right), Metropolitan Life and the Empire State

architect best known for
such buildings as the Dakota
(see p218) and the Plaza
(see p181). The 26-story
tower was built by the same
firm who designed Grand
Central Terminal. Near the
top of the tower, a 38-ft
(11.6-m) bronze lantern was
built as a memorial to Con
Ed's employees who died
in World War I. The tower
itself is not as tall as nearby
Empire State Building, but
when it is lit up at night, it
makes an attractive show-
piece, in addition to a potent
symbol of the company that
keeps Manhattan and the
other four boroughs shining.

Union Square ⓯

Map 9 A5. **M** *14th St-Union Sq.*
Farmers' Market ◯ *8am–6pm
Mon, Wed, Fri, Sat.*

Greenmarket day at Union Square

Opened in 1839, this park
joined Bloomingdale Road
(now Broadway) with the
Bowery Road (Fourth Avenue
or Park), and hence its name.
Later, the center of the square

was lifted up for a subway
to run beneath it. The park
became popular with soap-
box orators. During the
Depression in 1930, more
than 35,000 unemployed
people rallied here, before
marching on to City Hall to
demand jobs. The square
hosts a greenmarket and is
ringed by various shops from
discount department stores to
gourmet supermarkets.

The Little Church Around the Corner ⓰

1 E 29th St. **Map** 8 F3. *Tel* (212)
684-6770. **M** *28th St.* ◯ *8am–6pm
daily.* ✝ *12:10pm Mon–Fri; 8:30am,
11am Sun.* ◯ & ✉ *Sun, after
11am service.* **Lectures & concerts.**
www.littlechurch.org

Built from 1849 to 1856, the
Episcopal Church of the
Transfiguration is a tranquil
retreat. It has been known by
its nickname since 1870 when
Joseph Jefferson tried to
arrange the funeral of fellow
actor George Holland. The
pastor at a nearby church
refused to bury a person of so
lowly a profession. Instead, he
suggested "the little church
around the corner." The name
stuck and the church has had
special ties with the theater
ever since. Sarah Bernhardt
attended services here.

The south transept window,
by John La Farge, shows
Edwin Booth playing Hamlet.
Jefferson's cry of "God bless
the little church around the
corner" is commemorated in
a window in the south aisle.

CHELSEA AND
THE GARMENT DISTRICT

This was open farmland in 1750. By the 1830s it was a suburb, and in the 1870s, with the coming of the elevated railroads *(see pp26–7)*, it had become commercial. Music halls and theaters lined 23rd Street. Fashion Row grew in the shadow of the El, with department stores serving middle-class New York. As fashion moved uptown, Chelsea drifted downhill. It became a warehouse district, until the Els were removed and New Yorkers rediscovered its town houses. When Macy's arrived at Herald Square to the north, the retailing and garment districts grew around it, along with the flower district. Today Chelsea is filled with art galleries and antique shops and has a large gay community.

Statue of garment worker, at 555 7th Avenue

Inside Chelsea's Empire Diner

SIGHTS AT A GLANCE

Historic Streets and Buildings
Chelsea Historic District 12
Empire State Building pp136–7 2
General Post Office 7
General Theological Seminary 11
Hugh O'Neill Dry Goods Store 14

Churches
Marble Collegiate Reformed Church 1
St. John the Baptist Church 5

Modern Architecture
Chelsea Piers Complex 9
Jacob K. Javits Convention Center 8
Madison Square Garden 6

Monuments
Worth Monument 15

Parks and Squares
Herald Square 3

Landmark Hotels and Restaurants
Empire Diner 10
Hotel Chelsea 13

Landmark Stores
Macy's 4

GETTING THERE

To Chelsea, take the 1 subway train to 18th or 23rd St. The C and E trains go to 23rd St. Buses include the M11 and M20. For the area around Macy's, take the 1, 2, or 3 express trains to 34th St/Penn Station. The A, C, and E trains also stop at 34th St, and the B, D, F, V, N, R, Q, and W trains stop at Herald Sq.

KEY

- Street-by-Street map
- [M] Subway station
- Heliport

SEE ALSO

- ***Street Finder***, maps 7–8
- ***Where to Stay*** pp283–4
- ***Restaurants*** p304

Street by Street: Herald Square

Herald Square is named for the New York *Herald*, which had its office here from 1894 to 1921. Today full of shoppers, the area was once one of the raunchiest parts of New York. During the 1880s and '90s, it was known as the Tenderloin District and was filled with dance halls and bordellos. When Macy's opened in 1901, the focus moved from flesh to fashion. New York's Garment District now fills the streets near Macy's around Seventh Avenue, also known as Fashion Avenue. To the east on Fifth Avenue is the Empire State Building, with the city's best eagle's-eye views from the observation deck.

Manhattan Mall, the site of Gimbel's, Macy's former archrival, holds 90 stores, a huge food court, and a floor for children's wares.

Fashion Avenue is another name for the stretch of Seventh Avenue around 34th Street. This area is the heart of New York's garment industry. The streets are full of men pushing racks of clothes.

34th Street subway (1, 2, 3)

The Hotel Pennsylvania was a center for the 1930s big bands – Glenn Miller's song "Pennsylvania 6-5000" made its telephone number famous.

St. John the Baptist Church
A beautiful set of carved Stations of the Cross is hung on the walls of the white marble interior of this church 🄝

The SJM Building is at 130 West 30th Street. Mesopotamian-style friezes adorn the outside of the building.

The Fur District is at the southern end of the Garment District. Furriers ply their trade between West 27th and 30th streets.

The Flower District, around Sixth Avenue and West 28th Street, hums with activity in the early part of the day as florists pack their vans with their highly scented, brightly colored wares.

28th Street subway (lines N, R, W)

★ Macy's

The biggest department store in the world has something for everyone ❹

The Greenwich Savings Bank (now the HSBC) is a Greek temple to banking with huge columns on three sides.

34th Street subway (lines B, D, F, N, Q, R, V, W)

Herald Square
The New York Herald Building's clock now is situated where Broadway meets Sixth Avenue ❸

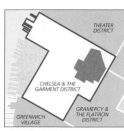

LOCATOR MAP
See Manhattan Map pp14–15

KEY

– – – Suggested route

| 0 meters | 100 |
| 0 yards | 100 |

Greeley Square is more of a traffic island than a square, but it does have a fine statue of Horace Greeley, founder of the New York Tribune.

★ Empire State Building

The observation deck of this quintessential skyscraper is a great place to view the city ❷

Little Korea is an area of Korean businesses. In addition to shops, there are restaurants nearby on West 31st and 32nd streets.

The Life Building at 19 West 31st Street housed *Life* magazine when it was a satirical weekly. Carrère & Hastings designed the building in 1894. It is now a hotel.

Marble Collegiate Church

This 1854 church was built in the Gothic Revival style. It became famous when Norman Vincent Peale was pastor here ❶

STAR SIGHTS

★ Empire State Building

★ Macy's

Marble Collegiate's Tiffany stained-glass windows

Marble Collegiate Reformed Church ❶

1 W. 29th St. **Map** 8 F3. **Tel** (212) 686-2770. Ⓜ 28th St. ◯ 8:30am–8:30pm Mon–Fri, 9am–4pm Sat, 8am–3pm Sun. ◉ public hols. ✝ 11:15am Sun. 🎤 during services. ♿ **Sanctuary** 3 W 29th St. ◯ 10am–noon, 2–4pm Mon–Fri. **www**.marblechurch.org

This church is best known for its former pastor Norman Vincent Peale, who wrote *The Power of Positive Thinking*.

Another positive thinker, future US president Richard M. Nixon, attended services here when he was a lawyer in his pre-White House days.

The church was built in 1854 using the marble blocks that give it its name. Fifth Avenue was then no more than a dusty country road, and the cast-iron fence was there to keep livestock out.

The original white and gold interior walls were replaced with a stenciled gold *fleur-de-lis* design on a soft rust background. Two stained-glass Tiffany windows, depicting Old Testament scenes, were placed in the south wall in 1893.

Empire State Building ❷

See pp136–7.

Herald Square ❸

6th Ave. **Map** 8 E2. Ⓜ 34th St-Penn Station. See **Shopping** p321.

Named after the New York *Herald*, which occupied a fine arcaded, Italianate Stanford White building here from 1893 to 1921, the square was the hub of the rowdy Tenderloin district in the 1870s and 1880s. Theaters, such as the Manhattan Opera House, dance halls, hotels, and restaurants kept the area humming with life until reformers clamped down on sleaze in the 1890s. The ornamental Bennett clock, named for James Gordon Bennett Jr., publisher of the *Herald*, is now all that is left of the Herald Building.

The Opera House was razed in 1901 to make way for Macy's and, soon after, other department stores followed, making Herald Square a mecca for shoppers. One such store was the now-defunct Gimbel Brothers Department Store, once arch rival to Macy's. (The rivalry was affectionately portrayed in the New York Christmas movie *A Miracle on 34th Street*.) In 1988 the store was converted into a vertical mall with a glittery neon front. Most of the old names have gone, but Herald Square is still a key shopping district packed with chain stores.

Macy's ❹

151 W. 34th St. **Map** 8 E2. **Tel** (212) 695-4400 Ⓜ 34th St-Penn Station. ◯ 10am–9:30pm Mon–Sat; 11am–8:30pm Sun. ◉ public hols. See **Shopping** p319. **www**.macys.com

The "world's largest store" covers a square block, and the merchandise inside covers just about any item you could imagine in every price range.

Macy's was founded by a former whaler named Rowland Hussey Macy, who opened a small store on West 14th Street in 1857. The store's red star logo came from Macy's tattoo, a souvenir of his sailing days.

By the time Macy died in 1877, his little store had grown to a row of 11 buildings. It was to expand further under two brothers, Isidor and Nathan Straus, who had operated Macy's china and glassware department. By 1902 Macy's had outgrown its 14th Street premises, and the firm acquired its present site. The eastern facade has a

Macy's 34th Street facade

The nave of St. John the Baptist Church

modern entrance but still bears the bay windows and Corinthian pillars of the 1902 design. The 34th Street facade still has its original caryatids guarding the entrance, along with the clock, canopy, and lettering. Inside, many of the original wooden escalators are still in good working order.

The sea featured again in Macy's history in 1912 – a plaque by the main entrance commemorates the death of Isidor and his wife in the sinking of the *Titanic*.

Macy's sponsors New York's renowned Thanksgiving Day parade and the Fourth of July fireworks. The store's popular Spring Flower Show draws thousands of visitors.

St. John the Baptist Church ❺

210 W 31st St. **Map** 8 E3. *Tel (212) 564-9070.* Ⓜ *34th St-Penn Station.* ◯ *6:15am–6pm daily.* ✝ *8:45am, 10:30am, 5:15pm daily.* 📷 ♿ 🛍

Founded in 1840 to serve a congregation of newly arrived immigrants, today this small Roman Catholic church is

almost lost in the heart of the Fur District. The exterior has a single spire. Although the brown-stone facade on 30th Street is dark with city soot, many treasures lie within this dull exterior. The entrance is through the modern Friary on 31st Street.

The sanctuary by Napoleon Le Brun is a marvel of Gothic arches in glowing white marble surmounted by gilded capitals. Painted reliefs of religious scenes line the walls; sunlight streams through the stained-glass windows. Also off the Friary is the Prayer Garden, a small, green and peaceful oasis with religious statuary, a fountain and stone benches.

Madison Square Garden ❻

4 Pennsylvania Plaza. **Map** 8 D2. *Tel (212) 465-6741.* Ⓜ *34th St-Penn Station.* ◯ *Mon–Sun, times vary according to shows.* 📽 *See Entertainment p360.* **www**.thegarden.com

There's only one good thing to be said for the razing of the extraordinarily lovely McKim, Mead & White Pennsylvania Station building in favor of this undistinguished 1968 complex: it so enraged city preservationists that they formed an alliance to ensure that such a thing would never be allowed to happen again.

Madison Square Garden itself, which sits atop underground Pennsylvania Station, is a cylinder of precast concrete, functional enough as a 20,000-seat, centrally located home for the famous

New York Knickerbockers (the Knicks) basketball, Liberty (women's basketball), and New York Rangers hockey teams. It has a packed calendar of other events: rock concerts, championship tennis and boxing, outrageously staged wrestling, the Ringling Bros. and Barnum & Bailey Circus, an antiques show, a dog show and more. There is also a 5,600-seat theater.

Despite renovation work, Madison Square Garden lacks the panache of its earlier location, which combined a stunning Stanford White building with extravagant entertainment *(see p126)*.

The massive interior of Madison Square Garden

General Post Office ❼

421 8th Ave. **Map** 8 D2. *Tel (800) ASK-USPS.* Ⓜ *34th St-Penn Station.* ◯ *24 hrs a day, every day (incl public hols). See Practical Information p377.*

Designed by McKim, Mead & White in 1913, in a style to complement their 1910 Pennsylvania Station across the street, the General Post Office is a perfect example of a public building of the Beaux Arts period. The imposing, two-block-long structure has a broad staircase leading to a facade with 20 Corinthian columns and a pavilion at each end. The 280-ft (85-m) inscription across it is based on a description of the Persian Empire's postal service, from around 520 BC: "Neither snow nor rain nor heat nor gloom of night stays these couriers from the swift completion of their appointed rounds."

The Corinthian colonnade of the General Post Office

Empire State Building ❷

Empire State Building

The Empire State Building is the tallest skyscraper in New York. Construction began in March 1930, not long after the Wall Street Crash, and by the time it opened in 1931, space was so difficult to rent that it was nicknamed "the Empty State Building." Only the immediate popularity of the observatories saved the building from bankruptcy – to date, they have attracted more than 120 million visitors – and the building soon became a symbol of the city the world over.

102nd-floor observatory

The Empire State was planned to be 86 stories high, but a then 150 ft (46 m) mooring mast for zeppelins was added. The mast, now 204 ft (62 m), transmits TV and radio to the city and four states.

Colored floodlighting of the top 30 floors marks special and seasonal events.

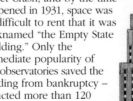

Symbols of the modern age are depicted on these bronze Art Deco medallions placed throughout the lobby.

CONSTRUCTION
The building was designed for ease and speed of construction. Everything possible was prefabricated and slotted into place at a rate of about four stories per week.

High-speed elevators travel at up to 1,000 ft (305 m) a minute.

The framework is made from 60,000 tons of steel and was built in 23 weeks.

Aluminum panels were used instead of stone around the 6,500 windows. The steel trim masks rough edges on the facing.

Ten million bricks were used to line the whole building.

Nine minutes 33 seconds is the record for racing up the 1,575 steps from the lobby to the 86th floor, in the annual Empire State Run-Up.

Sandwich space between the floors houses the wiring, pipes and cables.

Over 200 steel and concrete piles support the 365,000-ton building.

STAR FEATURES

★ Fifth Avenue Entrance Lobby

★ Views from the Observatories

★ Views from the Observatories
The 86th-floor outdoor observation decks offer superb views of Manhattan. The 102nd-floor observatory, 1,250 ft (381 m) high, can be visited for an additional fee payable only at the Visitors' Center on the second floor, not online.

A Head for Heights
As the building took shape, construction workers often showed great bravery. Here, a worker clings to a crane hook. The Chrysler Building and other skyscrapers in the background appear surprisingly small.

Lightning Strikes
The Empire State is a natural lightning conductor, struck up to 100 times a year. The observation deck is closed during unfavorable weather.

Empire State
1454 ft (443 m)
with mast

Eiffel Tower
1045 ft
(319 m)

Great Pyramid
350 ft (107 m)

Big Ben 220 ft
(67 m)

Pecking Order
New Yorkers are justly proud of their city's symbol, which towers above the icons of other countries.

★ Fifth Avenue Entrance Lobby
A relief image of the skyscraper is superimposed on a map of New York State in the marble-lined lobby.

ENCOUNTERS IN THE SKY

The Empire State Building has been seen in many films. However, the finale from the 1933 classic *King Kong* is easily its most famous guest appearance, as the giant ape straddles the spire to do battle with army aircraft. In 1945 a real bomber flew too low over Manhattan in fog and struck the building just above the 78th floor. The luckiest escape was that of a young elevator operator whose cabin plunged 79 floors. The emergency brakes saved her life.

Jacob K. Javits Convention Center ❽

655 W. 34th St. **Map** 7 B2. **Tel** *(212) 216-2000.* Ⓜ *34th St-Penn Station, 42nd St.* 🚌 *M34, M42.* ⭕ *only on show days – times vary.* 📷 🚻 ♿ 🍴 **www.**javitscenter.com

The Convention Center – modern New York architecture at its best

Strikingly modernistic in appearance, this glass building facing the Hudson, which opened in 1986, was designed by I.M. Pei to give New York the space for large-scale expositions. The 18-story building is constructed of 16,000 panes of glass, the two main halls can accommodate thousands of delegates, and the lobby is high enough to hold the Statue of Liberty. In 1989 the construction of the

Galleria River Pavilion added another 40,000 sq ft (3,750 sq m) of open space to the building, and two outdoor terraces overlooking the river.

Chelsea Piers Complex ❾

11th Ave (17th to 23rd Sts) **Map** 7 B5. **Tel** *(212) 336-6666.* Ⓜ *14th St, 18th St, 23rd St.* 🚌 *M14, M23.* ⭕ *daily.* 📷 **www.**chelseapiers.com

This mammoth complex converted four neglected piers into a center for a vast range of sports and leisure activities *(see p33).* The facilities include skating rinks, running tracks, a rock-climbing wall, a golf driving range, a marina, and TV and film production sound stages.

Empire Diner ❿

210 10th Ave. **Map** 7 C4. **Tel** *(212) 243-2736.* Ⓜ *23rd St.* ⭕ *24hrs daily.* ⭘ *4–8am Mon.* 🚌 *M11, M23.*

This Art Deco beauty is a faithful refurbishing of a classic 1929 American diner, complete with stainless steel bar and black and chrome trim. Bette Davis reputedly declared this to be her favorite diner. Both the cuisine and the clientele here are up-to-date New York style.

A 15th-century music manuscript in the General Theological Seminary

General Theological Seminary ⓫

175 9th Ave. **Map** 7 C4. **Tel** *(212) 243-5150.* Ⓜ *23rd St.* ⭕ *noon–3pm Mon–Fri, 11am–3pm Sat.* 🕚 *11:45am Mon, Wed–Fri, 6pm Tue, Sun.* 📷 ♿ **www.**gts.edu

Founded in 1817, this block-square campus accepts 150 students at a time to train for the priesthood. Clement Clarke Moore, a professor of Biblical Learning, donated the site, officially known as Chelsea Square. The earliest remaining building dates from 1836; the most modern, St. Mark's Library, was built in 1960 and holds the largest collection of Latin Bibles in the world.

The campus can be entered from Ninth Avenue only. Inside, the garden is laid out in two quadrangles like an English cathedral close: it is especially lovely in spring.

The Empire Diner before hungry club-goers arrive for breakfast

Chelsea Historic District ⑫

W. 20th St from 9th to 10th Aves.
Map 8 D5. Ⓜ *18th St.* 🚌 *M11.*

Although he is better-known as the author of the poem "A Visit from St. Nicholas" than as an urban planner, Clement Clarke Moore owned an estate here and divided it into lots in the 1830s, creating handsome rows of town houses. Restoration has since rescued many of the original buildings here.

Of these, the finest are seven houses known as Cushman Row, running from 406–418 West 20th Street, which were built from 1839–40 for Don Alonzo Cushman. He was a merchant who also founded the Greenwich Savings Bank. He joined Moore and James N. Wells in the development of Chelsea. Rich in detail and intricate ironwork, Cushman Row is ranked with Washington Square North as supreme examples of Greek Revival architecture. Look for cast-iron wreaths around attic windows and the pineapples on the newel posts of two of the houses – old symbols of hospitality.

Farther along West 20th Street, from 446–450, there are fine examples of the Italianate style for which Chelsea is also renowned.

A house on Cushman Row

The detailed brickwork arches of windows and fanlights subtly implied the wealth of the owner, being able to afford this expensive effect.

Hugh O'Neill Dry Goods Store

Hotel Chelsea ⑬

222 W. 23rd St. **Map** 8 D4.
Tel *(212) 243-3700.* Ⓜ *23rd St.*
www.hotelchelsea.com
See **Where to Stay** *p284.*

Few hotels can match the Chelsea for artistic and literary heritage – and notoriety. Many former guests have been commemorated in the brass plaques on the hotel's

A guest's-eye view of the Hotel Chelsea's cast-iron stairwell

facade. They include Tennessee Williams, Mark Twain, Jack Kerouac, and Brendan Behan. Dylan Thomas spent his last years here. In 1966 Andy Warhol's movie *Chelsea Girls* was set here, reviving its cult status, and in 1978 punk band member Sid Vicious killed his girlfriend in the hotel. The Chelsea still draws musicians, artists, and writers who hope their names will one day be remembered. Stop by the bar to soak in the decadence of this creative atmosphere.

Hugh O'Neill Dry Goods Store ⑭

655–671 6th Avenue. **Map** 8 E4.
Ⓜ *23rd St.*

Though the store is long gone, the 1876 cast-iron columned and pilastered facade clearly shows the scale and grandeur of the emporiums that once lined Sixth Avenue from 18th to 23rd streets, the area known as Fashion Row. O'Neill, whose sign can still be seen on the facade, was a showman and super-salesman whose trademark was a fleet of shiny delivery wagons. His customers came in droves via the conveniently close Sixth Avenue El. They were not the "carriage trade" enjoyed by Ladies' Mile *(see p127)*, but their numbers allowed the Row to flourish until the turn of the century, when the retailing district continued its move uptown. Now mostly restored, the buildings have turned into superstores and bargain places like Filene's Basement.

Worth Monument ⑮

5th Ave and Broadway. **Map** 8 F4.
Ⓜ *23rd St-Broadway.*

Hidden away behind a water meter on a triangle amid city traffic is an obelisk erected in 1857 to mark the grave of the one public figure to be buried under the streets of Manhattan. That honor belongs to General William J. Worth, a hero of the Mexican wars of the mid-1800s. A cast-iron fence of swords embedded in the ground surrounds the monument.

The Worth
Monument

THEATER DISTRICT

It was the move of the Metropolitan Opera House to Broadway at 40th Street in 1883 that first drew lavish theaters and restaurants to this area. In the 1920s, movie palaces added the glamour of neon to Broadway, the signs getting bigger and brighter until eventually the street became known as the "Great White Way." After World War II,

Lee Lawrie design in Rockefeller Center

the pull of the movies waned, and the glitter was replaced by grime. However, a redevelopment program has brought the public and the bright lights back. Pockets of calm also exist away from the bustle. Explore the Public Library or relax in Bryant Park. For the best of both worlds, though, visit the landmark Rockefeller Center.

The heart of the Theater District, around Times Square

SIGHTS AT A GLANCE

Historic Streets and Buildings
Alwyn Court Apartments 18
Group Health Insurance Building 12
New York Public Library 8
New York Yacht Club 5
Paramount Building 13
Shubert Alley 14
Times Square 10

Museums and Galleries
International Center of Photography 9
Intrepid Sea-Air-Space Museum 19
Museum of Arts and Design 20

Modern Architecture
MONY Tower 15
Rockefeller Center 1

Parks and Squares
Bryant Park 6

Famous Theaters
Carnegie Hall 17
City Center of Music and Dance 16
Lyceum Theater 3
New Amsterdam Theater 11

Landmark Hotels and Restaurants
Algonquin Hotel 4
Bryant Park Hotel 7

Landmark Stores
Diamond Row 2

GETTING THERE

Subway lines A, C, and E go to the Port Authority and connect to the 1, 2, 3, N, Q, R, W, S, and 7 at Times Sq. The B, D, F, V, and 7 lines stop at Bryant Park. The 1, N, R, W, C, and E lines also stop at the north end of Times Sq. Bus routes through the area are the M1–7, M10, M20, M27 and M104, and the M42, M50, M57 crosstown.

KEY

- Street-by-Street map
- [M] Subway station
- Riverboat boarding point

SEE ALSO

- ***Street Finder,*** maps 8, 11–12
- ***Where to Stay*** pp284–7
- ***Restaurants*** pp304–6

0 meters 500
0 yards 500

Street by Street: Times Square

Named for the 25-story New York Times Tower, which opened in 1906, Times Square has been at the heart of the city's theater district since 1899, when Oscar Hammerstein built the Victoria and Republic theaters. Since the 1920s, the glowing neon of theater billboards has combined with the *Times'* illuminated newswire and other advertising to create a spectacular lightshow. After a period of decline starting in the 1930s, which saw sex shows taking over many of the grand theatres, rejuvenation of the district began in the 1990s. Old-style Broadway glamour again rubs shoulders with modern entertainment in this enticing part of the city.

Paramount Hotel
Designed by Philippe Starck, this hotel is the hip haunt of the theater crowd who drink in the late-night Paramount Bar *(see p285).*

MTV Studios
Crowds gather outside around 3pm Monday through Friday to watch interviews being filmed in the second-floor studios. Roving cameras often seek reactions on the street.

Westin Hotel
This striking 45-story hotel consists of a prism split by a curving beam of light. Stunning views over the city.

★ E Walk
This entertainment and retail complex has a multiplex cinema, restaurants, a hotel, and the BB King Blues Club.

Sardi's
In Times Square since 1921, Sardi's walls are lined with caricatures of Broadway stars of yesterday and today.

W 45TH ST

W 43RD ST

W 41ST ST

SEVENTH AV

★ Times Square
Every New Year's Eve at midnight, the famed crystal ball drops from the top of One Times Square. There are great views from the front of this New York landmark ❿

0 meters	100
0 yards	100

★ New Victory Theater
This classic Broadway theater used as a young people's performance space

Electronic Ticker Tape
The figures on the Morgan Stanley LED tickertape are 10 feet (3 m) high. It is one of the many eye-catching lighting displays that illuminate Times Square day and night. City ordinances require office buildings to carry neon advertising.

LOCATOR MAP
See Manhattan Map pp14–15

KEY

– – – Suggested route

STAR SIGHTS

★ E Walk

★ New Victory Theater

★ Times Square

McGraw-Hill Building

J.P. Stevens Tower

Celanese Building

Duffy Square
A statue of actor, composer, and writer George M Cohan, responsible for many of Broadway's hits, stands proud in this small square. Duffy Square is named for World War I hero, "Fighting" Father Duffy, immortalized in a statue. It is also home to the **TKTS** booth, where cut-price theater tickets are sold daily.

GEORGE·M·COHAN
1878-1942

Times Square Information Center

Lyceum Theater
The oldest Broadway theater, the Lyceum has a beautifully ornate Baroque facade ❸

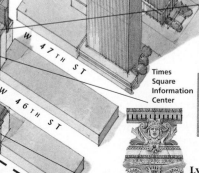

Belasco Theater
Built in 1907 by producer David Belasco, it was the most technically advanced theater of its time. Original Tiffany glass and Everett Shinn murals decorate the interior. It is rumored that Belasco's ghost still treads the boards some nights.

BROADWAY

AVENUE

SEVENTH

W 47TH ST

W 46TH ST

RD ST

Rockefeller Center, looking toward the General Electric Building

Rockefeller Center ❶

Map 12 F5. Ⓜ *47th–50th Sts.* **Tel** *(212) 332-6868 (information).* 📷 ♿ 🍴 📺 📽 *NBC, Rockefeller Center, daily.* **Tel** *(212) 664-7174 (reservations advised). Radio City Music Hall, daily.* **Tel** *(212) 247-4777. Top of the Rock, daily.* **Tel** *(212) 698-2000.* **www**.rockefellercenter.com **www**.nbc.com **www**.radiocity.com **www**.topoftherocknyc.com

When the New York City Landmarks Preservation Commission unanimously voted to declare Rockefeller Center a landmark in 1985, they rightly called it "the heart of New York . . . a great unifying presence in the chaotic core of midtown Manhattan."

It is the largest privately owned complex of its kind. The Art Deco design was by a team of top architects headed by Raymond Hood. Works by 30 artists can be found in foyers, on facades, and in the gardens. The site, once a botanic garden owned by Columbia University, was leased in 1928 by John D. Rockefeller, Jr., as an ideal central home for a new opera house. When the 1929 Depression scuttled these plans, Rockefeller, stuck with a long lease, went ahead with his own development. The 14 buildings erected between 1931 and 1940 provided jobs for as many as 225,000 people during the Depression; by 1973 there were 19 buildings.

In December 1932, Radio City Music Hall opened within

Wisdom by Lee Lawrie, on the GE Building

the complex. It still hosts its famous Christmas and Easter shows here. Later, NBC opened its TV studios here. Rockefeller Plaza is home to a well-known ice-skating rink in winter; it is also the site of a famous Christmas tree.

The Top of the Rock, an observatory on the 67th–70th floors of the center, offers a dizzying 360° panoramic view of the city.

Diamond Row ❷

47th St, between 5th and 6th Aves. **Map** 12 F5. Ⓜ *47th–50th Sts. See* **Shopping** *p328.*

Most shop windows on 47th Street glitter with gold and diamonds. The buildings are filled with booths and workshops where jewelers vie for customers while, upstairs, vast sums of money change hands. Diamond Row was born in the 1930s, when the Jewish diamond cutters of Antwerp and Amsterdam fled to the US to escape Nazism. Hasidic Jews with black hats, beards, and long earlocks are still an integral part of the scene. Although mainly a wholesale district, individual customers are

Diamond Row's main commodity

welcome. Bring cash, compare prices, haggle, and stay away if you know nothing about the value of diamonds.

Lyceum Theater ❸

149 W 45th St. **Map** 12 E5. **Tel** *Telecharge (212) 239-6200.* Ⓜ *42nd, 47th St, 49th St. See* **Entertainment** *p345.*

The oldest New York theater still active is a Baroque-style bandbox as frilly as a wedding cake. This 1903 triumph was the first theater by Herts and Tallant, later renowned for their extravagant style. The Lyceum made history with a record run of 1,600 performances of the comedy *Born Yesterday*. It was the first theater to be designated a historic landmark and though the Theater District has shifted westward, there are still many shows here.

The Rose Room in the Algonquin Hotel

Algonquin Hotel ❹

59 W 44th St. **Map** 12 F5.
Tel (212) 840-6800. Ⓜ 42nd St.
See **Where to Stay** p285.
www.algonquinhotel.com

No other hotel captures the city's formidable literary history quite like the Algonquin Hotel. For more than a century it has played host to home-grown talent and international luminaries. In the 1920s, the Rose Room was home to America's best-known luncheon club, the Round Table, with literary lights such as Alexander Woollcott, Franklin P. Adams, Dorothy Parker, Robert Benchley, and Harold Ross. All were associated with the *New Yorker* (Ross was the founding editor), whose 25 West 43rd Street headquarters had a back door opening into the hotel.

Renovations have preserved the old-fashioned, civilized feel of the Rose Room, as well as the cozy, paneled lobby where publishing types and theater-goers still like to gather for drinks, settling into comfortable armchairs and ringing a brass bell in order to summon the waiters.

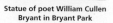

Statue of poet William Cullen Bryant in Bryant Park

New York Yacht Club ❺

37 W 44th St. **Map** 12 F5.
Tel (212) 382 1000. Ⓜ 42nd St.
⬤ to the public (members only).
www.nyyc.org

A whimsical 1899 creation, this private club has the carved sterns of 16th-century Dutch galleons in the three bay windows. The prows of the ships are borne up by sculpted dolphins and waves that spill over the windowsills and splash down to the pavement. This is the birthplace of the Americas Cup yacht race, which was based in the US from 1857 to 1983. That was the year the much coveted prize was taken from the table where it had stood for more than a century, when the *Australia II* sailed to a historic victory.

The Americas Cup, the coveted yachting prize

Bryant Park ❻

Map 8 F1. Ⓜ 42nd St.
www.bryantpark.org

In 1853, with the New York Public Library site still occupied by Croton Reservoir, Bryant Park (then Reservoir Park) housed a dazzling Crystal Palace, built for the World's Fair of that year (*see p25*).

In the 1960s the park was a hangout for drug dealers and other undesirables. In 1989 the city renovated the park, reclaiming it for workers and visitors to relax in. In spring and fall, world-famous fashion shows take place here; in the summer, classic movies are screened.

Over seven million books lie in storage stacks beneath the park.

Bryant Park Hotel ❼

40 W 40th St. **Map** 8 F1.
Tel (212) 869-0100. Ⓜ 42nd St.
www.bryantparkhotel.com

The American Radiator building (now the Bryant Park Hotel) was the first major New York work by Raymond Hood and John Howells, who went on to design the Daily News Building (*see p155*), the McGraw-Hill building, and Rockefeller Center. The 1924 structure is reminiscent of one of Hood's best-known Gothic buildings, Chicago's Tribune Tower. Here, the design is sleeker, giving the building the illusion of being taller than its actual 23 stories. The black brick facade is set off by gold terracotta trim, evoking images of flaming coals: a comparison that would have suited its original owners well, since they made heating equipment. The building is now a luxury hotel (*see p288*) across the street from Bryant Park and boasts the New York outpost of trendy LA eatery Koi.

The Bryant Park Hotel, formerly the American Radiator Building

The New York Public Library ⑧

5th Ave and 42nd St. **Map** 8 F1.
Tel (212) 930-0830. M *42nd St-Grand Central, 42nd St-5th Ave.* ○ *11am-6pm Mon–Thu.* ● *public hols.* 🄯 ♿ ☑
Lectures, workshops, readings. 📷

Doorway leading to New York Public Library's Main Reading Room

In 1897 the coveted job of designing New York's main public library was awarded to architects Carrère & Hastings. The library's first director envisaged a light, quiet, airy place for study, where millions of books could be stored and yet be available to readers as promptly as possible. In the hands of Carrère & Hastings, his vision came true, in what is considered the epitome of New York's Beaux Arts period.

Built on the site of the former Croton Reservoir *(see p24)*, it opened in 1911 to immediate acclaim, despite having cost the city \$9 million.

Barrel vaults of carved white marble over the stairs in the Astor Hall

The vast, paneled Main Reading Room stretches two full blocks and is suffused with daylight from the two interior courtyards. Below it are 88 miles (140 km) of shelves, holding over seven million volumes. A staff of over 100 and a computerized dumb-waiter can supply any book within 10 minutes.

The Periodicals Room holds 10,000 current periodicals from 128 countries. On its walls are murals by Richard Haas, honoring New York's great publishing houses. The original library combined the collections of John Jacob Astor and James Lenox. Its collections today range from Thomas Jefferson's hand-written copy of the Declaration of Independence to T.S. Eliot's typed copy of "The Waste Land." More than 1,000 queries

One of the library's two stone lions, named Patience and Fortitude by Mayor LaGuardia

The Main Reading Room, with its original bronze reading lamps

are answered daily, using the vast database of the CATNYP and LEO computer catalogs.

This library is the hub of a network of 82 branches, with nearly seven million users. Some branches are very well known, such as the New York Public Library for the Performing Arts at the Lincoln Center *(see p212)* and the Schomburg Center in Harlem *(see p229)*.

International Center of Photography ⑨

1133 Avenue of the Americas (43rd St). **Map** 8 F1. **Tel** *(212) 857-0000.* Ⓜ *42nd St.* ⏱ *10am–6pm Tue–Thu, Sat & Sun; 10am–8pm Fri.* ◐ *4 Jul.* 🈲 ♿ 🛈 *10am–5pm Tue–Sun.* 🖥 www.icp.org

This museum was founded by Cornell Capa in 1974 to conserve the work of such photojournalists as his brother Robert, who was killed on assignment in 1954. The collection of 12,500 original prints contains work by top photographers such as Ansel Adams, Henri Cartier-Bresson, and W. Eugene Smith. Special exhibitions are organized from the ICP'S archive as well as from outside sources. There are also films, lectures, and classes.

Times Square ⑩

Map 8 E1. Ⓜ *42nd St-Times Sq.* 🛈 *Times Square Information Center, 1560 Broadway (46th St) 8am–8pm daily.* 🎦 *noon Fri, (212) 869-1890.* **www**.timessquarenyc.org

The 1990s saw a transformation in Times Square, reversing a decline that began during the Depression. The square is now a safe and vibrant place where Broadway traditions comfortably coexist with modern innovations.

Although the *New York Times* has moved on from its original headquarters at the south end of the square, the glistening ball (now of Waterford crystal) still drops at midnight on New Year's Eve, as it has since the building opened with fanfare and fireworks in 1906. New buildings, such as the Bertelsmann and the fashionably minimalist Condé Nast offices, sit comfortably alongside the classic Broadway theaters.

Broadway's fortunes have also revived. Many theaters have been renovated and are again housing new productions; theatergoers

throng the area's bars and restaurants each evening.

One of the newer landmarks is the 57-story skyscraper designed by Miami architects Arquitectonica, that tops the E Walk entertainment and retail complex at 42nd Street and Eighth Avenue *(see p142).* Other attractions include an outpost of Madame Tussaud's Wax Museum at 42nd Street, between Seventh and Eighth Avenues; ESPN Zone, a huge sports bar and video game complex at 1472 Broadway and 42nd Street; and Toys 'R' Us at 1514 Broadway.

W.C. Fields (far left) and Eddie Cantor (holding top hat, right) in the 1918 *Ziegfeld Follies* **at the New Amsterdam Theater**

New Amsterdam Theater ⑪

214 W 42nd St. **Map** 8 E1. **Tel** *(212) 282-2900.* Ⓜ *42nd St-Times Sq.* 🎦 *10am–3pm Mon–Tue, 10am–11am Thu–Sat, 10am Sun; (212) 282-2907.*

This was the most opulent theater in the United States when it opened in 1903, and the first to have an Art Nouveau interior. It was owned for a time by Florenz Ziegfeld, who produced his famous *Follies* revue here between 1914 and 1918 – with Broadway's first $5 ticket price. He remodeled the roof garden into another theater, the Aerial Gardens. This is one of the fine early theaters on 42nd Street that fell on hard times. With the rehabilitation of Times Square its fortunes rose again and it is once more in Show Business.

Art Deco top of the Paramount Building

Group Health Insurance Building ⑫

330 W 42nd St. **Map** 8 D1. Ⓜ *42nd St-8th Ave.* ◐ *office hours.*

This 1931 design by Raymond Hood was the only New York building selected for the influential International Style survey of 1932 *(see p43).* Its unusual design gives it a stepped profile seen from east and west, but a slab effect viewed from the north or south. The exterior's horizontal bands of blue-green terracotta have earned it the nickname "jolly green giant." Step inside to see the classic Art Deco lobby of opaque glass and stainless steel.

One block west is Theater Row, a pleasant group of Off-Broadway theaters and cafés.

Paramount Building ⑬

1501 Broadway. **Map** 8 E1. Ⓜ *34th St.*

The fabulous ground-floor movie theater where bobby-soxers stood in line in the 1940s to hear Frank Sinatra perform is gone, but there's still a theatrical feel to the massive building designed by Rapp & Rapp in 1927. On each side 14 symmetrical setbacks rise to an Art Deco crown – a tower, clock, and globe. In the heyday of the "Great White Way," the tower was lit, with an observation deck at the top. The Hard Rock Cafe is now here, along with a retail store and a concert area.

Shubert Alley ⓮

Between W 44th and W 45th St.
Map 12 E5. Ⓜ *42nd St-Times Sq.*
See *Entertainment p342.*

The playhouses on the streets
west of Broadway are rich in
theater lore – and in notable
architecture. Two classic
theaters built in 1913 are the
Booth (222 West 45th Street),
named after actor Edwin
Booth, and the Shubert
(225 West 44th), after theater
baron Sam S. Shubert. They
form the west wall of Shubert
Alley, where aspiring actors
lined up, hoping for a casting
in a Shubert play.

A Chorus Line ran at the
Shubert until 1990, for a record
6,137 performances; Katharine
Hepburn starred earlier in *The
Philadelphia Story.* Across from
the 44th Street end of the
alley is the St. James, where
Rodgers and Hammerstein
made their debut with
Oklahoma! in 1941, followed
by *The King and I.* Nearby is
Sardi's, the restaurant where
actors waited for opening-
night reviews. Irving Berlin
staged *The Music Box Revue*
opposite the other end of the
alley in 1921. His Music Box
Theater has since housed
many famous shows.

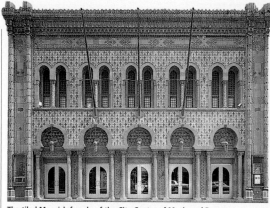
The tiled Moorish facade of the City Center of Music and Dance

MONY Tower ⓯

1740 Broadway. **Map** 12 E4.
Ⓜ *57th St.* Ⓞ *to the public.*

Built in 1950, the head office
of the Mutual of New York
insurance company (now
MONY Financial Services) has
a weather vane that tells you
everything except the wind
direction. The mast turns green
for fair, orange for cloudy,
flashing orange for rain and
white for snow. Lights moving
up the mast mean warmer
weather; lights going down
mean get out your overcoat!

City Center of Music and Dance ⓰

131 W 55th St. **Map** 12 E4.
Tel *(212) 581-1212.* Ⓜ *57th St.*
Ⓧ Ⓖ See *Entertainment p346.*
www.citycenter.org

This highly ornate Moorish
structure with its dome of
Spanish tiles was designed in
1924 as a Masonic Shriners'
Temple. It was saved from
the developers by Mayor
LaGuardia, becoming home
to the New York City Opera
and Ballet in 1943. When the
troupes moved to Lincoln
Center, City Center lived on
as a major venue for dance.
Renovation work has
preserved the delightful
excesses of the architecture.

Carnegie Hall ⓱

154 W 57th Street. **Map** 12 E3. **Tel**
(212) 247-7800. Ⓜ *57th St, 59th St.*
Museum Ⓞ *11am–4:30pm daily &
during concert intermissions.* Ⓞ
Wed. Ⓧ Ⓖ Ⓒ *11:30am, 12:30pm,
2pm & 3pm Mon–Fri; 11:30am &
12:30pm Sat; 12:30pm Sun.* Ⓒ
See *Entertainment p350.*
www.carnegiehall.org

Financed by millionaire philanthropist Andrew Carnegie,
New York's first great concert
hall opened in 1891. The
terracotta and brick
Renaissance-style building has
among the best acoustics in
the world. On opening night,
Tchaikovsky was a guest
conductor and New York's

Auditorium of the Shubert Theater, built by Henry Herts in 1913

Carnegie Hall offering some of the best acoustics in the world

finest families attended. For many years Carnegie Hall was home to the New York Philharmonic, under conductors such as Arturo Toscanini, Bruno Walter, and Leonard Bernstein. Playing Carnegie Hall quickly became an international symbol of success for both classical and popular musicians.

In the 1950s, a campaign by violinist Isaac Stern saved the site from redevelopment, and in 1964 it was made a national landmark. Renovation in 1986 brought the bronze balconies and the ornamental plaster back to their original splendor. In 1991, a museum opened next to the first-tier level, telling the story of the first 100 years of "The House that Music Built." In 2003, the Judy and Arthur Zankel Hall re-established the lower level as a performance venue.

Millionaire Andrew Carnegie

Top orchestras and performers from around the world still fill Carnegie Hall, and the corridors are lined with memorabilia of artists who have performed here.

Alwyn Court Apartments ⑱

180 W 58th St. **Map** 12 E3.
Ⓜ 57th St. ◑ to the public.

You can't miss it – not with the fanciful crowns, dragons, and other French Renaissance-style terracotta carvings covering the exterior of this 1909 Harde and Short apartment building. The ground floor has lost its cornice, but the rest of the building is intact, and it's one of a kind in the city.

The facade follows the style of François I, whose symbol, a crowned salamander, can be seen above the entrance to the building.

The interior courtyard features a dazzling display of the illusionistic skills of artist Richard Haas, in which plain walls are transformed into "carved" stonework.

The crowned salamander, symbol of François I, on Alwyn Court

Intrepid Sea-Air-Space Museum ⑲

Pier 86, W 46th St. **Map** 11 A5. ⬛
(877) 957-SHIP. 🚌 M16, M42, M50.
◑ Apr–Sep: 10am–5pm Mon–Fri;
10am–6pm Sat, Sun and hols; Oct–
Mar: 10am–5pm Tue–Sun and hols.
📷 📗 www.intrepidmuseum.org

Exhibits on board this World War II aircraft carrier include fighter planes from the 1940s, the A-12, the world's fastest spy plane, and the *Growler*, a guided-missile submarine.

The workings of today's super-carriers are traced in Stern Hall, while Technologies Hall looks at the rockets of the future and includes two flight simulators. Mission Control offers live coverage of NASA shuttle missions.

Photographs, film footage, and archive material explore the lives of the crew.

The flight deck of the Intrepid with fighter and spy planes on display

Museum of Arts and Design ⑳

2 Columbus Circle. **Map** 12 D3. **Tel**
(212) 956-3535. Ⓜ 5th Ave-53rd St.
◑ 10am–6pm daily (to 8pm Thu). ◑
public hols. 📷 📗 🔊 📗 **Lectures,
films.** 📗 www.madmuseum.org

The leading American cultural institution of its kind, this museum housed in a modern, bold, eyecatching building is dedicated to contemporary objects in an array of media from clay and glass to wood, metal, and fiber. The permanent collection includes over 2,000 artifacts by international craftsmen and designers. Items by top-class American designers are also on sale.

LOWER MIDTOWN

From Beaux Arts to Art Deco, this section of midtown boasts some fine architecture. Quiet, residential Murray Hill was named for a country estate that once occupied the site. By the turn of the century, it was home to many of New York's first families, including the financier J.P. Morgan, whose library,

Brass door, Fred F. French Building

now a museum, reveals the grandeur of the age. The commercial pace quickens at 42nd Street, near Grand Central Terminal, where tall office buildings line the streets. However, few of the newer buildings have equaled the Beaux Arts Terminal itself or such Art Deco beauties as the Chrysler Building.

SIGHTS AT A GLANCE

Historic Streets and Buildings
Chanin Building ❹
Chrysler Building ❺
Daily News Building ❻
Fred F. French Building ⑫
Grand Central Terminal pp156–7 ❷
Helmsley Building ❽
Home Savings of America ❸
Sniffen Court ⑮
Tudor City ❼

Museums and Galleries
Japan Society ⑪
Morgan Library & Museum pp164–5 ⑭

Modern Architecture
MetLife Building ❶
Nos. 1 and 2 United Nations Plaza ❾
United Nations pp160–63 ❿

Churches
Church of the Incarnation ⑬

GETTING THERE
By subway, take the crosstown S or 7 or the Lexington Avenue 4, 5, or 6 trains to 42nd Street–Grand Central. Buses M15, M101/102, M1, M2, M3, and M4 run along the area's avenues, while the M34 and M42 are the crosstown buses.

0 meters 500
0 yards 500

SEE ALSO

- *Street Finder,* maps 9, 12, 13
- *Where to Stay* pp287–8
- *Restaurants* p306

KEY

■ Street-by-Street map

Ⓜ Subway station

◁ **The stainless-steel–coated spire of the Chrysler Building**

Street by Street: Lower Midtown

A walk in the neighborhood allows you to see an eclectic mix of New York's architectural styles. Step back to appreciate the contours of the tallest skyscrapers, and step inside to experience the many fine interiors, from modern atriums such as those in the Philip Morris Building and Ford Foundation buildings to the ornate details of the Home Savings Bank and the soaring spaces of Grand Central Terminal.

MetLife Building
This skyscraper, built by Pan Am in 1963, towers above Park Avenue ❶

★ Grand Central Terminal
The vast, vaulted interior is a splendid reminder of the heyday of train travel. This historic building also features specialty shops and gourmet restaurants ❷

Grand Central-42nd St. subway (lines S, 4, 5, 6, 7)

STAR SIGHTS

- ★ Chrysler Building
- ★ Daily News Building
- ★ Grand Central Terminal
- ★ Home Savings of America

Chanin Building
Built for self-made real estate mogul Irwin Chanin in the 1920s, this building has a fine Art Deco lobby ❹

PARK AVENUE

E 41ST ST

LEXINGTON AVENUE

Brass door, Home Savings Bank

★ Home Savings of America
Formerly the headquarters of the Bowery Savings Bank, this is one of the finest bank buildings in New York. Architects York & Sawyer designed it to resemble a Romanesque palace ❸

The Mobil Building
has a self-cleaning stainless steel facade that is embossed in geometric patterns to prevent it from warping. It was built in 1955.

Helmsley Building
Straddling Park Avenue between 45th and 46th, its ornate entrance symbolized the wealth of its first occupants, New York Central Railroad ❽

Mailbox in the Chrysler Building

★ Chrysler Building
Ornamented with automotive motifs, this Art Deco delight was built in 1930 for the Chrysler car company ❺

Worker resting during construction of the Chrysler Building

The Ford Foundation Building is the headquarters of Ford's philanthropic arm. It has a lovely interior garden surrounded by a cube-shaped building made of pinkish gray granite, glass, and steel.

Ralph J. Bunche Park

★ Daily News Building
The Art Deco former home of the newspaper has a revolving globe in the lobby ❻

Tudor City
This 1928 private residential complex has 3,000 apartments. Built in the Tudor style, it features fine stonework details ❼

MetLife Building ❶

200 Park Ave. **Map** 13 A5.
Ⓜ *42nd St-Grand Central.*
◯ *office hours.* 🍽 🚻

Lobby of the MetLife Building

Once, the sculptures atop the Grand Central Terminal stood out against the sky. Then this colossus, formerly called the Pan Am Building and designed by Walter Gropius, Emery Roth and Sons, and Pietro Belluschi, rose up in 1963 to block the Park Avenue view. It dwarfed the terminal and aroused universal dislike. At the time it was the largest commercial building in the world, and the dismay over its scale helped thwart a later plan to build a tower over the terminal itself.

It is ironic that the New York skies were blocked by Pan Am, a company that had opened up the skies as a means of travel for millions of people. When the company began in 1927, Charles Lindbergh, fresh from his solo trans-atlantic flight, was one of their pilots and an adviser on new routes. By 1936, Pan Am managed to introduce the first trans-Pacific passenger route, and in 1947 they introduced the first round-the-world route.

The building's famous roof-top heliport was abandoned in 1977 after a freak accident showered debris on to the surrounding streets. Now Pan Am itself has gone, too, and in 1981 the entire building was sold to the Metropolitan Life organization.

Grand Central Terminal ❷

See pp156–7.

Home Savings of America ❸

110 E 42nd St. **Map** 9 A1. Ⓜ *42nd St-Grand Central.* ◯ *by appt only.* **Cipriani** *Tel (646) 723-0826.*

Many consider this 1923 building the best work of the best bank architects of the 1920s. York & Sawyer chose the style of a Romanesque basilica for the uptown offices of the venerable Bowery Savings Bank (now Home Savings of America). An arched entry leads into the vast banking room, with a high beamed ceiling, marble mosaic floors, and marble columns that support the stone arches that soar overhead.

Facade of Home Savings of America building

Between the columns are unpolished mosaic panels of marble from France and Italy. The rich detailing includes symbolic animal motifs, such as a squirrel representing thrift and a lion for power.

Chanin Building ❹

122 E 42nd St. **Map** 9 A1.
Ⓜ *42nd St-Grand Central.*
◯ *office hours.*

Stonework detail on the Chanin Building

Once the headquarters of Irwin S. Chanin, one of New York's leading real estate developers, the 56-story tower was the first skyscraper in the Grand Central area, a harbinger of things to come. It was designed by Sloan & Robertson in 1929 and is one of the best examples of the Art Deco period. A wide bronze band, patterned with birds and fish, runs the full length of the facade; the terracotta base is decorated with a luxuriant tangle of stylized leaves and flowers. Inside, Radio City's sculptor René Chambellan worked on the reliefs and the bronze grills, elevator doors, mailboxes, clocks, and pattern of waves in the floor. The vestibule reliefs chart the career of Chanin, who was a self-made man.

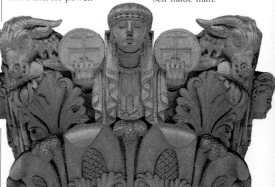

Carved detail in the banking hall of Home Savings of America

Chrysler Building ❺

405 Lexington Ave. **Map** 9 A1.
Tel *(212) 682-3070.* **M** *42nd St-Grand Central.* ◯ *office hours (7am–6pm), lobby only.* 📷 ♿

Stainless-steel gargoyle on the Chrysler Building

Walter P. Chrysler began his career in a Union Pacific Railroad machine shop, but his passion for the motor car helped him rise swiftly to the top of the new industry, to found, in 1925, the corporation bearing his name. His wish for a headquarters in New York that symbolized his company led to a building that will always be linked with the golden age of motoring. Following Chrysler's wishes, the stainless-steel Art Deco spire resembles a car radiator grill; the building's series of stepped setbacks are emblazoned with winged radiator caps, wheels and stylized automobiles; and there are gargoyles modeled on hood ornaments from the 1929 Chrysler Plymouth.

It stands at 1,046ft (320 m) but it lost the title of tallest building in the world to the Empire State Building a few months after its completion in 1930. William Van Alen's 77-story Chrysler Building and its shining crown are still among the city's best-known and most-loved landmarks.

The crowning spire was kept a secret until the last moment, when, having been

built in the fire shaft, it was raised into position through the roof, ensuring that the building would be higher than the Bank of Manhattan, then just completed downtown by Van Alen's great rival, H. Craig Severance.

Van Alen was poorly rewarded for his labors. Chrysler accused him of accepting bribes from contractors and refused to pay him. Van Alen's career never recovered from the slur.

The stunning lobby, once used as a showroom for Chrysler cars, was perfectly restored in 1978. It is lavishly decorated with patterned marbles and granite from around the world and has chromed steel trim. A vast painted ceiling by Edward

Elevator door at the Chrysler Building

Trumball shows transportation scenes of the late 1920s.

Although the Chrysler Corporation never occupied the building as their headquarters, their name remains, as firm a fixture as the gargoyles.

Entrance to the Daily News Building

Daily News Building ❻

220 E 42nd St. **Map** 9 B1.
M *42nd St-Grand Central.*
◯ *8am–6pm Mon–Fri.*

The *Daily News* was founded in 1919, and by 1925 it was a million-seller. It was known, rather scathingly, as "the servant girl's bible," for its concentration on scandals, celebrities, and murders, its readable style and heavy use of illustration. Over the years it has stuck to what it does best, and the formula paid off handsomely. It revealed stories such as the romance of Edward VIII and Mrs. Simpson, and has become renowned for its punchy headlines. Its circulation figures are still among the highest in the United States.

Its headquarters, designed by Raymond Hood in 1930, has rows of brown and black brick alternating with windows to create a vertical striped effect. Hood's lobby is familiar to many as that of the *Daily Planet* in the 1980s *Superman* movies. It includes the world's largest interior globe, and bronze lines on the floor indicate the direction of world cities and the position of the planets. At night, the intricate detail over the front entrance of the building is lit from within by neon. The newspaper's offices are now on West 33rd Street, but this building has been designated as a national historic landmark.

Grand Central Terminal ❷

In 1871 Cornelius Vanderbilt opened a railway station on 42nd Street. Although often revamped, it was never large enough and was finally demolished. The present station opened in 1913. This Beaux Arts gem has been a gateway to and symbol of the city ever since. Its glory is the soaring main concourse and the way it separates pedestrian and train traffic. The building has a steel frame covered with plaster and marble. Reed & Stern were in charge of the logistical planning; Warren & Wetmore for the overall design. The restoration by architects Beyer Blinder Belle is awesome.

42nd Street colonnaded facade

Statuary on the 42nd Street Facade
Jules-Alexis Coutans sculptures of Mercury, Hercules, and Minerva crown the main entrance.

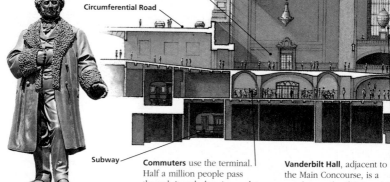

Main Concourse Level

Circumferential Road

Subway

Cornelius Vanderbilt
The railroad magnate was known as the "Commodore."

Commuters use the terminal. Half a million people pass through it each day. An escalator leads up into the MetLife Building, where there are specialty shops and restaurants.

Vanderbilt Hall, adjacent to the Main Concourse, is a good example of Beaux Arts architecture. It is decorated with gold chandeliers and pink marble.

Grand Central Oyster Bar
This popular spot (see p306), with its yellow Guastavino tiles, is one of the many eateries in the station. The dining concourse is enormous, with food, snacks, and drinks to suit all tastes.

STAR SIGHTS

★ Central Information

★ Grand Staircases

★ Main Concourse

★ **Main Concourse**
This vast area with its vaulted ceiling is dominated by three great arched windows on each side.

Vaulted Ceiling
A medieval manu-script provided the basis for French artist Paul Helleu's zodiac design containing over 2,500 stars. Lights pinpoint the major constellations.

The Lower Level
is linked to the other levels by stairways, ramps, and brand new escalators.

Grand Staircase
There are now two of these double flights of marble steps, styled after the staircase in Paris' Opera House, and a vivid reminder of the glamorous days of early rail travel.

★ **Central Information**
This four-faced clock tops the travel information booth on the main concourse.

Tudor City **7**

E 41st–43rd St between 1st and 2nd Aves. **Map** 9 B1. Ⓜ *42nd St-Grand Central.* 🚌 *M15, M27, M42, M50, M104.* **www**.tudorcity.com

Dating from 1925–8, this early urban renewal effort by the Fred F. French Company was designed as a middle-class city within the city. Rents were modest, thanks to the "large-scale production." There are 12 buildings containing apartments, a hotel, shops, restaurants, a post office, and two small private parks, all built in the Tudor Gothic style.

In the mid-19th century the area was the haunt of gangs and criminals and was known as Corcoran's Roost, after Paddy Corcoran, the leader of the notorious "Rag Gang." The East River shore was lined with glue factories, slaughter-houses, breweries, and a gasworks. Some were still there when Tudor City was planned, so its buildings have only a few outward-facing windows from which residents might enjoy what is now a great view of the river.

Upper stories of Tudor City

Helmsley Building **8**

230 Park Ave. **Map** 13 A5. Ⓜ *42nd St-Grand Central.* ◯ *office hours.*

One of the great New York views looks south down Park Avenue to the Helmsley Building straddling the busy traffic flow beneath. There is just one flaw – the monolithic MetLife Building (which was built by Pan Am as its corporate headquarters

Performance at the Japan Society

in 1963) that towers behind it, replacing the building's former backdrop, the sky.

Built by Warren & Wetmore in 1929, the Helmsley Building was originally the headquarters of the New York Central Rail-road Company. Its namesake, the late Harry Helmsley, was a billionaire who began his career as a New York office boy for $12 per week. His wife Leona, who passed away in 2007, was a prominent feature in all the advertise-ments for their hotel chain – until her imprisonment in 1989 for tax evasion on a grand scale. Many observers believe that the extravagant glitter of the building's face-lift is due to Leona's over-blown taste in decor.

1 & 2 United Nations Plaza **9**

Map 13 B5. Ⓜ *42nd St-Grand Central.* 🚌 *M15, M27, M42, M50, M104.*

These two great columns of blue-green mirrored glass are set at an angle to each other; the play of light and reflec-tions on their gleaming sides and sloping setbacks make them seem a giant, ever-changing, work of modern art. The marble and mirrored interiors are also stunning. They house streamlined modern offices and, in No. 1, the Millennium United Nations Plaza Hotel. Here, the guest list frequently includes many UN delegates from all over the world as well as a number of visiting heads of state. Even the stresses of international diplomacy must ease when one is floating lazily in the glassed-in swimming pool, enjoying the bird's-eye views of the city and the United Nations itself.

United Nations **10**

See pp160–63.

Japan Society **11**

333 E 47th St. **Map** 13 B5. ***Tel** (212) 832-1155.* Ⓜ *42nd St-Grand Central.* 🚌 *M15, M27, M50.* ***Gallery*** ◯ *11am–6pm Tue–Thu, 11am–9pm Fri, 11am–5pm Sat–Sun.* 🚫 ♿ 📷 **www**.japansociety.org

The headquarters of the Japan Society, founded in 1907 to foster understanding and cultural exchange between Japan and the US, was built with the help of

Roman gods reclining against the Helmsley Building clock

John D. Rockefeller III, who underwrote costs of some $4.3 million. The striking black building with its delicate sun grilles was designed by Tokyo architects Junzo Yoshimura and George Shimamoto in 1971. It includes an auditorium, a language center, a research library, a museum gallery, and traditional Oriental gardens.

Changing exhibits include a variety of Japanese arts, from swords to kimonos to scrolls. The society offers programs of Japanese performing arts, lectures, language classes, and many business workshops for American and Japanese executives and managers.

Fred F. French Building ⑫

521 5th Ave. **Map** 12 F5.
Ⓜ *42nd St-Grand Central.*
◯ *office hours.*

Built in 1927 to house the best-known real estate firm of the day, this is a fabulously opulent creation.

It was designed by French's chief architect, H. Douglas Ives, in collaboration with Sloan & Robertson, whose

Tiffany stained-glass window in the Church of the Incarnation

other work included the Chanin Building *(see p154)*. They handsomely blended Near Eastern, ancient Egyptian and Greek styles with early Art Deco forms.

Multicolored faïence ornaments decorate the upper facade, and the water tower is hidden in a false top level of the building. Its disguise is an elaborate one, with reliefs showing a rising sun flanked by griffins and bees and symbols of virtues such as integrity and industry. Winged Assyrian beasts ride on a bronze frieze over the entrance. These exotic themes continue into the vaulted lobby, with its elaborate polychrome ceiling decoration and 25 gilt-bronze doors.

This was the first building project to employ members of the Native Canadian Caughnawaga tribe as construction workers. They did not fear heights and soon became highly sought-after as scaffolders for many of the city's most famous skyscrapers.

Church of the Incarnation ⑬

209 Madison Ave. **Map** 9 A2. *Tel (212) 689-6350.* Ⓜ *42nd St-Grand Central, 33rd St.* ◯ *11:30am–2pm Mon–Fri (also 4–7pm Tue, 5–7pm Wed), 1–4pm Sat, 8:15am–12:30pm Sun.* ✝ *12:15pm & 6:30pm Wed, 12:45pm Fri, 8:30am & 11am Sun.* 📷 ♿ 📿 *By appointment.* **www**.churchoftheincarnation.org

This Episcopal church dates from 1864, when Madison Avenue was home to the elite. Its patterned sandstone and brownstone exterior is typical of the period. The interior has an oak communion rail by Daniel Chester French; a chancel mural by John La Farge; and stained-glass windows by La Farge, Tiffany, William Morris and Edward Burne-Jones.

Morgan Library & Museum ⑭

See pp164–5.

Sniffen Court ⑮

150–158 E 36th St. **Map** 9 A2.
Ⓜ *33rd St.*

Here is a delightful, intimate courtyard of ten brick Romanesque revival carriage houses, built by John Sniffen in the 1850s. They are perfectly and improbably preserved off a busy block in modern New York. The house at the south end was used as a studio by the American sculptor Malvina Hoffman, whose plaques of Greek horsemen decorate the exterior wall.

Lobby of the Fred F. French Building

Malvina Hoffman's studio

United Nations ⑩

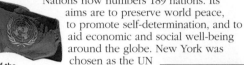

Founded in 1945 with 51 members, the United Nations now numbers 189 nations. Its aims are to preserve world peace, to promote self-determination, and to aid economic and social well-being around the globe. New York was chosen as the UN headquarters, and John D. Rockefeller, Jr. donated $8.5 million for the purchase of the site. The chief architect was American Wallace Harrison, who worked with an international Board of Design Consultants. The 18-acre (7-ha) site is an international zone, with its own stamps and post office. In 2006, the UN's General Assembly approved a $1.6-billion renovation of the complex that will take several years to complete; visitors should phone ahead to check access.

Flag of the United Nations

United Nations headquarters

Secretariat building

The Conference Building houses meeting rooms for the Security Council, the Trusteeship Council and the Economic and Social Council.

★ Security Council
Delegates and their assistants confer around the horseshoe-shaped table while verbatim reporters and other UN staff members sit at the long table in the center.

Trusteeship Council

Economic and Social Council

★ Peace Bell
Cast from the coins of 60 nations, this gift from Japan hangs on a cypress pagoda shaped like a Shinto shrine.

Rose Garden
Twenty-five varieties of roses adorn the manicured gardens on the East River.

STAR FEATURES

★ General Assembly

★ Peace Bell

★ Reclining Figure

★ Security Council

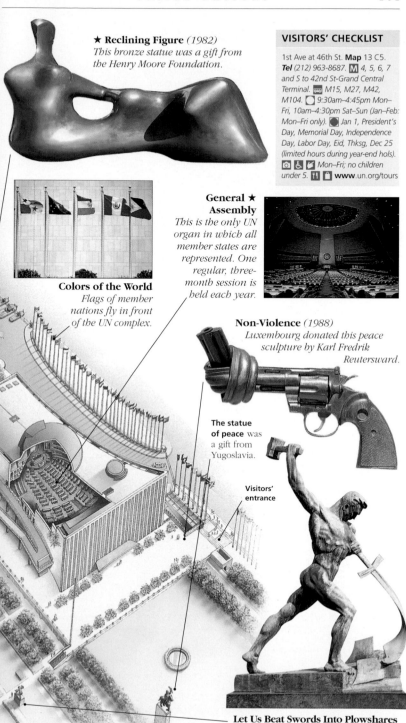

★ **Reclining Figure** (1982)
This bronze statue was a gift from the Henry Moore Foundation.

General ★ Assembly
This is the only UN organ in which all member states are represented. One regular, three-month session is held each year.

Colors of the World
Flags of member nations fly in front of the UN complex.

Non-Violence (1988)
Luxembourg donated this peace sculpture by Karl Fredrik Reutersward.

The statue of peace was a gift from Yugoslavia.

Visitors' entrance

Let Us Beat Swords Into Plowshares
This bronze statue (1958) by Soviet sculptor Evgeny Vuchetich symbolizes the main goal of the United Nations.

The Work of the United Nations

The goals of the United Nations are pursued by three UN councils and a General Assembly comprising all of its member nations. The Secretariat carries out the administrative work of the organization. Guided tours allow visitors to see the Security Council Chamber. Often there is a chance to briefly observe a meeting.

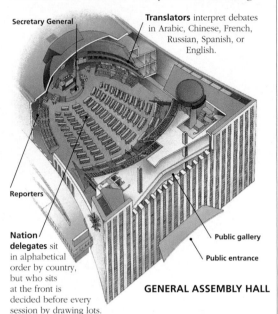

Secretary General

Translators interpret debates in Arabic, Chinese, French, Russian, Spanish, or English.

Reporters

Nation delegates sit in alphabetical order by country, but who sits at the front is decided before every session by drawing lots.

Public gallery

Public entrance

GENERAL ASSEMBLY HALL

GENERAL ASSEMBLY

The General Assembly is the governing body of the UN and has regular sessions each year from mid-September to mid-December. Special sessions are also held when the Security Council or a majority of members request one. All member states are represented with an equal vote, regardless of size. The General Assembly may discuss any international problem raised by the members or by other UN bodies. Although it cannot enact laws, recommendations strongly influence world opinion; these require a two-thirds majority vote.

Lots are drawn before each session to determine the seating in the chamber for the delegations. All 1,898 seats in the chamber are equipped with earphones that offer simultaneous translations in

several languages. The General Assembly also appoints the Secretary General (on the recommendation of the Security Council), approves the UN budgets and elects the non-permanent members of

Foucault's Pendulum (Holland); its slowly rotating swing is proof of the earth's rotation on its axis

the Councils. Together with the Security Council, it also appoints the judges of the International Court of Justice, based in the Netherlands.

SECURITY COUNCIL

The most powerful part of the UN is the Security Council. It strives to achieve international

Mural symbolizing peace and freedom by Per Krohg (Norway)

peace and security and intervenes in crises such as the fighting in Iraq and Afghanistan. It is the only body whose decisions member states are obliged to obey as well as the only one in continuous session.

Five of its members – China, France, the Russian Federation, the United Kingdom, and the United States – are permanent. The other nations are elected by the General Assembly to serve two-year terms.

When international conflicts arise, the Council first tries to seek agreement by mediation. If fighting breaks out, it may issue cease-fire orders and impose military or economic sanctions. It could also decide to send UN peace-keeping missions into troubled areas to separate opposing factions until issues can be resolved through diplomatic channels.

Military intervention is the Council's last resort. UN forces may be deployed, and peace-keeping forces are resident in such places as Cyprus and the Middle East.

TRUSTEESHIP COUNCIL

The smallest of the councils, this is the only UN body whose workload is decreasing. The council was established in 1945 with the goal of fostering peaceful independence for non-self-governing territories or colonies. Since then, more than 80 colonies have gained self-rule, and the number of people living in dependent territories has been reduced from 750 million to about 3 million. The Trusteeship Council currently consists of the five permanent members of the Security Council.

Zanetti mural (Dominican Republic) in the Conference Building depicting the struggle for peace

Trusteeship Council Chamber

ECONOMIC AND SOCIAL COUNCIL

The 54 members of this Council work to improve the standard of living and social welfare around the world, goals that consume 80% of the UN's resources. It makes recommendations to the General Assembly, to each member nation and to the UN's specialized agencies. The Council is assisted by commissions dealing with regional economic problems, human rights abuses, population, narcotics, and women's rights. It also works with the International Labor Organization, the World Health Organization, UNICEF, and other global welfare organizations.

SECRETARIAT

An international staff of 16,000 works for the Secretariat to carry out the day-to-day work of the United Nations. The Secretariat is headed by the Secretary General, who plays a key role as a spokesperson in the organization's peace-keeping efforts. The Secretary

General is appointed by the General Assembly for a five-year term. On January 1, 2007, Ban Ki-moon of South Korea became the latest Secretary General.

IMPORTANT EVENTS IN UN HISTORY

Soviet premier Krushchev speaking to the General Assembly in 1960

The UN depends on voluntary compliance and military support from its members to keep the peace in the event

of disputes. In 1948, the UN declared South Korea the legitimate government of Korea; two years later, it played a major role in defending South Korea against North Korea. In 1949, the UN helped negotiate a cease-fire between Indonesia and the Netherlands and set up a conference that led to the Dutch granting independence to Indonesia.

In 1964 a UN military force was sent to Cyprus to keep peace between the Greeks and Turks, and still remains. Persistent issues in the Middle East have kept UN forces in the area since 1974, the year that China – long refused membership in favor of Taiwan – gained UN membership. In the 1990s, the UN was involved in the break-up of Yugoslavia, and more recently in the conflicts in Afghanistan and Iraq. A 2004 UN mission to Congo was plagued by accusations of sexual abuse by UN peace-keepers. In 2006–7 there were arrests over kickbacks in the UN oil-for-food program to Iraq.

At any given time at least half a dozen missions are active somewhere in the world. The UN was awarded the Nobel Peace Prize in 1988 and 2001.

WORKS OF ART AT THE UN

The UN Building has acquired numerous works of art and reproductions by major artists; many have been gifts from member nations. Most of them have either a peace or international friendship theme. The legend on Norman Rockwell's *The Golden Rule* reads "Do unto others as you would have them do unto you." Marc Chagall designed a large stained-glass window as a memorial to former Secretary General Dag Hammarskjöld, who was accidentally killed while on a peace mission in 1961. There is a Henry Moore sculpture in the grounds (limited access) and many other sculptures and paintings by the artists of many nations.

The Golden Rule (1985), a large mosaic by Norman Rockwell

Morgan Library & Museum ⑭

The Morgan Library reopened in 2006 after an expansion program. The collection, accumulated by banker Pierpont Morgan, is housed in a magnificent palazzo-style 1902 building by architects McKim, Mead & White. Morgan's son, J.P.Morgan, Jr., made it a public institution in 1924. One of the world's finest collections of rare manuscripts, prints, books, and bindings is on display in a complex that includes the original library and the home of J.P. Morgan, Jr.

Exterior of the original library building

The Song of Los *(1795)*
Mystic poet William Blake designed and engraved this plate for one of his most innovative works.

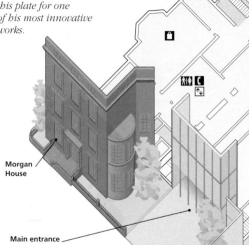

Morgan House

KEY TO FLOOR PLAN

☐ Exhibition space

☐ Non-exhibition space

Main entrance

Gutenberg Bible *(1455)*
Printed on vellum, this volume is one of only eleven surviving copies.

Gallery

The Nursery Alice
Lewis Carroll's characters are immortalized in John Tenniel's classic illustrations (c. 1865).

STAR EXHIBITS

★ The West Room

★ The Rotunda

★ East Room

LIBRARY GUIDE

Mr. Morgan's Study and the original library contain some of his favorite paintings, objets d'art and rare acquisitions. Changing exhibitions feature a wide variety of impressive cultural artifacts.

Mozart's Horn Concerto in E-flat Major

The six surviving leaves of this score are written in different colored inks.

VISITORS' CHECKLIST

225 Madison Ave. **Map** 9 A2.
Tel *(212) 685-0008.*
M 6 to 33rd St; 4, 5, 6, 7,
S to Grand Central Terminal;
B, D, F, V to 42nd St.
M1–5 crosstown M16, M34.
10:30am–5pm Tue–Thu,
10:30am–9pm Fri, 10am–6pm
Sat, 11am–6pm Sun.
Mon, Jan 1, Thanksgiving,
Dec 25. free 7–9pm Fri.
www.themorgan.org

West Room (Mr. Morgan's study)

★ **East Room**
The walls are lined from floor to ceiling with triple tiers of bookcases. Murals show historical figures and their muses, and signs of the zodiac.

★ **The Rotunda** *(1504)*
The entrance foyer of the Library has marble columns and pilasters; the marble floor is modeled on the floor in Villa Pia in the Vatican gardens.

★ **The West Room**
Renaissance art and an antique, Florentine wooden ceiling adorn this room.

PIERPONT MORGAN

Pierpont Morgan (1837–1913) was not only a leading financier but also one of the great collectors of his time. Rare books and original manuscripts were his passion, and inclusion in his collection was an honor. In 1909, when Morgan requested the donation of the manuscript of *Pudd'nhead Wilson*, Mark Twain responded, "One of my high ambitions is gratified."

UPPER MIDTOWN

Upscale New York in all its diversity is here, in this district of churches and synagogues, clubs and museums, grand hotels and famous stores, as well as trend-setting skyscrapers and pockets of luxury living. For almost 30 years from 1833, Upper Midtown was home to society names such as Astor and Vanderbilt. In the 1950s, architectural history was made when the Lever and Seagram buildings were erected. These first great modern towers marked midtown Park Avenue's change from a residential street to a prestigious office address.

1946 Cisitalia in the MoMA

SIGHTS AT A GLANCE

Historic Streets and Buildings
Beekman Place 18
Fuller Building 21
General Electric Building 11
Roosevelt Island 19
Sutton Place 17
Villard Houses 9

Modern Architecture
Citigroup Center 15
IBM Building 3
Lever House 13
Seagram Building 14
Trump Tower 2

Museums and Galleries
American Folk Art Museum 6
Museum of Modern Art (MoMA) pp172–5 5
The Paley Center for Media 7

Churches and Synagogues
Central Synagogue 16
St. Bartholomew's Church 10
St. Patrick's Cathedral pp178–9 8
St. Thomas Church 4

Landmark Hotels
Plaza Hotel 22
Waldorf–Astoria 12

Landmark Stores
Bloomingdale's 20
Fifth Avenue 1

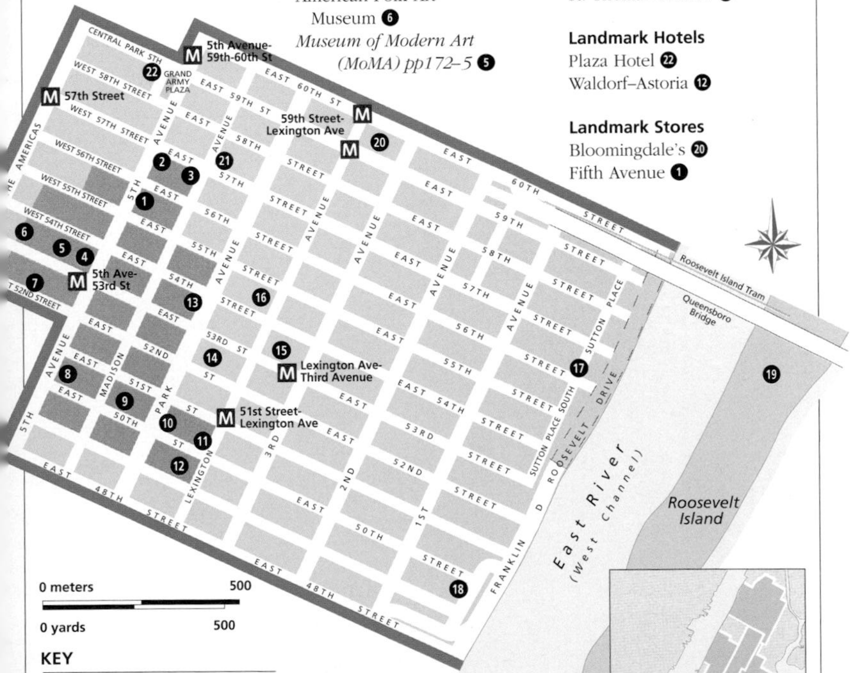

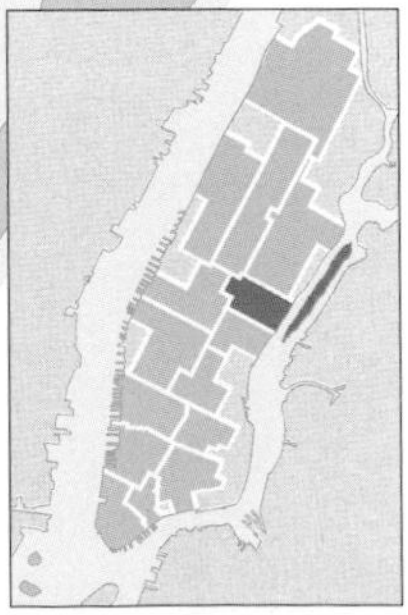

KEY
Street-by-Street map
[M] Subway station

SEE ALSO

- ***Street Finder,*** maps 12, 13–14
- ***Where to Stay*** pp288–9
- ***Restaurants*** pp306–8

GETTING THERE
Take the 6 subway to 51st St or the 4, 5, or 6 to 59th St, the N, R, or W to 60th St, or the E or V to 53rd St-5th Ave or 53rd St-Lexington. Bus routes are the M1–4, M15, or M101–3. Crosstown buses are the M27 and M50, and the M31 and M57.

◁ **The façade of St. Patrick's Cathedral on Fifth Avenue**

Street by Street: Upper Midtown

The luxury stores that are synonymous with Fifth Avenue first blossomed as society moved on uptown. In 1917, Cartier's acquired the mansion of banker Morton F. Plant in exchange for a string of pearls, setting the style for other retailers to follow. But this stretch of midtown is not simply for shoppers. There are three distinctive museums and an equally diverse assembly of architectural styles to enjoy, too.

Fifth Avenue
The popular carriage rides offer tourists a taste of past elegance and a leisurely way to view some of the main sights around this thoroughfare ❶

The University Club was built in 1899 as an elite club for gentlemen.

W 55TH ST

St. Thomas Church
Much of the interior carving was designed by sculptor Lee Lawrie ❹

★ Museum of Modern Art
One of the world's finest collections of modern art ❺

The Paley Center for Media
Exhibitions, seasons of special screenings, live events and a vast library of historic broadcasts are offered at this media museum ❼

Fifth Avenue subway (lines E, V)

Saks Fifth Avenue has offered goods in impeccable taste to generations of New Yorkers. (*See p319.*)

★ St. Patrick's Cathedral
This, the largest Catholic cathedral in the United States, is a magnificent Gothic Revival building ❽

Olympic Tower
combines offices, apartments and a skylit atrium within its sleek walls.

Villard Houses
Five handsome brownstone houses now form part of the New York Palace Hotel ❾

STAR SIGHTS

* ★ Museum of Modern Art

* ★ St. Patrick's Cathedral

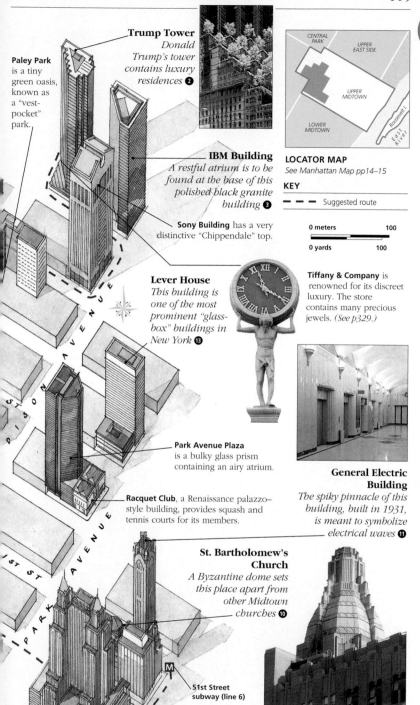

Trump Tower
Donald Trump's tower contains luxury residences ❷

Paley Park is a tiny green oasis, known as a "vest-pocket" park.

IBM Building
A restful atrium is to be found at the base of this polished black granite building ❸

Sony Building has a very distinctive "Chippendale" top.

Lever House
This building is one of the most prominent "glass-box" buildings in New York ⓭

Tiffany & Company is renowned for its discreet luxury. The store contains many precious jewels. *(See p329.)*

Park Avenue Plaza is a bulky glass prism containing an airy atrium.

Racquet Club, a Renaissance palazzo–style building, provides squash and tennis courts for its members.

General Electric Building
The spiky pinnacle of this building, built in 1931, is meant to symbolize electrical waves ⓫

St. Bartholomew's Church
A Byzantine dome sets this place apart from other Midtown churches ❿

51st Street subway (line 6)

Waldorf-Astoria
Old-world elegance has attracted many famous guests to this hotel, including the late Duke and Duchess of Windsor ⓬

CENTRAL PARK

UPPER EAST SIDE

UPPER MIDTOWN

LOWER MIDTOWN

Roosevelt I.

East River

LOCATOR MAP
See Manhattan Map pp14–15

KEY

– – – Suggested route

0 meters   100

0 yards   100

**Window display at Bergdorf
Goodman** *(see p319)*

Fifth Avenue ❶

Map 12 F3–F4. M *5th Ave-53rd St,
5th Ave-59th St.*

In 1883, when William Henry
Vanderbilt built his mansion
at Fifth Avenue and 51st Street,
he started a trend that resulted
in palatial residences stretching
as far as Central Park, built
for top families such as the
Astors, Belmonts, and Goulds.
Only a few remain to attest
to the grandeur of the era.

One of these is the Cartier
store at 651 Fifth Avenue, once
the home of Morton F. Plant,
millionaire and commodore
of the New York Yacht Club.
As retailers swept
north up the avenue
– a trend that began
in 1906 – society
gradually moved
uptown. In 1917,
Plant moved to a
mansion at 86th
Street, and legend
has it that he traded
his old home to
Pierre Cartier for a
perfectly matched
string of pearls.

Fifth Avenue has
been synonymous
with luxury goods
ever since. From
Cartier at 52nd Street
to Henri Bendel at
56th and Tiffany and
Bergdorf Goodman
at 57th, you will
find many brands
symbolizing wealth
and social standing
today, just as Astor
and Vanderbilt did
over a century ago.

Trump Tower ❷

725 5th Ave. **Map** 12 F3. *Tel (212)
832-2000.* M *5th Ave-53rd St, 5th
Ave-59th St.* **Garden level** ◻
*10am–6pm Mon–Sat, noon–5pm
Sun.* **Building** ◯ *8am–10pm daily.*
◎ ᵻ ᴨ ▱ ᵇ

This glittering, exorbitantly
expensive apartment and office
tower rises above a lavish
six-story atrium. Designed in
1983 by Der Scutt of Swanke,
Hayden, Connell & Partners,
the public space has pink
marble, mirrors and glitz
throughout. There is an
impressive 80-ft (24-m) high
indoor waterfall, while the
exterior is lined with hanging
gardens. The tower is a
flamboyant monument to
affluence by the developer
Donald Trump, a symbol of
the excesses and grandeur
of the 1980s *(see p33).*

Next door, 727 Fifth Avenue
is a complete contrast: the
location of Tiffany & Co., the
prestigious jewelers founded
in 1837. Famed for exquisite
window displays, the store
uses understated but elegant
blue packaging as a status
symbol in itself. Tiffany's was
immortalized by Truman
Capote in his 1958 novel
Breakfast at Tiffany's.

**Entrance to Tiffany & Co., the
exclusive jewelry emporium**

IBM Building ❸

590 Madison Ave. **Map** 12 F3.
M *5th Ave.* **Garden Plaza**
◯ *8am–10pm daily.* ◎ ᵻ

Completed in 1983, this 43-
story tower was designed by
Edward Larrabee Barnes. It is
a sleek, five-sided prism of
gray-green polished granite,
with a cantilevered corner at
57th Street. The
Garden Plaza, with
its bamboo trees, is
open to the public
and has been
redubbed "The
Sculpture Garden."
Eight new works,
which change four
times a year, are
on view at any
one time. Near the
atrium is a work
by American
sculptor Michael
Heizer, entitled
Levitated Mass.
Inside a low,
stainless-steel tank
is a huge slab of
granite that seems
to float on air.

On the corner
of 57th Street and
Madison Avenue is
Saurien, a bright-
orange abstract
sculpture by
Alexander Calder.

Interior of the Trump Tower atrium

St. Thomas Church ❹

1 W 53rd St. **Map** 12 F4. **Tel** (212) 757-7013. Ⓜ 5th Ave-53rd St. ○ 7am–6pm daily. ✝ frequent. 🚫 ♿ 📷 after 11am service & concerts. **www**.saintthomaschurch.org

This is the fourth home for this parish and the second on this site. Today's church was built between 1909 and 1914 to replace an earlier structure destroyed in a fire in 1905. The previous building had provided the setting for many of the glittering high-society weddings of the late 19th century. The most lavish of these was in 1895 when heiress Consuelo Vanderbilt married the English Duke of Marlborough.

The limestone building, in French–Gothic style, has a single asymmetrical tower and an off-center nave, novel solutions to the architectural problems posed by its corner position. The richly carved, shimmering white screens behind the altar were designed by architect Bertram Goodhue and sculptor Lee Lawrie. Carvings in the choir stalls, dating from the 1920s, include modern inventions such as the telephone, Presidents Roosevelt and Wilson, and Lee Lawrie himself.

Museum of Modern Art ❺

See pp172–5.

American Folk Art Museum ❻

45 W 53rd St. **Map** 12 F4. **Tel** (212) 265-1040. Ⓜ 5th Ave-53rd St. ○ 10:30am–5:30pm Tue–Sun (7:30pm Fri). 🚫 ♿ 📷 💻 📷 **www**.folkartmuseum.org

The permanent home for the appreciation and study of American folk art is here, in the first free-standing art museum built in New York since 1966. Designed by the innovative architectural firm of Tod Williams Billie Tsien & Associates and built in 2001,

Beatles Paul, Ringo and John on the "Ed Sullivan Show" in 1964

the structure is clad in panels of white tombasil, a white bronze alloy. The museum has 30,000 sq ft (2,787 sq m) of exhibition space on eight levels. The museum still retains the Eva and Morris Feld Gallery at the Lincoln Square location (see p214).

The American Folk Art Museum

The Paley Center for Media ❼

25 W 52nd St. **Map** 12 F4. **Tel** (212) 621-6800. Ⓜ 5th Ave-53rd St. ○ noon–6pm Wed–Sun (to 8pm Thu). ● public hols. 🚫 📷 ♿ 📷 📷 **www**.paleycenter.org

In this one-of-a-kind repository museum, visitors can watch and listen to news and a collection of entertainment and sports documentaries from radio and television's earliest days to the present. Pop fans can see the

early Beatles or a young Elvis Presley making his television debut. Sports enthusiasts can relive classic Olympic competitions. World War II footage might be chosen by students of history or by those who lived through the war. Six choices at any one time can be selected from a computer catalogue that covers a library of over 50,000 programs. The selections are then played on small private areas. There are larger screening areas and a theater for 200, where retrospectives of artists and directors are shown. There are also photo exhibits and memorabilia.

The museum was the brain-child of William S. Paley, a former head of the CBS TV network. It opened in 1975 as the Museum of Broadcasting on East 53rd Street. It proved so popular that in 1991 it moved into this hi-tech $50 million home in a building reminiscent of an antique radio set.

1960s television star Lucille Ball

The Museum of Modern Art ❺

Museum facade on 54th Street

MoMA contains one of the world's most comprehensive collections of modern art. Founded in 1929, it set the standard for museums of its kind. Following an expansion program, MoMA in Midtown reopened in 2004. The renovated building provides gallery space over six floors, almost twice that of the old museum. Expanses of glass allow abundant natural light both to penetrate inside the building and to bathe the sculpture garden.

Sculpture Garden
The Abby A. Rockefeller Sculpture Garden has a peaceful atmosphere.

STAR PAINTINGS

★ Les Demoiselles d'Avignon by Pablo Picasso

★ Portrait of the Postman Joseph Roulin by Vincent Van Gogh

Christina's World
(1948) Andrew Wyeth contrasts an overwhelming horizon with the minutely-studied surroundings of his handicapped neighbor.

Bird in Space *(c. 1928)*
Constantin Brancusi's elegant bronze sculpture captures the sheer essence of flight.

Sculpture garden

GALLERY GUIDE

The sculpture garden is on the first floor. The contemporary art, print, and media galleries are on the second floor. Painting and sculpture are exhibited on the second, fourth, and fifth floors. Architecture and design, photography, and drawings are all on the third floor. Changing exhibitions are displayed on the third and sixth floors. Films are shown on the lower level.

First floor

Main entrance

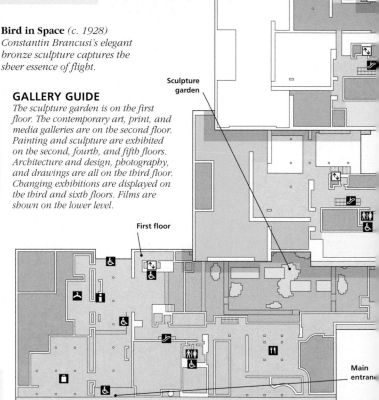

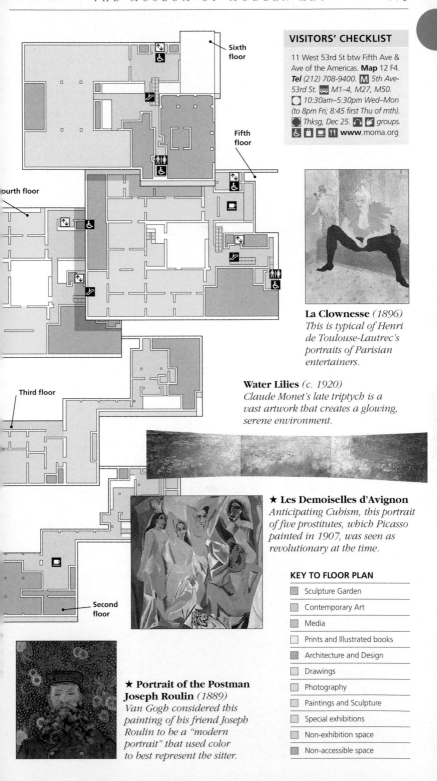

Sixth floor

Fifth floor

Fourth floor

Third floor

Second floor

VISITORS' CHECKLIST

11 West 53rd St btw Fifth Ave & Ave of the Americas. **Map** 12 F4. **Tel** (212) 708-9400. M 5th Ave-53rd St. M1–4, M27, M50. 10:30am–5:30pm Wed–Mon (to 8pm Fri; 8:45 first Thu of mth). Thksg, Dec 25. groups. www.moma.org

La Clownesse (1896)
This is typical of Henri de Toulouse-Lautrec's portraits of Parisian entertainers.

Water Lilies (c. 1920)
Claude Monet's late triptych is a vast artwork that creates a glowing, serene environment.

★ Les Demoiselles d'Avignon
Anticipating Cubism, this portrait of five prostitutes, which Picasso painted in 1907, was seen as revolutionary at the time.

KEY TO FLOOR PLAN

- Sculpture Garden
- Contemporary Art
- Media
- Prints and Illustrated books
- Architecture and Design
- Drawings
- Photography
- Paintings and Sculpture
- Special exhibitions
- Non-exhibition space
- Non-accessible space

★ Portrait of the Postman Joseph Roulin (1889)
Van Gogh considered this painting of his friend Joseph Roulin to be a "modern portrait" that used color to best represent the sitter.

Exploring the Collection

The Museum of Modern Art has approximately 150,000 works of art ranging from Post-Impressionist classics to an unrivaled collection of modern and contemporary art, from fine examples of design to early masterpieces of photography and film.

1880S TO 1940S PAINTING AND SCULPTURE

The Persistence of Memory by the Surrealist Salvador Dalí (1931)

abstract art of the Constructivists is included in a strong representation of Lissitzky, Malevich, and Rodchenko: De Stijl's influence is seen in paintings by Piet Mondrian, such as *Broadway Boogie Woogie*. There is a large body of work by Matisse, such as *Dance I* and *The Red Studio*. Dalí, Miró, and Ernst feature among the bizarre, strangely beautiful Surrealist works.

Paul Cézanne's monumental *The Bather* and Vincent Van Gogh's *Portrait of the Postman Joseph Roulin* are two of the seminal works in the museum's collection of late 19th-century painting. Both Fauvism and Expressionism are well represented with works by Matisse, Derain, Kirchner, and others, while Pablo Picasso's *Les Demoiselles d'Avignon* marks a transition to a new style of painting.

The collection also has an unparalleled number of Cubist paintings, providing an overview of a movement that radically challenged our perception of the world. Among the vast range are Picasso's *Girl with a Mandolin*, Georges Braque's *Man with a Guitar* and *Soda*, and *Guitar and Flowers* by Juan Gris. Works by the Futurists, who brought color and movement to Cubism to depict the dynamic modern world, include *Dynamism of a Soccer Player* by Umberto Boccioni, plus works by Balla, Carrà, and Villon. The geometric

POSTWAR PAINTING AND SCULPTURE

The extensive collection of postwar art includes works by Bacon and Dubuffet, and has a particularly strong representation of American artists. The collection of Abstract Expressionist art, for example, includes Jackson Pollock's *One [Number 31, 1950]*, Willem de Kooning's *Women, I*, Arshile Gorky's *Agony*, and *Red, Brown,*

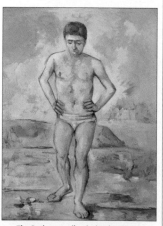

The Bather, an oil painting by French Impressionist artist Paul Cézanne

and Black by Mark Rothko. Other notable works include Jasper Johns' *Flag*, Robert Rauschenberg's *First Landing Jump*, composed of urban refuse, and *Bed*, which consists of bed linen. The Pop Art collection includes Roy Lichtenstein's *Girl with Ball* and *Drowning Girl*, Andy Warhol's famous *Gold Marilyn Monroe*, and Claes Oldenburg's *Giant Soft Fan*.

Works after about 1965 include pieces by Judd, Flavin, Serra, and Beuys, among many others.

DRAWINGS AND OTHER WORKS ON PAPER

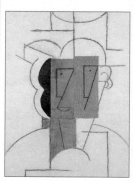

Man with a Hat by Pablo Picasso (1912), a collage with charcoal

More than 7,000 artworks ranging in size from tiny preparatory pieces to large mural-sized works are among MoMA's holdings. Many drawings use conventional materials, such as pencil, charcoal, pen and ink, pastel, and watercolor. However, there are also collages and mixed-media works composed of paper ephemera, natural products, and man-made goods.

The collection provides an overview of Modernism, from the late 19th century to the present day, including movements such as Cubism, Dadaism, and Surrealism. Drawings by famous and well-established artists, such as Picasso, Miró, and Johns, are exhibited alongside a growing number of works by talented emerging artists.

PRINTS AND ILLUSTRATED BOOKS

American Indian Theme II by Roy Lichtenstein (1980)

All significant art movements from the 1880s onward are represented in this extensive collection, which provides a fascinating overview of printed art. With more than 50,000 items in the department's holdings, there are wide-ranging examples of historical and contemporary printmaking. Works created in such traditional media as etchings, lithographic prints, screenprints, and woodcuts are displayed alongside pieces created using more experimental techniques.

There are some particularly fine examples of works by Andy Warhol, who is widely considered to be the most important printmaker of the 20th century. There are also many illustrations and prints by other artists including Redon, Munch, Matisse, Dubuffet, Johns, Lichtenstein, Freud, and Picasso.

PHOTOGRAPHY

The photography collection begins with the invention of the medium around 1840. It includes pictures by fine artists, journalists, scientists, and entrepreneurs, as well as amateur photographers.

Among the highlights of the collection are some of the best-known works by American and European photographers including Atget, Stieglitz, Lange, Arbus, Steichen, Cartier-Bresson, and Kertesz. There is also a range of contemporary practitioners,

FILM DEPARTMENT

With a collection of over 22,000 films and four million stills, the collection can offer a wide range of programs, including retrospectives of individual directors and actors, films in specific genres and experimental work, as well as a broad range of other exhibitions. Film conservation is a key part of the department's work. Today's top directors are donating copies of their films to help fund this expensive but vital work.

Film still of Charlie Chaplin and Jackie Coogan in *The Kid* (1921)

most notably Friedlander, Sherman, and Nixon.

The photographers have covered an extensive variety of subject matter in both colour and black and white– delicate landscapes, scenes of urban desolation, abstract imagery, and stylish portraiture, including some

Sunday on the Banks of the Marne, photographed by Henri Cartier-Bresson in 1939

beautiful silver-gelatin print nudes by the French Surrealist Man Ray. Together, they form a complete history of photographic art and represent one of the finest collections in existence.

ARCHITECTURE AND DESIGN

The Museum of Modern Art was the first art museum to include utilitarian objects in its collection. These range from household appliances such as stereo equipment, furniture, lighting, textiles, and glassware to industrial ball bearings and silicon chips. Architecture is represented in the collection of photographs, scale models, and drawings of buildings that have been or might have been built.

Graphic design is shown in typography and posters. Larger exhibits that look as if they belong in a museum of transportation include Willys-Overland Jeep and the Bell helicopter.

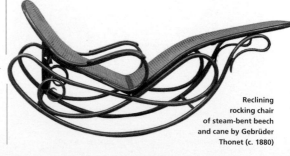

Reclining rocking chair of steam-bent beech and cane by Gebrüder Thonet (c. 1880)

St. Patrick's Cathedral ⑧

See pp178–9.

Villard Houses ⑨

457 Madison Ave (New York Palace Hotel). **Map** 13 A4. **Tel** *(800) NY PALACE.* Ⓜ *51st St.* www.newyork palace.com **Municipal Art Sociey Urban Center** ☐ *10am–7pm Mon–Thu, 10am–6pm Fri, 10am–5:30pm Sat.* **Tel** *(212) 935 3960.* ⬛ ♿ 🚻 www.mas.org

Henry Villard was a Bavarian immigrant who became publisher of the *New York Evening Post* and founder of the Northern Pacific Railroad. In 1881, he bought the land opposite St. Patrick's Cathedral and hired McKim, Mead & White to design town houses on the site. The inspired result has six four-story houses set round a central court opening to the street and the church, though financial difficulties forced Villard to sell and ownership passed to the Roman Catholic archdiocese. When the church outgrew its space in the 1970s the houses were saved when the Helmsley chain purchased air rights for the 51-story Helmsley (now New York) Palace Hotel.

The center wing comprises the hotel's formal entrance and the Villard Bar & Lounge. The **Municipal Art Society Urban Center** occupies the north wing, and its bookshop is the best place in New York for architectural books on the city. The Municipal Art Society also organizes excellent architectural tours, from Harlem to Brooklyn and Staten Island.

St. Bartholomew's Church

St. Bartholomew's Church ⑩

109 E 50th St. **Map** 13 A4. **Tel** *(212) 378-0222.* Ⓜ *51st St.* ☐ *8am–6pm daily (to 7:30pm Thu & 8:30pm Sun).* 🕇 *frequent.* ⬛ ♿ **Lectures, concerts.** 🕇 🎵 *after 11am Sunday services.* 🍴 *(212) 888-2664.* www.stbarts.org

Known fondly to New Yorkers as "St. Bart's," this Byzantine structure with its ornate detail, pinkish brick, open terrace and a polychromed gold dome brought color and variety to Park Avenue in 1919.

Architect Bertram Goodhue incorporated into the design the Romanesque entrance portico created by Stanford White for the original 1903 St. Bartholomew's on Madison Avenue, and marble columns from the earlier church were used in the chapel.

St. Bartholomew's program of concerts is well known, as is its theater group, which mounts three productions here each year.

Villard Houses, now the entrance to the New York Palace Hotel

General Electric Building ⑪

570 Lexington Ave. **Map** 13 A4. Ⓜ *Lexington Ave.* ⬛ *to the public.*

In 1931 architects Cross & Cross were commissioned to design a skyscraper that would be in keeping with its neighbor, St. Bartholomew's Church. Not an easy task, but the result won unanimous acclaim. The colors were chosen to blend and contrast, and the design of the tower complemented the church's polychrome dome.

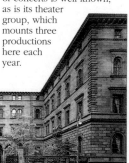

The General Electric Building on Lexington Avenue

View the pair from the corner of Park and 50th to see how well it works. However, the General Electric is no mere backdrop but a work of art in its own right and a favorite part of the city skyline. It is an Art Deco gem from its chrome and marble lobby to its spiky "radio waves" crown.

Walk one block north on Lexington Avenue to find a place much cherished by movie fans. It is right at this spot that Marilyn Monroe, in a billowing white frock, stood so memorably in the breeze from the Lexington Avenue subway grating in the movie *The Seven-Year Itch*.

Waldorf–Astoria @

301 Park Ave. **Map** 13 A5.
Tel (212) 355-3000. Ⓜ *Lexington Ave, 53rd St. See **Where to Stay** p288.* **www**.waldorf.com

This Art Deco classic, which covers an entire city block, was designed by Schultze & Weaver in 1931. The original Hotel at 34th Street was demolished to make way for the Empire State Building.

Winston Churchill and New York philanthropist Grover Whalen at the Waldorf–Astoria in 1946

Still deservedly one of New York's most prestigious hotels, the Waldorf–Astoria serves, too, as a reminder of a more glamorous era in the city's history. The 625-ft (190-m) twin towers, where the Duke and Duchess of Windsor lived, have hosted numerous celebrities, including every US president since 1931. The giant lobby clock, executed for the Chicago World's Fair of 1893, is from the original hotel, and the piano in the Peacock Alley cocktail lounge belonged to Cole Porter when he was a resident of the hotel's exclusive Towers.

Lever House @

390 Park Ave. **Map** 13 A4.
Ⓜ *5th Ave-53rd St.* **Lobby and building** ⬤ *to the public.* 🍴

Imagine a Park Avenue lined with sturdy, residential buildings – and then imagine the sensation when they were suddenly reflected here in the first of the city's glass-walled skyscrapers, one of the most influential buildings of the modern era. The design, by Skidmore, Owings & Merrill, is simply two rectangular

The pool at the Four Seasons in the Seagram Building

slabs of stainless steel and glass, one laid horizontally, the other stacked to stand tall above it, to allow light in from every side. The crisp and bright design was in-tended to symbolize many of the Lever Brothers' products – they make soaps and other cleaning products. Revolutionary though it was in 1952, Lever House is now dwarfed by its many imitators, but its importance as an architectural pacesetter remains undiminished. The Lever House restaurant is a VIP scene.

Lever House on Park Avenue

Seagram Building @

375 Park Ave. **Map** 13 A4. Ⓜ *5th Ave-53rd St.* ◯ *9am–5pm Mon–Fri.* 🍴 *See **Where to Eat** p307.*

Samuel Bronfman, the late head of Seagram distillers, was prepared to put up an ordinary commercial building until his architect daughter, Phyllis Lambert, intervened and persuaded him to go to the best – Mies van der Rohe.

The result, which is widely considered the finest of the many Modernist buildings of the 1950s, consists of two rectangles of bronze and glass that let the light pour in.

Within is the exclusive Four Seasons Restaurant *(see p307)*, a landmark in its own right. Designer Philip Johnson has created a remarkable space, with the centerpiece of one room a pool, and another a bar topped by a quivering Richard Lippold sculpture.

Office workers at lunch in the spacious Citigroup Center atrium

Citigroup Center @

153 E 53rd St. **Map** 13 A4. Ⓜ *53rd St-Lexington Ave.* ◯ *7am–11pm daily.* 🍴 🍴 **St. Peter's Lutheran Church** 619 Lexington Ave. *Tel (212) 935-2200.* ◯ *9am–9pm daily.* ✝ *12:15pm Mon–Fri, 6pm Wed, 8:45am & 11am Sun.* **Jazz vespers** *5pm Sun.* **Concerts** *noon Wed.* **York Theater at St. Peter's;** *Tel (212) 935-5820.* **www**.saintpeters.org

An aluminum-clad spire built on ten-story stilts with a sliced-off roof, Citigroup Center is unique; it caused a sensation when it was completed in 1978. The unusual base design had to incorporate St. Peter's Lutheran Church. The church is separate both in space and design, a granite sculpture below a corner of the tower. Step inside to see the striking interior and the Erol Beker Chapel by sculptor Louise Nevelson. The church is well known for its organ concerts, jazz vespers, and theater presentations. Citigroup's slanting top never functioned as a solar panel as intended, but it is an unmistakable landmark on the skyline.

St. Patrick's Cathedral ❽

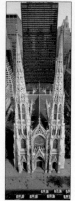

The Roman Catholic Church originally intended this site for use as a cemetery, but in 1850 Archbishop John Hughes decided to build a cathedral instead. Many thought that it was foolish to build so far beyond the (then) city limits, but Hughes went ahead anyway. Architect James Renwick built New York's finest Gothic Revival building, the largest Catholic cathedral in the United States. The

The cathedral's Fifth Avenue facade

cathedral, which seats 2,500 people, was completed in 1878, though the spires were added from 1885 to 1888.

★ Lady Chapel
This chapel honors the Blessed Virgin. The stained-glass windows portray the mysteries of the rosary.

Pietà
American sculptor William O. Partridge created this Pietà in 1906. The statue stands at the side of the Lady Chapel.

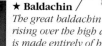

★ Baldachin
The great baldachin rising over the high altar is made entirely of bronze. Statues of the saints and prophets adorn the four piers supporting the canopy.

STAR FEATURES

- ★ Baldachin
- ★ Great Bronze Doors
- ★ Great Organ and Rose Window
- ★ Lady Chapel

Cathedral Facade
The exterior wall is built of white marble. The spires rise 330 ft (101 m) above the pavement.

Stations of the Cross

Carved of Caen stone in Holland, these reliefs won first prize in the field of religious art at the Chicago World's Fair in 1893.

VISITORS' CHECKLIST

5th Ave and 50th St. **Map** 12 F4. **Tel** (212) 753-2261. M 6 to 51st St; E, V to Fifth Ave. M1–4, M27, M50. 7:30am–8:45pm daily. frequent Mon–Sat; 7, 8, 9, 10:15am & noon, 1, 4 (in Spanish) & 5:30pm Sun. *Concerts, recitals, lectures.* www.saintpatrickscathedral.org

Saint Elizabeth Ann Seton Shrine

The bronze statue and screen depict the life of the first American to be canonized a saint. She founded the Sisters of Charity (see p76).

★ Great Organ and Rose Window

Measuring 26 ft (8 m) in diameter, the rose window shines above the great organ, which has more than 7,000 pipes.

Main entrance

★ Great Bronze Doors

The massive doors weigh 20,000 lb (9,000 kg) and are adorned with important religious figures in New York.

Central Synagogue ⑯

652 Lexington Ave. **Map** 13 A4.
Tel *(212) 838–5122.* Ⓜ *51st St,*
Lexington Ave. ◯ *noon–2pm Tue–*
Wed. 📷 *12:45 Wed.* ♿ ✡ *6pm*
Fri, also 10am Sat (Jul–Aug),
10.30am Sat (Sep–Jun).
www.centralsynagogue.org

This is New York's
oldest building in
continuous use as a
synagogue. It was
designed in 1870 by
Silesian-born Henry
Fernbach, America's
first prominent Jewish
architect. He also
designed some of
SoHo's finest cast-iron
buildings. Restored
after a 1999 fire, the
Synagogue is considered
the city's best example
of Moorish-Islamic
Revival architecture.
The congregation was
founded in 1846 as
Ahawath Chesed (Love
of Mercy) by 18 new
immigrants, most of
them from Bohemia,
on Ludlow Street on
the Lower East Side.

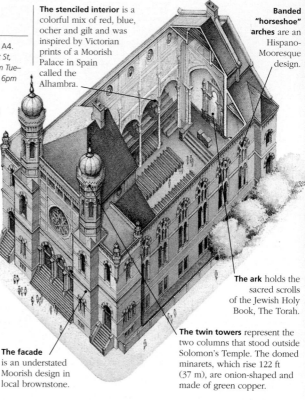

The stenciled interior is a
colorful mix of red, blue,
ocher and gilt and was
inspired by Victorian
prints of a Moorish
Palace in Spain
called the
Alhambra.

**Banded
"horseshoe"
arches** are an
Hispano-
Mooresque
design.

The ark holds the
sacred scrolls
of the Jewish Holy
Book, The Torah.

The facade
is an understated
Moorish design in
local brownstone.

The twin towers represent the
two columns that stood outside
Solomon's Temple. The domed
minarets, which rise 122 ft
(37 m), are onion-shaped and
made of green copper.

Sutton Place ⑰

Map 13 C3. Ⓜ *59th St, 51st St.*
🚌 M15, M31, M57

Sutton Place is a posh and
pleasant neighborhood,
delightfully devoid of busy
traffic, made up of elegant
low-rise apartment houses

and town houses designed by
noted architects. The arrival of
New York society in the 1920s
transformed an area that had
once been the province of
factories and tenements.
Three Sutton Square is the
residence of the secretary-
general of the United Nations.
Look beyond Sutton Square

and 59th Street for a glimpse
of Riverview Terrace, a
private street of five ivy-
covered brownstones fronting
on the river. The tiny parks
at the end of 55th Street and
jutting out at 57th Street offer
views of the river and the
Queensboro Bridge.
    After much neighborhood
opposition, Bridgemarket
opened in 2000. Located
between the huge vaults
under the Queensboro
Bridge, there is an upscale
Terence Conran's for
housewares and a Food
Emporium supermarket.

Beekman Place ⑱

Map 13 C5. Ⓜ *59th St, 51st St.*
🚌 M15, M31, M57.

Smaller than Sutton Place,
and even more tranquil, is
Beekman Place, a virtually
private two-block enclave
of 1920s town houses and

**Park at Sutton Place, looking toward Queensboro Bridge and
Roosevelt Island**

small-scale apartments. Famous residents here have included Gloria Vanderbilt, Rex Harrison, Irving Berlin and members of the large Rockefeller family.

At Turtle Bay Gardens, restored brownstone houses dating from the 1860s hide a charming Italianate garden. Among the residents enticed by this privacy have been the film stars Tyrone Power and Katharine Hepburn, composer Stephen Sondheim, and writer E.B. White.

Roosevelt Island

Map 14 D2. **M** *59th St. Tram, Roosevelt Island station (F).* www.rioc.com

Since 1976 a Swiss cable car has offered a quick ride across the East River to Roosevelt Island, with eagle's-eye views of the city and the Queensboro Bridge.

Near the tram station the remains of the Blackwell Farmhouse, which stood from 1796 to 1804 and gave the island its name until real estate development began in the 1920s. From then until the 1970s, the island housed a succession of hospitals, an almshouse, a jail, a workhouse and an insane asylum, and became known as Welfare Island. In 1927, Mae West was held in the penitentiary here after a "lewd performance." The ruins of 19th-century hospitals still remain, as does an 1872 lighthouse built by an asylum inmate.

The tram departs from 2nd Avenue at 60th Street and affords a thrilling ride and some fine city views.

Bloomingdale's store sign

Bloomingdale's ⑳

1000 3rd Ave. **Map** 13 A3. **Tel** *(212) 705-2000.* **M** *59th St.* ◻ *10am–8:30pm Mon–Fri, 10am–7pm Sat, 11am–7pm Sun. See* **Shopping** *p319.* www.bloomingdales.com

For a while in the booming 1980s, "Bloomies" was synonymous with the good life. Founded by Joseph and Lyman Bloomingdale in 1872, this famous department store had a bargain-basement image until the 3rd Avenue El was taken down in the 1960s. Then came the store's transformation to the epitome of trendy, sophisticated shopping. But the late 1980s brought new ownership and eventual bankruptcy. While not as flashy as in the past, Bloomingdale's is open every day and remains one of the city's best-stocked stores. A second store has opened in SoHo at 504 Broadway.

Fuller Building ㉑

41 E 57th St. **Map** 13 A3. *Peter Findlay Gallery.* **Tel** *(212) 644-4433; James Goodman Gallery.* **Tel** *(212) 593-3737.* ◻ *10am–6pm Tue–Sat.* **M** *59th St.*

This slim-towered black, gray and white 1929 beauty by Walker & Gillette is a prime example of geometric Art Deco design. The striking statues on either side of the clock above the entrance are by Elie Nadelman. Step inside to admire the intricate mosaic tile floors; one panel shows the Fuller Company's former home in

The clock statues above the Fuller Building entrance

the famous Flatiron Building on Fifth Avenue *(see 127).* The Fuller Building is a hive of exclusive art galleries, most of which are open to the public daily.

French Renaissance–style facade of the Plaza Hotel

Plaza Hotel ㉒

5th Ave & Central Park South. **Map** 12 F3. **M** *59th St.*

The city's grande dame of hotels was designed by Henry J. Hardenbergh, known for the Dakota *(see p218)* and the original Waldorf–Astoria. Completed in 1907 at the exorbitant cost of $12.5 million, the Plaza was proclaimed "the best hotel in the world," with 800 rooms, 500 baths, a two-story ballroom, five marble staircases, and 14- to 17-room apartments for such families as the Vanderbilts and the Goulds *(see p49).*

The 18-story cast-iron structure resembles a French Renaissance château. Much of the interior decoration came from Europe. The Palm Court still has mirrored walls and Italian carvings of the four seasons, and is a lovely place for afternoon tea.

Already lavishly restored by its former owner Donald Trump, the building underwent a $400-million conversion into a mix of apartments, hotel condominiums, and a 130-room hotel. There are also six floors of luxury retail and upscale dining, including the famous Oak Room.

UPPER EAST SIDE

At the turn of the century, New York society moved to the Upper East Side – and stayed. Many of the Beaux-Arts mansions in this district are now museums and embassies, but the well-to-do still occupy the grand apartment buildings on Fifth and Park avenues. Chic shops and galleries line

African urn, Metropolitan Museum of Art

Madison Avenue. Farther east, the area includes what is left of German Yorkville in the East 80s, Hungarian Yorkville to the south, and little Bohemia, with its Czech population, below 78th Street. Although many of these ethnic groups no longer inhabit the area, their churches, restaurants, and shops still remain.

Bird's-eye view of the lobby at the Solomon R. Guggenheim Museum

SIGHTS AT A GLANCE

Historic Streets and Buildings
Gracie Mansion **16**
Henderson Place **14**
Seventh Regiment Armory **10**

Museums and Galleries
Asia Society **9**
Cooper-Hewitt National Design Museum **3**
Frick Collection pp202–3 **8**
Jewish Museum **2**
Metropolitan Museum of Art pp190–97 **6**
Mount Vernon Hotel Museum and Garden **13**
Museum of the City of New York **19**
National Academy Museum **4**
Neue Galerie New York **1**
Society of Illustrators **12**
Solomon R. Guggenheim Museum pp188–9 **5**
Whitney Museum of American Art pp200–1 **7**

Churches and Synagogues
Church of the Holy Trinity **17**
St. Nicholas Russian Orthodox Cathedral **18**
Temple Emanu-El **11**

Parks and Squares
Carl Schurz Park **15**

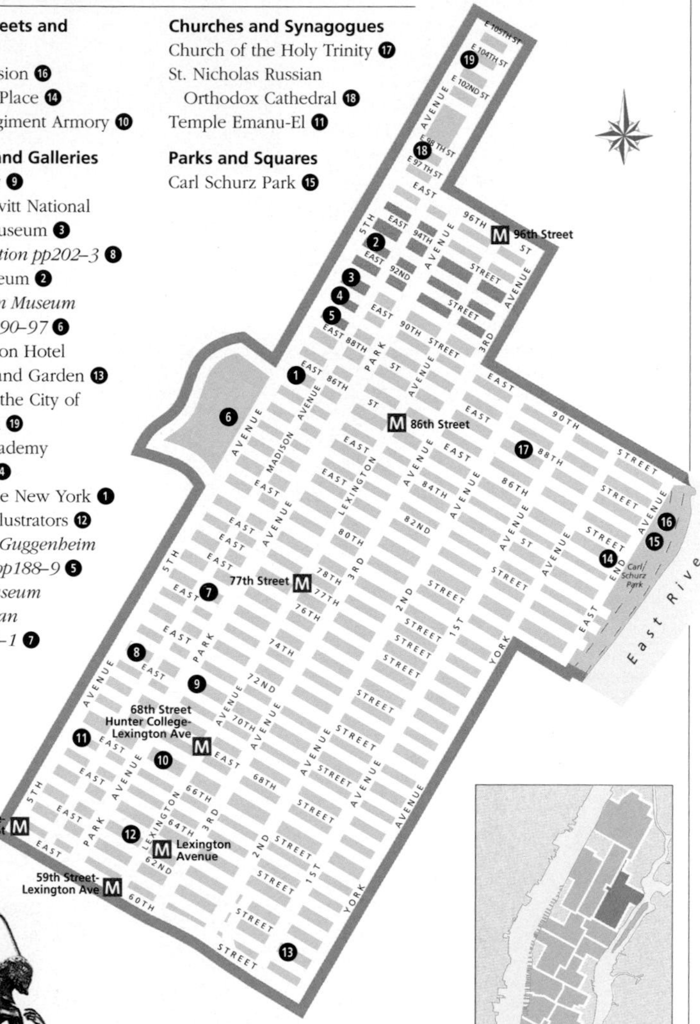

Statue of Diana, National Academy of Design

KEY

Street-by-Street map

M Subway station

SEE ALSO

- *Street Finder,* maps 12–13, 16–18, 21
- *East Side Walk* pp264–5
- *Where to Stay* pp289–90
- *Restaurants* pp308–9

GETTING THERE
The Lexington Ave 4 and 5 express trains stop at 59th and 86th sts. The local (No. 6) also stops at 68th, 77th, and 96th sts. The F stops at 63rd St, the N, R, and W at 5th Ave and 59th St. Buses include: M1, M2, M3, and M4 on Fifth/Madison aves, M101–3 on Lexington/ Third and M15 on First/Second. The crosstown buses are the M66, M72, M79, M86, and M96.

Street by Street: Museum Mile

Many of New York's museums are clustered on the Upper East Side, in homes ranging from the former Frick and Carnegie mansions to the modernistic Guggenheim, designed by Frank Lloyd Wright. The displays are as varied as the architecture, running the gamut from Old Masters to photographs to decorative arts. Presiding over the scene is the vast Metropolitan Museum of Art, America's answer to the Louvre. Some of the museums stay open late one day a week.

Jewish Museum
The most extensive collection of Judaica in the world is housed here. It includes coins, archaeological objects, and ceremonial and religious artifacts ❷

★ Cooper-Hewitt National Design Museum
Ceramics, glass, furniture and textiles are well represented here ❸

The Church of the Heavenly Rest was built in 1929 in the Gothic style. The madonna in the pulpit is by sculptor Malvina Hoffman.

National Academy Museum
The Academy, founded in 1825, moved here in 1940. Its fine collection includes paintings and sculptures by its members ❹

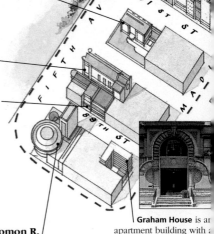

Graham House is an apartment building with a splendid Beaux Arts entrance. It was built in 1892.

★ Solomon R. Guggenheim Museum
Architect Frank Lloyd Wright's building, which is in the form of a spiral, is floodlit at dusk. Take the elevator to the top and walk down to see one of the world's best collections of modern art ❺

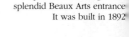

STAR SIGHTS

★ Cooper-Hewitt Museum

★ Solomon R. Guggenheim Museum

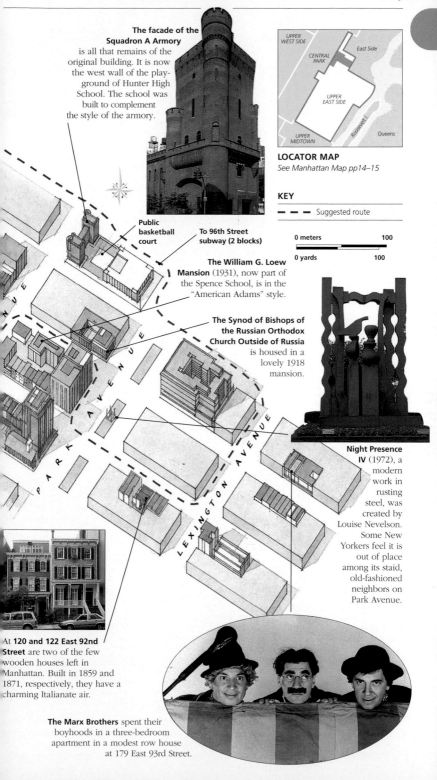

The facade of the Squadron A Armory is all that remains of the original building. It is now the west wall of the playground of Hunter High School. The school was built to complement the style of the armory.

UPPER WEST SIDE

CENTRAL PARK

East Side

UPPER EAST SIDE

Roosevelt I.

UPPER MIDTOWN

Queens

LOCATOR MAP
See Manhattan Map pp14–15

KEY

– – – Suggested route

0 meters   100

0 yards   100

Public basketball court

To 96th Street subway (2 blocks)

The William G. Loew Mansion (1931), now part of the Spence School, is in the "American Adams" style.

The Synod of Bishops of the Russian Orthodox Church Outside of Russia is housed in a lovely 1918 mansion.

Night Presence IV (1972), a modern work in rusting steel, was created by Louise Nevelson. Some New Yorkers feel it is out of place among its staid, old-fashioned neighbors on Park Avenue.

At **120 and 122 East 92nd Street** are two of the few wooden houses left in Manhattan. Built in 1859 and 1871, respectively, they have a charming Italianate air.

The Marx Brothers spent their boyhoods in a three-bedroom apartment in a modest row house at 179 East 93rd Street.

Neue Galerie New York ❶

1048 5th Ave at E 86th St. **Map** 16 F3. **Tel** *(212) 628-6200.* Ⓜ *86th St.* 🚌 *M1–4.* 🕐 *11am–6pm Mon–Thu.* 🌑 *public hols.* 💺 ⓘ ⭕ 🍽 *Café 9am–6pm daily (to 9pm Thu–Sun).* ⓘ 🔊 www.neuegalerie.org

This museum was founded by art dealer Serge Sabarsky and philanthropist Ronald Lauder. Its objective is to collect, research, and exhibit the fine and decorative arts of Germany and Austria from the early 20th century.

The Louis XIII-style Beaux-Arts structure was completed in 1914 by Carrère & Hastings, who also designed the New York Public Library *(see p146)*. The building, a designated landmark, is considered one of the most distinguished buildings on Fifth Avenue. Once occupied by Mrs. Cornelius Vanderbilt III, the mansion was purchased by Lauder and Sabarsky in 1994. The ground floor houses the entrance, a bookshop, and the Café Sabarsky, which draws its inspiration from the Viennese cafés of old and also plays host to chamber, cabaret, and classical music concerts. The second floor is devoted to the works of Klimt, Schiele, and Wiener Werkstätte objects. The upper floors feature works from Der Blaue Reiter (artists such as Klee, Kandinsky), the Bauhaus (Feininger, Schlemmer), and Die Brücke (Mies van der Rohe, Breuer).

Jewish Museum ❷

1109 5th Ave. **Map** 16 F2. **Tel** *(212) 423-3200.* Ⓜ *86th St, 96th St.* 🚌 *M1–4.* 🕐 *11am–5:45pm Sun–Wed, 11am–8pm Thu.* 🌑 *Sat, public & Jewish hols.* 💺 ⭕ 🔊 🎞 🖥 ⓘ www.thejewishmuseum.org

The exquisite château-like residence of Felix M. Warburg, financier and leader of the Jewish community, was designed by C. P. H. Gilbert in 1908. It now houses one of the world's largest collections of Jewish fine and ceremonial art, and historical Judaica. The stonework in a new extension is by the stonemasons of St. John the Divine *(see pp226–7)*.

Objects have been brought here from all over the world, some at great risk of persecution to the donors. Covering 4,000 years, artifacts include Torah crowns, candelabras, kiddush cups, plates, scrolls, and silver ceremonial objects.

There is a Torah ark from the Benguiat Collection, the exquisite faience entrance wall of a 16th-century Persian synagogue, and the powerful *Holocaust* by sculptor George Segal. Changing exhibitions reflect Jewish life and experience around the world.

19th-century ewer and basin from Istanbul at the Jewish Museum

Cooper-Hewitt National Design Museum ❸

2 E 91st St. **Map** 16 F2. **Tel** *(212) 849-8400.* Ⓜ *86th St, 96th St.* 🚌 *M1–4.* 🕐 *10am–5pm Mon–Sat (to 9pm Fri & 6pm Sat), noon–6pm Sun.* 🌑 *Jan 1, Thksg, Dec 25.* 💺 ⭕ 🔊 🎞 ⓘ 🖥 www.cooperhewitt.org

One of the largest design collections in the world, this museum occupies the former home of industrialist Andrew Carnegie. The collection was amassed by the Hewitt sisters, Amy, Eleanor, and Sarah. The museum opened in 1897 at Cooper Union *(see p120)*; the Smithsonian Institution acquired the collections in 1967, and the Carnegie Corporation offered the mansion.

Carnegie asked for "the most modest, plainest, and most roomy house in New York," but the house set new trends

Cooper-Hewitt Museum entrance

with central heating, private elevator, and air-conditioning. Note the wooden staircase, rich paneling and carving, and the sunny solarium.

National Academy Museum ❹

1083 5th Ave. **Map** 16 F3. **Tel** *(212) 369-4880.* Ⓜ *86th St.* 🚌 *M1–4.* 🕐 *noon–5pm Wed–Thu, 11am–6pm Fri–Sun.* 🌑 *public hols.* 💺 ⭕ 🔊 ⓘ www.nationalacademy.org

More than 6,000 paintings, drawings, and sculptures, including works by Thomas Eakins, Winslow Homer, Raphael Soyer, and Frank Lloyd Wright, comprise the collection of the National Academy Museum, founded in 1825 by a group of artists. The group's mission was (and is) to train artists and exhibit their work.

In 1940, Archer Huntington, an art patron and philanthropist, donated his house, an attractive building with patterned marble floors and decorative plaster ceilings. The grand entrance foyer has a statue of Diana by sculptor Anna Hyatt Huntington.

Statue of Diana in the National Academy Museum entrance foyer

Solomon R. Guggenheim Museum ❺

See pp188–9.

Metropolitan Museum of Art ❻

See pp190–97.

Whitney Museum of American Art ❼

See pp200–01.

Frick Collection ❽

See pp202–03.

Asia Society ❾

725 Park Ave. **Map** 13 A1. *Tel (212) 288-6400.* Events: (212) 517-ASIA. Ⓜ 68th St. ◯ *11am–6pm Tue–Sun (to 9pm Fri).* ● *public hols.* 🎦 📷 *12:30pm and 2pm Tue–Sat, 6:30pm Fri, 2:30pm Sun.* 🚫 ♿ 🏠 🖥 www.asia society.org

Founded by John D. Rockefeller III in 1956 to increase understanding of Asian culture, the society is a forum for 30 countries from Japan to Iran, Central Asia to Australia. The 1981 eight-story building was designed by Edward Larrabee Barnes and is made of red granite. After a renovation in 2001, the museum has increased gallery space. One gallery is permanently devoted to Rockefeller's own collection of Asian sculptures, amassed by him and his wife on frequent trips to the East.

Changing exhibits show a wide variety of Asian arts, and the society has a full program of films, dance, concerts, and lectures and a well-stocked bookshop.

Entrance Hall of the Seventh Regiment Armory

South Asian sculpture at the Asia Society

Seventh Regiment Armory ❿

643 Park Ave. **Map** 13 A2. *Tel (212) 616-3930.* Ⓜ 68th St. ◯ *call for opening times.* 🚫 ♿ www.armoryonpark.org

From the War of 1812 through two world wars, the Seventh Regiment, an elite corps of "gentlemen soldiers" from prominent families, has played a vital role. Within the fortress-like exterior of their armory are extraordinary rooms filled with lavish Victorian furnishings, *objets d'art*, and regimental memorabilia.

The design by Charles W. Clinton, a veteran of the regiment, had offices facing Park Avenue, with a vast drill hall stretching behind to Lexington Ave. The reception rooms include the Veterans' Room and the Library by Louis Comfort Tiffany. The drill hall is now the site of the Winter Antiques Show *(see p53)* and a favorite venue for charity balls. A massive renovation is under way, after which the Armory will open its doors as a center for arts and education.

Temple Emanu-El ⓫

1 E 65th St. **Map** 12 F2. *Tel (212) 744-1400.* Ⓜ 68th St, 63rd St. ◯ *10am–5pm Sun–Fri (last adm on Fri 3:30pm), 12:30–4:45pm Sat.* ● *Jewish hols.* ⭐ *5:30pm Sun–Thu, 5:15pm Fri, 10:30am Sat.* 📷 ♿ 🎦 🏠 www.emanuelnyc.org

This impressive limestone edifice of 1929 is the largest synagogue in the world, with seating for 2,500 in the main sanctuary alone. It is home to the oldest Reform congregation in New York, and the wealthiest members of Jewish society worship here.

Among the synagogue's many fine details are the bronze doors of the Ark, which represent an open Torah scroll. The Ark also has stained glass depicting biblical scenes and showing the tribal signs of the houses of Israel. These signs also appear on a great recessed arch that frames a magnificent wheel window, the dominant feature of the Fifth Avenue facade.

The synagogue stands on the site of the palatial home of Mrs. William Astor, the legendary society hostess. Lady Astor moved to the Upper East Side after a feud with her nephew, who lived next door. Her wine cellar and three marble fireplaces still remain at the synagogue.

The Ark at Temple Emanu-El

Solomon R. Guggenheim Museum ❺

Home to one of the world's finest collections of modern and contemporary art, the building itself is perhaps the museum's greatest masterpiece. The exterior of the museum was beautifully restored in celebration of the 50th anniversary of the building in 2009. Designed by Frank Lloyd Wright, the shell-like facade is a veritable New York landmark. The spiral ramp curves down and inward from the dome, passing works by major 19th-, 20th-, and 21st-century artists along the way.

Fifth Avenue facade

Paris Through the Window
The vibrant colors of Marc Chagall's 1913 masterpiece illumine the canvas, conjuring up images of a magical and mysterious city where nothing is quite what it appears to be.

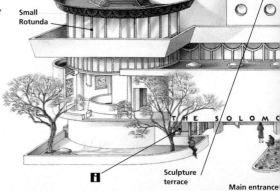

Small Rotunda

THE SOLOMC

ℹ️

Sculpture terrace

Main entrance

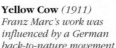

Yellow Cow *(1911)*
Franz Marc's work was influenced by a German back-to-nature movement.

Woman Ironing *(1904)*
A work from Pablo Picasso's Blue Period, this painting is his quintessential image of hard work and fatigue.

Nude *(1917)*
This sleeping figure is typical of Amedeo Modigliani's stylized work.

MUSEUM GUIDE

The Great Rotunda features special exhibitions. The Small Rotunda shows some of the museum's celebrated Impressionist and Post-Impressionist holdings. The Tower galleries feature exhibitions of work from the permanent collection as well as contemporary pieces. A fifth-floor sculpture terrace overlooks Central Park. Not all of the collection is on display at any one time.

Tower

Great Rotunda

VISITORS' CHECKLIST

1071 5th Ave at 89th St. **Map** 16 F3. **Tel** *(212) 423-3500.* 4, 5, 6 to 86th St. M1, M2, M3, M4. 10am–5:45pm Fri–Wed (to 7:45pm Fri). Jan 1, Dec 25. *Performing art series, concerts, lectures.* www.guggenheim.org

Before the Mirror *(1876)*
In trying to capture the flavor of 19th-century society, Edouard Manet often used the image of the courtesan.

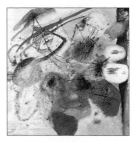

Woman Holding a Vase
Fernand Léger incorporated elements of Cubism into this work from 1927.

Black Lines *(1913) This is one of Vasily Kandinsky's earliest examples of his work in "non-objective" art.*

Woman with Yellow Hair
(1931) The gentle, voluptuous figure of Picasso's mistress often appears in his work.

FRANK LLOYD WRIGHT

During his lifetime, Wright was considered the great innovator of American architecture. Characteristic of his work are Prairie-style homes and office buildings of concrete slabs, glass bricks, and tubing. Wright received the Guggenheim commission in 1942 and it was completed after his death in 1959, his only New York building.

Interior of the Guggenheim's Great Rotunda

Metropolitan Museum of Art ❻

Founded in 1870 by a group of artists and philanthropists who dreamed of an American art institution to rival those of Europe, this collection is thought to be the most comprehensive in the Western world. Works date from prehistoric times to the present. The museum opened here in 1880 and houses collections from all continents. The Roman Court and Etruscan gallery on the first floor draws one quarter of the Met's visitors.

The entrance of the Metropolitan Museum of Art

★ Gertrude Stein *(1905–6)*
This portrait of the American writer Gertrude Stein is by Pablo Picasso. The masklike face is evidence of his debt to African and Roman art.

Ground floor

Pendant Mask
The kingdom of Benin (now part of Nigeria) was renowned for its art. This mask was made in the 16th century.

Seated Man with Harp
This statuette was made in the Cyclades c. 3,000 BC.

GALLERY GUIDE

Most of the collections are housed on the two main floors. Works from 19 curatorial areas are in the permanent galleries, with designated sections for temporary exhibitions. Central on the first and second floors are European painting, sculpture, and decorative art. The Costume Institute is situated on the ground level, directly below the Egyptian galleries on the first floor.

The Marriage Feast at C
This rare 16th-century p painting by Juan de Fla is part of the Linsky Colle

Bust of Diderot *(1773)*
Jean Antoine Houdon's bust was made for a Russian count.

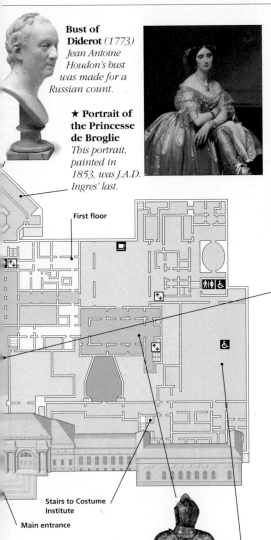

★ **Portrait of the Princesse de Broglie**
This portrait, painted in 1853, was J.A.D. Ingres' last.

First floor

Byzantine Galleries
This marble panel with a griffin is from Greece or the Balkans (c.1250). It is just one of the pieces on display in the Byzantine Galleries.

STAR EXHIBITS

★ Byzantine Galleries

★ Gertrude Stein by Pablo Picasso

★ Portrait of the Princesse de Broglie by Ingres

★ Temple of Dendur

Stairs to Costume Institute

Main entrance

KEY TO FLOOR PLAN

- Robert Lehman Collection
- European painting, sculpture and decorative arts
- Art of Africa, Oceania, and the Americas
- Modern art
- American art
- Egyptian art
- Greek and Roman art
- Medieval and Byzantine art
- Arms and armor
- Grace Rainey Rogers Auditorium
- Non-exhibition space

English Armor
This was made for Sir George Clifford around 1580.

★ **Temple of Dendur** *(15 BC)*
The Roman emperor Augustus built this three-room temple. He is shown in its reliefs making offerings.

Metropolitan Museum of Art: Upper Levels

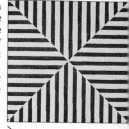

Marrakech
*This 1964 work
is one of Frank
Stella's "Moroccan"
paintings. Within
a square format,
fluorescent strips
form the painting's
main focus.*

Sculpture Garden
*These modern
sculptures, on top
of the Modern Art
wing, are changed
annually.*

Card Players *(1890)*
*Paul Cézanne departed here from his
traditional landscapes, still lifes and
portraits to paint this scene of
peasants intently playing cards.*

★ **Cypresses** *(1889)*
*Vincent Van Gogh painted
this the year before he died.
The heavy brushstrokes and
the swirling style mark his
later work.*

First floor

Second floor

STAR EXHIBITS

- ★ Cypresses by
  Vincent Van Gogh

- ★ Diptych by
  Jan van Eyck

- ★ George Washington
  Crossing the Delaware
  by Leutze

- ★ Self-portrait (1660)
  by Rembrandt

**Eagle-headed Winged
Being Pollinating the
Sacred Tree** *(about 900 BC)*
*This relief comes from an
Assyrian palace.*

★ Diptych
(1425–30)
Flemish painter Jan van Eyck was one of the earliest masters of oil painting. These scenes of the Crucifixion and Last Judgment show him to be a forerunner of realism, too.

★ Washington Crossing the Delaware
In 1851 Emanuel Gottlieb Leutze painted this romanticized – and inaccurate – view of the famous crossing.

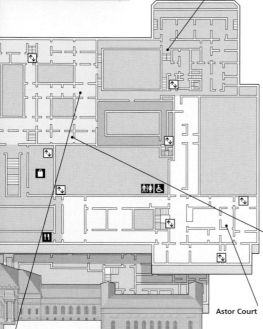

KEY TO FLOOR PLAN

- European painting, sculpture and decorative arts
- Art of Africa, Oceania, and the Americas
- Ancient Near Eastern, and Islamic art
- Modern art
- American art
- Asian art
- Cypriot art
- Musical instruments
- Drawings, prints and photographs
- Non-exhibition space
- Special exhibitions

Astor Court

The Death of Socrates *(1787)*
Jacques-Louis David shows Socrates about to take poison rather than renounce his beliefs.

★ Self-portrait *(1660)*
Rembrandt painted almost 100 self-portraits. This one shows him at the age of 54.

THE ASTOR COURT

In 1979, 27 crafts-people from China, responsible for the care of Souzhou's historic gardens, came to New York to replicate a Ming-style scholar's garden in the Metropolitan Museum. They used centuries-old techniques and hand-made tools that had been passed down for generations. It was the first cultural exchange between the United States and the People's Republic of China. The result is a quiet garden for meditation, a Western parallel to Souzhou's Garden of the Master of the Fishing Nets.

Exploring the Metropolitan

The treasures of "the Met" include a vast collection of American art and more than 2,500 European paintings, including masterpieces by Rembrandt and Vermeer. There are also many Islamic exhibits, plus the greatest collection of Egyptian art outside Cairo.

AFRICA, OCEANIA, AND THE AMERICAS

A painted gold funerary mask (10th–14th century) from the necropolis of Batán Grande, Peru

Nelson Rockefeller built the Michael C. Rockefeller Wing in 1982 in memory of his son, who lost his life on an art-finding expedition in New Guinea. The wing showcases a superb collection of over 1,600 objects from Africa, the islands of the Pacific and the Americas.

Among the African works, the ivory and bronze sculptures from the royal kingdom of Benin (Nigeria) are outstanding, as is the wooden sculpture by the Dogon, Bamana and Senufo peoples of Mali. From the Pacific come carvings by the Asmat people of New Guinea and decorations and masks from the Melanesian and Polynesian islands. From Mexico and Central and South America come pre-Columbian gold, ceramics and stonework. The wing also contains fine Native American artifacts by the Inuit and other groups.

AMERICAN ART

Gilbert Stuart's portrait of George Washington, George Caleb Bingham's *Fur Traders Descending the Missouri*, John Singer Sargent's notorious portrait of *Madame X,* and the monumental *Washington Crossing the Delaware* by Emanuel Leutze are among the icons in the American Wing. It holds not only one of the world's finest collections of American painting and sculpture but also of decorative arts from Colonial times to the beginning of the 20th century. Highlights range from elegant Neo-Classical silver vessels made by Paul Revere to innovative glassware by Tiffany & Co. In the furniture section are settees, dining chairs, tables, bookcases, and desks from major centers of American cabinetmaking such as Boston, Newport, and Philadelphia.

Period rooms, with their original decorative woodwork and furnishings, range from the saloon hall in which George Washington celebrated his last birthday to the elegant prairie-style living room that Frank Lloyd Wright designed for Francis W. Little in Wayzata, Minnesota, in 1912.

The Charles Engelhard Court is an indoor sculpture garden with large-scale architectural elements, including the lovely stained-glass and mosaic loggia from Louis Comfort Tiffany's Long Island estate and the facade of an 1824 United States Branch Bank that once stood on Wall Street.

ANCIENT NEAR EASTERN AND ISLAMIC ART

Massive stone sculptures of winged, human-headed animals, once the guardians of the 9th-century BC Assyrian

Mysterious in identity and origin, a rare 5,000-year-old copper head from the Near East

palace of Ashurnasirpal II, stand at the entrance to the Ancient Near Eastern galleries. Inside is a collection spanning 8,000 years, rich in Iranian bronzes, Anatolian ivories and Sumerian sculptures, and Achaemenian and Sassanian silver and gold. An adjacent area contains Islamic art of the 7th to the 19th centuries; glass and metalwork from Egypt, Syria and Mesopotamia; royal miniatures from Persia and Mughal India; 16th- and 17th-century rugs; and an 18th-century room from Syria.

ARMS AND ARMOR

Mounted knights in full armor charge at each other across the equestrian court here. These galleries are a favorite with children and anyone moved by medieval romance or thrilled by power.

There are suits of armor, rapiers and sabers with hilts of precious stones and gold, firearms inlaid with ivory and mother-of-pearl, plus colorful heraldic banners and shields.

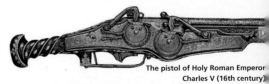

The pistol of Holy Roman Emperor Charles V (16th century)

Highlights include the armor of gentleman-pirate Sir George Clifford, a favorite of Queen Elizabeth I. The rainbow-colored armor of a 14th-century Japanese shogun and a collection of Wild West revolvers that once belonged to gunmaker Samuel Colt are also exhibited here.

ASIAN ART

The Old Plum, a Japanese paper screen from the early Edo period (about 1650)

Many outstanding galleries contain masterpieces of Chinese, Japanese, Korean, Indian, and Southeast Asian art, dating from the second millennium BC to the 20th century. A full-scale Ming-style Chinese scholar's garden was built by craftspeople from Souzhou as part of the first cultural exchange between the United States and the People's Republic of China. The museum also has one of the finest collections of Sung and Yuan paintings in the world, Chinese Buddhist monumental sculptures, fine Chinese ceramics and jade, and an important display of the arts of ancient China.

The full range of Japanese arts is represented in a breathtaking suite of 11 galleries featuring chronological and thematic displays of Japanese lacquer, ceramics, painting, sculpture, textiles, and screens. Indian, Southeast Asian, and Korean galleries display superb sculptures and other arts from these regions.

COSTUME INSTITUTE

The 31,000-piece collection of costumes and accessories has expanded by over 23,000 items under an agreement with the Brooklyn Museum *(see pp250–53)*. There is no permanent display due to the fragility of the objects, but there are two special exhibitions a year.

The collection spans five centuries from the 17th century to the present and is a definitive compendium of fashionable dress, from the elaborately embroidered dresses of the late 1600s to gowns from the Napoleonic era. The designs of Elsa Schiaparelli, Worth, and Balenciaga are also included, along with Ballets Russes costumes and even David Bowie's sequined jockstrap.

The *Art of Dress* audio tour, narrated by actress Sarah Jessica Parker, focuses on how artists have used clothing to express identity and power.

The Institute is sophisticated in its understanding of conservation techniques, with a state-of-the-art laboratory.

A 17th-century European silk-and-satin doublet

DRAWINGS, PRINTS, AND PHOTOGRAPHS

This eclectic gallery regularly displays selections from the museum's incredible holdings of drawings, prints, etchings, and photographs. The

Michelangelo's studies of a Libyan Sibyl for the ceiling of the Sistine Chapel (1508)

drawings collection is especially rich in Italian and French art from the 15th to the 19th century. Specific exhibits of the drawings in this collection are shown on a rotating basis because of the light-sensitive nature of works on paper.

Highlights among the 11,000 drawings include works by Michelangelo, Leonardo da Vinci, Raphael, Ingres, Goya, Rubens, Rembrandt, Tiepolo, and Seurat.

The encyclopedic print collection of nearly 1.5 million images and over 14,000 illustrated books includes major works by virtually every master printmaker, from an early German woodcut called *Virgin and Child* to some of Dürer's most accomplished works and Goya's *The Giant*. Influential gallery-owner Alfred Stieglitz's donation of his own extensive collection of photographs brought here such gems as Edward Steichen's *The Flatiron*. It formed the core of a photography collection that is now also particularly strong in Modernist works dating from between the world wars.

Ephemera such as posters and advertisements form another part of this collection.

EGYPTIAN ART

One of the museum's best-loved areas is the ancient Egyptian wing, which displays every one of its thousands of holdings – from the prehistoric period to the 8th century AD. Objects range from the fragmented jasper lips of a 15th-century BC queen to the massive Temple of Dendur. Other amazing archaeological finds, most of them originating from museum-sponsored expeditions undertaken early in the 20th century, include sculptures of the notorious Queen Hatshepsut, who seized the Theban throne in the 16th century BC; 100 carved reliefs of Amenhotep IV's reign; and tomb figures like the blue faïence hippo that has become the museum's mascot.

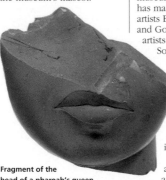

Fragment of the head of a pharoah's queen

EUROPEAN PAINTING, SCULPTURE, AND DECORATIVE ARTS

The heart of the museum is its awe-inspiring collection of over 3,000 European paintings. The Italian works include

Young Woman with a Water Jug (1660) by Johannes Vermeer

Botticelli's *Last Communion of Saint Jerome* and Bronzino's *Portrait of a Young Man*. The Dutch and Flemish canvases are among the world's finest, with Brueghel's *The Harvesters*, several works by Rubens, Van Dyck, and Rembrandt, and more Vermeers than any other museum. The collection also has masterpieces by Spanish artists El Greco, Velázquez, and Goya, and by French artists Poussin and Watteau. Some of the finest Impressionist and Post-Impressionist canvases reside here: 34 Monets, including *Terrace at Sainte-Adresse;* 18 Cézannes; and several Van Goghs, including *Cypresses.* In the Kravis wing and adjacent galleries are works from the 60,000-object collection of European sculpture and decorative arts, such as Tullio Lombardo's marble statue of Adam; a bronze statuette of a rearing horse, after a model by Leonardo; and dozens of pieces by Degas and Rodin. Period settings include the patio from a 16th-century

Spanish castle and a series of ornate 18th-century French domestic interiors known as the Wrightsman Rooms. The Petrie European Sculpture Court features French and Italian sculpture in a beautiful garden setting reminiscent of Versailles in France.

GREEK AND ROMAN ART

A Roman sarcophagus from Tarsus, donated in 1870, was the first work of art in the Met's collections. It can still be seen in the museum's Greek and Roman galleries, along with breathtaking wall panels from a villa that was buried under the lava of Vesuvius in AD 79, Etruscan mirrors, Roman portrait busts, exquisite objects in glass and silver, and hundreds of Greek vases. A monumental 7th-century BC statue of a youth shows the movement toward naturalism in sculpture, and the Hellenistic *Old Market Woman* demonstrates how the Greeks had mastered realism by the 2nd century BC.

An amphora by Exekias, showing a wedding (6th century BC)

LEHMAN COLLECTION

What had been one of the the finest private art collections in the world, that of investment banker Robert Lehman, came to the museum in 1969. The Lehman Wing is a dramatic glass pyramid housing an extraordinarily varied collection rich in Old Masters and 19th-century French paintings, drawings, bronzes,

EGYPTIAN TOMB MODELS

In 1920, a Met researcher's light illuminated a room, which had been closed for 2,000 years, in the tomb of the nobleman Meketre. Within were 24 tiny, perfect replicas of his daily life: his house and garden, fleet of ships and herd of cattle. Meketre is there, too, on his boat, inhaling a lotus's scent and enjoying the music of his singer and harpist. The museum has 13 of these delightful replicas.

A panel from the stained-glass *Death of the Virgin* window, from the 12th-century cathedral of Saint Pierre in Troyes, France

Renaissance majolica, Venetian glass, furniture, and enamels. Among the canvases are works by north-European masters; Dutch and Spanish paintings, French masterworks, Post-Impressionists and Fauves.

MEDIEVAL ART

The Metropolitan's medieval collection includes works dating from the 4th to the 16th century, roughly from the fall of Rome to the beginning of the Renaissance. The collection is split between the main museum and its uptown branch, the Cloisters *(see pp236–9)*. In the main building are a chalice once thought to be the Holy Grail, six silver Byzantine plates showing scenes from the life of David, a 1301 pulpit by Giovanni Pisano in the shape of an eagle, and several monumental sculptures of the Virgin and Child. Other exhibits include Migration jewelry, liturgical vessels, stained glass, ivories, and 14th- and 15th-century tapestries.

MUSICAL INSTRUMENTS

The world's oldest piano, Andrés Segovia's guitars and a sitar shaped like a peacock are some of the features of a broad and sometimes quirky collection of musical instruments that spans six continents and dates from prehistory to the present. The instruments illustrate the history of music and performance, and most of them are conserved to remain in playable condition.

Worth particular mention are instruments from the European courts of the Middle Ages and the Renaissance; rare violins, harpsichords; instruments inlaid with precious materials; and a fully equipped traditional violin-maker's work-shop; there are also African drums, Asian *pi-pas*, or lutes; and Native American flutes. Visitors can use audio equipment to hear many of the instruments playing the music of their day.

Stradivari violin from Cremona, Italy (1691)

MODERN ART

Since its foundation in 1870, the museum has been acquiring contemporary art, but it was not until 1987 that a permanent home for 20th-century art was built – the Lila Acheson Wallace Wing. Other museums in New York have larger collections of modern art, but this display space is considered among the finest. European and American works from 1900 onward are featured on three levels, starting with Europeans such as Picasso, Kandinsky, Braque, and Bonnard. The collection's greatest strength lies in its collection of modern American art, with works by New York school "The Eight," including John Sloan; such Modernists as Charles Demuth and Georgia O'Keeffe; American Regionalist Grant Wood; Abstract Expressionists Willem de Kooning; and such Color Field painters as Clyfford Still.

Grant Wood's view of *The Midnight Ride of Paul Revere* (1931)

Special areas of the wing house Art Nouveau and Art Deco furniture and metalwork; a large collection of works on paper by Paul Klee; and the Sculpture Gallery, with its large-scale sculptures and canvases.

Gems of the collection include Picasso's portrait of Gertrude Stein, Matisse's *Nasturtiums* and *"Dance,1"* Demuth's *I Saw the Figure 5 in Gold*, Jackson Pollock's *Autumn Rhythm*, and Andy Warhol's last self-portrait.

Each year the Cantor Roof Garden at the top of the wing features a new installation of contemporary sculpture, especially dramatic against the backdrop of the New York skyline and Central Park.

Book cover (1916) by illustrator N. C. Wyeth

Society of Illustrators ⓬

128 E 63rd St. **Map** 13 A2. *Tel (212) 838-2560.* Ⓜ *Lexington Ave.* ◯ *10am–8pm Tue, 10am–5pm Wed–Fri, noon–4pm Sat.* ⬤ *public hols.* 🖼 ♿ *restricted.* 🎫 📷
www.societyillustrators.org

Established in 1901, this society was formed to promote the illustrator's art. Its notable roster included Charles Dana Gibson, N. C. Wyeth, and Howard Pyle. It was at first concerned with education and public service, and still holds monthly lectures. In 1981, the Museum of American Illustration opened in two galleries. Changing thematic exhibitions show the history of book and magazine illustration, with an annual exhibition of the year's finest American illustrations.

Mount Vernon Hotel Museum ⓭

421 E 61st St. **Map** 13 C3. *Tel (212) 838-6878.* Ⓜ *Lexington Ave, 59th St.* ◯ *11am–4pm Tue–Sun.* ⬤ *Aug, public hols.* 🖼 📷 🎫 📷
www.mvhm.org

Built in 1799, the Mount Vernon Hotel Museum and Garden was once a country day hotel for New Yorkers who needed to escape from the crowded city, then only at the south end of the island. The stone building sits on land once owned by Abigail Adams Smith, daughter of President John Adams.

It was acquired by the Colonial Dames of America in 1924 and turned into a charming re-creation of a Federal home. Costumed guides show visitors through the rooms, pointing out the treasures, including Chinese porcelain, Aubusson carpets, Sheraton chests, and a Duncan Phyfe sofa. In one bedroom there is even a baby's cradle and children's toys. An 18th-century-style garden has been planted around the house.

Henderson Place ⓮

Map 18 D3. Ⓜ *86th St.* 🚌 *M31, M86.*

Queen Anne row houses at Henderson Place

Now surrounded by modern apartment blocks, this enclave of 24 red-brick Queen Anne row houses was built in 1882. The row houses were commissioned by John C. Henderson, a hat-maker, as a self-contained community. The elegant Lamb & Rich design has gray slate roof gables, pediments, parapets, chimneys and dormer windows forming patterns, and a turret marking the corner of each block.

Carl Schurz Park promenade

Carl Schurz Park ⓯

Map 18 D3. Ⓜ *86th St.* 🚌 *M31, M86.*

Laid out in 1891, this park along the East River has a wide promenade over the East River Drive. It offers fine vistas of the river and the turbulent waters of Hell Gate, where the river meets Long Island Sound. It is named after Carl Schurz, a native who became Secretary of the Interior (1869–75). The first part of the promenade is the John Finlay Walk, named for an editor of the *New York Times* known for his hiking prowess. One of the city's most pleasant green escapes, the park's grassy areas are filled with basking New Yorkers on sunny days.

Gracie Mansion ⓰

East End Ave at 88th St. **Map** 18 D3. *Tel (212) 570-4751.* Ⓜ *86th St.* 🚌 *M31, M86.* ◯ *10am, 11am, 1pm, 2pm most Weds for prebooked guided tours only.* 🖼 📷 ♿ 📷

This gracious, balconied wooden 1799 country home is the official mayor's residence. Built by wealthy merchant Archibald Gracie, it is one of the best Federal houses left in New York.

Acquired by the city in 1887, it was the first home of the Museum of the City of New York. In 1942 it became the official Mayoral Residence. When Fiorello LaGuardia

Front view of Gracie Mansion

moved in after nine years in office, preferring it to a 75-room palace on Riverside Drive, he said that even the modest Gracie Mansion was too fancy for him. "The Little Flower" (from Fiorello) had fought corruption in the city.

Church of the Holy Trinity ⑰

316 E 88th St. **Map** 17 B3. **Tel** (212) 289-4100. M 86th St. ◯ 9am–5pm Mon–Fri, 7:30am–2pm Sun. 🔔 8:45am Tue, Thu; 8am, 10:30am, 6pm Sun. 📷 **www**.holytrinity-nyc.org

Arched doorway of the Church of the Holy Trinity

Delightfully placed in a serene garden setting, this church was constructed in 1889 of glowing golden brick and terracotta in French Renaissance style. It boasts one of New York's best bell towers, which holds a handsome wrought-iron clock with brass hands. The arched doorway is richly decorated with carved images of the saints and prophets.

The complex was donated by Serena Rhinelander in memory of her father and grandfather. The land was part of the Rhinelander farm, which the family had owned for 100 years.

Farther down at 350 E. 88th Street is the Rhinelander Children's Center, also a gift, and the headquarters of the Children's Aid Society.

St. Nicholas Russian Orthodox Cathedral ⑱

15 E 97th St. **Map** 16 F1. **Tel** (212) 876-2190. M 96 St. ◯ by appt. 🔔 throughout the week, including 10am & 6pm Wed & Sun. 📷 **www**.russianchurchusa.org

Built in Muscovite Baroque style in 1902, this church has five onion domes crowned with crosses, and blue and yellow tiles on a red brick and white stone facade. Among the early worshipers were White Russians who had fled the first uprisings at home, mostly intellectuals and aristocrats who soon became a part of New York society. Later, there were more waves of refugees, dissidents, and defectors.

The cathedral now serves a scattered community, and the congregation is small. Mass is celebrated in Russian with great pomp and dignity.

The cathedral is filled with the scent of incense. The high central sanctuary has marble columns with blue and white trim above. Ornate wooden screens trimmed with gold enclose the altar. It is unique, an unexpected find on a side street in this staid part of Manhattan.

Facade and domes of St. Nicholas Russian Cathedral

Facade of the Museum of the City of New York

Museum of the City of New York ⑲

1220 5th Ave at 103rd St. **Map** 21 C5. **Tel** (212) 534-1672. M 103rd St. ◯ 10am–5pm Tue–Sun. ● Jan 1, Thanksgiving, Dec 25. 🎞 📷 ♿ 🎁 📕 🎫 **www**.mcny.org

Founded in 1923 and at first housed in Gracie Mansion, this museum is dedicated to New York's development from its earliest beginnings up to the present and on to the future.

Housed in a handsome Georgian Colonial building since 1932, the museum has expanded its public space, with special exhibitions throughout the year. These cover subjects such as fashion, architecture, theater, social and political history, and photography. In addition there is a collection of toys, including the famed Stettheimer Dollhouse, with original works of art in miniature, painted by such luminaries as Marcel Duchamp and Albert Gleizes.

A core exhibition of the museum is the film *Timescapes: A Multimedia Portrait of New York* (every 30 mins, 10:15am–4:45pm). It uses images from the museum's collection and historic maps to chart the growth of New York, from its early days as a tiny settlement to its current status as one of the largest cities in the world.

Whitney Museum of American Art ❼

The Whitney Museum is the foremost showcase for American art of the 20th and 21st centuries. It was founded in 1930 by sculptor Gertrude Vanderbilt Whitney after the Metropolitan Museum of Art turned down her collection of works by living artists such as Bellows and Hopper. In 1966 the museum moved to the present inverted-pyramid building designed by Marcel Breuer. The Whitney Biennial, held in even years, is the most significant survey of new trends in American art.

The cantilevered facade of the Whitney Museum

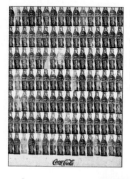

Green Coca-Cola Bottles
Andy Warhol's 1962 work is a commentary on mass production and monopoly.

Children Meeting *(1978)*
This painting by Elizabeth Murray reveals her interest in the use of color and form.

Little Big Painting
The 1965 work by Roy Lichtenstein is a comic critique of Abstract Expressionist painting.

Early Sunday Morning *(1930)*
Edward Hopper's paintings often convey the emptiness of American city life.

MUSEUM GUIDE
The Leonard and Evelyn Lauder galleries on the fifth floor have permanent collections, showing works by Calder, O'Keeffe, and Hopper. Changing exhibitions occupy the lobby and the second, third, and fourth floors.

Dempsey and Firpo
In 1924, George Bellows depicted one of the most famous prizefights of the century.

VISITORS' CHECKLIST

945 Madison Ave. **Map** 17 A5.
Tel (212) 570-3600. M 6 to
77th St. M1–4, 30, M72,
M79. ○ 11am–6pm Wed–Thu,
Sat, Sun, 1–9pm Fri. ● public
hols. **Lectures,
film/video presentations**.
www.whitney.org

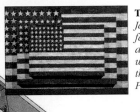

Three Flags (*1958*)
Jasper Johns's use of familiar objects in an abstract form was influential in the development of Pop Art.

Painting Number 5
The early modernist artist Marsden Hartley painted this oil on canvas between 1914 and 1915.

Circus (*1926–31*)
Alexander Calder's fanciful creation is usually on display.

Tango (*1919*)
This is considered Polish-born Elie Nadelman's greatest wood sculpture.

Gertrude Vanderbilt Whitney (*1916*)
Robert Henri's oil shows the Whitney Museum's founder.

Frick Collection ❽

The art collection of steel magnate Henry Clay Frick (1849–1919) is exhibited in a residential setting amid the furnishings of his opulent mansion, which provides a rare glimpse of how the extremely wealthy lived in New York's gilded age. Henry Frick intended the collection to be a memorial to himself, and on his death he bequeathed the entire house to the nation. The collection includes important Old Master paintings, major works of sculpture, French furniture, rare Limoges enamels, and beautiful Oriental rugs.

Fifth Avenue facade of the Frick Collection

The Harbor of Dieppe *(1826)*
J.M.W. Turner was criticized by some skeptical contemporaries for depicting this northern European port suffused with light.

Garden
Court

Library

West
Gallery

The Polish Rider
The identity of the rider in this equestrian portrait, painted by Rembrandt in 1655, is unknown. The somber, rocky landscape creates an eerie atmosphere of unknown danger.

Living
Hall

STAR PAINTINGS

★ Lady Meux by James McNeill Whistler

★ Mall in St. James's Park by Thomas Gainsborough

★ Officer and Laughing Girl by Johannes Vermeer

★ Sir Thomas More by Hans Holbein

★ **Sir Thomas More** *(1527)*
Holbein's portrait of Henry VIII's Lord Chancellor was painted eight years before More's execution for treason.

GALLERY GUIDE
Of special interest are the West Gallery, with oils by Vermeer, Hals, and Rembrandt; the East Gallery, featuring Van Dyck and Whistler; the Oval Room, featuring Gainsborough; the Library and Dining Room, with English works; and the Living Hall, with works by Titian and Holbein.

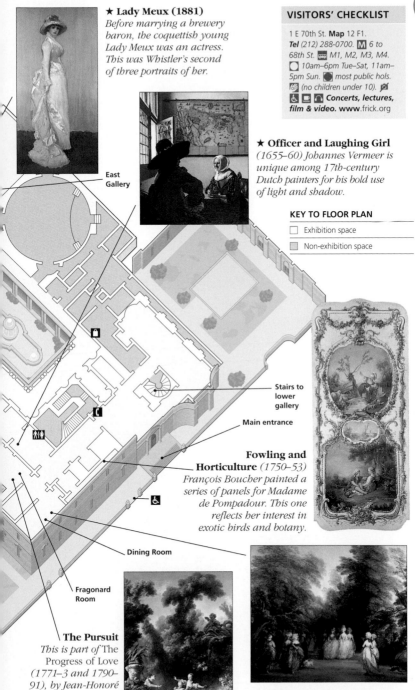

★ Lady Meux (1881)
Before marrying a brewery baron, the coquettish young Lady Meux was an actress. This was Whistler's second of three portraits of her.

East Gallery

VISITORS' CHECKLIST

1 E 70th St. **Map** 12 F1.
Tel (212) 288-0700. Ⓜ 6 to 68th St. 🚌 M1, M2, M3, M4. ◯ 10am–6pm Tue–Sat, 11am–5pm Sun. ◯ most public hols. 🏷 (no children under 10). 📷 ♿ 🔲 ⌂ **Concerts, lectures, film & video.** **www**.frick.org

★ Officer and Laughing Girl
(1655–60) Johannes Vermeer is unique among 17th-century Dutch painters for his bold use of light and shadow.

KEY TO FLOOR PLAN

☐ Exhibition space

▨ Non-exhibition space

Stairs to lower gallery

Main entrance

Fowling and Horticulture *(1750–53) François Boucher painted a series of panels for Madame de Pompadour. This one reflects her interest in exotic birds and botany.*

Dining Room

Fragonard Room

The Pursuit
This is part of The Progress of Love *(1771–3 and 1790–91), by Jean-Honoré Fragonard. The series of paintings depicts the events of an idealized courtship.*

★ Mall in St. James's Park *(1783) The three central figures in Thomas Gainsborough's London landscape may be the daughters of George III.*

CENTRAL PARK

The city's "backyard" was created in 1858 by Frederick Law Olmsted and Calvert Vaux on an unpromising site of quarries, pig farms, swampland and shacks. Ten million cartloads of stone and earth turned it into the lush 843-acre (340-ha) park of today. There are scenic hills, lakes and lush meadows, dotted throughout with out-crops

Statues, Delacorte Theater *(see p206)*

of Manhattan bedrock, and planted with more than 500,000 trees and shrubs. Over the years the park has blossomed, with playgrounds and skating rinks, plus ball fields and spaces for every activity from chess and croquet to concerts and events. Cars are banned on weekends, giving bicyclists, in-line skaters and joggers the right-of-way.

SIGHTS AT A GLANCE

Historic Buildings
Belvedere Castle ❸
The Dairy ❶

Monuments and Statues
Bethesda Fountain and
   Terrace ❺
Bow Bridge ❹
Strawberry Fields ❷

Lakes and Gardens
Central Park Wildlife
   Center ❼
Conservatory Garden ❽
Conservatory Water ❻

SEE ALSO

• **Street Finder,** maps 12, 16, 21

• **www**.centralparknyc.org

GETTING THERE

Subway lines A, B, C, and D run the length of the park on the Upper West Side, with stops at 59th, 72nd, 81st, 86th, 96th, and 103rd Sts. The 59th St/Columbus Circle stop is served by the 1; the 2 and 3 stop at 110th Street; the N, R, Q, and W stop at 57th St and 5th Ave at the southern end of the park. Bus routes M1, M2, M3, and M4 run along the eastern edge of the park; M10 to the west, and M5 to the south.

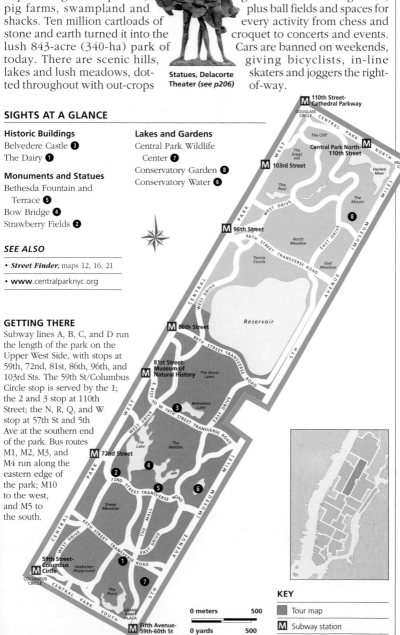

KEY

▨ Tour map

Ⓜ Subdway station

| 0 meters | 500 |
| 0 yards | 500 |

◁ **Bird's-eye view of the park**

A Tour of Central Park

On a short visit, a walking tour from
59th to 79th streets takes in some
of Central Park's loveliest features,
from the dense wooded Ramble
to the open formal spaces of
Bethesda Terrace. Along the way,
you will see artificial lakes and
some of the 30 graceful bridges and
arches that link around 58 miles (93 km)
of footpaths, bridle paths, and roads in the
park. In summer the park is often several
degrees cooler than the city streets around
it, and thus is a favorite retreat.

★ **Strawberry Fields**
*One of the park's most
visited spots, this
peaceful area was
created in memory
of John Lennon,
who lived nearby* ❷

★ **Bethesda Fountain and Terrace**
*The richly ornamented formal terrace
overlooks the Lake and the wooded shores
of the Ramble* ❺

Wollman Rink was restored
in the 1980s for future
generations of skaters by
tycoon Donald Trump.

**Central Park
Wildlife
Center**
*Three climate
zones are home
to over 100
species of
animals* ❼

**The
Pond**

Plaza Hotel
(see p181)

Frick Collection
(see pp202–3)

★ **The Dairy**
*This Victorian Gothic building
houses the Visitor Center. Make
it your first stop and pick up a
calendar of park events* ❶

Hans Christian Andersen's
statue is a favorite Central
Park landmark for children.
It is on the west side of
Conservatory Water
and is a popular
site for
storytelling
in the
summer.

Bow Bridge
This cast-iron bridge links the Ramble with Cherry Hill by a graceful arch, 60 ft (18 m) above the Lake ④

LOCATOR MAP
See Manhattan Map pp14–15

Alice in Wonderland is immortalized in bronze at the northern end of Conservatory Water, along with her friends the Cheshire Cat, the Mad Hatter and the Dormouse. Children love to slide down her toadstool seat.

STAR SIGHTS

★ The Dairy

★ Strawberry Fields

★ Belvedere Castle

★ Bethesda Fountain

★ Conservatory Water

...ota ...ing *(p218)*

San Remo Apartments *(see p214)*

American Museum of Natural History *(see pp216–17)*

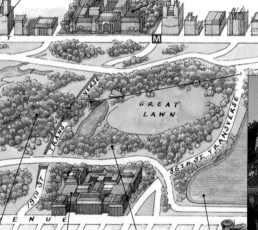

GREAT LAWN

Metropolitan Museum *(see pp190–97)*

Obelisk

The Ramble is a wooded area of 37 acres (15 ha), crisscrossed by paths and streams. It is a paradise for birdwatchers. Over 250 species of birds have been spotted in the park, which is on the Atlantic migration flyway.

Reservoir

Guggenheim Museum *(see pp188–9)*

★ Belvedere Castle
From the terraces there are unequaled views of the city and surrounding park. Within the stone walls is the Central Park Learning Center ③

★ Conservatory Water
From March to November, this is the scene of model boat races each Saturday. Many of the tiny craft are stored in the boathouse that adjoins the Lake ⑥

The Carousel, part of the park's Children's District

The Dairy ❶

Map 12 F2. *Tel* (212) 794-6564.
Ⓜ *Fifth Ave.* ◯ *10am–5pm Tue–Sun.* **Slide show.** 📷
www.centralparknyc.org

Now used as Central Park's Visitor Center, this charming building of natural stone was planned as part of the "Children's District" of the park, which included a playground, the Carousel, a Children's Cottage, and stable. In 1873, there were cows grazing on the meadows in front of the Dairy, a ewe and her lambs feeding nearby, and chickens, guinea fowl, and peacocks roaming the lawn. City children could get fresh milk and other refreshments here. Over the years, the Dairy deteriorated, being used as a shed until restoration in 1979, done according to original photographs and drawings. The Dairy is the place to begin exploring the lush and leafy park; maps and details of events can be obtained here. The less energetic can rent chess and checkers sets for use on the pretty inlaid boards of the *kinderberg*, the charming little "children's hill" nearby.

Strawberry Fields ❷

Map 12 E1. Ⓜ *72nd St.*

The restoration of this teardrop-shaped section of the park was Yoko Ono's tribute in memory of her slain husband, John Lennon. They lived in the Dakota apartments overlooking this spot *(see p218)*. Gifts for the garden came from all over the world. A mosaic set in the pathway, inscribed with the word *Imagine* (named for Lennon's famous song), was a gift from the city of Naples in Italy.

This broad expanse of the park's landscape was designed by Vaux and Olmsted. Now it is an international peace garden, with 161 species of plants (one from every country of the world), including jetbead, roses, witch hazel, birches – and strawberries.

Belvedere Castle ❸

Map 16 E4. *Tel* (212) 772-0210.
Ⓜ *81st St.* ◯ *10am–5pm Tue–Sun.*
📷 ♿ *to main floor only.*

This stone castle atop Vista Rock, complete with tower and turrets, offers one of the best views of the park and the city from its lookout on the rooftop. Inside is the Henry Luce Nature Observatory, with a delightful exhibit telling inquisitive young visitors about the surprising variety of wildlife to be found in the park.

The view to the north from the castle allows you to look down into

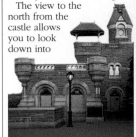

Belvedere Castle with its lookout over the park

the Delacorte Theater, home to the free productions of Shakespeare in the Park every summer, often featuring big-name stars *(see p347)*. The theater was the gift of George T. Delacorte. Publisher and founder of Dell paperbacks, Delacorte was a delightful philanthropist who was responsible for many of the park's pleasures.

Bow Bridge ❹

Map 16 E5. Ⓜ *72nd St.*

This is one of the park's seven original cast-iron bridges and is considered one of the finest. It was designed by Vaux as a bow tying together the two large sections of the Lake. In the 19th century, when the Lake was used for ice skating, a red ball was hoisted from a bell tower on Vista Rock to signal that the ice was safe. The bridge offers expansive views of the park and the buildings bordering it on both the east and west sides.

A tranquil scene in Central Park, overlooked by exclusive apartments

An 1864 print of Bethesda Fountain and Terrace

Bethesda Fountain and Terrace ❺

Map 12 E1. Ⓜ *72nd St.*

Situated between the Lake and the Mall, this is the architectural heart of the park, a formal element in the naturalistic landscape. The fountain was dedicated in 1873. The statue, *Angel of the Waters*, marked the opening of the Croton Aqueduct system in 1842, bringing the city its first supply of pure water; its name refers to a biblical account of a healing angel at the pool of Bethesda in Jerusalem. The Spanish-style detailing, such as the sculptured double staircase, tiles, and friezes, is by Jacob Wrey Mould.

The terrace is one of the best spots to relax and take in some people-watching.

Conservatory Water ❻

Map 16 F5. Ⓜ *77th St.*

Better known as the Model Boat Pond, this stretch of water is home to model yacht races every weekend.

At the north end of the lake, a sculpture of Alice in Wonderland is a delight for children. It was commissioned by George T. Delacorte in honor of his wife. He himself is immortalized in caricature as the Mad Hatter. On the west bank, free story hours are held at the Hans Christian Andersen statue. The author is portrayed reading from his own story, "The Ugly Duckling," while its hero waddles at his feet. Children like to climb on the statue and snuggle in the author's lap. Conservatory Water's literary links continue into adolescence: it is here that J. D. Salinger's Holden Caulfield comes to tell the ducks his troubles in *The Catcher in the Rye*.

Each spring, birdwatchers gather at the pond to see the city's most famous red-tailed hawk, Pale Male, nest on the roof of 927 Fifth Avenue.

Central Park Wildlife Center ❼

Map 12 F2. *Tel* (212) 439-6500. Ⓜ *Fifth Ave between 63rd and 66th sts.* ⬤ *10am–5pm Mon–Fri, 10am–5:30pm Sat–Sun & hols; Nov–Mar: 10am–4:30 daily. Last adm: 30 mins before closing.* 📷 ⬤ 📧 📱 www.centralparkzoo.com

This imaginative zoo has won plaudits for its creative and humane use of small space. More than 130 species of animals are represented in three climate zones, the Tropics, the Polar Circle, and the California coast. An equatorial rain forest is home to monkeys and free-flying birds, while penguins and polar bears populate an Arctic landscape that allows views both above and under water.

At the Tisch Children's Zoo children can get close to goats, sheep, alpacas, cows, and pot-bellied pigs. By its entrance is the much-loved Delacorte Clock, which plays nursery rhymes every half hour, as bronze musical animals (such as a goat playing pan pipes) circle around it. Toward Willowdell Arch is another favorite – the memorial to Balto, leader of a team of huskies that made a heroic journey across Alaska with serum for a diphtheria epidemic.

Statue of Balto, the heroic husky dog, Central Park Wildlife Center

Conservatory Garden ❽

Map 21 B5. Ⓜ *Central Pk N, 103rd St.* *Tel* (212) 860-1382. ⬤ *8am–dusk.* ♿

The Vanderbilt Gate on Fifth Avenue is the entry to a 6-acre (2.4-ha) park containing three formal gardens. Each one represents a different national landscape style. The Central Garden, with a large lawn, yew hedges, crabapple trees, and a wisteria pergola recreates an Italian style. The South Garden, spilling over with perennials, represents an English style, with a bronze statue in the reflecting pool of Mary and Dickon, from Frances Hodgson Burnett's *The Secret Garden*. Beyond is a slope with thousands of native wildflowers, spreading into the park beyond. The North Garden, in the French style, centers around the bronze *Fountain of the Three Dancing Maidens*. It puts on a brief but brilliant display of annuals each summer.

Polar bear in the Central Park Wildlife Center

UPPER WEST SIDE

This district of New York became residential in the 1870s, when the Ninth Avenue elevated railroad *(see pp26-7)* made commuting to midtown possible. The Dakota, the city's first luxury apartment house, was built here in 1884, and the streets were graded and leveled. Buildings sprang up on Broadway and Central Park West, and cross streets, dating from the 1890s, still retain fine brownstone row houses. The area is bustling and diverse, with many cultural institutions, including the American Museum of Natural History, Lincoln Center, and Columbus Circle complex for Time Warner and CNN.

Indian mask, Museum of Natural History

SIGHTS AT A GLANCE

Historic Streets and Buildings
Columbus Circle ❼
Pomander Walk ⓭
Riverside Drive and Park ⓮
The Dakota ❾
The Dorilton ⓱
Twin Towers of Central Park West ❶

Museums and Galleries
American Museum of Natural History pp216–17 ⓫
Children's Museum of Manhattan ⓯
Hayden Planetarium ⓬
New-York Historical Society ❿

Famous Theaters
Avery Fisher Hall ❻
Lincoln Center for the Performing Arts ❷
Lincoln Center Theater ❺
Metropolitan Opera House ❹
New York State Theater ❸

Landmark Hotels and Restaurants
Hotel des Artistes ❽
The Ansonia ⓰

GETTING THERE
By subway, take the A, B, C, D, or 1 to Columbus Circle, the 1, 2, or 3 along Broadway, or the B and C along Central Park West. Buses include the M10 (Central Park West), M7, M11, M104, and M5 or M66 or M72 crosstown buses.

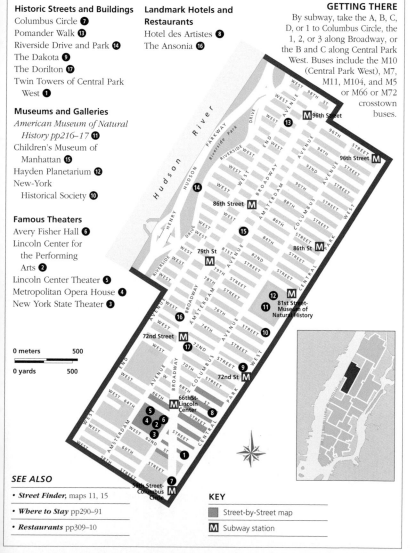

0 meters 500
0 yards 500

SEE ALSO

KEY
▢ Street-by-Street map
Ⓜ Subway station

◁ The facade of 14 Riverside Drive

Street by Street: Lincoln Center

Lincoln Center was conceived when both the Metropolitan Opera House and the New York Philharmonic required homes, and a large tract on Manhattan's west side was in dire need of revitalization. The notion of a single complex where different performing arts could exist side by side seems natural today, but in the 1950s it was considered both daring and risky. Today Lincoln Center has proved itself by drawing audiences of five million each year. Proximity to its halls prompts both performers and arts lovers to live nearby.

★ Lincoln Center for the Performing Arts
Dance, music, and theater come together in this fine contemporary complex. It is also a great place to sit around the reflecting fountain and people-watch ❷

Lincoln Center Theater
The Vivian Beaumont and the Mitzi E. Newhouse theaters are both housed in this building ❺

Composer Leonard Bernstein's famous musical *West Side Story*, which was based on the Romeo and Juliet theme, was set in the impoverished streets around what is now Lincoln Center. Bernstein was later instrumental in setting up the large music complex.

The Guggenheim Bandshell in Damrosch Park is the site of free concerts.

The New York State Theater
This is the home of the New York City Ballet, as well as an opera company ❸

The College Board Building is an Art Deco delight that now houses condominiums and the administrative offices of the College Board, developers of the college entrance exam.

Metropolitan Opera House
Lincoln Center's focus is the Opera House. The café at the top of the lobby offers wonderful plaza views ❹

American Folk Art Museum Quilting, pottery, and furniture are some of the arts displayed here.

Early American quilt

James Dean once lived in a one-room apartment on the top floor at 19 West 68th Street.

LOCATOR MAP
see Manhattan Map pp14–15

KEY

– – – Suggested route

| 0 meters | 100 |
| 0 yards | 100 |

★ **Hotel des Artistes**
Artists Isadora Duncan, Noël Coward, and Norman Rockwell once lived here ❽

To 72nd Street subway (4 blocks)

W 67TH STREET

65TH STREET

CENTRAL PARK WEST

CENTRAL PARK

An ABC-TV sound stage for soap operas is housed in this castle-like building, formerly an armory.

55 Central Park West is the Art Deco apartment building that featured in the film *Ghostbusters*.

The Society for Ethical Culture was one of the city's first Art Nouveau buildings. It also houses a school.

To 59th Street subway (2 blocks)

Central Park West is home to many celebrities, who like the privacy of its exclusive apartments.

Century Apartments
The Century's twin towers are visible from the park, making it a New York landmark ❶

STAR SIGHTS

★ Lincoln Center

★ Hotel des Artistes

The San Remo, a twin-towered apartment house designed by Emery Roth

Twin Towers of Central Park West ❶

Map 12 D1, 12 D2, 16 D3, 16 D5.
Ⓜ *59th St-Columbus Circle, 72nd St, 81St, 86th St.* ☐ *to the public.*

A familiar landmark on the New York skyline, the four twin-towered apartment houses on Central Park West were built between 1929 and 1931, before the Great Depression halted all luxury construction. They are among the most sought-after residences in New York.

Admired today for their grace and architectural detail, they were designed in response to a city planning law allowing taller apartments if setbacks and towers were used.

Emery Roth designed the San Remo (145 CPW), whose tenants have included Dustin Hoffman, Paul Simon, and Diane Keaton. Turned down by the residents' committee, Madonna went to live close by at 1 West 64th Street. The towers of the Eldorado (300 CPW), also by Roth, were home to Groucho

Marx, Marilyn Monroe, and Richard Dreyfuss. The Majestic (115 CPW) and the Century (25 CPW) are both sleek classics by Art Deco designer Irwin S. Chanin.

Lincoln Center for the Performing Arts ❷

Map 11 C2. *Tel (212) 546-2656.*
Ⓜ *66th St.* ♿ 🅿 *(212) 875-5350.*
🎫 🏛 *See Entertainment pp350–51.* **www**.lincolncenter.org

In May 1959, President Eisenhower traveled to New York to turn a shovelful of earth, Leonard Bernstein lifted his baton, the New York Philharmonic and the Juilliard

Choir broke into the Hallelujah Chorus – and the city's major cultural center was born. It soon covered 15 acres (6 ha) on the site of the slums that had been the setting for Bernstein's classic musical *West Side Story.* The plaza fountain is by Philip Johnson, and the sculpture, *Reclining Figure,* is by Henry Moore.

Jazz at the Lincoln Center has developed a state-of-the-art facility dedicated to a wide range of jazz performances. It forms part of a major complex at Columbus Circle *(see p215).*

New York State Theater ❸

Lincoln Center. **Map** 11 D2.
Tel (212) 870-5570. Ⓜ *66th St.*
♿ 🅿 🎫 🏛 *See Entertainment pp346–7.* **www**.nycballet.com

The home base for the highly acclaimed New York City Ballet and the New York City Opera, a troupe devoted to presenting opera at popular prices, is a Philip Johnson design. It was inaugurated in 1964.

Gargantuan white marble sculptures by Elie Nadelman dominate the vast four-story foyer. The theater seats 2,800 people. Because of its rhinestone lights and chandeliers both inside and out, some have described the theater as "a little jewel box."

Metropolitan Opera House ❹

Lincoln Center. **Map** 11 D2. *Tel (212) 362-6000.* Ⓜ *66th St.* ♿ 🅿 🎫 🏛 *See Entertainment pp350–51.* **www**.metopera.org; **www**.abt.org

Home to the Metropolitan Opera Company and the American Ballet Theater, "the Met" is the most spectacular of Lincoln Center's buildings. Five great arched windows offer views of the opulent foyer and two murals by Marc Chagall. (You can't see them in the mornings when they are protected from the sun.) Inside there are

Central plaza at Lincoln Center

curved white marble stairs, red carpeting, and exquisite starburst crystal chandeliers that are raised to the ceiling

Concert at Guggenheim Bandshell, Damrosh Park, near the Met

just before each performance. All the greats have sung here, including Maria Callas, Jessye Norman, and Luciano Pavarotti. First nights are glittering, star-studded occasions.

The Guggenheim Bandshell, in Damrosch Park next to the Met, is a popular concert site. The high point of the season is the Lincoln Center Out-of-Doors Festival, which takes place in August and features global music, dance, and spoken-word performances.

Lincoln Center Theater ➎

Lincoln Center. **Map** 11 C2. **Tel** *(212) 362-7600 (Beaumont and Newhouse), (212) 870-1630 (Library).* *800-432 7250 (tickets).* M *66th St.* ⏶ ⏷ ⏸ *See* ***Entertainment*** *pp350–51.* **www**.lct.org

Two theaters make up this innovative complex, where eclectic and often experimental drama is presented.

The theaters are the 1,000-seat Vivian Beaumont and the more intimate 280-seat Mitzi E. Newhouse. Works by some of New York's best modern playwrights have featured at the Beaumont. Among these was Arthur Miller's *After the Fall,* the theater's inaugural performance in 1962.

The size of the Newhouse suits workshop-style plays, but it can still make the news with theatrical gems such as Robin Williams and Steve Martin in a production

of Samuel Beckett's *Waiting for Godot.* The complex also houses the New York Public Library for the Performing Arts, which has exhibits including audio cylinders of early Met performances and original scores and playbills.

Avery Fisher Hall ➏

Lincoln Center. **Map** 11 C2. **Tel** *(212) 875-5030.* M *66th St.* ⏶ ⏷ ⏸
⏹ *See* ***Entertainment*** *pp350–51.* **www**.newyorkphilharmonic.org

Located at the northern end of the Lincoln Center Plaza, Avery Fisher Hall is home to America's oldest orchestra, the New York Philharmonic. It also provides a stage for some of the Lincoln Center's own performers, and the Mostly Mozart Festival.

When the venue opened in 1962 as the Philharmonic Hall, critics initially complained about the acoustics. Several structural modifications, however, have rendered the hall an acoustic gem, comparing favorably with other great classical concert halls around the world. For a small fee, the public can attend rehearsals on Thursday mornings in the 2,738-seat auditorium.

Columbus Circle ➐

Columbus Circle, New York. **Map** 12 D3. M *59th St.* **Concerts** *(212) 258 9800.* **www**.jazzatlincolncenter.org

Presiding over this urban plaza at the corner of Central Park is a marble statue of explorer Christopher Columbus, perched on top of a tall granite column. The statue is one of the few remaining original features in this circle – which has become one of the largest building projects in New York's history.

Multi-use skyscrapers have been erected, attracting national and international businesses. Global

media company Time Warner has its headquarters in an 80-story skyscraper. The 2.8 million sq ft (260,000 sq m) building provides a retail, entertainment, and restaurant facility. Facilities include shops such as Hugo Boss, Williams-Sonoma, Borders Books, and Whole Foods Market; dining at Per Se and Masa; and a Mandarin Oriental hotel.

The Time Warner Center is also home to Jazz at the Lincoln Center. The two venues here – The Frederic P. Rose Concert Hall and The Allen Room – together with a jazz club and education center, comprise the world's first performing arts facility dedicated to jazz.

Other notable buildings in Columbus Circle include Hearst House, designed by British architect Norman Foster, Trump International Hotel, the Maine Monument, and the eye-catching Museum of Arts and Design, formerly the American Craft Museum.

Hotel des Artistes ➑

1 W 67th St. **Map** 12 D2. **Tel** *(212) 877-3500 (café).* M *72nd St.*

Built in 1918 by George Mort Pollard, these two-story apartments were intended to be working artists' studios but they have attracted a variety of interesting tenants, including Alexander Woollcott, Norman Rockwell, Isadora Duncan, Rudolph Valentino, and Noël Coward. The Café des Artistes is well known for its misty, romantic Howard Chandler Christy murals and its fine cuisine.

Decorative figure on the Hotel des Artistes

American Museum of Natural History ⑪

This is one of the world's largest natural history museums. Since the original building opened in 1877, the complex has grown to cover four city blocks, and today holds more than 30 million specimens and artifacts. The most popular areas are the dinosaurs and the Milstein Hall of Ocean Life. The Rose Center for Earth and Space includes the Hayden Planetarium *(see p218)*.

The facade
on 77th Street

STAR EXHIBITS

★ Barosaurus

★ Blue Whale

★ Great Canoe

★ Star of India

★ Star of India

This 563-carat gem is the world's largest blue star sapphire. Found in Sri Lanka, it was given to the museum by J. P. Morgan in 1900.

GALLERY GUIDE

Enter at Central Park West onto the second floor to view the Barosaurus exhibit, African, Asian, Central and South American peoples and animals. First floor exhibits include ocean life, meteors, minerals and gems, and the Hall of Biodiversity. North American Indians, birds, and reptiles occupy the third floor. Dinosaurs, fossil fishes, and early mammals are on the fourth floor.

★ Blue Whale

The blue whale is the largest animal, living or extinct. Its weight can exceed 100 tons. This replica is based on a female captured off South America in 1925.

★ Great Canoe

This 63-ft (19.2-m) seafaring war canoe from the Pacific Northwest was carved from the trunk of a single cedar. It stands in the Grand Gallery.

Entrance on
W. 77th St

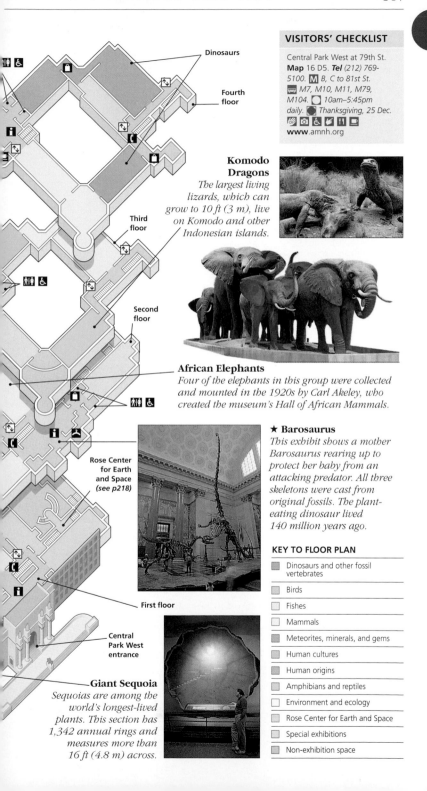

Dinosaurs

Fourth floor

Third floor

Second floor

Rose Center for Earth and Space
(see p218)

First floor

Central Park West entrance

VISITORS' CHECKLIST

Central Park West at 79th St.
Map 16 D5. *Tel* (212) 769-
5100. Ⓜ B, C to 81st St.
🚌 M7, M10, M11, M79,
M104. ☐ 10am–5:45pm
daily. ● Thanksgiving, 25 Dec.
www.amnh.org

Komodo Dragons
The largest living lizards, which can grow to 10 ft (3 m), live on Komodo and other Indonesian islands.

African Elephants
Four of the elephants in this group were collected and mounted in the 1920s by Carl Akeley, who created the museum's Hall of African Mammals.

★ Barosaurus
This exhibit shows a mother Barosaurus rearing up to protect her baby from an attacking predator. All three skeletons were cast from original fossils. The plant-eating dinosaur lived 140 million years ago.

KEY TO FLOOR PLAN

▢	Dinosaurs and other fossil vertebrates
▢	Birds
▢	Fishes
▢	Mammals
▢	Meteorites, minerals, and gems
▢	Human cultures
▢	Human origins
▢	Amphibians and reptiles
▢	Environment and ecology
▢	Rose Center for Earth and Space
▢	Special exhibitions
▢	Non-exhibition space

Giant Sequoia
Sequoias are among the world's longest-lived plants. This section has 1,342 annual rings and measures more than 16 ft (4.8 m) across.

The Dakota ➒

1 W 72nd St. **Map** 12 D1.
Ⓜ *72nd St.* ◒ *to the public.*

The name and style reflect
the fact that this apartment
building was truly "way out
West" when Henry J. Hardenbergh, the architect responsible
for the Plaza Hotel, designed
it in 1880–84. It was New
York's first luxury apartment
house and was originally
surrounded by squatters'
shacks and wandering farm
animals. Commissioned by
Edward S. Clark, heir to the
Singer sewing machine
fortune, it is one of the city's
most prestigious addresses.

The Dakota's 65 luxurious
apartments have had many
famous owners, including
Judy Garland, Lauren Bacall,
Leonard Bernstein, and Boris
Karloff, whose ghost is said
to haunt the place. It was the
setting for the film *Rosemary's
Baby,* and the site of the
tragic murder of former Beatle
John Lennon. His widow,
Yoko Ono, still lives here.

**Carved Indian head over the
entrance to the Dakota**

New-York
Historical Society ➓

170 Central Park West. **Map** 16 D5.
Tel (212) 873-3400. Ⓜ *81st St.*
Galleries ◒ *10am–6pm Tue–Sat
(to 8pm Fri), 11am–5:45pm Sun.* 🖼
Library ◒ *10am–5pm Tue–Sat (Tue–
Fri in summer).* ◒ *public hols.* ∅
♿ 🖼 🎁 🏛 www.nyhistory.org

Founded in 1804, this society
houses a distinguished research
library and the city's oldest

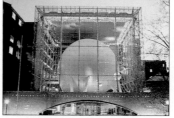

The Rose Center for Earth and Space

museum. Its collections include
historical material relating to
slavery and the Civil War, an
outstanding collection of
18th-century newspapers, all
435 watercolors of Audubon's
Birds of America, and the
world's largest collection of
Tiffany lamps and glasswork.
There are also fine displays of
American furniture and silver.

American Museum
of Natural History ⓫

See pp216–17.

Hayden
Planetarium ⓬

Central Park West at 81st St. **Map**
16 D4. **Tel** *(212) 769-5100.* Ⓜ *81st
St.* ◒ *10am–5:45pm daily. IMAX
show: every hour on the half-hour
10:30am–4:30pm; Space show:
every half-hour 10:30am–4:30pm
(from 11am Wed, to 5pm Sat & Sun).*
www.amnh.org/rose

On the northern side of the
American Museum of Natural
History *(see pp216–17)* is the
Hayden Planetarium, centerpiece of the spectacular Rose
Center for Earth and Space.
Housed within an 87-ft (26-m)
sphere, the Planetarium
contains a technologically
advanced Space Theater, the
Cosmic Pathway, a 350-ft (107-
m) spiral ramp with a timeline
chronicling 13 billion years
of evolution, and a Big Bang
Theater, where the origins of
the universe are explained.

The Hall of Planet Earth,
centered around rock samples
and using state-of-the-art
computer and video displays
explaining how the Earth
works, explores our geologic
history. Exhibits in the Hall of

the Universe present
the discoveries of
modern astrophysics.
Four zones have
hands-on interactive
exhibits. Seen from
the street at night, the
Rose Center is breath-
taking; the exhibits
inside prove that,
as Carl Sagan said,
"We are starstuff."

Pomander Walk ⓭

261–7 W 94th St. **Map** 15 C2.
Ⓜ *96th St.*

Look through the gate for a
delightful surprise – a double
row of tiny town houses built
in 1921 to look like the London
mews setting of a popular play
of the same name. It was much
favored as a home by movie
actors, including Rosalind
Russell, Humphrey Bogart,
and the Gish sisters.

Facade of a house on Pomander Walk

Riverside Drive
and Park ⓮

Map 15 B1–B5, 20 D1–D5.
Ⓜ *79th St, 86th St, 96th St.*

Riverside Drive is one of the
city's most attractive streets –
broad, with shaded and
lovely views of the Hudson
River. It is lined with the
opulent original town houses
as well as newer apartment
buildings. At 40–46, 74–77,
81–89, and 105–107 Riverside
Drive are houses designed in
the late 19th century by local
architect Clarence F. True.
The curved gables, bays and

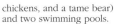

arched windows seem to suit the curves of the road and the flow of the river.

The bizarrely named Cliff Dwellers' Apartments at 243 (between 96th and 97th streets) is a 1914 building with a frieze showing early Arizona cliff dwellers, complete with masks, buffalo skulls, mountain lions, and rattlesnakes.

Riverside Park was designed by Frederick Law Olmsted in 1880. He also laid out Central Park (see pp204–7).

Children's Museum entrance

Soldiers' and Sailors' monument in Riverside Park

Children's Museum of Manhattan ⓯

212 W 83rd St. **Map** 15 C4.
Tel (212) 721-1234. Ⓜ 79th St, 81st St, 86th St. ⬤ 10am–5pm Tue–Sun. ⬤ Jan 1, Thanksgiving, Dec 25. 🏛 📷 ♿ 🛈
www.cmom.org

This particularly imaginative participatory museum was founded in 1973 and is based on the premise that children learn best through play. The exhibit called "Gods, Myths & Mortals" allows children to learn about Ancient Greece, its gods, and its impact on the modern world, while in "Block Party" they can build castles, towns, and bridges out of wooden blocks. Children also delight in the exhibit on Dora the Explorer and her adventurous cousin Diego, where they learn about

travel and cultures around the world.

On weekends and holidays there are guest performers, from puppeteers to storytellers, in the 150-seat theater. There is also a gallery for free play fun events, like "Pajama Day," as well as lively, theme-based tours of the museum.

The Ansonia ⓰

2109 Broadway. **Map** 15 C5.
Ⓜ 72nd St. ⬤ to the public.

This Beaux Arts gem was built in 1899 by William Earl Dodge Stokes, heir to the Phelps Dodge Company fortune, who brought French architect Paul E.M. Duboy to design a building to rival the Dakota. The hotel was converted to a condominium in 1992. The most prominent features are the round corner tower and the two-story mansard roof adorned with single and double dormers. The building had a roof garden (complete with Dodge's menagerie: ducks,

chickens, and a tame bear) and two swimming pools.

The hotel's thick, sound-muffling walls soon made it a favorite with the musical stars of yesteryear. Florenz Ziegfeld, Arturo Toscanini, Enrico Caruso, Igor Stravinsky, and Lily Pons were once regular guests there.

The Dorilton ⓱

171 W 71st St. **Map** 11 C1.
Ⓜ 72nd St. ⬤ to the public.

Opulent detail and an impressive high mansard roof adorn this apartment house. On the West 71st Street side of the building is a nine-story-high gateway. To the modern eye, the Dorilton is gloriously elaborate, but when it was first built in 1902 it provoked this reaction, reported by the *Architectural Record*: "The sight of it makes strong men

Balcony on the Dorilton, supported by groaning figures

swear and weak women shrink affrighted."

What would the critics have made of the Alexandria Condominium, at 135 West 70th Street, just a block away? Built in 1927 as the Pythian Temple, its current name stems from the lavish Egyptian-style motifs that adorned this former Masonic lodge. Many were stripped away when the building was converted to a condominium, but you can still see what the polychrome designs were like. There are lotus leaves, hieroglyphics, ornately carved columns, mythical beasts, and, in majestic splendor on the roof, two seated pharaohs.

Distinctive rounded turret of the Ansonia Hotel

MORNINGSIDE HEIGHTS AND HARLEM

Morningside Heights, near the Hudson River, is home to Columbia University and two of the city's finest churches. Farther east is Hamilton Heights, situated on the border of Harlem, America's most famous black community. One way to see the district's highlights, which are spread over a large

St. Francis of Assisi, Museo del Barrio

area, is by taking one of the tours offered, including a Sunday morning tour *(see p387)*. Many tours start in Hamilton Heights, move east to the St. Nicholas Historic District, stop to enjoy the gospel choir at the Abyssinian Baptist Church, and end with a southern-style brunch at Sylvia's, Harlem's best-known restaurant.

Louis Armstrong in a stained-glass window at the Cotton Club

SIGHTS AT A GLANCE

Historic Streets and Buildings
City College of the City University of New York **7**
Columbia University **1**
Grant's Tomb **6**
Hamilton Grange National Memorial **8**
Hamilton Heights Historic District **9**
Low Library **3**
Mount Morris Historic District **17**
St. Paul's Chapel **2**
St. Nicholas Historic District **10**

Museums and Galleries
Museo del Barrio **19**
Schomburg Center for Research into Black Culture **12**
Studio Museum in Harlem **16**

Famous Theaters
Apollo Theater **15**
Harlem YMCA **13**

Churches
Abyssinian Baptist Church **11**
Cathedral of St. John the Divine pp226–7 **4**
Riverside Church **5**

Parks and Squares
Marcus Garvey Park **18**

Landmark Restaurants
Sylvia's **14**

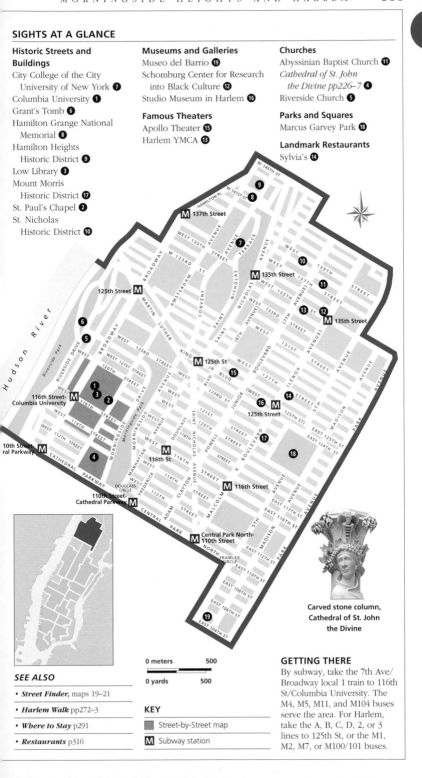

Carved stone column,
Cathedral of St. John
the Divine

SEE ALSO

• *Street Finder,* maps 19–21

• *Harlem Walk* pp272–3

• *Where to Stay* p291

• *Restaurants* p310

0 meters   500
0 yards   500

KEY

Street-by-Street map

M Subway station

GETTING THERE
By subway, take the 7th Ave/ Broadway local 1 train to 116th St/Columbia University. The M4, M5, M11, and M104 buses serve the area. For Harlem, take the A, B, C, D, 2, or 3 lines to 125th St, or the M1, M2, M7, or M100/101 buses.

Street by Street: Columbia University

A great university is as much spirit as buildings. After admiring the architecture, linger awhile on Columbia's central quadrangle in front of the Low Library, where you will see the jeans-clad future leaders of America meeting and mingling between classes. Across from the campus on both Broadway and Amsterdam Avenue are the coffee-houses and cafés where students engage in lengthy philosophical arguments, debate the topics of the day or simply unwind.

Alma Mater was sculpted by Daniel Chester French in 1903 and survived a bomb blast in the 1968 student demonstrations.

116th St/Columbia University subway (line 1) ── Ⓜ

The School of Journalism is one of Columbia's many McKim, Mead & White buildings. Founded in 1912 by publisher Joseph Pulitzer, it is the home of the Pulitzer Prize awarded for the best in letters and music.

Butler Library is Columbia's main library.

Low Library
With its imposing facade and high dome, the library dominates the main quadrangle. McKim, Mead & White designed it in 1895–97 ❸

★ **Central Quadrangle**
Columbia's first buildings were designed by McKim, Mead & White and built around a central quadrangle. This view looks across the quad toward Butler Library ❶

St. Paul's Chapel

*designed by the architects Howells &
Stokes in 1907, this church is known
for its fine woodwork and magnificent vaulted interior. It is full of
light and has fine acoustics* ❷

**The Sherman
Fairchild
Center** was
built in 1977
to house the
university's
life sciences
departments.

LOCATOR MAP
See Manhattan Map pp14–15

KEY

– – – Suggested route

| 0 meters | 100 |
| 0 yards | 100 |

Student demonstrations put Columbia
University in the news in 1968.
The demonstrations were sparked
by the university's plan to build a
gymnasium in nearby Morningside
Park. The protests forced the
university to build elsewhere.

The Église de Notre Dame was built for a
French-speaking congregation. Behind
the altar is a replica of the grotto at
Lourdes, France, the gift of a woman
who believed her son was healed there.

MORNINGSIDE DRIVE

116TH ST

★ Cathedral of St. John the Divine

*If this Neo-Gothic
cathedral is ever
finished, it will be
the largest in the
world. Although one third of the
structure has not yet been built, it
can hold 10,000 parishioners* ❹

**Carved
stonework**
decorates the
facade of the
Cathedral.

STAR SIGHTS

★ Cathedral of
St. John the Divine

★ Central
Quadrangle

Alma Mater statue at the Low Library, Columbia University

Columbia University ❶

Main entrance at W 116th St and Broadway. **Map** 20 E3. **Tel** (212) 854-1754. Ⓜ 116th St-Columbia University. **Visitors' Center** ◯ 9am–5pm Mon–Fri. 🎞 1pm Mon–Fri. **www**.columbia.edu

This is the third location of one of America's oldest universities. Founded in 1754 as King's College, it was first situated close to where the World Trade Center stood.

In 1814, when a move uptown was proposed, the university approached the authorities for funding but was instead given a plot of land valued at $75,000, on which to build a new home. The university never built on the land itself, but leased it out and spent the years from 1857 to 1897 in buildings nearby. It finally sold the plot in 1985 to the leaseholders, Rockefeller Center Inc., for $400 million.

The present campus was begun in 1897 on the site of the Bloomingdale Insane Asylum. Charles McKim, the architect, placed the university on a terrace, serenely above street level. Its spacious lawns and plazas still create a sense of contrast in the busy city.

Columbia is noted for its law, medicine, and journalism schools. Its distinguished faculty and alumni, past and present, include over 50 Nobel laureates. Famous alumni include Isaac Asimov, J.D. Salinger, James Cagney, and Joan Rivers. Across the street is the affiliated Barnard College, a highly selective liberal arts college for women.

St. Paul's Chapel ❷

Columbia University. **Map** 20 E3. **Tel** (212) 854-1487, for concert info. Ⓜ 116th St-Columbia Univ. ◯ 10am–11pm Mon–Sat (term time), 10am–4pm (breaks). 🕇 Sun. 📷 ♿

Interior brick vaulting of St. Paul's Chapel dome

Columbia's most outstanding building, built in 1904, is a mix of Italian Renaissance, Byzantine, and Gothic. The interior Guastavino vaulting is of intricate patterns of aged red brick; the whole chapel is bathed in light from above.

The free organ concerts are an exceptionally fine way to appreciate the beauty and acoustics of this church. The Aeolian-Skinner pipe organ is renowned for its fine tone.

Facade of St. Paul's Chapel

Low Library ❸

Columbia University. **Map** 20 E3. Ⓜ 116th St-Columbia University.

A Classical, columned building atop three flights of stone stairs, the library was donated by Seth Low, a former mayor and college president. The statue in front of it, *Alma Mater* by Daniel Chester French, became familiar as the backdrop to the many 1968 anti-Vietnam War student demonstrations. The building is now used as offices, and its rotunda for a variety of academic and ceremonial purposes. The books were moved in 1932 to the Butler Library, across the quadrangle. The university's library collections total more than six million volumes.

Cathedral of St. John the Divine ❹

See pp226–7.

Riverside Church ❺

490 Riverside Dr at 122nd St. **Map** 20 D2. **Tel** (212) 870-6700. Ⓜ 116th St-Columbia Univ. ◯ 10:30am–5pm Tue–Sun. 🕇 10:45am Sun. 📷 with prior permission. ♿ 🎞 **Carillon bell concerts**; (212) 870-6784; noon, 3pm Sun. **Theater**; (212) 864-2929. ⬜ **www**.theriversidechurchny.org

A 21-story steel frame with a Gothic exterior, the church design was inspired by the cathedral at Chartres. It was lavishly funded by John D. Rockefeller, Jr., in 1930. The Laura Spelman Rockefeller Memorial Carillon (in honor

Columbia University's main courtyard and the Low Library

of Rockefeller's mother) is the largest in the world, with 74 bells. The 20-ton Bourdon, or hour bell, is the largest and heaviest tuned carillon bell ever cast. The organ, with its 22,000 pipes, is among the largest in the world.

At the rear of the second gallery is a figure by Jacob Epstein, *Christ in Majesty*, cast in plaster and covered in gold leaf. Another Epstein statue, *Madonna and Child*, stands in the court next to the cloister. The panels of the chancel screen honor eight men and women whose lives have exemplified the teachings of Christ. They range from Socrates and Michelangelo to Florence Nightingale and Booker T. Washington.

For quiet reflection, enter the small, secluded Christ Chapel, patterned after an 11th-century Romanesque church in France. For views, take the elevator to the 20th floor and then walk the 140 steps to the top of the 392-ft (120-m) bell tower for a fine panorama of Upper Manhattan from the observation deck.

Mosaic mural in Grant's Tomb showing Grant (right) and Robert E. Lee

Grant's Tomb ⑥

W 122nd St and Riverside Dr. **Map** 20 D2. *Tel (212) 666-1640.* 116th St-Columbia Univ. M5. 9am–5pm daily. in bad weather (call ahead), Jan 1, Thanksgiving, Dec 25. www.nps.gov/gegr

This grandiose monument honors America's 18th president, Ulysses S. Grant, the commanding general of the Union forces in the Civil War.

The mausoleum contains the coffins of General Grant and his wife, in accordance with the president's last wish that they be buried together. After Grant's death in 1885, more than 90,000 Americans contributed $600,000 to build the sepulcher, which was inspired by Mausoleus's tomb at Halicarnassus, one of the Seven Wonders of the Ancient World.

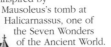

General Grant on a Civil War campaign

The tomb was dedicated on what would have been Grant's 75th birthday, April 27, 1897. The parade of 50,000 people, along with a flotilla of 10 American and 5 European warships, took more than seven hours to pass in review.

The interior was inspired by Napoleon's tomb at Les Invalides in Paris. Each sarcophagus weighs 8.5 tons. Two exhibit rooms feature displays on Grant's personal life and his presidential and military career.

Surrounding the north and east sides of the building are 17 sinuously curved mosaic benches that seem totally out of keeping with the formal architecture of the tomb. They were designed in the early 1970s by the Chilean-born Brooklyn artist Pedro Silva and were built by 1,200 local volunteers, who worked under his supervision. The benches were inspired by the work of Spanish architect Antonio Gaudi in Barcelona. The mosaics depict subjects ranging from the Inuit to New York taxis to Donald Duck.

A short walk north of Grant's Tomb is another monument. An unadorned urn on a pedestal marks the resting place of a young child who fell from the riverbank and drowned. His grieving father placed a marker that simply reads: "Erected to the memory of an amiable child, St. Clair Pollock, died 15 July 1797 in his fifth year of his age."

The 21-story Riverside Church, from the north

Cathedral of St. John the Divine ❹

Cram's Gothic West Front

Started in 1892 and still only two-thirds finished, this will be the largest cathedral in the world. The interior is over 600 ft (180 m) long and 146 ft (45 m) wide. It was originally designed in Romanesque style by Heins and LaFarge; Ralph Adams Cram took over the project in 1911, devising a Gothic nave and west front. Medieval construction methods, such as stone on stone supporting buttresses, continue to be used to complete the cathedral, which is also a venue for theater, music, and avant-garde art.

Choir
Each of the choir's columns is 55 ft (17 m) tall and made of polished gray granite.

Nave
Rising to a height of over 100 ft (30 m), the piers of the nave are topped by graceful stone arches.

Rose Window ★
Completed in 1933, the stylized motif of the Great Rose is symbolic of the many facets of the Christian Church.

★ West Front Entrance
The portals of the cathedral's west front are adorned with many fine stone carvings. Some are recreations of medieval religious sculpture, but others have modern themes. This apocalyptic vision of New York's skyline, by local stonemason Joe Kincannon, seems almost to predict the events of September 11, 2001 (see p54).

STAR FEATURES

- ★ Bay Altars
- ★ Peace Fountain
- ★ Rose Window
- ★ West Front Entrance

★ Peace Fountain
*The sculpture is the
creation of Greg
Wyatt and represents
nature in its many
forms. It stands
within a granite basin
on the Great Lawn,
south of the cathedral.*

VISITORS' CHECKLIST

1047 Amsterdam Ave at W 112th
St. **Map** 20 E4. **Tel** *(212) 316-7590.*
M 1 to Cathedral Pkwy (110th St).
M4, M11, M60, M104. ☐
7am–6pm Mon–Sat, 7am–7pm
Sun (6pm Jul, Aug). ✝ *Vespers*
6pm Sun. **Donations** ⚲ ♿ ☐
(212) 932-7347. ☐ **Concerts,
plays, exhibitions, gardens.**

Baptistry
*The Gothic Baptistry
has Italian, French and
Spanish influences.*

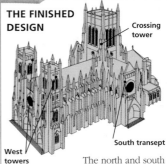

**THE FINISHED
DESIGN**

Crossing
tower

West
towers

South transept

The north and south
transepts, the crossing tower,
and the west towers have yet to be
finished. When the money to fund
their construction is raised, the
proposed design will still take at least
another 50 years to complete.

Pulpit

★ Bay Altars
*The bay altar windows
are devoted to human
endeavor. The sports
window shows feats
of skill and strength.*

Bishop's Chair
*This is a copy from the Henry VII
chapel in Westminster Abbey.*

St. Ambrose Chapel
*Named after a 4th-century
Italian bishop, the
chapel is decorated
with Renaissance-
style ironwork.*

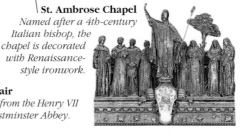

TIMELINE					
1823 Cathedral planned for Washington Square	**1891** Site chosen and designated Cathedral Parkway	**1909** Pulpit designed by Henry Vaughan **1911** Cram design replaces earlier ones		**2001** Major fire destroys interior and roof of north transept	
1800	**1850**	**1900**	**1950**	**2000**	**2010**
1873 Charter granted **1888** Competition to design cathedral won by Heins & LaFarge **1892** December 27 (St. John's Day), cornerstone laid		**1916** Ground broken for nave **1941** Work halted by World War II and does not resume until 1978		**1978–89** Third phase of building. Stonemasons' Yard opened and south tower heightened	

City College of the City University of New York ❼

Main entrance at W 138th St and Convent Ave. **Map** 19 A2. **Tel** *(212) 650-7000.* Ⓜ *137th St-City College.* **www**.ccny.cuny.edu

Set high on a hill adjoining Hamilton Heights, the original Gothic quadrangle of this college, built between 1903 and 1907, is very impressive. The material used for the buildings is Manhattan schist, a stone that had been excavated in building the IRT subway. Later, contemporary buildings were added to the school, which enrolls nearly 15,000 students.

Once free to all residents of New York, City College still offers an education at low tuition rates. Three-quarters of the students are from minority groups, and a large number of them are the first in their families to attend college.

Shepard Archway at City College of the City University of New York

Hamilton Grange National Memorial ❽

Saint Nicholas Park, 414 141st St. **Map** 19 A1. **Tel** *(212) 283-5154.* Ⓜ *137th St-City College.* ⏰ *9am–5pm Fri–Sun.* ⚫ *public hols.* 📷 🎥 *hourly.* **www**.nps.gov/hagr

Squeezed between a church and apartments is the 1802 country home of Alexander Hamilton. He was one of the architects of the federal government system, First Secretary of the treasury and founder of the National Bank. His face is on the $10 bill.

Statue of Alexander Hamilton at Hamilton Grange

Hamilton lived in The Grange for the last two years of his life. He was killed in a duel with political rival Aaron Burr in 1804.

The house was acquired by St. Luke's Episcopal Church in 1889 and moved two blocks to this "temporary" site. After extensive restoration work to the house and gardens, the site reopened in 2010.

Hamilton Heights Historic District ❾

W 141st–W 145th St and Convent Ave. **Map** 19 A1. Ⓜ *137th St-City College.*

Originally this was a setting for the impressive country estates of the wealthy. Also known as Harlem Heights, it was developed during the 1880s following the extension of the El line *(see p26)* into the neighborhood. The privacy of the enclave, on a high hill above Harlem, made it a very desirable location.

The section of Hamilton Heights known as Sugar Hill was highly favored by Harlem's elite – US Supreme Court Justice Thurgood Marshall, notable jazz musicians Count Basie, Duke

Ellington, and Cab Calloway, and world champion boxer Sugar Ray Robinson have all lived there.

The handsome three- and four-story stone row houses were built between 1886 and 1906 mixing Flemish, Romanesque and Tudor influences. In fine condition, many are used as residences by the faculty of City College.

Row houses in Hamilton Heights

St. Nicholas Historic District ❿

202–250 W 138th & W 139th St. **Map** 19 B2. Ⓜ *135th St (B, C).*

A startling contrast to the rundown surroundings, the two blocks here, known as the King Model Houses, were built in 1891 when Harlem was considered a neighborhood for New York's gentry. They still comprise one of the city's most distinctive examples of row townhouses.

The developer, David King, chose three leading architects, who succeeded in blending their different styles to create a harmonious whole. The most famous of these was the firm of McKim, Mead & White,

Houses in St. Nicholas district

Adam Clayton Powell, Jr. addressing a civil rights campaign

designers of the Pierpont Morgan Library *(see pp164–5)* and Villard Houses *(see p176)*, who were responsible for the northernmost row of solid brick Renaissance palaces. Their homes featured ground floor entrances rather than the typical New York brownstone stoops. Also, the elaborate parlor floors have ornate wrought-iron balconies below, as well as carved decorative medallions above their windows.

The Georgian buildings designed by Price and Luce are built of buff brick with white stone trim. James Brown Lord's section of buildings, also Georgian in architectural style, feels much closer to Victorian, with outstanding red-brick facades and bases constructed of brownstone.

Successful blacks were attracted here in the 1920s and 1930s, giving it the nickname Strivers' Row. Among them were celebrated musicians W. C. Handy and Eubie Blake.

Abyssinian Baptist Church ⓫

132 W 138th St. **Map** 19 C2. **Tel** *(212) 862-7474.* Ⓜ *135th St (B, C, 2, 3).* 🚹 *9am, 11am Sun. Groups of 10 or more need reservations.* **www**.abyssinian.org

Founded in 1808, New York's oldest black church became famous through its charismatic pastor Adam Clayton Powell, Jr. (1908–72), a congressman and civil rights leader. Under his leadership it became the most powerful black church in America. A room in the church houses memorabilia from his life.

The church, a fine 1923 Gothic building, welcomes properly dressed visitors to Sunday services and to hear its superb gospel choir.

Schomburg Center for Research into Black Culture ⓬

515 Malcolm X Blvd. **Map** 19 C2. Ⓜ *135th St (2, 3).* **Tel** *(212) 491-2200.* 🕐 *hours vary.* ⬤ *Mon, Sun, public hols.* 📷 *(212) 491-2207.* ♿ 📷 **www**.schomburgcenter.org

Housed in a sleek contemporary complex opened in 1991, this is the largest research center of black and African culture in the United States. The immense collection was assembled by the late Arthur Schomburg, a black man of Puerto Rican descent, who was told by a teacher that there was no such thing as "black history." The Carnegie

Kurt Weill, Elmer Rice, and Langston Hughes at the Schomburg Center

Corporation bought the collection in 1926 and gave it to the New York Public Library; Schomburg was made curator in 1932.

The library was the unofficial meeting place for writers involved in what later became known as the black literary renaissance of the 1920s, including Langston Hughes, W.E.B. Du Bois, Zora Neale Hurston, and many other great writers of the day. It also hosted many literary gatherings and poetry readings.

The Schomburg Library has excellent facilities for conserving and making available the archive's treasures, which include rare books, photos, movies, art, and recordings. The library was planned and designed to double as a cultural center and includes a theater and two art galleries, which feature changing shows of art and photography.

Harlem YMCA ⓭

180 W 135th St. **Map** 19 C3. **Tel** *(212) 281-4100.* Ⓜ *135th St (2, 3).*

Sociologist W. E. B. Du Bois

Paul Robeson and many others made their first stage appearances here in the early 1920s. The Krigwa Players, organized by W.E.B. Du Bois in the basement in 1928, was founded to counter the derogatory images of blacks often presented in Broadway reviews of the time. The "Y" also provided temporary lodgings for some notable new arrivals in Harlem, including writer Ralph Ellison.

Gospel singers performing at Sylvia's during Sunday brunch

Sylvia's ⑭

328 Lenox Ave. **Map** 21 B1.
Tel (212) 996-0660. Ⓜ 125th St
(2, 3). **www**.sylviassoulfood.com

Harlem's best-known soul food restaurant serves up southern-fried or smothered chicken, spicy ribs, black-eyed peas, collard greens, candied yams, sweet potato pie, and other comforting Southern

Sylvia's

delicacies. Sunday brunch here is served to the accompaniment of Gospel singers.

Take some time to explore the market at the corner of 125th Street and Lenox Avenue (opposite Sylvia's), extending for a block or more in either direction. It sells African clothing, jewelry, and art of varying quality.

Apollo Theater ⑮

253 W 125th St. **Map** 21 A1.
Tel (212) 531-5304/5 (events); (212)
531-5337 (tours). Ⓜ 125th St.
◯ at showtimes. ⓖ Groups only.
♿ ⓘ See **Entertainment** p353.
www.apollotheater.com

The Apollo opened in 1913 as a whites-only opera house. Its great fame came when Frank Schiffman, a white entrepreneur, took over in 1934. He then opened the

theater to all races and turned it into Harlem's best-known showcase, with great artists such as Bessie Smith, Billie Holiday, Duke Ellington, and Dinah Washington.

Wednesday Amateur Nights, (begun in 1935) with winners

Apollo Theater

determined by audience applause, were famous, and there was a long waiting list for performers. These amateur

nights launched the careers of Sarah Vaughan, Pearl Bailey, James Brown, and Gladys Knight, among others, and they still attract hopefuls.

The Apollo was *the* place during the swing band era; following World War II, a new generation of musicians, such as Charlie "Bird" Parker, Dizzy Gillespie, Thelonius Monk, and Aretha Franklin, continued the tradition.

Rescued from decline and refurbished in the 1980s, the Apollo once again features top black entertainers and hosts Amateur Nights.

Studio Museum in Harlem ⑯

144 W 125th St. **Map** 21 B2.
Tel (212) 864-4500. Ⓜ 125th St
(2, 3). ◯ 12–6pm Wed–Fri & Sun,
10am–6pm Sat. ● public hols.
🎟 Donations. ⤧ ♿ ✓ **Lectures,
children's programs, films,
video presentations.** ⓘ ▯
www.studiomuseum.org

The museum was founded in 1967 in a loft on upper Fifth Avenue with the mission of becoming the premier center for the collection and exhibition of the art and artifacts of African-Americans.

The present premises, a five-story building on Harlem's main commercial street, was donated to the museum by the New York Bank for Savings in 1979. There are galleries on two levels for changing exhibitions featuring artists and cultural themes, and three galleries are devoted to the permanent collection of works by major black artists.

The photographic archives comprise one of the most

Exhibition space at the Studio Museum in Harlem

complete records in existence of Harlem in its heyday. A side door opens onto a small sculpture garden.

In addition to its excellent exhibitions, the Studio Museum also maintains a national artist-in-residence program, and offers regular lectures, seminars, children's programs, and film festivals. An excellent shop sells a range of books, unique prints, and various African crafts.

Mount Morris Historical District ⑰

W 119th–W 124th Sts.
Map 21 B2. Ⓜ *125th St (2, 3).*

You can plainly see that the late 19th-century Victorian-style town houses near Marcus Garvey Park were once grand. This was a favorite neighborhood of German Jews moving up in the world from the Lower East Side. Time has not been kind, and this district shows how the area has deteriorated.

A few impressive churches, such as St. Martin's Episcopal Church, remain. There are also some interesting juxta-positions of faiths to be seen: the columned Mount Olivet Baptist Church, at 201 Lenox Avenue, was once Temple Israel, one of the most imposing synagogues in

St. Martin's Episcopal Church on Lenox Avenue

the city; and at the Ethiopian Hebrew Congregation, 1 West 123rd Street, housed in a former mansion, the choir sings in Hebrew on Saturdays.

Marcus Garvey Park ⑱

120th–124th Sts. **Map** 21 B2.
Ⓜ *125th St (2, 3).*

The flamboyant black nationalist leader Marcus Garvey

This hilly, rocky, two-block square of green is the site of New York's last fire watch-tower, an open cast-iron structure built in 1856, with spiral stairs leading to the observation deck. The bell below the deck sounded the alarm. It may be best to view it from a distance, however, if you have any doubts about your safety.

Previously known as Mount Morris Park, it was renamed in 1973 in honor of Marcus Garvey. He came to Harlem from Jamaica in 1916 and founded the Universal Negro Improvement Association, which promoted self-help, racial pride and a back-to-Africa movement.

Museo del Barrio ⑲

1230 5th Ave. **Map** 21 C5. *Tel (212) 831-7272.* Ⓜ *103rd St, 110th St.* ⏰ *11am–6pm Wed–Sun.* ⬤ *Jan 1, Jul 4, Thanksgiving, Dec 25.* 🎫 ▢ 🅿 ♿ ▢ *www.elmuseo.org*

Founded in 1969, this is North America's only museum devoted to Latin American art. It specializes in the culture of Puerto Rico. Exhibitions feature contemporary painting and sculpture, folk art, and historical artifacts. The stars of the permanent collection are about 240 wooden Santos, (carved figures of saints), and a reconstructed *bodega,* or Latino corner grocery. Exhibits change often, but some of the Santos are often on display. The Pre-Columbian collection contains rare artifacts from the Caribbean. Situated at the far end of Museum Mile, this unusual museum attempts to bridge the gap between the lofty Upper East Side and the cultural heritage of El Barrio (Spanish Harlem).

Folk art at the Museo del Barrio: one of the Three Wise Men (left) and the Omnipotent Hand

FARTHER AFIELD

Though officially part of New York City, the boroughs outside Manhattan are quite different in feel and spirit. They are residential and don't have the famous skyscrapers that are associated with New York. The difference is evident even in the way residents describe a trip to Manhattan as "going into the city." Yet the outlying areas boast many attractions, including the city's biggest zoo, botanical gardens, museums, beaches, and sports arenas. For a guided walk around Brooklyn see pages 266–7.

SIGHTS AT A GLANCE

Historic Streets and Buildings
Alice Austen House ㉗
George Washington Bridge ❸
Grand Army Plaza ⓲
Historic Richmond Town ㉔
Morris-Jumel Mansion ❷
Park Slope Historic District ⓳
Wave Hill ❺
Yankee Stadium ❿

Museums and Galleries
Audubon Terrace ❶
Brooklyn Children's Museum ⓰
Brooklyn Museum pp250–53 ㉑

Jacques Marchais Museum of Tibetan Art ㉕
Museum of the Moving Image and Kaufman Astoria Studio ⓮
New York Hall of Science ⓭
PS1 Museum of Modern Art (MoMA), Queens ⓯
Snug Harbor Cultural Center ㉖
The Cloisters pp236–9 ❹
Van Cortlandt House Museum ❻

Parks and Gardens
Bronx Zoo pp244–5 ❾
Brooklyn Botanic Garden ㉒
Flushing Meadow-Corona Park ⓬

New York Botanical Garden pp242–3 ❽
Prospect Park ⓴

Famous Theaters
Brooklyn Academy of Music ⓱

Cemeteries
Woodlawn Cemetery ❼

Beaches
City Island ⓫
Coney Island ㉓
Jamaica Bay Wildlife Refuge Center ㉘
Jones Beach State Park ㉙

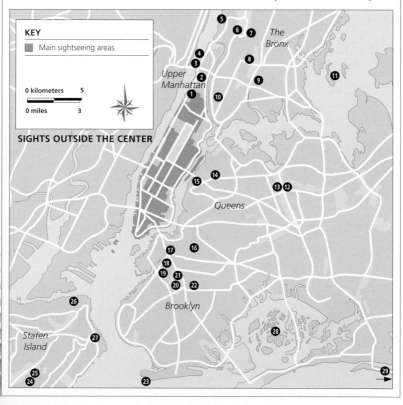

KEY

◼ Main sightseeing areas

0 kilometers 5
0 miles 3

SIGHTS OUTSIDE THE CENTER

The Bronx
Upper Manhattan
Queens
Brooklyn
Staten Island

◁ Jamaica Bay

Upper Manhattan

It was in Upper Manhattan that the 18th-century Dutch settlers established their farms. Now a suburban area with little of the bustle of downtown Manhattan, it is a good place to escape the inner city for some relaxed museum and landmark sightseeing. The Cloisters *(see pp236–9)* displays a magnificent collection of medieval art, housed within original European buildings of the period. A piece of New York history is found at the Morris-Jumel Mansion in north Harlem. From his headquarters here, George Washington mounted the defense of Manhattan in 1776.

Facade of the American Academy of Arts and Letters

Audubon Terrace ●

Broadway at 155th St. **M** *157th St.* **American Academy of Arts and Letters**; *(212) 368-5900.* ☐ *1–4pm Thu–Sun.* **Ⓘ Hispanic Society of America**; *(212) 926-2234.* ☐ *10am–4:30pm Tue–Sat, 1–4pm Sun.* ● *public hols.* **Donations.** ◙ Ⓘ *2pm Sat.* ☐ **www.**hispanicsociety.org

This 1908 complex of Classical Revival buildings by Charles Pratt Huntington is named for the great naturalist John James Audubon, whose estate once included this land. Audubon is buried in nearby Trinity Cemetery. His gravestone, a Celtic cross, bears the symbolic images of his adventurous career: the birds he painted, his palette and brushes, and his rifles.

The complex was funded by the architect's cousin, civic benefactor Archer Milton Huntington. His dream was that it should be a center of culture and study. A central plaza contains statues by his wife, sculptress Anna Hyatt Huntington.

Audubon Terrace contains two themed museums that are worth seeking out. The American Academy of Arts and Letters was set up to honor American writers, artists, and composers, and 75 honorary members from overseas. On this illustrious roll are writers John Steinbeck and Mark Twain, painters Andrew Wyeth and Edward Hopper, and composer

Aaron Copland. Exhibitions feature members' work. The library (for scholars, by appointment) has old manuscripts and first editions.

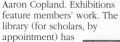

The Hispanic Society of America is a public museum and library based upon a personal collection amassed by Archer M. Huntington. The main gallery, in Spanish Renaissance style, holds works by Goya, El Greco, and Velázquez. There are also extensive collections of

Bronze door, American Academy

Spanish sculpture, decorative arts, prints, and photographs, with changing exhibits throughout the year.

Nearby, the Church of Our Lady of Esperanza stands on a knoll at 624 W 156th Street, which was once part of Audubon Park. It was built at the instigation of Señora de Barril, wife of the Spanish Consul-General in New York, as a church for the Spanish-speaking peoples of New York City. Built with funds provided by railroad magnate Archer Milton Huntington, the church was completed in 1912, and enlarged in the 1920s.

Statue of El Cid by Anna Hyatt Huntington at Audubon Terrace

Morris-Jumel Mansion ❷

Corner W 160th St and Edgecombe Ave. *Tel* (212) 923-8008. Ⓜ 163rd St. 🕙 10am–4pm Wed–Sun. ⬤ public hols. 🏷 🖻 🎫 noon Sat by appt. 🏠 **www.** morrisjumel.org

This is one of New York's few pre-Revolutionary buildings. Now a museum with nine restored period rooms, it was built in 1765 for Roger Morris. His former military colleague George Washington used it as temporary headquarters while defending Manhattan in 1776. In 1810 it was bought and updated by Stephen Jumel, a merchant of French-Caribbean descent, and his wife Eliza.

The pair furnished the house with souvenirs of their many visits to France. Her boudoir has a "dolphin" chair, reputedly bought from Napoleon. Eliza's social climbing and love affairs scandalized New York society. It was rumored that she let her husband bleed to death in 1832 so she could inherit his fortune. She later married Aaron Burr, aged 77, and divorced him three years later on the day he died.

The exterior of the Palladian-style, wood-sided Georgian house with classical portico and octagonal wing has been restored. The museum exhibits include many original Jumel pieces.

The 3,500-ft (1,065-m) span of the George Washington Bridge

George Washington Bridge ❸

Ⓜ 175th St. **www.**panynj.gov

French architect Le Corbusier called this "the only seat of grace in the disordered city." While not as famous a landmark as its Brooklyn equivalent, this bridge by engineer Othmar Ammann and his architect Cass Gilbert has its own character and history. Plans for a bridge linking Manhattan to New Jersey had been in the pipeline for more than 60 years before the Port of New York Authority raised the $59 million to fund the project. It was Ammann who suggested a road bridge rather than the more expensive rail link. Work began in 1927 and the bridge was opened in 1931: first across were two young roller skaters from the Bronx. Today it is a vital link for commuter traffic and is in constant use.

The lighthouse under Washington Bridge

Cass Gilbert had plans to clad the two towers with masonry but funds did not permit it, leaving an elegant skeletal structure 600 ft (183 m) high and 3,500 ft (1,065 m) long.

Ammann had also allowed for a second deck in his plan, and this lower deck was added in 1962, increasing the bridge's capacity enormously. Now the eastbound toll collection shows a traffic level of over 53 million cars per year.

Below the eastern tower is a lighthouse that was saved from possible demolition in 1951 by public pressure. Many thousands of young New Yorkers and children all around the world have loved the bedtime story *The Little Red Lighthouse and the Great Gray Bridge,* and wrote letters to save the lighthouse. Author Hildegarde Hoyt Swift wove the tale around her two favorite New York landmarks.

The bridge is also home to the world's largest free-flying American flag, which is hung out on major federal holidays.

The Cloisters ❹

See pp236–9.

Morris-Jumel Mansion, built in 1765, with its original colossal portico

The Cloisters ❹

The Cloisters seen from Fort Tryon Park

This world-famous museum of medieval art resides in a building constructed from 1934 to 1938, incorporating medieval cloisters, chapels, and halls. Sculptor George Grey Barnard founded the museum in 1914; John D. Rockefeller, Jr. funded the Metropolitan Museum of Art's 1925 purchase of the collection and donated the site at Fort Tryon Park and also the land on the New Jersey side of the Hudson River, directly across from The Cloisters.

Tomb Effigy of Jean d'Alluye
This tomb immortalizes the 13th-century Crusader.

Langon
Chapel

Pontaut
Chapter
House

Gothic
Chapel

★ Unicorn Tapestries
The set of beautifully preserved tapestries, woven in Brussels around 1500, depicts the quest and capture of the mythical unicorn.

Boppard Stained-Glass Lancets *(1440–47)*
Below the lancet of St Catherine, angels display the arms of the coopers' guild, of which Catherine was patron.

STAR EXHIBITS

★ Annunciation
Triptych by
Robert Campin

★ Belles Heures de Jean,
Duc de Berry

★ Unicorn Tapestries

Bonnefort Cloister

Glass
Gallery

Trie
Cloister

★ Annunciation Triptych *(about 1425)*
The Campin Room is the location of this Robert Campin of Tournai small triptych, a magnificent example of early Flemish painting.

Saint-Guilhem Cloister
Intricate floral ornamentation can be found on the capitals of this cloister.

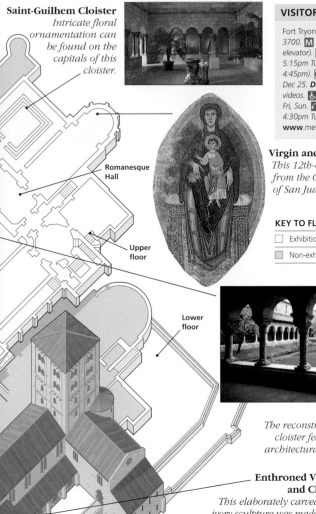

Romanesque Hall

Upper floor

Lower floor

Main entrance

VISITORS' CHECKLIST

Fort Tryon Park. **Tel** (212) 923-3700. M A to 190th St (exit via elevator). M4. ⬤ 9:30am–5:15pm Tue–Sun (Nov–Feb: to 4:45pm). ⬤ Jan 1, Thanksgiving, Dec 25. **Donations**. ⬤ No videos. ♿ limited. ⬤ 3pm Tue–Fri, Sun. ⬤ ⬤ May–Oct: 10am–4:30pm Tue–Sun. ⬤ **Concerts**. **www**.metmuseum.org/cloisters

Virgin and Child Frescoes
This 12th-century fresco is from the Catalonian church of San Juan de Tredós.

KEY TO FLOOR PLAN

☐ Exhibition space

▨ Non-exhibition space

Cuxa Cloister
The reconstructed 12th-century cloister features Romanesque architectural detail and motifs.

Enthroned Virgin and Child
This elaborately carved ivory sculpture was made in England during the late 13th century.

GALLERY GUIDE
The museum is organized roughly in chronological order. It starts with the Romanesque period (AD 1000) and moves to the Gothic (1150 to 1520). Sculptures, stained glass, paintings, and the gardens are on the lower floor. The Unicorn Tapestries are on the upper floor.

★ Belles Heures
This book of hours, commissioned by Jean, Duc de Berry, is among a rotating installation of exquisite illuminated books and folios.

Exploring The Cloisters

Known particularly for its Romanesque and
Gothic architectural sculpture, The Cloisters
collection also includes illuminated manuscripts,
stained glass, metalwork, enamels, ivories, and
paintings. Among its tapestries is the renowned
Unicorn series. The Cloisters' splendid medieval
complex is unrivaled in North America.

ROMANESQUE ART

**A lifesized 12th-century Spanish
crucifix portraying Christ as the
King of Heaven**

Fanciful beasts and people,
acanthus blossoms and
scrollwork top the columns
around The Cloisters. Many
are in the Romanesque style
that flourished in the 11th
and 12th centuries. The
museum has numerous
masterpieces of Romanesque
art and architecture, showing
the style's powerful rounded
arches and intricate details.
Highly embellished capitals
and warm, pink marble typify
the 12th-century Cuxa Cloister
from the Pyrenees in France.
A griffin, a dragon, a centaur,
and a basilisk are among the
creatures parading over the
Narbonne Arch nearby.

In a more solemn style, the
apse from the church of
Saint-Martín in Fuentidueña,
Spain, is a massive rounded
vault constructed from 3,300
blocks of limestone. It is
decorated with a 12th-century
fresco of the Virgin and Child
and has a golden-crowned
Christ depicted as triumphant
over death.

More than 800 years ago,
Benedictine and Cistercian
monks sat on the cold stone
benches in the Pontaut Chapter
House. By the 19th century it
had become so neglected that
it was used as a stable. Its
ribbed vaulting is a foretaste of
the Gothic style to come.

**A 16th-century Flemish boxwood
rosary bead from the Treasury**

GOTHIC ART

Where Romanesque art was
solid, the Gothic style that
followed (from 1150 to
around 1520) was open, with
pointed arches, glowing
stained-glass windows, and
three-dimensional sculpture.
Gothic depictions of the Virgin
and Child display exquisite
craftsmanship.

The Gothic Chapel's
brilliantly colored windows
show scenes and figures from
biblical stories. Lifesized tomb
sculptures include the effigy
of the Crusader knight Jean
d'Alluye. During the 1790s,

Vaulted ceiling of the Pontaut Chapter House

the statue's original home, La Clarté-Dieu Abbey in France, was vandalized, and the statue was used to bridge a stream.

In the Boppard Room, the lives of the saints are told in marvelous late Gothic stained glass from Germany.

Robert Campin's Flemish masterwork, the *Annunciation* altarpiece, is the focus of the Campin Room. It is an intimate room with furnishings that might have belonged to a wealthy 15th-century family.

MEDIEVAL GARDENS

More than 300 varieties of plants grown in the Middle Ages can be found in The Cloisters' gardens. The Bonnefont Cloister has many species of aromatic, magic, medicinal, and culinary herbs. The Trie Cloister features plants shown in the *Unicorn Tapestries* and reveals the use of flowers in medieval symbolism: roses (for the Virgin Mary), pansies (the Holy Trinity), and daisies (the eye of Christ).

Bonnefont Cloister

THE TAPESTRIES

The Cloisters' tapestries are full of rich imagery and symbolism, and are among the museum's most highly prized treasures. The four *Nine Heroes Tapestries* bear the coat of arms of Jean, Duc de Berry, who was a brother of the King of France and one of the greatest art patrons of the Middle Ages. These tapestries are one of only two sets that survived from the late 14th century; the other set belonged to Jean's brother, Louis, Duc d'Anjou.

Nine great heroes of the past – three pagan, three Hebrew, three Christian – are shown with members of the medieval court, from cardinals, knights, and damsels to musicians.

In an adjacent room is the magnificent *Hunt of the Unicorn*, a series of seven tapestries woven in Brussels around 1500. It depicts the symbolic hunt of the mythical unicorn and capture by a maiden.

Although they were misused in the 19th century to protect fruit trees from frost damage,

the tapestries are remarkably well preserved. They are also astonishing in detail, with

Julius Caesar, entertained by court musicians, in a *Nine Heroes* tapestry

literally hundreds of minutely observed plants and animals. Their story can be read as a tale of courtly love, but the series is also an allegory of the Crucifixion and the Resurrection of Christ.

THE TREASURY

In medieval times, precious objects were stored for safe-keeping in sanctuaries. At The Cloisters, they are found in the Treasury.

The collection includes several Gothic illuminated "books of hours." These were used for the private devotions of the nobility, such as the Limbourg brothers' *Belles Heures*, made for Jean, Duc de Berry, in 1410, and the tiny, palm-sized version by Gothic master Jean Pucelle for the Queen of France, around 1325.

Other religious artifacts range from a 13th-century English ivory Virgin to the 14th-century silver gilt and enamel reliquary shrine thought to have belonged to Queen Elizabeth of Hungary, along with censers, chalices, candlesticks, and crucifixes.

Curiosities here include the "Monkey Cup," an enameled beaker probably made for the 15th-century Burgundian court, showing mischievous monkeys robbing a sleeping peddler; an intricately carved rosary bead the size of a walnut; a 13th-century boat-shaped, jeweled saltcellar; and a full set of playing cards dating to the 15th century.

Hunting images and symbols depicted on a 15th-century deck of playing cards

The west parlor of the Van Cortlandt House Museum

The Bronx

Once a prosperous suburb with a famous Grand Concourse lined with apartment buildings for the wealthy, the Bronx has now become an unfortunate symbol of urban decay. Still, diverse ethnic communities, unique resources, and charming areas, such as Riverdale at the northern end, remain.

Two main attractions are the Bronx Zoo and New York Botanical Garden. There is also a golf course at Ferry Point Park, and Fulton Fish Market has relocated here. The much-loved Yankees baseball team's *(see p360)* main stadium is located here.

Wave Hill ❺

W 249th St and Independence Ave, Riverdale. *Tel (718) 549-3200.* Ⓜ *231st St, then bus Bx7, 10, or museum shuttle bus hourly 9:10am–3:10pm.* ◯ *10am–5:30pm Tue–Sun (to 4:30pm mid-Oct–mid-Apr).* 🈚 *free Tue (Jul, Aug & Nov–Apr), 9am–noon Tue (May, Jun, Sep & Oct), 9am–noon Sat (all year).* 📷 *2:15pm Sun.* 🖥 www.wavehill.org

This 28-acre (11-ha) oasis of beauty boasts fine views over to the New Jersey Palisades across the Hudson River. The former estate of financier and conservationist George W. Perkins, Wave Hill has had many distinguished tenants,

including Theodore Roosevelt, Mark Twain, and Arturo Toscanini. Perkins also owned neighboring estates, underneath which he built a recreation center complete with bowling alley, and a tunnel leading into the main building.

The house is frequently used for concerts. They often take place in the grand Armor Hall, designed in 1928 for Bashford Dean, who was then the curator of the collection of arms and armor at the Metropolitan Museum of Art.

The gardens were originally designed by Viennese landscape gardener Albert Millard. There are also greenhouses, lawns, an herb garden, and woodlands. Exhibitions range from sculpture to horticulture.

The adjoining Riverdale Park, which is also open to the public, has attractive woodland and paths along the river.

The interior of the grand Armor Hall at Wave Hill

Van Cortlandt House Museum ❻

Van Cortlandt Park. *Tel (718) 543-3344.* Ⓜ *242nd St, Van Cortlandt Park.* ◯ *10am–3pm Tue–Fri, 11am–4pm Sat, Sun (last adm: 30 mins before closing).* ◑ *public hols & Nov 26.* 🈚 *free Wed.* 📷 📷 📷 *See The History of New York pp20–21.* www.vancortlandthouse.org

The facade of Van Cortlandt House

A restored 1748 Georgian Colonial country manor built of rough stone, the Bronx's oldest building was the family home of Frederick Van Cortlandt, a New Yorker who inherited great wealth and was related to many influential families of his day.

The dining room was used as one of General George Washington's headquarters; the ground behind the house was once the scene of skirmishing during the Revolutionary War.

The interior has American period furnishings as well as a superb collection of delftware and a complete 17th-century Dutch bedroom.

On the exterior, look for the carved faces in the keystones over the windows.

Woodlawn Cemetery ❼

Webster Ave and E 233rd St.
Tel (718) 920-0500. Ⓜ Woodlawn.
◯ 8:30am–5pm daily.
◯ public hols. 🚫 ♿ 🎥
www.thewoodlawncemetery.org

For a glimpse into another kind of social history, visit Woodlawn Cemetery, burial place of many a wealthy and distinguished New Yorker. Memorials and tombstones are set in beautiful grounds. F.W. Woolworth and many members of his family are interred in a mausoleum only a little less ornate than the building that carries the family name. The pink marble vault of meat magnate Herman Armour is oddly reminiscent of a ham.

Entrance to the Woolworth mausoleum

Other New York notables buried here include Mayor Fiorello LaGuardia, Rowland Hussey Macy, the founder of the great department store, author Herman Melville, and jazz legend Duke Ellington.

New York Botanical Garden ❽

See pp242–3.

Bronx Zoo/Wildlife Conservation Park ❾

See pp244–5.

Yankee Stadium ❿

E 161st St at River Ave, Highbridge.
Tel (718) 293-6000. Ⓜ 161st St.
🎥 noon daily (except on game afternoons); reservation advised.
See **Sport** p360. **www**.yankees.com

This has been the home of the New York Yankees baseball team since 1923. Among Yankee heroes are two of the greatest players of all time: Babe Ruth and Joe DiMaggio (who was also famous for marrying the actress Marilyn Monroe in 1954). In 1921 left-hander Babe Ruth, wearing the Yankees' distinctive pinstripes, hit the stadium's first home run – against the Boston Red Sox, his former team. The stadium was completed two years later by Jacob Ruppert, the owner of the Yankees, and became known as "the house that Ruth built".

Joe DiMaggio in action at Yankee Stadium in 1941

The stadium had a facelift in the mid-1970s, and now seats up to 54,000 people who come for sports, concerts, and other events. One of the largest annual gatherings has been that of the Jehovah's Witnesses and in 1950, 123,707 people attended in a single day. In 1965 Pope Paul VI celebrated mass before a crowd of more than 80,000. It was the first visit to North America by a pope – the second was made in 1979 when John Paul II also visited the stadium.

The Yankees remain one of the top teams in the American League. There are five Yankee Clubhouse stores in New York where tickets for tours and games can be purchased.

The New York Yankee Stadium is now located parallel to the old stadium at 161st and 164th streets.

City Island ⓫

Ⓜ 6 to Pelham Bay Park, then Bx29 to City Island.
Museum 190 Fordham St.
◯ 1–5pm Sat–Sun. **Tel** (718) 885-0008. **www**.cityislandmuseum.org

Situated off the northeast shore of the Bronx and surrounded by Long Island Sound, City Island is a small nautical outpost with a very New England feel and offers a refreshing change of pace. Its scenic marinas are filled with sailboats, and its seafood restaurants would satisfy any sailor's appetite. Several Americas Cup winners have been built in its boatyards.

The **City Island Museum** is in one of the island's most historic buildings, the old Public School 17, built on an Indian burial ground at a high point on the island. City Island is linked to the Bronx by bridge. To the north on the mainland is Orchard Beach, a crescent of white sand edged with bathing huts. The beach is popular with area residents, and it can be crowded.

An old tugboat moored at one of City Island's piers

The New York Botanical Garden ⑧

Hibiscus

The New York Botanical Garden is 250 acres (100 ha) of dazzling beauty and hands-on enjoyment. From the nation's most glorious Victorian glasshouse to the 12-acre (5-ha) Everett Children's Adventure Garden, it is alive with things to discover. One of the oldest and largest botanical gardens in the world, it has 50 gardens and plant collections, and 50 acres (20 ha) of uncut forest. The spectacular Enid A. Haupt Conservatory has been wonderfully restored as *A World of Plants*, with misty tropical rain forests and dramatic deserts.

Entrance to Enid A. Haupt Conservatory

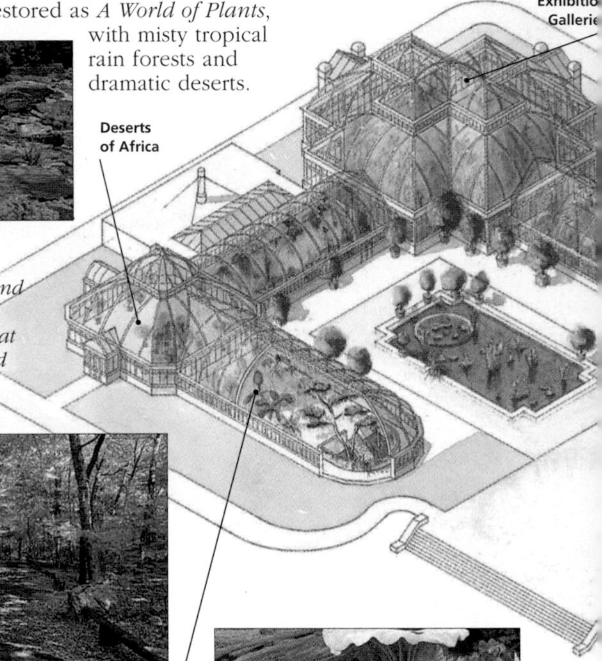
Season
Exhibitio
Gallerie
Deserts of Africa
Deserts of the Americas

Rock Garden
Rock outcroppings, streams, a waterfall, and a flower-rimmed pond create an alpine habitat for plants from around the world ④

Historic Forest
One of New York City's last surviving natural forest areas includes red oak, white ash, tulip trees, and birch ⑤

Everett Children's Adventure Garden *Kids can discover the wonders of ecology and plants* ⑧

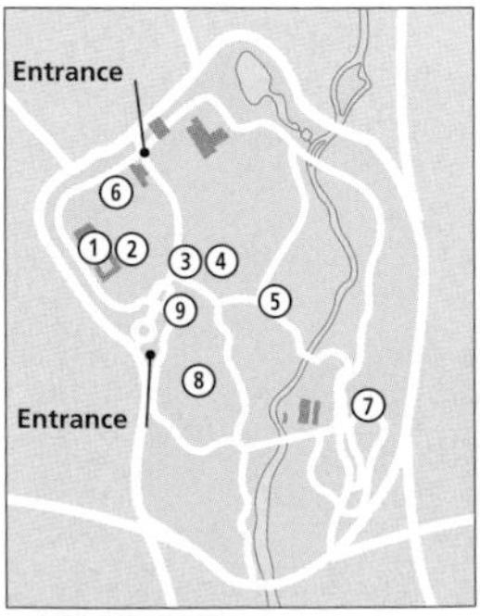
Entrance
⑥
①②
③④
⑨
⑤
⑧
Entrance
⑦

LOCATOR MAP

Peggy Rockefeller Rose Garden
Over 2,700 rose bushes have been planted in the Rose Garden, laid out in 1988 according to the 1916 design ⑦

Palms of the Americas Gallery

100 majestic palms soar into a 90-ft (27-m) glass dome. A tranquil reflecting pool is surrounded by tropical plants.

The Enid A. Haupt Conservatory consists of 11 interconnecting glass galleries housing *A World of Plants*, including rain forests, deserts, aquatic plants, and seasonal exhibitions ①

Garden Cafe

This is a delightful spot to enjoy a meal. You can eat outside on terraces overlooking beautiful gardens ⑥

Conservatory

Jane Watson Irwin Perennial Garden

Flowering perennials are arranged in dramatic patterns according to height, shade, color and blooming time ②

Tropical Lowland Rain Forest Gallery

Courtyard Pool

Leon Levy Visitor Center

This modern pavilion, which opened in 2004, has a shop, a cafe, and a visitor orientation facility ⑨

Aquatic Plants and Vines Gallery

Tropical Upland Rainforest Gallery

Tram

The half-hour tour of the gardens provides information about horticultural, educational, and botanical research programs. Passengers can alight at a number of stops to explore the gardens before reboarding ③

Bronx Zoo ❾

Opened in 1899, the Bronx Zoo is the largest urban zoo in the United States. It is home to more than 4,000 animals of 500 species, which live in realistic representations of their natural habitats. The zoo is a leader in the perpetuation of endangered species, such as the Indian rhinoceros and the snow leopard. Its 265 acres of woods, streams, and parklands include, in season, a children's zoo a butterfly garden, and a shuttle train that transports visitors around the sprawling park. Visitors are also free to walk around. For the best overview of the zoo's park areas take the SkyFari cable car (which also operates seasonally).

★ The Congo Gorilla Forest
This award-winning replica of a central African rainforest is home to the largest population of Western Lowland gorillas in the US, as well as a family of pygmy marmosets, the world's smallest monkeys.

★ African Plains
Wild dogs, zebras, lions, cheetahs, and gazelles roam the African Plains. Predators and prey are separated by a moat.

Carter Giraffe Building

Asia entrance

Camel Rides
Children enjoy such seasonal experiences as camel rides and other attractions.

Wild Asia Monorail

World of Darkness

SkyFari cable

★ JungleWorld
A climate-controlled tropical rain forest harbors mammals, birds, and reptiles from South Asia. The animals are kept apart from visitors by ravines, streams and cliffs.

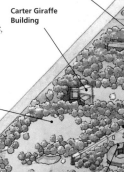

Monkeys in JungleWorld

Baboon Reserve
Visitors walk along a dry riverbed to see wildlife in an Ethiopian mountain habitat.

Children's Zoo
Kids can crawl through a prairie dog tunnel, try on a turtle shell, and pet and feed the animals.

VISITORS' CHECKLIST

Fordham Rd/Bronx River Pkwy. *Tel* (718) 367-1010. Ⓜ 2, 5 to E Tremont Ave. 🚉 to Fordham Station. 🚌 Bx9, Bx12, Bx19, Bx22, Bx39, BxM11 express bus, Q44. ◻ Nov–Mar: 10am–4:30pm daily; Apr–Oct: 10am–5pm daily (5:30pm Sat–Sun). 🎦 Wed by donation. 📷 ♿ ✍ 🍴 🛍 *Children's Zoo* ◻ Apr–Oct. www.bronxzoo.com

STAR FEATURES

★ African Plains

★ Congo Gorilla Forest

★ JungleWorld

★ Tiger Mountain

★ Wild Asia

★ World of Birds

World of Reptiles

The Zoo Center

Madagascar!

Butterfly Garden

Aquatic Bird House

Southern Boulevard entrance

Sea Bird Colony

wl

Rainey Gate entrance

Monkey House

★ World of Birds
Exotic birds soar free in the lush surroundings of a rain forest. An artificial waterfall rushes down a 50-ft (15-m) fiberglass cliff in this walk-through habitat.

Great hornbill

Mouse-House

Bronx Parkway entrance

Himalayan Highlands
Endangered species, such as snow leopards and red pandas, are here.

★ Wild Asia
From May to October, the monorail journeys through forests and meadows, where rhinos, tigers, and Mongolian wild horses roam free.

★ Tiger Mountain
Amur tigers are on view all year. Only one inch of glass separates visitors from these magnificent wild cats.

Queens

A big, sprawling borough, Queens has a wide variety of attractions and residential and commercial areas, including Long Island City, where exciting museums and restaurants are springing up all over. Development of the borough accelerated after 1909, when the construction of Queensboro Bridge made commuting easier. The city's main airports are here, and there are many different ethnic enclaves including the Greek neighborhood of Astoria and the various Asian communities in Flushing.

A 1900 Mutoscope at the Museum of the Moving Image

Flushing Meadow–Corona Park ⑫

Ⓜ *Willets Point-Shea Stadium.* See **Sports** *p361.*

The site of New York's two World's Fairs now offers expansive waterside picnic grounds and a multitude of attractions. These include the 50,000-seat Shea Stadium, the home of the New York Mets baseball team and a popular site for rock concerts. Flushing Meadow is also home to the US Tennis Center, where the prestigious United States Open is played. The courts are open for would-be Agassis, Grafs, and Everts for the remainder of the year. In the 1920s this area was known as the Corona Dump, a nightmarish place of salt marshes and great piles of smoldering trash. In *The Great Gatsby*, author F. Scott Fitzgerald dubbed it the "valley of ashes." It reeked of rotting garbage and glowed red at night. New York's Parks' Commissioner Robert Moses was the driving force behind its transformation. A whole mountain of rubbish was removed and the river was totally re-channeled. The marsh was drained and sewage works were built, helping to restore the area. This site was to serve as the site for the 1939 World's Fair, at which a world on the brink of war saluted the elusive notion of world peace.

The Unisphere, symbol of the 1964 fair, still dominates the remains of the fairground. This giant hollow ball of green steel, built by the US Steel Corporation, is 12 stories high and weighs a massive 350 tons.

New York Hall of Science ⑬

46th Ave and 111th St Flushing Meadow, Corona Park. *Tel* (718) 699-0005. Ⓜ *111th St.* ⬛ *Sep–Jun: 9:30am–2pm Mon–Thu, 9:30am–5pm Fri, 10am–6pm Sat, Sun; Jul–Aug: 9:30am–5pm Mon–Fri, 10am–6pm Sat, Sun.* ⬤ *Labor Day, Dec 25.* 🖼️📷♿🚻🎧 **www**.nyscience.org

The science pavilion was built for the 1964 World's Fair, with stained glass set in concrete. It is now a hands-on museum of science and technology, with exhibits on color, light, and physics. Kids love the giant video screens and laser optical exhibits.

The concrete curtain wall of the New York Hall of Science

Museum of the Moving Image and Kaufman Astoria Studio ⑭

35th Ave at 36th St, Astoria. **Museum** (718) 784-0077. Ⓜ *36th St.* **Steinway Museum** ⬛ *11am–5pm Wed, Thu, 11am–8pm Fri, 11am–6:30pm Sat, Sun. Screenings: 7:30pm Fri, afternoon and eves Sat–Sun.* 🖼️ *(free 4–8pm Fri).* 🎫 *2pm Sat, Sun.* ⬤ *Memorial Day, Thanksgiving, Dec 25.* **Studio.** ⬤ *to public.* 📷 ♿🖥️🚻 **www**.movingimage.us

In New York's filmmaking heyday, Rudolph Valentino, W.C. Fields, the Marx Brothers, and Gloria Swanson all made films in the Astoria Studio, which was opened in 1920 by Paramount Pictures. When the movies went west, the army took over, making training films from 1941 to 1971. The complex stood empty until 1977 when Astoria Motion Picture and Television

The 1964 World's Fair Unisphere at Flushing Meadow-Corona Park

Poster at the Museum of the Moving Image

Foundation was founded to preserve it. *The Wiz*, a musical starring Michael Jackson and Diana Ross, was made here, helping to pay for restoration.

Today, the studios house the largest moviemaking facilities on the East Coast.

In 1981 one of the studio buildings was transformed into the Museum of the Moving Image, with interactive displays on production and theaters for the screening of movies and television, as well as a special lecture hall.

There is a lot of memorabilia on display, from Ben Hur's chariot to *Star Trek* costumes. The main gallery draws from the permanent collection of over 85,000 movie artifacts. A major expansion of the museum has created a 254-seat theater, a video screening ampitheater and an educational 71-seat screeening room.

PS1 MoMA, Queens ⑮

22–25 Jackson at 46th Ave, Long Island City. *Tel* (718) 784-2084. M E, V to 23rd St-Ely Ave; 7 to 45 Road-Courthouse Square; G to Court Sq or 21 St-Van Alst. ▦ B61, Q67. ◯ noon–6pm Thu–Mon. ◉ Jan 1, Dec 25. 🎫 ♿ ▭ www.ps1.org

Housed in an elementary school, PS1 was founded in 1971 under a scheme to transform abandoned New York City buildings into exhibition, performance, and studio spaces for artists. The museum is affiliated to the Museum of Modern Art *(see pp172–5)* and is one of the oldest art organisations in the US devoted solely to modern art. Temporary exhibitions are hosted alongside permanent works and many pieces are interactive. In summer, music is performed in the courtyard.

Brooklyn

The bandstand at Prospect Park *(see p248)*

If Brooklyn were a separate city, it would be the country's fourth largest. It has a character all of its own. Many entertainment greats – Mel Brooks, Phil Silvers, Woody Allen, and Neil Simon among them – celebrate their birthplace with great affection and humor. Brooklyn is the ultimate melting pot, with West Indians, Hasidic Jews, Russians, Italians, and Arabs living side by side. Among the diverse neighborhoods are the historic residential districts of Park Slope and Brooklyn Heights.

Brooklyn Children's Museum ⑯

145 Brooklyn Ave. *Tel* (718) 735-4400. M Kingston (C, 3). ◯ 11am–6pm Sat–Sun; Sep–Jun: 1–6pm Wed–Fri; Jul–Aug: noon–6pm Tue–Thu, noon–6:30pm Fri. ◉ public hols.
Rooftop Theater ◯ 6:30–8pm Fri, 10am–5pm Sat, Sun. ◉ public hols.
🎫 ♿ ▭ 🅿 www.bchildmus.org

The Brooklyn Children's Museum was the first to be designed especially for children and was founded in 1899. Since then, it has been a model, inspiration, and consultant to the development of more than 250 museums for children across the country and all over the world. Housed in a high-tech, specially designed under-ground building dating from 1976, it is one of the most imaginative children's museums anywhere.

The layout of the building, which has doubled in size and is a maze of complex interconnected passageways running off the main "people tube" – a huge drainage pipe that connects the four levels. The emphasis here is on involvement and hands-on exhibits and everywhere you look there are curiosities to be discovered, experienced, made, or played with. There is even a walk-on piano like the one in the film *Big* – children of every age find it quite irresistible.

Special exhibitions and events are designed to help children learn about the planet, resolve their fears or problems, under-stand other cultures, and discover the past. The squeals of laughter that are always heard are a sign of this museum's success in teaching both children and the young at heart.

A mask at the Brooklyn Children's Museum

The facade of the Brooklyn Academy of Music

Brooklyn Academy of Music ⑰

30 Lafayette Ave. *Tel (718) 636 4100.* Ⓜ *Atlantic Ave, Nevins St (M, N, Q, R, W, 2, 3, 4, 5).* 🅿 ♿ 📷 💻 🎧 **www**.bam.org *See Classic and Contemporary Music p350.*

Home to the Brooklyn Philharmonic, the Academy of Music (BAM) is Brooklyn's leading cultural venue and the oldest, founded in 1858. It offers outstanding performances, often tending toward the innovative and avant-garde.

The classic 1908 building, designed by Herts & Tallant, was inaugurated with a production of Gounod's opera *Faust* featuring the Neapolitan tenor Enrico Caruso. Among the greats who have performed here are actress Sarah Bernhardt, ballerina Anna Pavlova, musicians Pablo Casals and Sergei Rachmaninoff, poets Edna St. Vincent Millay and Carl Sandburg, and statesman Winston Churchill. Many international touring groups have made appearances here, including Britain's Royal Shakespeare Company.

The BAM Next Wave Festival, which usually runs over the last three months of the year, has presented contemporary artists such as musicians

David Byrne and Philip Glass and choreographers Pina Bausch and Mark Morris. The BAM also runs the Harvey Theater nearby, a movie theater now used for dance, drama, and music events. BAM Rose Cinemas show first-run independent films and BAMcinématek has classics, retrospectives, festivals, and sneak previews.

Grand Army Plaza ⑱

Plaza St at Flatbush Ave. Ⓜ *Grand Army Plaza (2, 3).* **Arch** ⬜ *for occasional exhibitions.*

The Soldiers' and Sailors' Arch at Grand Army Plaza

Frederick Law Olmsted and Calvert Vaux laid out this grand oval in 1870 as a gateway to Prospect Park. The Soldiers' and Sailors' Arch and its sculptures were added in 1892 as a tribute to the Union Army. The bust of John F. Kennedy here is the only official New York monument to him.

In June, the plaza is the center of the Welcome Back to Brooklyn Festival for the famous – and not-so-famous – people born in Brooklyn.

Park Slope Historic District ⑲

Streets from Prospect Park W below Flatbush Ave, to 8th/7th/5th Aves. Ⓜ *Grand Army Plaza (2, 3), 7th Ave (F).*

Relief work on the Montauk Club

This wonderful enclave of beautiful Victorian town houses was developed on the edge of Prospect Park in the 1880s. It served the upper-middle-class professionals who were able to commute into Manhattan after the Brooklyn Bridge was opened in 1883. The shady streets are lined with two- to five-story houses in every architectural style popular in the late 19th century, some with the towers, turrets, and curlicues so representative of the era. Particularly fine examples are in Romanesque Revival style, with rounded entry arches.

The Montauk Club at 25 Eighth Avenue combines the style of Venice's Ca' d'Oro palazzo with the friezes and gargoyles of the Montauk Indians, for whom this popular 19th-century gathering place was named.

Prospect Park ⑳

Ⓜ *Grand Army Plaza, Prospect Park (B, Q).* 📷 *& information (718) 287 3400.* 💻 🎧 **www**.prospectpark.org

Olmsted and Vaux considered this park, opened in 1867, better than their earlier Central Park *(see pp203–09).* The Long Meadow, a sweep of broad lawns and grand vistas, is the longest unbroken swath of green space in New York.

Olmsted's belief was that "a feeling of relief is experienced by entering them [the parks] on escaping from the cramped, confining and controlling circumstances of the streets of the town."

The facade of the Brooklyn Public Library on Grand Army Plaza

That vision is still as true today as it was a century ago.

Among the many notable features are Stanford White's colonnaded Croquet Shelter, and the pools and weeping willows of the Vale of Cashmere. The Music Grove bandstand shows Japanese influences and hosts both jazz and classical music concerts throughout the summer.

A favorite feature of the park is the Camperdown Elm, an ancient and twisted tree planted in 1872. The Friends of Prospect Park raise money to keep it and all the park trees healthy. This old elm has inspired many poems and paintings. Prospect Park has a wide variety of landscapes, from classical gardens dotted with statues to rocky glens with running brooks. A guided tour with a ranger is the best way to see the park.

Carousel horse in Prospect Park

Brooklyn Museum ㉑

See pp250–53.

Brooklyn Botanic Garden ㉒

900 Washington Ave. **Tel** (718) 623-7200. Ⓜ Prospect Pk (B, Q), Eastern Pkwy (2, 3). **Grounds** ◯ Apr–Sep: 8am–6pm Tue–Fri (10am Sat–Sun & public hols); Oct–Mar: 8am–4:30pm (10am Sat–Sun & public hols). ◯ Jan 1, Labor Day, Thanksgiving, Dec 25. 🎟 Mar–mid-Nov: free Tue & 10am–noon Sat; mid-Nov–late Feb: free for under-16s Mon–Fri. 📷 ♿ 🖾 🛈 🖾 www.bbg.org

Though it is not vast, you will find that this 50-acre (20-ha) garden holds many delights. The area was designed by the

An Atlantic green turtle at the New York Aquarium, on Coney Island

Olmsted Brothers in 1910 and features an Elizabethan-style "knot" herb garden and one of North America's largest collections of roses.

The central showpiece is a Japanese hill-and-pond garden, complete with a teahouse and Shinto shrine. In late April and early May the park promenade is aglow with delicate Japanese cherry blossoms, which have prompted an annual festival featuring typical Japanese culture, food, and music.

April is also the time for tourists to appreciate Magnolia Plaza, where some 80 trees display their beautiful, creamy blossoms against a backdrop of daffodils on Boulder Hill.

The Fragrance Garden is planted in raised beds, where the heavily scented, textured and flavored plants are all labeled in Braille, giving blind visitors an opportunity to identify them as well.

The conservatory houses one of America's largest bonsai collections and some rare rain forest trees, whose extracts allow scientists to produce life-saving drugs.

Brooklyn Botanic Garden lily pond

Coney Island ㉓

Ⓜ Stillwell Ave (D, F, N, Q), W 8th St (F, Q). **New York Aquarium** Surf Ave and W 8th St, Coney Island. **Tel** (718) 265-FISH. ◯ 10am–5pm Mon–Fri, 10am–5:30pm Sat, Sun & hols (Jun–Aug: to 6pm Mon–Fri & 7pm Sat, Sun & hols; Nov–Mar: to 4:30pm daily). 🎟 last adm: 45 mins before closing. 🖾 www.nyaquarium.com **Coney Island Museum** 1208 Surf Ave, nr W 12th St. **Tel** (718) 372 5159. ◯ noon–5pm Sat, Sun. 🖾 www.coneyislandusa.com

In the mid-19th century, Brooklyn poet Walt Whitman composed many of his works on Coney Island, at that time untamed Atlantic coastline. By the 1920s, Coney Island was billing itself as the "World's Largest Playground." Three huge fairgrounds built by 1904 (Luna Park, Dream-land, and Steeplechase Park) provided a combination of hair-raising rides and nearby beaches. The subway arrived in 1920, and the 1921 boardwalk ensured Coney Island's popularity throughout the Depression.

A main attraction is the **New York Aquarium**, on 14 acres (6 ha) by the sea, with over 350 species. The **Coney Island Museum** has memorabilia, relics of old rides, and souvenirs. Coney Island is still exciting: the boardwalk yields ocean views, and the Cyclone roller coaster is an official city landmark. The Mermaid Parade in June is a major annual event.

Brooklyn Museum ㉑

When it opened in 1897, the
Brooklyn Museum building,
designed to be the largest cultural
edifice in the world, was the
greatest achievement of New York
architects McKim, Mead & White.

North facade, designed by McKim, Mead & White

Though only one-sixth completed, the museum
is today one of the most impressive cultural institutions
in the United States, with a permanent encyclopedic
collection of some one million objects, which are housed
in a grand structure of 560,000 sq ft (41,805 sq m).

KEY TO FLOOR PLAN

- Arts of Africa and the Americas
- Asian art
- Prints, drawings, and photographs
- Williamsburg Murals
- Egyptian and Classical art
- Decorative arts
- Painting and sculpture
- Special exhibitions
- Non-exhibition space

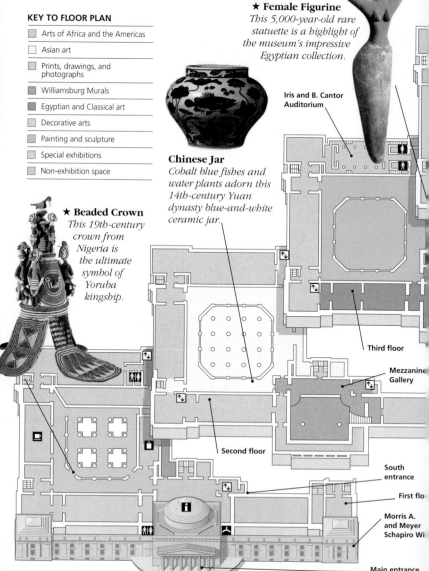

★ Female Figurine
*This 5,000-year-old rare
statuette is a highlight of
the museum's impressive
Egyptian collection.*

Iris and B. Cantor
Auditorium

Chinese Jar
*Cobalt blue fishes and
water plants adorn this
14th-century Yuan
dynasty blue-and-white
ceramic jar.*

★ Beaded Crown
*This 19th-century
crown from
Nigeria is
the ultimate
symbol of
Yoruba
kingship.*

Third floor

Mezzanine
Gallery

Second floor

South
entrance

First floor

Morris A.
and Meyer
Schapiro Wing

Main entrance

★ **An Out of Doors Study** (1889)
Sargent's portrait of French artist Paul Helleu and his wife Alice was painted during the couple's visit to the Sargent family at Fladbury.

Fifth floor

ce visible rage

Luce Center for American Art

Fourth floor

VISITORS' CHECKLIST

200 Eastern Pkwy, Brooklyn. **Tel** (718) 638-5000. Ⓜ 2, 3 to Eastern Parkway/Brooklyn Museum. 🚌 B41, B48, B67, B71. ⬜ 10am –5pm Wed–Fri, 11am–6pm Sat & Sun; 11am–11pm (free programs 5–11pm) 1st Sat in month. ⬤ Jan 1, Thanksgiving, Dec 25. **Donation expected.** 🖼 ♿ 🎧 📷 💻 🎁 *Concerts, lectures*. www.brooklynmuseum.org

★ **Winter Scene in Brooklyn** (1820)
Francis Guy's depiction of downtown Brooklyn is from the American Identities Collection.

The Dinner Party (1970s) This is the centerpiece of the Elizabeth A. Sackler Center for Feminist Art.

Moorish Smoking Room (1865)
This room is from a house on West 54th Street, bought by J. D. Rockefeller in 1884.

Alexander the Great
The military leader was portrayed in alabaster in the 1st century BC.

Ibis Coffin (332–330 BC)
The sacred bird of ancient Egypt merited a splendid coffin of gold leaf and silver.

GALLERY GUIDE
The collection is on five floors, with African and New World art on the first; prints, drawings, and Asian art on the second; Egyptian, Classical, and European painting and sculpture on the third; decorative art on the fourth; and American art on the fifth. There is special exhibition space on the first and fourth floors.

STAR EXHIBITS

★ An Out of Doors Study, by John Singer Sargent

★ Beaded Crown

★ Female Figurine

★ Winter Scene in Brooklyn, by Francis Guy

Exploring the Collection

The Brooklyn Museum houses one of the finest art collections in the United States. Its strengths include an outstanding collection of Native American art from the Southwest; American period rooms; exquisite pieces of ancient Egyptian and Islamic art; and important American and European paintings.

ARTS OF AFRICA, THE PACIFIC, AND THE AMERICAS

The Brooklyn Museum set a precedent in the United States in 1923 by exhibiting African objects as works of art rather than artifacts. Since then, the African art collection has grown steadily in both importance and size.

Exhibits include a rare intricately carved ivory gong from the Benin kingdom of 16th-century Nigeria, one of only five in existence.

The museum also has a notable collection of Native American work, including totem poles, textiles, and pottery. A 19th-century deerskin shirt, once worn by a chief of the Blackfoot tribe, depicts his brave and daring exploits in battle.

Ancient American artistic traditions are represented by Peruvian textiles, Central American gold, and Mexican sculpture. A beautifully preserved tunic from Peru, dating from AD 600, is so tightly woven that its vibrant symbolic designs appear to have been painted onto the cloth rather than woven in the traditional manner.

The Oceanic collection includes sculpture from the Solomon Islands, Papua New Guinea, and New Zealand.

Seated Buddha torso in limestone, from India (late 3rd century AD)

ASIAN ART

Changing exhibitions from the museum's permanent collection of Chinese, Japanese, Korean, Indian, Southeast Asian, and Islamic art are always on display. Japanese and Chinese paintings, Indian miniatures, and Islamic calligraphy complement the Asian sculpture, textiles, and ceramics. The collections of Japanese folk art, Chinese cloisonné (enamel work), and Oriental carpets are of particular note. Good examples of Buddhist art range from a variety of Chinese, Indian, and Southeast Asian Buddhas to a mandala-patterned temple banner from 14th-century Tibet, painted in rich, luminous watercolors.

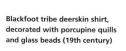

Blackfoot tribe deerskin shirt, decorated with porcupine quills and glass beads (19th century)

DECORATIVE ARTS

The decorative arts collection reflects changes in domestic life and design from the 17th century to the present.

The Moorish Smoking Room, from John D. Rockefeller's brownstone house, embodies elegant New York living in the 1880s. There is also a 1928–30 Art Deco study from a Park Avenue apartment, including a walk-in bar that was hidden behind paneling during the Prohibition era (see pp30–31).

More than 350 items from the museum's collection of silver, furniture, ceramics, and textiles are featured in the Luce Center for American Art. Although centered mostly on American art, the selection also includes pieces of Native American and Spanish colonial art.

Normandie chrome pitcher, by Peter Müller-Munk (1935)

The Luce galleries are arranged thematically and explore crucial moments and ideas in American visual culture over the past 300 years. Among the collection are pieces by John Singer Sargent, Frank Lloyd Wright, and Georgia O'Keeffe.

EGYPTIAN, CLASSICAL, AND ANCIENT MIDDLE EASTERN ART

Recognized as among the world's finest, the Egyptian collection holds many masterpieces. It begins with an early female figure dating from 3500 BC, and encompasses sculptures, statues, tomb paintings, and reliefs as well as funerary paraphernalia. Of the latter, the most unusual is the coffin of an ibis, probably recovered from the vast animal cemetery of Tuna el-Gebel in Middle Egypt. The ibis was a sacred bird representing the god Thoth, and this coffin is made of solid silver and wood overlaid with gold leaf, with rock crystal for the bird's eyes. These galleries have been renovated into a state-of-the-art, high-tech installation.

Among the artifacts from the Greek and Roman civilizations are statuary, pottery, bronzes, jewelry, and mosaics.

Among the Ancient Near and Middle Eastern exhibits are an extensive collection of pottery and 12 alabaster reliefs from the Assyrian palace of King Ashurnasirpal II. These date from around 883-859 BC and depict the king fighting, overseeing his crops, and purifying the "sacred tree," a major icon in Assyrian religion.

PAINTING AND SCULPTURE

This section contains works from the 14th century to the present, including a well-known and outstanding 19th-century French art collection with works by Degas, Rodin, Monet, Cézanne, Matisse, and Pissarro. It also boasts one of the largest holdings of Spanish

Pierre de Wiessant (about 1886) by Auguste Rodin, from his *Burghers of Calais* group

Colonial paintings and one of the best collections of North American paintings to be found in the United States.

The museum's 20th-century American collection includes, appropriately, *Brooklyn Bridge* by Georgia O'Keeffe.

The Sculpture Garden holds architectural ornamentation taken from demolished New York buildings, including statues rescued from the original Penn Station, and a replica of the Statue of Liberty.

PRINTS, DRAWINGS, AND PHOTOGRAPHS

The museum has an important collection of prints, drawings, and photographs that are constantly rotated for conservation purposes. The range includes a rare woodcut print by Dürer entitled *The Great Triumphal Chariot* and works by Piranesi. The Impressionist and Post-Impressionist collection includes works by Toulouse-Lautrec and Mary Cassatt, the only American woman associated with the Impressionist movement. There are lithographs by James McNeill Whistler, Winslow

Rotherhithe, an etching by James McNeill Whistler (1860)

Homer engravings, and a superb selection of drawings by Fragonard, Paul Klee, Van Gogh, Picasso, and Gorky, among others, many of them in black and white.

The photography collection consists mainly of works by major 20th-century American photographers, including a 1924 portrait of Mary Pickford by Edward Steichen and work by Margaret Bourke-White, Berenice Abbott, and Robert Mapplethorpe.

Sandstone reliefs from Thebes in Egypt (around 760–656 BC), depicting the great god Amun-Re and his consort Mut

Staten Island

Apart from the famous ferry ride, Staten Island and its attractions are not well known to New Yorkers in general. Residents feel so ignored, in fact, that they've talked about seceding from the city. Visitors who venture beyond the ferry terminal, however, will be pleasantly surprised to find hills, lakes, and greenery, with expanses of open space, amazing harbor views, and well-preserved early New York buildings. One of the biggest surprises here is a cache of Tibetan art that is hidden away in a replica of a Buddhist temple.

Historic Richmond Town 24

441 Clarke Ave. *Tel (718) 351-1611.*
S74 from ferry. ☐ Sep–Jun:
1–5pm, Wed–Sun; Jul–Aug: 10am–
5pm Wed–Sat, 1–5pm Sun.
☐ Jan 1, Easter Sun, Thanksgiving,
Dec 25. 🖼 🖸 ♿ 🚻 🎞 🏠
www.historicrichmondtown.org

Cologne at the General Store

There are now 29 buildings, 14 of which are open to the public, in New York's only restored village and outdoor museum. The village was first named Coccles-town, after the local shellfish, but was soon corrupted to "Cuckoldstown," much to the annoyance of the residents. By the end of the Revolutionary War the new name of Richmondtown had been adopted. It was the county seat until Staten Island was made part of the city in 1898, and has been preserved as an example of an early New York settlement.

The Voorlezer House, built in the Dutch era before 1696, is the oldest elementary school to be found in the country. The Stephens General Store, which opened in 1837, doubled as the local post office. It has been well restored, right down to the contents of the shelves. The complex, set on 100 acres (40 ha), includes wagon sheds, a courthouse built in 1837, houses, several shops, and a tavern. There are also seasonal workshops where traditional rural crafts are demonstrated to visitors.

St. Andrew's Church, dating to 1708, and its old graveyard are just across the Mill Pond stream, and the Historical Society Museum is in the County Clerk's and Surrogate's Office. The toy room is a delight.

Jacques Marchais Museum of Tibetan Art 25

338 Lighthouse Ave. *Tel (718) 987-3500.* S74 from ferry. ☐ 1–5pm
Wed–Sun. ☐ public hols. 🖼 🖸
🏠 www.tibetanmuseum.org

A hilltop provides a tranquil setting for one of the largest collections of privately owned Tibetan art of the 15th to the 20th centuries outside Tibet. The main building is a replica of a mountain monastery with an authentic altar in three

Sacred sculpture at the Jacques Marchais Center of Tibetan Art

The Voorlezer House at Richmond Town

tiers, crowded with gold, silver, and bronze figures.

The second building is used as a library. The soothing garden has some stone sculptures, including life-size Buddhas. The museum was built in 1947 by Mrs. Jacques Marchais, a dealer in Asian art. The Dalai Lama paid his first visit here in 1991.

A gezebo at the Snug Harbor Cultural Center

Snug Harbor Cultural Center 26

1000 Richmond Terrace.
Tel (718) 448-2500. S40 from
ferry to Snug Harbor Gate.
Grounds ☐ dawn–dusk daily.
Art Gallery ☐ 10am–5pm Tue–Sun.
🖼 donation. **Children's Museum**
☐ noon–5pm (summer 11am–5pm)
Tue–Sun. ☐ Jan 1, Thanksgiving,
Dec 25. ♿ limited. 🎞 🏠
www.snug-harbor.org

Founded in 1801 as a haven for aged sailors, Snug Harbor is now an arts center, with a complex of 28 buildings in various stages of restoration. There are five stately Greek Revival gems dating from 1831 to 1880, the finest such collection in the US. The oldest, the Main Hall, is the

Visitors' Center. This leads through to the **Newhouse Center for Contemporary Art**, but the ships in the stained-glass windows are a reminder of its origins. Other buildings house the award-winning **Staten Island Children's Museum** and Veterans Memorial Hall, used for indoor performances. A sculpture festival and summer shows are held on the lawns. The Staten Island Botanical Garden has a noted orchid collection and a beautiful rose garden.

Snug Harbor is the legacy of a Scottish sailor, Robert Richard Randall, who became rich in the Revolutionary War and bequeathed this property to be used by seamen, enabling them to enjoy its harbor views.

Clear Comfort, Alice Austen's lifetime residence

Alice Austen House ㉗

2 Hylan Blvd. *Tel (718) 816-4506.*
S 51 from ferry to Hylan Blvd.
noon–5pm Thu–Sun; grounds:
to dusk. Jan, Feb, public hols.
Donation limited.
www.aliceausten.org

This small cottage built around 1690 has the delightful name of Clear Comfort. It was the home of the photographer Alice Austen, who was born in 1866 and who lived in this house for most of her life. She documented life on the island, in Manhattan, and also on trips to other parts of the country and on her travels to Europe. She lost all her money in the stock market crash of 1929, and her poverty forced her into a public poorhouse at the age of 84. One year later, her photographic talent was finally recognized by *Life* magazine, which published an article about her, earning her enough money to enter a nursing home. She left 3,500 negatives dating from 1880 to 1930. Today, the Friends of Alice Austen House mounts exhibitions of her best work.

Even Farther Afield

The village of Broad Channel at Jamaica Bay

Jamaica Bay Wildlife Refuge Center ㉘

Cross Bay Blvd at Broad Channel. *Tel*
(718) 318-4340. M *Broad Channel*
(A). sunrise to sunset; visitor center:
8:30am–5pm daily. seasonal (call
ahead) www.nps.gov/gate

The marshes and uplands of the Refuge cover an area almost the size of Manhattan. Over 300 species of birds live here either seasonally or all year round. On the main Atlantic migratory path, the Refuge is at its best in spring and autumn, when the skies are filled with skeins of geese and ducks. The park rangers lead hikes and nature walks for weekend visitors – wear suitable shoes and clothes, and take along a zoom-lens camera or binoculars to get the best from your visit. The only village is Broad Channel, a small collection of houses on pilings on the Cross Bay Boulevard. The Refuge and a 10-mile (16-km) stretch of beach and boardwalk at Rockaway, are accessible by subway from Manhattan.

Jones Beach State Park ㉙

Beaches. all year. late
May–Labor Day. *Tel (516) 785-1600.*
www.nysparks.state.ny.us/parks
Long Island Railroad: Penn Station
to Jones Beach; train schedule (late
May–Labor Day); (718) 217-5477.
Jones Beach Theater; (516) 221-
1000. www.jonesbeach.com

Jones Beach was the creation of Robert Moses, New York's Parks' Commissioner *(see p246)*, who transformed this narrow spit of land into Long Island's most accessible and popular beach in 1929. There are sand dunes, surf on the Atlantic side, and sheltered water in the bay. There is also miniature golf, swimming pools, restaurants, and the **Jones Beach Theater**, which hosts concerts in the summer.

Robert Moses State Park is on the next island to the east, Fire Island, which is over 30 miles (48 km) long, yet less than 900 yds (800 m) across. Areas of the island are totally unspoiled, with long stretches of white sands, making it a great place for walking and bicycling in peaceful surroundings. Fire Island also has one of the few remaining forests on the Eastern Seaboard.

Fire Island's communities are small and varied. Some are favored by singles looking for the company of the opposite sex, others are sedate and family-orientated, and still others are favorites with New York's large gay community.

Sunbathers basking at Jones Beach

SEVEN GUIDED WALKS

Walking in New York is an excellent way to discover the human scale of the city. The following 16 pages explore the unique character and charm of New York through seven thematic walks. These range from an exploration of Greenwich Village and SoHo's literary and artistic connections (*see pp260–61*)

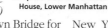

Sculpture outside US Custom House, Lower Manhattan

to a trip across the Brooklyn Bridge for spectacular views and a glimpse of 19th-century New York (*see pp266–7*).

In addition, each of the 15 areas of Manhattan described in the *Area by Area* section of this book has a

short walk on its *Street-by-Street* map, taking you past many of the interesting sights in that area.

Various organizations run walking tours of the city. These range from serious appraisals of architectural history to a guide to the ghosts of Broadway. Details of tour organizers are listed on page 387. Although New York's crime rate has dropped to a record low, as in any major city take extra care of your personal belongings while walking (*see p372–3*). Plan your route ahead and walk only during daylight hours.

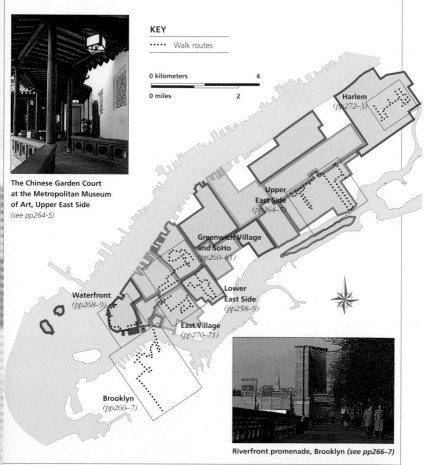

The Chinese Garden Court at the Metropolitan Museum of Art, Upper East Side
(see pp264–5)

KEY

••••• Walk routes

0 kilometers   4

0 miles   2

Harlem
(pp272–3)

Upper East Side
(pp264–5)

Greenwich Village and SoHo
(pp260–61)

Waterfront
(pp268–9)

Lower East Side
(pp258–9)

East Village
(pp270–71)

Brooklyn
(pp266–7)

Riverfront promenade, Brooklyn (see pp266–7)

◁ Relaxing on Grove Street, Greenwich Village (see pp260–61)

A 90-Minute Walk in the Lower East Side

This walk is through old immigrant neighborhoods that have given New York its unique flavor, and illustrates the ever-changing texture of the city as neighborhoods are rediscovered and one set of newcomers replaces another. Along the way you can experience a variety of cultures and cuisines. Sunday is the best day for local color. See more about Lower East Side on pages 92–101.

The Lower East Side

Begin on East Houston Street, the border between the Lower East Side and the East Village, where some of the best traditional Jewish cuisine can be found at Yonah Schimmel Knish Bakery ① (137) and Russ & Daughters ② (179), run by the great-grandson of the founder and famed for smoked fish and caviar. Katz's Delicatessen ③ (205) has been a fixture for over 100 years. Continue to Norfolk Street and turn right to see the Angel Orensanz Center ④ (172), housed in New York's oldest synagogue building.

Turn right on Rivington for another synagogue survivor, the Shaarai Shomoyim First Romanian-American Congregation ⑤ (89) in a handsome 1890 brick building. The interior, while shabby, is still impressive.

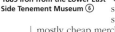

An 1885 iron from the Lower East Side Tenement Museum ⑥

The Lower East Side has been discovered by hip young New Yorkers and is now home to cutting-edge boutiques, trendy clubs, and restaurants. On Rivington cool fashion shops share the blocks with the old. Make a left onto Orchard Street, the traditional center of the Jewish Lower East Side. Pushcarts that lined the block are gone and the sidewalk stands sell mostly cheap merchandise, but many stores offer discount designer leather and fashion. All are closed on Saturday, so Sunday is the busiest day.

A must stop for historians is the Lower East Side Tenement Museum ⑥ (108 Orchard). An original tenement has been restored to show how three immigrant families lived from 1874 to the 1930s.

A detour across Broome Street on Orchard brings you to Guss' Pickle Company ⑦ (85–7), which was the inspiration for the 1988 film *Crossing Delancey*. Customers still line up for the crunchy pickles sold from barrels.

Come back to Broome and turn left for another unique survivor, the Kehila Kedosha Janina Synagogue and Museum ⑧ (280 Broome), a small but fascinating congregation with a little upstairs museum.

Another left along Eldridge will take you, beyond Canal Street, to the grand Eldridge Street Synagogue ⑨ (12), the first Eastern European synagogue in New York, which also houses a museum on the Jewish community.

TIPS FOR WALKERS

Starting point: *East Houston St.*
Length*: 2 miles (3.2 km).*
Getting there: *Take the subway F or V to Second Avenue; exit East Houston at Eldridge. Other stops: F to Delancey, J, M, Z to Essex. The M15 bus stops on East Houston and on the corner of Delancey and Allen Streets, M14A and M9 run along Essex Street. Returning from Chinatown-Little Italy, Canal Street station is served by the J, M, N, Q, R, W, and 6 trains.*
Stopping-off points: *Little Italy's cafés are perfect for coffee and cakes. For more substantial fare, Sweet-n-Tart at 20 Mott Street is good for Chinese food, or for Italian on Mulberry Street, Il Cortile (125) or Il Palazzo (151). Il Laboratorio del Gelato, at 95 Orchard Street, is a popular spot in summer, offering dozens of flavors of ice cream and sorbet.*

KEY

••• Walk route

✲ Good viewing point

[M] Subway station

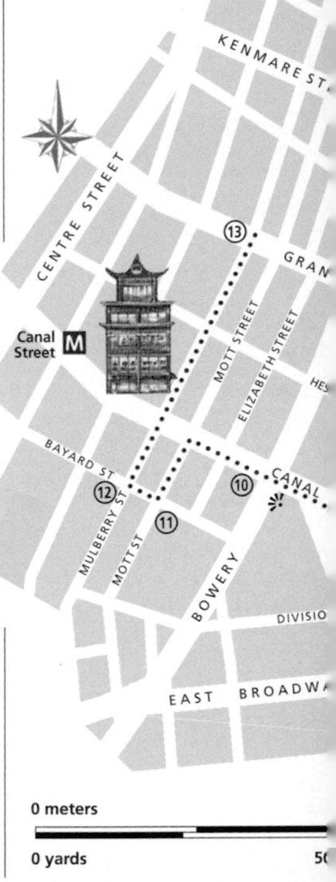

Clothes vendors at Orchard Street market

Guss' Pickle Company ⑦

M Essex
Street

M Delancey
Street

M East Broadway

EAST BROADWAY

Chinatown

Turn around and return to Canal Street, pausing to admire the spire of the Chrysler Building and the city skyline in view in the distance from Eldridge. Turn left and cross the Bowery, where many jewelry shops remain, remnants of the city's original Diamond District ⑩ (1). As you continue, the shops give way to stalls selling an exotic array of vegetables, and butcher shops

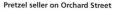

Pretzel seller on Orchard Street

with rows of roast ducks in the windows. At 200 Canal Street is Kam Man Food Products. One of the largest Chinese markets in the area, it is a fascinating place to explore. Turn left from Canal to Mott Street and you'll know you are right in the heart of Chinatown by all the Chinese neon signs. There are hundreds of restaurants here, from holes-in-the-wall to haute cuisine, all offering a chance to taste

Kam Man Food Products at 200 Canal Street

unusual fare. For spiritual sustenance. visit the Eastern States Buddhist Temple ⑪ in Mott Street (64b).

At Bayard Street, turn left to see all the Chinese political posters and messages on the Wall of Democracy, then turn back and walk to Mulberry Street. The curve next to Columbus Park was Mulberry Bend ⑫, once notorious for gang murders and mayhem.

An Italian deli in Little Italy ⑬

Little Italy

Walk up Mulberry Street toward Grand Street and you are suddenly in Little Italy ⑬. Small in area though it is, and encroached on by Chinatown, this is a colorful few blocks of old-world restaurants, coffee shops, and stores selling homemade pasta, sausages, breads, and pastries. The Italian population has dwindled over the years, but a staunch group of merchants remain, determined to retain the area's Italian atmosphere. Their stronghold is Mulberry Street between Broome and Canal streets, with a few shops holding their own on Grand Street near Mulberry. If you continue to walk on Grand, however, you are quickly back into Chinatown.

The big event of the year is the Feast of San Gennaro, named for the patron saint of Naples. For 11 nights in September, Mulberry Street is jammed with locals and visitors enjoying the parades and the Italian food, with rows of sizzling sausages stalls.

A 90-Minute Walk in Greenwich Village and SoHo

A stroll through the patchwork quilt of streets in Greenwich Village takes you to where New York's best-known writers and artists have lived, worked, and played. It ends with a tour of SoHo's galleries and museums, where established artists show their work. For more details on sights in Greenwich Village, see pages 108–15, and for SoHo sights, *see pages 102–07.*

Author Mark Twain, who lived on 10th Street

West 10th Street

The junction of 8th Street and 6th Avenue ① has many book, music, and clothing stores nearby. Walk up Sixth to West Ninth Street to see (on the left at 425) Jefferson Market Courthouse ②.

Turn right at West 10th Street ③ to the Alexander Onassis Center for Hellenic Studies (58). A passageway at the front once led up to the Tile Club, a gathering place for the artists of the Tenth Street Studio, where Augustus Saint-Gaudens, John LaFarge, and Winslow Homer lived. Mark Twain lived at 24 West 10th Street, and Edward Albee at 50 West 10th.

Back across Sixth Avenue is Milligan Place ④, with 19th-century houses, and Patchin Place ⑤, where the poets E. E. Cummings and John Masefield both lived. Farther on is the site of the Ninth Circle bar ⑥ which when it opened in 1898 was known as "Regnaneschi's." It was the subject of John Sloan's painting *Regnaneschi's Saturday Night*. Playwright Edward Albee first saw the question "Who's afraid of Virginia Woolf?" scrawled on a mirror here.

TIPS FOR WALKERS

Starting point: *8th St/6th Ave.*
Length: *2 miles (3.2 km).*
Getting there: *Take subway train A, B, C, D, E, F or V to West Fourth Street-Washington Square station (Eighth Street exit). Fifth Avenue buses M2 and M3 stop at Eighth Street. From here, walk one block west to Sixth. The M5 bus loops around Washington Square back to Sixth Avenue and Eighth Street.*
Stopping-off points: *The Pink Tea Cup, 42 Grove Street, is good for lunch. Fanelli's Café, 94 Prince Street, has been serving customers since 1847 and was once a speakeasy.*

The unusual exterior of Twin Peaks ⑨

Greenwich Village

Turn left at Waverly Place past the Three Lives Bookstore (154 West 10th St), a typical literary gathering spot, to Christopher Street and the Northern Dispensary ⑦.

Follow Grove Street along Christopher Park to Sheridan Square, the busy hub of the Village. The Circle Repertory Theater ⑧, which premiered plays by Pulitzer Prizewinner Lanford Wilson, is now closed.

Facade in Washington Mews ⑬

Cross Seventh Avenue and bear left on to Grove Street. At the corner of Bedford Street, you can't miss "Twin Peaks" ⑨ (102 Bedford), a home for artists in the 1920s.

Turn back around to look at the northeast corner of Bedford and Grove streets ⑩: the exterior of this edifice had a recurring role in the TV sitcom *Friends* as the characters' apartment building. 75½ Bedford is the narrowest house in the Village, and was once the home of feminist poet Edna St. Vincent Millay.

Walk up Carmine to Sixth Avenue and turn right at Waverly Place. At 116 Waverly ⑪, Anne Charlotte Lynch, an English teacher, held weekly gatherings in her town house for such eminent friends as Herman Melville and Edgar Allan Poe, who gave his first reading of *The Raven* here.

A detour left of just half a block will bring you to MacDougal Alley ⑫, a lane of carriage houses in which Gertrude Vanderbilt Whitney had her studio. She opened the first Whitney Museum here in 1932, just behind the studio.

Washington Square

Back on MacDougal, turn left to Washington Square North, to see the finest Greek Revival houses in the United States. Built of red brick, they have marble balustrades and entrances flanked by columns. Writer Henry James set his *Washington Square* in No. 18, his grandmother's home.

Washington Square Park and Arch

SoHo

Walk south on Thompson, a typical Village street lined with bars, cafés, and shops. Turn left at Houston, SoHo's northern limit, and right on West Broadway, lined with some of the city's most famous galleries along with a large number of chic and arty boutiques.

Turn left at Spring Street for yet more tempting shops, then right at Greene Street ⑮, which is the heart of the Cast-Iron Historic District. Many of these fine buildings now house art galleries.

Turn left at the end of Greene Street to Canal Street, the end of SoHo, to see how quickly the atmosphere of New York can change. This noisy street is full of hawkers and discount electronics stores. You can explore bargains for the next two blocks and then turn left up Broadway. Keen shoppers can turn right on Spring Street and head for the NoLita district, featuring clothes by trendy, aspiring designers.

Pause at Fifth Avenue to look back at Washington Square Park, with its famous Washington Square Arch. Go across to Two Fifth Avenue; opposite is Washington Mews ⑬, an elegant carriage house complex. John Dos Passos, Edward Hopper, and Rockwell Kent lived in the studio at No. 14a at various times.

Go back up Washington Square North, past some elegant houses. Writer Edith Wharton lived at 7 Washington Square North. Now walk beneath the arch and across Washington Square Park. On the left as you leave the park, is the fine Judson Memorial Church and Tower ⑭ by Stanford White and the NYU Loeb Student Center. The Center was once a boarding house, known as the "house of genius," and is where Theodore Dreiser wrote *An American Tragedy*.

0 meters　　　　　500

0 yards　　　　　500

KEY

• • • Walk route

⁂ Good viewing point

Ⓜ Subway station

Cast-iron facade, Greene Street ⑮

Subway entrance in wintertime, near Bryant Park ▷

A Two-Hour Walk in the Upper East Side

A promenade along upper Fifth Avenue and its environs will take you past the best remaining examples of New York's turn-of-the-century gilded age. A detour through the old German district of Yorkville leads to a riverside stroll to Gracie Mansion, official residence of the city's mayor, dating from 1799. For details on Upper East Side sights, *see pages 182–203*.

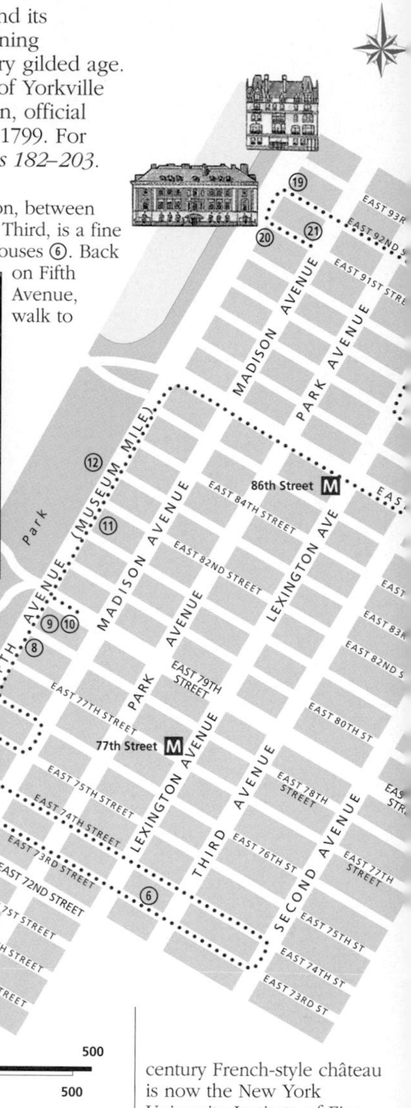

From the Frick to the Met

Begin at the Frick mansion ①, built in 1913–14 for coal magnate Henry Clay Frick and home to an exquisite art collection *(pp202–3)*. Many such mansions were built as New York's first families outdid each other with miniature Versailles châteaux and Venetian palazzos. Most of those still standing have now become either institutions or museums. The apartment building opposite the Frick is typical of those where today's affluent New Yorkers live.

Church of the Holy Trinity ⑰

East on 70th are two of the city's top art galleries, Knoedler & Co (19) and Hirschl & Adler ② (21). Walk up Madison to the corner of 72nd Street, to the big Polo-Ralph Lauren store ③, the 1898 French Renaissance home of Gertrude Rhinelander Waldo. Wander inside to see the elegant restored interior.

Walk back toward Fifth on the north side of 72nd, past two limestone beauties that once housed the Lycée Français de New York ④. Continue along Fifth Avenue to 73rd Street. Turn east to 11, Joseph Pulitzer's former home ⑤. A few blocks on, between Lexington and Third, is a fine row of town houses ⑥. Back on Fifth Avenue, walk to 75th Street, to see No. 1, the former residence of Edward S. Harkness, son of a founder of Standard Oil. It is now the Commonwealth Fund ⑦. At 1 East 78th, the tobacco millionaire James B. Duke's 18th-century French-style château is now the New York University Institute of Fine Arts ⑧.

At 79th Street and Fifth, the former home of financier Payne Whitney, is the French Embassy ⑨, and 2 East 79th is the Ukrainian Institute of America ⑩. On the southeast corner of 82nd Street is Duke-Semans House ⑪, one of the few grand Fifth Avenue residences that are still privately owned. Save another full day for The Metropolitan Museum of Art ⑫ at 82nd.

Ukrainian Institute of America ⑩

◁ Entrance to subway station in wintertime in Bryant Park

Carl Schurz Park Promenade

TIPS FOR WALKERS

Starting point: *Frick Collection.*
Length: *3 miles (4.8 km).*
Getting there: *Take subway train 6 to 68th Street and Lexington, then walk west (left) three blocks to Fifth Avenue. Or take the M1, M2, M3, or M4 bus up Madison Avenue to 70th Street and walk one block west.*
Stopping-off points: *Try the cafés at the Whitney and Guggenheim museums. Head to Café Sabarsky at the Neue Galerie (5th Ave/ 86th St) for Austrian food, or try the Heidelberg Café (2nd Ave off 86th St) for authentic Bavarian. Madison Avenue between 92nd and 93rd has many places to eat, including Sarabeth's Kitchen, with its excellent weekend brunch.*

Yorkville

Turn east on 86th Street for what is left of German Yorkville – Bremen House ⑬, cross Second Avenue, then turn right to the Heidelberg Café and German deli Schaller & Weber ⑭ for a break, or try Papaya King's hot dogs (179 East 86th Street).

East River and Gracie Mansion

Henderson Place ⑮ at East End Avenue is a cluster of 24 Queen Anne town houses. Carl Schurz Park opposite was named for the city's most prominent German immigrant, editor of *Harper's Weekly* and the *New York Post*. The park promenade atop East River Drive leads to a view of Hell Gate, where the Harlem River, Long Island Sound, and New York harbor meet. From the walkway you can see the back of Gracie Mansion ⑯, the mayor's official residence. Walk west on 88th Street past the Church of the Holy Trinity ⑰ and at Lexington Avenue go to 92nd Street and west past two of the few wooden houses left in Manhattan ⑱.

KEY

• • • Walk route

⚜ Good viewing point

Ⓜ Subway station

The Cooper-Hewitt Museum ⑳

Carnegie Hill

Back on Fifth Avenue, turn downtown past the Felix Warburg Mansion of 1908, now the Jewish Museum ⑲, and continue to 91st Street and the huge Andrew Carnegie home, now the Cooper-Hewitt Museum ⑳. Built in 1902 in the style of an English country manor, it gave the area the unofficial name of Carnegie Hill. The James Burden House ㉑ at 7 East 91st Street, built for Vanderbilt heiress Adele Sloan in 1905, has a spiral staircase under a stained-glass skylight that was known in society as "the stairway to heaven." At 1 East 91st, the financier Otto Kahn's Italian Renaissance-style residence was a show-place with a drive-through porch and interior courtyard. It is now the Convent of the Sacred Heart School.

Wooden houses on 92nd Street ⑱

A Three-Hour Walk in Brooklyn

A trip across New York's most famous crossing leads to Brooklyn Heights, the city's first suburb. This neighborhood has a 19th-century feel, mixed with a hint of Middle Eastern cultures. The riverfront promenade has unrivaled views of Manhattan. For more details on sights in Brooklyn, *see pages 247–53.*

Fire Station on Old Fulton Street

Fulton Ferry Landing

About 3,580 ft (1 km) long, the Brooklyn Bridge span yields thrilling views of the lower New York skyline and prize photo opportunities. Take a taxi, or if you have time, walk across to Brooklyn.

On the far side, follow the Tillary Street sign to the right, turn right at the bottom of the stairs, then take the first path through the park and walk down Cadman Plaza West ① under the Brooklyn-Queens Expressway; here Cadman becomes Old Fulton Street. You can see the bridge on the right as you head to the river at Water Street and the Fulton Ferry landing ②. During the Revolutionary War, George Washington's troops fled to Manhattan from here. In 1814, this was the depot for the ferry connecting Brooklyn and Manhattan Island. This transformed Brooklyn Heights from a predominantly farming area to a residential district. The area is full of character and is still a very popular place to live. To the right is the River Café ③. This restaurant's fine cuisine and spectacular views of the Manhattan skyline make it one of New York's most exceptional dining spots. Double back past the former Eagle Warehouse ④ of 1893.

Eagle Warehouse ④

Brooklyn Heights

From the landing, turn right to steep Everitt Street up Columbia Heights, on to Middagh Street, and along the streets of Brooklyn Heights. 24 Middagh ⑤ is one of the oldest, built in 1824.

Next turn right on Willow and left on Cranberry; here the town houses range from wooden clapboards to brick Federal-style to brownstones. Except for cars and a few modern buildings, you could be in the 19th century.

Many famous people have lived here. Truman Capote wrote *Breakfast at Tiffany's* and *In Cold Blood* in the basement of 70 Willow, and Arthur Miller once owned 155 Willow. Walt Whitman lived on Cranberry Street when he was editor of the *Brooklyn Eagle*. He set the type for his *Leaves of Grass* at a print shop near the corner of Cranberry and Fulton. The town houses now on the site are called Whitman Close.

Turn right along Hicks. The Hicks family, local farmers, inspired the name "hick" for a yokel. Turn left on Orange Street to the Plymouth Church ⑥, home of Henry Ward Beecher, an antislavery preacher. His sister, Harriet

Entrance to the River Café ③

Truman Capote with feathered friend

Beecher Stowe, wrote *Uncle Tom's Cabin*. Meander along Henry and Pineapple streets. At Clark Street are marquees of once-luxurious hotels, such as the Towers. Follow Clark Street to 142 Columbia Heights, where Norman Mailer lived ⑦. Washington Roebling, architect of the Brooklyn Bridge, lived at 110.

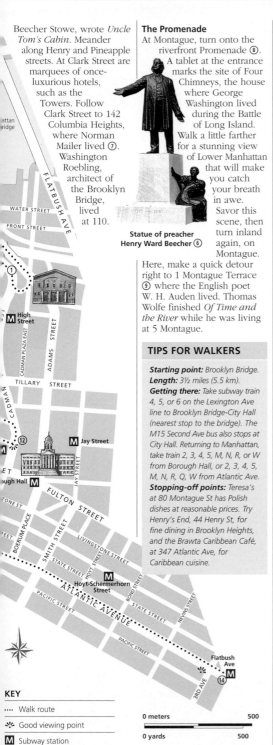

Statue of preacher Henry Ward Beecher ⑥

The Promenade

At Montague, turn onto the riverfront Promenade ⑧. A tablet at the entrance marks the site of Four Chimneys, the house where George Washington lived during the Battle of Long Island. Walk a little farther for a stunning view of Lower Manhattan that will make you catch your breath in awe. Savor this scene, then turn inland again, on Montague. Here, make a quick detour right to 1 Montague Terrace ⑨ where the English poet W. H. Auden lived. Thomas Wolfe finished *Of Time and the River* while he was living at 5 Montague.

TIPS FOR WALKERS

Starting point: Brooklyn Bridge.
Length: 3½ miles (5.5 km).
Getting there: Take subway train 4, 5, or 6 on the Lexington Ave line to Brooklyn Bridge-City Hall (nearest stop to the bridge). The M15 Second Ave bus also stops at City Hall. Returning to Manhattan, take train 2, 3, 4, 5, M, N, R, or W from Borough Hall, or 2, 3, 4, 5, M, N, R, Q, W from Atlantic Ave.
Stopping-off points: Teresa's at 80 Montague St has Polish dishes at reasonable prices. Try Henry's End, 44 Henry St, for fine dining in Brooklyn Heights, and the Brawta Caribbean Café, at 347 Atlantic Ave, for Caribbean cuisine.

The old Montague Street trolley, which led to the river and the ferry

Montague and Clinton Streets

Once back on Montague Street, walk to the heart of Brooklyn Heights, with all its cafés and boutiques. The baseball team, the Brooklyn Dodgers, got their name from dodging the trolley cars that once ran down the street. Walk to the intersection of Montague and Clinton to see the stained glass of the 1834 Church of St. Ann and the Holy Trinity ⑩. Walk a block left on Clinton to Pierrepont Street for the Brooklyn Historical Society ⑪. A block farther, at Court Street, is the 1849 Borough Hall ⑫, and the subway taking you back to Manhattan.

Brooklyn's Dodgers, who got their name from dodging trolley cars

Atlantic Avenue

Another option is to stay on Clinton Street and walk the five short blocks to Atlantic Avenue. A left turn here leads to a whole string of Middle Eastern emporia, such as Sahadi Imports ⑬ at 187 Atlantic Avenue, which stocks a huge selection of foods. The Damascus Bakery at 195 makes the most delicious filo pastries. Various other shops here sell Arabic books, tapes, DVDs, and CDs.

At Flatbush Avenue, look left to the Brooklyn Academy of Music ⑭ and the grand front of the Williamsburg Savings Bank. Watch for signs to the subway for your journey back to Manhattan.

KEY

···· Walk route

☆ Good viewing point

Ⓜ Subway station

0 meters   500

0 yards   500

A 90-Minute Waterfront Walk

From the breezy Battery Park City Esplanade with its sweeping river views and upscale condos to the magnificent schooners moored at South Street Seaport, this waterfront amble introduces you to New York's formidable maritime legacy. The concrete jungle may lie just a few blocks inland, yet it seems worlds away, as the bleating horns and hiss of the crosstown buses are blessedly muffled. Stroll the green tip of Battery Park for a startling reminder that Manhattan is, in fact, an island. For more details on sights in Lower Manhattan, *see pp64–79.*

View of the Statue of Liberty from the waterfront promenade

The many photographs at the Museum of Jewish Heritage ⑤

Battery Park City

Begin your walk on the Esplanade ① near Rector Place Park, just west of the Rector Street subway stop. Across the Hudson River looms the New Jersey skyline. Stroll toward the South Cove ②, where you'll catch sight, as did more than 100 million immigrants on their arrival, of Lady Liberty herself. Explore Robert F. Wagner, Jr. Park ③, named after a former New York City mayor. The leafy acres of grassy slopes, linden trees, and inviting pavilions are an important link in Lower Manhattan's waterfront "greenbelt". Climb to the Wagner Park lookout point ④ for vistas of the Hudson River. Here, information panels chronicle New York City's seafaring history when grand schooners and coastal packets plied these waters.

Battery Place

On Battery Place, visit the Museum of Jewish Heritage ⑤ *(see p77)* and its outdoor Garden of Stones, a calm, elegant space of dwarf oak saplings growing out of boulders. Since Manhattan is the undisputed king of tall buildings, pay homage at the sleek Skyscraper Museum ⑥, a marvel in stainless steel. Admire skyscraper history and current designs from around the world, as well as the original model, created in 1971, of the former World Trade Center.

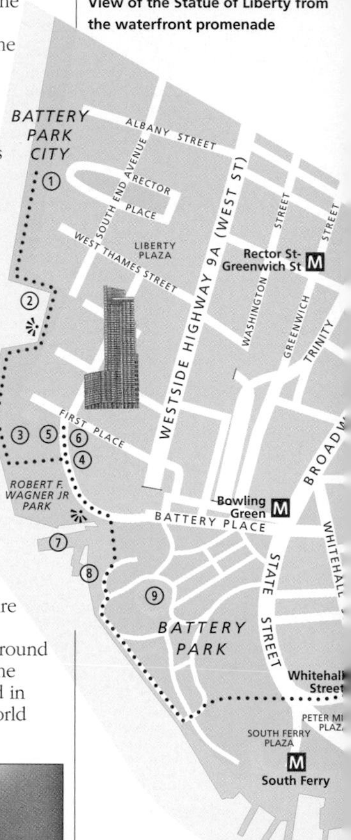

Shiny surfaces and sharp angles at the Skyscraper Museum ⑥

Castle Clinton, an early 19th century fort built to defend the harbor ⑨

Battery Park

On your way to nearby Battery Park, check out Pier A ⑦, which is all that remains of the 1886 grand marine firehouse. Important visitors who arrived by sea were once greeted with festive jets of water pumped into the sky by the fireboats. The clock on the pier tower used to keep time to the maritime system – eight bells and all's well. Continue along the waterfront, looking out for the American Merchant Mariners Memorial ⑧, a haunting sculpture of soldiers pulling a desperate comrade out of the waters, based on photographs of a World War II attack on an American ship. Head past Castle Clinton

Enjoying a well-earned rest at a café, South Street Seaport ⑬

monument ⑨, a fort built during the War of 1812. It later became an opera house, theater, and aquarium, but is now a museum. Stroll through the park where you can relax on benches in the shade of trees. Continue on to State Street, turn right on Whitehall, and then left onto South Street, passing the graceful Beaux Arts Battery Maritime Building ⑩.

South Street Seaport

Follow South Street, with the Brooklyn Bridge in the distance. Walk through the Vietnam Veterans Memorial Plaza ⑪ with its glass memorial etched with the poignant words from soldiers to their loved ones. Head north on Water Street, so named because it marks what was once the water's edge, and past Old Slip; all streets named "slip" are where boats used to dock between piers. Look west up the famed Wall Street ⑫ *(see pp66–7)* as you

cross it, for a view of the spires of Trinity Church *(see p68)*. Turn right at Maiden Lane, then left onto the quaint and cobblestoned Front Street, which feeds into South Street Seaport ⑬ *(see pp82–5)*, marked by the wooden masts and sails of the tall ships in the harbor. Explore New York's seafaring history at the South Street Seaport Museum, and then wander the shop-lined Fulton Street to Water Street. Take a peek into Bowne & Co Stationers at 211 ⑭, a charming old-fashioned print shop with 19th-century antique hand presses. Amble toward Pier 16 for a further glimpse of the past at the Maritime Crafts Center ⑮ where painters and carvers work at figureheads and carvings. Continue on to Pier 17 ⑯, bustling with shops and cafés. As you walk the wooden pier, look back for a memorable view of Manhattan – the masts of ancient schooners against the city's towering skyscrapers. Finish up at the inviting Paris Café in the 1873 Meyer's Hotel *(see p83)*.

TIPS FOR WALKERS

Starting point: The Esplanade near Rector Place.
Length: 2 miles (3.2 km).
Getting there: Take subway train 1, R, or W to Rector Street. Head west on Rector Street, cross the bridge over West Street to Rector Place, and walk to the Esplanade.
Stopping-off points: Gigino, on Wagner Park at 20 Battery Place, offers savory Italian fare outdoors.

KEY

• • • Walk route

☆ Good viewing point

Ⓜ Metro station

0 meters	300
0 yards	300

A 90-Minute Walk in the East Village

Originally the farm or *bouwerie* of the Stuyvesant family, this historic area now has a different appeal with its musical and artistic associations, as well as many of the city's interesting and affordable ethnic bars and restaurants. It also manages to balance a peaceful residential area with business and creativity, which is reflected in the constantly changing funky record shops, vegan cafés, craft stores, and live music clubs. For more details on sights in the East Village, *see pp116–21.*

Astor Place

Adjacent to the Astor Place subway stop is a black steel cube called the *Alamo* ① – a meeting point for students and skateboarders. Walk towards Third Avenue through the large buildings that comprise Cooper Union ② *(see p120).* This scholarship college was founded in 1859 by Peter Cooper, an illiterate but successful businessman and proponent of free education. Across the street is the Continental ③, a live music venue that has hosted groups such as Iggy Pop and Guns N' Roses. In the East Village, 8th Street becomes St. Mark's Place ④, a former jazz, then hippie, then punk hangout. With so many sidewalk cafés and street vendors, this is one of the busiest pedestrian areas of Manhattan. St. Mark's Ale House ⑤ on the right, formerly The Five Spot, was where musicians and poets got together in the 1960s. A few steps down is Trash and Vaudeville ⑥, a clothing store that was once the Bridge Theater. The venue was repeatedly shut down due to controversial acts, then reopened. Yoko Ono held "happenings," and the US flag was burned as an anti-war protest in 1967. At 19–25 St. Mark's Place ⑦, there was a Jewish hangout, then the Italian mafia ruled, until Andy Warhol turned the space into the infamous nightclub Electric Circus in the 1960s. The Velvet Underground was among the bands who played here. To check out their albums, stop at Kim's Video ⑧ nearby, which stocks obscure music and movies.

Locals enjoying celebrations on Ukrainian Day

Little Ukraine

Turn left onto Second Avenue, home of the largest and longest-standing Ukrainian population in the US, with restaurants, bars, and centers such as the Ukrainian National Home ⑨ on the right (140), and the good-value,

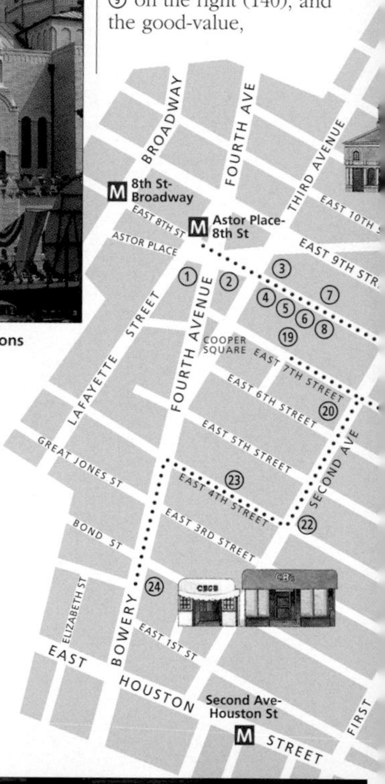

Trash and Vaudeville store, once a venue known for controversial acts ⑥

TIPS FOR WALKERS

Starting point: *The Alamo.*
Length: *1.75 miles (2.8 km).*
Getting there: *Take the subway train 6 to Astor Place. Or take M101, M102, or M103 buses.*
Stopping-Off Points: *Many good-value places on St. Mark's Place, but try Jules Bistro (French) between 1st and 2nd avenues, and Caracas Arepa Bar (cheap Venezuelan) at 93½ East 7th St.*

The style and elegance of an earlier century at Veniero's ⑫

Tompkins Square Park

Built in 1834, this square has seen political activism of all kinds. It is also where a sacred elm tree in the middle of the park ⑮ commemorates the first Hare Krishna ceremony on American soil. Jazz great Charlie Parker lived across the street from the park from 1950–55 ⑯. Walk to the southwestern corner on 7th Street where 7A ⑰ serves breakfast 24 hours a day. Down the block, Turntable Lab 04 ⑱ sells DJ equipment and vinyl. If thirsty, continue west toward Second Avenue to McSorley's Old Ale House ⑲, one of the oldest bars in the city. Then get back onto Second Avenue and turn right to see where the old Fillmore East Auditorium ⑳ used to be (105). This classic rock scene featured such legends as The Doors, Jimi Hendrix, Janis Joplin, and Pink Floyd. The Who even premiered their rock opera *Tommy* here. Look left at 6th Street – "Indian Restaurant Row" ㉑ – where Bengali curry houses compete for business. Go down Second Avenue to number 80 ㉒; this was the home of Joe "The Boss" Masseria, head of the Italian mob in the 1920s. Turn right onto 4th Street where KGB bar ㉓, on the right, is a literary institution. A final left on Bowery leads to the former site of CBGB & OMFUG ㉔, or Country, Bluegrass, Blues & Other Music For Uplifting Gormandizers, birthplace of American rock band Talking Heads.

24-hour Ukrainian eaterie Veselka ⑩ on the corner. Farther up Second Avenue, at East 10th Street, sits the St. Mark's-in-the-Bowery Church ⑪ *(see p121)*. Erected in 1795, this church was Dutch governor Peter Stuyvesant's private chapel and he is buried here. More recently, the Black Panthers and Young Lords gathered here, and Allen Ginsberg and other notable writers contributed to The Poetry Project that exists to this day. A right on 11th Street leads to Veniero's ⑫, a stylish Italian bakery that still has many of its original details, such as hand-stamped metal ceilings. Make a right and then a left onto 10th Street, past the three-story Russian and Turkish Bath House ⑬, to the northern edge of Tompkins Square Park ⑭ *(see p121)*.

Elm tree in Tomkins Square Park, a Hare Krishna memorial ⑮

KEY

••• Walk route

Ⓜ Metro station

| 0 meters | 200 |
| 0 yards | 200 |

"Indian Restaurant Row", lined with curry houses ㉑

A 90-Minute Walk in Harlem

Few neighborhoods in New York are as rich in cultural history as Harlem, a haven for African-American heritage. This walk starts in Strivers' Row, one of the few areas that provided affordable housing during the 1920s and 1930s when the area flourished with creative and intellectual expression. It takes you past renowned gospel churches, jazz and blues clubs, and ends at the Apollo Theater, Harlem's famous showcase for new artists. For more details on sights in Harlem, *see pp220–31*.

Apollo Theater, famous for televised shows and legendary acts ⑭

Strivers' Row

The tree-lined area on 138th Street between Seventh and Eighth avenues is the St. Nicholas Historic District, commonly known as Strivers' Row ①. In the 1920s and 1930s wealthy and influential black professionals aiming for better lives moved into homes designed by such great architects as James Brown Lord and McKim, Mead & White. Signs on some of the gates still read "Private road walk your horses." A short detour left on Seventh Avenue (Adam Clayton Powell, Jr. Boulevard) and right on 139th Street leads to West 139th Street ②, where in 1932 16-year-old Billie Holiday moved into No. 108 shortly before landing her first singing job at a club in nearby "Jungle Alley."

An ornate doorway in Strivers' Row ①

Abyssinian Baptist Church

Turn right at Lenox Avenue and right back onto 138th Street toward the striking Abyssinian Baptist Church ③ *(see p229)*, which is internationally renowned for its magnificent Sunday gospel service. Founded in 1921 and named for the East African Americans of its first congregation, this church has hosted such notable pastors as Adam Clayton Powell, Jr. A stone's throw away on West 137th Street is the Mother Zion church ④, New York's first black church and one of America's oldest. While part of the Underground Railroad (an escape route for slaves), it acquired the nickname "Freedom Church." Continue to the Countee Cullen Regional Library where Madam C.J. Walker founded the Walker School of Hair ⑤. With her successful cosmetics line and hair-smoothing system, Walker was one of the first self-made female millionaires in the country. An active philanthropist, she donated to many African-American charities such as the National Association of Colored People (NAACP) and Tuskegee Institute. After her death in 1919, her daughter A'Leila turned the salon into an intellectual center for artists, scholars, and activists. It was named "The Dark Tower" after Harlem writer Countee Cullen's protest poem. Around the corner on Lenox Avenue is the Schomburg Center for Research into Black Culture ⑥ *(see p229)*, a national research library named for the Puerto Rican-born black scholar who donated his personal collection to the library and served as its curator for six years. Down West 136th Street is Montgomery ⑦, a whimsical women's clothing store with one-of-a-kind designs. Farther down at No. 267 is "Niggerati Manor" ⑧, an artist's rooming house, so-named by Zora Neale Hurston, who lived here while collaborating with Wallace Thurman, Aaron Douglas, and Bruce Nugent on *Fire!!*, a magazine devoted

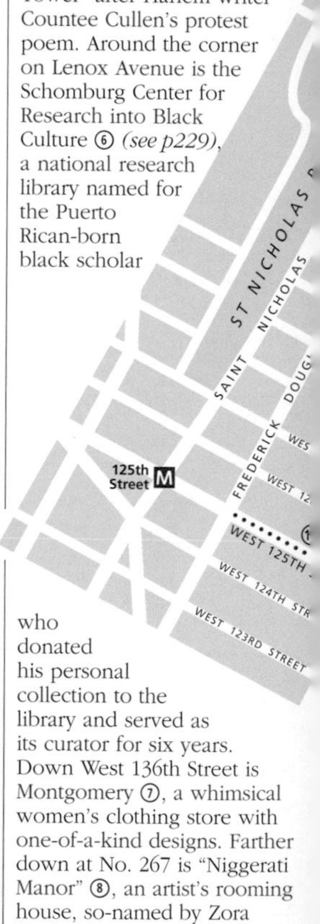

The famous Sylvia's restaurant, providing authentic soul food ⑪

to young black artists. Get back on Adam Clayton Powell, Jr. Boulevard and follow it down to "Jungle Alley" ⑨, the former highlight of Harlem nightlife, which once contained numerous bars, clubs, cabarets, and speakeasies. A detour across 131st Street will bring you to Marcus Garvey's house ⑩ (235), a major leader and fierce proponent of black unity, economic independence, and

Art displays at the Schomberg Center for Research into Black Culture ⑥

The great jazz singer Billy Holiday ②

"Jungle Alley," where Billie Holiday first performed ⑨

all performed. It is also home to the Zebra Room, a jazz spot that James Baldwin and Malcolm X frequented. In the middle of the next block is The Studio Museum in Harlem ⑬ (see pp230–31), with a variety of contemporary art exhibits, programs, lectures, and performances by artists of African descent. Its store is also worth a browse for its array of posters and books.

Apollo Theater

On West 125th Street is the famous Apollo Theater ⑭ (see p230), where since 1934, "stars are born and legends are made." These performers have ranged in style from Ella Fitzgerald to James Brown. Since 1987, "Amateur Night at the Apollo" has been televised nationwide and the theater has become the third-most popular tourist destination in Manhattan.

pride. Return to Adam Clayton Powell, Jr. Boulevard and make a left on 127th Street until you reach Sylvia's Restaurant ⑪ (see p230), the self-proclaimed "Queen of Soul Food." Family-owned since 1962, Sylvia's serves authentic southern favorites, such as fried chicken, catfish, and BBQ ribs. Stay on Lenox Avenue until 125th Street; here you'll find Lenox Lounge ⑫ where Billie Holiday, Miles Davis, and John Coltrane have

KEY

••• Walk route

M Metro station

TIPS FOR WALKERS

Starting point: Strivers' Row.
Length: 1.75 miles (2.8 km)
Getting there: Take subway train 2 or 3 to 135th St and Lenox Ave, then walk north to 138th St and west to Seventh Ave. Or take M2, M7, or M10 bus to 135th St and walk to Seventh Ave.
Stopping-off Points: Sylvia's on 127th and Lenox is the famous soul food place in Harlem. It is the perfect place to refuel.

TRAVELERS' NEEDS

WHERE TO STAY

With over 75,000 hotel rooms available, New York offers something for everyone. The city's top hotels are the most expensive in the US, but the best news for visitors is the increase in budget and mid-priced hotels. While many of these are basic rather than charming, they offer good value. Other budget options are furnished apartments and studios, and bed and breakfasts, as well as youth hostels and YMCAs. From an inspection of over 200 hotels in New York, we have selected the best of their kind. The hotels listed on pp280–91 contain detailed descriptions of facilities, which will help you select the one best suited to your needs. Most hotels have a website address to enable you to book a room online.

Cole Porter's piano, in the Waldorf Astoria bar *(see p288)*

luxury hotels, as prices drop *(see Special Rates p278)*. There are a growing number of good value all-suite hotels available in every price category. Suites offer extra space plus cooking facilities and a refrigerator. Most suites can accommodate up to four people, which makes them popular with families.

HIDDEN EXTRAS

When calculating the cost of hotels in New York, it is not enough simply to take into consideration the quoted room price. Hotel rooms have long been subject to extra taxes, but the former sliding scale, which favored rates under $100, has now given way to a blanket 13.375% hotel tax, plus $3.50 per night per room fee.

Several hotels now include continental breakfast in the room price. This is a big saving, since standard hotel continental breakfast prices, before tax and tip, start at about $5 and soar to around

Rooftop terrace at the Peninsula New York *(see p289)*

WHERE TO LOOK

The East Side, roughly between 59th and 77th streets, is the traditional location for luxury hotels, but the renovation of certain landmark midtown properties, such as the St. Regis, and the arrival of new hotels in famous chains, such as the Peninsula Group and Jumeirah Hotels, have considerably increased the competition in this price range.

Business travelers tend to favor midtown, especially the moderately priced hotels lining Lexington Avenue near Grand Central Terminal. Those seeking relative quiet with access to midtown should look in the Murray Hill area, while theater-lovers should note the revival of the Times Square area, where there are many hotels within walking distance of the Theater District.

There are a number of good, inexpensive hotels around Herald Square, which is convenient for shopping.

Trendy boutique hotels have flourished in SoHo and the Meatpacking District, where there are also plenty of good bars, restaurants, and upscale shops *(see pp320–21)* as well as trendy nightclubs.

New York & Co. (the Convention and Visitors Bureau) publishes a free, annually updated leaflet called "The New York Hotel Guide," listing current rates and toll-free numbers. Staff will offer advice about hotels but do not make reservations on your behalf.

HOTEL PRICES

Some hotels offer seasonal promotional rates and other off-peak reductions. For example, business travelers vacate hotels at the end of the working week, and you can take advantage of bargain weekend deals, even in

Antique furnishings, Inn at Irving Place *(see p283)*

◁ Tourists consult map on busy New York street

The Tribeca Grand lobby *(see p281)*

$25 in some of the luxury hotels. To save money, head for the nearest deli or coffee shop and leave the hotel to business people having power breakfasts.

Hotel telephone charges are always high; it is much less expensive to use the pay phone in the lobby, particularly when you are calling overseas.

Tips are expected. Staff who take your luggage to the room are usually tipped a minimum of $1 per bag – more in a luxury hotel. The concierge need not be tipped for normal services such as arranging transportation or making dinner reservations, but should be rewarded for exceptional services. When you order from room service,

check the menu to see whether a service charge will also be included in the bill; if not, a 15–20% tip is customary. Solo travelers will find that single room rates are usually at least 80% of the double rate and are sometimes the same as for two people.

FACILITIES

Although you'd expect hotel rooms in New York City to be noisy, most windows are double- or even triple-glazed to keep out the noise. Air-conditioning is a standard feature, so there is no need to open the windows in hot weather. Even so, some rooms are obviously quieter than others, especially if they are at the back of the hotel or overlooking a courtyard – check when reserving. Light sleepers may also want to request a room away from the elevator.

Television, radio, and at least one telephone are usually provided in every room, even in modest lodgings, and most hotel bedrooms have private bathrooms. In budget and mid-priced hotels a shower, rather than a tub, is the norm. Many hotels offer fax outlets and machines in each room, internet access, a business center, and a health club or exercise room. Luxury facilities include minibars in the room, dual phones, private phone message systems, and electronic checkout.

Most of the hotels listed here are within a few minutes' walk of shops and restaurants. Few hotels have their own parking, but valets may park your car in nearby garages. A reduced (but still expensive) daily parking fee is normally offered. If there is no concierge at the hotel, front desk staff will always help to answer any queries.

Understated elegance at the stylish Kitano *(see p288)*

DIRECTORY

HOW TO RESERVE

It is advisable to make hotel reservations at least one month in advance, otherwise you may well find that the best rooms and suites have been taken. The busiest periods are at Easter, the New York Marathon week in late October or early November, Thanksgiving and Christmas.

Reserve directly with the hotel online, or by telephone, letter, or fax. Internet bookings on Expedia.com and Hotels.com often yield the best deals. Written confirmation of your telephone booking will be required, probably with a deposit as a guarantee of your arrival; any cancellation fees may be deducted from this. You can pay by credit card, international bank draft or money order, or US traveler's check. Advise the staff if you are going to arrive at the hotel after 6pm or you will lose your reservation, unless you have prepaid with a credit card.

You can also book a hotel through your travel agent or airline. Most hotels have a toll-free telephone number for use in the United States, but these numbers do not work from Europe and the UK. If the hotel is part of an international chain, an affiliated hotel in your country should be able to reserve a room for you.

SPECIAL RATES

Hotels are busiest during the week, when business travelers are in the city, so most of them offer budget weekend packages. It's often possible to move from a standard to a luxury room for the weekend at the same rate. A lower corporate rate is usually available to employees of large companies. Quite often, reservation clerks will grant corporate discounts on request without asking for a company affiliation. It is also worth checking a hotel website for special deals and promotions.

Some reservation agencies offer discount rates. A good travel agent should be able to get the best rates, but compare prices by contacting directly a discount reservation service such as Hotel con-x-ions or Quikbook *(see p277)*, which offers discounts of 20–50%, depending on the time of year. You reserve by credit card and receive a voucher, which you present to the hotel. Sites such as www.kayak.com offer "private sales" of discounted hotel rooms.

Lobby of the St. Regis Hotel *(see p289)*

Package tours can also provide savings. Their rates may not oblige you to stay with a tour group, only to use their air and hotel arrangements. They may also include airport transfers, an additional saving. Airlines frequently have special deals, particularly during slow travel seasons. A knowledgeable travel agent should be able to tell you the current best deals, but newspapers often advertise special, limited offers that can be booked directly. At off-peak times you may net even bigger savings than with the package plans.

DIRECTORY

DISABLED TRAVELERS

Mayor's Office for People with Disabilities
100 Gold St,
2nd floor, NY,
NY 10038.
Tel *(212) 788-2830.*
www.nyc.gov/mopd

BED & BREAKFAST

At Home in NY
Tel *(212) 956-3125.*
www.athomeny.com

Bed and Breakfast Network of New York
Tel *800-900-8134.*
www.bedandbreakfast
netny.com

CountryInn The City
Tel *(212) 580-4183.*
www.countryinnthe
city.com

YOUTH HOSTELS AND DORMITORIES

Big Apple Hostel
119 W 45th St,
NY, NY 10036.
Map 12 E5.
Tel *(212) 302-2603.*
www.bigapplehostel.com

Hosteling International, NY
891 Amsterdam Ave at W 103rd St, NY, NY 10025.
Map 20 E5.
Tel *(212) 932-2300.*
www.hinewyork.org

New York's Jazz Hostels
Tel *(212) 722-6252.*
www.jazzhostels.com

92nd St Y
1395 Lexington Ave,
NY, NY 10128.
Map 17 A2.
Tel *(212) 415-5650.*
www.92y.org

YMCA-Vanderbilt
224 E 47th St,
NY, NY 10017.
Map 13 A5.
Tel *(212) 756-9600.*
www.ymcanyc.org

YMCA-West Side
5 W 63rd St, NY,
NY 10023.
Map 12 D2.
Tel *(212) 875-4273.*
www.ymcanyc.org

DISABLED TRAVELERS

By law, new hotels must provide facilities for disabled visitors. Many older buildings have also been renovated so as to comply with this regulation.

To find out which hotels offer the best facilities, check their websites. These are provided for all the hotels listed on pp280–91. When booking, let the hotel know of any specific needs. Guide dogs are allowed in most hotels, but it is also advisable to check in advance.

The **Mayor's Office for People With Disabilities** also offers information about hotels.

TRAVELING WITH CHILDREN

American hotels are generally very welcoming toward children. Cots or cribs as well as lists of reliable baby-sitters are usually available, and most hotel restaurants are happy to cater to young guests.

Traveling with children can be cheaper than anticipated. Many hotels do not charge for children if they stay in their parents' room, or make only a small charge for an extra bed. There is usually a limit of one or two children per room in these cases, and most hotels stipulate that the children must be under a certain age, most often 12. Parents of older children are expected to pay the full price, although the age limit is occasionally extended to 18. Ask about family rates when you make your reservation.

BED-AND-BREAKFAST

An increasing number of bed-and-breakfast accommodations in private apartments is available in New York. These can vary from a room in an apartment with an owner-host in residence to an entire self-contained apartment with its own kitchen and bathroom, which you have to yourself while the owner is away.

Staying in a private apartment has certain advantages. It enables you to feel at home in a New York neighborhood and to visit local restaurants,

Entrance to the Peninsula Hotel *(see p289)*

which are usually far more reasonably priced than those in tourist areas.

Bed-and-breakfast lodgings can be found through many free booking services. Some booking agencies have a two-or-more-night minimum.

Rates for unhosted apartments vary from about $100 to $300, and for a double room start at $100 a night, depending on whether you have a private bathroom. There is a wide range of apartments, from spacious and luxurious to cramped and dowdy. Be aware that, if the address is remote or inconveniently far from bus routes or subway stations, your costs will rise, as you will need frequent cabs. Ask about location and amenities when you reserve.

YOUTH AND BUDGET ACCOMMODATIONS

New York's youth hostel and its many **YMCA** dormitories offer lodgings for those on a tight budget. For the longer-term visitor, the **92nd Street Y**, a nonsectarian hostel in the Upper East Side, has good-value rooms, with prices starting from around $35 to $50 a night.

Sky-high swimming pool at a luxury hotel

There are no campsites in Manhattan, and, sadly, youth hostels are not as prevalent in New York as they are in large European cities.

For budget-minded travelers looking for the bare essentials, inexpensive rooms are available in several areas of New York, particularly in Chelsea, the Garment District, and the Upper West Side, and to a lesser extent in such prime neighborhoods as the Upper Midtown. Although some of these budget-price rooms are reasonably comfortable, with private baths or showers, others may be rather small, perhaps with no air conditioning, and you may have to share a bathroom.

Other interesting sources for budget lodgings are websites like www.couchsurfing.com, which has many member-hosts in New York, and www.airbnb.com, where locals offer accommodation in their homes for a very reasonable fee.

Finally, another way to make your budget go further is to avoid having breakfast in your hotel. Even its coffee shop is likely to be more expensive than an outside coffee shop or deli.

BEYOND MANHATTAN

As New York City becomes safer – and Manhattan more expensive – accommodation options are emerging in the outer boroughs for savvy travelers. Indeed, areas such as Williamsburg and Dumbo in Brooklyn have become destinations in their own right over the past few years, thanks to a rising number of cool bars, good restaurants, and trendy stores.

For a little over $300, which buys an average room in Manhattan, you can book a king room at the Marriott Brooklyn Bridge in Brooklyn Heights *(see p291)*, or a room with flat-screen TV and wireless internet access at the four-star boutique hotel Le Bleu, in the up-and-coming area of Gowanus, close to Park Slope (www.hotellebleu.com).

As always, cheaper deals can often be negotiated or found on hotel websites.

Choosing a Hotel

These hotels have been selected across a wide price range for their good value, excellent facilities, and location. This chart lists the hotels by area of the city in the same order as the rest of the guide. Within each area, entries are listed alphabetically within each price category, from the least expensive to the most expensive.

PRICE CATEGORIES
For a standard double room per night, inclusive of breakfast, service charges, and any additional taxes:

$ under $150
$$ $150–$250
$$$ $250–$350
$$$$ $350–$450
$$$$$ over $450

LOWER MANHATTAN

Best Western Seaport Inn Downtown $$

33 Peck Slip, 10038 **Tel** *(212) 766-6600* **Fax** *(212) 766-6615* **Rooms** *72*   **Map** *2 D2*

You'll feel like you're stepping into a 19th-century sailor's haunt at this property with views of Brooklyn Bridge. Families enjoy the deluxe breakfast and the lounge with coffee and tea. The 24-hour fitness center is large. Upgrade to a room with a terrace if you can. **www.seaportinn.com**

Embassy Suites New York $$$

102 North End Ave, 10282 **Tel** *(212) 945-0100* **Fax** *(212) 945-3012* **Rooms** *463*   **Map** *1 A2*

This all-suite hotel is a great bet for families. Two-room accommodations feature fold-out couch beds. Fantastic views of the harbor and discounted weekend rates. The hotel is located near Battery Park City and the Statue of Liberty ferry, but is quite far from the subway. **www.embassysuites.com**

Gild Hall $$$

15 Gold St, 10038 **Tel** *(212) 232-7700* **Fax** *(212) 425-0330* **Rooms** *126*   **Map** *2 D2*

This luxury hotel boasts, among other features, a bi-level private library, an elegant champagne bar, a modern English tavern, and über-sleek guest rooms. The mini bars are stocked by Dean & DeLuca, and the king suites even have chandeliers. **www.thompsonhotels.com**

Marriott New York City Financial Center $$$

85 West St, 10006 **Tel** *(212) 385-4900* **Fax** *(212) 227-8136* **Rooms** *497*   **Map** *1 B3*

This hotel in the heart of Financial District is modern and grand, and even offers an indoor pool. All rooms have luxurious bedding, and some offer views of the Statue of Liberty and New York Harbor. Primarily a business hotel, this property sometimes offers great weekend rates. **www.nycmarriottfinancial.com**

Ritz Carlton Battery Park $$$

2 West St, 10004 **Tel** *(212) 344-0800* **Fax** *(212) 344-3801* **Rooms** *298*   **Map** *1 B4*

Telescopes in the elegantly modern rooms offer spectacular close-up views of the Statue of Liberty and New York Harbor. Bathrooms are sleek and large, while business travelers are well catered for with numerous programs and amenities. Afternoon tea is served in the bar. **www.ritzcarlton.com**

The Wall Street Inn $$$

9 South William St, 10004 **Tel** *(212) 747-1500* **Fax** *(212) 747-1900* **Rooms** *46*   **Map** *1 C3*

Rates can drop to bargain levels on weekends at this business-targeted hotel. The early-American interiors keep it from feeling stuffy, and the professional service is first class. While rooms can feel small, the beds are comfortable. Score a corner room for a whirlpool tub. Continental breakfast included. **www.thewallstreetinn.com**

LOWER EAST SIDE

Off SoHo Suites Hotel $$

11 Rivington St, 10002 **Tel** *(212) 979-9808* **Fax** *(212) 979-9801* **Rooms** *38*   **Map** *5 A3*

Trendy downtown neighborhoods have enveloped this budget spot making it a good choice for those wanting to be near SoHo or the Lower East Side. Small suites share facilities, while the larger ones come with private bathrooms and full kitchens, making it a good choice for bigger groups or families. **www.offsoho.com**

Blue Moon Hotel $$$

100 Orchard St, 10002 **Tel** *(212) 533-9080* **Fax** *(212) 533-9148* **Rooms** *22*   **Map** *5 A3*

The spacious rooms, views, and amenities would amaze former residents of this one-time Lower East Side tenement. Located on a historic block, it mixes memorabilia and nostalgia with modern luxuries that include hydro-massage baths, flatscreen TVs, and free Wi-Fi. A good base for exploring a resurgent neighborhood. **www.bluemoon-nyc.com**

Key to Symbols *see back cover flap*

Hotel on Rivington
⤵ 🅿 🍴 📺 ⓦ $$$

105 Rivington St, 10002 **Tel** *(212) 475-2600* **Fax** *(212) 475-5959* **Rooms** *110*   **Map** 5 A3

Even the glass-enclosed showers have a view in this chic, 21-story tower offering oversize rooms with floor-to-ceiling windows and a 360-degree vista. Guests enjoy a private lounge, a state-of-the-art fitness center, and many other amenities. A sign of the changes on the Lower East Side. **www.hotelonrivington.com**

Howard Johnson Express Inn
⤵ $$$

135 East Houston St, 10002 **Tel** *(212) 358-8844* **Fax** *(212) 473-3500* **Rooms** *46*   **Map** 5 A3

This hotel offers small yet clean budget rooms for checking out the trendy cafés and boutiques just outside. Steps away from the subway line and cheap eats, the location for young hipsters is hard to beat. Some rooms have microwaves and small fridges. The famous Katz's Deli is just a block away. **www.hojo.com**

SOHO AND TRIBECA

Cosmopolitan Hotel
⤵ ⓦ $

95 West Broadway, 10007 **Tel** *(212) 566-1900* **Fax** *(212) 566-6909* **Rooms** *125*   **Map** 1 B1

This budget gem is located in the heart of trendy TriBeCa. While rooms are small, they are well maintained, with equally tiny but clean bathrooms; most have complimentary Wi-Fi. The many top restaurants nearby and easy access to public transport make this a top budget recommendation. Also great for shopping. **www.cosmohotel.com**

Duane Street Hotel
⤵ 🅿 🍴 ⓦ $$$

130 Duane St, 10013 **Tel** *(212) 964-4600* **Fax** *(212) 964-4800* **Rooms** *45*   **Map** 1 B1

This intimate hotel features sleek minimalist decor. Rooms have flatscreen TVs, all the latest amenities, and walk-in showers. The 'Beca restaurant, offering New American fare, is small and inviting. Convenient for City Hall and the many restaurants of TriBeCa, plus SoHo and Chinatown. **www.duanestreethotel.com**

Holiday Inn Downtown
⤵ 🍴 🏃 $$$

138 Lafayette St, 10013 **Tel** *(212) 966-8898* **Fax** *(212) 941-5832* **Rooms** *227*   **Map** 4 F5

This basic property is a longtime favorite of those wishing to be close to New York's bustling downtown area. SoHo, Chinatown, the Lower East Side, and Little Italy are just steps away with boutique shops and restaurants galore. Rooms are simple but comfortable, and the in-house restaurant is good at a pinch. **www.hidowntown-nyc.com**

Smyth Tribeca
⤵ 🍴 🏃 ⓦ $$$

85 West Broadway, 10007 **Tel** *(212) 587-7000* **Rooms** *100*   **Map** 1 B1

Smyth Tribeca features a sleek modern design with classic touches. A high-ceilinged lobby with plush, fabric walls gives way to ample rooms with pale and dark woods, crisp linens, and marble bathrooms. Ease into the evening over a cocktail at the elegant hotel bar. **www.thompsonhotels.com**

Tribeca Grand Hotel
⤵ 🍴 🏃 📺 ⓦ $$$

2 Sixth Ave, 10013 **Tel** *(212) 519-6600* **Fax** *(212) 519-6700* **Rooms** *203*   **Map** 3 E5

The atrium lobby gives this hotel a grand look. The private screening room downstairs has long made this a favorite of celebrities. Rooms are sleekly designed and the bathroom amenities first-rate. Score a corner room or studio suite for the most space, and make sure to sip a drink in the lounge to maximize star sightings. **www.tribecagrand.com**

60 Thompson
⤵ 🍴 🏃 📺 ⓦ $$$$

60 Thompson St, 10012 **Tel** *(877) 431-0400* **Fax** *(212) 431-0200* **Rooms** *100*   **Map** 4 D4

This chic boutique hotel has an excellent Thai restaurant, Kittichai, and a summertime rooftop lounge/deck available only to guests and certain trendsetters. Rooms are minimalist yet comfortable with a pleasing palette tone, and have all the latest high-tech gadgets. Location is the star here. **www.60thompson.com**

SoHo Grand Hotel
⤵ 🍴 🏃 📺 ⓦ $$$$

310 West Broadway, 10013 **Tel** *(212) 965-3000* **Fax** *(212) 965-3200* **Rooms** *363*   **Map** 4 E4

Entertainment moguls and celebrities as well keep returning to this boutique favorite. Located in the middle of happening SoHo, the rooms are small and can seem dark despite the high windows offering views of downtown. A 24-hour room service and pet amenities keep guests happy. **www.sohogrand.com**

Greenwich Hotel
🍽 🅿 📺 ⓦ $$$$$

377 Greenwich St, 10013 **Tel** *(212) 941-8900* **Fax** *(212) 941-8600* **Rooms** *88*   **Map** 1 B1

Robert DeNiro and partners spared nothing in their luxurious eight-story hotel, which opened in 2008. Part rustic, part elegant eclectic style mixes Tibetan rugs, Moroccan tiles, old wood beams, and antique Asian art. Rooms are light and spacious, and there's a large salon and an outdoor terrace. Worth the splurge. **www.thegreenwichhotel.com**

The Mercer Hotel
⤵ 🍴 🏃 📺 $$$$$

147 Mercer St, 10012 **Tel** *(212) 966-6060* **Fax** *(212) 965-3838* **Rooms** *75*   **Map** 4 E3

This discreet boutique property comes at luxury prices, and celebrities seeking a bit more privacy have made this their choice. Rooms are designed as lofts with exposed brick and wooden floors. Bathroom tubs are large enough for two. Children are welcome – cribs featuring Frette linens are available. **www.mercerhotel.com**

GREENWICH VILLAGE

Washington Square Hotel
103 Waverly Place, 10011 *Tel* (212) 777-9515 *Fax* (212) 979-8373 *Rooms* 160 | | $$ | Map 4 D2

Just steps away from NYU, this hotel faces bustling Washington Square Park. The marble lobby leads to fresh, boutique-like rooms. The central location means higher-than-average rates, but great bars and restaurants are just around the corner. The on-site restaurant also offers good meals. **www.wshotel.com**

Abingdon Guest House
13 Eighth Ave, 10014 *Tel* (212) 243-5384 *Fax* (212) 807-7473 *Rooms* 9 | $$$ | Map 3 C1

This lovely guesthouse is located on one of the West Village's most beautiful brownstone- and boutique-lined streets. Each room has unique decor and is fitted with classic comforts. No on-site full-time staff means this gem is best suited to independent travelers. No breakfast, but there are coffee facilities. **www.abingdonguesthouse.com**

Gansevoort Hotel
18 Ninth Ave, 10014 *Tel* (212) 206-9700 *Fax* (212) 255-5858 *Rooms* 210 | $$$$ | Map 3 B1

A 45-ft (13.5-m) rooftop pool and Ono, an indoor-outdoor restaurant, are among the features that draw models and celebrities to this sleek, high-rise addition to the hip Meatpacking District. Rooms are a good size with plush feather beds, while bathrooms are luxurious, and the hotel spa lavish. **www.hotelgansevoort.com**

Soho House
59 Ninth Ave, 10014 *Tel* (646) 253-6122 *Rooms* 24 | $$$$$ | Map 3 B1

Sister to London's exclusive private club, the New York version is also a hotel where guests enjoy all facilities, including rooftop pool, sitting rooms, library, restaurant, and the Cowshed spa. Rooms with names like Playpen and Playground range from large to gigantic, with prices to match. **www.sohohouseny.com**

EAST VILLAGE

Union Square Inn
209 East 14th St, 10003 *Tel* (212) 614-0500 *Fax* (212) 614-0512 *Rooms* 40 | $ | Map 4 F1

All the standard comforts come at reasonable prices in this hotel. Rooms have no views and are nothing to write home about, but the beds are comfortable and bathrooms clean. European breakfast is on offer at the in-house café (limited hours). Union Square nearby is great for peoplewatching and shopping. **www.unionsquareinn.com**

Second Home on Second Avenue
221 Second Avenue, 10003 *Tel* (212) 677-3161 *Rooms* 7 | $$ | Map 4 F1

A guesthouse with a home-like feel and a loyal following, this well-priced lodging has private or shared baths and provides TV, air conditioning, and free Wi-Fi. An excellent home base for exploring the East Village and downtown neighborhoods, but you'll need to reserve well ahead. **www.secondhomessecondavenue.com**

The Bowery Hotel
335 Bowery, 10003 *Tel* (212) 505-9100 *Rooms* 135 | $$$$ | Map 4 F3

From the same duo who developed the Maritime in Chelsea comes this luxury lodging. An opulent 17-story hotel, it features lobby fireplaces and wood-paneled elevators, floor-to-ceiling windows in every room, and seven rooms with private terraces, hot tubs, and outdoor showers. The bar attracts a VIP scene. **www.theboweryhotel.com**

GRAMERCY AND THE FLATIRON DISTRICT

Hotel 17
225 East 17th St, 10003 *Tel* (212) 475-2845 *Fax* (212) 677-8178 *Rooms* 120 | $ | Map 9 B5

Young travelers love the location of this very basic budget option. Rooms are tiny with not much flair and some share baths. Woody Allen popularized this hotel in *Manhattan Murder Mystery* and supposedly Madonna stayed here as a young singer. Some cheap eats are nearby as is good mainstream shopping. **www.hotel17ny.com**

Hotel 31
129 East 31st St, 10016 *Tel* (212) 685-3060 *Fax* (212) 532-1232 *Rooms* 60 | $ | Map 9 A3

This sister property to Hotel 17 features 60 rooms, each decorated differently, although the style is typical chic floral print. Rooms have the basics such as air conditioning, televisions with cable, and some share baths. This area is a little quieter at night. **www.hotel31.com**

Key to Price Guide *see p280* **Key to Symbols** *see back cover flap*

Gershwin Hotel

$$

7 East 27th St, 10016 **Tel** *(212) 545-8000* **Fax** *(212) 684-5546* **Rooms** *150* **Map** *8 F3*

An original Andy Warhol *Campbell's Soup Can* in the lobby sets the tone of this pop art-inspired hotel. More art can be found on every floor. Rooms are bright and stylishly decorated. A tourist bargain, as it's just steps to the Empire State Building. Many reasonable restaurants nearby. **www.gershwinhotel.com**

Thirty Thirty

$$

30 East 30th St, 10016 **Tel** *(212) 689-1900* **Fax** *(212) 689-0023* **Rooms** *253* **Map** *9 A3*

The stylish rooms here are perfect for sophisticated travelers on a budget. While small, the rooms are quite comfortable with many twin-bedded rooms available as well as some with kitchenettes. The restaurant and lounge add to its attractions. Several trendy restaurants and shops nearby as well. **www.thirtythirty-nyc.com**

Hotel Roger Williams

$$$

131 Madison Ave, 10016 **Tel** *(212) 448-7000* **Fax** *(212) 448-7007* **Rooms** *193* **Map** *9 A3*

A stylish option for those with a little more to spend, and the amenities make it worth the price – free breakfast, all-day serve-yourself coffee and treats, and a DVD library. The rooms are soothing in blond woods and warm colors. Fifteen rooms have garden terraces. Seasonal discounts can make this more affordable. **www.hotelrogerwilliams.com**

Hotel Giraffe

$$$$

365 Park Ave South, 10016 **Tel** *(212) 685-7700* **Fax** *(212) 685-7771* **Rooms** *73* **Map** *9 A4*

Perhaps the Flatiron District's finest full-service luxury hotel, the rooms are decorated with custom furnishings invoking the Moderne style. Suites have French doors opening onto a Juliet balcony. A restaurant two doors down from the hotel offers superb cuisine and potent cocktails with a lounge scene. **www.hotelgiraffe.com**

Inn at Irving Place

$$$$

56 Irving Place, 10003 **Tel** *(212) 533-4600* **Fax** *(212) 533-4611* **Rooms** *12* **Map** *9 A5*

Edith Wharton would be proud of these antique brownstones buildings, run impeccably as a luxury inn. Each room features beautiful bathrooms, as well as modern technology such as CD players. Complimentary breakfast is served in the salon, and don't miss the high tea. **www.innatirving.com**

The Marcel at Gramercy

$$$$

201 East 24th Street, 10010 **Tel** *(212) 696-3800* **Fax** *(212) 696-0077* **Rooms** *135* **Map** *9 B4*

The Marcel reopened in 2008 after a makeover that added four floors, the Inoteca restaurant, and an airy lounge. Rooms have clean, modern decor; many were combined to offer larger spaces. Compact baths have walk-in showers with rainfall shower heads. Complimentary morning newspaper and coffee. **www.marcelatgramercy.com**

Gramercy Park Hotel

$$$$$

2 Lexington Ave, 10010 **Tel** *(212) 920-3300* **Fax** *(212) 673-5890* **Rooms** *185* **Map** *9 A4*

The Gramercy Park Hotel is an "eclectic-Bohemian" extravagance, oozing modern art, wood paneling, velvet, and state-of-the-art gadgets. Guests can relax on the private rooftop garden at the elegant Rose and Jade bars or in Gramercy Park itself (yes, the keys are available). **www.gramercyparkhotel.com**

CHELSEA AND THE GARMENT DISTRICT

Americana Inn

$

69 West 38th St, 10018 **Tel** *(212) 840-6700* **Fax** *(212) 840-1830* **Rooms** *50* **Map** *8 F1*

This is the place for the budget-minded traveler looking for the bare minimum essentials. Rooms have private sinks, and each floor features a shared kitchenette. The central location and friendly staff make a winning combination. Just be aware that the area is always busy and can get hectic and loud. **www.theamericanainn.com**

Chelsea International Hostel

$

251 West 20th St, 10011 **Tel** *(212) 647-0010* **Fax** *(212) 727-7289* **Rooms** *57* **Map** *8 D5*

Considered one of the city's best hostels, this complex features a series of low-rise buildings looking out on a central courtyard. Both private bunkbed rooms and shared dorm beds are available; all bathrooms are shared. Facilities include two fully-equipped kitchens, laundry machines, and TVs. **www.chelseahostel.com**

Chelsea Lodge

$

318 West 20th St, 10011 **Tel** *(212) 243-4499* **Fax** *(212) 243-7852* **Rooms** *22* **Map** *8 D5*

A lovingly restored townhouse in the Chelsea Historic District is the setting for this budget find. The small rooms have private sinks and showers, so guests only share toilet facilities. Perfect for independent travelers looking for a true NYC experience. **www.chelsealodge.com**

Chelsea Star Hotel

$

300 West 30th St, 10011 **Tel** *(212) 244-7827* **Fax** *(212) 279-9018* **Rooms** *34* **Map** *8 D3*

The interiors of this hotel are bright and upbeat if a bit garish. A life-size statue of Betty Boop greets you at the lobby, and there are plenty of contemporary art galleries nearby. Rooms here range from dormitory style to more upscale chic with four-poster beds and DVD players. Free Wi-Fi. **www.starhotelny.com**

Colonial House Inn

W $

318 West 22nd St, 10011 **Tel** *(212) 243-9669* **Fax** *(212) 633-1612* **Rooms** *20*   **Map** *8 D4*

While the owners of this lovely brownstone-turned-inn cater mostly to a gay male clientele, everyone is welcome. The well-maintained rooms have modern decor and Wi-Fi; almost half have private baths, and a few feature working fireplaces. Seasonal discounts apply. **www.colonialhouseinn.com**

Broadway Plaza Hotel

P W $$

1155 Broadway, 10001 **Tel** *(212) 679-7665* **Fax** *(212) 679-7694* **Rooms** *69*   **Map** *8 F3*

The renovations in 2007 nicely updated and modernized all rooms in this budget find. New bed linens, drapes, and carpets give each room a fresh look, with extras such as high-speed internet access. Complimentary breakfast. The neighborhood can be noisy at times. **www.broadwayplazahotel.com**

Chelsea Savoy Hotel

$$

204 West 23rd St, 10011 **Tel** *(212) 929-9353* **Fax** *(212) 741-6309* **Rooms** *90*   **Map** *8 E4*

One of the more modern options in Chelsea, this hotel has a devoted following of those who appreciate the consistent service. The rooms are pleasant though lacking in any extra touches. A good choice for those who appreciate the Chelsea restaurant, bar, and club scene. **www.chelseasavoynyc.com**

Comfort Inn Chelsea

$$

18 West 25th St, 10010 **Tel** *(212) 645-3990* **Fax** *(212) 633-8952* **Rooms** *121*   **Map** *8 F4*

Budget travelers enjoy the location of this modest find in hip Chelsea. The 1901 brick building offers clean rooms with TVs and refrigerators. The restaurant and coffee bar in the lobby are a draw, as are the nearby restaurants and art galleries. The suites, which sleep up to six, are a bargain. **www.choicehotels.com**

Hotel Chelsea

$$

222 West 23rd St, 10011 **Tel** *(212) 243-3700* **Fax** *(212) 675-5531* **Rooms** *400*   **Map** *8 E4*

Music history was made when punk legend Sid Vicious killed girlfriend Nancy Spungen here. Since then, famous personalities such as Sandra Bernhardt and post-Uma Ethan Hawke have stayed here. Some claim the large rooms and privacy are the draw, while others enjoy the bohemian, if somewhat dusty, furnishings. **www.hotelchelsea.com**

Hotel Metro

$$

45 West 35th St, 10001 **Tel** *(212) 947-2500* **Fax** *(212) 279-1310* **Rooms** *179*   **Map** *8 F2*

This Art Deco-inspired jewel is one of the best-priced mid-range hotels in midtown. Rooms are large and better decorated than most in this range. Rates include breakfast, and many enjoy the restaurant ambience and food. The real draw is the rooftop terrace with dramatic views of the Empire State Building. **www.hotelmetronyc.com**

Hotel Wolcott

$$

4 West 31st St, 10001 **Tel** *(212) 268-2900* **Fax** *(212) 563-0096* **Rooms** *250*   **Map** *8 F3*

The large rooms, low rates, and central location makes this a good choice for budget-minded travelers. While the rooms are plain, they are clean, and internet access is available. There are laundry facilities on the premises, and though there is no restaurant, cheap eats abound in the area. **www.wolcott.com**

Inn on 23rd

$$

131 West 23rd St, 10011 **Tel** *(212) 463-0330* **Fax** *(212) 463-0302* **Rooms** *14*   **Map** *8 E4*

This inn offers a perfect blend of bed-and-breakfast charm and full hotel service. Rooms and suites are uniquely decorated with extra touches such as pillow-top beds and plush Turkish terry towels in the bathrooms. Sumptuous breakfast served each morning. Highly recommended. **www.innon23rd.com**

Ace Hotel

P $$$

20 West 29th St, 10001 **Tel** *(212) 679-2222* **Rooms** *260*   **Map** *8 F3*

The Ace Hotel channels a youthful rock-n-roll vibe: many of the large rooms come with vintage furniture, full-size refrigerator, and even a turntable and guitar. The loft corner room has plenty of light and a large bathroom with claw-foot tub. Those on a budget can opt for the relatively cheap bunkbed rooms. **www.acehotel.com**

Four Points by Sheraton

$$$

160 West 25th St, 10001 **Tel** *(212) 627-1888* **Fax** *(212) 627-1611* **Rooms** *158*   **Map** *8 E4*

This budget-conscious hotel appeals to sophisticated travelers and business executives who are willing to spend a little more. Rooms are well designed and some have balconies with views of downtown, plus good service as you'd expect from this chain. **www.starwoodhotels.com/fourpoints**

The Maritime

$$$

363 West 16th St, 10011 **Tel** *(212) 242-4300* **Fax** *(212) 242-1188* **Rooms** *125*   **Map** *8 D5*

You can't help noticing the nautical theme of this hotel, since every room is centered around a porthole window with views of the Hudson River. This hip and happening place has rooms that are small but well designed, and several restaurants and bars, including the noted Matsuri. Lots of outdoor space too. **www.themaritimehotel.com**

Radisson/Martinique on Broadway

$$$

49 West 32nd St, 10001 **Tel** *(212) 736-3800* **Fax** *(212) 277-2702* **Rooms** *532*   **Map** *8 F3*

The landmarked French-Renaissance building houses this outpost of the reliable Radisson chain. Past the ornate lobby, the rooms have been restored to an elegant finish. Affordable Asian dining lines the blocks around the hotel, just steps away from some of the best tourist sites on the island. **www.radisson.com/newyorkny_broadway**

Key to Price Guide *see p280* **Key to Symbols** *see back cover flap*

THEATER DISTRICT

Best Western President Hotel
234 West 48th St, 10036 **Tel** *(212) 246-8800* **Fax** *(212) 974-3922* **Rooms** *334*   **Map** *12 E5*

Families prefer the junior suites with fold-out sofas for children, while the standard rooms work well for the typical traveler. This outpost of the chain hotel is well run with simple but clean rooms in a good location. Be aware that the area is always busy, so light sleepers might look elsewhere. **www.bestwestern.com**

Big Apple Hostel
119 West 45th St, 10036 **Tel** *(212) 302-2603* **Fax** *(212) 302-2605* **Rooms** *39*   **Map** *12 E5*

For prime location, this hostel is perfect for young travelers. While most beds are dormitory style (both single-sex and co-ed), a few private rooms with queen-size beds are available. Full kitchen facilities, and the backyard garden provide a respite from the harried streets of Manhattan. Book well in advance. **www.bigapplehostel.com**

Park Savoy Hotel
158 West 58th St, 10019 **Tel** *(212) 245-5755* **Fax** *(212) 765-0668* **Rooms** *70*   **Map** *12 E3*

While this very plain hotel offers the most basic of accommodation, it does so only a block away from Central Park. The rooms are clean, but they tend to be a little ragged and spartan. Expect friendly but limited service at the front desk. Grab a sandwich to go at one of the delis nearby and head to the park. **www.parksavoyhotelny.com**

414 Inn
414 West 46th St, 10036 **Tel** *(212) 399-0006* **Fax** *(212) 957-8716* **Rooms** *22*   **Map** *11 C5*

This small and stylish hotel has accommodating staff and complimentary Wi-Fi. King-size rooms tend to be nicer than the double rooms, with better beds and linens. Make sure you snag a room overlooking the private garden courtyard for less noise. **www.414inn.com**

Amsterdam Court Hotel
226 West 50th St, 10019 **Tel** *(212) 459-1000* **Fax** *(212) 265-5070* **Rooms** *125*   **Map** *12 D4*

This stylish property is perfect for the sophisticated traveler with a few extra dollars to spend. Rooms are decorated in soothing whites and khakis, and they offer Belgian linens with down comforters and CD players. A rooftop terrace is delightful in summer. There are many good restaurants nearby, on Ninth Avenue. **www.nychotels.com**

Belvedere Hotel
319 West 48th St, 10036 **Tel** *(212) 245-7000* **Fax** *(212) 245-4455* **Rooms** *400*   **Map** *12 D5*

This quality mid-range hotel is a great choice over many hotels in this price range and location. Rooms are larger than average and relatively attractive. A very popular Brazilian steakhouse is located on the premises, a good addition to the many quality eateries just outside. A family favorite. **www.belvederehotelnyc.com**

Da Vinci Hotel
244 West 56th St, 10019 **Tel** *(212) 489-4100* **Fax** *(212) 399-0434* **Rooms** *20*   **Map** *12 D3*

This European-style, intimate boutique property prides itself on good service. Rooms are on the small side, but well stocked and comfortable. A good choice for those who want to be close to the theater and don't mind the heavily touristed street. Meals in this area can be pricey, so opt for coffee shops and diners. **www.davincihotel.com**

Holiday Inn New York City-Midtown-57th St
440 West 57th St, 10019 **Tel** *(212) 581-8100* **Fax** *(212) 581-7739* **Rooms** *596*   **Map** *11 C3*

This solid choice from the famous American chain is a favorite with families thanks to the outdoor pool, and the fact that children enjoy a free breakfast. The rooms are all that you'd expect – clean, comfortable, and wired for internet access. Just blocks away from Central Park and the Theater District. **www.hi57.com**

Hotel Skyline Motor Inn
725 10th Ave, 10019 **Tel** *(212) 586-3400* **Fax** *(212) 582-4604* **Rooms** *230*   **Map** *11 C5*

Unique in the area, this motel-style inn is ideal for families, offering spacious rooms, a big heated indoor swimming pool, and moderate prices. Broadway shows and many restaurants are a short stroll away. The on-site facility has the city's lowest parking rates. **www.skylinehotelnyc.com**

Algonquin
59 West 44th St, 10036 **Tel** *(212) 840-6800* **Fax** *(212) 944-1419* **Rooms** *174*   **Map** *12 F5*

The home of Dorothy Parker's literary "Round Table" of the 1920s has been fully refurbished and still draws literati to its doors. The comfortable rooms are small, so if possible, splurge on a literary-themed suite. The well-preserved mahogany-paneled lobby provides access to the legendary Oak Room cabaret. **www.algonquinhotel.com**

Blakely Hotel
136 West 55th St, 10019 **Tel** *(212) 245-1800* **Fax** *(212) 582-8332* **Rooms** *115*   **Map** *12 E4*

This hotel has been done up in a boutique tradition with an eye on service. From the duo who developed Mercer, the Blakely offers superb value and location in this price range. The nicely appointed rooms include details such as Egyptian linens, while the restaurant serves top-notch Italian fare. **www.blakelynewyork.com**

Casablanca Hotel
🔲 ⅱ ⓦ $$$

147 West 43rd St, 10036 **Tel** *(212) 869-1212* **Fax** *(212) 391-7585* **Rooms** *48*   **Map** *8 E1*

This Moroccan-themed hotel is ideal for theatergoers. The rooms are small, and feature fun touches such as polished rattan fixtures. Complimentary breakfast is served in the fireplace lounge. Great peoplewatching for the fashionistas heading in and out of *Vogue* headquarters across the street. **www.casablancahotel.com**

Chambers
🔲 ⅱ 🏋 🖥 ⓦ $$$

15 West 56th Street, 10019 **Tel** *(212) 974-5656* **Fax** *(212) 974-5657* **Rooms** *77*   **Map** *12 F3*

A little downtown style livens up this strip of midtown with a sleek design. The smallish rooms feature original modern art, Frette bathrobes, and cashmere throws. The excellent Town restaurant downstairs serves modern French cuisine. A perfect spot to take a break from shopping on Madison Avenue. **www.chambershotel.com**

Hotel Mela
🅿 ⓦ $$$

120 West 44th St, 10036 **Tel** *(877) 452-MELA* **Fax** *(212) 704-9680* **Rooms** *228*   **Map** *12 D5*

This hotel aims to offer boutique luxury that reminds its guests of home, beginning with a foyer that is less "hotel" and more a discreet welcoming area. The rooms are small but clean, with comfortable beds, nice bathroom amenities, flatscreen TVs, and complimentary wireless internet access. **www.hotelmela.com**

Mansfield
🔲 ⓦ $$$

12 West 44th St, 10036 **Tel** *(212) 277-8700* **Fax** *(212) 764-4477* **Rooms** *124*   **Map** *12 E5*

This 1905 hotel has been made over as a boutique property with rooms featuring complimentary internet access and down comforters. The bar is a quiet spot for a drink after a hectic New York day. Tucked away on a busy street, the hotel's location is very convenient to theatergoers. **www.mansfieldhotel.com**

Michelangelo
🔲 ⅱ 🖥 ⓦ $$$

152 West 51st St, 10019 **Tel** *(212) 765-0505* **Fax** *(212) 581-7618* **Rooms** *178*   **Map** *12 F4*

Italian Renaissance is the name of the game at this boutique gem that features classic rugs and weavings throughout the property. Italian espresso and pastries for breakfast start the day and Baci chocolates at bedtime finish it off. Bathrooms make good use of Italian marble. We say *la dolce vita*. **www.michaelangelohotel.com**

Millennium Broadway
🔲 🅿 ⅱ 🖥 ⓦ $$$

145 West 44th St, 10036 **Tel** *(212) 768-4400* **Fax** *(212) 768-0847* **Rooms** *752*   **Map** *12 E5*

Comfortable rooms are good value at this business-oriented skyscraper hotel that is also ideally located for Broadway. The separate Premier Tower is a more luxurious option, and also has a women's floor. The bar is a nice stop for after-theater drinks. **www.millennium-hotels.com**

Roosevelt Hotel
🔲 ⅱ 🏋 🖥 ⓦ $$$

45 East 45th St, 10017 **Tel** *(212) 661-9600* **Fax** *(212) 885-6161* **Rooms** *1013*   **Map** *13 A5*

Built in 1924 and meticulously renovated and restored for its 80th birthday, this "grand dame of Madison Avenue" is still a favorite of business and leisure travelers. Rooms are well appointed with comfortable beds, and the lobby will make you feel like you've stepped into history. **www.theroosevelthotel.com**

The Time
🔲 ⅱ 🖥 $$$

224 West 49th St, 10019 **Tel** *(212) 320-2900* **Fax** *(212) 245-2305* **Rooms** *200*   **Map** *12 D5*

The Time has been renovated by the celebrated designer Adam Tihany, who has used a primary color palette to create a multi-sensory experience. Many of the rooms are small, especially for the price. The lobby bar can be a scene, so stop by for a cocktail. Some can find the noise level too distracting. **www.thetimeny.com**

Doubletree Guest Suites
🔲 ⅱ 🏋 🖥 ⓦ $$$$

1568 Broadway, 10036 **Tel** *(212) 719-1600* **Fax** *(212) 921-5212* **Rooms** *460*   **Map** *12 E5*

What this all-suite hotel lacks in charm, it more than makes up for in location and superior facilities. Some suites are designed for families, while others are perfect for business travelers. A special kids' play area makes it a favorite of families with toddlers. **www.nyc.doubletreehotels.com**

Hilton Times Square
🔲 ⅱ 🖥 ⓦ $$$$

234 West 42nd St, 10036 **Tel** *(212) 840-8222* **Fax** *(212) 840-5516* **Rooms** *444*   **Map** *8 E1*

You could easily miss this oasis of serenity in the midst of the Times Square madness, but don't. The design of the hotel goes way beyond chain mentality with oversize rooms and modern amenities. Rooms begin on the 23rd floor, assuring great views of the area. The upscale restaurant is a winner. **www.timessquare.hilton.com**

Le Parker Meridien
🔲 🅿 ⅱ 🏊 🖥 ⓦ $$$$

118 West 57th St, 10019 **Tel** *(212) 245-5000* **Fax** *(212) 307-1776* **Rooms** *730*   **Map** *12 E3*

With outstanding service and one of the best restaurants and gyms in town, this sleek and modern hotel offers the best value in this price category. Try the cheap burger joint after going for a rooftop swim. Rooms are large, with high design and the latest technology. **www.parkermeridien.com**

The London, NYC
🔲 🅿 ⅱ 🖥 ⓦ $$$$

151 West 54th St, 10019 **Tel** *(212) 307-5000* **Fax** *(212) 765-6530* **Rooms** *561*   **Map** *2 E4*

A charming mural of Hyde Park marks this 54-story tower, an all-suite hotel with some of the city's largest accommodations, and smartly refurbished by British designer David Collins. The London, NYC boasts the well-reviewed debut in the United States of British star chef Gordon Ramsay. **www.thelondonnyc.com**

Key to Price Guide *see p280* **Key to Symbols** *see back cover flap*

Sofitel
⇅ [P] 🍴 🍸 [W] $$$$

45 West 44th St, 10036 ***Tel*** *(212) 354-8844* ***Fax*** *(212) 354-2480* ***Rooms*** *398* ***Map*** *12 F5*

This 30-story property blends modern and classic design and was an instant hit in the Theater District, with warm decor, helpful service, and a pleasant brasserie. High floor rooms facing the front have fabulous views and some of the top tier suites have terraces. A favorite with both business and leisure travelers. **www.sofitel.com**

W Times Square
⇅ 🍴 👪 🍸 [W] $$$$

1567 Broadway, 10036 ***Tel*** *(212) 930-7400* ***Fax*** *(212) 930-7500* ***Rooms*** *507* ***Map*** *12 E5*

This hip hotel from the Starwood Group continues to draw crowds and fans for its high-design and ultra-modern rooms – although somewhat dark, they offer fantastic views of midtown. The lounges and restaurants are always happening places. Make sure to check out Blue Fin, for great sushi. **www.whotels.com**

Ritz-Carlton, New York, Central Park
⇅ 🍴 👪 🍸 [W] $$$$$

50 Central Park South, 10019 ***Tel*** *(212) 308-9100* ***Fax*** *(212) 207-8831* ***Rooms*** *260* ***Map*** *12 F3*

Fans rave that this is the best hotel for service in the entire Ritz-Carlton chain. Traditional in style, the large rooms are extremely comfortable and filled with the latest technology. The full-service spa and location across from Central Park make it a true winner. **www.ritzcarlton.com**

LOWER MIDTOWN

Hotel Grand Union
⇅ 👪 $

34 East 32nd St, 10016 ***Tel*** *(212) 683-5890* ***Fax*** *(212) 689-7397* ***Rooms*** *95* ***Map*** *9 A3*

Extreme budget travelers of all ages find the Grand Union of good value for the level of service it offers. While rooms can be downright unattractive, they are well maintained and have all the necessary comforts. Some rooms are large enough for families. **www.hotelgrandunion.com**

Courtyard New York
⇅ 🍴 👪 🍸 [W] $$

3 East 40th St, 10016 ***Tel*** *(212) 447-1500* ***Fax*** *(212) 683-7839* ***Rooms*** *185* ***Map*** *8 F1*

This neighborhood location can be pricey, but this hotel offers good value for its price range. It has been taken over by the Marriott chain and substantially renovated. Families appreciate the location since it is close to the New York Public Library and the Theater District without the noise. **www.courtyard.com**

70 Park
⇅ 🍴 👪 🍸 [W] $$$

70 Park Ave, 10016 ***Tel*** *(212) 973 2400* ***Fax*** *(212) 973-2401* ***Rooms*** *205* ***Map*** *9 A1*

This smart addition in the boutique category from the well-regarded Kimpton Group is stylish and well executed. Pets are welcome, and they provide extra amenities for the little critters. Business travelers appreciate the free extras such as Wi-Fi and high-speed internet. Rooms can be small, but comfortable. **www.70parkave.com**

Affinia Dumont
⇅ 👪 🍸 [W] $$$

150 East 34th St, 10016 ***Tel*** *(212) 481 7600* ***Fax*** *(212) 889-8856* ***Rooms*** *248* ***Map*** *9 A2*

This all-suite hotel is perfect for travelers who want space and comfortable design. Amenities include full kitchens with microwave ovens, and the helpful staff will even do grocery shopping for you. The on-site spa is a winner and will help travelers stay healthy. **www.affinia.com**

Dylan
⇅ 🍴 🍸 [W] $$$

52 East 41st St, 10017 ***Tel*** *(212) 338-0500* ***Fax*** *(212) 338-0569* ***Rooms*** *107* ***Map*** *9 A1*

This boutique property is the former home of the Chemists Club, a 1903 Beaux-Arts building. The lobby may feel a little antiseptic, but the rooms are spacious by city standards. An excellent restaurant is on the premises, which is good, because there aren't too many good options nearby. **www.dylanhotel.com**

Library Hotel
⇅ [W] $$$

299 Madison Ave, 10017 ***Tel*** *(212) 983-4500* ***Fax*** *(212) 499-9099* ***Rooms*** *60* ***Map*** *9 A1*

This unique boutique hotel features cleverly designed rooms organized around a library theme. From fairy tales to erotic literature, choose your room based upon mood, and you'll get the books to go with it. A lovely rooftop terrace and all-day snacks make this a winning choice. **www.libraryhotel.com**

W The Court / W The Tuscany
⇅ 🍴 👪 🍸 [W] $$$

120–130 East 39th St, 10016 ***Tel*** *(212) 686-1600* ***Fax*** *(212) 779-8352* ***Rooms*** *320* ***Map*** *9 A1*

This matched set of club-like properties offers boutique-style hotels with much better service. Rooms are equipped with the latest technology, and many offer free movie downloads. The Court has a trendier lounge scene, while the Tuscany is a little more relaxed. Both are recommended in this price range. **www.whotels.com**

Bryant Park
⇅ 🍸 [W] $$$$

40 West 40th St, 10018 ***Tel*** *(212) 869-0100* ***Fax*** *(212) 869-4446* ***Rooms*** *128* ***Map*** *8 F1*

Wonderful pedigree and great location makes this midtown find a winner. The stunning American Radiator Building (with all the gold leaf) is home to minimalist design luxury across from Bryant Park. The Cellar Bar is filled with fashionistas; it also has a 70-seat screening room. **www.bryantparkhotel.com**

Fitzpatrick Grand Central Hotel $$$$
141 East 44th St, 10017 **Tel** *(212) 351-6800* **Fax** *(212) 818-1747* **Rooms** *155*   **Map** *13 A5*

An elegant hotel with charming service only steps away from Grand Central Terminal. Rooms go beyond business comforts with luscious colors, and some have canopied beds. A genuine pub on-site offers after-hours fun. Its location near many subway lines make it a good base for exploring. **www.fitzpatrickhotels.com**

Kitano $$$$
66 Park Ave, 10016 **Tel** *(212) 885-7000* **Fax** *(212) 885-7100* **Rooms** *149*   **Map** *9 A2*

Buttoned-up Japanese-style service is the name of the game at this elegant midtown hotel, which caters primarily to a business crowd. Hotel rooms are havens of serenity with complimentary Japanese green tea. The restaurant also draws a crowd. This part of Park Avenue can seem amazingly serene. **www.kitano.com**

UPPER MIDTOWN

Hotel 57 $$
130 East 57th St, 10022 **Tel** *(212) 753-8841* **Fax** *(212) 869-9605* **Rooms** *220*   **Map** *13 A3*

The hotel lives up to the label "cheap chic," effortlessly combining high design with low prices. While the rooms can be narrow and often share baths in the hallway, it's hard to beat the price with such a great midtown location, close to all major shopping. Great views from the 17th-floor bar. **www.hotel57.com**

The Pod Hotel $$
230 East 51st St, 10022 **Tel** *(212) 355-0300* **Fax** *(212) 755-5029* **Rooms** *320*   **Map** *13 B4*

Even after a major refurbishing, The Pod's prices are very reasonable, especially for the prime neighborhood. Be sure to inquire about private baths and the exact size of the room, as many can be tiny. But all are clean, and the hotel runs exceedingly well. Single rooms are a bargain. There is also a rooftop terrace. **www.thepodhotel.com**

Courtyard by Marriott Midtown East $$$
866 Third Ave, 10022 **Tel** *(212) 644-1300* **Fax** *(212) 317-7940* **Rooms** *308*   **Map** *13 B4*

The spacious rooms make this a good choice for families that need to be in this neighborhood. Rooms are modern and have in-room coffee makers and free high-speed internet access. Free Wi-Fi is available in a special lounge. The neighborhood can be much quieter at night. **www.marriott.com**

Doubletree Metropolitan Hotel $$$
569 Lexington Ave, 10022 **Tel** *(212) 752-7000* **Fax** *(212) 758-6311* **Rooms** *722*   **Map** *13 A4*

This former Loews property is now being managed by the Doubletree group, which means service remains strong with a special catering to families. Rates are reasonable, and while rooms can be small, they are well cared for. Restaurants on-site are good family dining options. **www.metropolitanhotelnyc.com**

Kimberly Hotel $$$
145 East 50th St, 10022 **Tel** *(212) 755-0400* **Fax** *(212) 486-6915* **Rooms** *185*   **Map** *13 A5*

For large space and great value, this low-profile establishment is perhaps the best choice. The one- and two-bedroom apartments feel like apartments with full-size kitchens and well-appointed furniture. The location is wonderful for a little peace and quiet, yet close to good shopping. **www.kimberlyhotel.com**

Roger Smith $$$
501 Lexington Ave, 10022 **Tel** *(212) 755-1400* **Fax** *(212) 758-4061* **Rooms** *130*   **Map** *13 A5*

This low-key property has a few high-design touches that separate it from the rest of the pack. Rooms are larger than normal and individually decorated. Rates include breakfast. Draws a diverse crowd, from businessmen to arty folk. The neighborhood calms down a bit when the sun goes down. **www.rogersmith.com**

The Benjamin $$$$
125 East 50th St, 10022 **Tel** *(212) 715-2500* **Fax** *(212) 715-2525* **Rooms** *209*   **Map** *13 A4*

The modern rooms in this low-key hotel are designed for comfort. The work stations are perfect for business travelers. Each room has a kitchenette, and comes with a varied pillow menu to guarantee you a perfect night's sleep. Restaurant and small spa on site as well. **www.thebenjamin.com**

Omni Berkshire Place $$$$
21 East 52nd St, 10022 **Tel** *(212) 753-5800* **Fax** *(212) 754-5018* **Rooms** *396*   **Map** *12 F4*

The decor is designed for comfort at this understated hotel. Service earns high marks and the wealth of business facilities make it a great choice for the business traveler. But the hotel also caters to families, so make sure you check for discounted weekend rates. The area is a little less hectic than most. **www.omnihotels.com**

Waldorf-Astoria / Waldorf Towers $$$$
301 Park Ave, 10022 **Tel** *(212) 355-3000* **Fax** *(212) 872-7272* **Rooms** *1,242*   **Map** *13 A5*

This New York legend is still kicking, despite complaints about indifferent service. Rates can be reasonable because the hotel is enormous, but it does have a historical feel about it. Rooms are large, and if you score one in the exclusive Towers, you can expect 24-hour butler service. **www.waldorfastoria.com**

Key to Price Guide *see p280* **Key to Symbols** *see back cover flap*

Four Seasons New York 🔌 P 🅿 🍴 🏋 📺 $$$$$

57 East 57th St, 10022 **Tel** *(212) 758-5700* **Fax** *(212) 758-5711* **Rooms** *368*   **Map** *13 A3*

One of the crown jewels in the Four Seasons chain is this I.M. Pei-designed tower that rises 52 stories above midtown – the tallest hotel in Manhattan. The lobby reeks of New York power and elegance and is worth a look. Rooms are large and extremely comfortable with fabulous views of Central Park. **www.fourseasons.com/newyorkfs**

New York Palace 🔌 🍴 🏋 📺 W $$$$$

455 Madison Ave, 10022 **Tel** *(212) 888-7000* **Fax** *(212) 303-6000* **Rooms** *896*   **Map** *13 A4*

This splendid hotel, housed in a landmark 1882 house, is a wonderfully lavish establishment with old-world style and good service. Many think it's the most serene and calming spot in NYC. The location is terrific and the views, notably of St. Patrick's Cathedral, are splendid. **www.newyorkpalace.com**

Peninsula New York 🔌 ♒ 🏋 📺 W $$$$$

700 Fifth Ave, 10019 **Tel** *(212) 956-2888* **Fax** *(212) 903-3949* **Rooms** *239*   **Map** *12 F4*

Expect legendary Peninsula service at the small Asian chain's Big Apple outpost. Rooms are designed for ultimate comfort with the latest technology integrated seamlessly. The spa is one of the best in New York, and the rooftop bar and terrace is a prime choice for sunset drinks. Highly recommended. **www.peninsula.com**

The Plaza 🔌 P 🍴 🏋 📺 W $$$$$

Fifth Ave and Central Park South, 10019 **Tel** *(212) 759-3000* **Fax** *(212) 759-3001* **Rooms** *282*   **Map** *12 F3*

New York's 1907 Grande Dame has emerged from a $400-million face-lift agleam with Baccarat chandeliers, vast expanses of marble, and large, luxurious rooms. Additions include a condominium tower, elaborate spa, and a two-story shopping center. The Palm Court, Oak Room, and Oak Bar remain. **www.fairmonthotels.com/theplaza**

St. Regis New York 🔌 P 🍴 🏋 📺 W $$$$$

2 East 55th St, 10022 **Tel** *(212) 753-4500* **Fax** *(212) 787-3447* **Rooms** *408*   **Map** *12 F4*

This 1904 Beaux-Arts landmark is filled with luxury and old-world glamour, with chandeliers, expensive rugs, and a butler assigned to each floor. Service is very formal, but you would expect this of a grand dame. A favorite spot for weddings. The historic King Cole bar is known for its splendid Bloody Marys. **www.stregis.com**

UPPER EAST SIDE

Franklin 🔌 W $$$

164 East 87th St, 10128 **Tel** *(212) 369-1000* **Fax** *(212) 369-8000* **Rooms** *50*   **Map** *17 A3*

Rooms may be tiny at this modern hotel, but they are well appointed with romantic canopied beds, flatscreen TVs, complimentary Wi-Fi, and the like. The limited space makes it the choice for short-term travelers or light packers. Continental breakfast included. Check for seasonal rates. **www.franklinhotel.com**

Hotel Wales 🔌 🍴 🏋 📺 $$$

1295 Madison Ave, 10028 **Tel** *(212) 876-6000* **Fax** *(212) 860-7000* **Rooms** *88*   **Map** *17 B2*

A cozy, comfortable hotel that is well located for Museum Mile. The decor and furnishing feature some nice touches, such as mahogany furniture, Belgian linen on the beds, and fresh flowers in the rooms. There are some wonderful city views from the rooftop terrace. **www.waleshotel.com**

Surrey Hotel 🔌 🍴 🏋 $$$$

20 East 76th St, 10021 **Tel** *(212) 288-3700* **Fax** *(212) 628-1549* **Rooms** *130*   **Map** *17 A5*

This all-suite hotel is a lovely choice for those willing to spend extra on dramatically more space. Each suite has a fully-equipped kitchen, but the reason to stay here is the in-suite dining from the famous Café Boulud downstairs. Cheaper diners and pizzerias are all around the area. **www.affinia.com**

Carlyle 🔌 🍴 🏋 📺 $$$$$

35 East 76th St, 10021 **Tel** *(212) 744-1600* **Fax** *(212) 717-4682* **Rooms** *187*   **Map** *17 A5*

You'll feel like a true Upper Eastsider in a room at this legendary hotel. The elegant rooms and phenomenal service have drawn heads of state and movie stars alike. Afternoon tea attracts the who's who of New York socialites. Central location just one block from Central Park but away from the hustle and bustle. **www.thecarlyle.com**

The Pierre 🔌 🍴 🏋 📺 W $$$$$

2 East 61st St, 10021 **Tel** *(212) 838-8000* **Fax** *(212) 940-8109* **Rooms** *203*   **Map** *12 F3*

Inviting service makes this sophisticated and beautifully renovated hotel seem not so intimidating. The interiors are grand, but the rooms have a residential touch. Royalty feels right at home here with gloved elevator operators. The bar and restaurant are both recommended. **www.tajhotels.com/pierre**

Sherry-Netherland 🔌 🍴 🏋 📺 W $$$$$

781 Fifth Ave, 10022 **Tel** *(212) 355-2800* **Fax** *(212) 319-4306* **Rooms** *50*   **Map** *12 F3*

A little less stuffy than next-door neighbor The Pierre, this old-world style hotel defines residential living in New York City. Suites are enormous, and the service is top-of-the-class. Breakfast at the downstairs Cipriani's is included in the price, if you can handle sitting with fellow powerbrokers. **www.sherrynetherland.com**

UPPER WEST SIDE

Amsterdam Inn — $

340 Amsterdam Ave, 10024 ***Tel*** *(212) 579-7500* ***Fax*** *(212) 545-0103* ***Rooms*** *25* — ***Map*** *15 C5*

All rooms are well cared for in this budget establishment, but the rooms can be narrow. Some share baths, but the private ones are good value. Be sure to verify that a "double" is actually a real bed for two, rather than a single and pull-out trundle. Excellent location near Upper West Side museums. **www.amsterdaminn.com**

Hostelling International – New York — ⇅ [W] — $

891 Amsterdam Ave, 10025 ***Tel*** *(212) 932-2300* ***Fax*** *(212) 932-2574* ***Rooms*** *628* — ***Map*** *20 E5*

You will feel like you've gone back to college in this mammoth building that feels exactly like a dormitory. The good news is that it features all the upside of campus living – cafeteria, game room, laundry, internet access, and picnic tables. The establishment is at least 18 years old. **www.hinewyork.org**

Hotel Newton — ⇅ 🧒 [W] — $

2528 Broadway, 10025 ***Tel*** *(212) 678-6500* ***Fax*** *(212) 678-6758* ***Rooms*** *110* — ***Map*** *15 C2*

One of the best options for the price, this well-run hotel has clean and attractive rooms with nice bathrooms. Service is pleasant and professional. Guests have access to a state-of-the-art fitness club across the street. While there's no restaurant on the premises, there are many options up and down Broadway. **www.thehotelnewton.com**

Jazz on the Park — $

36 West 106th St, 10025 ***Tel*** *(212) 932-1600* ***Fax*** *(212) 932-1700* ***Rooms*** *220* — ***Map*** *21 A5*

This arty hostel is extremely popular and brings a downtown feel to the sometimes staid Upper West Side. Don't miss the coffeehouse with live music that can be a little rowdy. Dorm rooms are very basic and so are the bathrooms. Very international crowd. The area keeps getting better and better. **www.jazzonthepark.com**

Milburn — ⇅ 🧒 🏋 [W] — $

242 West 76th St, 10023 ***Tel*** *(212) 362-1006* ***Fax*** *(212) 721-5476* ***Rooms*** *114* — ***Map*** *15 C5*

This all-suite hotel is exceedingly well priced and offers all the comforts of home, including size. While not particularly smart, the rooms come with well-equipped kitchenettes and nice bathrooms. Staff are helpful and laundry facilities are also available. Good restaurants around the corner. **www.milburnhotel.com**

West End Studios — ⇅ — $

850 West End Ave, 10025 ***Tel*** *(212) 749-7104* ***Fax*** *(212) 865-5130* ***Rooms*** *85* — ***Map*** *15 B1*

Blocks away from Riverside Park, this is a good budget choice for those who want to experience neighborhood living. A little way from the main subway lines, the hotel offers very basic and quite small rooms with shared baths. The family room comes with two beds and a bunkbed. **www.westendstudios.com**

Excelsior Hotel — ⇅ [P] 🏋 [W] — $$

45 West 81st St, 10024 ***Tel*** *(212) 362-9200* ***Fax*** *(212) 580-3972* ***Rooms*** *200* — ***Map*** *16 D4*

Welcoming Old World ambience awaits at this traditional hotel with comfortable rooms, a warm library/sitting room/breakfast room, and a well-equipped fitness center. The American Museum of Natural History is across the street, Central Park and a subway to midtown are on the corner. A good family choice. **www.excelsiorhotelnyc.com**

Hotel Beacon — ⇅ 🧒 [W] — $$

2130 Broadway, 10023 ***Tel*** *(212) 787-1100* ***Fax*** *(212) 724-0839* ***Rooms*** *236* — ***Map*** *15 C5*

Families enjoy the extra-large rooms and laundry facilities on offer at this great-value hotel. The rooms aren't the best in town, but they have kitchenettes and often can accommodate four people. Larger groups should inquire about the two-bedroom/two-bath suites. **www.beaconhotel.com**

Lucerne — ⇅ 🍴 🧒 🏋 [W] — $$

201 West 79th St, 10024 ***Tel*** *(212) 875-1000* ***Fax*** *(212) 579-2408* ***Rooms*** *184* — ***Map*** *15 C4*

This lovely jewel of a mid-priced hotel is housed in an elegant 1903 building. The rooms are very well maintained and feature Americana furnishings. Rates include Continental breakfast, and don't miss the live jazz and blues in the stylish bar and grill. Other good restaurant options are just blocks away. **www.thelucernehotel.com**

On the Ave — ⇅ [W] — $$

2178 Broadway, 10024 ***Tel*** *(212) 362-1100* ***Fax*** *(212) 787-9521* ***Rooms*** *251* — ***Map*** *15 C5*

Style is the name of the game at this mid-range budget hotel filled with modern design. Rooms have modular furniture in natural hues. A great deck offers beautiful views of the city. If possible, spring for a deluxe room, otherwise you might be too cramped. Good dining options up and down the avenue. **www.ontheave-nyc.com**

6 Columbus — ⇅ [P] 🍴 [W] — $$$

6 Columbus Circle, 10019 ***Tel*** *(212) 204-3000* ***Fax*** *(212) 204-3030* ***Rooms*** *88* — ***Map*** *12 D3*

The former West Park Hotel has been transformed by the trendy Thompson Hotel group with retro 1960s decor, four added floors and an uptown outpost of SoHo's popular Blue Ribbon Sushi restaurant. The Time Warner Center and Central Park are very close, Broadway and Lincoln Center a short walk away. **www.thompsonhotels.com**

Key to Price Guide *see p280* **Key to Symbols** *see back cover flap*

Empire Hotel

$$$

44 West 63rd St, 10023 **Tel** (212) 265-7400 **Fax** (212) 265-7401 **Rooms** 420 **Map** 12 D2

Only the 1920s metal canopy remains of the old Empire, there is now a dramatic entry, chic lobby and bar, stunning rooftop setting for cocktails, and an outdoor plunge pool for guests. Modernistic room decor is in earth tones. Most baths have shower only, but they are walk-ins with rain shower heads. **www.empirehotelnyc.com**

Inn New York City

$$$$

266 West 71st St, 10023 **Tel** (212) 580-1900 **Fax** (212) 580-4437 **Rooms** 4 **Map** 11 C1

Nothing but the best will do at this small, intimate, and charming guesthouse, a renovated 19th-century townhouse with four rooms, each with its own theme – Opera, Library, Vermont, or Spa. All rooms are equipped with top-notch amenities, and the in-suite breakfast is delightful. An over-the-top treat to be sure. **www.innnewyorkcity.com**

Mandarin Oriental New York

$$$$$

80 Columbus Circle, 10023 **Tel** (212) 805-8800 **Fax** (212) 805-8888 **Rooms** 248 **Map** 12 D3

Asian opulence comes at quite a price in this dramatic hotel. Rooms are modern-Oriental and feature terrific views of Central Park and the Hudson, if on a high floor. The spa is wonderful, but pricey. The bar and restaurants offer the same view and can be quite a scene in the evening. **www.mandarinoriental.com**

Trump International Hotel & Tower

$$$$$

1 Central Park West, 10023 **Tel** (212) 299-1000 **Fax** (212) 299-1150 **Rooms** 167 **Map** 12 D3

This modern luxury hotel tower prides itself on its exclusivity, discretion, and style. Lovely rooms are decorated in soothing tones and offer the latest technology. The unobstructed views of Central Park is the real draw, as is the Jean-Georges restaurant downstairs. **www.trumpintl.com**

MORNINGSIDE HEIGHTS AND HARLEM

Astor on the Park

$

465 Central Park West, 10025 **Tel** (212) 866-1880 **Fax** (212) 316-9555 **Rooms** 112 **Map** 21 A5

On Central Park West at 106th Street, the convenient location of this hotel more than makes up for the small, basic rooms. It is an ideal choice for visitors on a budget who plan to be out for most of the day (and night!). The bathrooms are clean, and the staff friendly.

Morningside Inn Hotel

$

235 West 107th St, 10025 **Tel** (212) 316-0055 **Fax** (212) 864-9155 **Rooms** 96 **Map** 20 E5

This hotel is modern and fresh, although it still retains the air of a dormitory. Best for students or single travelers, try and score a double deluxe, which will assure you a private bath and air conditioning. All rooms are clean and well cared for. **www.morningsideinn-ny.com**

Sugar Hill Harlem Inn

$$

460 West 141st St, 10031 **Tel** (212) 234-5432 **Fax** (212) 234-5432 **Rooms** 5 **Map** 19 A2

Attractive rooms in this Victorian town house have names like Miles and Ella for the jazz greats who once favored this neighborhood. Two accommodations are studios with kitchens, one is a two-bedroom apartment. Most have fireplaces; all have private bathrooms, TV, DVD player, and air conditioning. **www.sugarhillharleminn.com**

FARTHER AFIELD

BROOKLYN Best Western Gregory Hotel Brooklyn

$$

8315 Fourth Ave, 11209 **Tel** (718) 238-3737 **Fax** (718) 680-0827 **Rooms** 70

While this hotel is a little off the beaten path, it is a good choice for those who need to be in Brooklyn. The subway is only a few blocks away. Rooms can be small, but are well maintained. Past service problems seem to have been fixed with a change in management. Several cheap eats around the corner. **www.bestwestern.com**

BROOKLYN Marriott Brooklyn Bridge

$$

333 Adams St, 11201 **Tel** (718) 246-7000 **Fax** (718) 246-0563 **Rooms** 355

The only full-service hotel in Brooklyn, this is a wonderful option for business and leisure travelers who want to explore this borough but be close to Financial District. Nine major subway lines converge outside the hotel, and the rooms are nicely decorated. Lobby is grand, and there's a large fitness center with a pool. **www.marriott.com**

QUEENS Sheraton LaGuardia East Hotel

$$

135–20 39th Ave, 11354 **Tel** (718) 460-6666 **Fax** (718) 445-2655 **Rooms** 173

A comfortable, full-service 16-story hotel in the heart of Flushing's booming Chinatown, offering free transportation to LaGuardia airport and easy access to Mets games at Shea Stadium or the Arthur Ashe Tennis Center. Features include fitness and business centers, in-room coffee makers, and free Wi-Fi. **www.sheraton.com/laguardia**

RESTAURANTS AND BARS

New Yorkers love to eat well, and in the five boroughs there are more than 25,000 restaurants catering to their wishes. City dwellers avidly read restaurant reviews in magazines such as *New York* to ensure that they are seen in the latest fashionable eatery. "In" places and cuisine change with great regularity, while some favorite places simply remain popular.

The classic Manhattan cocktail

The restaurants cited in our listings have been selected as the best that New York can offer across a wide price range. While the information on pages 296–311 will help you to select a suitable restaurant, there are details of lighter refreshments on pages 312–14. *New York's Bars* on pages 315–17 highlights some of the city's best drinking spots.

RESTAURANT MENUS

Meals in most of the better restaurants consist of three courses: an appetizer (starter), an entrée (the main course), and a dessert. In some fine restaurants you may be offered a complimentary appetizer, such as a small dollop of mousse or a tiny triangle of quiche. Appetizers at the better restaurants are often the chef's most creative dishes – some diners request two appetizers and no entrée. Italian menus offer a pasta

Street-corner hot dog stand

dish as a course before the main course, but in many places pasta is seen as a main course. Coffee or tea and a dessert ordinarily conclude the meal in restaurants above the coffee-shop level. Your coffee cup may be refilled until you refuse any more. Some of the better establishments feature a cheeseboard on the menu.

To get a sense of a restaurant's cuisine, visit www.menupages.com, which features the menus of several thousand Manhattan eateries. Other local websites, including the *New York Magazine*'s (www.nymag.com), often have links to restaurant menus.

PRICES

You will always find a restaurant in New York to suit your budget. At inexpensive coffee shops, diners and fast-food chains, $10–$15 will buy you a filling meal. There are also hundreds of acceptable, even first-rate, restaurants where you can eat well at a moderate cost – around $25 per person for a filling and decent meal, not including drinks – in attractive surroundings.

For dinner at a trendy New American venue with a star chef, the bill could be upward of $80 to $100 per person, excluding drinks. Many top restaurants do, however, offer fixed-price (or, as they are known in New York, prix-fixe) meals. This is normally a much cheaper way of enjoying a good meal than choosing dishes from the à la carte menu. Lunch is also less expensive than dinner in such places and, because of the profusion of business diners, lunch is also the busiest period of the day.

TAXES AND TIPPING

New York city sales tax of 8.625% will be added to your bill. Service is not usually included. Tipping can run from 10% at a coffee shop to 20% at the fanciest places, with 15% an average fair tip. Many people just double the sales tax for a tip.

A typical New York deli *(see p312)*

The bill is known as the "check" in the US. The most commonly accepted credit cards are VISA, MasterCard and American Express. Traveler's checks are taken in many restaurants. Diners and coffee shops may accept cash only. In fast-food chains, you order at the counter and pay cash in advance. Some other types of establishment also take only cash.

DINING ON A BUDGET

Despite the tales of $200 business lunches, there are ways to stretch a meal budget in New York.

Order fewer courses than you would normally. American portions are huge, and an appetizer is often big enough for a light main course. You could share one with your companion or choose two appetizers and no entrée.

Ask your waiter if there is a prix-fixe menu. Many of the more expensive restaurants offer this at lunch and dinner – in the early evening it may often be called the pre-theater menu. Or try a prix-fixe lunch buffet. These are popular in Indian

McSorley's Old Ale House *(see p315)* restaurants,

and other, places and are very reasonably priced meals.

Other options for a quick, tasty, and restorative meal are the less expensive Chinese, Thai, and Mexican restaurants, and some Jewish delis. Italian pizzerias and French bistros, as well as the small eateries that serve hamburgers or sandwiches and desserts also offer good value. Alternatively, go to bars featuring "happy hours." They often offer a variety of substantial hors d'oeuvres, like Spanish *tapas*, which can make a meal in themselves.

If you simply want to see inside the restaurants every visitor has heard about, just go to have a drink and soak up the atmosphere. Many restaurants post their menus or will let you see them before you are seated, good for checking prices in advance. During Restaurant Week (usually in January and July), you can dine in some of the city's restaurants for a fraction of the usual cost – visit www. nycgo.com/restaurantweek.

Dining in style at the Oyster Bar in Grand Central Terminal *(see p306)*

Poolside dining at Four Seasons *(see p307)*

HOURS

Breakfast hours are usually from 7 to 10:30 or 11am. Sunday brunch, a popular meal, is served at most better restaurants between about 11am and 3pm. Lunch runs from 11:30am or noon to 2:30pm at most places, but the busiest time of the day is 1pm. Dinner is usually served from 5:30 to 6pm onward. The most popular time is around 7:30 to 8pm.

Some restaurants stop serving at 10pm during the week, or 11pm on Friday and Saturday. Certain informal restaurants are open from 11:30am to 10pm. Coffee shops are open long hours, from 7am to midnight or even 24 hours.

DRESS CODES

Few restaurants demand that male diners dress formally, though a jacket is required at classy restaurants, and a jacket and tie at the very best. At most restaurants, for both men and women, smart "business casual" suffices.

Women tend to dress up when dining at the more expensive restaurants. If you are unsure, check what the dress code is when you make your reservation.

RESERVATIONS

It is wise to make reservations at any restaurant above the diner/fast-food level, especially on weekends. A few of the trendiest restaurants won't even accept reservations less than two months in advance. Be sure to make reservations for lunch at a midtown restaurant. You may still have to wait at the bar, even if you have booked. Waits of an hour at the most popular spots are not unusual.

SMOKING

Smoking is now illegal in all bars and restaurants in New York. The only exceptions are owner-operated bars that have special smoking rooms.

CHILDREN

When eating out with children, ask if there's a child's menu with half-portions. The prices are reduced, sometimes by half. Children are accepted in most New York restaurants, but if yours are unpredictable

stick to casual spots, Chinatown Chinese or family-run Italian restaurants, burger bars, delis, cafés, fast food chains and diners. A few of the better restaurants have facilities for babies or toddlers; others may not be so well equipped. Dining out in the more formal New York restaurants is certainly not a family affair.

WHEELCHAIR ACCESS

While many restaurants may be able to accommodate a wheelchair, always mention your requirements when making your reservation. Many of the smaller places cannot cater to disabled customers because of lack of space.

CELEBRITY CHEFS

New York City attracts top chefs from around the world, all of whom are determined to make their mark and win over the local diners and the *New York Times*' influential restaurant reviewer.

A meal in a top restaurant will not come cheaply, but it can be worth the splurge. Booking a table can be difficult, and reservations should be made as early as two months in advance. Some reservations can be made online through Opentable (www.opentable.com).

Among the best names and signature venues are Thomas Keller (Per Se), Daniel Bouley (Daniel), Jean-Georges Vongerichten (Jean-Georges), Gordon Ramsay (London NYC), Mario Batali (Babbo), Alain Ducasse (Adour), and Nobu Matsuhisa (Nobu New York).

The Flavors of New York

Few cities can match the diversity of New York's restaurants. Reflecting the city's melting pot of nationalities, foods range from the "hautest" of French and continental cuisine to the freshest sushi outside of Tokyo. Caribbean, Mexican, Thai, Vietnamese, Korean, Greek, Indian – all are well represented, and every block seems to have an Italian restaurant. The quality of the city's top restaurants is unsurpassed and their chefs are superstars, as well-known and revered as movie idols. Yet, because so many nationalities are represented in its culinary culture, only a few foods are native to the city itself.

Dim sum

Fresh, local produce on display at the Greenmarket

DELI DINING

A large Jewish population has given rise to some of New York's best known specialties, now enjoyed by all – overstuffed corned beef and pastrami sandwiches, dill pickles, matzo ball soup, herrings, blintzes, and bagels served with cream cheese

and smoked salmon. The bagel, once synonymous with New York, has become a universal American food, but a true New York bagel is nothing like the bready imitations found in the hinterlands. It is shaped by hand, and the dough is cooked briefly in boiling water before being baked, resulting in a unique firm and chewy texture. A relative, and another New York specialty, is the bialy,

a flat, chewy flour-dusted roll with a center indentation filed with toasted onions. The finest examples of each are to be found in the kosher bakeries of the Lower East Side (see pp92–101).

THE GREENMARKET

You may well find yourself next to a well-known chef browsing at New York's greenmarkets, open-air markets where farmers from

Pastrami on rye

Blintzes

Bagels with smoked salmon and cream cheese

Pickle herring

Dill pickles

Selection of classic foods available at any New York deli

NEW YORK SPECIALTIES

Pretzels

While New York dining may span all nations, a few special dishes are closely associated with the city. Manhattan Clam Chowder, prepared with tomatoes rather than cream, has been popular ever since it was introduced at Coney Island beach stands in the 1880s. In the city's many steak houses, a prime selection is the "New York strip steak," a boneless sirloin cut from the short loin, the tenderest portion of beef. Italian cuisine has often been given a New York spin. Rich and creamy New York cheesecake is made with cream cheese rather the Italian ricotta. And, since traditional wood-burning ovens were impractical in New York, the first Italian immigrant chefs used coal ovens. Though these are rare today, purists still insist they are necessary for a true New York pizza.

Manhattan clam chowder
This is a rich blend of potatoes, onions, tomatoes, oyster crackers crumbs and clams.

Fast food cart on a Manhattan street corner, selling hots dogs and sodas

upstate New York sell fresh-picked fruits and vegetables, as well as meat, poultry and dairy products. Over 105 city restaurants patronize the greenmarkets, so you'll find ultra-fresh local produce on many menus in the city. As many as 70 vendors attend the biggest of the markets in Union Square on Monday, Wednesday, Friday, and Saturday *(see p129)*.

STREET FOOD

Street food is a favorite choice in a fast-moving city. Hot dogs and oversize soft pretzels are classic New York choices, along with some surprisingly good food cart specialties, from falafel to soup to barbecue to Texas chile, all ready to eat on the run. In winter, vendors all over town offer hot roasted chestnuts.

SOUL FOOD

Harlem is America's largest African-American community, and restaurants here are the place to sample specialties from the Deep South, such as fried chicken, ribs, collard

An Oriental produce store in New York's Chinatown

greens, yams, flaky biscuits or cornbread. A popular Harlem dish, fried chicken and waffles, is said to have originated to serve musicians leaving jazz clubs in the wee hours.

ASIAN FOOD RIVALS

Chinese restaurants and dim sum parlors have long been found throughout the city, but lately they have been challenged by the arrival of many excellent Thai and Vietnamese restaurants. All these, however, take second place to the multiplying sushi bars and high-profile, highly praised Japanese chefs.

DELICATESSEN CLASSICS

Babkas Slightly sweet, yeasted coffee cakes.

Blintzes Crêpes filled with sweetened soft white cheese and/or fruit and sautéd.

Chopped liver Chicken livers mashed with minced onion, hard-cooked eggs and *schmaltz* (chicken fat).

Gefilte fish Minced white fish dumplings poached in fish broth. A holiday dish.

Knishes Soft dough shells filled with oniony mashed potatoes.

Latkes Grated potato, onion and matzo-meal pancakes.

Rugelach Rich, cream-cheese-dough pastries filled with jam, chopped nuts and raisins.

New York-style pizza *Thick-or thin-crusted, a true New York pizza must be baked in a coal-fired oven.*

New York Strip Steak *Served with creamed spinach, fries or hash-browns, this tender steak is hard to beat.*

New York cheesecake *This is a dense, rich, baked cake with a crust of pastry or graham crackers (digestives).*

Choosing a Restaurant

The restaurants in this section have been selected for their good value and exceptional food. Within each area, entries are listed alphabetically within each price category, from the least to the most expensive. Details of *Light Meals and Snacks* are on pages 312–14 and for some of New York's best *Bars* see pages 315–17.

LOWER MANHATTAN

Adrienne's Pizza Bar $$
87 Pearl St, 10004 **Tel** *(212) 248-3838*   **Map** *1 C4*

The setting on a quaint street straight out of Old New York adds to the appeal of this popular spot, which is known for its thin-crust rectangular pizzas. An ideal stop for a tasty, inexpensive lunch while touring Lower Manhattan, but if you happen to be in the neighborhood at dinner, the mood is more serene.

Les Halles $$
15 John St between Broadway and Nassau St, 10038 **Tel** *(212) 285-8585*   **Map** *1 C2*

The Financial District meets a Parisian-style brasserie at this sister restaurant of the Park Avenue Les Halles, made famous by its celebrity chef Anthony Bourdain. Expect well-executed dishes such as mussels and *frites*. A heaven for carnivores, with a wide selection of grilled meats.

Battery Gardens $$$
17 State St, Battery Park, 10004 **Tel** *(212) 809-5508*   **Map** *1 C4*

It's worth a trip to the tip of Manhattan for the fantastic vistas of the harbor and the Statue of Liberty from this haven in Battery Park. The American-Continental menu is adequate, but the view is the lure. On a balmy day when you can sit on the terrace, there's no place like it.

Fraunces Tavern $$$
54 Pearl St, corner of Broad Street, 10004 **Tel** *(212) 968-1776*   **Map** *1 C4*

This historic tavern has been in operation since 1762 and was where George Washington bid a fond farewell to his officers, on the eve of his retirement in 1783. Classic American steak and fish dishes are on offer, along with wholesome pot roasts and soups. In winter warm up in the snug lounge.

Harry's Café $$$
1 Hanover Sq, 10004 **Tel** *(212) 785-9200*   **Map** *1 C3*

The former Bayard's has been restyled as a clubby steakhouse offering first-rate food and wine. If you don't have an expense account and your budget is limited, you can still enjoy the atmosphere of this landmark heritage building by choosing from a short and reasonably priced café menu. One of the few Wall Street spots open at the weekend.

Roy's New York $$$$
130 Washington St, Marriot Financial Center, 10005 **Tel** *(212) 266-6262*   **Map** *1 B3*

Noted Hawaiian chef Roy Yamaguchi brings his winning fusion formula to this New York outpost of a worldwide chain. That means the freshest ingredients flavored with island and Asian spices. Seafood is the specialty, with unusual Pacific fish flown in weekly. Attentive service and interesting dishes.

SEAPORT AND THE CIVIC CENTER

Acqua at Peck Slip $$$
21–23 Peck Slip, 10038 **Tel** *(212) 349-4433*   **Map** *2 D2*

Amid the tourist traps of South Street Seaport, this Italian restaurant stands out like a beacon, serving up New American-tinged Italian dishes prepared with organic ingredients. Service can be a little slow, so just sit back and enjoy the vaulted ceilings and warm earthy tones that make this a cozy, romantic spot. The lasagna is fantastic.

Bridge Café $$$
279 Water St at Dover St, 10038 **Tel** *(212) 227-3344*   **Map** *2 D2*

A charming café located just below the Brooklyn Bridge, this age-old restaurant is worth a visit while in the area. Adventurers should try the specialty – buffalo steak with gnocchi. For the tamer, there are still plenty of options – from lobster pot pie and fresh fish to a grilled vegetables and goats' cheese plate.

Key to Symbols *see back cover flap*

Stella Maris ♿ ⬥ $$$

213 Front St, 10038 **Tel** *(212) 233-2437* **Map** *2 D2*

A welcome find in the Seaport area, Stella Maris is a pleasant bistro with sleek decor. The seasonal modern European menu puts the emphasis on seafood, including a superb black sole, and offers a few pub favorites. The Raw Bar features oysters, clams, and treats such as poached lobster. The outdoor terrace is a great place for brunch.

LOWER EAST SIDE

Grand Sichuan ▤⬥ $

125 Canal St at Bowery, 10002 **Tel** *(212) 625-9212* **Map** *4 E5*

A never-ending menu with all kinds of Sichuan, Hunang, and "Chinese-food American style," as well as all types of hot (including spicy) and cold noodles and fried rice. It also offers a wide variety of vegetarian dishes. Spotty service and scant decor may be the reason for the quite affordable prices.

Katz Delicatessen ⬥♿ $

205 East Houston St, 10002 **Tel** *(212) 254-2246* **Map** *5 A3*

A New York City classic, this Jewish deli continues to serve the best pastrami and corned beef towering sandwiches. Don't expect much from service or decor – it's all in the pastrami and the very affordable prices. Famous for sending salami to the army, way before *that* scene from *When Harry Met Sally* (which is commemorated with a sign).

San Loco Mexico ▤⬥ $

11 Stanton St, 10002 **Tel** *(212) 253-7580* **Map** *5 A3*

You'll be hard pressed to spend over $10 at this excellent value Mexican restaurant, which is popular with cost-conscious locals. All the Mexican favorites are on offer and come with a choice of four potencies of homemade sauce – mild, hot, serious, and stupid. Save room for the dessert.

Teany Café ⬥♿ $

90 Rivington St, 10002 **Tel** *(212) 475-9190* **Map** *5 A3*

Rock star Moby owns this famous café offering all vegan and vegetarian sandwiches, salads, and nibblers. Great desserts, too, such as the chocolate peanut butter bomb and the warm rhubarb pie. The "afternoon tea service" for one or two is worth a try. Service can be patchy.

Il Palazzo ⬥▦ $$

151 Mulberry St, 10013 **Tel** *(212) 343-7000* **Map** *4 F4*

Il Palazzo ranks among Little Italy's few good Italian restaurants, especially when it comes to service. A glassed-in garden boosts its charm. Homemade pastas and risotti are always good and inexpensive choices. Popular desserts include cannoli and tiramisu.

Joe's Shanghai ▤⬥ $$

9 Pell St, 10013 **Tel** *(212) 233-8888* **Map** *4 F5*

When visiting this famous local restaurant, don't miss the crab and pork soup dumplings. This dish is the main reason for long lines especially on weekends, but it's worth it. The rest of the menu is hit and miss but it's good value. Other locations may have better decor/service at the expense of food quality.

Sammy's Roumanian ⬥ $$

157 Chrystie St, 10002 **Tel** *(212) 673-0330* **Map** *5 A4*

The Jewish-inspired menu at Sammy's Roumanian offers traditional fare such as *latkes*, chopped liver, mashed potatoes with *schmaltz* (chicken fat), and a large selection of meat cuts. Try the garlic sausage with ice-cold vodka. Impromptu entertainment and singalongs add to the fun factor.

The Orchard ♿ $$$

162 Orchard St, 10002 **Tel** *(212) 353-3570* **Map** *5 A3*

Imaginative New American food is served up to a hip and young LES crowd. The decor is stylish, with subdued lighting. Don't miss the steak tartare flatbread. Wines come at a good range of price points, ensuring there is something for every budget.

The Stanton Social ♿ $$$

99 Stanton St, 10002 **Tel** *(212) 995-0099* **Map** *5 A3*

Groovy and gorgeous sums up the scene at this restaurant, where the atmosphere almost overshadows the food. The eclectic tapas menu has many mouthwatering options from French onion soup and dumplings to mini burger "sliders" – but beware: the cost adds up quickly. The cocktails are equally inviting.

wd-50 ♿ $$$$

50 Clinton St, 10002 **Tel** *(212) 477-2900* **Map** *5 B3*

Wylie Dufresne, a pioneer in the food revolution on the Lower East Side, serves serious food here but in a casual setting that suits the neighborhood. His eclectic modern American cuisine is known for innovative touches, like lamb flavored with banana consommé. If you can't get a reservation, walk-ins are welcome for bar dining.

SOHO AND TRIBECA

Lombardi's
$

32 Spring St, 10012 **Tel** *(212) 941-7994*   **Map** *4 F4*

Among the top pizzerias of the city, the brick-oven baked pies come thin, charred, and oozing a delectable mozzarella. Lombardi's pays the price for its popularity with big crowds and long lines, but a very welcome expansion now allows you and your friends to share the joy faster.

Peanut Butter & Co.
$

240 Sullivan St, 10012 **Tel** *(212) 677-3995*   **Map** *4 D2*

A sandwich shop worth the trip to see the unbelievable combinations available with peanut butter. Yes, you can even get the famous Elvis Presley-inspired sandwich. Thankfully, you can get milk too, and plenty of other yummy desserts. Invite friends and bring your kids and your wallet won't even notice it.

Pho Pasteur
$

85 Baxter St, 10013 **Tel** *(212) 608-3656*   **Map** *4 F5*

A tiny restaurant in the midst of Chinatown, offering a cheap and fast choice of noodles. Try the Vietnamese rolls with lettuce leaves and rice noodles. You can even see yourself sweat in the mirrored walls in case you order any of their spicy dishes. Also try the large variety of Asian beverages.

Aquagrill
$$$

210 Spring St, 10012 **Tel** *(212) 274-0505*   **Map** *4 D4*

Aquagrill is a seafood-lovers' paradise with very fresh ingredients. An oyster bar selection to die for, a reliable kitchen, and courteous service are all ingredients for success adding up to a busy dining room. The mussel soup with saffron comes highly recommended.

Balthazar
$$$

80 Spring St, 10012 **Tel** *(212) 965-1414*   **Map** *4 E4*

The jewel in restaurateur Keith McNally's crown remains a popular draw, thanks to the Parisian brasserie setting, good-quality food, superb wine selection, and lively bar scene – you'll find SoHo literati, VIPs, and tourists rubbing shoulders here. Balthazar is a good choice for both brunch and late-night dining. There is also an excellent on-site bakery.

The Harrison
$$$

355 Greenwich St, 10013 **Tel** *(212) 274-9310*   **Map** *4 D5*

A New England seafront house in the midst of TriBeCa offering good "re-engineered" American fare such as biscuits and gravy with chorizo and clams and a crispy chicken with chestnut stuffing. Very popular with the area's 30-somethings, which means long lines at times.

L'Ecole
$$$

462 Broadway, 10012 **Tel** *(212) 219-3300*   **Map** *4 E4*

This small and charming SoHo restaurant is used by the students of the French Culinary Institute to do their hands-on training. The place offers different tasting menus at reasonable prices considering the good quality of the food and unfailingly courteous service.

Lupa
$$$

170 Thompson St, 10012 **Tel** *(212) 982-5089*   **Map** *4 F3*

An Italian *trattoria* courtesy of celebrity chef Mario Batali offering a cheaper alternative to its flagship Babbo. Expect a wide variety of dishes such as smoked eggplant, excellent fresh pastas, and accomplished entrées such as pork *saltimbocca*. Excellent Italian wine list.

Minetta Tavern
$$$

113 MacDougal St, 10012 **Tel** *(212) 475-3850*   **Map** *4 D2*

This Italian bistro manages to be both casual and celebrity-friendly. The menu is short but perfectly formed, and each dish is prepared with great flair, from the *petite omelette*, frog's legs, and tasty bone marrow to the incredible range of steaks. Open only in the evenings (5:30pm–2am). Reservations recommended.

Odeon
$$$

145 West Broadway, 10013 **Tel** *(212) 233-0507*   **Map** *1 B1*

One of the first restaurants to open in TriBeCa back in the 1980s, this "faux-bistro" offers good quality French-American fare. Don't miss the steak tartare, but note that the burgers are also top notch. The decor is simple and the place is always packed with a mixed crowd.

Peep
$$$

177 Prince St, 10012 **Tel** *(212) 254-7337*   **Map** *4 D3*

A hip SoHo single set descends on this hot-pink restaurant for tasty Thai and exotic cocktails. Be sure to stop by the bathrooms that give the restaurant its name – don't worry, the mirrors are only one-way (looking out). Prix-fixe lunches and dinner specials are a bargain.

Key to Price Guide *see p296* **Key to Symbols** *see back cover flap*

Petite Abeille
👪 ♿ $$$

134 West Broadway, 10013 **Tel** *(212) 791-1360* — **Map** *1 B1*

European cartoon favorite Tintin lends charm to the decor at this branch of a reasonably priced Belgian mini-chain. The most popular dish is mussels and French fries, especially the all-you-can-eat offerings on Wednesdays. The list of imported beers is impressive. Also open for breakfast and weekend brunch, when Belgian waffles are a favorite.

Public
👪 $$$

210 Elizabeth St, 10012 **Tel** *(212) 343-7011* — **Map** *4 F3*

A taste of modern Down Under food with inventive creations such as Meyer lemon ceviche, and grilled kangaroo on falafel. Try fusion cocktails or the Australian beer on offer and enjoy the industrial-chic, high-ceilinged space that fills nightly with a stylish SoHo crowd.

Kittichai
♿ [T] $$$$

60 Thompson St, 10012 **Tel** *(212) 219-2000* — **Map** *4 D4*

A high-end Thai restaurant in a beautifully designed space of the 60 Thompson hotel *(see p281)*, Kittichai is a definite place to be seen. The menu offers an expensive selection, including "Thai tapas," as well as seafood dishes such as monkfish with ginger, and desserts like banana spring rolls drizzled with a burnt honey sauce.

Nobu
♿ [T] $$$$

105 Hudson St, 10013 **Tel** *(212) 219-0500* — **Map** *4 D5*

Chef Nobu Matsuhisa offers a menu of fantastic reach for those who can afford it and get a reservation. The menu features items such as tuna toro tartar, Peruvian-influenced ceviches and tempuras, not to mention a lengthy sushi menu. This high-profile spot attracts celebrities and mortals alike.

Bouley
👪 ♿ [T] $$$$$

163 Duane St, 10013 **Tel** *(212) 668-5829* — **Map** *1 C1*

The modern French cuisine of famed chef David Bouley has an impressive TriBeCa home, with vaulted ceilings and elegant decor worthy of the fine fare. For those who cannot manage the hefty tab, the four-course prix-fixe lunch menu is a worthy sampling of the master's talents.

Corton
👪 ♿ [T] $$$$$

239 West Broadway, 10013 **Tel** *(212) 219-2777* — **Map** *4 E5*

After a 20-year reign in TriBeCa, the much-loved Montrachet has been renamed (Corton is a noted wine district in Burgundy) and given a revamped look and menu. The decor is cool and modern, and the chef has introduced modern French cuisine, like the foie gras with beets and blood orange, that has critics singing. A worthwhile splurge.

Megu
👪 ♿ [T] $$$$$

62 Thomas St, 10013 **Tel** *(212) 964-7777* — **Map** *1 B1*

Joining the latest trend in behemoth Japanese restaurants, Megu has an impressively decorated menu offering an outrageous option of dishes to be shared. Prime ingredients can quickly add up in the tab but some consider it the equivalent of dinner and a show. Can be noisy, especially on weekends.

GREENWICH VILLAGE

A Salt & Battery
👪 ♿ $

112 Greenwich Ave, 10011 **Tel** *(212) 691-2713* — **Map** *3 B1*

Come here for the best fish-and-chips this side of the pond at rock-bottom prices. There are many different combinations of fish and platters to choose from. A vast selection of other side dishes as well makes the trip worth it, especially that infamously delicious deep-fried Mars bar.

Corner Bistro
📋 👪 $

331 West 4th St, 10014 **Tel** *(212) 242-9502* — **Map** *3 C1*

The line outside indicates this isn't your typical bistro food, but a dive that has developed a cult following for the juiciest and messiest burgers and the cheapest beer in town. Grab a spot in line that sometimes snakes by the bar and outside. Food is served on paper plates with lots of napkins.

Moustache
📋 👪 $$

90 Bedford St, 10014 **Tel** *(212) 229-2220* — **Map** *3 C2*

Middle-Eastern casual eatery with consistently good and cheap food, including Turkish *pitzas*, merguez sausages, and lamb. The space may be too small for the crowd and service can be slow. Try the sibling East Village spot at 265 East 19th Street that includes an indoor garden.

Westville
👪 [T] $$

210 West 10th St, 10014 **Tel** *(212) 741-7971* — **Map** *3 C2*

A no-thrills narrow eatery offering great-value meals of regional American cooking, aka comfort food staples, such as cod po'boys, burgers, mac 'n' cheese, and BLTs. Avoid rush hours since cheap prices can mean long lines. So popular it spawned an East Village sister, cleverly called Westville East.

10 Downing
⚐ $$$

10 Downing St, 10014 **Tel** *(212) 255-0300*
Map *4 D3*

Dine on *nouveau* French cuisine at this sleek restaurant that fills with a lively crowd of locals and visitors. Try the hearty *cassoulet* tossed with mini duck meatballs or *agnoletti* topped with peekytoe crab. For dessert the rich chocolate cake with a malt-flavored ice cream center is a real treat.

Blue Ribbon Bakery
⚐ $$$

33 Downing Street, 10014 **Tel** *(212) 337-0404*
Map *4 D3*

An extensive tapas-style menu made out of cheeses and cold cuts with fantastic bread is complemented with soups, salads, and entrées such as filet mignon and burgers. An accessible wine list makes this an ideal place to pass time with friends and family.

Centro Vinoteca
⚐ $$$

74 Seventh Ave, 10011 **Tel** *(212) 367-7470*
Map *8 E5*

This buzzing, split-level restaurant, with whitewashed brick walls and large picture windows, features creative Italian fare. Ease into the evening with *piccolino* (small plates), including fried cauliflower in a parmesan crust, followed by meaty main dishes such as lamb bolognese or rabbit stuffed with sausage and pine nuts.

One
♿ $$$

1 Little West 12th St, 10014 **Tel** *(212) 255-9717*
Map *3 B1*

The New American menu is designed around plates for one and plates to share, with a large selection of seafood platters as a group option. Most people come here for the hopping, trendy scene rather than the food, however. There are three different lounge areas: choose one according to your mood.

Otto
⚐♿ $$$

1 Fifth Ave, 10003 **Tel** *(212) 995-9559*
Map *4 E1*

An upscale and fashionable pizzeria from chef Mario Batali. An amazing wine list and an array of side dishes and antipasti can quickly raise your tab in this usually crowded and upbeat place. Try the famous lardo pizza, which is exactly what it sounds like – pig lard slathered on pizza crust. Don't miss the olive oil ice cream.

Pastis
⚐▥ $$$

9 Ninth Ave, 10014 **Tel** *(212) 929-4844*
Map *3 B1*

Among the pioneers in the Meatpacking District, this gorgeous Parisian bistro offers good-quality French fare in large portions. The ambience can be loud on weekends, with plenty of celebrity sightseeing. It also serves a good weekend brunch. If you can't get a reservation, just show up and take your chances.

Pearl Oyster Bar
⚐ $$$

18 Cornelia St, 10014 **Tel** *(212) 691-8211*
Map *4 D4*

Very successful raw bar in the Village with top-of-the-line fresh ingredients and bold flavors. The lobster roll is a smash hit as are the Prince Edward Island mussels. Unlike other places that use quality ingredients, service is amicable too, but be prepared for long lines at rush hours.

The Spotted Pig
⚐ $$$

314 West 11th St, 10014 **Tel** *(212) 620-0393*
Map *3 B2*

Londoners will feel at home in Brit chef April Bloomfield's Italian take on gastropub fare. This tiny spot fills up quickly, so get there early during peak times and enjoy drinks at the bar. Hand-cask beer from Brooklyn Brewery is great with the first-rate shepherd's pie – and delicious.

The Waverly Inn and Garden
♿ $$$

216 Bank St (Waverly Place), 10014 **Tel** *(212) 243-7900*
Map *3 C1*

The quaint name belies the social scene, which on any given night might include celebrities, fashion editors, and VIPs. The homespun, well-priced menu features a selection of American classic dishes: clam chowder, pork chops with roasted apples, and the much-talked-about mac and cheese with shaved truffles.

Babbo
⚐ $$$$

110 Waverly Place, 10011 **Tel** *(212) 777-0303*
Map *4 D2*

Chef Mario Batali's flagship restaurant is housed in this beautiful Village duplex – paradise for high-quality pasta and offal lovers alike. Hard to get reservations and service could see some improvement given the prices. A winning wine list and trendy crowd add the magic touch to a great dining experience.

Blue Hill
⚐♿▥ $$$$

75 Washington Place, 10011 **Tel** *(212) 539-1776*
Map *4 E4*

This New American kitchen is obsessed with the quality of its ingredients, especially with the addition of its own Stone Barns produce from upstate New York. The limited menu is a guarantee of the freshness and liveliness of the seasonal dishes. Taste the poached foie gras or the Berkshire pork with chestnuts.

Da Silvano
⚐♿▥ $$$$

260 Sixth Ave, 10014 **Tel** *(212) 982-2343*
Map *4 D3*

This Tuscan restaurant is popular more for the celebrities that dine here than the food itself, which covers a wide range of pastas, some seafood antipasti, salads, and traditional entrées such as lamb chops and stewed rabbit. The coveted outdoor seating is perfect for peoplewatching in the summer months.

Key to Price Guide *see p296* **Key to Symbols** *see back cover flap*

One if by Land, Two if by Sea ♿ 🎵 👔 [$][$][$][$]

17 Barrow St, 10014 ***Tel*** *(212) 228-0822* ***Map*** *3 C3*

Aaron Burr's carriage house made famous in the American Revolution is now arguably one of the most romantic and historical spots in town. To some, the decor seems a tad kitsch. The three-course prix-fixe of casual American dining is served right next to the fireplace and candles. Piano music daily.

Spice Market ♿ [$][$][$][$]

403 West 13th St, 10014 ***Tel*** *(212) 675-2322* ***Map*** *3 B1*

A beautiful behemoth of a place featuring Asian-inspired "street food" by chef Jean Georges Vongerichten. With a club-like atmosphere, it is *the* place for beautiful people (including waiters) to sip fancy cocktails. The menu, however, is a hit-and-miss affair.

Gotham Bar & Grill ♿ 👔 [$][$][$][$][$]

12 East 12th Street, 10003 ***Tel*** *(212) 620-4020* ***Map*** *4 E1*

A New York classic of modern American cuisine showcasing revolutionary chef Alfred Portale's creations such as gingerbread crusted foie gras or roasted pheasant in a ginger and juniper marinade. Some consider the place somewhat past its prime but the bargain $25 prix-fixe lunch is worth a try.

EAST VILLAGE

Blue 9 Burger 🚫 🧒 ♿ [$]

92 Third Ave, 10003 ***Tel*** *(212) 979-0053* ***Map*** *4 F1*

Tasty griddle hamburgers in the East Village at very affordable prices for when you get those fast-food cravings without the need to visit a chain. Plus, they offer a mango-chili sauce with your fries. Grab it to go and head to a park nearby for a good people-watching picnic.

Dumpling Man 🚫 🧒 [$]

100 St Mark's Place, 10009 ***Tel*** *(212) 505-2121* ***Map*** *5 A1*

Tiny yet trendy bar in the East Village, offering a wide variety of dumplings to meet your imagination. You get to watch what goes on behind the bar as the cooks handle the steamed or fried treasures. With rock-bottom prices, it doesn't get better than this dinner and a show.

Minca Ramen Factory 🚫 🧒 [$]

536 East 5th St, 10009 ***Tel*** *(212) 505-8001* ***Map*** *5 B2*

Minca is a Ramen-style noodle joint that is far away from your memories of microwave noodle cups. You can choose a variety of noodles with beef, pork, vegetarian, and more. Perfect spot for cold weather after a stroll through the East Village hip boutiques.

Caracas Arepa Bar 🧒 [$][$]

91 East 7th St, 10009 ***Tel*** *(212) 228-5062* ***Map*** *5 A2*

A kitschy restaurant with delicious Venezuelan fast food and slow service. *Arepas* (savoury corn cakes with a variety of fillings), sandwiches, and *tamales* are great fillers at rock-bottom prices. The premises are unbelievably small but the food keeps people coming. They also have a Brooklyn location.

Counter 🧒 [$][$]

105 First Ave, 10003 ***Tel*** *(212) 982-5870* ***Map*** *5 A2*

Inventive vegetarian cuisine worth the trip for non-vegetarians in a sophisticated dining room. An inviting environmentally sound, organic or biodynamic, wine list is also highly recommended. Caring but nevertheless spotty service from time to time.

Great Jones Café 🧒 [$][$]

54 Great Jones St, 10012 ***Tel*** *(212) 674-9304* ***Map*** *4 F2*

Get your fix of New Orleans cooking in this inexpensive, family-friendly, jukebox-equipped hole-in-the-wall. Staples include fried shrimp po'boys, andouille sausages, and jambalaya. Definitely down it all with a beer. Look for the colorful Elvis likeness in the window.

Il Bagatto 🧒 [$][$]

192 East 2nd St, 10009 ***Tel*** *(212) 228-0977* ***Map*** *5 B2*

Trendy and popular Italian eatery with inexpensive and well-executed food that has New Yorkers flocking to the East Village. However, be warned of long lines and rushed service as a consequence. The reservation policy is a bit of mystery, so call ahead and see. If staying locally, order take-away.

La Palapa 🧒 ⛱ [$][$]

77 St. Marks Place, 10003 ***Tel*** *(212) 777-2537* ***Map*** *5 A1*

Mexico City-style and regional Mexican cooking with authentic ingredients make this a good fiesta destination in the beautifully decorated dining room. It's easy on the wallet and serves great margaritas too. Don't miss the Zihuatanejo-style catfish or the duck in black mole sauce.

Lil' Frankies

19–21 First Ave, 10003 **Tel** (212) 420-4900   **Map** 5 A2 $$

Lil' Frankies is a neighborhood pizzeria with an oven that claims to have lava from Vesuvius! Despite the boasting, cheap and very good pizzas draw a hip young crowd. The place features a backyard garden for alfresco dining, and service is friendly, if a bit on the slow side.

Zum Schneider

107 Avenue C, 10009 **Tel** (212) 598-1098   **Map** 5 B2 $$

Oktoberfest all year round in this neighborhood favorite Bier Garten. Bring your lederhosen and enjoy the relaxed atmosphere and great sausages. Family-friendly, it usually draws big crowds on weekends when the service can be slow. As you might expect, a great selection of beer on tap from all over the world.

Casimir

103 Avenue B, 10009 **Tel** (212) 358-9683   **Map** 5 B2 $$$

Packed French bistro in the happening area of Alphabet City. Authentic fare brought by good-looking, not necessarily speedy, waiters includes black pudding sausage and steak *frites*. Try grabbing a table at the little outside garden for extra charm, and make sure to bring your American Express (the only card accepted).

The Elephant

58 East 1st St, 10003 **Tel** (212) 505-7739   **Map** 5 A3 $$$

A Thai-French place that is always happening with cute crowd and waiters alike. Inventive Thai cocktails and well-executed dishes such as sticky rice with chicken and pork, and duck breast with orange confit and cinnamon prepared in a wok. The decor is a mix of funky rattan with French accents.

Jules

65 St. Marks Place, 10003 **Tel** (212) 477-5560   **Map** 5 A2 $$$

A candle-lit Parisian brasserie vibe and live jazz nightly with no cover charge (a New York rarity) make this a fine East Village choice. The menu has familiar bistro offerings like steak *frites* as well as more classic French dishes. The swinging young crowd adds to the ambience. Be prepared; the band will ask for tips.

The Mermaid Inn

96 Second Ave, 10003 **Tel** (212) 674-5870   **Map** 5 A2 $$$

This hip seafood restaurant attracts a young foodie crowd delighting in a prime, fresh raw bar and New England-style fare such as lobster sandwiches and chowder. A no-reservation policy usually comes with long lines attached, but stick them out: it is worth it.

Momofuku Noodle Bar

171 First Ave, 10003 **Tel** (212) 475-7899   **Map** 5 A1 $$$

Celebrated Korean-American chef David Chang is at the helm of this airy restaurant. The menu changes daily and might include steamed pork buns or duck confit salad. The signature ramen comes soaked in a fragrant stock made from pork bones and chicken legs, and then laden with pork belly, snowpeas, and a poached egg.

Hearth

403 East 12th St, 10009 **Tel** (212) 602-1300   **Map** 5 A1 $$$$

A Tuscan-American restaurant with high-quality and audacious food in a romantic and chic-rustic setting. Chef Marco Canora (previously from Craft) offers interesting dishes such as *ribollita* (bean and cabbage soup), New Zealand venison, and olive oil cake. Tasting menu available.

Jewel Bako

239 East 5th St, 10003 **Tel** (212) 979-1012   **Map** 4 F2 $$$$

The battle for New York's best sushi got more heated with this high-end Japanese restaurant offering fresh-from-the-sea ingredients beautifully prepared. Courteous but erratic service and the extremely tiny premises take some shine out of the expensive experience. A more casual spot just opened around the corner.

GRAMERCY AND THE FLATIRON DISTRICT

Chat 'n' Chew

10 East 16th St, 10003 **Tel** (212) 243-1616   **Map** 8 F5 $$

Kitschy comfort food destination in the Union Square area that fills the spot and is gentle on the wallet. Staples include mac 'n' cheese, a year-round Thanksgiving roast-turkey dinner, and mama's meatloaf. Don't forget the mashed potatoes, and a changing selection of cakes and pies for dessert. Good brunch spot.

Chennai Garden

129 East 27th St, 10016 **Tel** (212) 689-1997   **Map** 9 A3 $$

The area known as "Curry Hill" has many Indian restaurants but this inviting spot is a bit different, offering well-prepared South Indian fare that also happens to be vegetarian and kosher. Although the decor is nothing special, the bargain-priced all-you-can-eat lunch buffet definitely impresses with its variety and freshness.

Pipa

$$

38 East 19th St, 10003 **Tel** *(212) 677-2233* **Map** *9 A5*

Popular Pipa features a spacious dining room with wooden tables, aged mirrors, heavy draperies, and twinkling chandeliers. The zesty Spanish *tapas* include *coca*, a Catalan flatbread topped with tart artichokes and *sobrasada*, a spicy Mallorcan sausage; and sautéed spinach studded with raisins. There are also pitchers of potent sangria.

Tong Thai Brasserie

$$

39 East 13th St, 10003 **Tel** *(212) 253-2696* **Map** *4 F1*

A former lumber store transformed into an elegant two-level Thai restaurant, Tong Thai offers an array of creative dishes, including mussels resting on pillows of rice batter, and salt-baked chicken sweetened with strips of mango. For a warm finish, sip aromatic tea served in little iron teapots.

Bamiyan

$$$

358 Third Ave, 10016 **Tel** *(212) 481-3232* **Map** *9 B3*

This Afghan restaurant offers a pleasant change of pace, with windows featuring tribal rugs and pillow seats around traditional low tables. The authentic menu features tasty curries, charcoal-grilled kebabs and yogurt dishes, along with more unusual dishes for adventurous diners.

Blue Smoke

$$$

116 East 27th St, 10016 **Tel** *(212) 447-7733* **Map** *9 A3*

Danny Meyer does down south BBQ in this hip joint. Expect luscious heavy-duty pulled pork sandwiches, full racks of ribs, corn muffins, and hushpuppies (deep-fried cornmeal batter). The place features a jazz club downstairs. The large bar offers beer from around the US, and is great for large groups.

Devi

$$$

8 East 18th St, 10003 **Tel** *(212) 691-1300* **Map** *8 F5*

A trendy newcomer from chefs Suvi Saran and Hemant Mathur, showcasing authentic regional Indian cuisine in a gracious environment full of Indian textiles and woodcarvings. Dishes include tandoori lamb chops with pear chutney and Masala-fried quail, and don't miss the delectable cauliflower!

I Trulli

$$$

122 East 27th St, 10010 **Tel** *(212) 481-7372* **Map** *9 A3*

An upscale Italian restaurant specializing in Pugliese (Southern Italian) cuisine, I Trulli is the ideal spot for a romantic dinner by the fireplace in winter or in the garden during summer. A great wine list is available both here and at Enoteca I Trulli, its wine bar next door.

Pure Food and Wine

$$$

54 Irving Place, 10003 **Tel** *(212) 477-1010* **Map** *9 A5*

New York's first restaurant dedicated to the raw-vegan movement – no food heated above 118°F. Expect produce with pedigree in creative dishes at this smart venue. A few examples include coconut noodles, cauliflower samosas, and an amaranth-crust pizza with hummus.

Tamarind

$$$

41–43 East 22nd St, 10010 **Tel** *(212) 674-7400* **Map** *8 F4*

A modern Indian restaurant with minimalist decorations, fantastic china, and friendly service. While pricier than your average Indian eatery, the quality of the ingredients and mix of flavors will transport you to India promptly. Ask the waiter to help you pair something from their extensive wine list.

Craft

$$$$

43 East 19th St, 10003 **Tel** *(212) 780-0880* **Map** *9 A5*

Executive chef Tom Colicchio from the acclaimed Gramercy Tavern offers a "deconstructed" menu of vibrant quality in this sleekly decorated venue. Diners have the option to "create" their entrée with a combination of ingredients and sides that can quickly push up the tab. If it seems stressful, just ask the waiter for advice.

Gramercy Tavern

$$$$

42 East 20th St, 10003 **Tel** *(212) 477-0777* **Map** *9 A5*

Acclaimed chef Tom Colicchio prepares outstanding food in a comfortable, always hopping, rustic ambience of a country inn house. An ideal place for a sophisticated dining experience without stuffy pretense. This is consistently one of the best dining experiences in the city.

Mesa Grill

$$$$

102 Fifth Ave, 10011 **Tel** *(212) 807-7400* **Map** *8 F5*

Star chef Bobby Flay's flagship restaurant showcases modern Southwestern cuisine and has pleased crowds since 1991. The creative menu includes cornmeal-crusted oysters, a "deconstructed" lamb taco, and chile- and honey-glazed salmon. The special margaritas are quite something, and the bar scene alone can get quite lively.

Tocqueville

$$$$

1 East 15th St, 10003 **Tel** *(212) 647-1515* **Map** *8 F5*

This tucked-away gem in Union Square offers French cuisine with Japanese touches, in a simple yet elegant and intimate room. Husband-and-wife team Marco Moreira and Jo-Ann Makovitsky put out well-executed quality ingredients. Great for a special occasion that does not require a house mortgage.

Union Square Café
🚻 $$$$

21 East 16th Street, 10003 **Tel** *(212) 243-4020* **Map** *9 A5*

Among the most popular of New York City restaurants, this Danny Meyer flagship serves modern American cuisine in comfortable surroundings, drawing ingredients from the greenmarket in Union Square. The prices are anything but market level. Courteous service.

11 Madison Park
🚹🚻🛗 $$$$$

11 Madison Ave, 10010 **Tel** *(212) 889-0905* **Map** *9 A4*

The Art Deco dining room with soaring ceilings and views of historic Madison Square Park make this the most elegant of Danny Meyer's restaurant empire. The chef has brought recent acclaim, with a modern French menu that gets high marks from critics. Note, however, that the *haute cuisine* comes at a correspondingly high price.

Veritas
🚻 $$$$$

43 East 20th St, 10010 **Tel** *(212) 353-3700* **Map** *9 A5*

A small sleek restaurant in the Flatiron District dedicated to wine. Wine-lovers may have a coronary when reading the 2,700 plus wine list. However, the food rises to the occasion with jewels such as foie gras with a quince-Armagnac sauce and a fragrant bouillabaisse of monkfish, skate, cauliflower, and saffron. Prix-fixe only.

CHELSEA AND THE GARMENT DISTRICT

Empire Diner
🚹🟦 $$

210 Tenth Ave, 10011 **Tel** *(212) 243-2736* **Map** *7 C4*

Landmark Chelsea Art Deco diner open 24 hours with standard comfort food. This is the place to have trashy American fare such as pigs in a blanket after 4am for the still-raving club-kids! A sidewalk café in the warm months is also popular for brunch, and checking out the hip Chelsea crowd.

Bottino
🟦 $$$

246 Tenth Ave, 10001 **Tel** *(212) 206-6766* **Map** *7 C4*

A Northern Italian restaurant in a restored 100-year-old hardware shop with minimalist decor. The place attracts a stylish crowd especially to its lovely backyard garden to enjoy traditional salads, pastas, and grilled meats. Try tasty dishes like spinach pasta with ricotta cheese or juicy New York strip steak with cannellini beans.

The Red Cat
$$$

227 Tenth Ave, 10011 **Tel** *(212) 242-1122* **Map** *7 C4*

Modern American food in a gorgeous barnhouse setting with red- and white-painted wood that will transport you to New England. The menu features some of the best quality dishes in the neighborhood such as crispy fried oysters, wild striped bass in white wine butter, and delicious risotto fritters with blueberries.

Sueños
🚹 $$$

311 West 17th St, 10011 **Tel** *(212) 243-1333* **Map** *8 D5*

Traditional Mexican regional cuisine served in a colorful mid-sized space. Great tequila and margarita bar and inventive food creations, including a chile-tasting menu, provide the necessary ingredients for a pleasant, if slightly above average-priced, dining experience.

Buddakan
🚻 $$$$

75 Ninth Ave, 10011 **Tel** *(212) 989-6699* **Map** *8 D5*

Philadelphia restaurateur Stephen Starr is repeating his success with a series of New York establishments. Buddakan is the jewel in his crown, featuring jaw-dropping decor in the main hall and a series of more intimate, smaller spaces. The Asian fusion cuisine is tasty, but not the main draw to this Chelsea restaurant. Hopping bar scene.

Matsuri
🛗 $$$$

369 West 16th St, 10011 **Tel** *(212) 243-6400* **Map** *8 D5*

An enormous and noisy dining space in the Maritime Hotel *(see p284)*, Matsuri features high-quality Japanese fare from chef Tadashi Ono. He offers a range of dishes prepared with prime ingredients such as Kobe beef, sweet shrimp, and sake-soaked black cod. There is also a great sake list.

THEATER DISTRICT

Burger Joint at Le Parker Meridien
📋🚹🚻 $

119 West 57th St, 10019 **Tel** *(212) 708-7414* **Map** *12 E3*

This kitsch joint inside the Parker Meridien hotel *(see p286)* serves freshly cooked, mouthwatering burgers, fries, shakes, beer, and little else at rock-bottom prices. There's nothing uptight about this midtown gem hidden behind curtains in the lobby.

Carnegie Deli 📋 👪 $
854 Seventh Ave, 10019 **Tel** *(212) 757-2245* **Map** *12 E4*

You'll have to wait in long lines to glimpse one of this deli's gargantuan sandwiches and history-making cheesecakes. You'll also have to endure hostile waiters in order to experience this "quintessential" New York experience. While expensive, you probably won't eat for over a week.

Carve Unique Sandwiches 👪 ♿ $
760 Eighth Ave, 10036 **Tel** *(212) 730-4949* **Map** *12 D5*

A small shop where you can get all your sandwich cravings fulfilled on the cheap in the Theater District. Hefty sandwiches include grilled lemon chicken, and a tomato, basil, and mozzarella combo. Lines are exasperatingly long at lunchtime, so try it in off hours.

Pam Real Thai Food 📋 👪 $
404 West 49th St, 10019 **Tel** *(212) 333-7500* **Map** *11 C5*

If you are looking for good, inexpensive Thai food in the area, and don't care about decor, then this is the place. The usual assortment of curries, soups, pad Thai and noodle and rice dishes come in a variety of spicy degrees to order. No reservations means long waits at rush hour.

Kodama Sushi 👪 ♿ $$
301 West 45th St, 10036 **Tel** *(212) 582-8065* **Map** *12 D5*

The convenient location, reliably fresh sushi, and other well-prepared Japanese favorites at good prices make Kodama a popular pre-theater choice. Regulars recommend the menu of rolls, with inventive ingredient combinations. Fast service ensures you will make the show on time, even at busy times.

Norma's 👪 $$
118 West 57th St, 10019 **Tel** *(212) 708-7460* **Map** *12 E3*

Brunch reaches its zenith here in Le Parker Meridien hotel *(see p286)*. The elaborate and creative menu, from lobster and asparagus omelette to chocolate French toast, will fulfill all of your desires. Pricey, but you won't eat anything else for the rest of the day, or have brunch anywhere quite like it. Weekends can see long lines. Very family-friendly.

Virgil's Real Barbecue 👪 ♿ $$
152 West 44th St, 10036 **Tel** *(212) 921-9494* **Map** *12 E5*

Hopping BBQ joint in the heart of Times Square with an always bustling clientele and fast service. Ideal for pre-theater dining, provided that the heavy meal doesn't make you sleepy. Staples include over 10 different meat platters from around America, and tasty side dishes such as biscuits, collard greens, grits, and mac 'n' cheese.

Becco 👪 $$$
355 West 46th St, 10036 **Tel** *(212) 397-7597* **Map** *11 D5*

Chef Lidia Bastianich is a co-owner of this standard Italian *trattoria* on restaurant row offering a decent selection of antipasti, salads, pastas, and main courses, as well as pre-theater menus. The $25 wine list is a great deal as well; for those with more to spend, check out the more extensive regular wine list.

Marseille 👪 ♿ $$$
630 Ninth Ave, 10036 **Tel** *(212) 333-3410* **Map** *12 D5*

Good dining in the Theater District is indeed possible at this romantic French-Mediterranean restaurant with modern twists, including roasted monkfish with a cream-and-green-apple purée. The vegetarian-friendly menu is served by a courteous staff. Check out the funky bar, Kemia, downstairs.

Molyvos 👪 ♿ $$$
871 Seventh Ave, 10019 **Tel** *(212) 582-7500* **Map** *12 E4*

An upscale Greek restaurant near Carnegie Hall. The warm Mediterranean decor is the perfect setting for fresh seafood and other Greek specialties justifying the above-average prices. Try the flashy (and flaming) saganaki appetizer for your own pre-theater experience. Prix-fixe available.

Osteria al Doge $$$
142 West 44th St, 10036 **Tel** *(212) 944-3643* **Map** *12 E5*

Venetian cuisine in a rustic dining room with a successful power-lunch clientele and popular with early evening theater-goers. Service is expeditious and warm. The menu includes pizza, great salads, and carpaccio as well as fresh pastas at prices and quality better than other venues in the area.

Blue Fin ♿ $$$$
1567 Broadway, 10036 **Tel** *(212) 918-1400* **Map** *12 E5*

Among the coolest places in the area, this is dedicated to seafood in a big way, including a raw and sushi bar. The two-story restaurant is always hopping and some may complain about the noise level, not just from the live music. A good place to flex the expense account.

db Bistro Moderne ♿ $$$$
55 West 44th St, 10036 **Tel** *(212) 391-2400* **Map** *8 F1*

Home of the famous $32 burger (filled with foie gras and wine-braised short ribs). This lively midtown restaurant offers another glimpse of Daniel Boulud's fine-dining experience with less damage to the wallet. Popular for power lunches with the publishing executive crowd who can afford it. Nice choice for upscale pre-theater dinner.

Esca

402 West 43rd St, 10036 **Tel** *(212) 564-7272*

$$$$

Map 8 D1

An upscale Italian seafood restaurant from the Batali-Bastianich partnership. A large variety of appetizers is followed by other dishes that reflect the great quality of its ingredients. Service can be unreliable and some think the atmosphere is a bit stale. A little formal, so not the best place for children.

Gordon Ramsay

151 West 54th St, 10019 **Tel** *(212) 468-8888*

$$$$

Map 12 E4

Despite UK chef Gordon Ramsay's brash reputation, his first US venture is a subdued affair. The 45-seat restaurant focuses on exquisite French cuisine with Asian accents, including roasted striped bass with bak choi and caramelized sweetbreads. The prix-fixe lunch is a bargain. Book well in advance, especially for the eight-seat kitchen table.

Osteria del Circo

120 West 55th St, 10019 **Tel** *(212) 265-3636*

$$$$

Map 12 E4

Northern Italian restaurant from the Maccioni family known for Le Cirque. The Adam Tihany-designed dining room is spacious and comfortable and the food is well executed amid very affable service. Save space for desserts, including the Tuscan doughnuts with cappuccino cream.

Triomphe

49 West 44th St, 10036 **Tel** *(212) 453-4233*

$$$$

Map 12 F5

A charming oasis of quiet from the bustle of Times Square, this French restaurant in the Iroquois Hotel pairs excellent food and wine with impeccable service. Tasting menus are available, as well as quirkier events, such as gathering between 10 and 20 of your friends to enjoy dinner and a movie in the private room.

Le Bernardin

155 West 51st St, 10019 **Tel** *(212) 554-1515*

$$$$$

Map 12 E4

A dream-come-true for seafood- and fish-lovers. This superb and elegant longstanding dining experience offers an outstanding dining experience with French *haute cuisine* from chef Eric Ripert. Service is flawless, including the sommelier advice. It's the place to propose.

Milos Estiatorio

125 West 55th St, 10019 **Tel** *(212) 245-7400*

$$$$$

Map 12 E4

Formidable Greek food with fresh-out-of-the-water seafood set in a spartan, airy dining room where guests select the fish from a beautifully decorated stand. The catch of the day depends on the luck of the fishermen purveyors for this upscale restaurant. Prices are some of the most expensive in town.

LOWER MIDTOWN

Ali Baba

212 East 34th St, 10016 **Tel** *(212) 683-9206*

$$

Map 9 B2

Kebabs and lamb dishes are the favorites at this unpretentious Turkish standby offering good food at moderate prices. Pita pizzas are among the house specialties, and all of the *meze* (appetizers), hot and cold, are tasty, as are the main dishes, such as the lamb kebabs. The outdoor dining area hidden in the back is a welcome oasis in midtown.

Artisanal

2 Park Ave, 10016 **Tel** *(212) 725-8585*

$$$

Map 9 A2

Sparkling upscale French bistro where the main topic is cheese, including a large selection to taste either by themselves or in fondues. Non-cheese lovers need not be afraid as there are plenty of non-dairy selections available. Service can be unreliable, and reservations aren't always respected on time.

Grand Central Oyster Bar

Grand Central, Lower Level, 42nd St, 10017 **Tel** *(212) 490-6650*

$$$

Map 9 A1

Cavernous space inside Grand Central where you'll be transported to the past. The very fresh seafood in simple preparations are not too pricey, and the menu features a long list of over a dozen kinds of oysters. The setting and decor is casual, so leave the fur coats at home and bring your appetite. Waiter service included.

Convivio

45 Tudor City Place, 10017 **Tel** *(212) 599-5045*

$$$$

Map 9 B1

The admirable L'Impero restaurant has become the more colorful, less formal, Convivio. While the mood is more casual, the excellent southern Italian menu is as good as ever, and the pasta dishes continue to please. The prix-fixe is reasonable for this quality. Still a special occasion choice and a good excuse to discover hidden Tudor City.

Michael Jordan's The Steakhouse NYC

Grand Central, North Balcony, 10017 **Tel** *(212) 655-2300*

$$$$

Map 9 A1

The celebrity player steakhouse located at the beautifully renovated mezzanine of Grand Central Terminal. Expect high-quality (and high-priced) dry, aged cuts. Avoid a hot summer day because the terminal is not air conditioned. Service is casual but knowledgable and you can't beat the view of the hectic train passengers below.

UPPER MIDTOWN

La Bonne Soupe

48 West 55th St, 10019 **Tel** *(212) 586-7650*

$ · Map 12 F4

A cozy midtown haven for the thrifty, with a longstanding French bistro menu including quiches, omelettes, soups, steaks, fondues, and crêpes. Service is on the slow side. Features a small terrace for outdoor dining in the warm months. A great low-cost option in this pricey and upscale neighborhood.

BLT Steak

106 East 57th St, 10022 **Tel** *(212) 752-7470*

$$$ · Map 13 A3

Bistro Laurent Tourondel (BLT) offers fancy steaks with prime ingredients and your choice of sauces, from tangy three-mustard to creamy Béarnaise, for your Angus-certified protein. A stylish room with toffee-colored booths, a zinc bar, and other eye-catching elements draws a hip, fashion-conscious crowd.

Dawat

210 East 58th St, 10022 **Tel** *(212) 355-7555*

$$$ · Map 13 B3

An attractive Indian restaurant with recipes from none other than famous Indian chef Madhur Jaffrey. Signature dishes include salmon rubbed with a coriander chutney and baked in a banana leaf. The clever touch is a snack car that parades to your table. If you're not an Indian food expert, ask the helpful staff for advice.

Rue 57

60 West 57th St, 10019 **Tel** *(212) 307-5656*

$$$ · Map 12 F3

The fusion fever does not stop at Rue 57, which offers a combination of a sushi bar and French cuisine in a popular sophisticated bistro. The succulent duck à l'orange comes highly recommended. It's good value as a breakfast option as well. Sidewalk tables available – a great people-watching spot in warm months.

Shun Lee Palace

155 East 55th St, 10022 **Tel** *(212) 371-8844*

$$$ · Map 13 A4

A handsome dining room considered one of the city's premier Chinese restaurants. The menu is a Cantonese/ Szechuan blend with casserole specialties. The Grand Marnier prawns can become a serious addiction. Another location is near the Lincoln Center at 43 West 65th Street.

Insieme

77 Seventh Ave, 10019 **Tel** *(212) 582-1310*

$$$$ · Map 12 E4

Chef Marco Canova introduces his inventive Italian cuisine to this corner of midtown. The spare, cool-toned restaurant features weathered white-oak tables, raw-silk drapes, and a menu that lists traditional Italian dishes on one side and modern, quirky takes on the other.

Marea

240 Central Park South, 10019 **Tel** *(212) 582-5100*

$$$$ · Map 12 D3

This Italian seafood palace features a superb menu – with a location to match, situated as it is at the crossroads of Central Park South and Columbus Circle. Delicacies include salt-crusted sea bass and razor clams with fennel fronds. There is also a small selection of non-fish dishes. Closed Fri lunch & Sun.

Pampano

209 East 49th St, 10017 **Tel** *(212) 751-4545*

$$$$ · Map 13 B2

A lovely, modern Mexican restaurant from chef Richard Sandoval and opera legend co-owner Placido Domingo. Inventive and fresh creations in a chic dining room will make you want to sing an aria or two. Don't miss the smoked swordfish appetizer or the halibut Pampano. A beautiful terrace is also available.

Aquavit

65 East 55th St, 10022 **Tel** *(212) 307-7311*

$$$$$ · Map 13 A4

The minimalist space for Aquavit serves as the home of inventive Scandinavian creations, including smoked Arctic char, from chefs Nils Noren and Marcus Samuelsson, with prime ingredients and several tasting menus available. The signature Aquavit cocktails are also a must.

Felidia

243 East 58th St, 10022 **Tel** *(212) 758-1479*

$$$$$ · Map 13 B3

TV star chef Lidia Bastianich offers upscale Italian fare in this charming, wood-paneled town house with exposed bricks and flower arrangements. Conducive to romance, the seasonal menu is creative and well executed. In line with Lidia's other restaurants, an impressive wine list is also available.

Four Seasons

99 East 52nd St, 10022 **Tel** *(212) 754-9494*

$$$$$ · Map 13 A4

Restaurants come and go, but this gracious New York institution with landmark decor by Philip Johnson seems to go on forever, always among the top-rated for American-Continental food. The Grill Room is still the prime place for power lunches, and the Pool Room is a perfect setting for special-occasion dinners.

La Grenouille
3 East 52nd St, 10022 **Tel** *(212) 752-1495*   🚻♿ ⑤⑤⑤⑤⑤

Map 12 F4

One of the last remaining classic French restaurants in the city, with outstanding food. The dining room walls are laden with silk and velvet blanquettes, beautiful floral arrangements abound making the eating experience a memorable one. A place for special occasions.

L'Atelier de Joel Robuchon
57 East 57th St, Four Seasons Hotel, 10022 **Tel** *(212) 350-6658*   🔲♿🚻 ⑤⑤⑤⑤⑤

Map 13 A3

Chef Joel Robuchon has brought his exquisite Asian-influenced French cuisine to the Four Seasons Hotel *(see p289)*. Just be prepared to pay dearly for these "small plates" of near perfection, from plump scallops in seaweed butter to quail stuffed with foie gras. A seat at the counter gives a view of the culinary team at work in the open kitchen.

The Modern
9 West 53rd St, 10019 **Tel** *(212) 333-1220*   ♿ ⑤⑤⑤⑤⑤

Map 12 F4

In a clean, modern space at the Museum of Modern Art, overlooking the Sculpture Garden, this restaurant serves an impeccable array of New American and French cuisine, alongside an extensive wine list. Expect a high level of service. The tasting menu is popular and can be enjoyed with a wine pairing if your wallet can take the strain.

Oceana
1221 Sixth Ave, 10020 **Tel** *(212) 759-5941*   🚻 ⑤⑤⑤⑤⑤

Map 12 E5

Ease into the evening with a crisp white wine and a platter of fresh seafood at this stylish vaulted restaurant. The menu features American cuisine with influences from as far afield as the Mediterranean and Asia. Excellent dishes include *branzino* (sea bass) stuffed with mushrooms, spinach, and black olives. There is also a Raw Bar.

UPPER EAST SIDE

Brother Jimmy's BBQ
1485 Second Ave, 10021 **Tel** *(212) 288-0999*   🏃 ⑤⑤

Map 17 B5

The original of the Brother Jimmy's chain promises a rowdy evening and some "finger-lickin'" ribs and Southern favorites. All-you-can-eat specials are a popular option. This is a good destination for carnivores, though there are a few options for vegetarians. Some quieter tables can be found at the rear.

Shanghai Pavilion
1378 Third Ave, 10021 **Tel** *(212) 585-3388*   🏃 ⑤⑤

Map 17 B5

Offering Shanghai cuisine, as authentic as you can get outside of Chinatown, the menu here has plenty of options at reasonable prices, making it a good value in this neighborhood. The service is friendly. Great dim sums, noodle dishes, and specialties such as velvet sea bass or lobster tropicana.

Via Quadronno
25 East 73rd St, 10021 **Tel** *(212) 650-9880*   🏃 ⑤⑤

Map 12 F1

A cute Italian-style "bar paninoteca" with a rainbow of delicious prime-ingredient sandwiches and salads worth a stop after a Museum Mile extravaganza. The small space inspired by a Milan paninoteca translates into waiting lines at peak hours. Definitely splurge on a glass of wine to go with the meal.

Beyoglu
1431 Second Ave, 10028 **Tel** *(212) 650-0850*   🏃♿ ⑤⑤⑤

Map 17 B5

Everyone raves about the *meze*, delicious Turkish appetizers, at this whimsically decorated, always crowded neighborhood favorite. Regulars make a meal of a selection of small treats like *borek* (filo stuffed with feta cheese), stuffed grape leaves, calf's liver, and eggplant salad; the daily seafood specials and lamb are also recommended.

Maya
1191 First Ave, 10021 **Tel** *(212) 585-1818*   🔲♿ ⑤⑤⑤

Map 13 C2

Chef Richard Sandoval serves sophisticated and delicate main courses at this upbeat Mexican restaurant in a peach-hued setting. The drawback comes in the sound level; dine early to avoid the din. Many rave about the seafood tacos, margaritas, and guacamole.

Sfoglia
1402 Lexington Ave, 10128 **Tel** *(212) 831-1402*   🔲🚻 ⑤⑤⑤

Map 17 A2

This popular restaurant specializes in Italian farmhouse fare. Start out with a bowl of plump, complimentary olives, followed by a pot of wild mussels steeped in garlic or braised duck with dried apricots. Top off the evening with a fine Italian wine, and don't miss the superb desserts, including homemade cookies and tangy gelato.

Café Boulud
20 East 76th St, 10021 **Tel** *(212) 772-2600*   ♿🚻 ⑤⑤⑤⑤

Map 16 F5

Chef Daniel Boulud creates a less formal dining room with solid creations inside the Surrey hotel. An interesting array of dinner options will keep any diner intrigued – "Le Tradition" (classic French), "Le Voyager" (world cuisines), "Le Potager" (vegetarian), and "La Saison" (seasonal specialties).

Key to Price Guide *see p296* **Key to Symbols** *see back cover flap*

Daniel
♿ [T] $$$$$

60 East 65th St, 10021 ***Tel*** *(212) 288-0033* — ***Map*** *13 A2*

Chef Daniel Boulud's flagship restaurant features a Venetian Renaissance-inspired dining room, one of the most luscious settings in town. His highly acclaimed creations celebrate the seasons: summer brings forth corn crêpes stuffed with chanterelles, while in autumn there are mushrooms in a white truffle sauce. Beware of the sky-high prices.

David Burke & Donatella
[T] $$$$$

133 East 61st St, 10021 ***Tel*** *(212) 813-2121* — ***Map*** *13 A3*

Creative New American dishes from chef David Burke and former Bellini hostess Donatella Arpaia. Diners cross a glamorous white gloss and stone bar to proceed to a cool dining area in bold colors and lacquered surfaces. Save room for the signature cheesecake "lollipop" dessert.

UPPER WEST SIDE

Whole Foods Market
👪 ♿ $

Time Warner Center, 10 Columbus Circle, 10019 ***Tel*** *(212) 823-9600* — ***Map*** *12 D3*

An enormous, environment-friendly supermarket with an impressive food hall stocking all sorts of cuisine from sushi to pizzas. The ideal spot to shop for your inexpensive picnic adventures in Central Park or eat in at the booths. A wine shop is available inside too. Beware of crowds at peak times. There are other branches throughout New York.

Gennaro
🥗 👪 ♿ $$

665 Amsterdam Ave, 10025 ***Tel*** *(212) 665-5348* — ***Map*** *15 C2*

An inexpensive small café serving consistently good Italian food with large servings. With a no-reservation policy, there can be lines at busy times. All the usuals are available here, including daily pasta specials and a wine list that is pretty reasonable. When busy, service can be annoyingly slow.

Olympic Flame Diner
👪 ♿ $$

200 West 60th St, 10023 ***Tel*** *(212) 581-5259* — ***Map*** *11 C3*

A classic New York diner, Olympic Flame is a find in the Lincoln Center area, where reasonable prices and tables without reservations are hard to come by. The enormous menu offers everything from omelettes, salads, and burgers to pastas, Greek specialties, and regular entrées. The efficient waiters will get you out in time for the curtain.

BLT Market
[T] $$$

Ritz-Carlton Hotel, 1430 Sixth Ave, 10019 ***Tel*** *(212) 521-6125* — ***Map*** *12 E3*

French chef Laurent Tourandel's epicurean empire expands with this venture that pays homage to seasonal produce and local purveyors. The impressive result is rustic fare with a French twist, from stuffed Amish chicken with shoestring potatoes to black cod with butternut squash purée. Daily brunch. Closed lunch; Sun & Mon.

Boathouse Restaurant Central Park
👪 ♿ ☂ $$$

Central Park, East 72nd St & Park Drive North, 10023 ***Tel*** *(212) 517-2233* — ***Map*** *12 E1*

The setting by Central Park's lake could not be any lovelier than this boathouse. An ideal place for brunch or lunch, and a romantic dinner is available April through October. Given the prices, it's unfortunate that the inevitable touristy nature has limited its potential to serve above-average food.

Café Fiorello
👪 $$$

1900 Broadway, 10023 ***Tel*** *(212) 595-5330* — ***Map*** *12 D2*

Boasting that it's "the longest running show on Broadway" this noisy Italian place features a bountiful antipasto bar. You can sample enough for a whole meal before crossing the street to the Lincoln Center. The menu also includes pizzas and standard Italian fare. Great for peoplewatching in the seasonal outside tables.

Café Luxembourg
👪 $$$

200 West 70th St, 10023 ***Tel*** *(212) 873-7411* — ***Map*** *11 C1*

A classic Art Deco Parisian bistro with a zinc-topped bar, antique mirrors, and a loyal, hip clientele with the occasional celebrity sighting. Standard bistro fare with weekly specials available but don't expect flawless service. The crowd and decor make it a good choice for business dinners.

Calle Ocho
👪 ♿ $$$

446 Columbus Ave, 10024 ***Tel*** *(212) 873-5025* — ***Map*** *16 D4*

It's a never-ending party in this loud and colorful Cuban restaurant filled with beautiful 20-somethings. The menu is an amalgam of Latin American dishes, all with varying degrees of success. A small kids' menu is also available. And since it's close to the American Museum of Natural History, take a break with your family and have a drink.

La Rural
🥗 👪 ☂ $$$

768 Amsterdam Ave, 10025 ***Tel*** *(212) 749-2929* — ***Map*** *15 C1*

Lively Argentine steakhouse La Rural serves a hearty *parrillada* (mixed grill) for two which includes steak, sweetbreads, ribs, sausage, salad, and one side dish. Meat is definitely the specialty here and you get lots of it, but leave room for dessert if you can.

Pasha

70 West 71st St, 10023 **Tel** *(212) 579-8751*

Map 12 D1

A serene and spacious, skylit, Turkish restaurant with friendly service ideal for a good conversation amid well-executed food. The lamb dumpling appetizers are delicious as well as the eggplant dishes, in particular the smoky *patlican salatasi*, mashed with garlic, olive oil, and lemon.

Rosa Mexicano

61 Columbus Ave, 10023 **Tel** *(212) 977-7700*

Map 12 D2

Popular and trendy upscale Mexican fine dining drawing a crowd of hip diners near Lincoln Center. Awesome pomegranate margaritas and sparkling sangrias, plus guacamole made to order at your table. Try the *cochinita pibil* tacos (achiote rubbed pork steamed in banana leafs) or the Veracruz fish in tomato sauce.

Ouest

2315 Broadway, 10024 **Tel** *(212) 580-8700*

Map 15 C4

Chef Tom Valenti offers his version of New American comfort cuisine – it's an elegant restaurant that still makes you feel comfortable. The menu features nightly specials such as traditional meatloaf and other creative dishes such as poached squab with foie gras *agnolotti*. An outstanding wine list is available as well.

Asiate

80 Columbus Circle, 35th Floor, 10019 **Tel** *(212) 805-8881*

Map 12 D3

Stellar views of Central Park are available from this Asian-influenced restaurant at the Mandarin Oriental hotel. Highlights include pan-seared foie gras with steamed sea eel and tamarind sauce and Wagyu beef with oxtail sauce. The bar includes an interesting array of cocktails.

Jean-Georges

1 Central Park West at Columbus Circle and West 60th St, 10023 **Tel** *(212) 299-3900*

Map 12 D3

Chef Jean-Georges's flagship temple for modern French cuisine with Asian nuances. An austere yet elegant, Adam Tihany-designed room is the stage for an impressive array of delicate dishes. Service is courteous and knowledgeable. One of the most memorable fine dining experiences in New York.

Masa

Time Warner Center, 10 Columbus Circle, 10019 **Tel** *(212) 823-9800*

Map 12 D3

Chef Masayoshi Takayama, of the famed LA Ginza Sushi-ko, has moved to New York to break the record of most expensive meal ever. It consists of a never-ending *kaiseki*-style (tasting) menu chosen by Mr Masa using incredibly fresh ingredients. Take a seat by the sushi bar to savor the show in every detail.

Per Se

Time Warner Center, 10 Columbus Circle, 10019 **Tel** *(212) 823-9335*

Map 12 D3

Call at least two months in advance to score a seat in the critically acclaimed restaurant from Thomas Keller of California's French Laundry fame. The tasting menus change daily, and many think the vegetarian option is the best. Plus, it offers spectacular views of Central Park. Service is impeccable.

Picholine

35 West 64th St, 10023 **Tel** *(212) 724-8585*

Map 12 D2

Terrance Brennan's elegant French-Mediterranean restaurant a few steps away from the Lincoln Center. Several prix-fixe, *à la carte*, and even tasting menus available with dishes such as John Dory with grapes, chanterelles, and truffle vinaigrette. Save room for their famous artisanal cheeses.

MORNINGSIDE HEIGHTS AND HARLEM

Amy Ruth's

113 West 116th St, 10026 **Tel** *(212) 280-8779*

Map 21 B3

Soul food at its best can be found at this Harlem classic, named after the owner's grandmother and decorated with portraits of jazz greats. Think fried or smothered chicken with waffles, spare ribs, catfish, collard greens, and sweet potatoes. Be sure to save room for Southern desserts like peach cobbler and "red velvet" chocolate cake.

FARTHER AFIELD: BROOKLYN

Chip Shop

383 Fifth Ave, 11215 **Tel** *(718) 832-7701*

An outpost of British comfort food in New York City, this inexpensive shop offers fish and chips, bangers and mash, and kidney pies in a kitschy dining room. Great to sit back with a group of friends and enjoy a pint of beer. Family-friendly as well. Don't forget to try the yummy fried Mars bar. There are several other locations in Brooklyn.

Key to Price Guide *see p296* **Key to Symbols** *see back cover flap*

Grimaldi's
19 Old Fulton St, 11201 **Tel** (718) 858-4300

Unbelievably good coal-oven pizzas made from the milkiest mozzarella and the freshest sauce. Definitely try the pepperoni. This place is worth the trip to Brooklyn and a walk back across the bridge. Bring your family and wait in line to taste the inexpensive pies at this buzzing pizzeria.

Planet Thailand
133 North 7th St, 11211 **Tel** (718) 599-5758

A trendy renovated warehouse featuring outstanding Thai specialties – try the beef and broccoli flat noodles – and a less successful sushi bar. A very hip place for large groups. Reserve ahead. Only one stop into Brooklyn on the L-train, this is the place to dine before bar-hopping in Williamsburg.

Ghenet Brooklyn
348 Douglass St, 11217 **Tel** (718) 230-4475

This Ethiopian restaurant in Park Slope features low, dark-wood tables flanked by caramel-hued banquettes, which invite grazing from circular platters. In place of utensils is spongy injera bread, which arrives like a row of tan, folded napkins. Try dishes such as tender chicken legs enveloped in sweet onions, or rosy chunks of tuna tartar.

Thomas Biesl
25 Lafayette Ave, Fort Greene, 11217 **Tel** (718) 222-5800

The location directly across from the Brooklyn Academy of Music is only one good reason to discover this touch of Old Europe, a warm café serving schnitzel, goulash, spaetzle, strudel, linzertorte, and other Viennese classics. The patio garden is a nice spot for brunch and on Mondays, when the theater is dark, prix-fixe dinners are a real bargain.

The Grocery
288 Smith St, 11231 **Tel** (718) 596-3335

A charming 30-seat restaurant in Carroll Gardens, offering a delightful seasonal menu such as whole boneless trout stuffed with spaetzle and asparagus or braised duck breast with bulghur, Swiss chard, and caramelized red wine. The romantic venue also features a lovely summer garden.

Peter Luger Steakhouse
178 Broadway, 11211 **Tel** (718) 387-7400

A New York institution serving "the discerning steak connoisseur" since 1887. Try their out-of-this-world meat. Just be aware that the decor's ambience is much like a beer-hall and the waiters can be snippy. Reserve ahead and still expect to wait for a table.

River Café
One Water St, 11201 **Tel** (718) 522-5200

Unrivaled for its location featuring stunning Manhattan skyline views, this upscale Brooklyn standout offers a New American three-course, prix-fixe menu. A tasting menu is also available. An unbeatable romantic place for special occasions. Save room for their signature chocolate Brooklyn Bridge dessert.

FARTHER AFIELD: QUEENS

Jackson Diner
37–47 74th St, 11372 **Tel** (718) 672-1232

This spacious Indian cafeteria-style restaurant pulls out all the stops for well-prepared Northern Indian (spicy) and Southern Indian (less spicy) food at very cheap prices and well worth the visit when you are at Jackson Heights. Magnificent lamb and tandoori chicken and prawn dishes, as well as samosas and great *lassi* to wash it all down.

Sripraphai
64-13 39th Ave, Woodside, 11377 **Tel** (718) 899-9599

Many believe the best, most authentic, and least expensive Thai food in New York is found in this plain café, 20 minutes from Manhattan, not far from the Woodside stop on the No.7 subway line. Well worth the trip, especially on a balmy night when you can enjoy the very pretty garden out back.

Elias Corner
24–02 31st St, 11102 **Tel** (718) 932-1510

Among the more popular Greek restaurants with a huge following and long lines. This no-thrills, expanded restaurant serves some of the freshest fish in town, prepared simply. A large garden also makes this a good place for group gatherings, if you don't mind the wait at rush hours, especially weekends.

S'Agapo
34–21 34th Ave, 11106 **Tel** (718) 626-0303

The name means "I love you" in Greek, and this taverna has a cheerful atmosphere where grilled fish is the specialty. Live music on weekends and a terrace for summer evenings enliven the inexpensive experience. The restaurant is close to the American Museum of the Moving Image.

Light Meals and Snacks

You can get a snack almost anywhere and anytime in Manhattan. New Yorkers seem to eat endlessly – on street corners, in bars, luncheonettes, delis, before and after work, and long into the night. Casual eating in New York might include soft pretzels or char-roasted chestnuts from a corner stand; a huge sandwich from a deli; a Greek gyro sandwich (roasted lamb in pita bread) from street vendors; a pre-theater snack at a café or coffee bar; or a post-party binge at an all-night diner or bistro. While street fare is generally cheap, the quality and culinary skills vary greatly.

DELIS

Delicatessens are a New York institution, not to mention a great source for a hefty lunchtime sandwich. Any visitor to the city should definitely try a deli's wonderful corned beef and pastrami sandwiches. While **Carnegie Delicatessen** in the Theater District is perhaps New York's most famous deli, **Katz's Deli** on the Lower East Side is much more authentic – and cheaper. Also deservedly popular is **Second Avenue Deli**, with its superb pastrami on rye and oozing blintzes.

Most deli business is takeout, and as a result, delis are bustling places serving huge sandwiches at relatively cheap prices. Counter staff are typically surly and impatient, and rudeness has almost become a trademark of the **Stage Deli**, which is now more of a tourist stop than the showbiz favorite it used to be.

For New York ethnic Jewish flavor, try **Barney Greengrass**, on the Upper West Side. In operation since 1929, the "Sturgeon King" serves up lox, salmon, pastrami, and, of course, sturgeon. **Zabar's** is a takeout heaven for yuppies who put up with the crowds for superb smoked fish, pickles, and salads.

CAFÉS, BISTROS, AND BRASSERIES

Cafés, bistros, and the larger brasseries have become "in" places in New York. Try the upscale **Balthazar** on Spring Street for "brilliantly faux" everything except the menu, which is stellar. Even more trendy is Balthazar's sister bistro, **Pastis**, in the Meatpacking District. The **Café Centro**, above Grand Central, is particularly busy and noisy during lunchtime, and is a favorite with business types. The Centro's Provençal/Mediterranean fare includes fish soups and some succulent desserts. **Brasserie** on East 53rd, a longtime landmark, has had an elegant remodeling. **Bistro du Nord** on Madison Avenue has a variety of French/American fare with an inventive flair. Downtown, **Odeon** is a TriBeCa favorite for its brasserie menu and late hours. **Raoul's** in SoHo is a French bistro with a relaxed ambience that keeps artists and other habitués coming back for reliable, informal food. **Elephant and Castle**, a minimally decorated café, is a Greenwich Village standby for soup-salad-omelette lunches and other light snacks. Its real forte is breakfast and brunch, served in ample portions at modest prices. The bar scene is lively too. Tiny **Chez Jacqueline** is also a favored Village spot. Its French bistro fare and proximity to several off-Broadway theaters make it popular with the young, hip, and international crowd for a moderately priced dinner or late supper.

In the Theater District, try the Cuban **Victor's Café**. Large, lively, and Latin, it is known for authentic Cuban food served in giant portions at medium prices. **Chez Josephine** is an exuberant bistro-cabaret with live jazz piano playing. The scene is the main attraction here, and the French food is excellent.

La Boite en Bois, small but delightfully French, serves delicious French bistro food and is conveniently close to Lincoln Center. In the same vicinity is **Vince and Eddie's**, a tiny gem known for reliable, often superb American food.

Sarabeth's, on the Upper West Side, defies categorizing, but might best be dubbed a café. Breakfast or weekend brunch is the best time to try waffles, French toast, pancakes, and omelettes. There are two other branches, one of which is located in the Whitney Museum of Art.

The Gramercy Park area's **Les Halles** is about as all-out French bistro as New York gets. At its late-night peak, the decibel level is high, but regulars think the *frites* and beef dishes are worth the noise and crowds.

PIZZERIAS

Pizza is available all over New York, from street stands and fast-food places that sell it by the slice to a traditional Neapolitan pizzeria.

Some pizzerias offer something more. **Arturo's Pizzeria** uses a coal oven for crisp, thin-crusted bases with the added inducement of live jazz. **Mezzogiorno** has a Tuscan menu and wonderful pizzas with unusual toppings. **Lombardi's** oven-baked pizzas are considered among the finest in Manhattan. The crowded **Mezzaluna** also specializes in brick-oven, thin-crusted pizza, as does **John's Pizzeria**, whose fans, including Woody Allen, consider it Manhattan's best.

Brooklyn boasts a top pizzeria in Coney Island's **Totonno Pizzeria**, which is well worth the trip for real pizza aficionados, though it also has a Manhattan branch. **Joe's Pizza** has made a name for itself in Brooklyn and Manhattan. It's often busy, but the lines move quickly.

Generally, pizza parlors are good places to go for a cheap, simple meal, particularly with children. Most places won't take reservations, so popular ones may have long lines.

HAMBURGER PLACES

Apart from the hot dog stands on the street, New York has many places selling better quality burgers, even though prices for a top grade all-beef burger can go up to $10.

Burgers have even gone "upscale" with famed New York restauranteur Danny Meyer creating the **Shake Shack** in Madison Square Park. It offers good-value eats from April to November. In Midtown, the stylish Le Parker Meridien Hotel opened the **Burger Joint**, which looks like a truck-stop, and has some of the best burgers in town.

Bright and basic, the five outlets of **Jackson Hole** offer fat, juicy, meaty burgers in 28 varieties popular with kids. Adults might prefer less glare and smarter decor, but they will like the low prices. Alternatively, sink your teeth into the juicy burgers on offer at the **Five Guys** chain.

The **Corner Bistro** in Greenwich Village offers New York's best burgers, tasty and reasonably priced. The beer selection is good, too, and the 4am closing makes this a great late-night stop.

DINERS AND LUNCHEONETTES

Diners and luncheonettes, also called sandwich or coffee shops, can be found all over New York City. Food is mostly bland but served in huge, cheap platefuls. They are usually open from breakfast until late evening, and you can stop in at almost any hour.

A favorite trend with diners has seen 1990s replicas of the old 1930s cheap-eats places. One such retro-diner is the chic **Empire Diner** (*see p138*), which is a popular spot for

club kids thanks to its 24-hour opening times. The kitsch 50s-style **Comfort Diner** serves large portions of comfort food and the best milkshakes in town. Theatergoers love **Junior's** diner in Brooklyn which is famous for its delicious cheesecake. **Big Nick's** on Broadway is the best place for a pizza, hamburger, or breakfast on the Upper West Side. The **Coffee Shop** in Union Square serves Brazilian-American fare and is open all night.

On the Upper East Side, Eli Zabar's **E.A.T.** sells excellent but pricey Jewish favorites – such as mushroom-barley soup and challah bread, as well as some sinful desserts. Another popular UES spot is **EJ's Luncheonette**, offering classic kid-friendly meals in a retro 1950s setting.

Devotees swear by **Viand**, a spic-and-span East Side luncheonette, with cheap, ample American breakfasts, good burgers, egg creams, and the best turkey sandwiches in town. **Veselka**, not the usual New York sandwich shop, serves Polish/Ukrainian food at rock-bottom prices and also has a second outlet, **Little Veselka**.

TEA ROOMS

The only place you can be absolutely sure of getting a cup of real, brewed tea is at a formal, prix-fixe afternoon tea in a lounge at one of New York's pricier hotels, from 3pm to 5pm.

For an extra-stylish tea, on Chippendale furniture, visit **Carlyle** in the Upper East Side. Another good buy in hotel prix-fixe tea is **Hotel Pierre**. Tea at the **Waldorf-Astoria** comes with Devonshire cream, while the elegant tea at **Stanhope** on Fifth Avenue is abundant enough to carry you through to a late dinner.

A variation on tea themes can be found in a chain of teahouses called **Saint's Alp**. These delightful spots, serving frothy, flavored, colorful tea drinks poured over crushed ice, can be

found at 51 Mott Street near Chinatown and in the Times Square area. Teatime, Japanese-style, can also be enjoyed at **The Tea Box**, in the Takashimaya department store on Fifth Avenue.

COFFEE AND CAKES

You can get a decent cup of coffee for as little as 75 cents, with endless free refills, at most diners, luncheonettes, and coffee shops. There is a popular trend for coffee bars that serve a variety of specialty coffees, such as cappuccino, espresso, and caffè latte. Ice-cream parlors and patisseries also serve good coffee, along with sinfully luscious pastries.

People wait in line at **Magnolia Bakery** to sample the decadent cakes. Magnolia has now opened a second spot on the Upper West Side. **Joe** boasts the world's best espresso machine, while **Caffè Ferrara**, going strong since 1892, has moderately priced Italian pastries, good coffee, and outdoor seating.

The Hungarian Pastry Shop has a range of Austro-Hungarian delights and views of St. John the Divine. Located in the Hotel Edison, **Café Edison** offers reasonably priced food in an Art Nouveau setting. **Sant Ambroeus** is a luxurious outpost of the Milanese pasticceria selling sumptuous desserts. In addition to home delivery of pies or cakes, **Dessert Delivery** has a nifty café for tasting the pastries and coffee. Try **Serendipity 3**, famous for its Victoriana, ice-cream creations – if you're an ice-cream aficionado don't miss the frozen hot chocolate – as well as coffee, and mid-afternoon snacks.

Barnes & Noble Café is a happy refuge for coffee and a pastry while browsing the bookstore. **Mudspot** is the permanent counterpart to the mobile, bright orange "Mudtrack" van that sells potent coffee. And, like them or not, you can't ignore **Starbucks**, which has dozens of locations around town.

DIRECTORY

LOWER MANHATTAN

Pastis
9 9th Avenue.
Map 3 B1.

LOWER EAST SIDE

Caffè Ferrara
195 Grand St. **Map** 4 F4.

Katz's Deli
205 E Houston St.
Map 5 A3.

Saint's Alp
51 Mott St. **Map** 4 F4.

SOHO AND TRIBECA

Lombardi's
32 Spring St. **Map** 4 F4.

Mezzogiorno
195 Spring St.
Map 4 D4.

Odeon
145 W Broadway.
Map 1 B1.

Raoul's
180 Prince St. **Map** 4 D3.

GREENWICH VILLAGE

Arturo's Pizzeria
106 W Houston St.
Map 4 E3.

Balthazar
80 Spring St. **Map** 4 E4.

Chez Jacqueline
72 MacDougal St.
Map 4 D2.

Corner Bistro
331 W 4th St. **Map** 3 C1.

Elephant and Castle
68 Greenwich Ave.
Map 3 C1.

Five Guys
296 Bleecker St.
Map 3 C3.

Joe
141 Waverly Place.
Map 3 C1.

Joe's Pizza
7 Carmine St. **Map** 4 D3.

Magnolia Bakery
401 Bleecker St.
Map 3 C2.
200 Columbus Ave.
Map 12 D1.

Sant Ambroeus
259 W 4th St.
Map 3 C1.

EAST VILLAGE

Little Veselka
75 E 1st St.
Map 4 F3.

Mudspot
307 E 9th St.
Map 4 F1.

Veselka
144 2nd Ave.
Map 4 F1.

GRAMERCY AND THE FLATIRON

The Coffee Shop
29 Union Square West
Map 9 A5.

Les Halles
411 Park Ave South
Map 9 A3.

CHELSEA AND THE GARMENT DISTRICT

Comfort Diner
25 W 23rd St.
Map 8 F4.

Empire Diner
210 10th Ave.
Map 7 C4.

THEATER DISTRICT

Café Edison
Edison Hotel, 228 W
47th St.
Map 12 D5.

Carnegie Delicatessen
854 7th Ave.
Map 12 E4.

Chez Josephine
414 W 42nd St.
Map 7 B1.

Junior's
Shubert Alley, enter on
45th St.
Map 12 E5.

Stage Deli
834 7th Ave.
Map 12 E4.

Victor's Café
236 W 52nd St.
Map 11 B4.

EAST SIDE MIDTOWN

Second Avenue Deli
162 E 33rd St.
Map 9 B2.

UPPER MIDTOWN

Barnes & Noble Café
Citicorp Building,
160 E 54th St.
Map 13 A4.

Brasserie
100 E 53rd St.
Map 13 A4.

Burger Joint
Le Parker Meridien Hotel,
118 W 57th St.
Map 12 E3.

The Tea Box
Takashimaya,
693 5th Ave.
Map 12 F2.

Waldorf-Astoria
301 Park Ave.
Map 13 A5.

UPPER EAST SIDE

Bistro du Nord
1312 Madison Ave.
Map 17 A2.

Carlyle
35 E 76th St. **Map** 17 A5.

Dessert Delivery
350 E 55th St.
Map 13 B4.
Tel 838-5411.

E.A.T.
1064 Madison Ave.
Map 17 A4.

EJ's Luncheonette
1271 3rd Ave.
Map 13 B1.

Hotel Pierre
2 E 61st St.
Map 12 F3.

Jackson Hole
232 E 64th St.
Map 13 B2.
One of five branches.

John's Pizzeria
408 E 64th St.
Map 13 C2.
One of three branches.

Mezzaluna
1295 3rd Ave.
Map 17 B5.

Payard Patisserie
1032 Lexington Ave.
Map 13 A1.

Serendipity 3
225 E 60th St.
Map 13 B3.

Shake Shack
Madison Square Park.
Map 8 F4.

Stanhope
995 5th Ave. **Map** 17 A4.

Viand
1011 Madison Ave.
Map 17 A5.
One of four branches.

UPPER WEST SIDE

Barney Greengrass
541 Amsterdam Ave.
Map 15 C3.

Big Nick's
2175 Broadway at 77th St.
Map 15 C5.

La Boite en Bois
75 W 68th St. **Map** 11 C1.

Sarabeth's
423 Amsterdam Ave.
Map 15 C4.

Whitney Museum
945 Madison Ave.
Map 17 A5.

Vince and Eddie's
70 W 68th St.
Map 11 C1.

Zabar's
2245 Broadway.
Map 15 C2.

MORNINGSIDE HEIGHTS AND HARLEM

The Hungarian Pastry Shop
Amsterdam & 109th St.
Map 20 E4.

BROOKLYN

Totonno Pizzeria
1524 Neptune Ave.
Map 7 C5.

New York Bars

New York bars play a huge role in the life and culture of the city. Many New Yorkers spend the evening in a succession of bars, because each usually offers something more than just alcohol. There may be additional inducements, like excellent food, live music, dancing, or a particularly large selection of beers. Brew pubs, which serve meals and brew beer on the premises, are also popular. Bars suiting every taste and budget are to be found in every corner.

RULES AND CONVENTIONS

Bars generally remain open from around 11am to midnight. Some stay open to 2 or 4am, when they must close by law. Many bars have a "happy hour" between 5pm and 7pm, when they offer twofers (two drinks for the price of one) and free snacks. Bartenders can refuse to serve anyone they consider having had too much to drink. Smoking is banned and is only allowed outside or in specially ventilated rooms.

The legal minimum drinking age is 21; if the bartender suspects you are younger, you'll be "carded," or asked for identification. Children aren't usually allowed in.

It is common to "run a tab" by giving the bartender a credit card and paying your bill just before you leave. Tipping the bartender is expected – 15 percent of the bill or about $1 per drink. Shots are not pre-measured, so if you want a bigger drink, it can help to "belly up" to the bar and tip the bartender accordingly for his or her generosity. If you sit at a table, you'll be served there and be charged more. A round of drinks can be expensive. Save money by buying a quart (95 cl) or a half gallon (190 cl) pitcher of beer.

Many bars have obtained liquor licenses under an oscure cabaret law that prohibits dancing. Bars are regularly closed down for ignoring this rule, so if staff ask you to refrain from dancing to music, they are serious and should be obeyed.

WHAT TO DRINK

Mainstream bars serve standard beers from big producers, such as Budweiser, Coors, and Miller, as well as high-profile imports including Becks, Heineken, and draft Guinness. Old pubs and chic bars have a much wider variety of beers, imported and small domestics. These include flavorful beers, usually based on traditional European styles, made by some of New York's microbreweries. The locally brewed Brooklyn Lager is highly rated.

Other popular drinks include "designer," or "fusion," cocktails, rum and coke, vodka-and-tonic, gin-and-tonic, dry Martinis, and Scotch or bourbon – either "straight up" (without ice) or "on the rocks" (with ice). The "Cosmopolitan" is very New York: vodka, cranberry juice, triple sec, and lime. Most of the bars serve a range of Martinis made with vodka.

Wine is widely available at bars, and the "wine bar" concept is making a comeback with options all over the city.

FOOD

Some bars serve food such as burgers, fries, salads, sandwiches, and spicy chicken wings throughout the day. If you are visiting the bar of a popular restaurant, you can often order bar snacks. Most bar kitchens stop serving food just before midnight.

FASHIONABLE BARS

To get into a hip bar, you will need to look glamorous and be prepared to wait in line, unless you arrive early. The Meatpacking District is lined with lively bars, including **Cielo**, a strobe-lit bar and club with potent cocktails and a soundtrack with everything from 1980s pop to hip-hop. Within stumbling distance is **Buddha Bar NYC**, a spinoff of the Paris original. The enormous restaurant has a bar that draws a hip crowd. The only serene elements are the massive Buddha and the jellyfish-stocked aquariums. Also incorporating a giant Buddha is **Tao Bar**, located in a former theater next to the Four Seasons Hotel. The venue is spread over three floors: the top two are devoted to pan-Asian cuisine and overlook the bar below.

The nightlife in the Lower East Side (LES) is growing in leaps and bounds, with numerous bars and clubs opening their doors. Enjoy cocktails and conversation at the lively **Schiller's Liquor Bar**. Formerly the Bowery Bar, the **B-Bar** still attracts a stylish crowd, though some claim its glory days are over. In the summer, the enormous outdoor space can't be beaten. **Pravda** is another favorite in nearby NoLIta. Subdued lighting creates a degree of calm in this subterranean spot decorated in Soviet chic. **The Odeon** on Broadway captures the lively SoHo-TriBeCa scene.

BARS WITH VIEWS

Top of the Tower, on the 26th floor of the Art Deco Beekman Tower, offers unsurpassed views of the city and great piano music. Also with great views are the **Rooftop Bar and Lounge** at the Empire Hotel, **Stone Rose Lounge** in the Time Warner Center, and **Rise** at the Ritz-Carlton in Battery Park. In warm weather, **Bryant Park Café** is a popular midtown scene, or you can sip cocktails and soak up the dazzling skyline views on **230 Fifth**'s vast wraparound terrace.

HISTORIC AND LITERARY BARS

If you sample only one New York bar, it should probably be **McSorley's Old Ale House**, an Irish saloon often dubbed "McSurly's" because of its staff. It opened in 1854, and is one of the city's oldest bars.

The Ear Inn dates from 1812 when the first tavern opened on this SoHo site. Its cramped interior and long wooden bar ooze authenticity. Another SoHo favorite is **Fanelli's Café**, a former speakeasy that opened its doors in 1922 (though locals have been visiting the watering hole on this site since 1847).

Greenwich Village has some of the city's oldest bars, such as Dylan Thomas's favorite, the **White Horse Tavern**, an unpretentious 1880s landmark still crowded with literary and collegiate types. It also has an outdoor café for warm weather. **Peculier Pub** is a beer-lover's paradise, with over 360 varieties of beer.

A good, if touristy, place for a drink in the financial district is **Fraunces Tavern**, first built in 1719 (see p76).

Pete's Tavern in the Gramercy Park area dates to 1864. Busy until 2am, it is known for Victoriana and the house brew called Pete's Ale. The typical Irish pub **Old Town Bar** has been serving stout since 1892, and is now favored largely by advertising types. No longer the celebrity scene it once was, **Sardi's** still appeals to *New York Times* reporters, and serves generous portions.

Hidden away in the balcony of Grand Central Terminal is **The Campbell Apartment**, the former private office of 1920s tycoon John W. Campbell. The spectacular space resembles a 13th-century Florentine palace. On the Upper East Side, the **Uptown Lounge** draws large crowds with its potent cocktails, tasty nibbles, and lively dance tunes.

A bustling saloon with Irish bartenders, **P. J. Clarke's** has been New York's favorite since the 1890s. **Elaine's**, also on the East Side, remains a haunt of mainly visiting literary types, though the food is so-so.

Near Carnegie Hall is **P. J. Carney's**, a watering hole for musicians and artists since 1927. It serves Irish ales and a good shepherd's pie.

YOUNG HANGOUTS

Brew pubs, where the house beer is brewed on the premises, are all the rage with the 20- and 30-somethings, as are bars that stock a variety of microbrews and imported beers. The **Chelsea Brewing Company** is a large, fun-filled brew pub in the Chelsea Piers sports complex. In the Gramercy neighborhood, you will find the **Heartland Brewery**, a bustling brew pub with five beers, including the outstanding India Pale Ale, and many seasonals, such as pumpkin ale. The cozy bar at **The Room**, in SoHo, has a good selection of beers and wine.

Serious beer drinkers will enjoy the 170 draft and bottled Belgian beers on offer at **Burp Castle**, while homesick Brits will likely head to **Manchester**. In a cozy, publike setting, you'll find Watneys or Newcastle Brown Ale on tap, just two of the 18 draft beers, and 40 bottled ones not widely available in New York.

In the East Village is bustling **d.b.a.**, which has 14 draft beers on tap, along with scores of microbrews and 50 single-malt whiskeys to choose from.

A popular beer stop uptown for the college-age crowd is the loud and noisy **Brother Jimmy's BBQ**, where you can snack on old-fashioned southern barbequed ribs.

Park Slope Ale House in Brooklyn is another brew pub favored by the young for its home brews and seasonal beers, as well as its decent pub grub and lively ambience.

GAY AND LESBIAN BARS

Gay bars can be found in Greenwich Village, Chelsea, and the East Village with a few on the Upper East and West Sides. Lesbian bars are mostly in Greenwich Village and East Village. For current listings, check the free weekly gay publication *Next* (www.nextmagazine.com).

HOTEL BARS

Centrally located, the **Algonquin Hotel** (see p145) was a famous literary haunt in the 1920s and early 1930s. Its Lobby Bar and Blue Bar are good places for a quiet pre-dinner or pre-theater drink.

The minimalist **Bar 44** in the lobby lounge of the Royalton Hotel is a perfect spot for a drink while watching the theatrical crowds drifting in and out. Also in the Theater District, the **Paramount Bar** has floor-to-ceiling windows and is usually frequented by fashion and theater types. In Upper Midtown there's the **Gilt Bar**, where you can recline on soft, plush red velvet seats.

The **Bull and Bear** in the Waldorf-Astoria, dating back to the Prohibition era, exudes comfort, charm, and a sense of history.

The stylish **King Cole Room** at St. Regis Hotel is named after a colorful mural behind the bar, by Maxfield Parrish.

Relax to downtempo tunes at the **Grand Bar**. One of New York's trendier nightspots, the Soho Grand's bar is a good place to people-watch. Its sister hotel, the Tribeca Grand, also draws a crowd to its **Church Lounge**.

With dark-wood panels, navy-blue color scheme, and a kitschy seafaring theme, the Maritime Hotel's **Lobby Bar** draws a young, trendy crowd. Special attractions include a roaring fire in winter and an outdoor terrace in summer.

The glass-floored **Hudson Bar** at Ian Schrager's trendy Hudson Hotel is a regular hot-spot. The **Rose** and **Jade** bars, in Schrager's Gramercy Park Hotel, are filled with fashion-istas drinking in the "eclectic-Bohemian" vibe. Equally popular are **Thom Bar** at the 60 Thompson Hotel and **Bookmarks** at the Library Hotel; both attract a sophisticated scene. For those interested in joining the *Sex and the City* crowd, there's Rande Gerber's **Whiskey Blue Bar** in one of the boutique W Hotels.

DIRECTORY

LOWER MANHATTAN

Fraunces Tavern
54 Pearl St. **Map** 1 C4.
www.fraancestavern.com

Rise
2 W St. **Map** 1 B4.

SOHO AND TRIBECA

Church Lounge
Tribeca Grand, 2 6th Ave.
Map 4 D4.
www.tribecagrand.com

The Ear Inn
326 Spring St. **Map** 3 C4.
www.earinn.com

Fanelli's Café
94 Prince St. **Map** 4 E3.

The Grand Bar
Soho Grand, 310
W Broadway. **Map** 4 E4.
www.sohogrand.com

The Odeon
145 W Broadway.
Map 1 B1. www.the
odeonrestaurant.com

Pravda
281 Lafayette St.
Map 4 F3.
www.pravdany.com

The Room
144 Sullivan St. **Map** 4 D3.

Thom Bar
60 Thompson Hotel, 60
Thompson St. **Map** 4 D4.
www.60thompson.com

GREENWICH VILLAGE

Buddha Bar NYC
25 Little W 12th St.
Map 3 B1.
www.buddhabarnyc.com

Cielo
18 Little W 12th St.
Map 3 B1.
www.cieloclub.com

Peculier Pub
145 Bleecker St.
Map 4 D3.
www.peculierpub.com

White Horse Tavern
567 Hudson St.
Map 3 C1.

EAST VILLAGE AND LOWER EAST SIDE

B-Bar
40 E 4th St. **Map** 4 F2.
www.bbarandgrill.com

Burp Castle
41 E 7th St.
Map 4 F2.
http://burpcastlenyc.
wordpress.com

d.b.a.
41 1st Ave. **Map** 5 A1.
www.drinkgoodstuff.com

**McSorley's
Old Ale House**
15 E 7th St. **Map** 4 F2.
www.mcsorleys
newyork.com

Schiller's Liquor Bar
131 Rivington St.
Map 5 B3.

GRAMERCY

Heartland Brewery
35 Union Square W.
Map 9 A5.
www.heartland
brewery.com

Jade Bar
Gramercy Park Hotel,
2 Lexington Ave.
Map 9 A4.
www.gramercypark
hotel.com

Old Town Bar
45 E 18th St.
Map 8 F5.
www.oldtownbar.com

Pete's Tavern
129 E 18th St.
Map 9 A5.
www.petestavern.com

Rose Bar
Gramercy Park Hotel,
2 Lexington Ave.
Map 9 A4.
www.gramercypark
hotel.com

CHELSEA AND THE GARMENT DISTRICT

**Chelsea Brewing
Company**
Pier 59, 11th Ave.
Map 7 B5. www.chelsea
brewingco.com

Lobby Bar
Maritime Hotel, 363
W 16th St. **Map** 8 D5.
www.themaritime
hotel.com

THEATER DISTRICT

Bar 44
Royalton Hotel, 44 W
44th St. **Map** 12 F5.

Bryant Park Café
Bryant Park. **Map** 8 F1.
www.bryantpark.org

Hudson Bar
Hudson Hotel, 356 W
58th St. **Map** 12 D3.
www.hudsonhotel.com

Paramount Bar
Paramount Hotel, 235 W
46th St. **Map** 12 E5.

P. J. Carney's
906 7th Ave. **Map** 12 E3.
www.pjcarneys.com

Sardi's
234 W 44th St. **Map**
12 F5. www.sardis.com

LOWER MIDTOWN

230 Fifth
230 Fifth Ave. **Map** 8 F3.

Bookmarks
The Library Hotel, 299
Madison Ave. **Map** 9 A1.

**The Campbell
Apartment**
Grand Central Terminal,
15 Vanderbilt Ave.
Map 9 A1.

UPPER MIDTOWN

Bull and Bear
Waldorf-Astoria Hotel,
Lexington Ave. **Map** 13
A5. www.bullbearbar.com

Gilt Bar
New York Palace Hotel,
455 Madison Ave.
Map 13 A4.
www.giltnewyork.com

King Cole Room
St. Regis Hotel, 2 E 55th
St. **Map** 12 F5.

Manchester
920 2nd Ave.
Map 13 B5.

P. J. Clarke's
915 3rd Ave.
Map 13 B4.

Stone Rose Lounge
10 Columbus Circle,
4th Floor.
Map 12 D3.
www.gerberbars.com

Tao Bar
42 E 58th St.
Map 13 A3.
www.taorestaurant.com

Top of the Tower
Beekman Tower,
3 Mitchell Place.
Map 13 C5.
www.thebeekman
hotel.com

Whiskey Blue Bar
541 Lexington Ave.
Map 13 A2.
www.gerberbars.com

UPPER EAST SIDE

**Brother Jimmy's
BBQ**
1485 2nd Ave.
Map 17 B5.
www.brotherjimmys.com

Elaine's
1703 2nd Ave.
Map 17 B4.

Uptown Lounge
1576 Third Ave.
Map 17 B3.
http://uptownlounge
nyc.com

UPPER WEST SIDE

**Rooftop Bar and
Lounge**
Empire Hotel, 44
W 63rd St.
Map 12 D2.
www.empirehotel
nyc.com

BROOKLYN

**Park Slope Ale
House**
356 6th Ave at 5th St.

SHOPPING

Visitors to New York will inevitably include shopping in their action plan. The city is the consumer capital of the world: a shopper's paradise and a constant source of entertainment, with dazzling window displays and a staggering variety of goods for sale. Everything is found here, from high fashion to rare children's books, state-of-the-art electronics and a mouthwatering array of exotic food. Whether you are looking for a personal Hovercraft, read-in-the-dark eyeglass attachments, a designer bed for your pet gerbil or a Wurlitzer jukebox, this is the city of your dreams. Whether you have $50,000 or $5, New York is the place to spend it.

Tiffany's clock

BEST BUYS

New York is a bargain hunter's dream, with huge discounts on anything from household goods to designer clothes. Some of the best shops are on Orchard Street and Grand Street on the Lower East Side, where designer goods are sold at considerably lower

The Bulgari entrance at Hotel Pierre (see p289)

The 1920s-style Henri Bendel store (see p319)

than the retail price. You can find just about every imaginable item of clothing here, in addition to tableware, shoes, home furnishings, and electronics. Some shops in this area are closed on Saturday – the Jewish Sabbath – but are usually open all day Sunday.

Another great area for fashion bargain hunters is the Garment District, roughly between Sixth and Eighth avenues from 30th to 40th Street. The main hub, Seventh Avenue, was renamed Fashion Avenue in the early 1970s. Several designers and manufacturers have showrooms here, some of which are open to the public. Many of their samples are put up for sales, announced on notices posted around the area. The best

time to visit them is just before one of the major gift-giving holidays. Top Button (www. topbutton.com) has comprehensive sales listings.

SALES

One word you'll come across all over the city, anytime of the year, is "sale." So check the sale goods before you pay full price for any purchase. The best sales are during New York's sale seasons, which generally run from June until end-July and from December 26 until February. Look up the local papers for ads. Along midtown Fifth Avenue you'll see signs announcing "Lost Our Lease" sales. Avoid them, as these signs have been up for years at many shops. Also keep your eyes peeled for "Sample Sales," where the top designers sell to the public the sample outfits they have created to show store buyers. Sample sales occur at different locations throughout the city, and are generally not advertised, so your best bet is to keep a lookout for signs announcing sample sales, particularly on Fifth Avenue and on Broadway.

HOW TO PAY

Most shops accept major credit cards, although there will often be a minimum purchase price. If you want to use your traveler's checks, identification is needed. Personal checks drawn in another currency will be refused. Some stores only take cash, especially during sales.

OPENING HOURS

Most shops are open from 10am to 6pm, Monday to Saturday. Many department stores are open through Sunday and until 9pm, at least two nights a week. Lunch hours (noon to 2:30pm), Saturdays, sales, and holidays will be the most crowded times.

Designer dress at a New York sale

TAXES

The New York City sales tax is 8.625 percent, although clothing and shoes under $110 are exempt. However, sales tax will be waived if the goods are shipped home.

SHOPPING TOURS

If you dread braving the stores alone, shopping tours are a good option. Apart from the main department stores, you could visit private designer showrooms, auction houses, and fashion shows. Some operators will customize tours to suit your requirements.

DEPARTMENT STORES AND MALLS

Most of the large department stores are in midtown Manhattan. Explore at leisure the

Window displays at Bloomingdale's *(see p181)*

ones you are interested in, since all these stores tend to be enormous, with a great range of goods. If possible, avoid weekends and vacation times when the crowds can be overwhelming. Prices are often high, but you may find some bargains during sales.

Stores such as Saks Fifth Avenue, Bloomingdale's, and Macy's provide a diverse and extraordinary range of shopping services, including actually shopping for you.

One of the biggest malls to open in Manhattan is the **Shops at Columbus Circle** in the Time Warner Center. Its stores include Williams-Sonoma, Coach, and men's clothier Hugo Boss.

Barney's New York, favored by young professionals, specializes in excellent,

though expensive, designer clothes.

Luxurious, elegant, and understated, **Bergdorf Goodman** sells contemporary clothes by European designers at high prices. The men's store is across the street.

A visit to New York isn't complete without **Bloomingdale's** *(see p181)*, the Hollywood film star of the department stores, with many eye-catching displays and seductive goods. New Yorkers young and old come here to seek out the newest in fashion. The linen and fine china departments have an undisputed reputation for quality. Check out the gourmet food section, which features a shop devoted entirely to caviar. Extensive shopping services and amenities include a noted restaurant, Le Train Bleu, with its view of the Queensboro Bridge. There is also a SoHo branch of Bloomingdale's on Broadway. Though much smaller than the main store, it stocks a similar selection of luxury goods.

At the exclusive **Henri Bendel**, everything from the Art Deco jewels to beautiful handmade shoes is displayed as a priceless work of art. The store, laid out in a series of 1920s-style boutiques, sells an excellent range of innovative women's fashions.

Lord & Taylor is renowned for its classic and much more conservative fashions for men and women, with an emphasis on US designers. You'll need comfortable shoes and plenty of time for browsing.

Macy's, the self-proclaimed largest store in the world *(see p134–5)*, has ten floors selling everything imaginable from can openers to antiques.

A magnificent display offering household goods

Saks Fifth Avenue, known for style and elegance, has long been considered one of the city's best department stores, with service to match. It sells stunning designerwear for adults as well as children.

ADDRESSES

Barney's New York
660 Madison Ave. **Map** 13 A3.
Tel (212) 826-8900.

Bergdorf Goodman
754 5th Ave. **Map** 12 F3.
Tel (212) 753-7300.

Bloomingdale's
1000 3rd Ave. **Map** 13 A3.
Tel (212) 705-2000.

Bloomingdale's SoHo
504 Broadway. **Map** 4 E4.
Tel (212) 729-5900.

Convention Tours Unlimited
Tel (212) 545-1160.

Elegant Tightwad
Tel (800) 808-4614.

Guide Service of New York
Tel (212) 408-3332.

Henri Bendel
712 5th Ave. **Map** 12 F4.
Tel (212) 247-1100.

Lord & Taylor
424 5th Ave. **Map** 8 F1.
Tel (212) 391-3344.

Macy's
151 W 34th St. **Map** 8 E2.
Tel (212) 695-4400.

Saks Fifth Avenue
611 5th Ave. **Map** 12 F4.
Tel (212) 753-4000.

Shop Gotham
Tel (866) 795-4200 or (212) 209-3370 to purchase tour tickets.

Shops at Columbus Circle
Time Warner Center. **Map** 12 D3.
Tel (212) 823-6300.

New York's Best: Shopping

Designer shoes from Madison Avenue

In a city where you can literally shop 24 hours a day, the best plan is to shop the way New Yorkers do, by neighborhood. Each has its own character and specialties. Here are highlights of the best shopping districts – where they are and what you will find in each. If time is very tight, head for one of the huge department stores *(see p319)*, or if window shopping is your preference, stroll along Fifth Avenue, home to Manhattan's most glittering stores *(see opposite)*. For great bargains in a truly ethnic area, try the Lower East Side.

Greenwich Village and the Meatpacking District
Quaint, eclectic, and antique choices in the Village, and gourmands will enjoy the myriad speciality food stores. Meander over to Meatpacking District for high fashion shopping (see pp112–13).

SoHo
The area bordered by Sixth Avenue, Lafayette, Houston, and Canal streets is bustling with antiques, crafts, and clothes from designer flagships. Weekend brunchtime gallery-hopping is very popular. Cross Broadway to NoLIta for even trendier, cutting-edge fashion (see pp104–5).

East Village and Lower East Side
Explore around St Mark's Place for shoes, avant-garde fashions, and ethnic goods (see pp118–19). Bargains are becoming harder to find in the Lower East Side, but trendy options increasing (see pp94–5).

South Street Seaport
This is a browser's paradise of crafts, gifts, souvenirs, books, and antiques with a seafaring connection (see pp82–3).

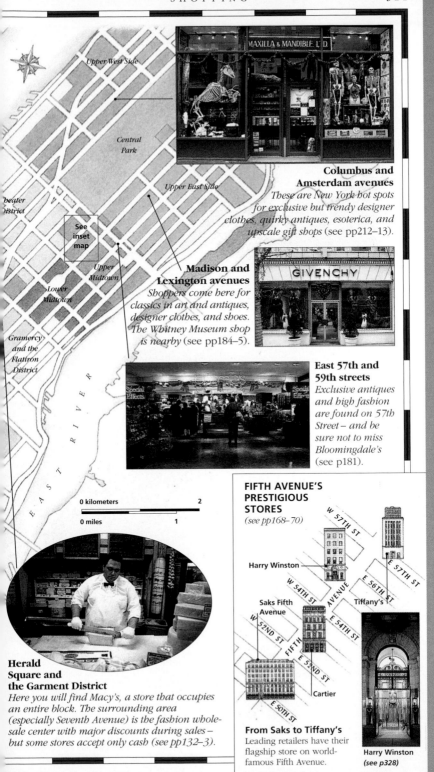

Columbus and Amsterdam avenues
These are New York hot spots for exclusive but trendy designer clothes, quirky antiques, esoterica, and upscale gift shops (see pp212–13).

Madison and Lexington avenues
Shoppers come here for classics in art and antiques, designer clothes, and shoes. The Whitney Museum shop is nearby (see pp184–5).

East 57th and 59th streets
Exclusive antiques and high fashion are found on 57th Street – and be sure not to miss Bloomingdale's (see p181).

Herald Square and the Garment District
Here you will find Macy's, a store that occupies an entire block. The surrounding area (especially Seventh Avenue) is the fashion whole-sale center with major discounts during sales – but some stores accept only cash (see pp132–3).

FIFTH AVENUE'S PRESTIGIOUS STORES
(see pp168–70)

Harry Winston

Saks Fifth Avenue

Tiffany's

Cartier

From Saks to Tiffany's
Leading retailers have their flagship store on world-famous Fifth Avenue.

Harry Winston
(see p328)

New York Originals

New York is a city where just about any kind of shop, no matter how esoteric, will always attract customers. Dozens of tiny shops scattered around the city specialize in unusual merchandise, from butterflies and bones to traditional Tibetan treasures and Shamrock sprigs from Ireland. Coming across these in some tucked-away corner is what makes shopping in New York such an entertaining and invigorating experience.

SPECIALTY SHOPS

For beautiful brass, onyx, and pewter chess sets, and the opportunity to play a decent game, make a move to the **Chess Shop**. For every type of pen **Arthur Brown & Bros.** stocks an enormous range, including such names as Mont Blanc and Schaeffer. For those with a bit more energy, **Blades Board & Skate** sells and rents out skates and also the trendiest skateboards plus all the safety equipment.

If you're looking for different or unusual buttons, a visit to **Tender Buttons**, which stocks millions, is a must. Whether you want enamel, wood, or Navajo silver buttons – or perhaps want your own buttons made into cuff links or earrings – here you'll find just what you want – and more. **Trash & Vaudeville** has been supplying punk and goth gear to New Yorkers for decades and is the HQ of Astor Place fashion.

Leo Kaplan Ltd. is the place to go if you are a keen collector of paperweights, while **Rita Ford's Music Boxes**, a 19th-century style shop, stocks a tuneful and extensive range of music boxes.

The **New York Firefighter's Friend** sells an intriguing range of items related to fire-fighting, including toy fire engines, firemen's jackets, badges, stuffed toy dalmatians and a wide selection of T-shirts, including a popular one with FDNY (Fire Department New York) on one side and "Keep back 200 feet" on the other.

Spies and conspiracy theorists will be enthralled with the extensive offering at **Quark Spy**, where you can simple choose from survival kits and camera pens up to audio intelligence rooms.

For the true romantic who wants to impress, everything sold by **Only Hearts** is heart-shaped, including pillows, soap, and jewelry. If you are artistic, or if you wish to buy a present for someone who is, visit **Pearl Paint**, which stocks everything you could need, from easels and brushes to modeling clay. **Forbidden Planet** is a science-fiction megastore with everything from comics to models for the true fan.

Cologne made especially for George Washington and the official soap of the White House during the Eisenhower era are just some of the many fascinating items for sale at **Caswell-Massey Ltd.**, which is the oldest pharmacy in the city.

Guitar gurus will want to visit **Rudy's**, Manny's, or Sam Ash's guitar shop. Not only is there a chance you'll bump into Eric Clapton or Lou Reed – both have their guitars made in this area – but you'll find the widest and best choice of instruments in the city.

Bibliophiles will find a range of gifts in both the **New York Public Library Shop** *(see p146)* (such as bookends of the lions guarding the main entrance) and the **Morgan Library Shop** *(see pp164–5)*, including bookmarks and writing paper.

University logos and college colors dominate the many knickknacks and accessories at **The Yale Club** gift shop and **The Princeton Club**. **Weisburg Religious Articles** carries one of the largest selections of Jewish religious items in the city.

The **Cathedral Shop** at the Cathedral of St. John the Divine on Amsterdam Avenue is a large store selling books, artworks, herbs, jewelry, and religious items made locally.

MEMORABILIA

At Lincoln Center, the **Metropolitan Opera Shop** has records, cards, librettos, small binoculars, and many other opera-related items. For theater fans, everything from scripts and vocal scores to CDs can be found at **One Shubert Alley**. For thousands of rare and classic film stills and posters visit **Jerry Ohlinger's Movie Material Store** on 242 W 14th Street.

The **Carnegie Hall Shop** carries musically themed cards, T-shirts, games, posters, tote bags, and much more. For something truly original and very American, be sure to visit **Lost City Arts** and **Urban Archaeology** in SoHo. Between these two shops, you'll unearth all sorts of relics from America's past, from Barbie Doll lunch boxes to salvaged furniture, including antique, claw footed bath tubs.

TOYS, GAMES, AND GADGETS

For children's gifts, don't miss the legendary **F.A.O. Schwarz**. This is a massive store crammed with luxury toy cars, enormous stuffed animals and every kind of electronic toy imaginable. There are shoulder-to-shoulder crowds at Christmas, when you might have to line up to get in.

The **Children's General Store** is one of the city's smarter toy stores, with a focus on educational and classic goods, while a trip to the **American Girl Place** doll store could entertain a young girl all day, with options such as a café, photo studio, and hair salon.

Penny Whistle Toys sells a huge selection of quality toys, games, and all kinds of dolls. **Red Caboose** is for fans of model railways. On three floors, the **Toys 'R' Us** flagship glass building on Broadway is the largest toy store in the world, with a 60-ft (20-m) ferris wheel.

Dinosaur Hill on Second Avenue offers handmade

puppets and toys, mobiles, and beautifully made children's clothes. It's expensive but worth it. Since 1848, **Hammacher Schlemmer** have been encouraging shoppers to buy gadgets for home, office, and recreation that they didn't know they wanted. The quirky **Kidrobot** in SoHo draws both kids and collectors for its urban, cartoony action figures and memorabilia.

MUSEUM SHOPS

Some of New York's best souvenirs can be found in the city's many museum shops. In addition to the usual range of books, posters, and cards, there are reproductions of the exhibits on display, including jewelry and sculpture. The **Museum of Arts & Design** (see p149) has an excellent selection of American crafts as well as original works for sale. In addition to realistic model dinosaurs, rubber animals, minerals, and rocks, the **American Museum of Natural History** (see pp216–17) has a variety of recycled products and earth-awareness gifts,

which include posters, bags, and T-shirts with environmental messages, and a large selection of Native American handicrafts. There is also a kids' shop with reasonably priced items such as shell sets, magnets, and toys.

The **Asia Society Bookstore and Gift Shop** (see p187) has a striking selection of Oriental prints, posters, art books, toys, and jewelry. Items related to interior design are offered at the **Cooper-Hewitt** (see p186). One of New York's largest collections of Jewish ceremonial objects, including menorahs and Kiddush cups, books, and jewelry, is found in the small shop at the **Jewish Museum** (see p186).

For reproduction prints of famous paintings and other exquisite gifts a visit to the **Metropolitan Museum of Art** (see pp190–97) gift shop is a must. There is also an enormous book department and a children's gift shop. The traditional **American Folk Art Museum** (see p171) prides itself on its American country crafts, including wooden toys, quilts, and weathervanes, which are

mostly original. Works by craftspeople who currently have pieces on display in the museum are also sold.

The **Museum of the City of New York** (see p199), specializes in pictures of old New York as well as books and unique prints and posters. The **Museum of Modern Art/MOMA Design Store** (see pp172–75) has a highly praised selection of innovative home furnishings, toys, and kitchenware inspired by international designers such as Frank Lloyd Wright and Le Corbusier.

For a selection of nautical items, including charts, maps, model ships, and scrimshaw, go to the **South Street Seaport Museum Shops** (see pp82–85). The **Whitney Museum's Shop** (see pp200–201) stocks American-made items, including jewelry, wooden toys, books, and posters complementing current exhibitions. The **Museum of Jewish Heritage** (see p77) has a gift shop with an unusual array of gifts, souvenirs, and educational material about Jewish life. Open to ticketed visitors only.

THE BEST OF THE IMPORTS

New York is a massive melting pot of ethnic groups, nationalities, and cultures. Many ethnic shops specialize in food or goods of a particular group. **Alaska on Madison** has a collection of Eskimo art and Northwest prints and hangings, as does **Alaska House** in SoHo. The **Chinese Porcelain Company** sells exquisite Chinese decorative arts and furniture. **Pearl River Mart** has been a staple for Asian goods for thirty years, from novelty items to tea and tote-bags, and **Himalayan Crafts and Tours** stocks everything from paintings to Tibetan rugs. **Sweet Life**, on the Lower East Side, is a tiny, old-fashioned candy shop with delicacies from around the world. **Things Japanese**

has beautifully made crafts and unusual books. **Surma** is a Ukrainian general store that sells hand-painted eggs and linens. **Common Ground** sells Native American arts, and **Astro Gems** has a large collection of jewelry and mineral specimens from Africa and Asia. Nearby, Chinatown is packed with shops selling everything from souvenirs to leather goods, all at low prices.

ADDRESSES

Alaska House
109 Mercer St. **Map** 4 E3.
Tel (212) 431-1580.

Alaska on Madison
937 Madison Ave. **Map** 17 A1.
Tel (212) 879-1782.

Astro Gems
185 Madison Ave. **Map** 9 A2.
Tel (212) 889-9000.

Chinese Porcelain Company
475 Park Ave. **Map** 13 A3.
Tel (212) 838-7744.

Common Ground
55 W 16th St. **Map** 8 F5.
Tel (212) 989-4178.

Himalayan Crafts and Tours
2007 Broadway. **Map** 11 C1.
Tel (212) 787-8500.

Pearl River Mart
477 Broadway. **Map** 4 E4.
Tel (212) 431-4770.

Sweet Life
63 Hester St. **Map** 5 B4.
Tel (212) 598-0092.

Surma
11 E 7th St. **Map** 4 F2.
Tel (212) 477-0729.

Things Japanese
127 E 60th St. **Map** 13 A3.
Tel (212) 371-4661.

DIRECTORY

SPECIALTY SHOPS

Arthur Brown & Bros.
2 W 46th St. **Map** 12 F5.
Tel (212) 575-5555.

Blades Board & Skate
120 W 72nd St.
Map 12 D1.
Tel (888) 552-5233.
One of several branches.

Caswell-Massey Ltd.
518 Lexington Ave.
Map 13 A5.
Tel (212) 755-2254.

The Cathedral Shop
Cathedral of St. John the
Divine, 1047 Amsterdam
Ave. **Map** 20 E4.
Tel (212) 316-7540.

Leo Kaplan Ltd.
114 E 57th St.
Map B A3.
Tel (212) 355-7212.

Morgan Library Shop
Madison Ave at 36th St.
Map 9 A2.
Tel (212) 685-0008.

New York Firefighter's Friend
263 Lafayette St.
Map 4 F3.
Tel (212) 226-3142.

New York Public Library Shop
5th Ave at 42nd St.
Map 8 F1.
Tel (212) 930-0869.

Only Hearts
386 Columbus Ave.
Map 15 D5.
Tel (212) 724-5608.

Pearl Paint
308 Canal St. **Map** 4 E5.
Tel (212) 431-7932.

The Princeton Club
15 W 43rd St. **Map** 8 F1.
Tel (212) 596-1200.

Quark Spy
240 E 29th St. **Map** 9 B3.
Tel (212) 683-9100.

Rita Ford's Music Boxes
19 E 65th St. **Map** 12 F2.
Tel (212) 535-6717.

Rudy's
169 W 48th St.
Map 12 E5.
Tel (212) 391-1699.

Tender Buttons
143 E 62nd St.
Map 13 A2.
Tel (212) 758-7004.

The Chess Shop
230 Thompson St.
Map 4 D3.
Tel (212) 475-9580.

Trash & Vaudeville
4 St. Mark's Pl.
Map 5 A4.
Tel (212) 982-3590.

Weisburg Religious Articles
45 Essex St. **Map** 5 B4.
Tel (212) 674-1770.

The Yale Club
50 Vanderbilt Ave.
Map 13 A5.
Tel (212) 661-2070.

MEMORABILIA

One Shubert Alley
1 Shubert Alley.
Map 12 E5.
Tel (212) 944-4133.

The Carnegie Hall Shop
881 7th Ave. **Map** 12 E3.
Tel (212) 903-9610.

Forbidden Planet
840 Broadway.
Map 4 E1.
Tel (212) 473-1576.

Jerry Ohlinger's Movie Material Store
253 W 35th St.
Map 8 D2.
Tel (212) 989-0869.

Lost City Arts
18 Cooper Square.
Map 4 F2.
Tel (212) 375-0500.

Metropolitan Opera Shop
Metropolitan Opera
House, Lincoln Center, 136
W 65th St. **Map** 11 C2.
Tel (212) 580-4090.

Urban Archaeology
143 Franklin St.
Map 4 D5.
Tel (212) 431-4646.

TOYS, GAMES, AND GADGETS

American Girl Place
609 Fifth Ave.
Map 12 F5.
Tel (877) 247-5223.

The Children's General Store
Lexington Concourse,
Grand Central Station.
Map 9 A1.
Tel (212) 682-0004.

Dinosaur Hill
306 E 9th St, 2nd Ave.
Map 4 F1.
Tel (212) 473-5850.

F.A.O. Schwarz
767 5th Ave.
Map 12 F3.
Tel (212) 644-9400.

Hammacher Schlemmer
147 E 57th St.
Map 13 A3.
Tel (212) 421-9000.
One of two branches.

Kidrobot
126 Prince St.
Map 4 E3.
Tel (212) 966-6688.

Penny Whistle Toys
448 Columbus Ave.
Map 16 D4.
Tel (212) 873-9090.
One of several branches.

Red Caboose
23 W 45th St.
Map 12 F5.
Tel (212) 575-0155.

Toys 'R' Us
1514 Broadway,
Times Square.
Map 8 E2.
Tel (646) 366-8800.

MUSEUM SHOPS

Museum of Arts & Design
40 W 53rd St.
Map 12 F4.
Tel (212) 956-3535.

American Folk Art Museum
45 W 53rd St.
Map 12 F4.
Tel (212) 265-1040.

American Museum of Natural History
W 79th St at Central
Park W. **Map** 16 D5.
Tel (212) 769-5100.

Asia Society Bookstore and Gift Shop
725 Park Ave.
Map 13 A1.
Tel (212) 288-6400.

Cooper-Hewitt
2 E 91st St. **Map** 16 F2.
Tel (212) 849-8400.

Jewish Museum
1109 5th Ave.
Map 16 F2.
Tel (212) 423-3200.

Metropolitan Museum of Art
5th Ave at 82nd St.
Map 16 F4.
Tel (212) 535-7710.

Museum of the City of New York
5th Ave at 103rd St.
Map 21 C5.
Tel (212) 534-1672.

Museum of Jewish Heritage
18 1st Place, Battery Park
City. **Map** 1 B4.
Tel (646) 437-4200.

Museum of Modern Art/MOMA Design Store
44 W 53rd St.
Map 12 F4.
Tel (212) 767-1050.

South St. Seaport Museum Shops
12 Fulton St.
Map 2 D2.
Tel (212) 748-8600.

The Whitney Museum's Store Next Door
943 Madison Ave.
Map 13 A1.
Tel (212) 570-3676.

Fashion

Whether you're looking for a secondhand pair of 501s or the kind of ballgown Ivana Trump would be proud to wear, you're sure to find it in New York. The city is the fashion capital of America and an important center of clothing manufacture and design. New York's clothing stores, like its restaurants, reflect the city's dramatically different styles and cultures. To save time it's probably best to visit one area at a time and wander from store to store. Alternatively, visit one of the major department stores for an excellent selection of fashion for everyone.

AMERICAN DESIGNERS

Many American designers sell their creations in boutiques within the large department stores, or have exclusive shops of their own. One of the most famous is Michael Kors, known for sophisticated looks that are classic and comfortable.

Bill Blass is the king of American fashion whose clothes feature loads of different colors, wild patterns, innovative shapes, and a lot of wit. Liz Claiborne's designs are always elegantly simple, casual, and reasonably priced, including everything you could possibly need from tennis whites to casual professional wear for women.

Marc Jacobs, known for his sportswear, has his own label and store in Greenwich Village. James Galanos is an exclusive designer for the rich and famous, making one-of-a-kind *couture* clothes, and Betsey Johnson is popular with women able to wear figure-hugging fashions in fabulous fabrics.

In the last decade, Donna Karan has become a name that appears everywhere. Her simple, stylish, and great-looking designs work for everything from work-out clothes to black tie wear. Calvin Klein now has his name on place settings and sunglasses in addition to underwear, jeans, and a whole range of clothes. He is renowned for comfortable, sensuous, and well-fitting – as well as very hip – looks. Ralph Lauren is very well known for his aristocratic and expensive clothes, a "look" favored by the exclusive and posh Ivy League, horsey set. For those with a taste for more experimental designs, Joan Vass specializes in moderately priced but exciting, colorful, and innovative knitwear.

DISCOUNT DESIGNER CLOTHES

If you're on the lookout for discount designer clothes, **Designer Resale**, **Encore**, and **Michael's** sell a wide range. Oscar de la Renta, Ungaro, and Armani are just some of the leading labels available. Clothes are either new or worn but near-perfect.

The designer discount emporium **Century 21** in Lower Manhattan sells European and American designer fashions discounted up to an amazing 75 percent off regular retail prices. **Filene's Basement**, one of Manhattan's longest-running discount department stores, offers designer clothes, shoes, and accessories at bargain prices. **Loehmann's** offers discounted fashion clothes, and it's the place to shop if you want top-of-the-line fashions at unbelievable discounts.

MEN'S CLOTHES

In the center of midtown, you'll find two of the city's most highly regarded menswear stores: **Brooks Brothers** and **Paul Stuart**. Brooks Brothers is something of a New York institution, famous for its traditional, conservative clothing such as smart button-down shirts and Chinos. There's an ultra-conservative woman's line too. Paul Stuart prides itself on its very British look and offers a stylish array of superbly tailored fashions. Go to the high-quality department store **Bergdorf Goodman Men** to find beautifully made Turnbull & Asser shirts and marvelous suits by Gianfranco Ferré or Hugo Boss.

Barney's New York has one of the most comprehensive men's departments in America, with a truly massive range of clothes and accessories.

The Custom Shop Shirtmakers specializes in custom-made suits and shirts in beautiful materials. Go to **Burberry Limited** if you are looking for classic British trenchcoats and traditional outdoor wear.

J. Press sells classic, conservative yet elegant clothes while **John Varvatos** is famous for luxurious, sporty designs with superb detail. Uptown designer menswear boutiques include the renowned **Beau Brummel** with a selection of very stylish European clothes and **Thomas Pink** whose bright colors and fine fabrics make this store a celebrity favorite. Many of these men's stores also carry striking women's fashions. The **Hickey Freeman** store on Fifth Avenue sells a wide range of men's traditional clothing.

CHILDREN'S CLOTHES

In addition to an excellent selection within the large department stores, there are several shops around the city that sell children's clothing exclusively. A good example is **Bonpoint**, which has a world of French-style charm. Also stocked with delightful outfits is **Bundle**, in SoHo.

GapKids and **BabyGap** shops, often in the **Gap** shops, have comfortable, long-lasting cotton overalls, sweat pants, denim jackets, sweatshirts, and leggings. Actress Phoebe Cates has opened a hip kids' clothing store on Madison Avenue called **Blue Tree**. **Space Kiddets** has everything from booties to Western wear.

WOMEN'S CLOTHES

Women's fashion is subject to design trends, and New York stores keep pace with them all. Most of the city's most fashionable shops are found in the midtown area around Madison and Fifth Avenues. These include some of the major department stores (see p319), which stock a range of American designers, including Donna Karan, Ralph Lauren and Bill Blass.

Leading international names such as **Chanel** and **Valentino** also have shops here, as does one of the outstanding American designers, **Michael Kors**. There is also a handful of popular ready-to-wear stores, including **Ann Taylor**, which is much favored by young, busy professionals looking for stylish, comfortable clothing.

Right at the heart of this area stands the pink-marbled Trump Tower, which houses a selection of exclusive shops.

Madison Avenue is packed with designers for the smart set, who have everything you could ever need, including **Givenchy**, who sells show-stopping formal gowns at phenomenal prices; Valentino, who has classic Italian clothes; and **Emanuel Ungaro**, who generally has something to suit most tastes and physiques from beautifully tailored jackets to more matronly full-figured and boldly patterned print dresses. **Missoni** is famous for richly textured sweaters in sumptuous wools and colorful patterns. **Yves St Laurent Rive Gauche** has evening gowns, one-of-a-kind jackets, silks and extravagant blouses, and beautifully cut pants suits.

Sophisticated Italian looks are also available from Italian style kings **Giorgio Armani** and **Gianni Versace**. **Dolce & Gabbana** sells unique, one-of-a-kind Italian clothing. **Gucci**, one of the oldest Italian shops in America, is only for the wealthy and status-conscious.

The Upper West Side has many shops competing for attention with contemporary fashions, including **Betsey Johnson**'s shop, with her whimsical, relatively inexpensive designs. **Calvin Klein** now has a store on the East Side, specializing in ultra-hip, casual fashions. **French Connection** is known for its affordable separates, both casual and for the office. **Scoop** is *the* place to get a little black dress.

The villages – the East Village in particular – are the best places to go for secondhand clothing and 1950s rock 'n' roll gear, with ever-changing interesting shops run by new and young designers and art school graduates. For a range of affordable, well-cut clothes from classic to casual, try **APC**.

Cheap Jack's carries a huge selection of secondhand Levi's as well as hundreds of denim and leather jackets. **Screaming Mimi's** is where you could unearth that pair of velvet bell-bottoms or go-go boots you've always dreamed of having. A more mainstream shop is **The Gap**, a chain store selling lots of moderately-priced, casual and comfortable clothes for men, women, and children.

Sotto and Notto/Nolita rival Madison Avenue for designer boutiques specializing in expensive but interesting clothes – the fashions here are far more avant-garde. The playful boutique **Kirna Zabete**, for example, features a unique range of clothes as well as accessories. You'll also find **Yohji Yamamoto** in this area, among other exclusive stores. **Comme des Garçons** in the Garment District sells minimalist Japanese chic.

Cynthia Rowley is a prominent New York designer who sells flirty fashions for women and **What Comes Around Goes Around** on West Broadway is the place to go for vintage jeans.

SIZE CHART

For Australian sizes follow the British and American conversions.

Children's clothing

American	2–3	4–5	6–6x	7–8	10	12	14	16 (size)
British	2–3	4–5	6–7	8–9	10–11	12	14	14+ (years)
Continental	2–3	4–5	6–7	8–9	10–11	12	14	14+ (years)

Children's shoes

American	7½	8½	9½	10½	11½	12½	13½	1½	2½
British	7	8	9	10	11	12	13	1	2
Continental	24	25½	27	28	29	30	32	33	34

Women's dresses, coats and skirts

American	4	6	8	10	12	14	16	18
British	6	8	10	12	14	16	18	20
Continental	38	40	42	44	46	48	50	52

Women's blouses and sweaters

American	6	8	10	12	14	16	18
British	30	32	34	36	38	40	42
Continental	40	42	44	46	48	50	52

Women's shoes

American	5	6	7	8	9	10	11
British	3	4	5	6	7	8	9
Continental	36	37	38	39	40	41	44

Men's suits

American	34	36	38	40	42	44	46	48
British	34	36	38	40	42	44	46	48
Continental	44	46	48	50	52	54	56	58

Men's shirts

American	14	15	15½	16	16½	17	17½	18
British	14	15	15½	16	16½	17	17½	18
Continental	36	38	39	41	42	43	44	45

Men's shoes

American	7	7½	8	8½	9½	10½	11	11½
British	6	7	7½	8	9	10	11	12
Continental	39	40	41	42	43	44	45	46

DIRECTORY

DISCOUNT DESIGNER CLOTHES

Century 21 Department Store
22 Cortland St.
Map 1 C2.
Tel (212) 227-9092.

Designer Resale
324 E 81st St.
Map 17 B4.
Tel (212) 734-3639.

Encore
1132 Madison Ave.
Map 17 A4.
Tel (212) 879-2850.

Filene's Basement
4 Union Square South.
Map 9 A5.
Tel (212) 358-0169.
One of several branches.

Loehmann's
101 7th Ave. **Map** 8 E1.
Tel (212) 352-0856.

Michael's
1041 Madison Ave.
Map 17 A5.
Tel (212) 737-7273.

MEN'S CLOTHES

Barney's New York
660 Madison Ave.
Map 13 A3.
Tel (212) 826-8900.

Beau Brummel
421 W Broadway.
Map 4 E3.
Tel (212) 219-2666.
One of several branches.

Bergdorf Goodman Men
754 5th Ave.
Map 12 F3.
Tel (212) 753-7300.

Brooks Brothers
346 Madison Ave.
Map 9 A1.
Tel (212) 682-8800.

Burberry Limited
9 E 57th St.
Map 12 F3.
Tel (212) 757-3700.

The Custom Shop Shirtmakers
618 5th Ave.
Map 12 F4.
Tel (212) 245-2499.
One of several branches.

Hickey Freeman
666 Fifth Ave.
Map 12 F4.
Tel (212) 586-6481.

J. Press
7 E 44th St. **Map** 12 F5.
Tel (212) 687-7642.

John Varvatos
149 Mercer St. **Map** 4 E3.
Tel (212) 965-0700.

Paul Stuart
350 Madison Ave.
Map 13 A5.
Tel (212) 682-0320.

Polo/Ralph Lauren
Madison Ave at 72nd St.
Map 13 A1.
Tel (212) 606-2100.

Thomas Pink
520 Madison Ave.
Map 13 A4.
Tel (212) 838-1928.

CHILDREN'S CLOTHES

Blue Tree
1283 Madison Ave.
Map 17 A2.
Tel (212) 369-2583.

Bonpoint
1269 Madison Ave.
Map 17 A3.
Tel (212) 722-7720.

Bundle
128 Thompson St.
Map 4 D3.
Tel (212) 982-9465.

GapKids
60 W 34th St. **Map** 8 F2.
Tel (212) 760-1268.
One of several branches.

Space Kiddets
46 E 21st St.
Map 8 F4.
Tel (212) 420-9878.

WOMEN'S CLOTHES

Ann Taylor
645 Madison Ave.
Map 13 A3.
Tel (212) 832-2010.
One of several branches.

APC
131 Mercer St.
Map 4 E3.
Tel (212) 966-9685.

Betsey Johnson
248 Columbus Ave.
Map 16 D4.
Tel (212) 362-3364.
One of several branches.

Calvin Klein
654 Madison Ave.
Map 13 A3.
Tel (212) 292-9000.

Chanel
15 E 57th St.
Map 12 F3.
Tel (212) 355-5050.

Cheap Jack's
841 Broadway.
Map 4 E1.
Tel (212) 777-9564.

Comme des Garçons
520 W 22nd St.
Map 8 F3.
Tel (212) 604-9200.

Cynthia Rowley
376 Bleecker St.
Map 3 C2.
Tel (212) 242-3803.

Dolce & Gabbana
434 W Broadway.
Map 4 E3.
Tel (212) 965-8000.

Emanuel Ungaro
792 Madison Ave.
Map 13 A2.
Tel (212) 249-4090.

French Connection
700 Broadway.
Map 4 E2.
Tel (212) 473-4486.
One of several branches.

The Gap
250 W 57th St.
Map 12 D3.
Tel (212) 315-2250.
One of many branches.

Gianni Versace
647 5th Ave.
Map 12 F4.
Tel (212) 317-0224.

Giorgio Armani
760 Madison Ave.
Map 13 A2.
Tel (212) 988-9191.

Givenchy
710 Madison Ave.
Map 13 A1.
Tel (212) 688-4005.

Gucci
685 5th Ave.
Map 12 F4.
Tel (212) 826-2600.

Kirna Zabete
96 Greene St.
Map 4 E4.
Tel (212) 941-9656.

Michael Kors
974 Madison Ave.
Map 17 A5.
Tel (212) 452-4685.

Missoni
1009 Madison Ave.
Map 13 A1.
Tel (212) 517-9339.

Saks Fifth Avenue
611 5th Ave.
Map 12 F4.
Tel (212) 753-4000.

Scoop
532 Broadway
(near Spring St).
Map 4 E4.
Tel (212) 925-2886.
One of two branches.

Screaming Mimi's
382 Lafayette St.
Map 4 F2.
Tel (212) 677-6464.

Valentino
747 Madison Ave.
Map 13 A2.
Tel (212) 772-6969.

What Comes Around Goes Around
351 W Broadway.
Map 4 E4.
Tel (212) 343-9303.

Yohji Yamamoto
103 Grand St.
Map 4 E4.
Tel (212) 966-9066.

Yves St Laurent Rive Gauche
855 Madison Ave.
Map 13 A1.
Tel (212) 517-7400.

Accessories

In addition to the following shops, all of the major
Manhattan department stores have extensive accessory
departments stocking a range of hats, gloves, bags,
jewelry, watches, scarves, shoes, and umbrellas.

JEWELRY

Midtown Fifth Avenue is
where to find the most
dazzling jewelers. By day,
windows glisten with gems
from around the world; by
night they are empty – the
jewels safely locked away.
The most sensational shops
are all within a couple of
blocks of one another and
include the museum-like
Harry Winston, which showcases its coveted jewels from
around the world. **Buccellati**
is well respected for its
innovative Italian creations
and excellent workmanship.
Bulgari has an impressive
collection that ranges in price
from a couple of hundred to
over a million dollars.

Housed in a Renaissance-
style palazzo, **Cartier** is a jewel
in itself and sells its beautiful
baubles at unthinkable prices.
Tiffany & Co. has ten floors of
glittering crystal, diamonds,
and other jewels just waiting
to be packed up for you and
taken away in the store's
signature sky blue boxes.

Diamond Row, a one-block
area on 47th Street (between
Fifth and Sixth Avenues), is
lined with shops displaying
hundreds of thousands of
dollars worth of diamonds,
gold, pearls, and other exotic
jewels from around the world.
Try not to miss the **Jewelry
Exchange**, a complex where
60 different crafts-people sell
their ware direct to the
public. Boisterous bargaining
is very much alive here, so be
prepared to play the game.

HATS

New York's oldest hat shop is
Worth & Worth, which also
has the largest collection of
hats in the city. You can get
anything here, from original
Australian bush hats to silk
toppers, to slouch hats and
boaters. **Suzanne Millinery** is
the hat-maker to the stars, as

she has proved very popular
with celebrities such as Ivana
Trump and Whoopi Goldberg.
Lids sells baseball caps in
dozens of varieties, with logos
ranging from sports teams to
the evergreen "I HEART NY".
For a wide range of fabulous
headgear, stop by **The Hat
Shop**, where you can find
everything from classic to
contemporary styles.

UMBRELLAS

The minute it starts to rain
in New York, hundreds
of street vendors selling
umbrellas seem to sprout like
mushrooms. Their umbrellas,
which sell at just a few
dollars, are without doubt the
cheapest in the city, but
unlikely to last much longer
than the downpour itself.
For good-quality umbrellas,
you'll find a fine selection of
Briggs of London at **Worth &
Worth**. There is a wide range
of different sizes, trendy
patterns, and traditional
tartans and stripes at **Barney's
New York**, and there's always
Macy's (see p319) for the
usual sizes and styles. World-
famous **Gucci** has umbrellas
to match its ties. Subway-
themed ones can be found at
the **NY Transit Museum Store**.

HANDBAGS AND
BRIEFCASES

Twice a year, during the
January and August sales,
a serpentine line of buyers
wraps around the corner
of 48th Street and Madison
Avenue waiting to get into
Crouch & Fitzgerald, an old
New York institution, selling
handbags, briefcases, and
luggage. All the well-known
brands are sold here, including
Judith Leiber, Ghurka, Dooney
& Bourke, and Louis Vuitton,
as well as the firm's own line.
Elsewhere in the city are such
exclusive shops as **Bottega
Veneta**, and **Prada**, where

handbags are displayed like
precious art, with prices to
match. Younger and trendier
places include **Furla**, well-
respected for its Italian
designs, and the stylish **Il
Bisonte**. Current must-have
designer Rafé Totengco's soft
suede pastel pouches are
found at **TG-170**. **The Coach
Store** is known for its simple,
classic leather handbags.
Designer **Kate Spade's** stylish
yet practical rectangular
handbags, in a plethora
of prints and colors, have
become modern classics,
and add a chic touch to
any woman's wardrobe.
Jack Spade designs similarly
unique bags for men.

For discount designer
handbags try the legendary
Fine & Klein, and for bargain
briefcases from slim enve-
lopes to thick lawyer's bags,
a visit to the **Altman Luggage
Company** is a must.

SHOES AND BOOTS

Manhattan shoe stores are
famous for their extensive
selections of shoes and boots,
and if you shop around, you
are sure to find what you
want at a reasonable price.

Most of the large depart-
ment stores in New York also
have shoe departments where
you can find designer-label
shoes in addition to other
brands. **Bloomingdale's** (see
p181) has a huge women's
footwear department, and
Brooks Brothers has one of
the best selections of traditional men's shoes in the city.

For both men's and
women's shoes, the most
exclusive shops are around
the midtown area. **Ferragamo**
sells classic styles crafted in
Florence. Go to **Botticelli** for
whimsical shoe fashions.
For stylish shoes at decent
prices, head for **Sigerson
Morrison** in Little Italy.

For cowboy boots, head for
Billy Martin's. There's a huge
selection of handmade boots,
from basic, no-frills "ropers,"
which real American cowboys
wear, to crocodile leather
boots that sell for thousands of
dollars. Billy Martin's stocks

western garb and accessories, so you can dress in western gear from head to toe. For beautiful custom-made boots, try **Buffalo Chips Bootery**.

Sneaker collectors should make a stop at **Alife Rivington Club** on the Lower East Side, which stocks several hard-to-find styles.

For the best in children's shoes, **East Side Kids** stocks the trendiest fashions for kids, while **Shoofly** has imported shoes in all styles.

The **Jimmy Choo** boutique offers a plethora of sexy, stylish heels. Popular among Manhattan's chic set are the beautiful women's shoes,

particularly the flattering heels, at **Manolo Blahnik**. **Christian Louboutin** rounds out the stiletto heavyweights. Spain's most popular brand, **Camper**, has an airy SoHo store featuring their signature comfy, funky, and colorful shoes for women and men.

For discounted shoes, go to West 34th Street and West Eight Street between Fifth and Sixth Avenues, and Orchard Street on the Lower East Side. The **DSW** store, on the third floor of 40 E 14th Street, sells brand-name shoes and boots at a fraction of the regular price. There's also a branch near Battery Park.

LINGERIE

Expensive imports from Europe, which are sexy yet elegant, can be found at **La Petite Coquette**.

More affordable is **Victoria's Secret** on 57th Street or SoHo, which offers beautifully made lingerie in satin, silk, and many other fine fabrics. **Henri Bendel's** lingerie department offers a sumptuous array of lingerie, from naughty to nice. The Italian **La Perla** features seductive lingerie and undergarments in sensual fabrics from tulle and chiffon to satin.

DIRECTORY

JEWELRY

Buccellati
46 E 57th Ave. **Map** 12 F3.
Tel (212) 308-2900.

Bulgari
730 5th Ave. **Map** 12 F3.
Tel (212) 315-9000.

Cartier
653 5th Ave. **Map** 12 F4.
Tel (212) 753-0111.

Harry Winston
718 5th Ave. **Map** 12 F3.
Tel (212) 245-2000.

Jewelry Exchange
15 W 47th St. **Map** 12 F5.

Tiffany & Co
5th Ave. **Map** 12 F3.
Tel (212) 755-8000.

HATS

The Hat Shop
120 Thompson St. **Map** 4 D3. *Tel (212) 219-1446.*

Lids
243 W 42nd St. **Map** 8 E1. *Tel (212) 575-1717.*

Suzanne Millinery
27 E 61 St. **Map** 13 A3.
Tel (212) 593-3232.

Worth & Worth
45 W 57th St, 6th floor, Suite Le02. **Map** 12 F3. *Tel (212) 265-2887.*

UMBRELLAS

Barney's New York
See p319.

Gucci
See p327.

NY Transit Museum Store
Grand Central Terminal.
Map 9 A1.
Tel (212) 878-0106.

HANDBAGS AND BRIEFCASES

Altman Luggage Company
135 Orchard St. **Map** 5 A3.
Tel (212) 254-7275.

Il Bisonte
120 Sullivan St. **Map** 4 D4. *Tel (212) 966-8773.*

Bottega Veneta
635 Madison Ave. **Map** 13 A3. *Tel (212) 371-5511.*

The Coach Store
595 Madison Ave. **Map** 13 A3. *Tel (212) 754-0041.*

Crouch & Fitzgerald
400 Madison Ave.
Map 13 A5.
Tel (212) 755-5888.

Fine & Klein
119 Orchard St. **Map** 5 A3. *Tel (212) 674-6720.*

Furla
727 Madison Ave.
Map 13 A3.
Tel (212) 755-8986.
One of two branches.

Jack Spade
56 Greene St. **Map** 4 E4. *Tel (212) 625-1820.*

Kate Spade
454 Broome St. **Map** 4 E4. *Tel (212) 274-1991.*

Prada
49 E 57th St. **Map** 12 F3.
Tel (212) 308-2332.

TG-170
170 Ludlow St. **Map** 5 A3.
Tel (212) 995-8660.

SHOES AND BOOTS

Alife Rivington Club
158 Rivington St. **Map** 5 B3. *Tel (212) 375-8128.*

Billy Martin's
220 E 60th St. **Map** 13 B3. *Tel (212) 861-3100.*

Botticelli
620 5th Ave. **Map** 12 F4. *Tel (212) 582-6313.*

Bloomingdale's
See p319.

Brooks Brothers
See p327.

Buffalo Chips Bootery
355 W Broadway. **Map** 4 E4. *Tel (212) 625-8400.*

Camper
125 Prince St. **Map** 4 E3. *Tel (212) 358-1842.*

Christian Louboutin
941 Madison Ave.
Map 17 A5.
Tel (212) 396-1884.

DSW
40 E 14th St. **Map** 9 A5. *Tel (212) 674-2146.*

East Side Kids
1298 Madison Ave. **Map** 17 A2. *Tel (212) 360-5000.*

Ferragamo
655 5th Ave. **Map** 12 F3. *Tel (212) 759-3822.*

Jimmy Choo
645 5th Ave. **Map** 12 F4. *Tel (212) 625-1820.*

Manolo Blahnik
31 W 54th St. **Map** 12 F4. *Tel (212) 582-3007.*

Shoofly
42 Hudson St. **Map** 1 B1. *Tel (212) 406-3270.*

Sigerson Morrison
28 Prince St. **Map** 4 F3. *Tel (212) 219-3893.*

LINGERIE

Henri Bendel
See p319.

La Perla
93 Greene St. **Map** 4 E3. *Tel (212) 219-0999.*

La Petite Coquette
51 University Place. **Map** 4 E1. *Tel (212) 473-2478.*

Victoria's Secret
34 E 57th St. **Map** 12 F3. *Tel (212) 758-5592.*
591–593 Broadway.
Map 4 E3.
Tel (212) 219-3643.

Beauty, Manicures and Pedicures, and Hair Salons

You can shop 'til you drop in New York City – and when you do, rest assured that rejuvenation (and a heavenly foot massage) is just around the corner. There are plenty of well-stocked beauty stores, manicure and pedicure specialists, and sleek hair salons. Many of the manicurists and salons cater to New Yorkers and their hectic schedules, so they often accept same-day appointments that can easily fitted in between rounds of sightseeing and shopping. After a pamper session or two (or three…), you'll be ready to hit the shops again, this time with the prettiest toes and silkiest hair around.

BEAUTY STORES

The French-owned **Sephora** is a cosmetics megastore that offers its shoppers row upon row of beauty products, from skin cleansers to cosmetics and fragrances, and, thankfully, a no-pressure sales staff. For all-natural essences and products, try **Erbe** ("herbs" in Italian), a soothing sanctuary with a plethora of hypoallergenic products, all made with fresh herbs and free from mineral oils, animal products, waxes, synthetic fragrances, or dyes. The royal jelly nutrient moisturizer and Pennywort exfoliating cream are popular choices.

The high-ceilinged **MAC Cosmetics** store is always busy. Their face powders, particularly the Studio Fix line, are unsurpassed. The promise of creamy Swedish skin (at a reasonable price) lures shoppers to **FACE Stockholm**, where they stock natural, botanical skin products plus lipstick and nail polish in a rainbow of colors. Since 1851, **Kiehl's** has been creating cleansers, toners, balms, and masques "in purposefully utilitarian" packaging as the natural ingredients speak for themselves.

The nature-friendly **Fresh** sells fragrant body creams and fruity perfume. **Sabon** sells a luxurious range of bath and beauty products that are 100 percent natural and irresistibly scented. Soaps can be bought by the pound here, and they are gift-wrapped for free.

For good quality makeup that stands the test of time, visit SoHo's stylish **Make Up for Ever**, which stocks everything from liquid face foundations and creamy lipsticks, to sparkling body powders. Head to earthy **Origins** and select from their plethora of plant-based lotions, an antioxidant moisturizer made with white tea, and body creams sensitive enough for a baby's skin. British beauty maven Nicky Kinnaird has opened her first outlet of **Space.NK** in SoHo. The shop also offers beauty services.

Most of New York's large department stores, including **Bloomingdale's**, **Lord & Taylor**, **Saks Fifth Avenue**, **Barney's New York**, and **Macy's** offer well-stocked makeup counters.

MANICURES AND PEDICURES

Young Korean entrepreneur Ji Baek's **Rescue Beauty Lounge** started out as a cozy SoHo salon, but it proved so popular that she had to open a second outpost. As well as manicures and pedicures, you can have waxing and browse hard-to-find makeup lines. **Eve's** may look somewhat bland and institutional, but appearances can be deceiving. Their long-lasting manicures and pedicures are top-notch. **Dashing Diva** not only offers excellent manicures and pedicures at a bargain price (starting at $10). The whole experience is made all the more alluring, however, as they offer treats with their treatments. On Thursdays and Fridays, they serve Cosmopolitans and turn up the music.

Experience the ultimate in hand and nail care at **Sweet Lily Natural Nail Spa & Boutique**. The range includes an intoxicating blend of warm milk and almond oil for your hands, and a moisturizing honey walnut mask with a honey walnut manicure ($40). The hot lavender cream manicure includes a wonderful conditioning treatment for cuticles that contains tea tree and citrus oil. The boutique is not just for adults, as there is also a manicure for little girls: the Little Miss Mani includes a choice of nail art.

HAIR SALONS

If you're in the mood for a new hair do, or just want to refresh your current cut, try one of New York City's cutting-edge hair salons.

The stylists at the downtown **Arrojo Studio** will update your style, so that you walk out of the salon looking as hip as they do. Arrojo colorists are also top-notch, and the salon offers a wide range of exellent color treatments. Follow the celebrities, and get your hair cut, styled, and/or colored by stylist Frederic Fekkai or one of his associates at the chic **Frederic Fekkai Beaute de Provence**. This top salon is very much a cut above the rest.

Korean stylist Younghee Kim, formerly of Vidal Sassoon, offers hip cuts and colors, as well as "hair spa treatments" and thermal conditioning, starting at $110 at her eponymous hair salon, **Younghee Salon** in TriBeCa. The stylists at the **Rumor Salon** are well-known to be czars with scissors, creating simple yet fashionable and flattering cuts amid a spare salon awash in warm lighting. Set in a classy, sun-flooded loft, the **Aveda Institute** offers superb cuts, colors, and scalp massages. Pick up one of their plant-based beauty and bath products. The institute also offers the opportunity to receive a discount haircut by one of the trainee hairdressers. A great choice for men is **La Boite a Coupe**, whose clientele includes many advertising and media personalities. Moroccan-French stylist Laurent De Louya has been cutting hair here since 1972. The upscale, Asian-accented **Le Salon Chinois**, never fails to create a sleek cut that will turn heads.

They also offer excellent scalp treatments, hair aromatherapy, and effective "Japanese straightening." Head to the lovely **TwoDo Salon**, where you can get an expert cut and color amid a rustic, colorful decor of fresh flowers and brick walls hung with paintings by local artists.

Styling stalwart **Vidal Sassoon** is still going strong. Visit the elegant downtown salon on Fifth Avenue where accomplished stylists and colorists – all of whom have gone through the company's rigorous training – turn out impeccable, eye-catching cuts and colors. **Toni & Guy**, a premiere hair salon from the UK, is renowned for its consistently good cuts. The NYC salon is the US training headquarters, where creative stylists offer the boldest cuts around. Toni & Guy colorists have also been lauded for their tinting and highlighting skill.

For more great cuts and colors, try the hip favorites **Antonio Prieto** and **Bumble & Bumble**, the refined **John Masters Organics**, and the elite **Oscar Blandi**.

DIRECTORY

BEAUTY STORES

Erbe
196 Prince St. **Map** 4 D3.
Tel (212) 966-1445.

FACE Stockholm
10 Columbus Circle.
Map 12 D3.
Tel (212) 823-9415.

110 Prince St, SoHo.
Map 4 E3.
Tel (212) 966-9110.

Fresh
57 Spring St at
Lafayette St. **Map** 4 F4.
Tel (212) 925-0099.
One of five branches.

John Masters Organics
77 Sullivan St near
Broome St. **Map** 4 D4.
Tel (212) 343-9590.

Kiehl's
109 3rd Ave. **Map** 9 B5.
Tel (212) 677-3171.

MAC Cosmetics
113 Spring St. **Map** 4 E4.
Tel (212) 334-4641.

Make Up for Ever
409 W Broadway at
Spring St. **Map** 4 E4.
Tel (212) 941-9337.

Origins
175 5th Ave at 23rd St.
Map 8 F4.
Tel (212) 677-9100.

Sabon
93 Spring St. **Map** 4 E4.
Tel (212) 925-0742.
One of three branches.

Sephora
555 Broadway.
Map 4 E3.
Tel (212) 625-1309.
One of several branches.

Space.NK
99 Greene St, near
Spring St. **Map** 4 E4.
Tel (212) 941-9200.

MANICURE AND PEDICURES

Barney's New York
660 Madison Ave.
Map 13 A3.
Tel (212) 826-8900.

Bloomingdale's
1000 3rd Ave.
Map 13 B3.
Tel (212) 705-2000.

Bloomingdale's SoHo
504 Broadway.
Map 4 E4.
Tel (212) 729-5900.

Dashing Diva
41 E 8th St. **Map** 4 E2.
Tel (212) 673-9000.

Eve
400 Bleecker St.
Map 3 C2.
Tel (212) 807-8054.

Lord & Taylor
424 5th Ave. **Map** 8 F1.
Tel (212) 391-3344.

Macy's
151 W 34th St.
Map 8 E2.
Tel (212) 695-4400.

Rescue Beauty Lounge
8 Centre Market Pl.
Map 4 F4.
Tel (212) 431-0449.
34 Gansevoort St.
Map 3 B1.
Tel (212) 206-6409.

Saks Fifth Avenue
611 5th Ave. **Map** 12 F4.
Tel (212) 753-4000.

Sweet Lily Natural Nail Spa & Boutique
222 W Broadway,
between N Moore &
Franklin sts. **Map** 4 E5.
Tel (212) 925-5441.

HAIR SALONS

Antonio Prieto
25 19th St, between 5th
& 6th aves. **Map** 8 F5.
Tel (212) 255-3741.

Arrojo Studio
180 Varick St.
Map 4 D3.
Tel (212) 242-7786.

Aveda Institute
233 Spring St. **Map** 4 D4.
Tel (212) 807-1492.

La Boite a Coupe
18 W 55th St.
Map 12 F4.
Tel (212) 246-2097.

Bumble & Bumble
415 13th St, near
9th Ave. **Map** 3 B1.
Tel (212) 521-6500.

Frederic Fekkai Beaute de Provence
15 E 57th St.
Map 12 F3.
Tel (212) 753-9500.

Oscar Blandi
746 Madison Ave.
Map 13 A2.
Tel (212) 988-9404.

Le Salon Chinois
44 W 55th St, 4th Floor.
Between 5th & 6th aves.
Map 12 F4.
Tel (212) 956-1200.

Rumor Salon
15 E 12th St, 2nd Floor.
Map 4 E1.
Tel (212) 414-0195.

Toni & Guy
673 Madison Ave,
Suite 2 at 61st St.
Map 13 A3.
Tel (212) 702-9771.

TwoDo Salon
210 W 82nd St,
between Broadway &
Amsterdam. **Map** 15 C4.
Tel (212) 787-1277.

Vidal Sassoon
90 5th Ave, Suite 90.
Between 14th & 15th sts.
Map 8 F5.
Tel (212) 229-2200.

Younghee Salon
64 N Moore St.
Map 4 D5.
Tel (212) 334-3770.

Books and Music

As the publishing capital of America, it's not surprising that New York has the country's best selection of bookstores. These range from vast general interest stores to hundreds of esoteric bookstores specializing in everything from sci-fi to suspense, selling new books and old. Music lovers will also find sounds for all tastes at reasonable prices, plus thousands of rare recordings.

GENERAL INTEREST BOOKSTORES

One of the most well-known of New York's bookstores – for best prices as well as selection of titles – is **Barnes & Noble** on Fifth Avenue, reputedly the world's largest bookstore and packed high with over three million books on every imaginable subject. There are branches all over the City, plus the sales annex across the street, with amazing bargains.

Several blocks away is the main branch of New York's famous **Strand Book Store**, with an astonishing two million copies of new and secondhand books. There is also a large rare book room for first editions.

Westsider Bookshop is as comprehensive as its music counterpart, as it stocks an enormous collection of used books and country/bluegrass LPs. **12th Street Books** has a good selection of new and used books, and art books. **Borders Books & Music** offers a choice of CDs and books of all genres. **Housing Works Bookstore Café** is a lovely, high-ceilinged bookstore-café with a wide range of gently used books. The friendly **McNally Jackson** stocks classics and contemporary fiction, and also has a café.

Rizzoli has a big selection of photography, foreign language, music, and art books, plus children's books and videos. **Shakespeare & Co.** offers a sensational selection of titles and is open late every night.

SPECIALTY BOOKSTORES

For the best selection of art books in the city, visit **Hacker-Strand Art Books**. **Urban Center Books** has titles on urban planning and other conservation issues. The city's largest selection of theatrical books and publications is found at **Drama Book Shop**. Jewish books and music abound at **J. Levine Judaica**. Rare books, books out-of-print, and old books about New York are the *raison d'être* of **JN Bartfield Books**. The **Biography Bookshop** is the only midtown store specializing in diaries, letters, biographies, and autobiographies. Theater buffs should try **Applause Theater & Cinema Books**.

Books on murder and suspense are the focus of **Mysterious Bookshop**. Try **Forbidden Planet** for old and new science-fiction books and comics. **Midtown Comics** has two spacious locations and offers a good range of comics at affordable prices, mostly from the late 1980s to the present. Vintage collectors might prefer **Jim Hanley's Universe**, across from the Empire State Building. Collectible merchandise here ranges from reasonable to "ask Santa" in price.

Bank Street Book Store has one of the best selections of current children's books; they also host storytime and other engaging events for kids. Visit **Books of Wonder** for a variety of hardcover and rare children's books.

The Complete Traveler stocks a wide selection of brand-new and antique travel books and guides for your trip. The staff is very knowledgeable and more than helpful.

For an excellent range of maps visit the **Hagstrom Map & Travel Store**. Cookbooks are on the menu at **Kitchen Arts & Letters**, with many out-of-print books and first editions. Radicals should head for **Revolution Books** or **St. Mark's Bookstore**, which also has an excellent selection of literary and art titles. The **Oscar Wilde Memorial Bookshop** has a wide selection of gay and lesbian texts.

Lots of educational toys and their book tie-ins can be found in the airy and bright **Scholastic Store**, downstairs from the publisher's SoHo offices.

RECORDS, TAPES, AND COMPACT DISCS

J&R Music World is a complete home-entertainment store with one of the best CD selections in the city.

For out-of-print records, go to **Westsider Records**, a treasure trove for collectors, with an excellent choice of classical, jazz, and opera recordings. **House of Oldies** has a massive stock of deleted and rare records to suit all tastes. **Bleecker Bob's Golden Oldies** record shop has everything from imports, rock, and punk to rare jazz. Try **Midnight Records** for imports, reissues, American garage rock, and psychedelia.

DJs and vinyl lovers still have options for deep house, breakbeat, and electronica. Check out **Turntable Lab** in Manhattan, while in Brooklyn there is **Earwax** or the lively **Halcyon**. True music enthusiasts should head to **Other Music**, which stocks obscure gems, from hot electronica to 1970s free jazz. **Disc-O-Rama** has some of the cheapest CD prices around.

SHEET MUSIC

Just behind Carnegie Hall is one of the best stores for classical sheet music, **Joseph Patelson Music House**. The **Frank Music Company** has a huge collection of classical music scores. **Charles Colin Publications** specializes in jazz. For chart music and pop tunes try **Colony Music Center** in the Brill Building on Broadway.

DIRECTORY

GENERAL INTEREST BOOKSTORES

Barnes & Noble
105 5th Ave. **Map** 8 F5.
Tel (212) 807-0099.
One of several branches.

Borders Books & Music
100 Broadway.
Map 1 C3.
Tel (212) 964-1988.
One of several branches.

Housing Works Bookstore Café
126 Crosby St. **Map** 4 F3.
Tel (212) 334-3324.

McNally Jackson
52 Prince St. **Map** 4 F3.
Tel (212) 274-1160.

Rizzoli
31 W 57th St.
Map 12 F3.
Tel (212) 759-2424.

Shakespeare & Co.
716 Broadway.
Map 4 E2.
Tel (212) 529-1330.
One of several branches.

Strand Book Store
828 Broadway.
Map 4 E1.
Tel (212) 473-1452.

12th Street Books
11 East 12th St.
Map 4 F1.
Tel (212) 645-4340.

Westsider Bookshop
2246 Broadway.
Map 15 C4.
Tel (212) 362-0706.

SPECIALTY BOOKSTORES

Applause Theater & Cinema Books
19 W 21st St.
Map 8 F4.
Tel (212) 575-9265.

Bank Street Book Store
610 W 112th St.
Map 21 A4.
Tel (212) 678-1654.

Biography Bookshop
400 Bleecker St.
Map 3 C2.
Tel (212) 807-8655.

Books of Wonder
16 W 18th St.
Map 8 E5.
Tel (212) 989-3270.

The Complete Traveler
199 Madison Ave.
Map 9 A2.
Tel (212) 685-9007.

Drama Book Store
250 W 40th St.
Map 8 E1.
Tel (212) 944-0595.

Forbidden Planet
840 Broadway.
Map 4 E1.
Tel (212) 473-1576.

Hacker-Strand Art Books
45 W 57th St.
Map 12 F3.
Tel (212) 688-7600.

Hagstrom Map & Travel Store
57 W 43rd St.
Map 8 F1.
Tel (212) 398-1222.

Jim Hanley's Universe
4 W 33rd St.
Map 8 F2.
Tel (212) 268-7088.

J. Levine Judaica
5 W 30th St.
Map 8 F3.
Tel (212) 695-6888.

JN Bartfield Books
30 W 57th St.
Map 12 F3.
Tel (212) 245-8890.

Kitchen Arts & Letters
1435 Lexington Ave.
Map 17 A2.
Tel (212) 876-5550.

Midtown Comics
200 W 40th St.
Map 8 E1.
459 Lexington Ave.
Map 13 A5.
Tel (212) 302-8192.

Mysterious Bookshop
58 Warren St.
Map 1 B1.
Tel (212) 582-1011.

Oscar Wilde Memorial Bookshop
15 Christopher St.
Map 3 C2.
Tel (212) 255-8097.

Revolution Books
9 W 19th St.
Map 7 C5.
Tel (212) 691-3345.

St. Mark's Bookshop
31 3rd Ave.
Map 5 A2.
Tel (212) 260-7853.

The Scholastic Store
577 Broadway.
Map 4 E4.
Tel (212) 343-6166.

Urban Center Books
457 Madison Ave.
Map 13 A4.
Tel (212) 935-3592.

RECORDS, TAPES, AND COMPACT DISCS

Bleecker Bob's Golden Oldies
118 W 3rd St.
Map 4 D2.
Tel (212) 475-9677.

Disc-O-Rama
186 W 4th St.
Map 4 D2.
Tel (212) 206-8417.

Earwax
218 Bedford Avenue, Brooklyn.
Tel (718) 486-3771.

Halcyon The Shop
57 Pearl St at Water St, Dumbo, Brooklyn.
Map 2 F2.
Tel (718) 260-WAXY.

House of Oldies
35 Carmine St.
Map 4 D3.
Tel (212) 243-0500.

J&R Music World
23 Park Row.
Map 1 C2.
Tel (800) 806-1115.

Midnight Records
263 W 23rd St.
Map 8 D4.
Tel (212) 675-2768.

Other Music
15 E 4th St.
Map 4 F2.
Tel (212) 477-8150.

Turntable Lab
120 E 7th St.
Map 5 A2.
Tel (212) 677-0675.

West Sider Records
233 W 72nd St.
Map 11 D1.
Tel (212) 874-1588.

SHEET MUSIC

Charles Colin Publications
315 W 53rd St.
Map 12 D4.
Tel (212) 581-1480.

Colony Music Center
1619 Broadway.
Map 12 E4.
Tel (212) 265-2050.

Frank Music Company
244 W 54th St.
Map 12 D4.
Tel (212) 582-1999.

Joseph Patelson Music House
160 W 56th St.
Map 12 E4.
Tel (212) 757-5587.

Art and Antiques

Any art-loving visitor to New York could easily spend several days gallery-hopping around the several hundred galleries found throughout New York. Antique lovers can find an exciting variety of goods, including Americana and many bargains, at the many flea markets; or they can browse through European and American fine antiques in one of the more exclusive antiques centers. To find out what's happening, pick up the free monthly *Art Now Gallery Guide*, available at most galleries, or check the local papers.

ART GALLERIES

One of the city's best-known galleries is **Leo Castelli**, an important showcase for Pop Art during the early 1960s and now spotlighting new artists. **Mary Boone Gallery** features Neo-Expressionist artists such as Julian Schnabel. **Pace Wildenstein Gallery** exhibits current stars, especially well-known painter-photographers. **Postmasters** features impressive changing shows of emerging artists. **Marian Goodman Gallery** focuses on the European avant-garde.

In Chelsea, the **Mathew Marks Gallery** and **Marianne Boesky Gallery** are usually worth a visit. **Paula Cooper** often hosts controversial shows in her beautiful loft space. The **Gagosian Gallery** exhibits paintings by modern masters, with great works by Lichtenstein and Johns. It also has an outlet in the Upper East Side where you can find **Knoedler & Company**, and the **Hirschl & Adler Galleries** with a good selection of European and American fine art. **Max Protech** is very architecture-friendly, while **Esso** displays Pop Art. **Barbara Gladstone** is another heavy hitter in the art scene, and **Exit Art** is famed for its multimedia exhibitions. The airy **Agora Gallery** shows memorable local and international works, including Art Nouveau pieces.

AMERICAN FOLK ART

If you're in the market for American folk art, **Susan Parrish Antiques** has a wide selection of hooked rugs and other Americana, but is open only by appointment. Similar goods are at **Laura Fisher Quilts** in Manhattan Art & Antiques Center, who sells everything from decoys to hooked rugs.

ANTIQUES CENTERS AND SECONDHAND ANTIQUES

In addition to hundreds of small shops selling every-thing from tiger teeth to multimillion-dollar paintings, Manhattan is home to **The Manhattan Art & Antiques Center**, which has dozens of dealers under one roof. The **Showplace Antique and Design Center** in Chelsea, featuring four floors of antiques, retro furnishings, and memorabilia, is also well worth a visit.

AMERICAN FURNITURE

For furniture from the 17th-, 18th-, and 19th-centuries, try **Bernard & S. Dean Levy**, or **Leigh Keno American Furniture**. **Judith & James Milne** sell early American country furniture as well as a splendid collection of quilts. Alternatively, go to **Woodard & Greenstein American Antiques & Quilts** for a truly wonderful selection of Shaker pieces.

Collectors of Art Deco or Art Nouveau furniture should pay a visit to **Alan Moss**, which is full of furniture and decorative items of all kinds. **Macklowe Gallery** on Madison Avenue has a massive collection of fine Art Nouveau furniture. Just a few blocks away, **Lillian Nassau** has Tiffany lamps and many Art Nouveau and Art Deco pieces.

New York has a handful of retro shops, including **Depression Modern**, which has treasures from the 1930s and 1940s.

INTERNATIONAL ANTIQUES

If you're looking for English antiques, try **Florian Papp** and **Kentshire Galleries**. For European pieces, you'll have plenty of choices; try **Betty Jane Bart Antiques**, **Kurt Gluckselig Antiques**, **Linda Horn Antiques**, and **Les Pierres**. **La Belle Epoque** stocks antique posters. Oriental dealers include luxury **Doris Leslie Blau**, **E. & J. Frankel**, and **Flying Cranes Antiques**.

FLEA MARKETS

New York has a number of year-round weekend markets. Most flea markets officially open at 9 or 10am. If you arrive early, you could unearth some valuable piece of cultural Americana like a Barbie lunch box or a Soupy Sales record.

Visit the **Annex Antiques Fair and Flea Market** for everything from secondhand clothing to antique furniture. The **Columbus Avenue Flea Market** has new and second-hand clothing and furniture. For information on all street fairs and flea markets, check Friday's *The New York Times* or *The Village Voice*.

AUCTION HOUSES

Manhattan's two most cele-brated auction houses are **Christie's** and **Sotheby's**, selling collectibles ranging from coins, jewels, and vintage wines to fine and decorative arts. Also worth a try are **Doyle New York** and **Phillips de Pury & Co**. both well-respected names for fine art, jewelry, and antiques. Bear in mind that items for sale are previewed several days before the auctions, so check the Friday and Sunday *Times* beforehand to see what's coming up. The venerable **Swann Galleries** auctions prints, books, maps, posters, autographs, and photographs.

DIRECTORY

ART GALLERIES

Agora Gallery
530 W 25th St. **Map** 7
C4. **Tel** *(212) 226-4151.*

Barbara Gladstone
515 W 24th St.
Map 7 C4.
Tel *(212) 206-9300.*

Esso Gallery
531 W 26th St, 2nd Floor.
Map 7 C4.
Tel *(212) 560-9728.*

Exit Art
475 10th Ave. **Map** 7 C2.
Tel *(212) 966-7745.*

Gagosian Gallery
555 W 24th St.
Map 7 C4.
Tel *(212) 741-1111.*
One of several galleries.

**Hirschl & Adler
Galleries**
21 E 70th St.
Map 12 F1.
Tel *(212) 535-8810.*

**Knoedler &
Company**
19 E 70th St.
Map 13 A1.
Tel *(212) 794-0550.*

Leo Castelli
18 E 77th St.
Map 17 A5.
Tel *(212) 249-4470.*

**Marian Goodman
Gallery**
24 W 57th St.
Map 12 F3.
Tel *(212) 977-7160.*

**Marianne Boesky
Gallery**
535 W 22nd St.
Map 7 C4.
Tel *(212) 680-9889.*

Mary Boone Gallery
745 5th Ave.
Map 12 F3.
Tel *(212) 752-2929.*
One of two galleries.

**Mathew Marks
Gallery**
523 W 24th St.
Map 7 C4.
Tel *(212) 243-0200.*

Max Protech
511 W 22nd St.
Map 7 C4.
Tel *(212) 633-6999.*

**Pace Wildenstein
Gallery**
534 W 25th St.
Map 7 C4.
Tel *(212) 929-7000.*
One of two galleries.

Paula Cooper
534 W 21st St.
Map 7 C4.
Tel *(212) 255-1105.*

Postmasters
459 W 19th St.
Map 7 C5.
Tel *(212) 727-3323.*

AMERICAN FOLK ART

Laura Fisher Quilts
Manhattan Art
& Antiques Center,
1050 2nd Ave.
Map 13 B4.
Tel *(212) 838-2596.*

**Susan Parrish
Antiques**
Tel *(212) 807-1561.*
By appointment only.

ANTIQUE CENTERS AND SECOND-HAND ANTIQUES

**The Manhattan
Arts & Antiques
Center**
1050 2nd Ave.
Map 13 A3.
Tel *(212) 355-4400.*

**The Showplace
Antique and Design
Center**
40 W 25th St. **Map** 8 F4.
Tel *(212) 633-6063.*

AMERICAN FURNITURE

Alan Moss
436 Lafayette St.
Map 4 F2.
Tel *(212) 473-1310.*

**Bernard &
S. Dean Levy**
24 E 84th St.
Map 16 F4.
Tel *(212) 628-7088.*

Depression Modern
150 Sullivan St.
Map 4 D3.
Tel *(212) 982-5699.*

**Judith & James
Milne**
506 E 74th St. **Map** 17
C5. **Tel** *(212) 472-0107.*
One of two branches.

**Leigh Keno
American Furniture**
127 E 69th St.
Map 17 A5.
Tel *(212) 734-2381.*

Lillian Nassau
220 E 57th St.
Map 13 B3.
Tel *(212) 759-6062.*

Macklowe Gallery
667 Madison Ave.
Map 13 A3.
Tel *(212) 644-6400.*

**Woodard &
Greenstein
American Antiques**
506 E 74th St.
Map 17 A5.
Tel *(212) 988-2906.*

INTERNATIONAL ANTIQUES

La Belle Epoque
280 Columbus Ave.
Map 12 D1.
Tel *(212) 362-1770.*

**Betty Jane Bart
Antiques**
1225 Madison Ave.
Map 17 A3.
Tel *(212) 410-2702.*

Doris Leslie Blau
724 5th Ave. **Map** 12 F3.
Tel *(212) 586-5511.*
By appointment only.

E. & J. Frankel
1040 Madison Ave.
Map 17 A5.
Tel *(212) 879-5733.*

Florian Papp
962 Madison Ave.
Map 17 A5.
Tel *(212) 288-6770.*

**Flying Cranes
Antiques**
1050 2nd Ave.
Map 13 B4.
Tel *(212) 223-4600.*

Kentshire Galleries
37 E 12th St. **Map** 4 E1.
Tel *(212) 673-6644.*

**Kurt Gluckselig
Antiques**
200 E 58th St. **Map** 13 B3.
Tel *(212) 758-1805.*

**Linda Horn
Antiques**
1015 Madison Ave.
Map 17 A5.
Tel *(212) 772-1122.*

Les Pierres
369 Bleecker St.
Map 3 C2.
Tel *(212) 243-7740.*

FLEA MARKETS

**Annex Antiques
Fair and Flea
Market**
26th St at 6th Ave, 112
W 25th St (Annex). **Map**
8 E4. **Tel** *(212) 243-5343.*
Open Sat and Sun.

**Columbus Avenue
Flea Market**
Columbus Ave, between
76th and 77th St.
Map 16 D5. **Tel** *(631)
873-4790. Open Sun.*

AUCTION HOUSES

Christie's
20 Rockefeller Plaza.
Map 12 F5.
Tel *(212) 636-2000.*

Doyle New York
175 E 87th St.
Map 17 A3.
Tel *(212) 427-2730.*

**Phillips de
Pury & Co.**
450 W 15th St.
Map 7 C5.
Tel *(212) 940-1200.*

Sotheby's
1334 York Ave.
Map 13 C1.
Tel *(212) 606-7000.*

Swann Galleries
104 E 25th St.
Map 9 A4.
Tel *(212) 254-4710.*

Gourmet Groceries, Specialty Food, and Wine Shops

New York's striking cultural and ethnic diversity is celebrated in its food – the city's food shops provide a truly international feast. There is also a dazzling array of coffee stores and wine shops available almost everywhere you turn.

GOURMET GROCERIES

Scattered around town are several famous food emporiums that are tourist attractions in themselves. Remember, too, to visit the department stores, which often rival the specialty food stores.

At **Dean & DeLuca** on Broadway, a chic delicatessen, food has been elevated to an art form – don't miss the huge selection of take-out food. **Russ & Daughters** on Houston Street, one of the oldest gourmet shops, is known as an "appetizing" store, full of ethnic food and famous for smoked fish, cream cheese, chocolates, and bagels. The **Gourmet Garage** on Broome Street sells all kinds of delicious fresh food, in particular organic produce. **Zabar's** on Broadway is perhaps the finest food store in the world, with huge crowds jostling for the excellent smoked salmon, bagels, caviar, nuts and candies, cheese, and coffee.

William Poll on Lexington Avenue offers picnic hampers as well as a great variety of prepared dishes. For pâté de foie gras, Scottish smoked salmon, beluga, and caviar, go to **Caviarteria**.

Whole Foods, famed for their superb selection of natural, organic, wholesome foods, draws devoted shoppers throughout the city. The Whole Foods in Columbus Circle is now the largest supermarket in Manhattan, with row upon gleaming row of quality food "in its purest state" with no artificial additives. There's also a popular central Whole Foods on Union Square. **Fairway Market** on Broadway offers premium groceries from fresh produce to smoked fish and baked goods.

SPECIALTY FOOD

Fabulous bread and cake shops abound but one of the best is **Poseidon Greek Bakery**, renowned for its filo pastry. **H & H Bagels** bakes 60,000 of the finest bagels every day. Try the delicious Chinese pastries at **Fung Wong**, or the pretzel croissants and great tarts at **City Bakery**. Instantly recognizable by the line of happy customers at the door, **Magnolia Bakery** is famed for its beautifully decorated and superb-tasting cupcakes. It has three locations in Manhattan.

Great confectionery shops include **Li-Lac** for handmade chocolates and **Mondel Chocolates** for chocolate animals. **Economy Candy** has a huge range of dried fruit but for a real treat go to **Teuscher Chocolates**, which has fresh champagne truffles flown in direct from Switzerland.

Myers of Keswick imports English food. For something more exotic, **Kam Man Market** is an Oriental grocery selling Chinese, Thai, and other oriental products. The **Italian Food Center** has great olive oils, dried pastas, and sausages. Go to **Jefferson Market** for meat and fish, and **Citarella** for its fine seafood. **Angelica's Herbs and Spices** has a selection of 2,000 varieties of herbs and spices.

For a wide choice of cheese, as well as olives and *charcuterie*, visit **Murray's Cheese Shop**. The intoxicating wafts that greet you at the front door are sure to lure you in. Named New York's Best Cheese Shop by many of the city's newspapers, it is heaven for cheese-lovers, with over 250 types of cheese from around the world, from bloomy rinds like Camembert to moist Ricotta. Feel free to sample; the friendly staff happily offers tastings from the mind-boggling selection. Make a picnic out of it, and pick up some of their fresh breads and olives to accompany your pungent purchases.

If you are looking for true old Eastern European pickle recipes then **The Pickle Guys** is the right place. In addition to pickles, they also store pickled tomatoes, mushrooms, olives, hot peppers, sweet kraut, sauerkraut, herring, and sun-dried tomatoes.

For fruit and vegetables at reasonable prices, visit a farmers' green market, but get there early if you want the pick of the crop. Among the most popular are **Upper West Side**, **St. Mark's in-the-Bowery**, and **Union Square**. For information on the city's markets, phone: (212) 788-7476.

COFFEE STORES

New York also has many fine coffee stores. Among the best are **Oren's Daily Roast** and **Porto Rico Importing Company**, each with a mouth-watering selection. **The Sensuous Bean** features a superb range of gourmet coffees and teas, as does the cozy **McNulty's Tea & Coffee Company**, one of the nation's oldest coffee stores.

WINE SHOPS

Acker, Merrall & Condit have been selling wines since 1820 and have an excellent selection. Go to **Garnet Liquors** for fine wines and champagnes at bargain prices. **Spring Street Wine Shop**, in the heart of SoHo, is a convenient, well-stocked spot to pop in for a bottle of fine wine. **Sherry-Lehmann** is New York's leading wine merchant. **Astor Wines & Spirits**, New York's largest wine store, features a massive selection of premium and discount wines and spirits. Every month they highlight their Top 10 choices under $10 – great for superb bargains. **Union Square Wines and Spirits** offers terrific a variety of wines, and features tastings every week.

DIRECTORY

GOURMET GROCERIES

Caviarteria
502 Park Ave.
Map 13 A3.
Tel (212) 759-7410.

Dean & DeLuca
560 Broadway.
Map 4 E3.
Tel (212) 226-6800.
One of several branches.

Fairway Market
2127 Broadway.
Map 15 C5.
Tel (212) 595-1888.

Gourmet Garage
453 Broome St.
Map 4 E4.
Tel (212) 941-5850.
One of several branches.

Russ & Daughters
179 E Houston St.
Map 5 A3.
Tel (212) 475-4880.

Whole Foods
10 Columbus Circle.
Map 12 D3.
Tel (212) 823-9600.
One of several branches.

William Poll
1051 Lexington Ave.
Map 17 A5.
Tel (212) 288-0501.

Zabar's
2245 Broadway.
Map 15 C4.
Tel (212) 787-2000.

SPECIALTY FOOD

Angelica's Herbs and Spices
147 1st Ave.
Map 5 A1.
Tel (212) 677-1549.

Citarella
2135 Broadway.
Map 15 C5.
Tel (212) 874-0383.

City Bakery
3 W 18th St.
Map 8 F5.
Tel (212) 366-1414.

Economy Candy
108 Rivington St.
Map 5 A3.
Tel (212) 254-1531.

Fung Wong
41 Mott St.
Map 4 F3.
Tel (212) 267-4037.

H & H Bagels
2239 Broadway.
Map 15 C4.
Tel (212) 595-8003.
One of two branches.

Italian Food Center
186 Grand St.
Map 15 C4.
Tel (212) 925-2954.

Jefferson Market
450 Ave of the Americas.
Map 12 E5.
Tel (212) 533-3377.

Kam Man Market
200 Canal St.
Map 4 F5.
Tel (212) 571-0330.

Li-Lac
120 Christopher St.
Map 3 C2.
Tel (212) 242-7374.

Magnolia Bakery
401 Bleecker St.
Map 3 C2.
Tel (212) 462-2572.

Mondel Chocolates
2913 Broadway.
Map 20 E3.
Tel (212) 864-2111.

Murray's Cheese Shop
257 Bleecker St.
Map 4 D2.
Tel (212) 243-3289.
One of two branches.

Myers of Keswick
634 Hudson St.
Map 3 C2.
Tel (212) 691-4194.

The Pickle Guys
49 Essex St.
Map 5 B4.
Tel (212) 656-9739.

Poseidon Greek Bakery
629 9th Ave.
Map 12 D5.
Tel (212) 757-6173.

St. Mark's in-the-Bowery Greenmarket
E 10th St at 2nd Ave.
Map 4 F1.
Open Tue.

Teuscher Chocolates
25 E 61st St.
Map 12 F3.
Tel (212) 751-8482.

620 5th Ave.
Map 12 F4.
Tel (212) 246-4416.

Union Square Greenmarket
E 17th St & Broadway.
Map 8 F5.
Open Mon, Wed, Fri, and Sat.

Upper West Side Greenmarket
Columbus Ave
at 77th St.
Map 16 D5.
Open Sun.

COFFEE STORES

McNulty's Tea & Coffee Company
109 Christopher St.
Map 3 C2.
Tel (212) 242-5351.

Oren's Daily Roast
1144 Lexington Ave.
Map 17 A4.
Tel (212) 472-6830.
One of several branches.

The Sensuous Bean
66 W 70th St.
Map 12 D1.
Tel 1-800-238-6845.

Porto Rico Importing Company
201 Bleecker St.
Map 3 C2.
Tel (212) 477-5421.
One of several branches.

WINE SHOPS

Acker, Merrall & Condit
160 W 72nd St.
Map 11 C1.
Tel (212) 787-1700.

Astor Wines & Spirits
399 Lafayette St.
Map 4 F2.
Tel (212) 674-7500.

Garnet Liquors
929 Lexington Ave.
Map 13 A1.
Tel (212) 772-3211.

Sherry-Lehmann
679 Madison Ave.
Map 13 A3.
Tel (212) 838-7500.

Spring Street Wine Shop
187 Spring St.
Map 4 D4.
Tel (212) 219-0521.

Union Square Wines and Spirits
33 Union Square West.
Map 9 A5.
Tel (212) 675-8100.

Electronics and Housewares

From flat-screen TVs and top-of-the-line sound systems to swanky designer home furnishings, New York City abounds with electronics and housewares stores. Perhaps the most competitive retailers in New York are the ones that sell electronics, so it pays to shop around. Be particularly careful with electronics stores on the heavily touristed streets and those around the major tourist sights, such as Fifth Avenue near the Empire State Building. Many of these stores sell mediocre, sometimes faulty equipment at inflated prices, and it's a hassle or near impossible to get a refund once you've returned home. If you're buying electronic goods to take to Europe, make sure they have compatible voltages and formats (many in the US are made to different standards).

SOUND SYSTEMS AND EQUIPMENT

For the latest in cutting-edge stereo equipment, head to **Sound by Singer**. **J&R Music World** sells competitively priced equipment and has the best jazz CD collection in the city. The Danish **Bang & Olufsen** showcases a range of sleek, minimalist sound systems that can dress up even the humblest flat. **Harvey Electronics** sells top-notch stereos and electronics with the bonus of a friendly, informative staff. Browse the quality systems at **Lyric Hi-Fi**, a longtime favorite that's been around since 1959. The perennially jam-packed **Sony Style** delivers on its wide assortment of top-shelf sound systems and plenty of impulse-buy gizmos. True to its name, the chain store **Best Buy** does offer some of the best buys on an enormous range of stereo systems and home-entertainment products. For high-end stereo equipment and components, check out **Innovative Audio Video Showrooms**. Also stop to look around at the wide range of both used and new stereos at the friendly **Stereo Exchange**.

PHOTOGRAPHY

B & H Photo is where amateur and professional photographers can find everything they need. **Willoughby's** has decent sales on photographic equipment and supplies. The appropriately named **Olden Camera** on Broadway eschews anything digital offering instead quality, old-school cameras and gear. Head to Chelsea's **Foto Care** for a wide range of cameras and accoutrements. **Alkit Pro Camera** offers a large assortment of cameras, components, and lighting equipment plus rentals and film developing and processing. Make for **Adorama** in the Flatiron District, and browse the spectacular displays of digital cameras and accessories, point-and-shoots, and disposables, and also affordable prices on film developing and processing. Don't miss the quality, high-end cameras and equipment at the elegant **The Photo Village**.

COMPUTERS

There are several Macintosh meccas in Manhattan, including the immense, airy **Apple Store SoHo** and the new, gleaming cube of a store on Fifth Avenue. Mac-philes flock to both to peruse and test-drive the latest models, plug in to iPods, and attend seminars geared to both novices and experts.

If you brought your computer from home and find that you need a repair, head to **Amnet PC Solutions**, where a tech whiz will – keep your fingers crossed – be able to fix whatever ails your computer. If you'd rather not haul your computer across town in a cab, they also do house calls starting at $125 an hour. The specialty at **Tekserve** is Mac repairs, where you can get a free estimate and also browse for upgrades.

KITCHENWARE

Most of the department stores offer a wide range of household goods. For a specialized shop, try **Broadway Panhandlers** on Broome Street, a cook's heaven with outstanding baking and pastry-making equipment. **Bridge Kitchenware** is a household name among most restaurateurs. **Williams-Sonoma** has a wide range of kitchenware, utensils, and cookbooks. The East Village, particularly on and around Bowery Street, has long been the nucleus for restaurant supply stores, where you can find top-quality kitchenware at bargain prices. **Leader Restaurant Equipment & Supplies** sells all the kitchenware you can think of, from heavy cutlery to sushi platters and chopsticks.

HOUSEWARES AND FURNISHINGS

Baccarat, **Lalique**, and **Villeroy & Boch** are where you'll find the finest crystal, china, and silverware. **Orrefors Kosta Boda** has beautiful glassware, from vases to candlesticks, and **Tiffany & Co.** is also a fashionable spot. Go to **Avventura** for crystal and china and, for the best of inexpensive, utilitarian china, visit **Fishs Eddy**. Try **Ceramica**, which stocks lovely handmade Italian pottery, and **La Terrine** and **Stuben Glass** for hand-painted ceramics. Browse the hip SoHo showcase of designer **Jonathan Adler**, whose eye-catching pottery of natural shades and primitive and organic shapes will stand out from everything else in your living room. His collection includes a "family" of playful decanters in the shapes of man, woman, and child, plump vases of smiling suns and fish plates, and a menagerie of pottery animals, including bookends shaped like the front and back of a charging bull. **ABC Carpet & Home** on Broadway has an enviable reputation for home furnishings. For low prices on housewares, shop on **Grand Street** on the Lower East Side.

For elegant furniture, from soft leather sofas to luxurious beds, and sleek tableware, try Giorgio Armani's posh **Armani Casa**. **Dune** on Franklin Street in TriBeCa offers chic furniture by contemporary designers, including wool sofas and convertible lounges. **Design Within Reach** is the source for fully licensed classics, such as Saarinen, Eames, and Bertoia. If you lean toward retro, make a beeline for **Restoration Hardware** on Broadway, where you can choose from updated Art Deco furnishings, lighting fixtures, and patinated bronze accessories.

LINENS

Linens can be found in most department stores, but for silk sheets and luxurious linens, visit **Porthault** and **Pratesi**. The Italian **Frette**, on Madison Avenue, sells thick towels and robes and wonderfully soft cotton sheets and bedding. **Bed, Bath & Beyond** offers a varied selection of bed linens, kitchen, and bath accessories.

DIRECTORY

ENTERTAINMENT IN NEW YORK

New York City is a non-stop entertainment extravaganza, every day, all year round. Whatever your taste, you can be sure the city will satisfy it on both a grand and an intimate scale. The challenge is to take advantage of as many of the entertainments as possible. If it's theater, you can enjoy a mainstream success on Broadway or take a chance on an experimental production

Performance by the New York City Ballet

in a loft. If it's music, there's the magnificence of opera at the Met or a jazz group blowing in a club in the Village. You can catch a spectacle of avant-garde dance in a café or try your own avant-garde dancing in one of the city's warehouse-sized clubs. Movie theaters abound. But perhaps best of all is wandering and watching the vast show that is New York.

PRACTICAL INFORMATION

Find out what events there are to choose from in the arts and leisure listings of *The New York Times* and the *Village Voice* newspapers and in *Time Out New York, New York,* and

TKTS discount ticket booth

The New Yorker magazines. Listings are updated on the websites of these magazines, such as www.nymag.com and http://newyork.timeout.com. At your hotel ask for *Where*, a free weekly magazine with maps and information on the many attractions.

Hotel staff may be able to answer some of your questions and should also carry a wide selection of brochures and leaflets. In addition, they may be willing to reserve tickets for you. Some hotel TVs have a New York visitor information channel.

At **NYC & Company**, touch-screen kiosks provide information and sell tickets to the city's top attractions. Multi-lingual counselors, discount coupons, free maps, brochures, tour information, and ATMs are available. **Broadway Inner Circle** gives brief descriptions of current

shows, schedules, and prices; **Moviefone** gives online information on all the films; and **ClubFone** has up-to-date information on nightlife.

BOOKING TICKETS

Popular shows may be sold out for weeks ahead, so book early. Box offices are open daily, except Sundays, from 10am until one hour after the performance begins. Call in person, or phone the box office or a ticket agency and order your seats by credit card. The biggest agencies are **Telecharge**, **Ticketmaster**, and **Ticket Central**; they charge a small fee. An independent ticket agent may also be able to find seats for you – try **Prestige Entertainment**; others are listed in the Yellow Pages. Fees vary according to demand. Broadway Ticket Center in

A band playing at a cozy New York jazz club

the Times Square Information Center *(see p371)* sells full-price tickets.

DISCOUNT TICKETS

Established in 1973 to the advantage of theaters and theatergoers alike, the non-profit **TKTS** company sells unsold tickets on the day of the performance for all Broadway shows. Discounts range from 25 to 50 percent, but the price will include a small handling fee and must be paid for in cash or by traveler's check.

The **TKTS** booth in Times Square (at Duffy Square under the red steps) sells matinée tickets from 10am to 2pm every Wednesday and Saturday, and from 11am to 3pm on Sundays; evening tickets are sold from 3pm to 8pm, and Sunday tickets from 11am until closing. The booths at Front and John streets, where lines are often shorter, sell evening tickets from 11am to 6pm Monday to Saturday. All matinée tickets and Sunday performances are sold the day before. There is also a TKTS booth in downtown Brooklyn.

The **Broadway Ticket Center** in Times Square offers same-day and advance tickets for both Broadway and Off-Broadway shows. They also have seating charts and, occasionally, video previews to help you choose a show.

You can purchase day-of-performance tickets from **Ticketmaster** at

The Booth Theater on Broadway *(see p345)*

discounts of 10 to 25 percent (with a small commission fee) by telephone. The **Hit Show Club** sells vouchers to its members (it's free to join) that can be exchanged at box offices for discounted tickets. Some shows offer standing-room tickets on the day at a bargain price. It's often the only way to catch a sold-out show on short notice, but you might not get the best view. You can also get discount tickets for shows at **Broadway Bucks**. **StubHub!** is the largest ticket resale site. Tickets for sports, music, and Broadway events are FedExed to you.

"SCALPERS" AND TOUTS

If you buy from a "scalper" (a ticket tout), you risk getting tickets for the wrong day, counterfeit tickets, and paying outrageous prices. The police often monitor sports and theater venues for scalpers and their customers.

FREE TICKETS

Free tickets to TV shows, concerts, and special events are sometimes offered at **NYC & Co.** (New York Convention & Visitors Bureau), which is open from 8:30am to 6pm Monday to Friday and 9am to 5pm on weekends. Free or deeply discounted tickets to film or theater premieres are often advertised in *The New York Times*, *Daily News*, or

Time Out New York. The "Cheap Thrills" section in the *Village Voice* lists poetry readings, recitals, and experimental films. The Shakespeare Festival at the **Delacorte Theater** in Central Park offers free tickets – one per person – on a first-come, first-served basis (be prepared to queue).

Neon lights of theaters in the heart of Broadway

DISABLED ACCESS

Broadway theaters reserve a few spaces and cut-price tickets for the disabled. Call **Ticketmaster** or **Telecharge** well in advance for information and to reserve your tickets. For Off-Broadway theaters, call their box offices. Some theaters offer special equipment for their hearing-impaired patrons. **Tap** can arrange sign language for Broadway theaters.

USEFUL CONTACTS

Broadway Bucks
226 W 47th St. **Map** 12 E5.
Tel 1-800-223-7565, ext. 214.
www.bestofbroadway.com

Broadway Inner Circle
Tel (212) 563-2929.
www.broadwayinnercircle.com

Broadway Ticket Center
Times Square Information Center,
1560 Broadway. **Map** 12 E5.

ClubFone
Tel (212) 777-2582.
www.clubfone.com

Delacorte Theater
Entrance via 81st St at Central
Park W. **Map** 16 E4.
Tel (212) 539-8750.
www.publictheater.org
Summer time only.

Hit Show Club
Tel (212) 581-4211.
www.hitshowclub.com

Movie Tickets Online
www.movietickets.com
www.fandango.com
www.moviefone.com

NYC & Co.
810 7th Ave. **Map** 12 E4.
Tel (212) 484-1222.
www.nycvisit.com

Prestige Entertainment
Tel 1-800-243-8849.

StubHub!
Tel (866) STUB-HUB.
www.stubhub.com

Tap (Theatre Access Project)
Tel (212) 221-1103 (Voice).
www.tdf.org

Telecharge
Tel (212) 239-6200,
1-800-432-7250.
www.telecharge.com

Ticket Central
Tel (212) 279-4200.
www.ticketcentral.org

Ticketmaster
Tel (212) 307-4100,
1-800-755-4000.
www.ticketmaster.com

TKTS
Tel (212) 221-0013.
Front & John Sts. **Map** 2 D2.
Duffy Square, Times Square.
47th St & Broadway. **Map** 12 E5.
Tel (212) 221-0885, ext. 446.
www.tdf.org/TKTS

25

New York's Best: Entertainment

Greenwich Village jazz club

New York is one of the great entertainment capitals of the world. Top names in every branch of the arts are drawn here to perform and often to live and work. Major sports events are a huge attraction and live music, theater, and comedy can be found throughout the year. In terms of nightlife, New York truly lives up to its reputation as "the city that never sleeps." From the huge choice offered, there are some venues and events that stand out as classics of their kind; this selection has been chosen from the listings on pages 344 to 363 as among those not to be missed. Even if you experience only one of them, you will have been part of something as essentially New York as the Empire State Building or the Brooklyn Bridge.

Madison Square Garden
Top sporting action is found at "the Garden," including home games for basketball's New York Knicks and ice hockey's Rangers, plus the Golden Gloves boxing tournament (see p360).

Chelsea and Garment Di...

Greenwich Village

SoHo and TriBeCa

Lower East Side

Seaport and the Civic Center

Lower Manhattan

HUDSON RIVER

Film Forum
At New York's most stylish arts movie theater you can see the latest foreign and American independent releases or catch up with a classic in a wide range of retrospectives (see p349).

Village Vanguard
The jazz clubs of Greenwich Village have played host to all the great names in jazz. Fans can catch the stars of today and tomorrow at the world-famous Village Vanguard and the Blue Note (see p352).

Philharmonic Rehearsals
The Wednesday- and Thursday-morning rehearsals at Avery Fisher Hall are often open to the public at a fraction of the normal ticket price (see p350).

Metropolitan Opera House
Reserve well ahead and prepare to pay high prices to see the giants of the opera world (see p350).

The Nutcracker
The Christmas event for children of every age is performed each year at Lincoln Center by the New York City Ballet (see p346).

Shakespeare in Central Park
If you are a summer visitor, set aside a time to get one of the rare free tickets for the Delacorte Theater's open-air Shakespeare featuring top Hollywood and Broadway names (see p344).

0 kilometers 2

0 miles 1

Public Theater
Founded in 1954, the Public has a mandate to create theater for all New Yorkers. Its year-round Shakespeare Festival is part of a commitment to classical works, but new plays are also developed here (see p120).

Carnegie Hall
Conveniently situated in the Theater District, Carnegie Hall is famous the world over as a show-case for the best in the musical arts. A backstage tour gives a fascinating insight into "the house that music built" (see p350).

Theater and Dance

New York is famous for its extravagant musicals and its ferocious critics. It is one of the world's greatest theater and dance centers, featuring every kind of production imaginable. Whether your preference is for the glitz and glamour of a Broadway blockbuster or something truly experimental, you'll find it here.

BROADWAY

Broadway has long been synonymous with New York's Theater District, but the majority of Broadway theaters are actually scattered between 41st and 53rd streets and from Sixth to Ninth Avenues, with a few around the much-improved Times Square. Most were built between 1910 and 1930, during the heyday of vaudeville and the famous Ziegfeld Follies. The **Lyceum** *(see p144)* is the oldest theater still in operation (1903), the **American Airlines Theater**, permanent home of the Roundabout Theater Co., is the newest, and the historic **Biltmore Theater** opened in 2003 after a 14-year closure.

Many Broadway theaters went through a slump in the 1980s but are now enjoying a revival, using big names to draw in the crowds. This is where you will find the "power productions" – the big, highly publicized dramas, musicals and revivals starring Hollywood luminaries in (it is hoped) sure-fire earners. Hits have included imports such as *Les Misérables;* New York originals such as *Cats* and *The Producers*; the popular children's favorite *The Lion King*; and great revivals like *42nd Street*. There have also been glitzy adaptations from popular movies, such as *Hairspray*; shows celebrating 60s and 70s pop favorites, such as ABBA in *Mamma Mia!* and Monty Python's *Spamalot*.

OFF-BROADWAY AND OFF-OFF-BROADWAY

There are about 20 Off-Broadway stages and 300 Off-Off-Broadway stages whose works will sometimes transfer to Broadway. Off-Broadway theaters have from 100 to 499 seats, and Off-Off-Broadway

showplaces have fewer than 100. Both range from the well-appointed to the improvised, sited in lofts, churches, and even garages. Off-Broadway became very popular during the 1950s as a reaction to the commercialism of Broadway. It was also an ideal place for cautious producers to try out works considered too avant-garde for Broadway at lower operating costs. During the past two decades, Off-Off-Broadway theaters have staged more experimental pieces by these same producers.

Off-Broadway theaters are found all over Manhattan – from the **Douglas Fairbanks Theater**, where the irreverent *Forbidden Broadway* plays, to Central Park's open-air **Delacorte Theater**. Some are even in the Broadway district, such as the **Manhattan Theater Club**. Farther afield are the **Brooklyn Academy of Music (BAM)** *(see p248)*, and the **92nd Street Y**. In these venues you will find lively, unusual, and experimental showcases for new talent as well as lots of uninhibited productions.

The Off-Broadway theaters mounted the first productions in New York of the works of playwrights Sean O'Casey, Tennessee Williams, Eugene O'Neill, Jean Genet, Eugene Ionesco, and David Mamet. Samuel Beckett's *Happy Days* premiered at the **Cherry Lane Theatre** in 1961, a venue that still promotes cutting-edge writing. Off-Broadway theaters host new and very often irreverent treatments of the classics.

Sometimes a more intimate, smaller Off-Broadway stage suits a production better than a larger more established theater would, as proved by such long-running successes as *The Fantasticks* along with the *Threepenny Opera*, which has been shown at the **Lucille Lortel Theater** since 1955.

PERFORMANCE THEATERS

This extremely avant-garde art form can be found in several Off- and Off-Off-Broadway locations. Accurate descriptions and categorizations are almost impossible, but expect the bizarre and outlandish. The most likely venues to find this are **La MaMa Experimental Theatre Club, P.S. 122, HERE, Baruch Performing Arts Center, 92nd Street Y, Symphony Space**, and the **Joseph Papp Public Theater** *(see p120)*. The latter is perhaps the most influential theater in New York. It was founded in the 1950s by the late director Joseph Papp, who introduced neighborhood tours to bring theater to people who had never seen it before.

The Public Theater created hits such as *A Chorus Line;* and *Hair;* it is most famous for its free summer performances of Shakespeare at the Delacorte Theater in Central Park *(see p208)*. It usually has several productions running, and at 6pm on the day of performance, "Quiktix" tickets (limited to two per person) are sold in the Public Theater lobby.

THEATER SCHOOLS

New York is the best place in the country to see actors learning their trade. Foremost among the acting schools is **The Actors' Studio**. The late Lee Strasberg, the advocate of method acting – in which the actor aims for complete identification with the character being played – was its guru. His students included Dustin Hoffman, Al Pacino, and Marilyn Monroe. "In progress" productions feature trainees and are open to the public and free. Sandy Meisner trained many actors, including the late Lee Remick, at the **Neighborhood Playhouse School of the Theater**. Its plays are not open to the public. The **New Dramatists** began in 1949 to develop new playwrights, helping the careers of the likes of William Inge. Play readings are open to the public and free.

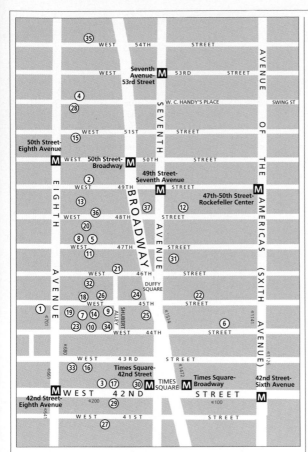

BROADWAY THEATERS

① Al Hirschfield
302 W. 45th St.
Tel (212) 239-6200.

② Ambassador
219 W. 49th St.
Tel (212) 239-6200.

③ American Airlines Theater
227 W. 42nd St.
Tel (212) 719-1300.

④ August Wilson
245 W. 52nd St.
Tel (212) 239-6200.

⑤ Barrymore
243 W. 47th St.
Tel (212) 239-6200.

⑥ Belasco
111 W. 44th St.
Tel (212) 239-6200.

⑦ Bernard B Jacobs
242 W. 45th St.
Tel (212) 239-6200.

⑧ Biltmore
261 W. 47th St.
Tel (212) 239-6200.

⑨ Booth
222 W. 45th St.
Tel (212) 239-6200.

⑩ Broadhurst
235 W. 44th St.
Tel (212) 239-6200.

⑪ Brooks Atkinson
256 W. 47th St.
Tel (212) 307-4100.

⑫ Cort
138 W. 48th St.
Tel (212) 239-6200.

⑬ Eugene O'Neill
230 W. 49th St.
Tel (212) 239-6200.

⑭ Gerald Schoenfeld
236 W. 45th St.
Tel (212) 239-6200.

⑮ Gershwin
222 W. 51st St.
Tel (212) 307-4100.

⑯ Helen Hayes
240 W. 44th St.
Tel (212) 239-6200.

⑰ Hilton
213 W. 42nd St.
Tel (212) 307 4100.

⑱ Imperial
249 W. 45th St.
Tel (212) 239-6200.

⑲ John Golden
252 W. 45th St.
Tel (212) 239-6200.

⑳ Longacre
220 W. 48th St.
Tel (212) 239-6200.

㉑ Lunt–Fontanne
205 W. 46th St.
Tel (212) 307-4747.

㉒ Lyceum
149 W. 45th St.
Tel (212) 239-6200.

㉓ Majestic
247 W. 44th St.
Tel (212) 239-6200.

㉔ Marquis
211 W. 45th St.
Tel (212) 307-4100.

㉕ Minskoff
200 W. 45th St.
Tel (212) 307-4100.

㉖ Music Box
239 W. 45th St.
Tel (212) 239-6200.

㉗ Nederlander
208 W. 41st St.
Tel (212) 307-4100.

㉘ Neil Simon
250 W. 52nd St.
Tel (212) 307-4100.

㉙ New Amsterdam
214 W. 42nd St.
Tel (212) 307 4100.

㉚ New Victory
209 W. 42nd St.
Tel (212) 239-6200.

㉛ Palace
1564 Broadway.
Tel (212) 307-4100.

㉜ Richard Rodgers
226 W. 46th St.
Tel (212) 307-4100.

㉝ St. James
246 W. 44th St.
Tel (212) 239-6200.

㉞ Shubert
225 W. 44th St.
Tel (212) 239-6200.

㉟ Studio 54
254 W. 54th St.
Tel (212) 719 3100.

㊱ Walter Kerr
219 W. 48th St.
Tel (212) 239-6200.

㊲ Winter Garden
1634 Broadway.
Tel (212) 239-6200.

For other theaters
see p347.

BALLET

At the heart of the dance world is Lincoln Center *(see p214)*, where the New York City Ballet performs pieces in the **New York State Theater**. This company was created by the legendary brilliant choreographer George Balanchine *(see p49)* and is probably still the best in the world. The current director, Peter Martins, was one of Balanchine's best dancers and continues the strict policy of ensemble dancing rather than "star turns." The season runs from November to February and late April to early June. The ballet school at the **Juilliard Dance Theater** also presents a spring workshop every year, and this is a good chance to see budding stars.

The American Ballet Theater appears at the **Metropolitan Opera House**, which also hosts many visiting foreign companies, such as the Kirov, Bolshoi, and Royal ballets. Its repertoire includes 19th-century classics, such as *Swan Lake,* and works by modern choreographers such as Twyla Tharp and Paul Taylor.

CONTEMPORARY DANCE

New York is the center of many of the most important movements in modern dance. The **Dance Theater of Harlem** is world famous for its modern, traditional, and ethnic productions. Other havens of experimental dance include the **92nd Street Y** and the **Merce Cunningham Studio** in Greenwich Village. The unique **Dance Theater Workshop** features contemporary dance and performance from around the world. **The Kitchen**, **La MaMa**, **Symphony Space**, and **P.S. 122** are all multimedia venues with the latest in contemporary dance, performance art and avant-garde music. Choreographer Mark Morris's company performs at the brand new **Mark Morris Dance Center** in Brooklyn; **City Center** *(see p148)* is a favorite spot for dance fans. It used to house the New York City Ballet and the American Ballet Theater before Lincoln Center was built. As well as featuring the Joffrey Ballet, City Center has held performances by all the great contemporary artists, including Alvin Ailey's blend of modern, jazz, and blues and the companies of modern dance masters Merce Cunningham and Paul Taylor. Avoid the mezzanine as the view is restricted.

The city's single most active venue for dance is probably the **Joyce Theater**, where such well-established companies as the Feld Ballet, along with bold newcomers and visiting troupes, perform.

Each spring the Festival of Black Dance at the **Brooklyn Academy of Music (BAM)** *(see p248)* features everything from ethnic dance to hip-hop. During autumn the "Next Wave" festival of music and dance is held, celebrating international and American avant-garde dance and music. During winter, the American Ballet Festival is held here.

During June, **New York University** *(see p115)* holds a Summer Residency Festival with lecture-demonstrations, rehearsals, and performances, and **Dancing in the Streets** organizes summertime dance performances all over the city.

Throughout the month of August, **Lincoln Center Out of Doors** has a program of free dance events on the plaza, with such experimental groups as the American Tap Dance Orchestra.

The **Duke Theater** presents many contemporary dance companies and participates in events such as the New York Tap Festival.

At different times of the year, **Radio City Music Hall** holds several spectacular shows, with different companies from all over the world. At Christmas and Easter, it features the famously precise Rockettes dance troupe.

Choreographers and dance companies frequently present works-in-progress and recitals to the public. Among the most interesting venues for these is **Alvin Ailey's Repertory Ensemble**, famous for promoting black cultural expression, which opened one of the country's largest dance facilities in 2004. The **Hunter College Dance Company** performs new works by its student choreographers, and the **Isadora Duncan Dance Foundation** recreates Duncan's original dances. To see contemporary choreographers the best place to go is **Juilliard Dance Theater**.

PRICES

Theater is extremely expensive to produce, and ticket prices tend to reflect this. Even Off- and Off-Off-Broadway tickets are not cheap anymore. Preview tickets are easier to get hold of, though, and it's fun to see a show before the reviews are in so you're able to make up your own mind.

For a Broadway theater ticket you can expect to pay $80 or more; for musicals, up to $100; Off-Broadway, $25 to $60. For dance, $20 to $50 is the usual range, with up to $115 for the American Ballet Theater.

TIMES OF PERFORMANCE

The general rules for theater-hours are: closed on Mondays (except for most musicals), with matinees on Wednesdays, Saturdays, and sometimes Sundays. Matinees usually begin at 2pm, with evening performances at 8pm. Be sure to check the correct dates and times of the performance beforehand, as tickets are usually non-refundable if you fail to turn up at the correct time.

BACKSTAGE TOURS AND LECTURES

For those interested in the mechanics and anecdotes of the theater, your best bet is to go on one of the theater tours. The **92nd Street Y** organizes insider's views of the theater, with famous directors, actors, and choreographers taking part. Writers are invited along to read or discuss their current works. **Radio City Music Hall** also holds tours.

DIRECTORY

OFF-BROADWAY

92nd Street Y
1395 Lexington Ave.
Map 17 A2.
Tel (212) 415-5500.

Baruch Performing Arts Center
55 Lexington Ave.
Map 9 A4.
Tel (646) 312-4085.

Brooklyn Academy of Music
30 Lafayette Ave,
Brooklyn.
Tel (718) 636-4100.

Cherry Lane Theatre
38 Commerce St.
Map 3 C2.
Tel (212) 239-6200.

HERE Art Center
145 6th Ave.
Map 4 D4.
Tel (212) 647-0202.

Circle in the Square
1633 Broadway.
Map 12 E4.
Tel (212) 307-0388.

Delacorte Theater
Central Park. (81st St.)
Map 16 E4.
Tel (212) 539-8750.
Summer time only.

Douglas Fairbanks Theater
432 W 42nd St.
Map 7 C1.
Tel (212) 239-6200.

Lambs Theater
130 W 44th St.
Map 12 E5.
Tel (212) 575-0300.

Lucille Lortel Theater
121 Christopher St.
Map 3 C2.
Tel (212) 924-2817.

Manhattan Theater Club
311 W 43rd St.
Map 8 D1.
Tel (212) 399-3000.

New York Theater Workshop
79 E 4th St. **Map** 4 F2.
Tel (212) 460-5475.

Public Theater
425 Lafayette St.
Map 4 F2.
Tel (212) 539-8500.

Symphony Space
2537 Broadway.
Map 15 C2.
Tel (212) 864-5400.

Vivian Beaumont
Lincoln Center.
Map 11 C2.
Tel (212) 362-7600.

OFF-OFF-BROADWAY

Bouwerie Lane Theater
330 Bowery.
Map 4 F2.
Tel (212) 677-0060.

The Kitchen
512 W 19th St.
Map 7 C5.
Tel (212) 255-5793.

Performing Garage
33 Wooster St.
Map 4 E4.
Tel (212) 966-3651.

York Theater at St. Peter's Church
Citigroup Center,
619 Lexington Ave.
Map 13 A4.
Tel (212) 935-5820.

PERFORMANCE THEATER

La MaMa Experimental Theatre Club
74a E 4th St.
Map 4 F2.
Tel (212) 475-7710.

P.S. 122
150 First Ave.
Map 5 A1.
Tel (212) 477-5288.

Public Theater
See Off-Broadway.

THEATER SCHOOLS

The Actors' Studio
432 W 44th St.
Map 11 B5.
Tel (212) 757-0870.

New Dramatists
424 W 44th.
Map 11 C5.
Tel (212) 757-6960.

DANCE

92nd Street Y
See Off-Broadway.

Alvin Ailey American Dance Center
405 West, 55th St.
Map 11 D4.
Tel (212) 405-9000.

Brooklyn Academy of Music
See Off-Broadway.

City Center
130 W 56th St.
Map 12 E4.
Tel (212) 581-1212.

Dance Theater of Harlem
466 W 152nd St.
Tel (212) 690-2800.

Dance Theater Workshop
219 W 19th St. **Map** 8 E5.
Tel (212) 924-0077.

Dancing in the Streets
55 6th Ave (offices).
Tel (212) 625-3505.

Hunter College Dance Company
695 Park Ave.
Map 13 A1.
Tel (212) 772-4490.

Isadora Duncan Dance Foundation
141 W 26th St.
Map 20 D2.
Tel (212) 691-5040.

Joyce Theater
175 Eighth Ave at 19th St.
Map 8 D5.
Tel (212) 242-0800.

Juilliard Dance Theater
60 Lincoln Center Plaza,
W 65th St.
Map 11 C2.
Tel (212) 769-7406.

PERFORMANCE VENUES

Duke Theater
229 W 42nd St.
Map 8 E1.
Tel (646) 223-3000.

The Kitchen
See Off-Off-Broadway.

La MaMa Experimental Theatre Club
See Performance Theater.

Lincoln Center Out of Doors
Lincoln Center, Broadway
at 64th St. **Map** 11 C2.
Tel (212) 362-6000.

Manhattan Center
311 W 34th St. **Map** 8 D2.
Tel (212) 279-7740.

Mark Morris
3 Lafayette Ave. (Brooklyn)
Tel (718) 624-8400.

Merce Cunningham Studio
55 Bethune St. **Map** 3 B2.
Tel (212) 255-8240.

Metropolitan Opera House
Lincoln Center, Broadway
at 65th St. **Map** 11 C2.
Tel (212) 362-6000.

New York State Theater
Lincoln Center, Broadway
at 65th St. **Map** 11 C2.
Tel (212) 870-5570.

New York University
Tisch School of the Arts
(TSOA), 111 2nd Ave.
Map 4 F1.
Tel (212) 998-1920.

P.S. 122
See Performance Theater.

Radio City Music Hall
50th St at Ave of the
Americas. **Map** 12 F4.
Tel (212) 307-7171.

Symphony Space
See Off-Broadway.

BACKSTAGE TOURS

92nd Street Y
See Off-Broadway.

Radio City Music Hall
Tel (212) 307-7171.

Events Guide
www.playbill.com
www.newyork.citysearch.
com

Movies

New York is a film buff's paradise. Apart from new US releases, which show months in advance of other countries, many classic and foreign films are screened here.

The city has always been the testing ground for new developments in films, and it continues to be a hotbed of new and innovative talent. Many of the movies' most famous directors – Spike Lee, Martin Scorsese, and Woody Allen – were born and raised in New York, and the city's influence can be seen in many of their films. They, and others, can often be seen filming on the streets of the city; many of New York's landmarks have become famous after appearing in films. Most of the TV networks based in New York offer free tickets to the taping of their shows. Watching a show, such as *The David Letterman Show*, is popular with visitors.

FIRST-RUN MOVIES

New York reviews and box office returns are so vital to a film's success that most major American films have their premieres in Manhattan's theaters. First-run films are shown mainly at the City Cinema chains, Loews, United Artists and Cineplex Odeon, which are scattered around the city. Some theaters have recorded information giving the names and duration of the different films showing, with starting times and ticket prices.

Programs start at 10am or 11am and are repeated every two to three hours until midnight. You should expect to line up for most evening and weekend performances of the more popular films. Making reservations using a credit card is possible at some theaters for an additional charge

of about $1 per ticket. Matinees (usually before 4pm) are easier to get into. Senior citizens pay a reduced price for tickets: the required age may be over 60, 62, or 65 depending on the policy of the theater.

NEW YORK FILM FESTIVAL

A high point of the year for film buffs is the New York Film Festival, now in its third decade. Organized by the **Film Society of Lincoln Center**, the festival starts in late September and continues for two weeks at the many Lincoln Center theaters. Outstanding new films from the US and abroad are entered in a competition for the huge prestige of winning an award. Many of the films shown during the festival are later released and can usually be seen only in art houses.

The **TriBeCa Film Festival**, created in part by director and actor Robert De Niro, was launched in 2002 to celebrate New York City as a filmmaking capital and to contribute to the long-term recovery of Lower Manhattan. The festival showcases a wide range of films, including classics, documentaries, and premieres, and usually takes place in late April and early May. Every spring, **Docfest** (the New York International Documentary Festival) presents five days of film and video documentaries from around the world, followed by panel discussions with the filmmaker.

FILM RATINGS

Films in the United States are graded as follows:
G General audiences; all ages admitted.
PG Parental guidance suggested; some material unsuitable for children.
PG-13 Parents strongly cautioned; some material inappropriate for children under age 13.
R Restricted. Children under 17 need to be accompanied by a parent or an adult guardian.
NC-17 No children under 17 admitted.

ON LOCATION

Many New York locations have played starring roles in films. Here are a few:

The Brill Building (1141 Broadway) contained Burt Lancaster's penthouse in *Sweet Smell of Success*.
The Brooklyn Bridge was a great backdrop in Spike Lee's *Mo' Better Blues*.
Brooklyn Heights and the **Metropolitan Opera** appeared in *Moonstruck*.
Central Park has shown up in countless films, including *Love Story* and *Marathon Man*.
55 Central Park West will be remembered as Sigourney Weaver's home in *Ghostbusters*.
Chinatown played a major role in *Year of the Dragon*.
The Dakota was where Mia Farrow lived in the classic *Rosemary's Baby*.
The Empire State Building is still standing after *King Kong*'s last battle. The observation deck is where Cary Grant waited in vain in *An Affair to Remember;* here Meg Ryan finally met Tom Hanks in *Sleepless in Seattle*.
Grand Central Station is famous for Robert Walker's meeting with Judy Garland in *Under the Clock* and for the magical ballroom sequence in *The Fisher King*.
Harlem hosted the jazz musicians and dancers in *The Cotton Club*.
Katz's Deli was the setting for the café scene between Billy Crystal and Meg Ryan in *When Harry Met Sally…*.
Little Italy appeared in *The Godfather I* and *II*.
Madison Square Garden was the setting for the dramatic climax of *The Manchurian Candidate*.
Tiffany & Co. was Audrey Hepburn's favorite shop in *Breakfast at Tiffany's*.
The United Nations Building featured and *North by Northwest* and *The Interpreter*.
Washington Square Park was where Robert Redford and Jane Fonda walked *Barefoot in the Park*.

FOREIGN FILMS AND ART HOUSES

For the latest foreign and independent films, go to the **Angelika Film Center**, which also has an upscale coffee bar. Other good places are the **Rose Cinemas** at the BAM, the **Film Forum**, and **Lincoln Plaza Cinema**. The Plaza has a busy program of art and foreign films. For Asian, Indian, and Chinese films, you should visit the **Asia Society**. The **French Institute** screens many French films with English subtitles on Tuesdays. The **Quad Cinema** shows a wide selection of foreign films, often quite rare. **Cinema Village** runs special film events, such as the Festival of Animation.

The **Walter Reade Theater** houses the Film Society of the Lincoln Center, offering retrospectives of international movies as well as celebrations of contemporary works, such as the popular annual Spanish Cinema Now festival.

CLASSIC FILMS AND MUSEUMS

Retrospectives of films by particular directors or featuring specific actors are shown at the **Public Theater** and the **Whitney Museum of American Art** *(see pp200–201)*. The **Museum of the Moving Image** *(see p246)* screens old films and also has many exhibits of memorabilia from the film industry. The **Paley Center for Media** *(see p171)* has regular screenings of classic films; you can also see or hear specific television or radio programs. Students interested in classic, new and experimental movies will appreciate the collection of the **Anthology Film Archives**.

The shows at the **Rose Center for Earth and Space** at the **American Museum of Natural History** are well worth a whole day's visit.

On summer evenings in Bryant Park, you can watch free classic movies, and on Saturday mornings, the **Film Society of Lincoln Center,** where special children's shows are held.

TELEVISION SHOWS

A number of TV programs originate in New York. The popular *David Letterman* and *Saturday Night Live* shows are almost impossible to get tickets for, but tickets for many other shows can be obtained online, by calling the networks such as **NBC**, **ABC**, and **CBS**, or sometimes on standby.

Another good source of free tickets is the Times Square Information Bureau *(see p368)*. On weekday mornings on Fifth Avenue around **Rockefeller Plaza**, free tickets for a number of TV programs are sometimes distributed by the program's production staff. There's absolutely no way that you can plan for this. It's simply a matter of good luck and being in the right place at the right time.

For those who want to get a glimpse behind the scenes of TV, NBC organizes tours of the studios, from 8:30am to 4:30pm Mon–Thu (depart every 30 mins), 9:30am to 5:30pm Fri–Sat, and 9:30am to 4:30pm on Sunday (depart every 15 mins).

CHOOSING WHAT TO SEE

If you feel bewildered by the huge range of films offered in New York, check the listings in *New York* magazine, the *New York Times*, the *Village Voice* and *The New Yorker*. The following Internet guides give show times and locations:
www.moviefone.com
www.movietickets.com

DIRECTORY

ABC
Tel (212) 580-5176.
www.abc.com.

American Museum of Natural History
Central Park W at 79th St.
Map 16 D5.
Tel (212) 769-5100.

Angelika Film Center
18 W Houston St.
Map 4 E3.
Tel (212) 995-2000.

Anthology Film Archives
32 2nd Ave at 2nd St.
Map 5 C2.
Tel (212) 505-5181.

Asia Society
725 Park Ave. **Map** 13 A1.
Tel (212) 517-2742.

CBS
Tel (212) 247-6497.

Cinema Village
22 E 12th St. **Map** 4 F1.
Tel (212) 924-3363.

Docfest
Tel (212) 668-1100.
www.docfest.org

Film Forum
209 W Houston St.
Map 3 C3.
Tel (212) 727-8110.

French Institute
55 E 59th St. **Map** 12 F3.
Tel (212) 355-6160.

Lincoln Plaza Cinema
1886 Broadway.
Map 12 D2.
Tel (212) 757-2280.

Museum of Modern Art
11 W 53rd St. **Map** 12 F4.
Tel (212) 708-9480.

Museum of the Moving Image
35th Ave & 36th St.
Astoria, Queens.
Tel (718) 784-0077.

NBC
30 Rockefeller Plaza at 49th St.
Tel (212) 664-3056.
www.nbc.com

The Paley Center for Media
25 W 52nd St. **Map** 12 F4.
Tel (212) 621-6600.

Public Theater
425 Lafayette St.
Map 4 F4.
Tel (212) 539-8500.

Quad Cinema
34 W 13th St.
Map 4 D1.
Tel (212) 255-8800.

Rockefeller Plaza
47th–50th St, 5th Ave.
Map 12 F5.

Rose Cinemas
Brooklyn Academy of Music (BAM), 30 Lafayette Ave, Brooklyn.
Tel (718) 636-4100.

TriBeCa Film Festival
Tel (212) 941-2400.
www.tribecafilmfestival.org

Walter Reade Theater
70 Lincoln Center Plaza.
Map 12 D2.
Tel (212) 875-5600.

Whitney Museum of American Art
945 Madison Ave.
Map 13 A1.
Tel 1-800-WHITNEY.

Classical and Contemporary Music

New Yorkers have a voracious appetite for music. Live concerts by the world's most celebrated musical performers may be enjoyed at famous halls throughout the year, and younger, newer artists, and exotic imports always find receptive audiences.

TICKETS

Find out what you can choose from in New York by checking out the listings in the *New York Times* and the *Village Voice* and in *Time Out New York* and *The New Yorker* magazines.

CLASSICAL MUSIC

The orchestra in residence at **Avery Fisher Hall** in Lincoln Center *(see p215)* is the New York Philharmonic. It is also the annual site for the popular "Mostly Mozart" series and Young People's Concerts. **Alice Tully Hall**, in Lincoln Center, is an acoustic gem and home to the Chamber Music Society.

One of the world's premier concert halls is the revamped **Carnegie Hall** *(see p148)*. Upstairs in the Weill Recital Hall there are quality performances for reasonable prices.

The **Brooklyn Academy of Music (BAM)** *(see p248)* is the home of the Brooklyn Philharmonic. Classical music, dance, opera, jazz, and world music all find an audience at the **New Jersey Performance Arts Center** in Newark.

The **Merkin Concert Hall** is host to some top chamber ensembles and soloists. For really excellent acoustics, go to the **Town Hall**. The **92nd Street Y's** Kaufmann Concert Hall also offers a lively menu of music and dance. There's also the **Frick Collection** and **Symphony Space**, both of which offer a varied program

ranging from gospel to Gershwin, classical to ethnic. The beautiful Grace Rainey Rogers Auditorium in the **Metropolitan Museum of Art** is for chamber music and soloists, while the well-equipped **Florence Gould Hall**, at the Alliance Française, presents a varied program of chamber music, orchestral pieces, concerts, and even classic French films.

The **Juilliard School of Music** and the **Mannes College of Music** are both considered excellent. Their students and faculties give free recitals, and there are shows by leading orchestras, chamber music groups, and opera companies. The **Manhattan School of Music** offers an excellent program of over 400 events per year, from classical to jazz.

At 9:45am on the Thursdays of the New York Philharmonic concerts, the evening show is rehearsed at **Avery Fisher Hall** in Lincoln Center. Audiences are often admitted to listen, and rehearsal tickets are available at low prices. The **Kosciuszko Foundation** hosts the annual Chopin Competition. **Corpus Christi Church** has an active concert schedule, presenting such groups as the Tallis Scholars.

OPERA

Dominating the city's operatic scene is **Lincoln Center** *(see p212)*, home to the New York City Opera, and the **Metropolitan Opera House**, which has its own opera company. The Met is the jewel in the crown, offering top international performers. More accessible and dynamic is the New York City Opera. Its performances range from *Madame Butterfly* to *South Pacific*, with subtitles above the stage to help the audience understand the plot. Lower-priced quality performances

are staged by the up-and-coming singers at the **Village Light Opera Group**, the **Amato Opera Theater**, the **Kaye Playhouse** at Hunter College, and the students at the **Juilliard Opera Center** in Lincoln Center.

CONTEMPORARY MUSIC

New York is one of the most important places in the world for contemporary music. Exotic, ethnic, and experimental music is played in many first-rate venues. The **Brooklyn Academy of Music (BAM)** is the standard-bearer of the avant-garde. Each autumn the Academy holds a festival of music and dance called "Next Wave," which has helped launch many musical careers.

An annual festival of serious modern music called "Bang on a Can" is performed at the **Ethical Culture Society Hall** and features works by Steve Reich, Pierre Boulez, and John Cage. Experimentalists, such as Davie Weinstein with his "audio-visual acid test" music – a mix of CD players, amplified instruments, keyboards, and sound effects – perform at the **Dance Theater Workshop**.

Other venues include the **Asia Society** *(see p187)*, with its jewel of a theater for many visiting Asian performers, and **St. Peter's Church**.

BACKSTAGE TOURS

Behind-the-scenes tours are offered by **Lincoln Center** and **Carnegie Hall**.

RELIGIOUS MUSIC

Few experiences are more moving than an Easter concert in the vast **Cathedral of St. John the Divine** *(see pp226–7)*. Seasonal music is also offered at many of the city's museums and in almost every other available space – from **Grand Central Terminal**'s main concourse *(see pp156–7)* to bank and hotel lobbies. For jazz vespers in a stunning modern building, visit **St. Peter's Church** *(see p177)*.

CLASSICAL RADIO

New York has three FM radio stations that broad-cast classical music: WQXR at 96.3, the National Public Radio station WNYC at 93.9 and WKCR 89.9.

Most of these concerts are free, but you are encouraged to contribute.

ALFRESCO

Free outdoor summer concerts occur in **Bryant Park**, **Washington Square**, and **Lincoln Center's Damrosch Park**. The annual concerts on Central Park's Great Lawn and in Brooklyn's Prospect Park are performed by the New York Philharmonic and the Metropolitan Opera. In good weather, strolling musicians perform at South Street Seaport, on the steps of the **Metropolitan Museum of Art** *(see pp190–97)*, and in the area around Washington Square.

MUSIC FOR FREE

Free musical performances are given at **The Cloisters** *(see pp236–9)* and the **Whitney Museum**'s Philip Morris Building *(see p152)*. Sunday-afternoon recitals are held at Rumsey Playfield and the Naumburg Bandshell in Central Park *(see p208)*, as well as the Summerstage. Call **The Dairy** for more information. You will also find music in the **Federal Hall** *(see p68)*, while at **Lincoln Center**, don't miss the exciting free performances held in the **Juilliard School of Music**. Other popular venues include the **Greenwich House Music School** (free student recitals) and the **Winter Garden** at the World Financial Center *(see p69)*. Numerous free concerts and talks take place in the city's churches, including **St. Paul's Chapel**, **Trinity Church** *(see p68)*, and St. Thomas Church *(see p171)*.

INTERNET EVENTS GUIDE

www.nymag.com
www.nytoday.com
www.newyork.citysearch.com
http://newyork.timeout.com

DIRECTORY

92nd Street Y
1395 Lexington Ave.
Map 17 A2.
Tel (212) 415-5500.

Amato Opera Theater
319 Bowery at 2nd St.
Map 4 F2.
Tel (212) 228-8200.

Asia Society
725 Park Ave.
Map 13 A1.
Tel (212) 517-2742.

Brooklyn Academy of Music
30 Lafayette Ave, Brooklyn.
Tel (718) 636-4100.

Bryant Park
Map 8 F1.
Tel (212) 768-4242.

Carnegie Hall
881 7th Ave. **Map** 12 E3.
Tel (212) 247-7800.

Cathedral of St. John the Divine
1047 Amsterdam Ave & 112th St. **Map** 20 E4.
Tel (212) 316-7540.

The Cloisters
Fort Tryon Park.
Tel (212) 923-3700.

Corpus Christi Church
529 W 121st St.
Map 20 E2.
Tel (212) 666-9350.

The Dairy
Central Park at 65th St.
Map 12 F2.
Tel (212) 794-6564.

Dance Theater Workshop
See Dance p347.

Ethical Culture Society Hall
2 W 64th St.
Map 12 D2.
Tel (212) 874-5210.

Federal Hall
26 Wall St.
Map 1 C3.
Tel (212) 825-6888.

Florence Gould Hall (at the Alliance Française)
55 E 59th St.
Map 13 A3.
Tel (212) 355-6160.

Frick Collection
1 E 70th St. **Map** 12 F1.
Tel (212) 288-0700.

Greenwich House Music School
46 Barrow St. **Map** 3 C2.
Tel (212) 242-4770.

Kaye Playhouse (Hunter College)
695 Park Ave. **Map** 13 A1.
Tel (212) 772-4448.

Kosciuszko Foundation
15 E 65th St. **Map** 12 F2
Tel (212) 734-2130.

Lincoln Center
155 W 65th St.
Map 11 C2.
Tel (212) 546-2656.
Tours of various venues at Lincoln Center can be arranged by calling:
Tel (212) 875-5350.

Alice Tully Hall
Tel (212) 875-5050.

Avery Fisher Hall
Tel (212) 875-5030.

Damrosch Park
Tel (212) 875-5000.

Juilliard Opera Center
Tel (212) 769-7406.

Juilliard School of Music
Tel (212) 799-5000.

Metropolitan Opera House
Tel (212) 362-6000.

Manhattan School of Music
120 Claremont Ave.
Map 20 E2.
Tel (212) 749-2802.

Mannes College of Music
150 W 85th St.
Map 15 D3.
Tel (212) 580-0210.

Merkin Hall
129 W 67th St.
Map 11 D2.
Tel (212) 501-3330.

Metropolitan Museum of Art
1000 5th Ave at 82nd St.
Map 16 F4.
Tel (212) 535-7710.

New Jersey Performance Arts Center
1 Center St, Newark, NJ.
Tel 1-888-466-5722.

St. Paul's Chapel
Broadway at Fulton St.
Map 1 C2.
Tel (212) 233-4164.

St. Peter's Church
619 Lexington Ave.
Map 13 A4.
Tel (212) 935-2200.

Symphony Space
2537 Broadway.
Map 15 C2.
Tel (212) 864-5400.

Town Hall
123 W 43rd St.
Map 8 E1.
Tel (212) 997-1003.

Trinity Church
Broadway at Wall St.
Map 1 C3.
Tel (212) 602-0800.

Village Light Opera Group
Perform at: Haft Auditorium, Fashion Institute of Technology, 227 W 27th St.
Map 8 E3.
Tel (212) 352-3101.

Washington Square
Map 4 D2.

Whitney Museum
Philip Morris Building, 120 Park Ave at 42nd St.
Map 9 A1.
Tel 1-800-944-8639.

Winter Garden
World Financial Center, West St.
Map 1 A2.
Tel (212) 945-2600.

Rock, Jazz, and World Music

There's every imaginable form of music in New York, from international stadium rock to the sounds of the 1960s, from Dixieland jazz or country blues, soul, and world music to talented street musicians. The city's music scene changes at a dizzying pace, with many new arrivals (and departures) almost daily, so there's no way to predict what you may find when you arrive. Musical standards also vary.

PRICES AND PLACES

At clubs, expect to pay a cover charge and possibly a one- or two-drink minimum (at $7 or more) requirement. The prices for concerts range from $50 to $150 for the major venues. Many of the smaller concert venues are arranged for seating in certain areas and dancing in others – often with different prices for each.

The top international bands are usually to be found in the huge arenas at the **Meadowlands** or **Madison Square Garden** (see p135). Here the likes of Elton John, Bruce Springsteen, and the Stones perform. Tickets for these events sell out very fast, so buy as many as you need as soon as you hear of a concert, unless you don't mind paying a lot for them through an agent or a scalper (see p341). During the summer, big outdoor concerts are held at Jones Beach (see p255) and **Central Park SummerStage**.

Medium-sized venues for mainstream bands include the Art Deco palace of **Radio City Music Hall**, the **Manhattan Center** (formerly the Hammerstein Ballroom), and the **Beacon Theater**. Booking an impressive lineup of acts is the **Nokia Theater** in Times Square. This state-of-the-art venue is known for its top-notch acoustics. The most popular live-music venues are in the Upper West Side area.

Many leading rock venues are basically bars with music. They will often book different bands every night, so check the listings in the *New York Times*, *Village Voice*, or *Time Out New York* or phone the place to find out what's happening and at what time during that particular week.

ROCK MUSIC

Rock comes in many forms: gothic, industrial, techno, psychedelic, post-punk funk, indie, and alternative music are among the latest crazes. If you prefer to see more of a band than a giant video screen, the following venues have a much more intimate, friendly atmosphere.

The **Knitting Factory** has live jazz and new music, while the **Mercury Lounge** is one of the most happening music spots, featuring hot new bands being groomed for MTV. **Irving Plaza** is where relatively unknown and sometimes known rock groups play, as do the occasional famous country and blues musicians.

The **Bowery Ballroom**, in the Lower East Side, boasts superior acoustics and sightlines and usually books well-known touring acts and local bands.

A converted bodega, **Arlene's Grocery** has been attracting a loyal crowd since 1995, thanks to acts ranging from rock to country and comedy. **Joe's Pub** draws those who appreciate the eclectic roster of rock, jazz, hip-hop, and lounge music. A more upscale venue **Crash Mansion** showcases up-and-coming talents of any musical persuasion, from rock and punk to Brazilian and jazz, as well as featuring established performers such as Norah Jones.

JAZZ

The original Cotton Club and Connie's Inn, which were once crucibles of jazz, are long gone, as are the former speakeasies of West 52nd Street. However, many talented performers carry on the old traditions of Dave Brubeck, Les Paul, Duke Ellington, Count Basie, and other big bands. In Harlem, the stylish yet informal **Lenox Lounge** features contemporary jazz on the weekends.

In Greenwich Village, jazz temples from the 1930s survive and continue to foster great music. Foremost among them is the **Village Vanguard**, where some of the most highly revered jazz memories linger and newer ones are being fashioned by such groups as the McCoy Tyner and Branford Marsalis trios. **Blue Note** hosts big bands at high prices but has a great atmosphere. **Smalls** offers cutting-edge jazz, with four sets a night from two different bands (Mon–Sat). The **Knitting Factory** features contemporary and avant-garde jazz.

Smoke is an intimate nightspot offering a divergent roster of musicians, and **Birdland** features ex-Mingus alumni and musicians such as Bud Shank.

Café Carlyle, an East Side spot once famed for late jazz pianist and singer Bobby Short, now sometimes features clarinetist-filmmaker Woody Allen playing with Eddy Davis and his New Orleans Jazz Band. **Jazz Standard**, with an ample underground performance space, showcases top-notch jazz performers most nights of the week.

A sophisticated club and restaurant, **Iridium** features progressive jazz. If you're in New York in June, don't miss the annual **JVC Jazz Festival**, where famous jazz and blues icons play at various clubs all around Manhattan.

Jazz at Lincoln Center events are scheduled throughout the year, including concerts by the renowned Lincoln Center Jazz Orchestra under the direction of Wynton Marsalis. The music ranges from Duke Ellington's New York sounds to Johnny Dodds' traditional New Orleans-style jazz. Jazz at Lincoln Center now has its own home since it moved into the world's first performing arts center specifically for jazz. It is housed in the Time Warner Center – a multiroom facility on Columbus Circle, perched above Central Park, with bandstands posed against sparing walls of glass and a dance floor beneath the moon and stars *(see p215)*. Finally, Friday night at the **Rose Center** (at **AMNH**) offers live jazz concerts.

FOLK AND COUNTRY MUSIC

Folk, rock music, and R&B (rhythm and blues) can be found at the rather faded **Bitter End**, which once showcased James Taylor and Joni

Mitchell but now specializes in promising new talent, as does **Kenny's Castaways**. Also worth checking out is the **Sidewalk Café**, with its wide range of emerging performers.

BLUES, SOUL, AND WORLD MUSIC

For blues, soul, and world music, options include the **Apollo Theater** in Harlem *(see p230)*. For more than 60 years the near-legendary Wednesday Amateur Nights have been responsible for discovering and launching stars, including James Brown and Dionne Warwick.

The **Cotton Club** is no longer located in its original spot, but the modern venue offers good blues, jazz, and a

Sunday real Gospel brunch on Harlem's main street. The **B.B. King's Blues Club** lineup often features legendary jazz and gospel performers. Food is also served, but can be pricy. Don't miss "Mambo Mondays" with Nestor Torres at **SOB's** (Sounds of Brazil), a world music club specializing in Afro-Latin rhythms.

Terra Blues's bar doubles as an interesting music venue. The blues artists that appear here range from authentic Chicago acoustic players to modern blues acts. In the East Village, **The Stone** showcases an eclectic range of artsy acts. Part community center and café, part jazz and experimental music space, the **5C Café** is a throwback to old New York and has a laidback vibe.

DIRECTORY

MUSIC VENUES

Beacon Theater
2124 Broadway.
Map 15 C5.
Tel *(212) 465-6500.*

Central Park SummerStage
Rumsey Playfield.
Map 12 F1.
Tel *(212) 360-2777.*

Continental Arena Meadowlands
50 Route 120 E
Rutherford, NJ.
Tel *(201) 935-3900.*

Madison Square Garden
7th Ave & 33rd St.
Map 8 E2.
Tel *(212) 465-6741.*

Manhattan Center
311 W 34th St. **Map** 8
D2. **Tel** *(212) 279-7740.*

Nokia Theater
1515 Broadway.
Map 12 E5.
Tel *(212) 930-1959.*

Radio City Music Hall
See p347.

ROCK MUSIC

Arlene's Grocery
95 Stanton St. **Map** 5 A3.
Tel *(212) 995-1652.*

Bowery Ballroom
6 Delancey St. **Map** 4 F3.
Tel *(212) 533-2111.*

Crash Mansion
199 Bowery. **Map** 4 F3.
Tel *(212) 982-7767.*

Joe's Pub
Public Theater, 425
Lafayette St. **Map** 4 F2.
Tel *(212) 539-8770.*

Knitting Factory
74 Leonard St. **Map** 4 E5.
Tel *(212) 219-3132.*

Mercury Lounge
217 E Houston St.
Map 5 A3.
Tel *(212) 260-4700.*

Irving Plaza
17 Irving Pl. **Map** 9 A5.
Tel *(212) 777-6800.*

JAZZ

Birdland
315 W 44th St. **Map** 12
D5. **Tel** *(212) 581-3080.*

Blue Note
131 W 3rd St. **Map** 4 D2.
Tel *(212) 475-8592.*

Café Carlyle
95 E 76th St. **Map** 17 A5.
Tel *(212) 744-1600.*

Iridium
1650 Broadway.
Map 12 D2.
Tel *(212) 582-2121.*

Jazz at Lincoln Center
Tel *(212) 258-9800.*

Jazz Standard
116 E 27th St. **Map** 9 A3
Tel *(212) 576-2232.*

JVC Jazz Festival
www.festivalnetwork.
com

Lenox Lounge
288 Malcolm X Blvd.
Map 21 B2.
Tel *(212) 427-0253.*

Rose Center
79th St at CPW. **Map** 16
D5. **Tel** *(212) 769-5100.*

Smalls
183 W 10th St. **Map** 3
C2. **Tel** *(212) 252-5091.*

Smoke
2751 Broadway. **Map** 20
E5. **Tel** *(212) 864-6662.*

Village Vanguard
178 7th Ave S. **Map**
3 C1. **Tel** *(212) 255-4037.*

FOLK AND COUNTRY

Bitter End
147 Bleecker St. **Map** 4
E3. **Tel** *(212) 673-7030.*

Kenny's Castaways
157 Bleecker St.
Map 4 E3.
Tel *(212) 979-9762.*

Sidewalk Café
94 Ave A. **Map** 5 B2.
Tel *(212) 473-7373.*

BLUES, SOUL, AND WORLD MUSIC

Apollo Theater
253 W 125 St.
Map 19 A1.
Tel *(212) 531-5305.*

B.B. King's Blues Club
237 W 42nd St.
Map 8 E1.
Tel *(212) 997-4144.*

Cotton Club
656 W 125th St. **Map** 22
F2. **Tel** *(212) 663-7980.*

5C Café
68 Avenue C. **Map** 5 C2.
Tel *(212) 477-5993.*

SOB's
204 Varick St. **Map** 4 D3.
Tel *(212) 243-4940.*

Terra Blues
149 Bleecker St.
Map 4 E3.
Tel *(212) 777-7776.*

The Stone
Avenue C at 2nd St.
Map 5 C2.
www.thestonenyc.com

Clubs, Dance Halls, and Gay and Lesbian Venues

New York's nightlife and club scene is legendary, and deservedly so. Whatever your preference – be it for a noisy disco, stand-up comedy, or the soothing melodies of a Harry Connick, Jr., sound-alike in a piano bar – you'll be really amazed at the choice. There was a rash of big discos in the 1980s, but relatively few of these have survived the more recent trend toward the comfort and style of supper clubs.

WHEN AND WHERE

The best and hippest time for clubbing is during the week – it's also a lot cheaper. Take a fair amount of money and some ID to prove that you're old enough to drink (which is over 21) – but beware, all the drinks are very expensive.

The trendiest clubs roll on until 4am or later. Fashions and club nights change all the time, so go to Tower Records on Broadway for all the latest leaflets, check club details in the listings magazines *(see p340)* and read the *Village Voice*. The most interesting places nowadays are often popularized by word of mouth. Your best bet is to go somewhere like **Pacha** and hope someone will tell you where to go on to. It's a well-known spot and often invitations to other clubs are given out there.

DANCING

New Yorkers thrive on music and dancing. The dance floors available all around the city range from the ever-popular **SOB's** – for jungle, reggae, soul, jazz, and salsa – to a few huge basketball-court-sized places, such as **Roseland**. This has ballroom dancing every Thursday and Sunday and is New York's classic Broadway ballroom, revealing a tantalizing glimpse of older Broadway culture. It also has a good megasize, 700-seater, restaurant with a fully stocked bar.

The legendary club **Pacha**, which started out in Ibiza, has opened a swanky four-floor venue in the heart of Times Square and is consistently booking top international DJs to make the most of the colossal sound system installed here. This is the place for those who enjoy pounding music, sweaty dance floors, and a lively crowd. **Marquee** is another A-list spot in Chelsea, with a glass-enclosed VIP mezzanine that draws Hollywood starlets. Bring some models if you want to be sure of getting in.

Those who prefer a more underground house scene should head to **Apt** for top DJ tunes. In Chelsea, **Home** buzzes with dance tunes and has plenty of VIP seating. **The Plumm** fills with trendy clubbers, celebrities, and those who have come to spot them. Join the crowd cutting moves on the dance floor to hip-hop, funk, rock, and classics. The door policy can be strict, so dress up in your hippest duds.

Also attracting a try-hard crowd is **The Pink Elephant**, with its swanky decor (a lot of pink lights, of course). Many of the girls here are on the lookout for a hedge-fund husband, so guys might be expected to pay for drinks. The tables all require bottle service, and house music is the mainstay. Even more elite is the **Hiro Ballroom** at the Maritime Hotel, a Sunday night must for the beautiful set. There are two levels to this Japanese-themed restaurant, with ample seating for poseurs who wish to see and be seen.

For those who are more interested in music and dancing, rather than decor, head to **Club Shelter**, New York's longest-running deep-house club, and **The Sullivan Room**, which draws the cream of techno talent and boasts a top-notch sound system and plenty of seating.

NIGHTCLUBS

Nightclubs are the places to see a show. NY shows are less flashy than in the 1940s and 1950s but they still boast a wide variety of acts. Expect to pay a cover charge; many of the clubs also require that you have at least two drinks.

The **Rainbow Grill** on the 65th floor of the RCA Building has a fine piano bar. The chic **Supper Club** surrounds you with gold lamé draperies and features big band music downstairs. Cabaret singers perform upstairs in their intimate Blue Room. **Joe's Pub** at the Public Theater has decent food and a wonderful array of performances and musical acts. **Feinstein's at the Regency** is the epitome of classic cabaret. Come here to enjoy everything from tinkling live piano shows to Broadway tributes and jazz trios.

GAY AND LESBIAN VENUES

The past two decades have seen the arrival of clubs and restaurants specifically geared to gay and lesbian clientele. Popular gay cabarets include the **Duplex**, which has a mix of stand-up comics, comedy sketches and singers. Often adorned with year-round Christmas lights, the long-running **Pieces** heats up most nights of the week with everything from drag shows to karaoke.

The very fashionable nightclubs and bars for men include the trendy uptown **Town House**, a piano bar with restaurant, and **Don't Tell Mama**, a long-established gay bar that presents good musical revues and spoofs. **Henrietta Hudson** caters solely to women, as does **Grolier**.

Magazines such as the *Village Voice*, *HX*, and *Next* have good listings of what's happening in the gay communities, and the *Gay Yellow Pages* covers the gay scene. If you need more information, phone the **Gay and Lesbian Switchboard**.

The Chelsea neighborhood, particularly around Eighth Avenue, is the bustling heart of New York's gay life. The Hell's Kitchen area, around the mid 40s between Eighth and 10th avenues, also thrums with gay nightlife –

Barrage is a hopping bar featuring a popular Friday happy hour. The inviting and stylish **G Lounge** serves a potent selection of cocktails and flavored coffees, and is the perfect spot for a drink before hitting the clubs.

Lively **Barracuda** features drag shows and draws a diverse crowd of regulars and newcomers. **Rawhide** stays hopping throughout the evening, with a popular happy hour every night until 10pm. **Stonewall Inn**, the famed site of the

Stonewall riots and birth of the modern gay movement, has undergone a multimillion-dollar refurbishment. The comfy neighborhood lounge **Posh** pulls in a friendly crowd for the popular happy hour 4–8pm.

Casual, friendly **Rubyfruit Bar and Grill** on Hudson Street fills with women who are out for cocktails and conversation. The imaginatively decorated **Cubby Hole** is a cozy lesbian bar where regulars often sing along to the jukebox.

DIRECTORY

DANCING

Apt
419 W 13th St.
Map 3 C1.
Tel (212) 414-4245.

Club Shelter
150 Varick St.
Map 4 D4.
Tel (646) 862-6117.

Hiro Ballroom
The Maritime Hotel, 371 W 16th St. **Map** 8 D5.
Tel (212) 727-0212.

Home
532 W 27th St.
Map 8 D4.
Tel (212) 273-3700.

Knitting Factory
74 Leonard St.
Map 4 E5.
Tel (212) 219-3132.

Marquee
289 10th Ave.
Map 7 C4.
Tel (646) 473-0202.

Pacha
618 W 46th St.
Map 12 E5.
Tel (212) 209-7500.

Roseland
239 W 52nd St.
Map 12 E4.
Tel (212) 247-0200.

SOB'S
204 Varick St.
Map 4 D3.
Tel (212) 243-4940.

Sullivan Room
218 Sullivan St.
Map 4 D2.
Tel (212) 252-2151.

The Pink Elephant
527 W 27th St.
Map 7 C3.
Tel (212) 463-0000.

The Plumm
246 W 14th St.
Map 3 C1.
Tel (212) 675-1567.

NIGHTCLUBS

Feinstein's at the Regency
540 Park Ave.
Map 13 A3.
Tel (212) 339-4095.

Joe's Pub
425 Lafayette St.
Map 4 F2.
Tel (212) 539-8777.

The Metropolitan Room
94 W 22nd St.
Map 7 4F.
Tel (212) 206-0440.

Rainbow Grill
30 Rockefeller Plaza.
Map 12 F4.
Tel (212) 632-5000.

The Supper Club
240 W 47th St.
Map 12 D5.
Tel (212) 921-1940.

GAY AND LESBIAN VENUES

Barracuda
275 W 22nd St.
Map 8 D4.
Tel (212) 645-8613.

Barrage
401 W 47th St.
Map 12 D5.
Tel (212) 586-9390.

Don't Tell Mama
343 W 46th St.
Map 12 D5.
Tel (212) 757-0788.

Duplex
61 Christopher St.
Map 3 C2.
Tel (212) 255-5438.

G Lounge
223 W 19th St.
Map 8 E5.
Tel (212) 929-1085.

Gay and Lesbian Switchboard
Tel (212) 989-0999.

Henrietta Hudson
438 Hudson St.
Map 3 C3.
Tel (212) 924-3347.

Phoenix
447 E 13th St.
Map 5 1A.
Tel (212) 477-9979.

Pieces
8 Christopher St.
Map 4 D2.
Tel (212) 929-9291.

Posh
405 W 51st St.
Map 11 C4.
Tel (212) 957-2222.

Rawhide
212 8th Ave.
Map 8 D4.
Tel (212) 242-9332.

Rubyfruit Bar and Grill
531 Hudson St.
Map 3 C2.
Tel (212) 929-3343.

Stonewall Inn
53 Christopher St.
Map 3 C2.
Tel (212) 488-2705.

The Cubby Hole
281 W 12th St.
Map 3 C1.
Tel (212) 243-9041.

Town House
236 E 58th St.
Map 13 B4.
Tel (212) 754-4649.

Comedy, Cabaret, and Literary Events

From Jack Benny and Rodney Dangerfield to Woody Allen and Jerry Seinfeld, New York has spawned almost as many comics as it has jokes about itself, including the requisite quips: on crime – "In New York crime is getting worse. When I was there the other day, the Statue of Liberty had both hands up"; and on driving – "Always look both ways when running a red light." Comedy is a cut-throat business here. This is good news for punters, because it means that no matter what comedy club you walk into, you'll be howling after just a few sets. NYC is also a consummate romancer, judging by its plethora of cabarets and lounges. An unforgettable New York experience is to be serenaded by a lounge singer in a dusky piano bar. New York also boasts a booming literary scene, with superb weekly readings and lectures.

COMEDY SHOWCASES

Many of New York's best current comedy clubs or showcases have evolved from earlier "improvisational" comedy. Part of the allure of New York comedy clubs is that you never know who might get behind the mic to deliver their spiel. Anyone from Dennis Miller and Roseanne Barr to Robin Williams could show up. A word of caution: if you don't want to be singled out and made fun of, sit away from the stage. Many of the larger comedy clubs offer meals, and at the more popular clubs, it's always a good idea to make reservations to ensure admission.

Leading the comedy club pack is the **Broadway Comedy Club** in the Theater District, which has formed from a merger of Chicago City Limits and NY Improv. As the city's largest club, it draws big names nightly. **Caroline's** also has big-name comics perform in elegant surroundings. The famous catchphrase of the bug-eyed New York comedian Roger Dangerfield was "I get no respect," but judging from the lasting fame of his **Dangerfield's Comedy Club**, which draws top acts from around the country, he seems to have gotten respect after all. The **Upright Citizens Brigade Theatre** has sassy, Chicago-style improvisation on various days of the week.

Many of the UCB's weekly late shows are free. The **Gotham Comedy Club** in the Flatiron District, presents a wide range of comics in a sophisticated setting. **Comic Strip Live**, on the East Side, has hosted a slew of top comics, including Eddie Murphy, and continues to introduce many new comics to the scene. The basement-level **Comedy Cellar** in Greenwich Village presents a nightly lineup of new and established comics. Also good are **Stand-Up New York**, **NY Comedy Club**, and **Laugh Lounge NYC**, which showcases two comedy shows a night, as well as offering nicely priced cocktails. **Underground Lounge** and **The Laugh Factory** are also good value.

CABARETS AND PIANO BARS

Cabarets have become a New York institution. Such cozy, just-for-listening places are often called "rooms" and are located in hotels. Most operate from Tuesday to Saturday (usually with a cover charge or a drink minimum), and most take credit cards.

The Algonquin's **Oak Room** has song stylists. For a classic piano lounge with a pano-ramic Manhattan view, visit the **Top of the Tower** at the Beekman Tower Hotel. The "long-distance hummer" award goes to the late Bobby Short, who played

his piano for over 25 years at the Café Carlyle in the **Carlyle Hotel**. Now Woody Allen plays there on Mondays with Eddy Davis's New Orleans Jazz Band.

Also in the Carlyle is **Bemelman's Bar**, with its whimsical murals; it attracts a relaxed crowd who enjoy first-class crooners. A jacket is required if you visit the **5757 Bar** at the Four Seasons Hotel, but the opulence of the place makes it worth dressing up.

The spirited cabaret **Don't Tell Mama** showcases emerging and established performers who belt out their songs with equal gusto. **Ars Nova** in Hell's Kitchen is an informal, anything-goes cabaret where you may see show tunes and experimental comedy, and has attracted the likes of Liza Minnelli and Tony Kushner.

For Manhattan's choicest cabaret, kick back and enjoy the show at lively **Duplex**, the longest-running cabaret venue in New York City. Relax to the tinkling of keys at the downstairs piano bar, or head upstairs for superlative classic cabaret shows, one-act plays, and top-notch comedy. A mixed crowd, including the talented staff, croons along at **Brandy's Piano Bar**. For a memorable evening of song and music, head to **Feinstein's at the Regency Hotel**, where top-of-the-line performers entertain an appreciative crowd. Enjoy sultry cabaret, theater, and musical ensembles at the plush showroom in **Dillon's Restaurant and Lounge**, nestled in the heart of the Theater District.

LITERARY EVENTS AND POETRY SLAMS

As the birthplace of some of the greatest American writers, from Herman Melville to Henry James, and the adopted home of countless others, New York has long been a writer's city. The literary tradition is celebrated often and throughout the year, with readings and talks that take place at bookstores, libraries, cafés, and community centers across the city. Readings are usually free, but expect long lines for the better known names. The **92nd Street Y** hosts readings by some of the greatest writers to pass through New York, including many Nobel- and Pulitzer-prize winning authors. Most NYC bookstores present a weekly or monthly reading series, including **Barnes & Noble** (the Fifth Avenue and Union Square branches usually attract the highest

profile authors) and **Borders Books and Music**. The **Mid-Manhattan Library** also presents readings, as does **Strand Bookstore**. Enjoy spirited readings by playwrights at the **Drama Book Shop**. Check out *The New Yorker* magazine, available in bookstores and at many newsstands, for current listings of readings and talks.

Poetry slams (sometimes called Spoken Word), are just what the name implies, an evening of freeform poems, raps, and storytelling, usually raucous and entertaining,

often unpredictable, and never boring. The **Nuyorican Poets Café** in Alphabet City, often heralded as the progenitor of spoken word in New York, serves up a nightly mix of poetry slams, readings, and performances. The **Bowery Poetry Club**, established as a performance space for spoken word in all its incarnations, presents an eclectic range of performances, from poetry jams to various performance arts. The **Poetry Project** at St. Mark's Church also hosts contemporary poetry readings, events, and workshops.

DIRECTORY

COMEDY SHOWCASES

Broadway Comedy Club
318 W 53rd St.
Map 12 E4.
Tel (212) 757-2323.

Caroline's
1626 Broadway.
Map 12 E5.
Tel (212) 757-4100.

Comedy Cellar
117 MacDougal St.
Map 4 D2.
Tel (212) 254-3480.

Comic Strip Live
1568 2nd Ave.
Map 17 B4.
Tel (212) 861-9386.

Dangerfield's
1118 1st Ave.
Map 13 C3.
Tel (212) 593-1650.

Gotham Comedy Club
208 W 23rd St.
Map 8 D4.
Tel (212) 367-9000.

Laugh Lounge NYC
151 Essex St.
Map 5 B3.
Tel (212) 614-2500.

NY Comedy Club
241 E 24th St.
Map 9 B4.
Tel (212) 696-5233.

Stand-up New York
236 W 78th St.
Map 15 C5.
Tel (212) 595-0850.

The Laugh Factory
303 W 42 St.
Map 8 D1.
Tel (212) 586-7829.

Underground Lounge
955 W End Ave.
Map 20 E5.
Tel (212) 531-4759.

Upright Citizens Brigade Theatre
307 W 26th St.
Map 8 D4.
Tel (212) 366-9176.

CABARETS AND PIANO BARS

5757 Bar
Four Seasons Hotel,
57 E 57th St.
Map 12 F3.
Tel (212) 758-5700.

Ars Nova
511 W 54th St.
Map 12 E4.
Tel (212) 489-9800.

Brandy's Piano Bar
235 E 84th St.
Map 17 B4.
Tel (212) 650-1944.

Carlyle Hotel
35 E 76th St.
Map 17 A5.
Tel (212) 744-1600.

Dillon's Restaurant and Lounge
245 W 54th St.
Map 12 D4.
Tel (212) 307-9797.

Don't Tell Mama
343 W 46th St.
Map 12 D5.
Tel (212) 757-0788.

Duplex
61 Christopher St.
Map 3 C2.
Tel (212) 255-5438.

Feinstein's at the Regency Hotel
540 Park Ave.
Map 13 A3.
Tel (212) 759-4100.

Oak Room
Algonquin Hotel,
59 W 44th St.
Map 12 F5.
Tel (212) 840-6800.

Top of the Tower
Beekman Tower Hotel,
3 Mitchell Pl.
Map 13 C5.
Tel (212) 355-7300.

LITERARY EVENTS AND POETRY SLAMS

92nd Street Y
1395 Lexington Ave.
Map 17 A2.
Tel (212) 415-5729.

Barnes & Noble
555 Fifth Ave.
Map 12 F5.
Tel (212) 697-3048.

33 E 17th St.
Map 9 A5.
Tel (212) 253-0810.

Borders Books and Music
461 Park Ave.
Map 17 A3.
Tel (212) 980-6785.

Bowery Poetry Club
308 Bowery.
Map 4 F3.
Tel (212) 614-0505.

Drama Book Shop
250 W 40th St.
Map 8 E1.
Tel (212) 944-0595.

Mid-Manhattan Library
455 Fifth Ave at 40th St.
Map 8 F1.
Tel (212) 340-0833.

Nuyorican Poets Café
236 E 3rd St.
Map 5 B2.
Tel (212) 505-8183.

Poetry Project
St. Mark's Church,
131 E 10th St.
Map 4 F1.
Tel (212) 674-0910.

Strand Bookstore
828 Broadway.
Map 4 E1.
Tel (212) 473-1452.

Late-Night New York

New York is indeed a city that never sleeps. If you wake up in the middle of the night – with a craving for fresh bread, a need to be entertained, or an urge to watch the sun rise over the Manhattan skyline – there are always plenty of options to choose from.

BARS

The best and friendliest bars are often the Irish ones. **O'Flanagan's** or **Scruffy Duffy's** are both loud, have late-night dancing, and cater to regulars. Go for a late-night dry martini at the **Temple Bar**. The best piano bars are in the hotels: try the Café Carlyle in the **Carlyle Hotel**, **Feinstein's at Loews Regency** *(see p357)*, or the Oak Room in the **Algonquin Hotel**.

For hot American jazz until 4am, go to **Joe's Pub** or the **Blue Note**. **Cornelia Street Café** is a lively nook for prose, poetry, and theater readings. Poetry, theater, and Latin music can be found at the **Nuyorican Poets Café**. If you're in the Village, stop in at **Rose's Turn** for open mike, piano bar, and late-night ambience.

MIDNIGHT MOVIES

Special midnight showings and a youthful crowd can be found the Angelika Film Center and the Film Forum *(see p349)*. New multi-plexes often show movies at midnight on weekends.

SHOPS

Shakespeare & Company Booksellers on Broadway and the St. Mark's Bookshop are open until late. The **Apple Store** on Fifth Ave is open 24 hours and well worth a visit at any time of the day. In the evening, DJs bring the store to life, while during the day, more than 300 Mac specialists are available for training and consultations. In SoHo, **H&M** sells affordable fashion until 9pm Monday to Saturday and until 8pm on Sundays.

Among the many Village clothing stores that stay open late is **Trash and Vaudeville** (open till 8pm Mon–Sat); **Macy's** at Herald Square is open daily until 9:30pm. For health essentials, numerous **Duane Reade**, **CVS**, and **Rite Aid** pharmacies are open 24 hours.

TAKE-OUT FOOD AND GROCERIES

A few take-out food stores are open 24 hours a day, including numerous **Gristedes** emporiums and the **West Side Supermarket**. Many Korean greengrocers also stay open all night. The **Food Emporium** is a supermarket chain usually open until midnight. Liquor stores are usually open until 10pm and many deliver.

For the best in bagels, go to **H & H Bagels**, **Bagels On The Square**, and **Jumbo Bagels and Bialys**. Many pizzerias and Chinese restaurants stay open late.

DINING

The trendy set often frequent **Balthazar**, and **Les Halles** for good French dishes. Twentysomethings will seek out the **Coffee Shop** for late-night beer and Brazilian food. You'll find delicious and legendary sandwiches at the **Carnegie Deli**. **Caffè Reggio** in Greenwich Village has been a favorite for late-night coffee and desserts since 1927. Other good options include **Blue Ribbon** and **Odeon**. **The Dead Poet** is a real Upper West Side neighborhood hangout, with a jukebox, a lively bar, and late-night bar food. Downtown, the party crowds flock to **Bereket Turkish Kebab House** for excellent kebabs, or to the **Empire Diner** in Chelsea. Both are open 24 hours a day.

SPORTS

There is late-night play at **Slate Billiards** until 4am on weekends. Have late-night beers and burgers with the New York University crowd at **Bowlmor Lanes** bowling alley. Also popular is the **Lucky Strike Lanes and Lounge**, featuring cocktails, bowling, and music in a retro atmosphere. **24–7 Fitness Club** offers a no-frill gym around the clock.

SERVICES

Midnight Express Cleaners picks up garments in Manhattan until midnight and has them ready the next day. Note that this service does not pick up or deliver to major hotels. On Thursdays hairdresser **George Michael of Madison Avenue/Madora** is open until 9pm and will also make house calls. Primarily for women, the no-nonsense Korean spa **Juvenex** provides massages and saunas at any time. If you are locked out, try **Mr Locks Inc**. For stamps, head to the General Post Office, open 24 hours. Upscale grocer **Dean & DeLuca**'s Kip's Bay branch is open till 10pm.

TOURS AND VIEWS

One of New York's most enjoyable walks is along the Hudson River at the World Financial Center's **Battery Park City**, open (and safe) at all hours. Piers 16 and 17 at South Street Seaport attract strollers and revelers all night long and the **Harbour Lights** restaurant on Pier 17 is often open until 2am for a middle of the night pick-me-up. Enjoy the city lights by taking a **Circle Line** two-hour tour of the nighttime harbor.

Try the Riverview Terrace at Sutton Place: the benches offer a peaceful place to watch the sun rise over the East River, Roosevelt Island, and Queens. Two of the most sensational views with the Manhattan backdrop are (looking west) from the **River Café** and (looking east) from **Arthur's Landing** restaurant.

Take a trip on the **Staten Island Ferry** *(see p76)* to see the Statue of Liberty and the Manhattan skyline in the dawn light, or a take a taxi across Brooklyn Bridge *(see* *pp86–9)* to watch the sun rise over New York Harbor. Go to the **Beekman Tower Hotel**'s Top of the Tower for some panoramas of the city's East Side up to 1am. The ultimate view is from the **Empire State Building**: its observation decks *(see pp136–7)* stay open until 2am. **Top of the Rock**'s observation decks *(see p144)* are open until midnight. **Rise**, the 14th-floor bar of the Ritz-Carlton Hotel in Battery Park has great views of the harbor and Statue of Liberty.

Château Stables has rides in horse-drawn carriages and **Liberty Helicopters** run flights over the city at sunset. If you want something a little bit different, try **Marvelous Manhattan Tours**' escorted evening barhopping walks. And if you still can't sleep, stroll along the Upper West Side and grab a couple of hot dogs at the famous **Gray's Papaya**.

DIRECTORY

BARS

Algonquin Hotel
See p357.

Blue Note
See p353.

Carlyle Hotel
See p357.

Cornelia Street Café
29 Cornelia St.
Map 4 D2.
Tel *(212) 989-9318.*

Joe's Pub
See p353.

Nuyorican Poets Café
236 E 3rd St. **Map** 5 A2.
Tel *(212) 505-8183.*

O'Flanagan's
1215 1st Ave. **Map** 13 C2.
Tel *(212) 439-0660.*

Rose's Turn
See p357.

Scruffy Duffy's
743 8th Ave. **Map** 12 D5.
Tel *(212) 245-9126.*

Temple Bar
332 Lafayette St.
Map 4 F4.
Tel *(212) 925-4242.*

SHOPS

Apple Store
767 5th Ave. **Map** 12 F3.
Tel *(212) 336-1440.*

CVS Pharmacy
158 Bleecker St. **Map** 4 D3. **Tel** *(212) 982-3133.*

Duane Reade Drugstores
224 W 57th (Broadway).
Map 12 D3.
Tel *(212) 541-9708.*

1279 3rd Ave at E 74th St.
Map 17 B5.
Tel *(212) 744-2668.*

H&M
558 Broadway. **Map** 4 E4. **Tel** *(212) 343-2722.*

Macy's
See p134.

RiteAid Pharmacy
See p373.

Trash and Vaudeville
See p324.

TAKE-OUT FOOD AND GROCERIES

Bagels On The Square
7 Carmine St. **Map** 4 D3.
Tel *(212) 691-3041.*

Gristedes Food Emporium
See the Yellow Pages for locations.

H & H Bagels
Broadway at 80th St.
Map 15 C4.
Tel *(212) 595-8003.*

H & H Midtown Bagels East
1551 2nd Ave. **Map** 17 B4. **Tel** *(212) 734-7441.*

Jumbo Bagels and Bialys
1070 2nd Ave. **Map** 13 B3. **Tel** *(212) 355-6185.*

West Side Market
2171 Broadway.
Map 15 C5.
Tel *(212) 595-2536.*

DINING

Balthazar
80 Spring St. **Map** 4 E4.
Tel *(212) 965-1414.*

Bereket Turkish Kebab House
187 E Houston St. **Map** 5 A3. **Tel** *(212) 475-7700.*

Blue Ribbon
See p300.

Caffè Reggio
119 MacDougal St. **Map** 4 D2. **Tel** *(212) 475-9557.*

Carnegie Deli
See p314.

Coffee Shop
See p314.

The Dead Poet
450 Amsterdam Ave. **Map** 15 C4. **Tel** *(212) 595-5670.*

Empire Diner
See p138.

Gray's Papaya
Broadway at 72nd St.
Map 11 C1.
Tel *(212) 260-3532.*

Les Halles
See p314.

Odeon
See p298.

SPORTS

24–7 Fitness Club
47 W 14th St. **Map** 4 D1.
Tel *(212) 206-1504.*

Bowlmor Lanes
110 University Pl. **Map** 4 E1. **Tel** *(212) 255-8188.*

Lucky Strike Lanes and Lounge
624–660 West 42nd St.
Map 7 B1.
Tel *(646) 829-0170.*

Slate Billiards
See p361.

SERVICES

Dean & DeLuca
576 2nd Ave. **Map** 9 B3.
Tel *(212) 696-1369.*
One of several branches.

General Post Office
See p135.

George Michael of Madison Avenue/ Madora
422 Madison Ave. **Map** 13 A5. **Tel** *(212) 752-1177.*

Juvenex Spa
25 W 32nd St, 5th Floor.

Map 8 F3.
Tel *(646) 733-1330.*

Midnight Express Cleaners
Tel *(718) 392-9200.*

Mr Locks Inc
Tel *(866) 675-6257.*

TOURS AND VIEWS

Arthur's Landing
Port Imperial Marina, Pershing Circle, Weehawken, NJ.
Tel *(201) 867-0777.*

Battery Park City
West St. **Map** 1 A3.

Beekman Tower Hotel
1st Ave 49th St. **Map** 13 C5. **Tel** *(212) 355-7300.*

Château Stables
608 W 48th St.
Map 15 B3.
Tel *(212) 246-0520.*

Circle Line
W 42nd St. **Map** 15 B3.
Tel *(212) 563-3200.*

Marvelous Manhattan Tours
Tel *(718) 846-9308.*

Harbour Lights
89 South St Seaport.
Pier 17. **Map** 2 D2.
Tel *(212) 227-2800.*

Liberty Helicopters
Tel *(212) 487-4777.*

Rise
Ritz-Carlton, Battery Park.
Map 1 B4.
Tel *(212) 344-0800.*

River Café
See p311.

Staten Island Ferry
See p76.

Top of the Rock
See p144.

Sports

Many New Yorkers are ardent sports fans, and you'll find a range of sports events, both to watch and participate in, going on throughout the year. The city boasts two professional baseball teams, two hockey teams, a basketball team, and two football teams. Madison Square Garden plays host to an extraordinary variety of spectator sports, including basketball, hockey, boxing, and track and field events. Tennis fans can take in the US Open and Virginia Slims tournaments, and those who follow track and field events swarm to the Millrose Games, where top runners and other athletes compete.

TICKETS

The easiest way to get hold of tickets is through **Ticketron** or **Ticketmaster**. For the big games, you may need a ticket agent. You can also buy tickets at the stadium box office itself, though these tickets often sell out quickly, so you'll have to call or stop by far in advance. Keep your eyes peeled for ticket offers in the free entertainment weeklies that are distributed throughout town, and check the local newspapers for upcoming sporting events.

FOOTBALL

The city's two professional football teams are the New York Giants and the New York Jets. They both play their home games across the river at the **Giants Stadium** in New Jersey, though there are plans in the works for the construction of a new Giants Stadium on the West Side of Manhattan. Tickets for the Giants, a popular team with an impressive number of NFL and Super Bowl championships under their belt, are near impossible to obtain, but they may be available for the Jets.

BASEBALL

To capture the essence of this American institution, baseball fans should try to see the famed New York Yankees, who moved to the new **Yankee Stadium** in 2009. The team's legendary accomplishments are manifold, and include winning the most World Series titles and

boasting such celebrated players as Joe DiMaggio and Jackie Robinson. The New York Mets, the other major baseball team, plays at **Shea Stadium** in Queens. Catching a game of "America's favorite pastime" on a crisp summer day is a memorable event, from the crack of the bat and the baseball soaring into the clear blue sky to the seemingly effortless slides into base and the roar of the crowd. If you can, try and catch a game when the Yankees are playing the Boston Red Sox. The baseball season runs from April to October.

BASKETBALL

The New York Knicks play their home games at **Madison Square Garden**; tickets are pricey and difficult to attain, so you'll need to reserve far in advance through Ticketron or Ticketmaster. The ever-popular Harlem Globetrotters also play their games at The Garden.

BOXING

Professional boxing matches are more often seen on Paramount's wide TV screen than in the flesh at Madison Square Garden. Also at the Garden are the Daily News Golden Gloves in mid-April, the largest and oldest amateur boxing tournament in the US, with boxers from New York's five boroughs competing. Past Golden Glove winners, many of whom have gone on to become Olympic gold medalists and world champions, have included Sugar Ray Robinson and Floyd Patterson.

HORSE RACES

A day at the races may not be quite the lavish affair it once was, but the high-stakes races still draw the society crowd – hats, summer dresses and all – along with lively crowds who have come to cheer, jeer, and bet on their lucky horse. Harness racing, in which horses pull sulkies (small carts), takes place year-round at the **Yonkers Raceway**. Flat races are held daily, except Tuesday, October to May, at the **Aqueduct Race Track** in Queens, and May to October at the **Belmont Park Race Track** in Long Island.

ICE HOCKEY

Fists and ice fly when the New York Rangers meet their competition at Madison Square Garden. The New York Islanders are also fierce hockey contenders, with exciting matches at the **Nassau Coliseum** in Long Island. The hockey season runs from October to April.

ICE-SKATING

There are a variety of good places to go ice skating out of doors. One is the **Rockefeller Plaza Rink**, which looks beautiful at Christmas. The others are in Central Park: **Wollman Memorial Rink** and **Lasker Ice Rink**. For indoor sites, try the Sky Rink at **Chelsea Piers**.

MARATHON

To be one of the 30,000 who enter the New York Marathon, you have to sign up six months in advance. The race is held on the first Sunday in November. Phone (212) 423-2249 for information.

TENNIS

The top tennis tournament in New York is the US Open, played each August at the **National Tennis Center**. Also good is the women's Virginia Slims Championships in November at **Madison Square Garden** (see p135). If you want to play tennis rather than watch it, look in the telephone directory under "Tennis Courts: Public and Private." For private courts, you can expect to pay about $50–70 an hour. The **Manhattan Plaza Racquet Club** offers both courts and lessons by the hour. For public courts, you will need a $50 permit, available from the **NY City Parks & Recreation Department**. You will also need an identity card and a reservation coupon.

TRACK AND FIELD

The Millrose Games, which draws top athletes from around the world, are normally held in early February at **Madison Square Garden**. The 100-meter sprint, pole vault, and high jump competitions are particularly exciting. The Amateur Athletic

Union (AAU) championships, where many renowned student athletes compete, are held in late February at the Garden. Chelsea Piers also has a complete track and field complex.

SPORTS BARS

New York City is crammed with sports bars, often unmissable for their big screens, sports banners, and cheering (or booing), beer-guzzling patrons. For a slice of American sports life, step into a sports bar when a big game is on, and you'll soon be whooping it up with the rest of them. Try **Mickey Mantle's**, which has a giant scoreboard. **ESPN Zone**, in Times Square, offers a plethora of screens so that you can follow the action no matter where you are. **Bounce**,

on the Upper East Side, is a boisterous sports lounge with drinks specials through the week. **Bar None** and the friendly, Irish **Pioneer Bar** are also favorites, and for soccer, try the amiable **Nevada Smith's** in the East Village, with friendly, Guinness-fueled crowds.

OTHER ACTIVITIES

In Central Park, options include renting rowboats from **Loeb Boathouse** or playing chess – pick up the pieces from The Dairy (see p208). Rent rollerblades at **Blades Board & Skate** and have a free lesson on stopping at Central Park before making a circuit. Bowling is available at **Chelsea Piers** and a few other lanes throughout the city. **Slate Billiards** and many bars offer pool and darts.

DIRECTORY

Aqueduct Race Track
Ozone Park, Queens.
Tel (718) 641-4700.

Bar None
98 3rd Ave. **Map** 4 F1.
Tel (212) 777-6663.

Belmont Park Race Track
Hempstead Turnpike,
Long Island.
Tel (718) 641-4700.

Blades Board & Skate
120 W 72nd St.
Map 12 D1.
Tel (212) 787-3911.

Bounce
1403 Second Ave.
Map 13 B1.
Tel (212) 535-2183.

Chelsea Piers Sports & Entertainment Complex
Piers 59–62 at 23rd St & 11th Ave (Hudson River).
Map 7 B4–5.
Tel (212) 336-6000.
www.chelseapiers.com

ESPN Zone
1472 Broadway at W 42nd St.
Map 8 E1.
Tel (212) 921-3776.

Giants Stadium
Meadowlands,
E Rutherford, NJ.
Tel (201) 935-8111.
www.giants.com

Tel (516) 560-8200.
www.newyorkjets.com

Lasker Ice Rink
Central Park Drive East at 108th St.
Map 21 B4.
Tel (212) 534-7639.

Loeb Boathouse
Central Park.
Map 16 F5.
Tel (212) 517-2233.

Madison Square Garden
7th Ave at 33rd St.
Map 8 E2.
Tel (212) 465-6741.
www.thegarden.com

Manhattan Plaza Racquet Club
450 W 43rd St.
Map 7 C1.
Tel (212) 594-0554.

Mickey Mantle's
42 Central Park South.
Map 12 E3.
Tel (212) 688-7777.

Nassau Coliseum
1255 Hempstead Turnpike.
Tel (516) 794-9303.
www.nassaucoliseum.com

National Tennis Center
Flushing Meadow Park, Queens.
Tel (718) 595-2420.
www.usta.com

Nevada Smith's
74 3rd Ave.
Map 4 F1.
Tel (212) 982-2591.

NY City Parks & Recreation Department
Arsenal Building,
64th St & 5th Ave.
Map 12 F2.
Tel (212) 408-0100.
www.nycgovparks.org

Pioneer Bar
218 Bowery.
Map 4 F3.
Tel (212) 334-0484.

Plaza Rink
1 Rockefeller Plaza,
5th Ave.
Map 12 F5.
Tel (212) 332-7654.

Shea Stadium
126th St at Roosevelt Ave,
Flushing, Queens.
Tel (718) 507-8499.

Slate Billiards
54 W 21st St.
Map 8 E4.
Tel (212) 989-0096.

Ticketmaster
Tel (212) 307-4100.
www.ticketmaster.com

Ticketron
Tel (212) 239-6200,
1-800-432-7250.
www.telecharge.com

Wollman Memorial Rink
Central Park,
5th Ave at 59th St.
Map 12 F2.
Tel (212) 439-6900.

Yankee Stadium
161st and 164th sts,
The Bronx.
Tel (718) 293-4300.

Yonkers Raceway
Yonkers,
Westchester County.
Tel (914) 968-4200.

Fitness and Wellbeing

New York City may be (in)famous for its concrete, crowds, and cacophony, but the urban jungle is a boon for sports and fitness aficionados. A host of possibilities beckon, from pedaling on the sun-washed riverfront and jogging under the shadow of Manhattan's signature skyline at the Central Park Reservoir to scaling a soaring climbing wall at one of the city's many upscale gyms, indulging in a massage at gorgeous spa strewn with rose petals and finding your inner Om in the lotus position at a yoga class.

CYCLING

There's nothing like being stuck in midtown traffic to make you long for pedaling the open road. While Manhattan may be one of the most crowded islands on the planet, it offers a surprising 120 km (75 miles) of bike trails. At the last count, Manhattan boasted more than 110,000 everyday cyclists. One of the most pleasant places to cycle is in Central Park during the weekend, when it's closed to cars. Bikes may be rented from **Central Park Bike Rentals** on Columbus Circle. If you would like to feel the river breeze in your hair, pedal the well-maintained bike path along the West Side Highway that runs parallel to the Hudson River, or hit the bike trails in Riverside Park. On summer weekends, the paths can get exasperatingly congested, but if you go early or late in the day, or in the winter months, you can often coast solo.

The friendly folks at **Bicycle Habitat** on Lafayette Street rent bikes and dole out tips on getting around New York by bike.

FITNESS CENTERS, GYMS, AND HEALTH CLUBS

In New York, a weekly workout has become almost de rigueur for even the most extreme workaholics. Gyms and health clubs have sprouted across the city to accommodate the demand, and serious sweating goes on at all hours, day and night. The options are endless: Get your aggression out with a punch bag, increase your heart rate on the stairmaster, or pump iron. Most major hotels have fitness centers. Many commercial gyms and health clubs are open only to members, but an increasing number of gyms now offer day passes. Check out the **Chelsea Piers Sports & Entertainment Complex** on Piers 59–62 near Hudson River; there's something for everyone at this enormous facility. It's one-stop shopping at the multilevel **May Center for Health, Fitness, and Sport at the 92nd Street Y**, with exercise studios, weight-training, racquetball courts, a boxing room, and an indoor track. Day passes start at around $35. With its well-maintained gym along with an array of personal diet and exercise programs, the **Casa Spa & Fitness at the Regency Hotel** on Park Avenue lives up to its promise to be "your health and fitness oasis when you're away from home".

You can enjoy a wide range of activities at **YMCA** (one in West Side and the other on 47th Street) fitness centers. The state-of-the-art training equipment, a number of gymnasiums, swimming pools, aerobics studios, running/walking tracks, and various courts for different games, add to your enthusiasm of working out. The center also has special programs for elderly people designed to suit their physical stature for a healthy life.

GOLF

Practice your swing at **Randalls Island Golf Center** on Randalls Island, **Chelsea Golf Club**, or play mini-golf at the **Wollman Memorial Rink** in Central Park. The city owns several courses in the boroughs, such as **Pelham Bay Park** in the Bronx and **Silver Lake** on Staten Island.

JOGGING

Some parks are safe for joggers, others are not, so be guided by your concierge. None is safe after dark, at dusk or before dawn. The most popular and beautiful route is around the reservoir in Central Park. The **NY Road Runners** on 89th Street have weekly running clinics and races, as does **Chelsea Piers Sports & Entertainment Complex**.

PILATES

All you have to lose are your love handles. Work your abs and torso for lean, toned muscles at a Pilates class. The philosophy behind Pilates is based on the premise that the body's core is the "powerhouse" for the peripheral parts of the body. Challenge your muscles at a **Grasshopper Pilates** class, which is taught by a professionally trained dancer in a TriBeCa loft. **Power Pilates** also hold strengthening classes throughout the city.

YOGA

It's easier to get in touch your spiritual center when you can do it in a place like the airy **Exhale Mind Body Spa** on Madison Avenue, with its high ceilings and hard-wood floors. "Journey into the Core", "Ride the Vinyasa Wave", and "Dance into Trance" at a variety of yoga sessions, the ideal antidote to the city's madness. And, lest you should think yoga isn't enough of a work-out, then you haven't tried the core fusion power pack abs session. **YogaMoves** on Sixth Avenue also offers a wide range of yoga classes, from beginner to advanced.

SPAS

Pamper yourself at one of New York City's choice spas and you'll emerge fresh as a daisy – and ready to take on the urban jungle once again. Most spas offer packages where you can enjoy several treatments at a lower price. If you're travelling with your significant other, bond over a couples' massage. The intoxicating wafts of incense that greet you at the front door of the fragrant, low-lit **Clay** are just a hint of the luxurious massage that awaits within.

At the comfy, casual **Oasis Day Spa** at Union Square, select from six aromatherapy massages ($100) in aromas of uplift, refresh, balance, passion, calm, or relief. Men's specials include a Dead Sea salt scrub, an algae facial, or a muscle meltdown massage ($100 for an hour). For a slice of heaven, Bali style, disappear into the **Acqua Beauty Bar** on 14th Street and enjoy a botanical purifying facial ($115), orchid pedicure ($45), or Indonesian ritual of beauty ($170), where your skin is scrubbed with ground rice and kneaded with fragrant oils. Enter **Bliss** on 57th Street and you'll soon discover that there's nothing a carrot and sesame body buff ($195) or fully loaded facial ($195) can't cure. Top it off with a decadent double chocolate pedicure, accompanied by a cup of creamy cocoa. Pure bliss.

Celebrities including Antonio Banderas and Kate Moss swear by **Mario Badescu** on 52nd Street whose facials and body scrubs, including the fresh fruit body scrub, with plump raspberries and strawberries, are as legendary as the beauty products, which are perfect to bring home as gifts.

SWIMMING

Many Manhattan hotels have pools with free access during your stay. It is also possible to purchase a day pass to use a hotel swimming pool and facilities – for example, at Le Parker Meridien *(see p286)*. You can also swim and surf at the Surfside 3 Maritime Center at **Chelsea Piers**. For a day trip, go to Jones Beach State Park *(see p255)* along Long Island's shoreline.

INDOOR SPORTS

Chelsea Piers has it all: roller rinks, bowling, indoor soccer, basketball, rock-climbing walls, fitness centers, golf, a field house for gymnastics, sports medicine, spa centers, and of course, swimming pools. This huge complex, which is spread over four old West Side piers, is open to everyone.

Apart from providing fitness centers, gymnasium facilities, and indoor sports activities **YMCA** also offers exercise, balance, and flexibility classes; organizes day trips; special events; and sports and volunteer opportunities. If you are planning an adventurous day out for your children with fitness on the agenda or for burning extra calories then the club is worth a visit.

DIRECTORY

Acqua Beauty Bar
7 E 14th St. **Map** 8 F5.
Tel (212) 620-4329.

Bicycle Habitat
244 Lafayette St.
Map 4 F3.
Tel (212) 431-3315.

Bliss
19 E 57th St.
Map 12 F3.
Tel (212) 219-8970.
(Also has a SoHo location).

Casa Spa & Fitness at the Regency Hotel
540 Park Ave.
Map 13 A3.
Tel (212) 223-9280.

Central Park Bike Rental
2 Columbus Circle.
Map 12 D3.
Tel (212) 541-8759.

Chelsea Piers Sports & Entertainment Complex
Piers 59–62 at 23rd St & 11th Ave (Hudson River).
Map 7 B4–5.
Tel (212) 336-6000.
www.chelseapiers.com

Clay
25 W 14th St.
Map 4 D1.
Tel (212) 206-9200.

Exhale Mind Body Spa
980 Madison Ave.
Map 17 A5.
Tel (212) 561-6400.

Grasshopper Pilates
116 Franklin St.
Map 4 E5.
Tel (212) 431-5225.

NY Road Runners
9 E 89th St.
Map 17 A3.
Tel (212) 860-4455.

Mario Badescu
320 E 52nd St.
Map 13 B4.
Tel (212) 758-1065.

May Center for Health, Fitness, and Sport at the 92nd Street Y
1395 Lexington Ave.
Map 17 A2.
Tel (212) 415-5729.

Oasis Day Spa
108 E 16th St.
Map 9 A5.
Tel (212) 254-7722.
One of several branches.

Pelham Bay Park
The Bronx,
870 Shore Rd.
Tel (718) 885-1461.

Power Pilates
49 W 23rd St,
10th floor.
Map 8 F4.
Tel (212) 627-5852.

Randalls Island Golf Center
Randalls Island.
Map 22 F2.
Tel (212) 427-5689.

YMCA West Side
1395 Lexington Ave.
Map 17 A2.
Tel (212) 415-5500.

Silver Lake
915 Victory Blvd.
Staten Island.
Tel (718) 447-5686.

Wollman Memorial Rink
Central Park, 5th Ave at 59th St. **Map** 12 F2.
Tel (212) 439-6900.

YMCA 47th St
224 E 47th St.
Map 13 B5.
Tel (212) 756-9600.

YogaMoves
1026 6th Ave.
Map 8 E1.
Tel (212) 278-8330.

CHILDREN'S NEW YORK

Young visitors soon catch the contagious excitement in the air in New York. Attractions for all ages abound, and plenty are designed especially for children. More than a dozen theater companies, two zoos, and plenty of imaginative museums are for just the young, backed up with special events at many museums and parks. The chance to visit a TV studio is a treat, and New York's own Big Apple Circus is a perennial delight. With more to do than can ever be squeezed into a single visit, you'll never hear the cry "I'm bored!" Best of all, there's no need to spend a fortune to have fun.

A young visitor making New York his very own playground

PRACTICAL ADVICE

New York is family-friendly. Many of its hotels allow children in parents' rooms free, and will supply cots or cribs if needed. Most museums charge half price or less for children, while others are free. Children under 112 cm (44 in) also ride free on subways and buses when accompanied by an adult. Travel between 9am and 4pm to avoid rush hours.

Supplies such as diapers and medicines are readily available, and the Rite Aid Pharmacy *(see p373)* is open 24 hours a day. Finding changing tables in public toilets is less easy, but no one objects if a counter is used. Best bets are the facilities in libraries, hotels, and department stores. Most hotels will arrange baby-sitters; try **Baby Sitters' Guild** or **Pinch Sitters**.

To find out more about the range of current activities for children, get a copy of the free quarterly calendar of events, available from the New York Convention and Visitors Bureau *(see p368)*. Weekly listings can be found in *New York* magazine or *Time Out New York*.

NEW YORK ADVENTURES

The city can seem like a giant amusement park for youngsters. Elevators whisk you sky-high for bird's-eye views from atop the world's highest buildings. You can set sail on the classic **Circle Line** tour around Manhattan; the sailboat **Pioneer** *(see p84)*, or charter your own paddle-wheeler from the marina at E. 23rd St; or the free round-trip on the Staten Island Ferry *(see p76)*. The Roosevelt Island Tram *(see p181)* is a Swiss cable car offering an airborne ride over the East River. Central Park *(see pp204–9)* is a source of rides of every kind – from the old-fashioned charm of the carousel to real horseback and ponycart rides. Children who prefer a faster

Skating with Santa at Rockefeller Center

pace can join the skate-boarders and in-line skaters who cruise around the traffic-free park every weekend.

Cooling off in a playground in Central Park

MUSEUMS

While many of New York's museums appeal to all ages, some are designed just for the young. High on the list are the Children's Museum of Art *(see p107)*, where kids can paint and sculpt, and the Children's Museum of Manhattan *(see p219)*, a multimedia world in which children produce their own videos and newscasts. Farther afield are the **Staten Island Children's Museum**, where a huge climb-through anthill is one of the favorite items, and the Brooklyn Children's Museum *(see p247)*. The *Intrepid* Sea-Air-Space Museum *(see p149)* is a real aircraft carrier. Finally, don't miss the dinosaur display at the American Museum of Natural History *(see pp216–17)*.

OUTDOOR FUN

In summer, all of New York comes out to play. Central Park is a child's wonderland, from skating rinks to boating lakes, bicycle paths to miniature golf. The park offers free entertainment – such as guided walks by park rangers on Saturdays, toy sailboat races and summer storytelling. The Central Park Wildlife Center and the Tisch Children's Zoo are favorites.

Children of all ages will be fascinated by the Bronx Zoo/ Wildlife Conservation Park which is home to over 500 species (see pp244–5).

Coney Island (see p249) is just a subway ride away. Winter brings the chance to skate at Rockefeller Center (see p144) or in Central Park on a rink fringed with views of skyscrapers.

INDOOR FUN

New York children's theater is of a quality and variety matching that for adults. Some favorite companies are the **Paper Bag Players** and **Theaterworks USA**, whose shows sell out fast; get schedules and reserve seats early.

The **Swedish Marionette Theater** in Central Park has shows at 10:30am and noon Tuesdays through Fridays, and Saturdays until 1pm.

The New York City Ballet's annual Christmas production of *The Nutcracker* at Lincoln Center (see p212) opens at the same time that the **Big Apple Circus** sets up its tent nearby. Ringling Brothers and Barnum & Bailey Circus is in action at Madison Square Garden (see p135) each spring.

Opportunities for youngsters to work off energy in winter are many, from indoor skating rinks to mini-golf and bowling alleys at **Chelsea Piers**. Kids can create video games, movies, and music for free at **Sony Wonder Technology Lab**.

Centerpiece clock at toy store
F.A.O. Schwarz

SHOPPING

There will be no complaints about shopping trips if they include the huge **F.A.O. Schwarz** or **Toys 'R' Us** for a vast range of wonderful toys and other items. For more information on other toystores see New York Originals on pages 322–4. Youngsters are welcomed for storytelling sessions at **Books of Wonder**.

EATING OUT

Hamburger-and-pasta joint **Ottomanelli's Café** is very popular with children, and even adults find it hard to finish their huge burgers. The colorful **S'Mac**, where the specialty is creamy macaroni and cheese, is also a hit with youngsters. The lively **Hard Rock Café** is also popular, and most children enjoy the foods sold around Chinatown and Little Italy. Drop into the **Chinatown Ice Cream Factory** for some strange and wonderful flavors. For a quick hot snack, try pizza-by-the-slice or pretzels and hot dogs from street vendors.

DIRECTORY

PRACTICAL ADVICE

Baby Sitters' Guild
Tel (212) 682-0227.

Pinch Sitters
Tel (212) 260-6005.

ADVENTURES

Circle Line
Pier 83, W 42nd St. **Map** 7 A1.
Tel (212) 563-3200.

MUSEUMS

Staten Island Children's Museum
1000 Richmond Terr, Staten Is.
Tel (718) 273-2060.

INDOOR FUN

Big Apple Circus
Tel (212) 268-2500.

Chelsea Piers
Tel (212) 336-6800.
www.chelseapiers.com

Paper Bag Players
Tel (212) 663-0390.

Sony Wonder Technology Lab
550 Madison Ave. **Map** 13 A3.
Tel (212) 833-8100.

Swedish Cottage Marionette Theater
Tel (212) 988-9093.

Theaterworks USA
787 7th Ave. **Map** 12 E4.
Tel (212) 627-7373.

SHOPPING

Books of Wonder
16 W 18th St. **Map** 8 C5.
Tel (212) 989-3270.

F.A.O. Schwarz
767 5th Ave. **Map** 12 F3.
Tel (212) 644-9400.

Toys 'R' Us
See p324.

EATING OUT

Chinatown Ice Cream Factory
65 Bayard St. **Map** 4 F5.
Tel (212) 608-4170.

Hard Rock Café
1501 Broadway. **Map** 8 E1.
Tel (212) 343-3355.

Ottomanelli's Café
1626 York Ave. **Map** 17 C3.
Tel (212) 772-7722.

S'Mac
345 E 12th St. **Map** 5 A1.
Tel (212) 358-7912.

Storytelling session at South Street Seaport

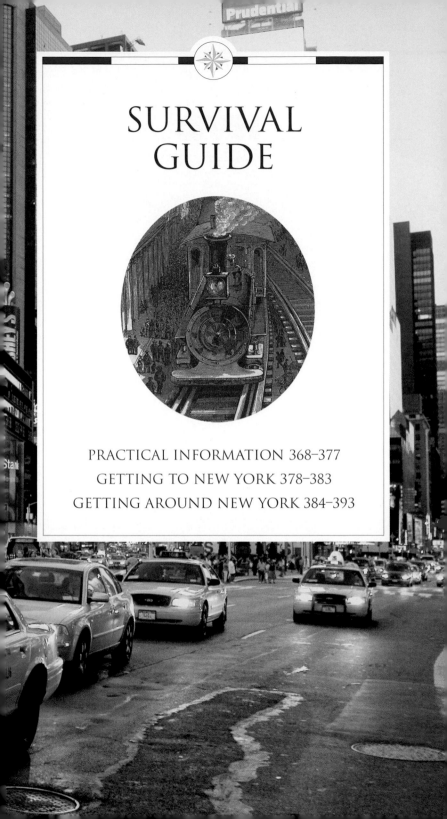

SURVIVAL GUIDE

PRACTICAL INFORMATION

New York is one of the most diverse and exciting cities in the world. The fast pace of Manhattan may seem daunting at first, but there are many services to help tourists, and you will find the city is safe and easy to explore. Midtown streets are straight and mostly laid out in an easy-to-follow grid pattern. Buses and subway trains *(see pp388–91)* are reliable and cheap; there are plenty of cash machines *(see p374)*, and money can be easily exchanged at banks and hotels. The wide range of prices offered by the many hotels *(see pp280–91)*, restaurants *(see pp296–311)*, and entertainment venues *(see pp340–65)* in the city means that your New York trip can be both fun and affordable.

New York City tourist office logo

Skaters at an ice rink in Central Park

WHEN TO GO

September and October are the prize months in New York, offering warm days, cool nights, and colorful leaves in the city parks. Late spring is also appealing, when the city is less crowded and humid. Summers can be unpleasantly hot, but there are attractions such as outdoor concerts, plays, and sporting events to keep visitors busy. Christmas in the city is wonderful, although you will have to share your experience with hundreds of other tourists. Weather-wise, any season can be unpredictable; always pack layers and be prepared for changes.

VISAS AND PASSPORTS

All visitors to the United States require passports valid for at least six months after the dates of travel. Citizens of Great Britain, Australia, New Zealand, and 32 other countries, including most EU countries, do not need visas if they are staying in the US for 90 days or less. However, they must apply and pay for entry online via the Electronic System for Travel Authorization (ESTA). The ESTA is valid for up to two years and can be used for multiple entries into the US (https://esta.cbp.dhs.gov/).

Canadians must show their passports when entering the US by air, and a passport or an enhanced driver's license proving citizenship when arriving by land or sea.

Those requiring a visa should apply in person at the nearest US embassy or consulate in their own country. It is vital to begin the process early, allowing sufficient time for processing the application. Some services will expedite the process for a fee. Visit http://travel.state.gov for more details.

CUSTOMS INFORMATION

Customs allowances per person when you enter the US are 200 cigarettes, 100 cigars, or 4.4 lb (2 kg) of tobacco; no more than 2 pints (1 liter) of alcohol; and gifts worth no more than $100. Many foods, including fruits and vegetables, are prohibited from entering the United States. Baked items, candy, chocolate, and cured cheese are exceptions, as are canned goods (other than those containing meat or poultry products) if being imported for personal use.

Upon arrival at one of New York's airports, follow signs stating "other than American passports" to immigration counters, where your passport will be stamped. Next, reclaim your bags from the appropriate area and proceed to a customs officer, who will examine the customs declaration that you should have received and filled in on your flight.

TOURIST INFORMATION

Advice on any aspect of life in New York City is available from the New York Convention & Visitors Bureau, known as **NYC & Co.** Its 24-hour touch-tone phone service *(see p371)* offers help

New York tourist information office

outside office hours. New York City has another free phone and Internet service, **311**, which provides government information and non-emergency general assistance. Calls are answered by a team 24 hours a day, with a translation service.

SMOKING AND ETIQUETTE

It is illegal to smoke in any public place or building in New York, including restaurants, and this law is taken very seriously.

When boarding buses, New Yorkers generally form a line rather than pushing to enter. Subway boarders are not so polite at rush hours, but do stand aside to let passengers exit before rushing in. Turning off cell phones in theaters, cinemas and museums is expected. Casual wear is accepted in many places in New York City, but some establishments may require formal dress, check when you make a reservation.

ADMISSION PRICES

New York can be expensive for visitors, though you can often find a way to avoid high charges. Museum prices can run from $12 to $20, but some galleries, such as the Metropolitan Museum, call their charge a "suggested donation," leaving it to the visitor to decide what to pay. On Friday evenings, the Museum of Modern Art, Whitney Museum, Folk Art Museum, and Guggenheim Museum are open late and are free or have a "pay what you wish" policy. The Jewish Museum is free all day Saturday, while the Brooklyn Museum offers free art and entertainment on the first Saturday of the month (5–11pm). Consult local listings for museums of interest to you. The **New York Pass** and **CityPass** *(see p370)*, offer discounted entry to some 50 attractions.

OPENING HOURS

Business hours are generally from 9am to 5pm, with no lunchtime closing. Many midtown stores stay open until 7pm to accommodate people in full-time jobs, and they may close even later on Thursdays, at 8:30 or 9pm. Most stores are also open from noon to 6pm on Sundays.

Typical banking hours run from 9am to 6pm, Monday to Friday; some banks also open on Saturdays from 9am to 3pm. ATM machines are available 24 hours for credit and debit card cash withdrawals *(see p374)*.

Closing days vary for the major museums, as do the evenings they are open late, although most tend to be closed on a Monday. The Museum of Modern Art is closed on Tuesdays however, while the Guggenheim closes on Thursdays. Phone ahead of your visit, or check the website, before planning your itinerary.

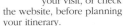
The New York Pass and CityPass

New York's traffic rush hours extend roughly from 8 to 10am and 4:30 to 6:30pm, Monday to Friday. During these times, every form of public transportation will be crowded, as will pedestrian streets.

PUBLIC CONVENIENCES

New York City does not provide public bathrooms. City information centers, department stores, large

The entrance to the Guggenheim Museum *(see pp188–9)*

bookstores (Barnes & Noble, Borders), and big restaurant chains (Starbucks, McDonald's) offer free restrooms, as do most hotels. Bathrooms are also available in train and bus stations, but these are not always the most pleasant options.

TAXES AND TIPPING

Sales tax in New York is 8.875%, and it is added to all purchases (including meals), except for clothing under $100. Tipping is an integral part of New York life: taxi drivers expect 10–15%; cocktail waiters 15%, hotel room service 10% (when not added to the bill); coat check $1; hotel maids $1 or $2 per day after the first day; hotel bellhops about $1 per bag; hairstylists 15–20%, and barbers 10–20%. Waiters generally receive 15–20% of the bill, not including tax. A quick way to calculate restaurant tips is simply to double the tax, adding up to about 18%.

Many stores have late opening hours to accommodate workers

City bus with access ramp lowered for a disabled passenger

TRAVELERS WITH SPECIAL NEEDS

All city buses have ramps for easy access. Subways, however, are a challenge for the disabled, as most stations are accessed via steps from the street. Only the busiest stops and stations, such as Grand Central and Penn stations and the Port Authority Bus Terminal, have elevators. A list of accessible stations is available on the Metropolitan Transit Authority website (www.mta.info).

Most hotels, restaurants, and attractions are equipped for disabled visitors, but do check in advance. It is also wise to ask about accessibility to the restrooms.

Some museums offer tours for deaf, blind, or disabled visitors, and all Broadway theaters have devices for the hearing-impaired. The *Official Accessibility Guide*, available free from the **Mayor's Office for People with Disabilities**, is a great resource, as is *Access for All*, published by **Hospital Audiences**. Both detail disabled access at public places such as museums, landmarks, theaters, and stadiums.

SENIOR TRAVELERS

Seniors are welcomed in New York, and they are eligible for many offers. They travel half-fare on all subways and buses and get discounted prices at museums, movie theaters, and many sightseeing attractions. City buses can lower the entry steps to make it easier for older passengers to board.

GAY AND LESBIAN TRAVELERS

New York has a large gay and lesbian population. Gay Pride Week in June brings celebrants from around the world for parties and a big parade, the annual Halloween parade in Greenwich Village has a large gay following. The **Lesbian, Gay, Bisexual & Transgender Community Center** is a good first stop for general information. Christopher Street in Greenwich Village is the epicenter of New York's gay scene. Eighth Avenue around Chelsea is an increasingly popular neighborhood, and Park Slope in Brooklyn is a hotspot for the lesbian community. **Next** (www.next magazine.com) is a free weekly publication that can be found in these areas. The monthly **GO Magazine** (www.gomag. com) covers the lesbian scene, and both *Time Out New York* (*see p377*) and the *New York Magazine* website (www. nymag.com) have gay and lesbian listings for venues.

Sign for the Lesbian, Gay, Bisexual & Transgender Community Center

STUDENT TRAVELERS

Many museums and theaters in New York offer discounted admission for students. To receive this, however, you will need to show proof of your student status. An **International Student Identity Card (ISIC)** can be purchased quite cheaply, provided you have the right credentials, from **STA Travel**, which has two branches in New York. At the same time, ask for a copy of the *ISIC Student Handbook*, which lists places and services that offer discounts to cardholders, including selected accommodations, various museums, tours, theaters, attractions, nightclubs, and restaurants.

Although it is very difficult to obtain permission to work in the US, students are eligible to work as part of exchange programs or as interns. Again, STA Travel can provide you with further details.

Note that the minimum age for drinking in New York is 21, and patrons may be asked for proof of age.

International Student Identity Card

TRAVELING ON A BUDGET

There are many ways to take advantage of the best of New York while on a budget. The TKTS booth (*see p341*), near Times Square, offers half-price admission to same-day Broadway shows, while pre-theater prix-fixe meals save on dining. The David Rubenstein Atrium, across from the Lincoln Center (*see p214*), offers discount tickets for same-day performances, in addition to a free concert in the Atrium itself on Thursdays at 8:30pm. The New York Philharmonic invites visitors to rehearsals for just $16, and the Juilliard School (*see p214*) also presents free concerts. In summer, free Shakespeare plays and music by the Philharmonic and the Metropolitan Opera are performed in Central Park. Many TV shows produced in the city are free if you request tickets in advance. The **New York CityPass**, while not cheap, is good value for those who plan to do a lot of sightseeing. It offers free entry to over 50 attractions, from museums to the Empire State Building and river cruises. It also offers a 15% discount on one- or two-day NBC studio tours.

TIME

New York is on Eastern Standard Time from early November to mid-March.

Eastern Daylight Time moves the American clock forward 1 hour the rest of the year.

Add 5 hours for the time in London, 8 hours for Moscow, 14 hours for Tokyo, and 16 hours for Sydney.

ELECTRICAL APPLIANCES

All American electric current flows at a standardized 110 to 120 volts AC (alternating current). You will need to bring an adapter plug and a voltage convertor that fits standard US electrical outlets. US plugs have two flat prongs.

Most New York hotels provide wall-mounted electric hair dryers in bathrooms. In addition, some hotels have wall plugs capable of powering both 110- and 220-volt electric shavers, but little else – not even radios. It can, in fact, be dangerous to connect anything more powerful.

Few New York hotel rooms provide coffee-makers; however, most have radios and clocks, and a large number have iPod docking stations. If you require an iron and ironing board but they are not in the room, ask room service.

CONVERSION CHART

Bear in mind that 1 US pint (0.5 liter) is a smaller measure than 1 UK pint (0.6 liter).

Imperial to Metric
1 inch = 2.5 centimeters
1 foot = 30 centimeters
1 mile = 1.6 kilometers
1 ounce = 28 grams
1 pound = 454 grams
1 US pint = 0.47 liter
1 US gallon = 3.8 liters

Metric to Imperial
1 millimeter = 0.04 inch
1 centimeter = 0.4 inch
1 meter = 3 feet 3 inches
1 kilometer = 0.6 mile
1 gram = 0.04 ounce

RESPONSIBLE TOURISM

New York is increasingly aware of "green issues." Proper recycling bins, with separate areas for paper and plastic, are widely available. Most hotels encourage guests to be ecologically aware and not request fresh towels every day. Shoppers tend to carry reusable cloth shopping bags, which are sold in almost every department store and

Fresh local produce for sale at one of New York's Greenmarkets

supermarket. Most markets carry organic foods, and the city's many neighborhood Greenmarkets are popular sources of locally grown produce. The **Greenmarket at Union Square** (Mon, Wed, Fri, and Sat) is one of the best. Opening times vary.

You can contribute to these green efforts by patronizing restaurants that use locally grown produce. **5 Points** and **Gramercy Tavern** are two popular restaurants that have been given the **Slow Food NYC** seal of approval.

DIRECTORY

EMBASSIES AND CONSULATES

Australia
150 E 42nd St. **Map** 9 A1.
Tel (212) 351-6500.
www.australianyc.org

Britain
845 Third Ave. **Map** 13 B4.
Tel (212) 745-0200.
www.britainusa.com/ny

Canada
1251 Sixth Ave at 50th St.
Map 12 E4.
Tel (212) 596-1628.
www.canada-ny.org

Ireland
345 Park Ave. **Map** 13 A4.
Tel (212) 319-2555.
www.irelandemb.org

New Zealand
37 Observatory Circle, NW,
Washington, DC, 20008.
Tel (202) 328-4800.
www.nzembassy.org

TOURIST INFORMATION

311
Tel 311.
www.nyc.gov/311

NYC & Co.
810 Seventh Ave. **Map** 12
E4. *Tel (212) 484-1222.*
www.nycgo.com

New York CityPass
www.citypass.com/city/ny

Times Square Information Center
1560 Broadway.
Map 12 E5.
www.timessquarenyc.org

TRAVELERS WITH SPECIAL NEEDS

Hospital Audiences
Tel (212) 575-7676.
www.hospital
audiences.org

Mayor's Office for People with Disabilities
Tel (212) 788-2830.
www.nyc.gov/mopd

GAY AND LESBIAN TRAVELERS

Lesbian, Gay, Bisexual & Transgender Community Center
208 West 13th St. **Map** 3
C1. *Tel (212) 620-7310.*
www.gaycenter.org

STUDENT TRAVELERS

International Student Identity Card (ISIC)
www.isic.org

STA Travel
30 Third Avenue.
Map 4 F1.
Tel (212) 473-6100.

Also at: 2871 Broadway.
Map 20 E4.
Tel (212) 865-2700.
www.statravel.com

BUDGET TRAVEL

www.nycgo.com/free
www.nyc.gov/nyculture

RESPONSIBLE TOURISM

5 Points
31 Great Jones St. **Map** 4
F2. *Tel (212) 253-5700.*
www.fivepoints
restaurant.com

Gramercy Tavern
42 East 20th St. **Map** 9 A5.
Tel (212) 477-6777.
www.gramercytaven.com

Greenmarket at Union Square
Union Square. **Map** 9 A5.
www.cenyc.org

Slow Food NYC
www.slowfoodnyc.org

Personal Security and Health

Police badge

New York is one of the US's safest large cities. There is a good level of security in midtown, the transportation system, and at airports, and the city's police force is very much in evidence around Manhattan. As in any major metropolis, there are places where travelers would be foolish to venture after dark alone, such as city parks and quiet streets. But if you keep your wits about you and stick to the following guidelines, you should enjoy a trouble-free and pleasant visit to New York City.

New York City police officers patrolling the streets

POLICE

The New York Police Department has around-the-clock foot, horse, bike, and car patrols. These are concentrated in specific areas at critical times – for instance, the Theater District after show times. There is also a police presence on the subways and buses, and this is reflected in the dramatic drop in crime statistics.

LOST AND STOLEN PROPERTY

There is no city-wide lost-and-found service, but the Metropolitan Transit Authority (MTA) *(see p391)* has a lost-and-found department for city buses and subways, and the Taxi Commission *(see p387)* will help passengers who have left their belongings in a cab. The lost-and-found rooms at Grand Central and Penn stations are well run, with helpful staff. If you don't know who to contact, phone 311 for guidance.

In the event of loss or theft of valuables, report all missing items to the police, or **Crime Victims Hot Line** and make sure you get a copy of the police report for your insurance claim. It is wise to keep the receipts of expensive items as proof of possession.

If your passport is stolen, report the theft immediately to your consulate *(see p371)*. Lost or stolen credit cards should also be reported promptly so that your account can be blocked. American Express *(see p375)* has offices in the city where new cards can be processed quickly, and other card companies can often provide replacements. It is always a good idea to separate your credit and debit cards so that if a wallet is lost, you have a backup card.

WHAT TO BE AWARE OF

Manhattan has become quite a safe place to roam, but pickpockets do operate and common sense still rules, as in any big city. Be alert, and walk as if you know where you're going. Avoid eye contact and confrontations with down-and-outs. If someone asks you for money, be careful and do not be drawn into conversation.

It is better to avoid deserted locations late at night. Even if there is no actual danger, empty streets may make you feel uneasy. Neighborhoods such as parts of the Lower East Side, Chinatown, or midtown west of Broadway bustle through dinner hours but feel empty after 10pm or so. The Financial District (except for the World Financial Center) is deserted after business hours, and even the very trendy TriBeCa and SoHo areas are empty late at night. Subways stay crowded until around 11pm but may not be advisable later. If you can't find or afford a taxi, try to travel with a group and keep to the main streets.

Parks are not recommended after dark, unless there is a concert or other event. If you want to go for a jog, ask your hotel concierge for a map of safe routes. In crowds, take precautions to avoid being pickpocketed.

When walking in the street, keep your wallet in an inconspicuous place, never in a back pocket, and have your MetroCard or change handy for bus fares – it's best not to have to dig into your purse or wallet while standing in line. Never stop to count your money on the street, and be

It is best to travel in groups and stick to the main streets and avenues

Police car

Ambulance

Fire engine

aware of strangers watching at bank ATMs. Defeat purse snatchers by carrying your bag with the clasp facing toward you and the shoulder strap across your body.

Wise travelers always leave valuable jewelry at home or stored at the hotel. Do not allow anyone except hotel and airport personnel to carry your luggage or parcels, and stow your valuables and camera in a locked suitcase or a closet safe when you leave your hotel room.

IN AN EMERGENCY

If you should be involved in a medical emergency, proceed at once to a hospital emergency room. Dial **411**, and ask the operator to give you the number of the nearest hospital. Should you need an ambulance, telephone **911**, and one will be sent. If you have time and a choice, avoid the crowded city-owned hospitals listed in the Blue Pages telephone book. Instead, choose one of the many private hospitals listed in the Yellow Pages (see also

Directory box). If your travel medical insurance is in order, you won't have to worry about costs, but remember that national insurance in other countries is not valid in the US.

If the situation is not urgent, ask your hotel to call a doctor or dentist to visit you in your room or to recommend one. You can find one yourself through the **NY Hotel Urgent Medical Services** or **NYU Dental Care**. The Beth Israel Medical Center has an excellent walk-in clinic, **DOCS**. For more general advice and information, call **Travelers' Aid**, a national organization geared to helping travelers. Note that the cost of prescriptions may be higher than in your home country.

HOSPITALS AND PHARMACIES

If you must visit a doctor or hospital, be prepared to undergo an expensive experience: some of the city's practitioners and facilities are among the best in the country, and they charge accordingly. The best way to protect yourself against large medical costs is with comprehensive travel insurance. Note that you will have to pay and then reclaim the money. Hospitals accept most credit cards, but physicians and dentists are more likely to want payment in cash. The city has many 24-hour pharmacies, some will often fill a prescription while you wait.

A 24-hour pharmacy, one of several in the city

TRAVEL INSURANCE

Travel insurance is highly recommended, mainly because of the high cost of medical care. There are many types and levels of coverage, with prices dependent on the length of your trip and the number of people covered.

Among the most important features are emergency medical and dental care, trip cancellation, baggage and travel-document loss, and accidental dismemberment or death. Many policies will cover all of these items.

DIRECTORY

POLICE

All Emergency Services
Tel 911 (or 0).

Crime Victims Hot Line
Tel (212) 577-7777.

IN AN EMERGENCY

DOCS
55 E 34th St. **Map** 8 F2.
Tel (212) 252-6000.
One of three branches.

NY Hotel Urgent Medical Services
Tel (212) 737-1212.

NYU Dental Care
345 E 24th St/First Ave.
Map 9 B4. *Tel* (212) 998-9800,
(212) 998-9828 (weekends and after 9pm).

Travelers' Aid
JFK Airport, Terminal 410.
Tel (718) 656-4870.

HOSPITALS AND PHARMACIES

Duane Reade
4 Times Square, near Broadway.
Map 8 E1. *Tel* (646) 366-8047.

Midtown Hospital Emergency Rooms
11th St and Seventh Ave.
Map 3 C1. *Tel* (212) 604-7998.

NYU Medical Center
560 First Avenue at 33rd Street.
Map 9 C3. *Tel* (212) 263-5550.

Rite Aid
50th St/Eighth Ave. **Map** 12 D4.
Tel (212) 247-8384.

St. Luke's Roosevelt
58th St and Ninth Ave. **Map** 12 D3.
Tel (212) 523-6800.

Banks and Currency

New York is the nation's banking center. It has a wealth of local, regional, and major national banks, plus some retail branches of the leading foreign banks. HSBC and Barclays are well represented in the city; the banks of Australia, Canada, Ireland, Scotland, Japan, and Turkey also all have offices or branches. Exchange bureaux are located in airports, the major train stations, and in various locations throughout the city, though you will probably get a better rate of exchange from a bank.

American Express charge cards

BANKING

New York banks are generally open weekdays from 9am to 6pm. Several banks open earlier or close later in the evening to suit commuters' needs, and many now stay open on Saturday 9am–3pm. Tellers are available to help customers inside the bank, or you can use a cash withdrawal machine (ATM). At most banks, all the tellers will cash traveler's checks and exchange your currency.

ATM (machine) for cash withdrawal

ATMS

Automated teller machines (ATMs) can be found in most bank lobbies. They enable you to obtain American currency 24 hours a day from your bank account using a debit card. ATMs usually issue American banknotes in $20 denominations. Among the many advantages of ATMs is the swift, secure exchange of your money at the whole-sale rate used between the banks. Bank fees are generally much lower than those charged by money-exchange offices. Before you leave for New York, ask your

bank which New York City banks and ATM systems will accept your bank card and what fees and commissions will be charged on each transaction. Most ATMs are part of either the Cirrus or the Plus network. They accept various US bank cards, MasterCard and Visa cards, and certain others.

On a more cautionary note, always be aware of your surroundings when using an ATM. Make sure you shield your PIN, and, if available, use a machine located within the bank. Be careful when removing your card at the machine.

CREDIT CARDS AND TRAVELER'S CHECKS

MasterCard, **American Express**, **Visa**, and **Diners Club** cards are widely accepted throughout the United States, regardless of which company or bank issued them. These cards can also be used for purchases, as well as to obtain cash advances from ATMs. Before you travel, it is a good idea to phone your card provider and inform them that you will be abroad, or you may find that your card gets blocked when you start using it in New York. Charges may be higher when using a credit card – check with your bank before you leave.

In the United States, you can use a credit card to pay for most purchases in store and online. Major expenses such as tours, travel packages, and expensive rentals are all best paid for by credit card. Using a card also means that you can avoid carrying large sums of money around with you.

Traveler's checks issued in dollars by American Express and **Thomas Cook** are widely accepted without a fee by most department stores, shops, hotels, and restaurants in New York. Traveler's checks in other currencies, including sterling, are not universally accepted. Major hotels may have cashiers that will exchange traveler's checks, but more often than not you will need to visit a bank. Exchange rates for foreign currency are printed daily in *The New York Times* and *Wall Street Journal* and may be posted in bank windows. American Express checks may also be exchanged without a fee at American Express offices.

Among the most well-established foreign-exchange brokers are **Travelex Currency Services Inc.** and American Express. All brokers are listed in the Yellow Pages under "Foreign Money Brokers." When you use the services of a foreign-exchange broker, you will have to pay a fee, which will vary widely from one place to the next. There will also be a commission.

Banking company **Chase** has over 400 locations where you can exchange money, and there are scores of hole-in-the-wall check-cashing shops in Manhattan. **TD Bank** also has branches throughout Manhattan, many of which are open on Saturdays and until 8pm on weekdays. Both Chase and TD Bank are listed in the Yellow Pages.

WIRING MONEY

In emergencies, you can arrange to have money wired to you through **MoneyGram** or **Western Union**, though there is a considerable fee.

Coins

American coins come in 1- , 5-, 10-, 25- and 50-cent pieces. A gold-tone $1 coin is also in circulation, as are the State quarters, which feature a historical scene on one side. One-dollar coins are not popular, however, and you will receive them mainly as change from vending machines. Each value of coin has a popular name: 25-cent pieces are called quarters, 10-cent pieces are called dimes, 5-cent pieces are called nickels, and 1-cent pieces are called pennies.

1-cent coin (a penny) **5-cent coin (a nickel)** **10-cent coin (a dime)** **25-cent coin (a quarter)**

Bank Notes (Bills)

The units of currency in the United States are dollars and cents. There are 100 cents to a dollar. Bank notes come in the following denominations: $1, $5, $10, $20, $50, and $100. Security features include subtle color hues and improved color-shifting ink in the lower right hand corner of the face of each note.

1-dollar bill ($1)

5-dollar bill ($5)

10-dollar bill ($10)

20-dollar bill ($20)

50-dollar bill ($50)

100-dollar bill ($100)

Communications and Media

Sign for public payphones

The wide use of cellular telephones and the Internet has changed the communications picture in most of the world, and New York is no exception. Though some public telephones may still be found in hotel lobbies, they have disappeared from city streets. Visitors will find the city is well supplied with mobile telephone stores, Internet cafés, and public access to computers and Wi-Fi. The variety of readily available local newspapers and magazines makes it easy for visitors to keep up with world news as well as the latest dining and entertainment options in the city. New York 1, the all-local TV outlet found at Channel 1, is a quick source for up-to-the minute weather reports and news.

Using a laptop in the New York Public Library

CELL PHONES

Visitors who wish to use their own cell phone in the US will need a tri-band phone and a SIM card that has been set up for "roaming." Ask your cell-phone provider if you are unsure whether your phone is ready to be used abroad.

Note that you are charged for the calls you receive as well as for the calls you make. However, some cell-phone companies offer "bundles" of calls to save costs while you are away.

If you are going to be in New York for some time, buy a sim card for better rates on local calls or rent a telephone. **Cellhire** offers rentals for $19 per week, with charges of 20 cents per minute and overseas rates from 49 cents.

PUBLIC TELEPHONES

If you can find a public tele-phone, you will see that the setup is standard. Few use credit cards, but you can buy prepaid phone cards from newsstands for long-distance calls; they can be bought in $5, $10, and $25 amounts. The cards offer good savings compared to standard rates. Most phones are coin-operated and take 5-, 10-, and 25-cent coins. In some locations the pay phone may belong to an independent company. The independents are often more expensive and less reliable. Regulations require each public pay phone to post information about charges, toll-free numbers, and how to make calls using other carriers. Look for the Verizon logo on the box to be sure the phone will reach all numbers at standard rates. Within all boroughs of New York City, the standard charge, around 25 cents, buys 3 minutes' talking time. International rates for calls dialed from a land line vary.

US Postal Service logo

REACHING THE RIGHT NUMBER

• Five area codes are used in New York: 212, 646, 917 (cell phones) are for Manhattan; the other boroughs use 718 and 347. Calls to 800, 888, 866, and 877 numbers are free.
• To call any number in Manhattan, even in your same area code, you must first dial 1.
• To make an international direct call, dial 011 followed by the country code (Australia: 61; New Zealand: 64; UK: 44), then the city or area code (minus the first 0) and the local number.
• International Directory Inquiries are on 00. International operator assistance is on 01.

INTERNET

Visitors will find many ways to access the Internet in New York. The **Times Square Information Center** provides free use, as does the **New York Public Library** at its main facilities and all 85 branches. Almost all hotels offer the use of computers, but some hotel business centers can be expensive. Most hotels also have Wi-Fi, though you may be charged to use it. (In hotels' public areas, however, Wi-Fi is often complimentary.) **FedEx Office Center** locations around town have computer rentals at 30 cents per minute. Rates are better at Internet cafés, which abound. Some, such as the **easyInternet café**, are huge; others, including **Cyber Café**, give more emphasis to the snacks and coffee available. Expect to pay about $6 for 30 minutes. **Web2Zone** offers cheap rates at quiet times.

There is free Wi-Fi at all libraries, Barnes & Noble stores, and in most city parks and plazas below 59th Street, including Bryant Park and Union Square. Cafés such as Starbucks has Wi-Fi for around 10 cents per minute.

POSTAL SERVICES

The city's main **General Post Office** is open 24 hours a day. Stamps can be bought here, from branch offices, and from some drugstores and newsstands. As well as at post offices, letters can be mailed at your hotel's concierge desk (which usually sells stamps too); in letter slots in office-building lobbies; and in street mailboxes. These are usually painted blue, or red, white, and blue. The mail is generally not picked up on Sundays. Post offices are shown on the Street Finder maps (see pp394–5).

All letters are sent first class. The post office also offers several special-delivery services: Express Mail service, for next-day delivery; Global Express Guaranteed, which delivers overseas in one–three days; and Express Mail International, with delivery in three–five days. Private express services such as **FedEx**, **UPS**, or **DHL** can be arranged through hotels. Online services are available.

NEWSPAPERS AND MAGAZINES

New York has one major daily newspaper, *The New York Times*, and two colorful tabloids, *The Daily News* and the *New York Post*. Two free morning tabloids are also available, *AM New York* and *Metro*. Both are useful for local events and a brief rundown of the news. The best entertainment listings are found in the Friday and Sunday editions of *The New York Times* and

in weekly magazines such as *Time Out New York*, *New York*, and *The New Yorker*. The *Village Voice*, a free weekly newspaper, also has entertainment listings, geared largely to a younger audience.

The free weekly *Where*, distributed through hotel concierges, lists major museums, their opening hours, locations, and any exhibitions. *Art Now/ New York Gallery Guide*, also free, is released in art galleries monthly. It lists current exhibitions and has maps showing where they are located.

You can buy foreign newspapers at **Universal News & Magazine**, **Hotalings**, **Barnes & Noble** bookstores, airports, and some hotels.

TELEVISION AND RADIO

TV program schedules for each day can be found in the local dailies. *The Daily News* on Sunday has a useful pull-out section of the next week's programs. The choice of TV stations in New York is vast. Major networks include CBS on channel 2, NBC on channel 4, ABC on channel 7, and WNYW (Fox) on channel 5. PBS offers cultural and educational fare on channel 13. Cable TV offers everything from the Arts & Entertainment Network (channel 46) to sports on ESPN (channel 28) and public-access programs.

AM radio stations include WCBS News (880AM), WINS News (1010AM), and WFAN Sports (660AM). Some FM stations are WWFS–contemporary (102.7FM), WBGO–jazz (88.3FM), and WQXR–classical (105.9FM).

DIRECTORY

USEFUL NUMBERS

Directory Inquiries
Tel 411 or 10-10-9000.
www.bigyellow.com
www.switchboard.com

CELL PHONES

Cellhire
45 Broadway, 20th Floor.
Map 1 C3. *Tel (888) 950-9391.*
www.cellhire.com

INTERNET

Cyber Café
250 W 49th St. **Map** 11 B5.
Tel (212) 333-4109.

easyInternetcafé
234 W 42nd St. **Map** 8 D1.

FedEx Office Center
www.fedex.com

Library for the Performing Arts
40 Lincoln Center Plaza.
Map 11 C2. *Tel (212) 870-1630.*

New York Public Library
5th Avenue and 42nd Street.
Map 8 F1. *Tel (212) 939-0653.*

Times Square Information Center
1560 Broadway. **Map** 12 E5.
www.timessquarenyc.org

Web2Zone
54 Cooper Square. **Map** 4 F2.

POSTAL SERVICES

DHL
Tel (800) 782-7892.

FedEx
Tel (800) 225-5345.

General Post Office
421 Eighth Ave. **Map** 8 D2.
Tel (800) ASK-USPS or (800) 222-1811.
Priority and Express Mail: *Tel (800) 463-3339.* www.usps.com

UPS
Tel (800) 742-5877.

NEWSPAPERS AND MAGAZINES

Barnes & Noble
1972 Broadway at 68th Street.
Map 11 C1.

Hotalings
630 W 52nd St. **Map** 11 B4.

Universal News & Magazine
977 Eighth Ave. **Map** 12 D3.

Express Mail

Priority Mail

Standard Mail

GETTING TO NEW YORK

Delta Airlines flight arriving in New York

A lot of global airlines run direct flights to New York. The city is also very well served by charter and domestic services. Price wars between airlines have reduced fares, and domestic flights are an affordable form of national travel. Early reservation and seat selection are good ways to ensure a more comfortable flight. New York City is also a regular docking point for many cruise ships.

The train network across the United States is not as extensive as that found in Europe, but Amtrak, the national carrier, has several comfortable and clean long-distance trains that run from New York. Interstate and long-distance buses are a cheaper way to travel and usually have air-conditioning and on-board toilets. For information on arriving in New York, see the map on *pages 382–3*.

Taxis heading into LaGuardia airport

AIR TRAVEL

New York can be reached by air direct from most major cities. The flight from London takes about 8 hours, however, there are no direct flights from Australia or New Zealand. Instead, the airlines fly to the West Coast or Asia, which takes around 10–14 hours, land, refuel, and then continue on to New York.

Allow extra time at the airport, for both arriving and departing, and for the careful passport and security checks in the United States.

Among the main airline carriers to New York are **Air Canada**, **Delta**, **British Airways**, **American Airlines**, **Virgin Atlantic**, and **United Airlines**. All international flights arrive at either JFK Newark airports.

TICKETS AND FARES

APEX (Advance Purchase Excursion) tickets for the scheduled airlines are usually the cheapest return fares apart from package tours. They must be bought at least 14 days in advance and are valid for a stay of 7–30 days. The least expensive international air fares to and from Europe are found from November to March, excluding holiday periods. Budget airlines flying within the US – such as **Southwest Airlines**, **JetBlue**, and **AirTran** – often have better fares than the major airlines.

Booking online can help save money. Websites such as www.lastminute.com, www. priceline.com, and www. expedia.com have flight-and-hotel deals that tend to be cheaper than booking the two separately. Search engines like www.kayak.com are useful for comparing the costs of all the different airlines and online travel stores.

ON ARRIVAL

Be prepared for extra security precautions when you visit the United States. Make sure that you leave ample time for checking in – ask your flight carrier what time you need to arrive at the airport for your flight. They can also give you details about any restrictions on hand luggage.

The airline you are flying with will give you an I-94 form to fill out before you land. It asks simple questions such as your name, birth date, country of citizenship, passport number, and current address.

Have this form and your passport ready for the Customs and Border Protection officer who will inspect your documents (get in the line that says "non-US passports"). The officer may ask you questions such as why you are visiting and how long and where you will stay. Your fingerprints will be taken, and you will be photographed with a digital camera. The I-94 is in two parts; one part will be for you to keep. This part must be returned on departing.

AirTrain en route to JFK

JOHN F. KENNEDY AIRPORT (JFK)

Every year, some 41 million passengers pass through New York's main airport, JFK. It serves over 100 airlines in nine terminals and is the main New York entry for international flights. JFK lies 15 miles (24 km) southeast of Manhattan, in the borough of Queens, about 45–60 minutes from midtown. However, airport traffic is often heavy, so the trip can take longer.

Larger carriers like American Airlines, British Airways, Delta, and United Airlines

Planes arriving at Newark airport

have their own arrivals and departure terminals, which they may share with some of their partners. Terminal 4 is the main arrival area for over 50 international airlines, and Terminal 1 serves many foreign carriers, including Air China, Air France, Alitalia, and Japan Airlines.

Foreign-exchange offices and ATMs are located in all terminals, and each terminal has a service desk to help book hotels and answer any transportation questions. Courtesy phones are also provided by car-rental companies.

Dispatchers regulate the line for the yellow taxis waiting outside each terminal. There is a flat fee of $45, plus tolls and tip. New York Airport Service buses go to Grand Central, Penn Station, and the Port Authority; tickets start at $13. The Express Shuttle Service ($14) stops at many midtown hotels. **SuperShuttle** runs shared vans that will go to specific addresses for about $23 for the first guest and $10 for each additional passenger. Advance reservations are needed for the trip back to the airport. Air-Link has a similar service for $19. Round-trip fares are cheaper.

A light-rail system, AirTrain JFK connects to the A train at Howard Beach, and to the E, J, and Z trains and Long Island Rail Road (for Penn Station) at Jamaica. The AirTrain costs $5, the subway $2.25.

If you are feeling rich **Helicopter Flight Services** offer a 10-minute helicopter ride for $850 to East 34th Street.

NEWARK LIBERTY AIRPORT (EWR)

Newark, New York's second-largest international airport, is about 16 miles (26 km) southwest of Manhattan, in New Jersey.

Most international flights into Newark arrive at Terminal B. Baggage trolleys are free for passengers arriving on international flights. Foreign-exchange desks and ATMs can also be found in the terminal, but there is no left-luggage room.

The Ground Transportation Services desk can help arrange private onward travel. Courtesy phones are provided by limousine and car-rental firms. Many of these have a free shuttle service to their rental offices.

As with JFK, there are taxi stands located outside most arrival areas, and uniformed taxi dispatchers will help you hail a cab. The taxi ride into Manhattan takes about 40–60 minutes and will cost you up to $50, plus tolls and tip.

Olympia Airport Express buses to Manhattan stop at the Port Authority Bus Terminal, 42nd Street near 5th Avenue, and Grand Central Station. The journey time is no longer than a cab, but the fare is only $15. Round-trip fares are cheaper.

AirTrain Newark links to NJ Transit and Amtrak trains; it then continues on to Penn station. The 25-minute journey costs about $12, as does the NJ Transit, while Amtrak costs $32.

Hotels can be booked on arrival through courtesy

phones in all terminals at Newark that link directly to various Manhatten hotels. Knowledgeable staff are on hand to help you make the best choice.

LAGUARDIA AIRPORT (LGA)

LaGuardia is a busy airport serving domestic carriers from all over the US. It lies 8 miles (13 km) east of Manhattan, on the north side of Long Island, in Queens. The trip to Manhattan averages 30 minutes.

Upon arrival, you can rent luggage trolleys from the baggage-claim area next to the luggage carousels. Skycaps, people who check in your luggage for you, are on hand to assist you. Baggage can also be left in the Tele-Trip business center on the departure level. A foreign-currency exchange desk and ATMs are located in the Central Terminal. A free bus service runs between each of the terminals and parking areas from 5am to 2am.

Buses and taxis into the city and its suburbs depart from the front of the terminal buildings. If you are approached by other taxis offering you transportation, do not accept. These drivers have no insurance, and you will be overcharged. A taxi fare starts at $3 and increases by $0.40 every fifth of a mile. A single bus ride is $2.25. The cost of tolls, plus a peak-hour surcharge of $1 (4–8pm) weekdays or a night surcharge of 50 cents (8pm–6am), will be added to the taxi fare shown on the meter.

Terminal at LaGuardia airport

Ocean liner anchored in Manhattan

ARRIVING BY SEA

Cruising past the Statue of Liberty into New York Harbor is a thrilling experience. The city's three cruise ports are popular stopping-off points for many major cruise lines sailing to the Caribbean, Bermuda, Canada, and Europe.

The main **New York Cruise Terminal**, on 12th Avenue between 46th and 54th streets, serves Carnival, Silversea, Holland America, MSC, and NCL lines. Taxis are available at the vehicle entrance, located at 55th Street and 12th Avenue. The M57 and M31 crosstown buses provide convenient, inexpensive access to midtown, and it is only a 15–20-minute walk to the heart of Manhattan.

The state-of-the-art **Brooklyn Cruise Terminal** was opened in 2006 in Red Hook. It is the port of choice for Cunard and Princess Cruise lines and the home port of the *QM2*, which sails to New York from Southampton several times a year. You can also take the *QM2* from New York to Australia and New Zealand. Taxis from the terminal can drop you in Manhattan or at convenient subway stops into the city.

Royal Caribbean and Celebrity cruise ships use the **Cape Liberty Cruise Port** in Bayonne, on the New Jersey side of New York Harbor. It is 7 miles (11 km) from New York City and about 15 minutes from Newark International Airport. The Hudson–Bergen Light Rail station at 34th Street, an easy taxi ride just 2 miles (3 km) from the port, connects to PATH trains, New Jersey Transit at Hoboken, and ferry services to and from New York. Visit www.njtransit.com for more information.

Passengers arriving by ship who remain in New York receive the same I-94 form as air passengers and go through the same procedures; *see p378* for more details.

ARRIVING BY LONG-DISTANCE BUS

Long-distance buses from all over the US arrive at the **Port Authority Bus Terminal**, on Eighth Avenue, between 40th and 42nd streets. The location is convenient to midtown, and many hotels are within walking distance. Taxis can be found on the Eighth Avenue side of the terminal; the A and C subway stops are located on the lower floors in the terminal; and a one-block-long tunnel leads to Times Square station and other subway connections. The M42 crosstown bus stops at the corner of Eighth Avenue and 42nd Street, and uptown buses are available on Eighth Avenue. Buses from the Port Authority connect with all three airports, and the terminal also serves many busy commuter bus lines to New Jersey. With over 6,000 buses arriving and departing daily, the atmosphere can be hectic at rush hour.

Buses can be an economical way to see the US. **Greyhound Lines** offer a Discovery Pass priced at $199 for seven days ($299 for 15 days). No advance reservations are necessary. Buses are comfortable and air-conditioned, and they have reclining seats, ample legroom, and usually bathrooms. Greyhound **NeOn** buses, available from New York to Boston, Toronto, and Montreal, are equipped with free Wi-Fi and plug-ins for devices such as iPods. The trip to Boston takes 4½ hours, to Montreal 8½ hours, and to Toronto 11½ hours.

Greyhound has a ticket office in the Port Authority Bus Terminal, but it is cheaper to buy tickets over the phone or online. APEX tickets save 25% off the regular price on shorter trips purchased at least 14 days in advance, and 10% (or more) for tickets bought seven days in advance. "Friends and family" rates offer savings of 50% for up to three companions with the purchase of a regular adult fare. Seniors, students, and military personnel have special discounts.

ARRIVING BY TRAIN

Amtrak, the US passenger rail service, connects New York with the rest of the country and Canada. Amtrak trains use **Penn Station** as their New York headquarters *(see p392)*. The Metro-North train service and the daily commuter service from upstate New York and Connecticut arrive at Grand Central Terminal *(see p392)*.

Amtrak has its own section in Penn Station for ticket sales and separate waiting rooms for coach and high-speed passengers. Tickets can be purchased in advance by phone or online and picked up at the station at the ticket

Imposing entrance hall of Grand Central Terminal

window or at automated kiosks. If you pick up tickets at the window, a photo ID will be requested.

Taxis are available from the station, and buses run downtown on Seventh Avenue and uptown on Eighth. The Lexington and Broadway lines also serve the station.

Amtrak trains are very comfortable, with ample legroom and snack-bar services, as well as dining cars on longer routes. Sleeping compartments are available on long-distance trips, some with showers and toilets ensuite.

Amtrak's USA Rail Pass allows unlimited travel for 15 days for $389; children pay half-fare. The most used train service from New York is Amtrak's Northeast Corridor route between Boston, New York, Philadelphia, and Washington, DC. Most of the trains on this route have unreserved seating, but high-speed Acela Express trains offer an hourly service with reserved first-class and business-class seating and electrical outlets for laptops.

ARRIVING BY CAR

Manhattan is an island, so it must be approached via bridge or tunnel. From the

Traffic approaching the George Washington Bridge

south, the entries are from New Jersey via the Holland Tunnel to the Financial District, or the Lincoln Tunnel to midtown. A more scenic approach is the George Washington Bridge, which arrives at 178th Street to the north of the city.

The Robert Kennedy Bridge (formerly known as the Triborough Bridge) has branches from two boroughs connecting to Manhattan. The bridge from Queens, east of the city, is used by those arriving at LaGuardia or JFK airports. The second branch, from the Bronx, approaches Manhattan from the north. The two bridges merge into one and offer a

striking view of the city skyline on the approach.

Those driving in from Queens can avoid tolls by taking the 59th Street Bridge. Queens is also connected to Manhattan by the Midtown Tunnel, which feeds into the Long Island Expressway.

The most famous approach to New York is via the Brooklyn Bridge, with its vistas of the skyscrapers of the downtown Financial District. Brooklyn is also connected to the city by the Brooklyn Battery tunnel.

BRIDGE AND TUNNEL TOLLS

Most of the major access routes in and out of New York City levy tolls. Tolls for the tunnels to and from Long Island and Brooklyn cost $5.50 each way, as does the Robert Kennedy Bridge. The Lincoln Tunnel, Holland Tunnel, and the George Washington Bridge between New York and New Jersey are free for those leaving New York, but they charge $8 coming into the city. Tolls must be paid in cash. Avoid E-Z Pass lanes, marked with purple signs, which are only for holders of pre-paid passes.

DIRECTORY

AIR TRAVEL

Air Canada
Tel (888) 247-2262.
www.aircanada.ca

Airport Information Service
Tel JFK: (718) 244-4444.
EWR: (973) 961-6000.
LGA (718) 533-3400.
www.panynj.gov/airports

AirTran
Tel (800) 247-8726.
www.airtran.com

American Airlines
Tel (800) 433-7300.
www.aa.com

British Airways
Tel (800) AIRWAYS.
www.british-airways.com

Delta
Tel (800) 241-4141.
www.delta.com

Helicopter Flight Services
Tel (212) 355-0801.
www.heliny.com

JetBlue
Tel (800) 538-2583.
www.jetblue.com

Olympia Airport Express
Tel 877-863-9275.
www.coachusa.com

Southwest Airlines
Tel (800) 435-9792.
www.southwest.com

SuperShuttle
Tel (212) 209-7000.
www.supershuttle.com

United Airlines
Tel (800) 241-6522.
www.united.com

Virgin Atlantic
Tel (800) 862-8621.

ARRIVING BY SEA

Brooklyn Cruise Terminal
Pier 12, Building 112,
Bowne Street, Red Hook.
Tel (718) 246-2794.
www.nycruise.com

Cape Liberty Cruise Port
14 Port Terminal Blvd,
Bayonne.
Tel (201) 823-3737.
www.cruiseliberty.com

New York Cruise Terminal
Pier 90, 711 12th Avenue.
Map 11 B4.
Tel (212) 246-5450.
www.nycruise.com

ARRIVING BY LONG-DISTANCE BUS

Greyhound Lines
Tel (800) 231-2222
www.greyhound.com

NeOn
www.neonbus.com

Port Authority Bus Terminal
Eighth Ave and W 40th St.
Map 8 D1.
Tel (212) 564-8484.
www.panynj.gov

ARRIVING BY TRAIN

Amtrak
Tel (800) 872-7245.
www.amtrak.com

Penn Station
Eighth Ave and 31st St.
Map 8 E3.
www.amtrak.com

Arriving in New York

This map shows the links between New York's three airports and the center of Manhattan. It also illustrates rail connections linking New York to the rest of the United States and Canada. Travel information, including times for bus, rail, and helicopter services, and connections to subway lines, is listed in each information box. The passenger ship terminal, New York's key point of arrival for the flood of post-war immigrants, is located on 55th Street. Port Authority Bus Terminal, on the West Side, provides services across the city.

Ships at the passenger terminal

KEY

✈ Airport *see pp378–9*	
⚓ Seaport *see p380*	
🚉 Rail link *see pp380–81*	
🚌 Bus station/link *see p380*	
🚁 Helicopter links *see p379*	
— New York Airport Service and Super Shuttle *see pp378–9*	
— Helicopters *see p379*	
— Long Island Rail Road *see pp392–3*	
— New Jersey Transit buses *see p379*	
— Olympia Airport Express *see p379*	
— AirTrain *see p379*	
— Subway A *see p389*	

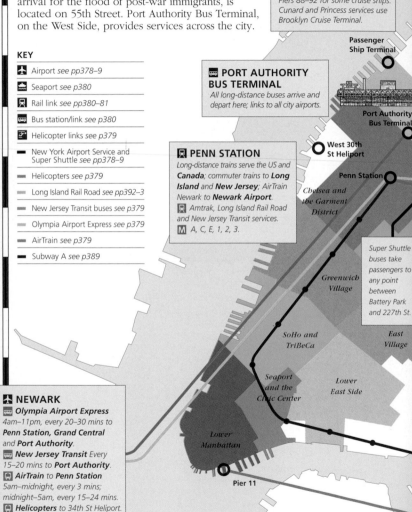

⚓ PASSENGER SHIP TERMINAL
Piers 88–92 for some cruise ships. Cunard and Princess services use Brooklyn Cruise Terminal.

Passenger Ship Terminal

🚌 PORT AUTHORITY BUS TERMINAL
All long-distance buses arrive and depart here; links to all city airports.

Port Authority Bus Terminal

West 30th St Heliport

🚉 PENN STATION
*Long-distance trains serve the US and **Canada**; commuter trains to **Long Island** and **New Jersey**; AirTrain Newark to **Newark Airport**.*
🚉 *Amtrak, Long Island Rail Road and New Jersey Transit services.*
Ⓜ *A, C, E, 1, 2, 3.*

Penn Station

Chelsea and the Garment District

Super Shuttle buses take passengers to any point between Battery Park and 227th St.

Greenwich Village

SoHo and TriBeCa

East Village

Seaport and the Civic Center

Lower East Side

Lower Manhattan

Pier 11

✈ NEWARK
🚌 ***Olympia Airport Express** 4am–11pm, every 20–30 mins to **Penn Station, Grand Central** and **Port Authority**.*
🚌 ***New Jersey Transit** Every 15–20 mins to **Port Authority**.*
🚉 ***AirTrain** to **Penn Station** 5am–midnight, every 3 mins; midnight–5am, every 15–24 mins.*
🚁 ***Helicopters** to 34th St Heliport.*

The Port Authority of New York and New Jersey, operator of JFK, Newark, and LaGuardia airports, has invested in the AirTrain, a rail link that connects JFK and Newark to the city subway system.

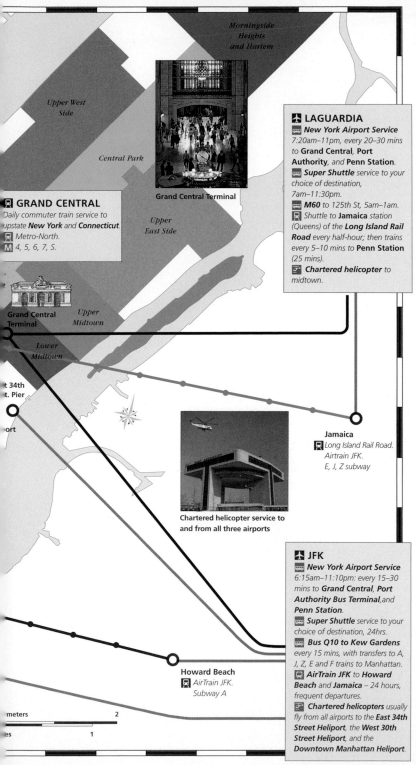

Morningside Heights and Harlem

Upper West Side

Central Park

Grand Central Terminal

✈ LAGUARDIA
🚌 *New York Airport Service*
7:20am–11pm, every 20–30 mins to **Grand Central**, **Port Authority**, and **Penn Station**.
🚌 *Super Shuttle* service to your choice of destination, 7am–11:30pm.
🚌 *M60* to 125th St, 5am–1am.
🚆 Shuttle to **Jamaica** station (Queens) of the **Long Island Rail Road** every half-hour; then trains every 5–10 mins to **Penn Station** (25 mins).
🚁 *Chartered helicopter* to midtown.

🚆 GRAND CENTRAL
*Daily commuter train service to upstate **New York** and **Connecticut**.*
🚆 Metro-North.
Ⓜ *4, 5, 6, 7, S.*

Upper East Side

Grand Central Terminal

Upper Midtown

Lower Midtown

t 34th t. Pier

ort

Jamaica
🚆 *Long Island Rail Road. Airtrain JFK. E, J, Z subway*

Chartered helicopter service to and from all three airports

✈ JFK
🚌 *New York Airport Service*
6:15am–11:10pm: every 15–30 mins to **Grand Central**, **Port Authority Bus Terminal**, and **Penn Station**.
🚌 *Super Shuttle* service to your choice of destination, 24hrs.
🚌 *Bus Q10 to Kew Gardens* every 15 mins, with transfers to A, J, Z, E and F trains to Manhattan.
🚆 *AirTrain JFK to **Howard Beach** and **Jamaica** – 24 hours, frequent departures.*
🚁 *Chartered helicopters* usually fly from all airports to the **East 34th Street Heliport**, the **West 30th Street Heliport**, and the **Downtown Manhattan Heliport**.

Howard Beach
🚆 *AirTrain JFK. Subway A*

meters   2

es   1

GETTING AROUND NEW YORK

With more than 6,000 miles (9,650 km) of streets, getting around New York might seem a problem, but the city is actually a network of small neighborhoods that are connected via subway or bus. Each one is also quite walkable or easy to get around on public transportation. Midtown Manhattan, for example, with many of the major sights, runs 25 blocks from 34th to 59th streets, and if you should tire, you can hop on a bus that goes down Fifth

Signs on a street corner

Avenue or up Sixth. Subways are the quickest way to get around. Service is frequent, they are inexpensive and reliable, and they make stops throughout Manhattan. The city's bus service is also reliable and convenient but can be slow in traffic. Weekly or unlimited MetroCards, valid for all public transportation, provide excellent value. Taxis are the best option for door-to-door transit, but they can be expensive if you are held up by traffic.

GREEN TRAVEL

New York is working hard to be more energy-efficient for those traveling around town. Back in the 1990s, the city was a pioneer in launching an alternative-fuel vehicle program aimed at cutting emissions and making its bus

Cyclist in Central Park

fleet one of the cleanest in the world. It was the first in the US to switch all diesel buses to ultra-low sulfur fuel. Cleaner-burning engines have been installed, and buses have been equipped with filters, cutting emissions by as much as 95 per cent. The MTA currently has around 2,000 hybrid-electric buses in operation. Numerous bicycle lanes have also been added around town for those brave enough to use them amid the heavy city traffic.

When it comes to leaving the city, the US train system is quite limited, but New York has some of the better connections, especially Amtrak's East Coast Metroliner and Acela trains (*see pp381 and 393*).

FINDING YOUR WAY AROUND NEW YORK

Manhattan's avenues run north to south; New Yorkers say "uptown" and "downtown." Streets (except in the older areas) run east to west, and are referred to as "crosstown." Fifth Avenue is the divider between East and West street addresses.

Most streets in midtown are one-way. In general, traffic is eastbound on even-numbered streets and westbound on odd-numbered streets. Avenues also tend to be one-way. First, Third (above 23rd Street), Madison, Avenue of the Americas (Sixth), Eighth, and Tenth avenues are northbound, while Second,

FINDING AN ADDRESS

A useful formula has been devised to help pinpoint any avenue address. By dropping the last digit of the address, dividing the remainder by 2, then adding or subtracting the key number given here, you will discover the nearest cross street. For example: to find No. 826 Lexington Avenue, you have to drop the 6; divide 82 by 2, which is 41; then add 22 (the key number). Therefore, the nearest cross street is 63rd Street.

Avenue Address	Key Number	Avenue Address	Key Number
1st Ave	+3	9th Ave	+13
2nd Ave	+3	10th Ave	+14
3rd Ave	+10	Amsterdam Ave	+60
4th Ave	+8	Audubon Ave	+165
5th Ave, up to 200	+13	Broadway above	
5th Ave, up to 400	+16	23rd St	-30
5th Ave, up to 600	+18	Central Park W, divide	
5th Ave, up to 775	+20	full number by 10	+60
5th Ave 775–1286, do not divide by 2	-18	Columbus Ave	+60
5th Ave, up to 1500	+45	Convent Ave	+127
5th Ave, up to 2000	+24	Lenox Ave	+110
(6th) Ave of the Americas	-12	Lexington Ave	+22
7th Ave below 110th St	+12	Madison Ave	+26
		Park Ave	+35
		Park Ave South	+8
7th Ave above 110th St	+20	Riverside Drive, divide full number by 10	+72
8th Ave	+10	St Nicholas Ave	+110
		West End Ave	+60

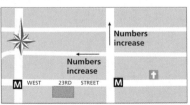

Walking through Chelsea

Lexington, Fifth, Seventh, and Ninth avenues and Broadway below 59th Street are southbound. There is two-way traffic on York, Park, 11th, and 12th avenues and on Broadway above 60th Street.

The grid of streets is rectangular rather than square, so crosstown blocks are longer than north–south avenue blocks. To gauge distances, 20 north–south city blocks equal about 1 mile (1.6 km); it takes only about six to ten crosstown (east–west) blocks to make up that distance.

Some streets have more than one name – for example, Avenue of the Americas is better known as Sixth Avenue. Park Avenue is called Park Avenue South below 34th Street and Fourth Avenue below 14th Street. The maps in this guide give the names most often used.

PLANNING YOUR JOURNEY

Buses and subways are busiest during the rush hours: 8–10am and 4:30–6:30pm, Monday to Friday. Throughout these periods, it may be easier to face the crowds on foot than attempt any journey by bus, taxi, or subway. At other times of day and during certain holiday periods (see p53), the traffic is often much lighter, and you should reach your destination quickly.

There are, of course, a few exceptions. When the president or other political celebrities visit, security measures can cause major disruption to the traffic. The area around Seventh Avenue, south of 42nd Street, is likely to be busy during the day with the

truck and handcart traffic of New York's garment industry.

Avoid Fifth Avenue on parade days, which often take place in spring and fall. On these days, and during the New York Marathon, it is difficult to get across town as bus services are disrupted. If such events are scheduled during your visit, plan to see other areas of the city on that day. Subway traffic will not be affected, though trains may be more crowded than usual.

DRIVING IN NEW YORK

Heavy traffic, lack of parking, and expensive rental cars make driving in New York a frustrating experience. If you decide to drive, you must wear a seat belt by law. Driving is on the right, and the speed limit is usually 30 mph (48 kmh) in midtown. Most streets are one-way, and there are traffic lights at almost every corner. Unlike the rest of New York State, you can never turn right on a red light unless there is a sign indicating otherwise.

To rent a car, you must be at least 25 years old. You will need a valid driver's license (foreign visitors need an International Driver's License), a passport, and a credit card.

CAR INSURANCE

Unless you are adequately covered by your own insurance policy, you should take out damage and liability protection when renting a car. Check with your insurance company before you travel.

Your car-rental agency will be able to provide you with a policy if necessary.

PARKING

Parking in Manhattan is costly and difficult. You can use parking garages, or see if your hotel includes overnight parking, but both options are very expensive.

The busiest streets in midtown do not allow parking. Other streets may have curbside meters for short-term (20–60 minutes) parking. Yellow street and curb markings mean no parking. "Alternate-side" parking applies on most of the city's side streets. Cars may usually be left all day and night, but they must be moved to the other side of the street before 8am the next day. For specific information, call 311.

Car-rental logos

PENALTIES

If you receive a parking ticket, you have seven days to pay the fine or to appeal. If you have any queries about your ticket, call the **Parking Violations Bureau**.

If you cannot find your car, call 311 to find out if it has been towed. The **Traffic Department Tow Pound** is open 24 hours a day, Monday to Saturday. Redeeming your car will cost $185 towing fee, $70 execution fee, and $10–15 per day storage fee. Traveler's checks, certified checks, money orders, and cash are accepted. If you have rented the car, the contract must be produced, and only the authorized driver may redeem the vehicle.

Traffic passing through Times Square at night

Taxis driving through an intersection in SoHo

TAXIS

There are more than 12,000 yellow cabs in New York, easily identified by their color, the distinctive logo on the door, and the light on top. A taxi can carry up to four passengers, with a single fare covering everyone on board. All taxis are metered and can issue printed receipts. Taxis can be hailed anywhere on the street, but taxi stands are scarce. The best places to find waiting cabs are outside Penn and Grand Central stations. Cabs indicate that they are available by turning on the top light. This goes off if the cab is occupied or if the side lights indicate "off duty."

Licensed taxis undergo periodic inspections and are insured against accidents and losses. Non-licensed, or "gypsy," cabs are unlikely to have these safeguards. They will have no meters and charge what they please.

Once the cab accepts a passenger, the meter starts ticking at $2.50, plus a state tax surcharge of 50 cents. The fare increases 40 cents after each additional one-fifth of a mile (292 yards/267 meters) or every 60 seconds of waiting time. There is an additional 50-cent charge from 8pm to 6am, and a $1 extra charge from 4 to 8pm on weekdays. It is customary to tip the driver about 15%. Taxi drivers will accept credit cards.

Make sure your driver understands where you want to go before you start your ride. If you have a map of the area, mark the locations you want. A driver should not ask you your destination until after you've sat down, and by law, they must take you anywhere in the city. They must follow your requests not to smoke or talk on a cell phone, to open or close a window, and to pick up or drop off passengers as you direct. Each yellow cab displays the driver's photograph and registered number next to the meter. If drivers don't comply with your requests, you can report them to the **Taxi & Limousine Commission**.

As an expensive alternative, radio-dispatched sedans can be hired for $40 per hour with a two hour minimum.

WALKING

All intersections have lamp-posts with clearly marked street names; most have electric traffic signals. The lights show red (stop) and green (go) for vehicles, and "Walk/Don't Walk" signals for pedestrians. Crossing while the "Don't Walk" sign is showing is not recommended, nor is crossing mid-block, referred to in the US as "jay-walking."

Vehicles in the US drive on the right, and there are no markings on the road for pedestrians indicating the direction of traffic. It is best to look both ways before you cross, and beware of cars, trucks, and taxis turning the corner behind you as you start to cross the street.

Signs in midtown

Midtown has several small parks and plazas where visitors can rest. In the Broadway area you can have a rest with a Times Square view on the high tier of steps behind the TKTS booth (Broadway and 47th St). Some of the surrounding blocks are traffic-free and furnished with chairs. The traffic islands around the Lincoln Center also offer seating *(as on p370)*.

FERRIES

The **Circle Line** runs several ferry services a day to the Statue of Liberty and Ellis Island from Battery Park, at the southern tip of Manhattan. The 24-hour **Staten Island Ferry**, also from Battery Park, travels the channel and offers splendid views of lower Manhattan, the Statue of Liberty, Ellis Island, the bridges, and Governors Island. The round trip is the best bargain in New York; it's free.

WATER TAXIS

The **New York Water Taxi** is mainly a commuter service, but it also offers various tours and a weekend hop-on/hop-off sightseeing boat (mid-Apr–mid-Oct). The route is around New York Harbor, between West 44th and East 34th streets, with stops including Chelsea Pier, World Financial Center, Battery Park, South Street Seaport, the Brooklyn river-front, and Long Island City. In summer, water taxis provide a service to a couple of man-made beaches in Long Island City and on Governors Island.

A water taxi crossing New York Harbor

GUIDED TOURS

Whichever way you choose to see New York – with the help of a knowledgeable guide, a photographer, a pre-recorded walk, or an exciting trip in a helicopter, boat, or horse-drawn carriage – organized sightseeing trips can save a lot of time and effort. Walking tours give in-depth background information about specific neighborhoods and the city's history and architecture that you might not get on your own. The **Municipal Art Society** is renowned for its knowledgeable guides. Fascinating behind-the-scenes tours are available for the New York Public Library, Metropolitan Opera, and Radio City Music Hall. Bus tours are also a great way to see the city, as you can hop on/hop off as you please (see also p391).

CYCLING

Hoping to cut down on auto traffic, the city is making a real effort to create bike paths, which cover over 90 miles (145 km) in Manhattan. It takes courage to travel beside heavy traffic on busy midtown streets; however, trails along the East River and far west side are pleasant and very popular, as are the many roads for bikers in Central Park, where auto traffic is banned on weekends. Visit www.nycbike maps.com for maps of bike routes. You can rent bikes at Columbus Circle or the Loeb Boathouse in Central Park (see p362).

DIRECTORY

CAR RENTAL AGENCIES

Avis
Tel (800) 331-1212.
www.avis.com

Budget
Tel (800) 527-0700.
www.drivebudget.com

Hertz
Tel (800) 654-3131.
www.hertz.com

National
Tel (800) CAR RENT.
www.nationalcar.com

PARKING

Alternate Side Parking Information
Tel 311.

Parking Violations and Towing Information
Tel 311.

Parking Violations Bureau
Tel (718) 802-3636.

Police
Tel 911.

Traffic Department Tow Pound
Pier 76, W 38th St and 12th Ave. **Map** 7 B1.
Tel 311.

TAXIS

Taxi & Limousine Commission
Tel 311.

Taxi Lost and Found
Tel 311.

Transportation Department
Tel 311.

FERRIES

Circle Line
www.circleline.com

Staten Island Ferry
www.siferry.com

WATER TAXIS

New York Water Taxi
Tel (212) 742-1969.
www.nywatertaxi.com

GUIDED TOURS

Bicycle Tours: Bite of the Apple Tours
2 Columbus Circle, 59th St & Broadway. **Map** 12 D3.
Tel (212) 541-8759.

Boat Tours: Circle Line Sightseeing Yachts
Pier 83, W 42nd St. **Map** 7 A1. **Tel** (212) 563-3200.

Spirit of New York
W 23rd and Eighth Ave. **Map** 8 D4.
Tel (866) 211-3805.

World Yacht, Inc.
Pier 81, W 41st St. **Map** 7 A1. **Tel** (212) 630-8100.

Building Tours: Grand Central Terminal
E 42nd St at Park Ave. **Map** 13 A5.
Tel (212) 883-2420.
www.grandcentral
terminal.com

Heritage Trails
Federal Hall, 26 Wall St.
Map 1 C3.
www.nps.gov/feha/

Metropolitan Opera Tours
Lincoln Center. **Map** 11 C2. **Tel** (212) 769-7020.
www.metoperafamily.org

NBC Studio Tour
30 Rockefeller Plaza.
Map 12 F5. **Tel** (212) 664-7174. www.
rockefellercenter.com

New York Public Library
Fifth Ave and 42nd St.
Map 8 F1.
Tel (917) 275-6975.
www.nypl.org

Radio City Music Hall Stage Door Tours
Sixth Ave. **Map** 12 F4.
Tel (212) 247-4777.

Walkin' Broadway
1619 Broadway. **Map** 12 E5. **Tel** (212) 997-5004.

Bus Tours: Gray Line of New York
42nd St and Eighth Ave.
Map 8 D1.
Tel (212) 397-2620.

Carriage Tours
59th St at Fifth Ave and along Central Park S.
Map 12 F3.

Helicopter Tours: Liberty
W 30th St and 12th Ave, South Ferry. **Map** 7 B3.
Tel (212) 967-6464.

Walking Tours: Adventures on a Shoestring
300 W 53rd St. **Map** 12 E4. **Tel** (212) 265-2663.

Big Apple Greeters
1 Centre St, Suite 2035.
Map 4 F4.
Tel (212) 669-8159.

Big Onion Walking Tours
76 13th St, Brooklyn.
Tel (212) 439-1090.
http://bigonion.com

Eldridge Street Synagogue
12 Eldridge St. **Map** 5 A5.
Tel (212) 227-8780.

Harlem Spirituals, Inc.
690 Eighth Ave. **Map** 8 D1. **Tel** (212) 391-0900.

Lower East Side Tenement Museum
108 Orchard St. **Map** 5 A4. **Tel** (212) 431-0233.

Municipal Art Society
457 Madison Ave. **Map** 13 A4. **Tel** (212) 980-1297.
www.mas.org

Wall Street Walks
Tel (212) 209-3379.
www.wallstreetwalks.com

CYCLING

Central Park Bike Rental
203 West 58th St.
Map 12 E3.
Tel (212) 541-8759.
www.centralpark
biketour.com

Traveling by Subway

New York City Subway

New York subway logo

The subway is the quickest and most reliable way to travel in the city. The vast system extends over 233 route miles (375 km) and has 468 stations. Most routes operate 24 hours a day throughout the year. In the past few years, the subway system has been upgraded, and the trains are now air-conditioned, well lit, safer, and (unless you are riding at rush hour) more comfortable. Since the 1980s, a portion of all station-improvement funds has gone to the Arts for Transit project, with some notable results. Keep an eye out for the mosaics, sculptures, and art that decorate many stations.

Passengers exiting from South Ferry Subway Station

TICKETS AND FARES

A MetroCard must be purchased in order to enter the subway. The fare is $2.25 no matter how far you travel. A 1-day FunPass ($8.25) offers all-day unlimited travel to visitors. Other money-saving tickets are the 7-day ($27) or 14-day ($51.50) Unlimited Ride MetroCard. If you purchase a Pay-Per-Ride MetroCard and put $8 or more on it, you will receive a 15 per cent bonus credit. MetroCards, which can also be used on buses (see pp390–91), are sold at newsstands, drugstores, and other locations around the city, as well as at all subway stations, where you can pay with cash. The machines take cash and debit and credit cards. One transfer per ride is allowed between the subway and bus; it must be used within 2 hours.

USING THE SUBWAY

Enter the subway by swiping your MetroCard at the turnstiles; the card is not needed to exit. Look for signs for uptown (northbound) and downtown (southbound) trains. Note that there are two types of trains: local trains stop at all stations, while faster express trains make fewer stops. Express lines have different letters or numbers than local ones; both types of stops are distinguished on every subway map.

SUBWAY STATIONS

Many subway entrances are marked by illuminated spheres: green where the station booth is manned around the clock, red where there is restricted entry. Others are marked simply by a sign bearing the name of the station and the numbers or letters of the routes passing through it. Although the subway system runs 24 hours a day, not all routes operate at all times. The basic service is between 6am and midnight. The most crowded periods are the weekday rush hours (6–8:30am and 4:30–6:30pm); it is best to avoid these times if you can. If not, during

READING THE SUBWAY MAP

Each route is identified on the subway map (see inside back cover) by color, by the names of the stations at each end of the line, and by a letter or number. Local and express stops and interchange points are also identified. The letters and numbers below the station names indicate which routes serve that particular station. A letter or number in heavy type indicates that trains on that route stop between 6am and midnight; letters in lighter type mean that the route is served by a part-time service only; a boxed letter or number shows the last stop on the line. Express trains are indicated on subway maps with a white (rather than solid) circle. The maps posted in all the subway stations have a comprehensive guide that explains the trains and timetable of each route.

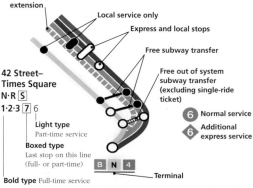

Part-time line extension

Local service only

Express and local stops

Free subway transfer

Free out of system subway transfer (excluding single-ride ticket)

42 Street–Times Square
N·R S
1·2·3 7 6

Light type
Part-time service

Boxed type
Last stop on this line (full- or part-time)

Bold type Full-time service

6 Normal service

6 Additional express service

B N 4

Terminal

TRAVELING BY SUBWAY

Subways run north–south up and down the city; the N, R, E, F, V, and W trains run east–west from Midtown to Queens. See "Subway Lines" for the most useful routes.

2 Buy a MetroCard from a station subway booth or MetroCard vending machine. The machines accept most credit and debit cards and bills up to $50, but no pennies. Vending machines can also be used to refill MetroCards.

1 There is a map of the subway system on the back inside cover of this book. Large-scale maps are also positioned in prominent areas in every station. Maps are also available at www.mta.info and at subway stations.

3 Use MetroCard to pass through the turnstile onto the platform.

4 Follow the directions for the train you want. For safety, stay in sight of the booth as you wait for your train; at night, stay in one of the yellow off-hours waiting areas.

6 On every platform, you will find a line map, while on each train there is a system map next to the door on both sides of the car. Newer trains have electronic route maps for that line that light up overhead. Stops are announced on the public address system, and you will see station names at each platform. The doors are operated by the conductor.

5 Each train displays its route number or letter in the appropriate color and the names of the terminal stations.

7 After leaving the train, look for signs giving directions to the exit. If you need to change trains, just follow the signs to the connecting platforms.

---

crowded times the first and last cars are usually less busy.

The subway is generally quite safe, but visitors may feel more secure riding during the day and until around 10pm, when there are many other passengers around. If you feel unsure, stand in the "Off-Hours Waiting Area" on the platforms. Avoid traveling alone late at night, but if you must ride when traffic is light, use the central cars. In an emergency, contact either the station agent in the station booth or a member of the train crew, who are located in the first car and in the middle of the train.

SUBWAY LINES

Subways run north–south up and down the city on Lexington Avenue, Sixth Avenue, Seventh Avenue/Broadway, and Eighth Avenue. The N, R, E, F, V, and 7 trains to Queens run east–west in Manhattan. A shuttle train connects Grand Central, East 42nd Street to Times Square, West 42nd Street. Trains mostly run along one avenue, but some stations, such as Times Square, Union Square, and Columbus Circle,

are convenient transfer points where several lines converge.

Each subway line has a distinct color, while the routes on each line are identified either by letter or number. For example, the Lexington Avenue line is green and the #6 is a local train, while #4 and #5 run express. The Eighth Avenue line is blue, and the A train is the express, while C and E are local trains. First and last stops are posted on track signs and on each car. Large system maps are posted in all stations. Free individual subway maps are usually available from booth attendants.

Some lines are especially useful for visitors. The Lexington Line is the only one serving the East Side and its many museums. The #6 train stops near the Guggenheim, the Metropolitan Museum of Art, and the Frick Collection. The red #1 Broadway/Seventh Avenue line on the West Side takes you to Lincoln Center, MOMA, Times Square,

Number 6 train at Brooklyn Bridge–City Hall station

Greenwich Village, SoHo, the Financial District, and South Ferry, where you can catch a ferry to the Statue of Liberty.

Note that track work on weekends can cause changes to the schedule. When you enter, ask the booth attendant about changes that may affect your journey.

DIRECTORY

MetroCard Customer Service
Tel (212) 638-7622.

MTA Automated Travel Planner
http://ripplanner.mta.info/

Subway Information
Tel (718) 330-1234.
www.mta.info

Traveling by Bus

Traveling by bus is a good way to take in many of New York's sights. The city's 4,000-plus blue-and-white buses cover more than 200 routes in the five boroughs. Many run 24 hours a day, every day. The buses are modern, clean, air-conditioned, and energy-efficient. They are also quite safe and tend not to get crowded, except during rush hours. Smoking and eating are forbidden on all public buses, and only service animals (guide dogs) are allowed on board.

Bus stop in midtown Manhattan

TICKETS AND FARES

You can pay the $2.25 fare on a bus using a MetroCard (see p388) or exact change in coins. Bus drivers cannot make change, and fare boxes do not accept dollar bills, half-dollars, or pennies. You can buy a MetroCard at any subway station booth or machine and at many other outlets around the city.

If you need to take more than one bus to reach your destination, you are eligible for a free transfer. If you pay your fare with a MetroCard, transfers to bus or subway are automatically electronically placed on the card. If you use cash, ask the driver for a transfer ticket when you pay. Transfers are good for 2 hours.

Senior citizens with proof of age and the disabled pay half-fare. All buses can "kneel," lowering the steps to help elderly people to board (see p370). They are also accessible to wheelchairs via a lift with ramp, at the rear or front depending on the bus design.

BUS STOPS

Buses will stop only at designated bus stops. They follow north–south routes on the major avenues, stopping every two or three blocks. Crosstown buses run east–west and usually stop at every block, with the exception of Park Avenue, which is skipped by some lines. Many routes run a 24-hour daily service.

Bus stops are marked by red, white, and blue signs and yellow paint along the curb. Most also have bus shelters; newer shelters provide seating and helpful signs giving the location. A route map and schedule is posted at each stop. Buses use letters to indicate the boroughs they serve: M for Manhattan, B for Brooklyn, Bx for the Bronx, and Q for Queens. Bus stops often serve several routes, so check the maps at the stop for your route, then look for that route number posted on the lighted strip above the windshield on the front of the bus.

Some buses will be marked "Limited," indicated by a flashing sign in the route number space and by a card in the front window. These buses are faster since they make fewer stops, but be sure the stops they do make are near your destination. Limited buses do stop at streets connecting to crosstown buses.

Free city bus maps are often available on board; ask the driver for a copy.

USING BUSES

Most buses run every 3–5 minutes during the morning and evening rush hours, and every 7–15 minutes from noon to 4:30pm and from 7 to 10pm. Bad traffic or adverse weather conditions can cause delays. Service is reduced on weekends and holidays.

Enter the bus at the front door. If you are unsure of your route, ask the driver if they will be stopping at your destination or close to it. The majority of New York's bus drivers are helpful and will call out your stop if you ask when you board. Put your MetroCard in the slot or drop the correct coins in the fare box, then look for a seat.

To request a stop when traveling on the bus, press the yellow vertical call strip between the windows. Some newer buses also have stop buttons on center poles. A "Stop Requested" sign near the driver will then light up. If the bus is crowded, it is wise to start moving toward the exit door when you are a few blocks from your stop.

Leave through the double door located toward the rear of the bus. The driver will activate the door release as soon as the bus has stopped, and a green light will go on above the door. You then push the yellow stripe on the door, and the doors will open automatically; they will stay open long enough for everyone to leave. If the strip does not work properly, just push the door and then hold it open for the passenger behind you as you leave.

The M86 crosstown bus traveling through Central Park

NIGHT BUSES

Most lines run 24 hours, but be sure to check the schedule posted at your stop. After 10pm, many buses run every 20 minutes or so. From midnight to 6am, expect to wait 30–60 minutes for a bus.

BUS TOURS

One of the most popular ways to see the sights is aboard a hop-on/hop-off bus tour that allows you to get off wherever you like, stay as long as you want, and catch another bus when you are ready. Gray Line *(see p387)* is the best-known company offering these tours aboard double-decker buses. Routes include a Downtown Loop, Uptown Loop, Brooklyn Loop, and Night/Holiday Lights Tour (not hop-on/hop-off). Buy a 48- or 72-hour pass, and you can see a great deal of New York. While you ride, narration is available in several languages through rented headsets.

MTA TRIP PLANNER

The MTA website has a useful feature known as the Trip Planner, which provides a map and directions by bus and/or subway between any two points in New York. Enter your starting and ending points, the time you expect to travel, preferred mode of transportation, how far you are willing to walk, and whether you need accessible vehicles, and you will get clear directions. Visit www. travel.mtanyct.info to access the planner; www.hopstop. com offers a similar service.

SIGHTSEEING BUSES

For a pleasant and cheap alternative to a tour bus, hop on a city bus and see New York with the New Yorkers. Recommended bus routes include routes 1 and 2, which run down Fifth Avenue alongside Central Park. Route 1 then continues south to SoHo and Greenwich Village, while route 2 returns north on Madison Avenue via the Empire State Building and the Rockefeller Center. From Broad Street, head north on route 15 to visit Brooklyn Bridge and the United Nations, or take routes 6 and 7 along Eighth Avenue for Times Square and Madison Square Garden.

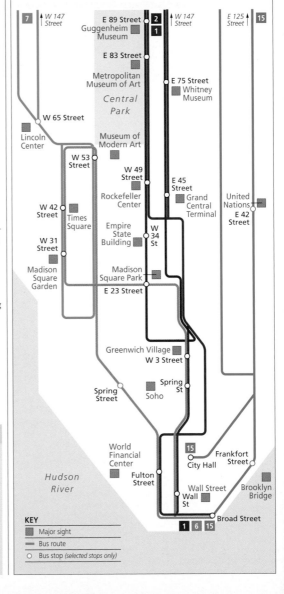

KEY
- ■ Major sight
- ▬ Bus route
- ○ Bus stop *(selected stops only)*

Day Trips from New York

For a change of pace and some beautiful scenery, it is worth taking a day trip from New York City to the surrounding areas. Public transport links are excellent, and there are many convenient and easy ways to travel to nearby destinations *(see pp232–55)*.

Departure board at Penn Station

MAIN TRAIN STATIONS

New York has two main train stations, serving commuters as well as long-distance travelers.

Grand Central Terminal *(see pp156–7)*, on Park Avenue at 42nd Street, is the main terminal for **Metro-North Railroad** trains (Hudson, New Haven, and Harlem lines), which run north and east of New York and serve southwest Connecticut and Westchester, Dutchess, and Putnam counties *(see pp380–81)*. From Grand Central, you can travel by train to the Bronx Zoo *(see pp244–5)*, the New York Botanical Garden, President Franklin D. Roosevelt's Hyde Park estate, and other mansions and towns overlooking the Hudson River.

The 4, 5, and 6 trains on the Lexington line and number 7 on the Flushing line serve Grand Central subway station. A shuttle train service links Grand Central to Times Square. Many bus lines stop near Grand Central, and taxis can usually be found in front of the station on 42nd Street or across from the side entrance on Vanderbilt Avenue at 43rd Street.

Penn Station, between Seventh and Eighth avenues and from 31st to 33rd streets, is a somewhat cramped underground terminal that was rebuilt in 1963 underneath the Madison Square Garden complex *(see p135)*. **Long Island Rail Road** (LIRR) and **New Jersey Transit** commuter trains, plus **Amtrak** trains from Canada and other parts of the US, terminate at this station. There are no luggage trolleys, but redcap porters will help.

Taxis can be found at street level. Buses run downtown on Seventh Avenue and uptown on Eighth Avenue. The Eighth Avenue subway lines A, C, and E run on the Eighth Avenue side of the station; the Broadway lines 1, 2, and 3 run on the Seventh Avenue side of the station.

COMMUTER RAIL LINES

Metro-North lines to upstate New York and Connecticut depart from Grand Central Station. These are mostly commuter trains but may be useful for trips to New Haven or Hartford, Connecticut, or to destinations along the Hudson River.

MTA
Long Island Rail Road
Long Island Rail Road logo

Long Island Rail Road and New Jersey Transit commuter rail lines depart from Penn Station. They can take you to New Jersey or Long Island beach resorts, or to the casinos at Atlantic City, New Jersey.

PATH trains are used mainly by commuters. They operate around the clock between New Jersey stations and Penn Station. From Penn Station they make stops at Christopher Street; the World Trade Center; Ninth, 14th, 23rd, and 33rd streets; and Avenue of the Americas.

TICKETS AND FARES

Train tickets are based on a one-way fare; a return fare is twice the single fare. Peak commuter fares are for trains arriving in New York weekdays between 6 and 10am or departing between 4 and 8pm. All other hours and weekend days are considered off peak and cost much less.

The Long Island Rail Road has many One-Day Getaway packages, with discounted rail fares and admissions to places such as the Hamptons, vineyards, historic sites, and New York Mets baseball games.

Metro-North and LIRR cars are all one class and have no reserved seating, while Amtrak trains offer both services. The conductor will ask to see your ticket after the train has left the station.

Long Island Rail Road train

BOOKING TICKETS

Ticketing offices at all train stations will accept most credit and debit cards, as well as cash. When there are lines for tickets, you can use the automated machines, which accept credit cards. Tickets can be purchased online by credit card. Savings are offered for those who buy in advance. Note that there is a surcharge for buying tickets after you board the train.

Yale University in New Haven, Connecticut

DAY TRIPS BY TRAIN

Many destinations near New York are worth a visit and easily reached by train. Below is a list of some recommended sights; for further details, call NYC & Co. (see p371).

Stony Brook is a peaceful North Shore village and the entrance to the Three Villages historic district. The journey takes 2 hours from Penn Station on a LIRR train.

The chic bars, clubs, and boutiques of the Hamptons are just under 3 hours from New York. Take a LIRR train from Penn Station.

Westbury House, John Phipps's 1906 re-creation of a Charles II mansion with English formal gardens, is 40 minutes from Manhattan. Take a LIRR train from Penn Station to Old Westbury.

Kykuit, the Rockefeller mansion; Washington Irving's home "Sunnyside;" and Jay Gould's mansion, "Lyndhurst", are all in Tarrytown. Take a Metro-North train from Grand Central Station, then a taxi. The journey should take 40–50 minutes.

Two hours outside of Manhattan is Hyde Park, where you can visit Franklin D. Roosevelt's Springwood estate and the Vanderbilt mansion. Take a Metro-North train from Grand Central to Poughkeepsie, then a bus.

Cold Spring, New York, is an antiquing mecca on the Hudson. The scenic riverside journey takes 70 minutes from Grand Central on the Metro-North Hudson Line.

New Haven, Connecticut, is home to the world-famous Yale University. The journey takes 1 hour and 45 minutes, again on a Metro-North train from Grand Central.

DAY TRIPS BY BUS

Many appealing destinations can be reached by bus from the Port Authority Bus Terminal (see p381) on Eighth Avenue. **Short Line Bus** offers popular day-out packages to the US Military Academy at West Point, Franklin D. Roosevelt's home at Hyde Park, and the Storm King Art Center. Also on offer is shopping at the Woodbury Common Outlet Center. Rates include round-trip bus fare and any admissions.

New Jersey Transit buses go to the casinos at Atlantic City; they also have stops on the Jersey shore. **Trans-Bridge Lines** has services to charming antiquing meccas such as Lambertville, New Jersey, and New Hope, Pennsylvania.

A number of budget bus lines have inexpensive fares to Philadelphia, a historic city with many attractions that is only 100 miles (160 km) from New York. Among the most reliable and comfortable of these are **Megabus** and **Bolt Bus**, both of which offer free Wi-Fi on board. For those with time to travel farther afield, these companies also serve Boston and Washington, DC.

Bus tickets are on sale in the main concourse of the Port Authority. The long-distance bus companies Greyhound (see p381), **Peter Pan**, and **Adirondacks** and the Short Line, Trans-Bridge, and New Jersey Transit commuter lines have their own ticket counters. No reservations are taken on any of these bus lines.

DAY TRIPS BY SUBWAY OR CITY BUS

The outer boroughs, served by New York's subway and bus system, are also worth exploring. Head for the Coney Island beaches (see p249) and the New York Aquarium on the D train, or take the M4 bus to the last stop and visit The Cloisters (see pp236–9), high above the Hudson River.

New York's fascinating ethnic neighborhoods are also easily reached by subway. At Grand Central Station, take the 7 Queens train to 74th Street in Jackson Heights, where you'll find a slice of India. Nearby, 37th Avenue is home to New York's Latin-American community. If you stay on the 7 train to the end of the line, you can explore a Chinatown that some say rivals the one in Manhattan, as well as the city's largest Korean neighbourhood.

In Brooklyn, the D train will take you to the Russian enclave of Brighton Beach, while the G train will let you sample a bit of Poland in Greenpoint. Take the N train to go Greek or Egyptian in Astoria, or the M train to the city's largest Orthodox Jewish community in Borough Park.

STREET FINDER

The map references given with all sights, hotels, restaurants, bars, shops, and entertainment venues described in this book refer to the maps in this section (*see* How the Map References Work *opposite*). These maps cover the whole of Manhattan. A complete index of street names and all the places of interest marked on the maps can be found on the following pages.

The key map *(below)* shows the areas covered by the *Street Finder*, within the various districts. The maps include all of Manhattan's sight-seeing areas (which are color-coded), with all the districts important for hotels, restaurants, bars, shops, theaters, and entertainment.

Browsing at South Street Seaport

0 kilometers   2

0 miles   1

Inset on Map 1

KEY TO STREET FINDER

Major sight

Other sight

Station building

Ⓜ Subway station

Heliport

Ferry terminal

Bus terminal

Ⓟ Parking

Tourist information office

Hospital with emergency room

Police station

Church

Synagogue

⊠ Post office

═══ Railroad line

▬▬▬ Pedestrian street

SCALE OF MAP PAGES

| 0 meters | 200 | |
| 0 yards | 200 | 1:11,500 |

Inset on Map 19

HOW THE MAP REFERENCES WORK

The first figure tells you which Street Finder map to turn to.

Theodore Roosevelt Birthplace ❼

28 E 20th St. **Map 9 A5**. **Tel** 260-1616. Ⓜ 14th St-Union Sq. ◯ 9am–5pm Wed–Sun (last adm: 4:30pm). ● public hols. 🎦 📷 📹 **Lectures, concerts, films & video** 🖥 www.nps.gov/thrb

A letter and number give the grid reference. Letters go across the map's top and bottom, numbers on its sides.

The map continues on map 5 of the *Street Finder*.

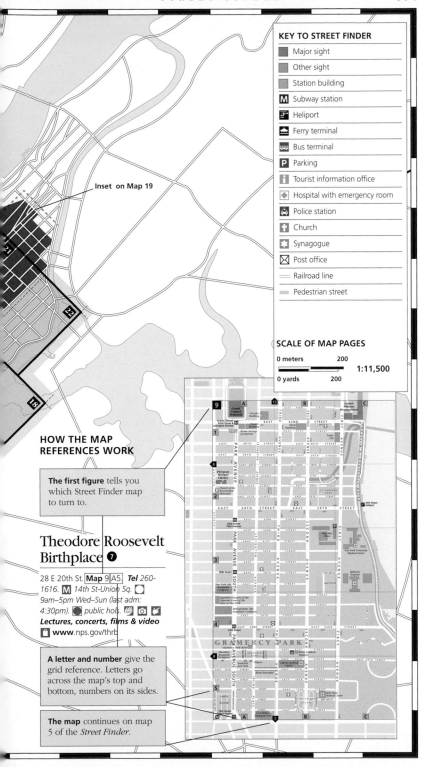

Street Finder Index

Each place name is followed by its borough (unless in Manhattan) and then by its Street Finder reference

Each place name is followed by its borough (unless in Manhattan) and then by its Street Finder reference

Each place name is followed by its borough (unless in Manhattan) and then by its Street Finder reference

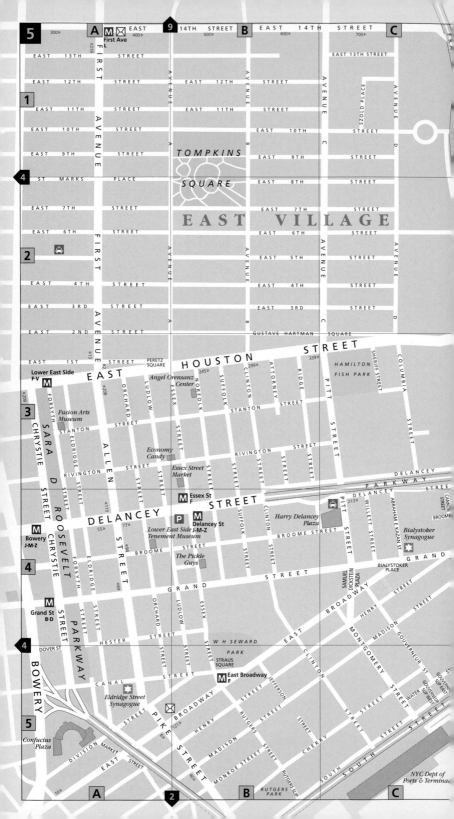

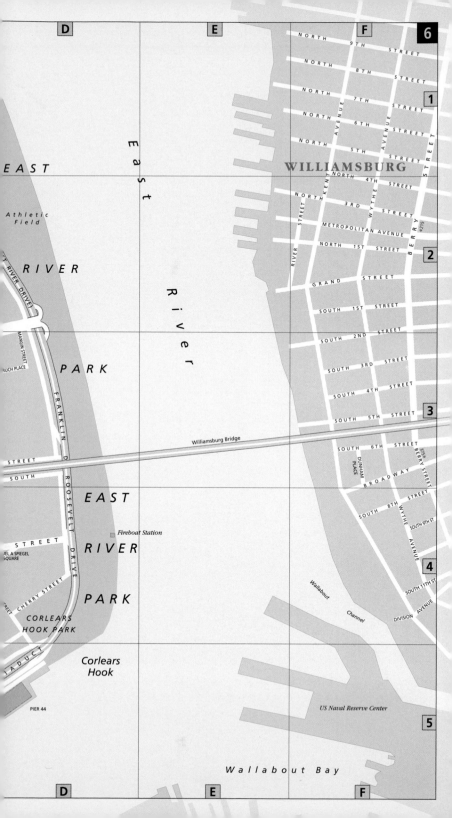

NORTH 9TH STREET

NORTH 8TH STREET

NORTH 7TH STREET

NORTH 6TH STREET

NORTH 5TH STREET

WILLIAMSBURG

NORTH 4TH STREET

NORTH 3RD STREET

METROPOLITAN AVENUE #215

NORTH 1ST STREET

GRAND STREET

SOUTH 1ST STREET

SOUTH 2ND STREET

SOUTH 3RD STREET

SOUTH 4TH STREET

SOUTH 5TH STREET

Williamsburg Bridge

SOUTH 6TH STREET

DUNHAM PLACE

#378 BERRY STREET

BROADWAY

SOUTH 8TH STREET

WYTHE AVENUE

SOUTH 9TH ST

SOUTH 11TH ST

DIVISION AVENUE

Wallabout

Channel

CORLEARS
HOOK PARK

Fireboat Station

EAST

RIVER

PARK

EAST

RIVER

PARK

Corlears
Hook

PIER 44

US Naval Reserve Center

Wallabout Bay

Athletic
Field

EAST

RIVER

East

River

River

FRANKLIN D. ROOSEVELT DRIVE

T RIVER DRIVE

MANGIN STREET

RUCH PLACE

STREET

SOUTH

EL A SPIEGEL
SQUARE

STREET

CHERRY STREET

STREET

IADUCT

KENT AVENUE

BERRY STREET

NORTH STREET

RIVER STREET

WYTHE STREET

BERRY STREET

13

A EAST 73RD STREET B C

✝ #760

EAST 72ND STREET
«100» «1250» EAST «300» #1344 72ND STREET #1353
«200» «400»

U P P E R   E A S T   S I D E

EAST 71ST STREET EAST 71ST STREET
«1231»

1 ✝ *Asia Society* ⊠ New York Hospital
EAST 70TH STREET EAST 70TH STREET

EAST 69TH STREET EAST 69TH STREET

Hunter College
EAST 68TH STREET EAST 68TH STREET Memorial Hospital

12 Ⓜ 68th Street-
Hunter College
6
EAST 67TH STREET EAST 67TH STREET

Seventh Regiment Armory
EAST 66TH STREET EAST 66TH STREET

✝ EAST 65TH STREET EAST 65TH STREET

2 EAST 64TH STREET EAST 64TH STREET

Lexington Avenue-
63rd Street
F
Ⓜ EAST 63RD STREET EAST 63RD STREET

Museum of American Illustration
Society of Illustrators EAST 62ND STREET EAST 62ND STREET #1102 62ND STREET *Mount Vernon Hotel Museum*

EAST 61ST STREET EAST 61ST STREET #1111

59th Street-
Lexington Ave
N·R·W
✝ #520 Ⓜ EAST 60TH STREET «991» EAST 60TH STREET
#502 «1010»

Bloomingdale's
Ⓜ EAST 59TH STREET EAST 59TH STREET

3 59th Street
4·5·6
EAST 58TH STREET EAST 58TH STREET

Fuller Building
EAST 57TH STREET EAST 57TH STREET
«100» «200» «300» «400»
#1066
#1083

EAST 56TH STREET EAST 56TH STREET
#421 #1006

EAST 55TH STREET EAST 55TH STREET
#915

Central Synagogue ✡
Lever House EAST 54TH STREET ⊠ EAST 54TH STREET

Citigroup Center ✝
Lexington Avenue-
53rd Street
E·V
Ⓜ EAST 53RD STREET EAST 53RD STREET

4 *Seagram Building*
EAST 52ND STREET EAST 52ND STREET

Villard Houses
General Electric Building
EAST 51ST STREET EAST 51ST STREET
Ⓜ 51st Street 🚕
6
St Bartholomew's Church ✝

12 EAST 50TH STREET EAST 50TH STREET BEEKMAN PLACE

Waldorf-Astoria
EAST 49TH STREET EAST 49TH STREET

EAST 48TH STREET EAST 48TH STREET

EAST 47TH STREET EAST 47TH STREET *Japan Society* ✝
HAMMARSKJOLD PLAZA

5 EAST 46TH STREET EAST 46TH STREET **United Nations Headquarters**
#240

Helmsley Building
EAST 45TH STREET EAST 45TH STREET
⊠

MetLife Building EAST #702 *1&2 United Nations Plaza*
#824
A EAST 9 44TH STREET B C

PARK AVENUE
MADISON AVENUE
LEXINGTON AVENUE
THIRD AVENUE
SECOND AVENUE
FIRST AVENUE
YORK AVENUE
SUTTON PLACE
SUTTON PLACE SOUTH
FRANKLIN D ROOSEVELT DRIVE (EAST RIVER DRIVE)
UNITED NATIONS PLAZA
VANDERBILT AVENUE

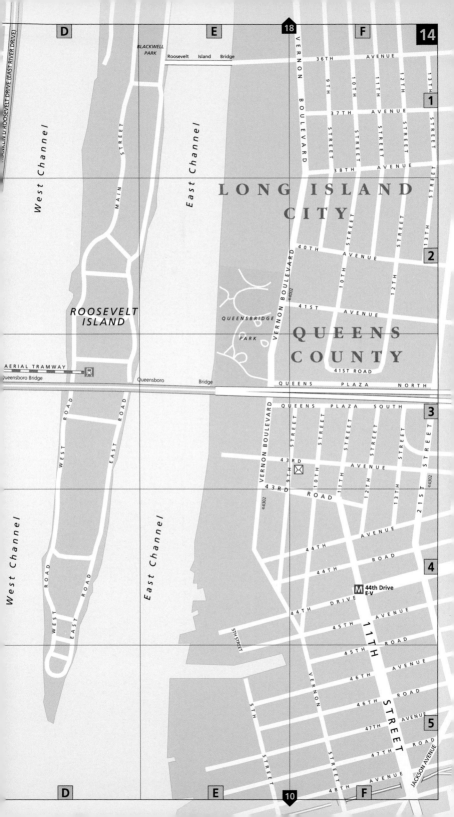

FRANKLIN D ROOSEVELT DRIVE (EAST RIVER DRIVE)

BLACKWELL
PARK

Roosevelt Island Bridge

West Channel

MAIN STREET

East Channel

36TH AVENUE

VERNON BOULEVARD

9TH STREET

10TH STREET

11TH STREET

12TH STREET

13TH STREET

37TH AVENUE

38TH AVENUE

**LONG ISLAND
CITY**

40TH AVENUE

VERNON BOULEVARD

#4202

10TH STREET

12TH STREET

13TH STREET

**ROOSEVELT
ISLAND**

QUEENSBRIDGE
PARK

41ST AVENUE

**QUEENS
COUNTY**

41ST ROAD

AERIAL TRAMWAY

Queensboro Bridge

Queensboro Bridge

QUEENS PLAZA NORTH

QUEENS PLAZA SOUTH

VERNON BOULEVARD

9TH STREET

10TH STREET

11TH STREET

12TH STREET

13TH STREET

21ST STREET

#4302

43RD

43RD ROAD

#4302

44TH AVENUE

44TH ROAD

West Channel

WEST ROAD

EAST ROAD

East Channel

44TH AVENUE

44TH DRIVE

M 44th Drive
E-V

45TH AVENUE

11TH STREET

WEST ROAD

EAST ROAD

5TH STREET

45TH ROAD

46TH AVENUE

VERNON

46TH ROAD

5TH STREET

47TH AVENUE

47TH ROAD

STREET

STREET

48TH AVENUE

JACKSON AVENUE

1

2

3

4

5

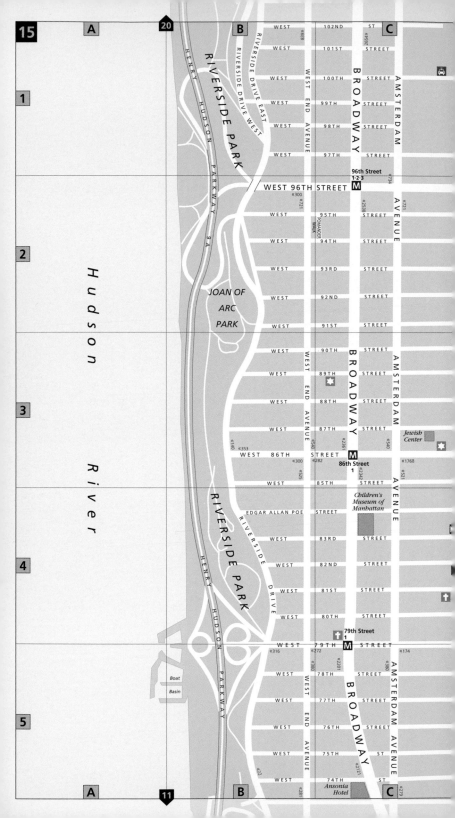

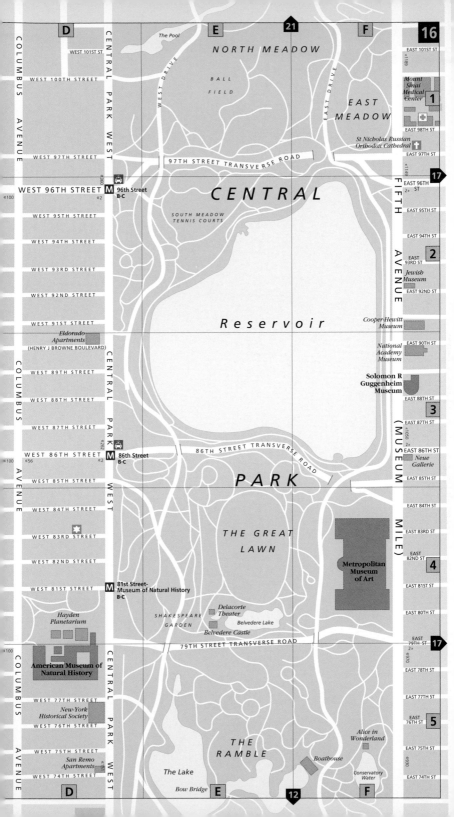

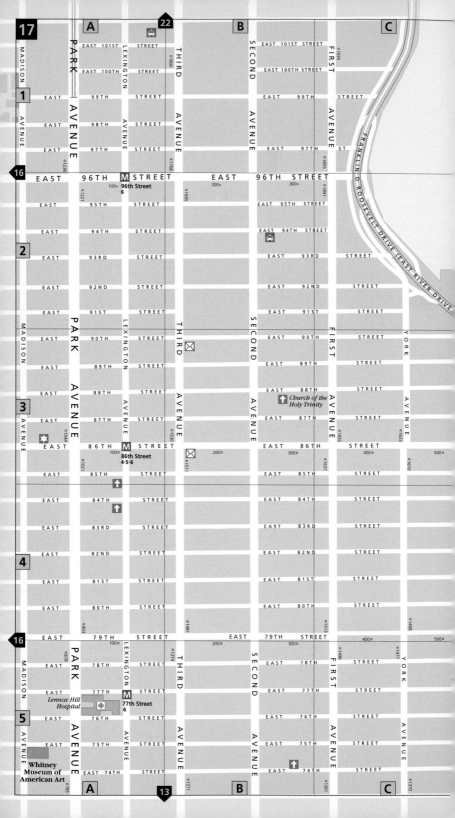

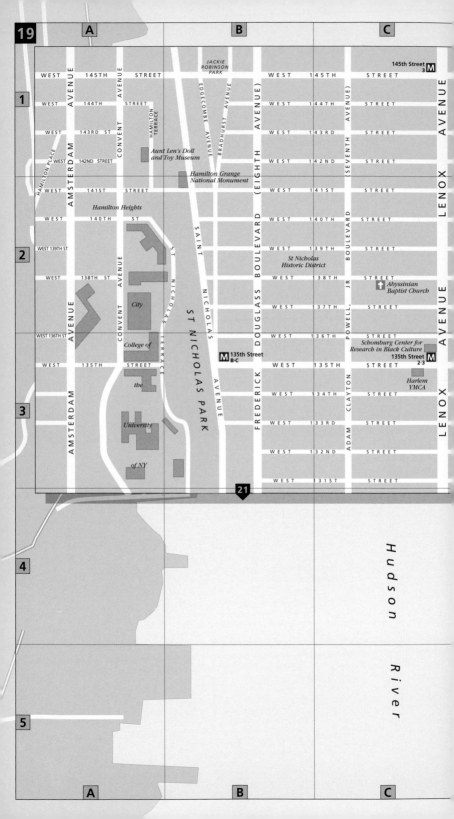

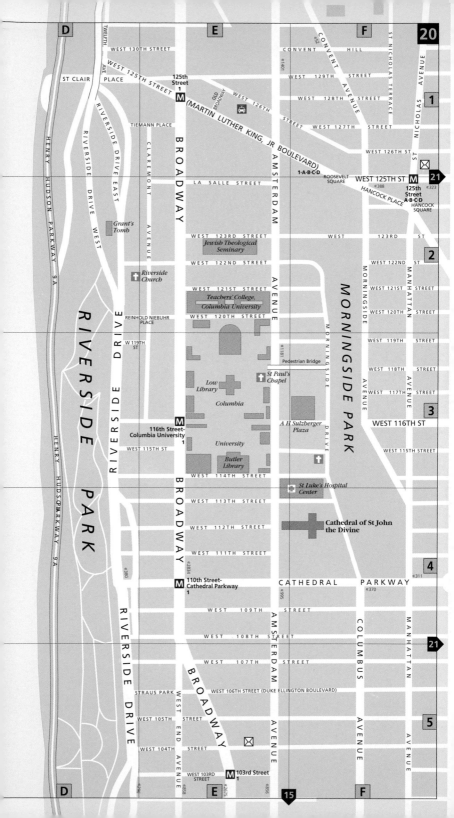

General Index

Acknowledgments

Dorling Kindersley would like to thank the many people whose help and assistance contributed to the preparation of this book.

Main Contributor
Eleanor Berman has lived in New York for almost 40 years. Her travel articles are widely published and she is the author of *Away for the Weekend: New York*, a favorite since 1982. Her other books include *Away for the Weekend* guides for the Mid-Atlantic, New England and Northern California, *Travelling on Your Own* and *Reflections of Washington, DC*.

Museum Contributors
Michelle Menendez, Lucy O'Brien, Heidi Rosenau, Elyse Topalian, Sally Williams.

Dorling Kindersley wishes to thank editors and researchers at Websters International Publishers: Sandy Carr, Matthew Barrell, Sara Harper, Miriam Lloyd, Ava-Lee Tanner, Celia Woolfrey.

Additional Photography
Rebecca Carman, Rachel Feierman, Andrew Holigan, Edward Hueber, Eliot Kaufman, Karen Kent, Dave King, Norman McGrath, Howard Millard, Angus Oborn, Ian O'Leary, Rough Guides/Nelson Hancock, Susannah Sayler, Paul Solomon, Chuck Spang, Chris Stevens, Peter Wilson.

Additional Illustrations
Steve Gyapay, Arshad Khan, Kevin Jones, Dinwiddie MacLaren, Janos Marffy, Chris D. Orr, Nick Shewring, John Woodcock.

Cartography
Maps Uma Bhattacharya, Andrew Heritage, Suresh Kumar, James Mills-Hicks, Chez Picthall, John Plumer (Dorling Kindersley Cartography), Kunal Singh. Advanced Illustration (Cheshire), Contour Publishing (Derby), Europmap Ltd (Berkshire). Street Finder maps: ERA-Maptec Ltd (Dublin) adapted with permission from original survey and mapping by Shobunsha (Japan).

Cartographic Research
Roger Bullen, Tony Chambers, Ruth Duxbury, Ailsa Heritage, Jayne Parsons, Laura Porter, Donna Rispoli, Joan Russell, Jill Tinsley, Andrew Thompson.

Design and Editorial
Managing Editor Douglas Amrine
Managing Art Editors Stephen Knowlden, Geoff Manders
Senior Editor Georgina Matthews
Series Design Consultant Peter Luff
Editorial Director David Lamb
Art Director Anne-Marie Bulat
Production Controller Hilary Stephens
Picture Research Susan Mennell, Sarah Moule
Dtp Designer Andy Wilkinson
Keith Addison, Emma Anacootee, Lydia Baillie, Eleanor Berman, Vandana Bhagra, Jon Paul Buchmeyer, Ron Boudreau, Linda Cabasin, Rebecca Carman, Michelle Clark, Sherry Collins, Carey Combe, Diana Craig, Maggie Crowley, Guy Dimond, Nicola Erdpresser, Rhiannon Furbear, Fay Franklin, Tom Fraser, Anna Freiberger, Jo Gardner, Camilla Gersh, Alex Gray, Michelle Haimoff, Marcus Hardy, Sasha Heseltine, Rose Hudson, Pippa Hurst, Kim Inglis, Jaqueline Jackson, Claire Jones, Priya Kukadia, Mathew Kurien, Maite Lantaron, Shahid Mahmood, Susan Millership, Jane Middleton, Helen Partington, Pollyanna Poulter, Leigh Priest, Pamposh Raina, Nicki Rawson, Marisa Renzullo, Amir Reuveni, Ellen Root, Liz Rowe, Sands Publishing Solutions, Anaïs Scott, Shailesh Sharma, Meredith Smith, AnneLise Sorensen, Anna Streiffert, Clare Sullivan, Andrew Szudek, Alka Thakur, Shawn Thomas, Ros Walford, Lucilla Watson.

Special Assistance
Beyer Blinder Belle, John Beatty at the Cotton Club, Peter Casey at the New York Public Library, Nicky Clifford, Linda Corcoran at the Bronx Zoo, Audrey Manley at the Morgan Library, Jane Fischer, Deborah Gaines at the New York Convention and Visitors Bureau, Dawn Geigerich at the Queens Museum of Art, Peggy Harrington at St. John the Divine, Pamela Herrick at the Van Cortlandt House, Marguerite Lavin at the Museum of the City of New York, Robert Makla at the Friends of Central Park, Gary Miller at the New York Stock Exchange, Laura Mogil at the American Museum of Natural History, Fred Olsson at the Shubert Organization, Dominique Palermo at the Police Academy Museum, Royal Canadian Pancake House, Lydia Ruth and Laura I. Fries at the Empire State Building, David Schwartz at the American Museum of the Moving Image, Joy Sienkiewicz at the South Street Seaport Museum, Barbara Orlando at the Metropolitan Transit Authority, the staff at the Lower East Side Tenement Museum, Msgr. Anthony Dalla Valla at St. Patrick's Cathedral.

Research Assistance
Christa Griffin, Bogdan Kaczorowski, Steve McClure, Sabra Moore, Jeff Mulligan, Marc Svensson, Vicky Weiner, Steven Weinstein.

Photographic Reference
Duncan Petersen Publishers Ltd.

Photography Permissions
Dorling Kindersley would like to thank the following for their kind permission to photograph at their establishments: American Craft Museum, American Museum of Natural History, Aunt Len's Doll and Toy Museum, Balducci's, Home Savings of America, Brooklyn Children's Museum, The Cloisters, Columbia University, Eldridge Street Project, Federal Hall, Rockefeller Group, Trump Tower.

Picture credits
t = top; tc = top center; tr = top right; cla = center left above; ca = center above; cra = center right above; cl = center left; c = center; cr = center right; clb = center left below; cb = center below; crb = center right below; bl = bottom left; bc = bottom center; br = bottom right.

Works of art have been reproduced with the permission of the following copyright holders: © ADAGP, Paris and DACS, London 2006: 67ca (April 1971–July 1972, by Jean Dubuffet), 107cl, 162tr (donated by the Norwegian Government, 1952), 172bl, 188cl, 189cra, 189crb; © ARS, NY and DACS, London 2006:185cr, 201crb; Jose de Creeft ©DACS, London/VAGA, New York 2006: 53cl, 207cl; © DACS, London 2006: 161cr, 163tc; *Charging Bull* © Arturo Di Modica 1998 73tl;

© Sucession Picasso/DACS, London 2006: 36tr, 115tc, 173cb, 174cr, 188bl, 189bl, 190cla; DK IMAGES: Judith Miller/Wallis & Wallis, Sussex 58br; © Kingdom of Spain, Gaia - Salvador Dali Foundation, DACS, London 2006: 174cl; © Marisol Escobar/DACS, London/VAGA, New York 2006: 55bc; © Jasper Johns/DACS, London/VAGA, New York 2006: 201ca; ©The Estate of Roy Lichtenstein/DACS, London 2006: 175tl, 200clb; © 1993 Frank Stella/ARS, New York and DACS, London: 192tr; By permission of E Jan Nadelman: 201br; Printed by permission of the Norman Rockwell Family Trust © 1961 the Norman Rockwell Family Trust: 163br; © Licensed by The Andy Warhol Foundation for the Visual Arts, Inc/ARS, New York and DACS, London 2006: 200ca; © The Whitney Museum of American Art: 37br, 200bl.

The Publishers are grateful to the following museums, companies and picture libraries for permission to reproduce their photographs:

AGENCE FRANCE PRESSE: Doug Kanter 33tr; ALAMY IMAGES: Ambient Images Inc./Joseph A. Rosen 171c; Sandra Baker 370tl; Peter Cavanagh 373cla; Comstock Images 295c; Wendy Connett 96cr; Kevin Foy 73tl; Jeff Greenberg 268cla; Blaine Harrington III 379tl; Bob Jones 111b; Richard Levine 381tc; Yadid Levy 366–7; Ian Marlow 373cl; Ellen McKnight 378cl; PCL 295tl; Pictures Colour Library 108; Alex Segre 294cla; Lana Sundman 373tl; tbkmedia.de 340bc; Hugh Threlfall 372cla; ALGONQUIN HOTEL, N.Y: 280bl; AMERICAN MUSEUM-HAYDEN PLANETARIUM, NY: D. Finnin 218t; AMERICAN MUSEUM OF THE MOVING IMAGE: Carson Collection © Bruce Polin 247t; AMERICAN MUSEUM OF NATURAL HISTORY, NY: 39bl, 216ca; D. Finnin 216bl; Angel Orensanz Center: Laszlo Regas 101cl; Aquarius, UK: 171cr; Ashmolean Museum, Oxford: 17tc; THE ASIA SOCIETY, NY: 187cl; ATTACHÉ COMMUNICATIONS: 392crb; AVERY FISHER HALL: © N McGrath 1976 351tr. AVIS BUDGET GROUP: 385crb; © THE GEORGE BALANCHINE TRUST: *Apollo*, choreography by George Balanchine, photo by P Kolnik 5tc; *Stravinsky Violin Concerto*, choreography by George Balanchine, photo by P Kolnik 340tc; George Balanchine's *The Nutcracker*, SM, photo by P Kolnik 343cb; The BETTMANN ARCHIVE, NY: 18cl, 19cra, 19cr, 19bl, 20cl, 22cbr, 22bl, 22–23, 25br, 27cra, 28cla, 28cra, 28crb, 32cla, 33tl, 43tl, 45cbl, 49c, 54-55b, 71tl, 74cla, 79crb, 79br, 111bl, 175cb, 185br, 209t, 212cl, 225cr, 231t, 241tr, 267tr; Bettmann Newsphotos/Reuters: 33tr; Bettmann/ UPI: 29cra, 29bc, 30bcr, 31br, 32cra, 32bl, 32br, 46cl, 48cl, 49bl, 72c, 78cl, 153c, 163c, 266br, 267cr; BLOOMINGDALE'S: 29cbr; © Roy Export Company Establishment 173tr; THE BRITISH LIBRARY, London: 16; BROOKLYN HISTORICAL SOCIETY: (detail) 89tl; THE BROOKLYN MUSEUM: 38bl, 39c, 250c, 250cra, 250bl, 251t, 251cra, 251c, 251bl, 251b, 252t, 252br, 253cr, 253bl; Lewis Wick Hine, *Climbing Into The Promised Land*, 1908 – 36clb; J Kerr 250c, 252bl; P Warchol: 251cr; The Cantor Collection 253cl; Adam Husted 250t; BROWN BROTHERS: 67br, 71bl, 82cra, 90t, 106br. CAMERA PRESS: 30cbr, 30bl, 33cb, 127cr; R Open 48tr; T Spencer 32cb; THE CARLYLE HOTEL, NY: 281tr; CARNEGIE HALL: © H. Grossman 343br; J ALLAN CASH: 303bl; CATHEDRAL OF ST. JOHN THE DIVINE: Greg Wyatt 1985, 227tl; CBS ENTERTAINMENT/DESILU TOO: "Vacation from Marriage" 171br; CHELSEA PIERS: Fred George 33bl; CHILDREN'S MUSEUM OF THE ARTS: 107cl; CITY PASS, INC: 2008 Vasily Goosieff 369cl; COLORIFIC!:

Colorific/ Black Star: 79cra; T Cowell 223cr; R Fraser 74t; D Moore 31bl; T Spiegel 15cr, 364tr; CORBIS: Bettmann 137cl, 273ca, 383c; Jacques M. Chenet 272tl; Randy Duchaine 99cl; Kevin Fleming 271tl; Bob Krist 10cra; Todd Gipstein 75t; Gail Mooney 207b, 269tr, 271br; Bill Ross 12t; Michael Setboun 268tr; Steven E. Sutton 51b; Bo Zaunders 376cl; Mike Zens 262–3. CULVER PICTURES, INC: (inset) 9, 19crb, 20cbl, 21bl, 23tl, 23br, 26tl, 26cl, 29cb, 29bl, 48br, 49tr, 74bl, 75cra, 75cb, 76tl, 78crb, 83c, 121bl, 124tc, 127bl, 137cr, 147c, 149cl, 229t, 229bc, 229cr, 261crb. DAILY EAGLE: (detail) 89cl; DAILY NEWS: 370tl, 370tr. ESTO: P Aaron 342bl; DELTA AIRLINES INC. CORPORTAE COMMUNICATIONS EMEA: 378tc; DOLLAR THRIFTY AUTOMOTIVE GROUP, Inc.: 385cra; MARY EVANS PICTURE LIBRARY: 24br, 87br, 106bl; CHRIS FAIRCLOUGH COLOUR LIBRARY: 385bcl; THE FORBES MAGAZINE COLLECTION, NY: 114tl; FOUR SEASONS HOTEL: Peter Vitale 281cr; FRAUNCES TAVERN MUSEUM, NY: From the exhibit "Come All You Gallant Heroes" The World of the Revolutionary Soldier December 4, 1991 to August 14, 1992: 22cla; Copyright THE FRICK COLLECTION, NY: 37bl (*St Francis In The Desert* by Giovanni Bellini), 202ca, 202cl, 202clb, 202b, 202tr, 203ca, 203cr, 203bc, 203br. GARRARD THE CROWN JEWELLERS: 145c; GETTY IMAGES: AFP/Stan Honda 392cla; Mitchell Funk 341cb; Michael Grimm 386tl; GREENMARKET FARMERS MARKET: 371tr; THE SOLOMON R GUGGENHEIM MUSEUM, NY: photo by D Heald 188tl, 188bl, 188bc, 188br, 189t, 189cra, 189crb, 189bl; ROBERT HARDING PICTURE LIBRARY: 378tc; HARPERS NEW MONTHLY MAGAZINE: 87tl; HARPERS WEEKLY: 367c; MILTON HEBALD: *Prospero and Miranda* 205t, *Romeo and Juliet* 343cr. THE IMAGE BANK: front endpaper bl, 89br; M Melford 393tl; P Miller 383tr; A Satterwhite 75br. THE JEWISH MUSEUM, NY: 184tr, 186c; THE KOBAL COLLECTION: 213tc; LEBRECHT MUSIC: Toby Wales 149t; THE LEISURE PASS GROUP: 369cla; THE LESBIAN, GAY, BISEXUAL & TRANSGENDER COMMUNITY CENTER: 370c; FRANK LESLIE'S ILLUSTRATED NEWSPAPER: 86br, 87tr, 275c; LIBRARY OF CONGRESS: 20bc, 23cla, 27bl, 27br; LIFE MAGAZINE © TIME WARNER INC/KATZ/A FEININGER: 8–9; Georg John Lober: *Hans Christian Andersen*, 1956, 206br; LEONARDO MEDIA LTD: 276br, 276cl, 277crb, 277tl; THE LOWELL HOTEL, NY: 281cl; MARY ANN LYNCH: 318bc, 372cl. MADISON SQUARE GARDEN: 134r, 342cr; MAGNUM PHOTOS: © H Cartier-Bresson 175c; Erwitt 35cr; G Peres 14br, 92; JACQUES MARCHAIS CENTER OF TIBETAN ART: 254bc; MASTERFILE UK: Gail Mooney 33br; METRO-NORTH COMMUTER RAILROAD: F English 156tr, 156cla; THE METROPOLITAN MUSEUM OF ART, NY: 35bl (*Young Woman With A Waterjug* by Johannes Vermeer), 37crb (*Figure of a Hippopotamus*, faience, Egypt, 12th Dynasty), 182tc, 190cla, 190clb, 190bc, 190br, 191tl, 191tr, 191cr, 191bl, (photo Al Mozell) 191br, 192tr, 192c, 192bl, 192br, 193tl, 193tr, 193c, 193bl, 194tl, 194tr, 194b, (detail) 195tl, 195tr, 195b, 196t, 196cl, 196cr, 196b, 197tl, 197cr, 197bl, 236tr, 236cl, 236cr, 236b, 237ca, 237cr, 237bl, 237br, 238tl, 238tr, 239tr, 239c, 239b; METROPOLITAN TRANSIT AUTHORITY: 388tl, 392bl; MTA/Patrick Cashin 388cl, all 389, 390tr, 390bl; COLLECTION OF THE MORGAN LIBRARY, NY: 36cr (*Blanche of Castille and King Louis IX of France, author dictating to a scribe*, moralized Bible, c1230), 164br, *Song of Los* David A. Loggie (gift of Mrs Landon K Thorne) 164la, *Biblia Latina* David A. Loggie 164lb, 165cl, 165bl, 165br; Morris-Jumel Mansion, Inc NY: 19tl; A Rosario 23crb; THE MUSEUM OF THE CITY OF NEW YORK: 17b,

18cra, 18–19, 19tr, 20ca, 21crb (photo J Parnell), 22tl, 22cbl, 24tl (attributed to Samuel Lovett Waldo), 24cla, 24clb, 25cr, 25crb, 25bc, 26cb, 27tl, 27crb, 27cb, 28bl, 29tr, 30tl, 30cr, 31tc, 31c, 32tr, 37tr (silver porringer), 87cr (Talfour); THE MUSEUM OF MODERN ART, NY: 172c, 172bl, 173tc, 173cra, 173crb, 173cb, 173bl, 174cl, 174cr, 175tl, 175b; *The Bather*, c. 1885, Paul Cézanne 174bc; Cisitalia "202" GT car 167tc; © 2004 Photo Elizabeth Felicella, architectural rendering Kohn Pedersen Fox Associates, digital composite Robert Bowen 172tl; ©2005 Timothy Hursley 168cr, 172tr; *The Goat* by Pablo Picasso, 1950, 36t; *Portrait of the Postman Joseph Roulin* by Vincent Van Gogh, 1889, 35ca. NATIONAL BASEBALL LIBRARY, COOPERSTOWN, NY: 4tr, 25bl, 30cl; NATIONAL CAR RENTAL: 385cr; NATIONAL MUSEUM OF THE AMERICAN INDIAN/SMITHSONIAN INSTITUTION: 18c; NATIONAL PARK SERVICE: Ellis Island Immigration Museum 78ca, 78br; Statue of Liberty National Monument 75bl; THE NEW MUSEUM OF CONTEMPORARY ART, NY: 107cl; NEW YORK BOTANIC GARDEN: Tori Butt 242b, 243t/cl/b; Jason Green 242cr; Muriel Weinerman 243b; NEW YORK CITY FIRE DEPARTMENT: 359br; NEW YORK CITY TRANSIT AUTHORITY: 390bc; Phil Bartley 391tc, 391ca, 391cl; THE NEW YORKER MAGAZINE INC: Cover drawing by Rea Irvin, © 1925, 1953, All rights reserved, 30bcl; THE NEW YORK PALACE, NY: 27tr; NEW YORK POST: 370tl; NEW YORK PUBLIC LIBRARY: Special Collection Office, Schomburg Center for Research in Black Culture 30ca, 31cla; Stokes Collection 23tr; NEW YORK STATE DEPARTMENT OF MOTOR VEHICLES: 386b; NEW YORK STOCK EXCHANGE: 71ra; THE NEW YORK TIMES: 370tl; NPA: © CNES 1993 12b; NYC & COMPANY: 368br, 368tc; Julienne Schaer, 2009 372br; Stefano Giovannini 369br; THE PENINSULA, NY: 279bc; PERFORMING ARTS LIBRARY: Clive Barda 212bl; The Pickle Guys: Alan Kaufman 100bl; PHOTOLIBRARY: Renaud Visage 166; PLAZA HOTEL, NY: 280tr; POPPERFOTO: 31cra, 31cr, 262cla; THE PORT AUTHORITY OF NEW YORK & NEW JERSEY: 379br; COLLECTION OF THE QUEENS MUSEUM OF ART: purchased with funds from the George and Mollie Wolfe World's Fair Fund 31cbr; Official souvenir, purchase 32cbr; RENSSELAER POLYTECHNIC INSTITUTE: 86–87, 87bl; REX FEATURES LTD: Sipa-Press 52tr, 52br; Courtesy of the Rockefeller Center © THE ROCKEFELLER GROUP, Inc: 31cbl. LUIS SANGUINO: *The Immigrants*, 1973, 258b; THE ST. REGIS, NY: 278c; Scientific American: 18 May 1878 edition 86tr; 9 November 1878 edition 88bl; THE SHERMAN GROUP/NEW YORK WATER TAXI: 386br; SKIDMORE, OWINGS & MERRILL LLP, Chicago: 54cr; SKYSCRAPER MUSEUM: Robert Polidori 55tl; 72br; 268bl; THE SOCIETY OF ILLUSTRATORS: 198tl; SOUTH STREET SEAPORT MUSEUM: R.B. Merkel 83bl, 84bl; FRANK SPOONER PICTURES: Gamma 160cl; Liaison/Gamma/ Anderson front endpaper clb,

160tl, 161cla; Liaison/Levy/Halebian: 44tr, 47c; STA TRAVEL GROUP: 370br; THEATER DEVELOPMENT FUND: David LeShay 340cl; TURNER ENTERTAINMENT COMPANY: 137br, 185br. UNITED NATIONS, NY: 161cra, 162tr, 162bc, 163tc, 163cla, 163br; UNITED NATIONS PHOTO: 160tr; Used with permission UN PLAZA HYATT HOTEL, NY: 281bl. © JACK VARTOOGIAN, NY: 61bc, 158t. JUDITH WELLER: *The Garment Worker* 130t; LUCIA WILSON CONSULTANCY: Ivar Mjell 2–3, 15br; COLLECTION OF THE WHITNEY MUSEUM OF AMERICAN ART, NY: 200cla, 200clb, 201t, 201ca, 201crb (purchase with funds from a public fundraising campaign in May 1982. One half of the funds were contributed by the Robert Wood Johnson Jr. Charitable Trust. Additional major donations were given by The Lauder Foundation; the Robert Lehman Foundation, Inc.; the Howard and Jean Lipman Foundation, Inc; an anonymous donor; The TM Evans Foundation, Inc.; MacAndrews & Forbes Group Incorporated; the DeWitt Wallace Fund, Inc; Martin & Agnes Gruss; Anne Phillips; Mr and Mrs Laurance S. Rockefeller; the Simon Foundation, Inc.; Marylou Whitney; Bankers Trust Company; Mr and Mrs Kenneth N Dayton; Joel and Anne Ehrenkranz; Irvin and Kenneth Feld; Flora Whitney Miller. More than 500 individuals from 26 states and abroad also contributed to the campaign); 201br (purchased with funds from the Mr and Mrs Arthur G Altschul Purchase Fund, the Joan and Lester Avnet Purchase Fund, the Edgar William and Bernice Chrysler Garbisch Purchase Fund, the Mrs Robert C Graham Purchase Fund in honour of John I H Baur, the Mrs Percy Uris Purchase Fund and the Henry Schnakenberg Purchase Fund in honor of Juliana Force); 200tr Krause/Johansen; 201bc gift of Flora Whitney Miller 86.70.3; 200c purchase, with funds from the Louis and Bessie Adler Foundation, Inc., Seymour M. Klein, President 78.34; 201cr gift of an anonymous donor 58.65. WHEELER PICTURES: 78t; WILDLIFE CONSERVATION SOCIETY, BRONX ZOO: Dennis DeMello 244bl; Julie Maher 244tr, 244cl, 245br, 245bl; ROBERT WRIGHT: 43t, 140b, 142tr, 142cr, 142bl; 143tl/br, 156br, 157tl/r, 293tr. YU YU YANG: *Untitled*, 1973, 57br.

All other images © Dorling Kindersley. See www. dkimages.com for further information.

Front Endpapers
ALAMY IMAGES: Pictures Colour Library ftl; MAGNUM PHOTOS: G. Per bl; PHOTOLIBRARY: Renaud Visage tr.
Jacket
Front - PHOTOLIBRARY: Index Stock Imagery/Henryk T. Kaiser. Back - ALAMY IMAGES: Patrick Batchelder cla; Russell Kord clb; DORLING KINDERSLEY: Dave King bl; Robert Wright tl. Spine - PHOTOLIBRARY: Index Stock Imagery/Henryk T. Kaiser t.

SPECIAL EDITIONS OF DK TRAVEL GUIDES

DK Travel Guides can be purchased in bulk quantities at discounted prices for use in promotions or as premiums. We are also able to offer special editions and personalized jackets, corporate imprints, and excerpts from all of our books, tailored specifically to meet your own needs.

To find out more, please contact:
(in the United States) **SpecialSales@dk.com**
(in the UK) **TravelSpecialSales@uk.dk.com**
(in Canada) DK Special Sales at **general@tourmaline.ca**
(in Australia) **business.development@pearson.com.au**

The Manhattan Subway

HOW TO USE THIS MAP

MTA New York City Transit subway service operates 24 hours a day. On this map, bold identification letters or numbers below station names indicate a full-time service. A light letter or number shows a part-time service at the station. For more information, and to check the latest opening times, call (718) 330-1234 or visit www.mta.info. Throughout this guide, the subway station closest to each sight is listed. For more details on traveling on the New York subway, see pages 390–1.

WHEELCHAIR ACCESSIBLE STATIONS *(See table below)*

For further information on accessible service, call (718) 596-8585 (6am–9pm daily). For information regarding the accessibility status of elevators and escalators, call (800) 734-6772 (24 hours).

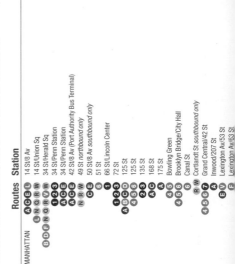

	Routes	Station
MANHATTAN	A C E L	14 St/8 Av
	L N Q R W	14 St/Union Sq
	B D F N Q R W	34 St/Herald Sq
	1 2 3	34 St/Penn Station
	A C E	34 St/Penn Station
	A C E	42 St/8 Av (Port Authority Bus Terminal)
	N R W	49 St *northbound only*
	C E	50 St/8 Av *southbound only*
	6	51 St
	1	66 St/Lincoln Center
	1 2 3	72 St
	A B C D	125 St
	1	125 St
	2 3	135 St
	2 3	168 St
	A	175 St
	4 5	Bowling Green
	4 5 6	Brooklyn Bridge/City Hall
	6	Canal St
	R W	Cortlandt St *southbound only*
	4 5 6 7	Grand Central/42 St
	A	Inwood/207 St
	E M	Lexington Av/53 St
	F	Lexington Av/63 St

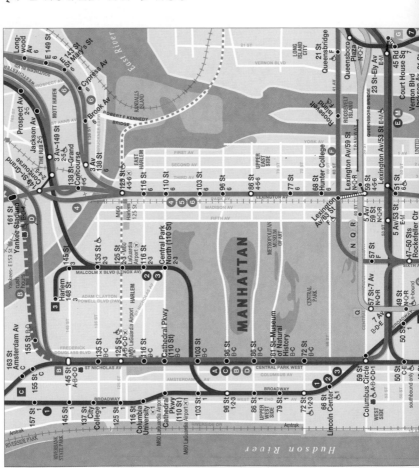